From Max Weber

Max Weber is the most distinguished sociologist of modern times. He died in 1920, leaving behind him a considerable amount of material, which has been assembled in volumes of collected essays on politics, methodology, general sociology, and the sociology of religion. Now, in the volume before us, H. H. Gerth and C. Wright Mills have produced a translation of a further selection from his work, preceded by an illuminating introduction . . . Instructive and a great intellectual pleasure. – *The Listener*

Max Weber (1864–1920) was one of the most prolific and influential sociologists of the twentieth century. This classic collection draws together his key papers. This edition contains a new preface by Professor Bryan S. Turner.

Bryan S. Turner is a leading Weber scholar and contemporary sociologist. He has edited *Max Weber: Critical Responses* (Routledge 1999) and *Max Weber on Economy and Society*, with Robert Holton (Routledge 1989), and is the founding editor with John O'Neill of the *Journal of Classical Sociology*.

From Max Weber

Essays in Sociology

Translated, edited, with an Introduction by H.H. Gerth and C. Wright Mills With a New Preface by Bryan S. Turner

Routledge
Taylor & Francis Group

LONDON AND NEW YORK

First published 2009
by Routledge
2 Park Square, Milton Park, Abingdon, Oxon OX14 4RN

Simultaneously published in the USA and Canada
by Routledge
270 Madison Avenue, New York, NY 10016

*Routledge is an imprint of the Taylor & Francis Group,
an informa business*

© 2009 H.H. Gerth and C. Wright Mills for selection Preface Bryan Turner

Printed and bound in Great Britain by
CPI Antony Rowe, Chippenham, Wiltshire

British Library Cataloguing in Publication Data
A catalogue record for this book is available from the British Library

Library of Congress Cataloging-in-Publication Data
Weber, Max, 1864–1920.
[Selected works. English]
From Max Weber : essays in sociology / edited, with an introduction by
H. H. Gerth and C. Wright Mills with a new preface by Bryan S. Turner.
p. cm. – (Routledge classics in sociology)
1. Social sciences.   I. Gerth, Hans Heinrich, 1908–1979.   II. Mills, C.
Wright (Charles Wright), 1916–1962.   III. Title.
H33.W3613 2009
301–dc22
2008034087

ISBN 978–0–415–48269–1 pbk
ISBN 0–415–48269–0 pbk

Table of Contents

PART III: RELIGION

PART IV: SOCIAL STRUCTURES

Preface

ONE HUNDRED AND FIFTY YEARS AGO A. F. Tytler set forth three *Principles of Translation:* To give a complete transcript of the original ideas; to imitate the styles of the original author; and to preserve the ease of the original text. In presenting selections from Max Weber to an English-reading public, we hope we have met the first demand, that of faithfulness to the original meaning. The second and the third demands are often disputable in translating German into English, and, in the case of Max Weber, they are quite debatable.

The genius of the German language has allowed for a twofold stylistic tradition. One tradition corresponds to the drift of English towards brief and grammatically lucid sentences. Such sentences carry transparent trains of thought in which first things stand first. Friedrich Nietzsche, Georg Christoph Lichtenberg, and Franz Kafka are eminent among the representatives of this tradition.

The other tradition is foreign to the tendency of modern English. It is often felt to be formidable and forbidding, as readers of Hegel and Jean Paul Richter, of Karl Marx and Ferdinand Tönnies may testify.

It would hardly do to classify the two traditions as 'good' and 'bad.' Authors representing the first believe in addressing themselves to the ear; they wish to write as if they were speaking. The second group address themselves to the eye of the silent reader. Their texts cannot easily be read aloud to others; everyone has to read for himself. Max Weber once compared German literary humanism to the education of the Chinese Mandarin; and Jean Paul Richter, one of the greatest of German writers, asserted that 'a long period bespeaks of greater deference for the reader than do twenty short sentences. In the end the reader must make them over into one by rereading and recapitulation. The writer is no speaker and the reader is no listener. . .'[1]

[1] *Vorschule der Aesthetik,* p. 382, Sämmtliche Werke, Vol. 18 (Berlin, 1841).

It is obvious that this school of writing is not what it is because of the inability of its practitioners to write well. They simply follow an altogether different style. They use parentheses, qualifying clauses, inversions, and complex rhythmic devices in their polyphonous sentences. Ideas are synchronized rather than serialized. At their best, they erect a grammatical artifice in which mental balconies and watch towers, as well as bridges and recesses, decorate the main structure. Their sentences are gothic castles. And Max Weber's style is definitely in their tradition.

Unfortunately, in his case this style is further complicated by a tendency to Platonize thought: he has a predilection for nouns and participles linked by the economic yet colorless forms of weak verbs, such as 'to be,' 'to have,' or 'to seem.' This Platonizing tendency is one of Weber's tributes to German philosophy and jurisprudence, to the style of the pulpit and the bureaucratic office.

We have therefore violated the second of Tytler's rules for translators. Although we have been eager to retain Weber's images, his objectivity, and of course his terms, we have not hesitated to break his sentence into three or four smaller units. Certain alterations in tense, which in English would seem illogical and arbitrary, have been eliminated; occasionally the subjunctive has been changed into the indicative, and nouns into verbs; appositional clauses and parentheses have been raised to the level of equality and condemned to follow rather than herald the main idea. As Weber has not observed Friedrich Nietzsche's suggestion that one should write German with an eye to ease of translation, we have had to drive many a wedge into the structure of his sentences. In all these matters, we have tried to proceed with respect and measure.

But we have also broken the third rule: Whatever 'ease' Weber may have in English is an ease of the English prose into which he is rendered and not any ease of the original work.

A translator of Weber faces a further difficulty. Weber frequently betrays a self-conscious hesitancy in the use of loaded words such as democracy, the people, environment, adjustment, etc., by a profuse utilization of quotation marks. It would be altogether wrong to translate them by the addition of an ironical 'so-called.' Moreover, Weber often emphasizes words and phrases; the German printing convention allows for this more readily than does the English. Our translation, in the main, conforms to the English convention: we have omitted what to the English reader would seem self-conscious reservation and manner of emphasis. The same holds for the accumulation of qualifying words, with which the English language dispenses without losing in exactitude, emphasis, and meaning. Weber pushes German academic tradition to its extremes. His major theme often seems to be lost in a wealth of footnoted digressions, exemptions, and comparative illustrations. We have taken some footnotes into the text and in a few instances we have relegated technical cross-references which stand in the original text to footnotes.

We have thus violated Tytler's second and third rules in order to fulfil the first. Our constant aim has been to make accessible to an English-reading public an accurate rendering of what Weber said.

* * *

We wish to thank the editorial staff of Oxford University Press for their encouragement of our efforts. Special thanks are due Mrs. Patricke Johns Heine who assisted revisions of the first drafts of chapters IV, X, and XII; and to Mr. J. Ben Gillingham who performed the same task in connection with section 6 of chapter XIII. Miss Honey Toda partially edited and retyped many pages of almost illegible manuscript and we are grateful for her diligence.

We are grateful for the valuable assistance of Dr. Hedwig Ide Gerth and Mrs. Freya Mills. The administrative generosity of Professor Carl S. Joslyn, chairman of the Department of Sociology, the University of Maryland, and the support of Professor Thomas C. McCormick, chairman at the University of Wisconsin, have greatly facilitated the work. Professor E. A. Ross has been kind enough to read chapter XII and to give us his suggestions.

One of our translations, 'Class, Status, Party,' has been printed in Dwight Macdonald's *Politics* (October 1944) and is included in this volume by his kind permission. We are grateful to the publishers, Houghton Mifflin Company, for permission to reprint a revision of Max Weber's paper given before the Congress of Arts and Science, St. Louis Exposition of 1904.

Responsibility for the selections and reliability of the German meanings rendered is primarily assumed by H. H. Gerth; responsibility for the formulation and editorial arrangement of the English text is primarily assumed by C. Wright Mills. But the book as a whole represents our mutual work and we are jointly responsible for such deficiencies as it may contain.

HANS H. GERTH
C. WRIGHT MILLS

Preface to the new edition

INTRODUCTION: APPROACHING MAX WEBER

IN THE Preface to the 1991 edition of *From Max Weber* I wrote that there had been a great revival of interest in Weber and Weberian sociology. Writing now from the first decade of a new century, scholarly interest in Weber shows no sign of abatement. At the same time, disputes about the character of Weber's sociology are still unresolved. He has been attacked as a reactionary prophet of despair, as a bourgeois sociologist whose views on domination were part of the background of fascism, as one of the greatest minds of the twentieth century, or as a philosopher of modernity whose views on rationalization prepared the way towards the disputes between modernists and postmodernists.

In the context of debates about the meaning and importance of Weber's work, perhaps the enduring merit of Hans Gerth and C. Wright Mills' introduction to Weber which first appeared in 1946 is its focus on core issues—power, social stratification, social structure and religion. Their selections and translations from Weber remain therefore one of the most balanced introductions to Weber, in English, which we possess. Furthermore, given the notorious difficulties of Weber's German, they have offered us a lucid, but accurate translation. At the time of the publication of their selections little of Weber's sociology had appeared in English translation, apart from Parsons' translation of *The Protestant Ethic and the Spirit of Capitalism* (Weber 1930). In 1944, J.P. Mayer published a valuable study of Weber's political sociology in his *Max Weber and German Politics* (Mayer 1944). Of course, more than half a century after *From Max Weber* appeared, we have access to a far greater range of Weber's sociological publications, including the monumental *Economy and Society* (Weber 1978a). There have also been re-translations of major parts of Weber's opus, such as the 'science as a vocation' lecture (Lassman and Velody 1989) and various *Selections in Translation* (Runciman 1978). There have also been new translations of the essays on the Protestant ethic by Stephen Kalberg (2002) and by Peter Baehr and Gordon Wells (2002). There are also available collections on the 'critical responses' to Weber's work (Turner 1999).

Although there have been great advances in Weber scholarship, Gerth and Mills' approach to Weber has retained an originality and freshness which continues to command respect. Anticipating later commentary, it is valuable to mention three aspects of their approach to Weber, namely their awareness of the importance of the German philosopher Friedrich Nietzsche on Weber's world view, the signifi- cance of Weber's interest in military and political questions for his general sociology of historical change, and finally the centrality of the analysis of power to Weber's sociology as a whole.

The other accidental (so to speak) interest of *From Max Weber* is the insight it gives us into the intellectual career of C. Wright Mills. The translations from Weber had been largely the responsibility of Gerth— a scholar whose first language was German. Mills, who had first met Gerth in 1940 at the University of Wisconsin at Madison, was respon- sible for editing the English version. They were later to collaborate in writing *Character and Social Structure* (1953). However, when Oxford University Press announced the publication of *From Max Weber* the credit in their catalogue unfortunately listed Mills' name before Gerth's. The problem was compounded by a review of their interpret- ation of Weber by Meyer Schapiro in politics (1945) in which he also reversed the order of their names. Mills apologized to Gerth describing him as 'the senior author in all that we have done with Max Weber' (Mills and Mills 2000: 86). Apart from the minor embarrassment caused by the order of names, the Schapiro review objected to the view propounded by Mills that Weber was a prophetic political thinker. The selections and translations by Gerth and Mills clearly emphasized the importance of social structure, power conflicts and politics in Weber's sociology and hence Mills was critical of Talcott Parsons' approach to Weber's sociology and in reference to Parsons' translation of *Wirtschaft und Gesellschaft* as *The Theory of Social and Economic Organization* (1947). Mills famously declared that, 'The son of a bitch translated it so as to take all the guts, the radical guts, out of it, whereas our translation doesn't do that!' (Mills and Mills 2000: 53). Mills went on to become a trenchant critic of the sociology of Parsons, especially the idea of social equilibrium in *The Social System* (1951). The influence of Weber in Mills' criticisms of Parsons are most obvious in *The Sociological Imagination* (Mills 1959) and in such works as *The Power Elite* (Mills 1956) in which the Weberian distinctions between class, status and power are most self evident. Thus, while Parsons is often credited with the introduction of Weber into American sociology, we should not neglect the role of Gerth and Mills in representing an alternative vision of Weberian sociology. These early conflicts with Parsons and Edward Shils were the beginning of a more permanent alienation of Mills from professional American sociology (Brewer 2004). We might summarize Gerth and Mills' perspective by saying that in *From Max Weber* they presented Weber's work as essentially the historical and comparative sociology of class, status and power.

WEBER'S LIFE

Weber's life has been the subject of a number of major inquiries. It is important to stress the fact that the biography by Weber's wife is both an essential text for any scholarly understanding of Weber, and a work of considerable literary and historical merit in its own right (Marianne Weber 1926 and 1975). There are also a number of major general discussions of Weber's life in relation to his intellectual development, In this context it is necessary to refer to Rheinhard Bendix's *Max Weber, An Intellectual Portrait* (1960), Paul Honigsheim's *On Max Weber* (1968) and, more recently, Dirk Käsler's *Max Weber* (1988). In addition, there are a number of interpretations of Weber's sociology which give prominence to certain (alleged) psychological problems in Weber's development which are held to explain, or at least throw light on, aspects of his intellectual development. For example, Weber's religion and sexuality are often seen in terms of the tensions between his mother's spirituality and father's secularity. Weber's early letters, especially to his mother, give us a wonderful insight into his develop-ment. Unfortunately, the *Jugendbriefe* have yet to be translated into English (Weber 1936). Arthur Mitzman's *The Iron Cage* (1971) has been influential in identifying the intellectual consequences of Weber's rift with his father, the death of his father and his separation from Emmy Baumgarten in 1887. What emerges from these commentaries is a general understanding of Weber's tender but problematic relationship with women (his mother, Emmy Baumgarten, Marianne Weber and the von Richthofen sisters), and how these emotional issues form a part of his analysis of asceticism and the religious calling in his sociology of religion. Although the history of Max Weber and Marianne Weber in the rise of German feminism has yet to be written adequately, a valuable insight into the ambiguities of Weber's attitudes is offered in Green's study of the von Richthofen sisters (Green 1974).

Subsequent interpretations of Weberian sociology have drawn attention to the contradictions between the discipline of intellectual life, the practical commitments which are necessary for a life in politics, and the ecstatic intensity of sexual and religious experience (Lepenies 1985; Mommsen and Osterhammel 1987; Turner 1987). In this perspective, many of the oppositions and dichotomies in Weberian social theory can be seen as reflections upon the difference between the Apollonian principles (of order, form and rationality) and the Dionysian principles (of ecstasy, energy and creativity) which were explored by Nietzsche in the will-to-power problematic, and which were subsequently analysed in the literary masterpieces of Thomas Mann (Megill 1985; Stauth and Turner 1988). The degree to which these questions in Weber's academic work can be understood as a direct consequence of these psychoanalytic constellations is, of course, a matter of intense dispute.

There is little to be gained from merely repeating the personal and academic details of Weber's life, many of which are in any case discussed in the short but excellent 'biographical view' which is presented by Gerth and Mills in this volume. However, while Weber's biographical details are relatively well known, it is still the case that many commentaries on Weber's sociology manage to divorce his sociology from its specific historical context. In my own approach to Weber's sociology, I take a strong position in the sociology of knowledge that Weber's conceptual apparatus is actually meaningless once divorced from the political issues which he sought to address in, for example, his political sociology. To take one crucial issue, Weber's views on leadership, bureaucracy and class structure were developed as part of a debate about the future of Germany and the legacy of Bismarck's chancellorship. Weber's apparently formal discussion of ideal types of leadership and bureaucracy are to be understood as contributions to an (initially) German political problem: clearly this claim does not in principle preclude the usefulness of Weber's conceptual apparatus in other contexts.

It is another feature of the merits of *From Max Weber* that Gerth and Mills took this historical and social location of Weber's sociology very seriously. They noted for example that 'Max Weber's life and thought are expressions of political events and concerns' (Gerth and Mills 1948: 32). One of Weber's major political anxieties was for the future of a strong Germany in view of the political vacuum following Bismarck's resignation in 1890 (Gall 1986). Thus, Weber's arguments in favour of the value-neutrality and value-freedom of sociology should not mislead us into assuming that either Weber or Weber's sociology were somehow politically disengaged. On the contrary, even Weber's discussion of the value-neutrality of sociology has to be understood in the context of specific problems in the development of the German university system (Shils 1976). Thus, in order to understand Weber's sociology, we have to understand his aspirations in the context of the changing national and international situation of Germany.

Max Weber was born in Erfurt, Thuringia in 1864 into an influential and affluent family, whose background and development exhibit many of the virtues which Weber came to explore in his famous Protestant Ethic theses (Weber 1930), and which Thomas Mann developed in his novel *Buddenbrooks*. Weber's father, himself a member of a linen merchant family from Bielefeld, Westphalia, was a Councillor of Berlin, deputy of the Prussian Diet, and National-Liberal member of the Reichstag. Weber grew up in the Charlottenburg suburb of Berlin in an atmosphere of practical engagement with politics, and throughout his life was torn between a career in politics and the world of science—a conflict which he came to summarize brilliantly in his two lectures in 1919 on science as a vocation and politics as a vocation (Turner and Factor 1984; Roth and Schluchter 1979).

Weber's mother Helene Fallenstein Weber came from south Germany with a Huguenot background, and it was her austere Puritanism which came ultimately to shape Weber's ethical view of discipline, rectitude and personal ethics. Although he claimed to be 'religiously unmusical', it would be difficult to understate the continuous influence of religious ideas on his career, personality and sociological concerns. Weber's deep interest in the impact of religion on America, and in the Christian separation of politics and church was associated with his personal sympathy for the religious doctrines of W.E. Channing; his sociological analysis of religious institutionalization was a product of the influence of church historians like Ernst Troeltsch (1912); his conceptualization of charisma and his detailed knowledge of Old Testament prophecy (Weber 1966) testify not only to his profound understanding of the Abrahamic faiths but also to the moral influence of Israelite prophecy on his own view of history; and finally, Weber's view of the tragic character of the times in which he was living was shaped, above all else, by Nietzsche's own prophetic proclamation that God was dead in *Thus Spake Zarathustra* in 1883–5 (Hollingdale 1973).

Although Weber's health was often poor, he undertook his compulsory military service in Strassburg, becoming an *Unteroffizier* in 1884, but he was clearly relieved to return to his academic studies at the universities of Berlin and Göttingen, where he continued with his studies of law and history. Under Professor Goldschmidt, he began to prepare for his doctoral thesis on the history of commercial societies in the Middle Ages (*Zur Geschichte der Handelgesellschaften im Mittelalter*) and he eventually completed his habilitationschrift on the meaning of the history of Roman agrarian institutions for private and public law (*Die römische Agrargeschichte in ihrer Bedeutung für das Staatsrecht und Privatrecht*).

Very few commentaries on Weber's intellectual orientations have taken sufficient notice of his abiding focus on legal issues (Berman and Reid 2000) It is not enough, for example, merely to take note of the fact that Weber undertook many important historical studies in law, which are reflected in the collection *Max Weber on Law and Society* (Rheinstein 1954), or that Weber treated legal rationalization as an important foundation of modern capitalist activity. Among recent evaluations of Weber as a legal theorist, only Anthony T. Kronman (1983), after Talcott Parsons (1971), has fully understood that Weber's notions of personality and rationality were deeply dependent on legal ideas of personality and responsibility (Berman and Reid 2000; Holton and Turner 1989).

Weber's legal training should also alert us to the fact that throughout his academic career he was hesitant about employing the word 'sociology' to describe his intellectual endeavours. Nevertheless, an involvement with social theory and social questions always shaped his approach to religion, law, politics and history. Thus, Weber joined the Association for Social Policy (*Verein für Sozialpolitik*) which had been founded in 1873 primarily by a group of German economists (including Wagner, Schmoller and Brentano). On behalf of the Association, Weber plunged into a survey of the position of rural workers in the East-Elbian region of Germany (*Die Lage der Landarbeiter im ostelbischen Deutschland*). In eastern Germany, the agricultural economy depended heavily (partly because of the continuity of traditional social relations on the Junker estates) on the influx of Polish and Russian migrant labour. Weber was interested in and concerned by the political and social implications of this dependency on foreign labour.

This apparently factual study of conditions in agricultural production in fact reflected two aspects of Weber's political orientation, but also the underlying assumptions of his sociology. First, Weber was intensely nationalistic, and much of his sociology is based on an assumption about the cultural superiority of German values. Weber feared that the dependence on Polish and Russian labour would eventually weaken the dominance of German culture on its eastern border. In his later political commentaries Weber was much exercised by the issue of Germany's foreign policy in a period when Britain and America appeared to be on the verge of a global monopoly of power (Eliaeson 2000). Weber's writing on economics, international relations and sociology not only presupposes a strong German state, but actually requires it. Second, Weber assumes that one of the great threats to German (and finally western) civilization is a Russian (Cossack) invasion. Weber was acutely aware of the military history of the flatlands of northern Europe, extending from Holland through Germany and Poland to the steppes of Asia. Germany's eastern sector had to be defended against such a threat, otherwise all attempts to reform and strengthen Germany would be pointless. Weber was impressed by the proposition that social policy, however excellent, was useless if the danger of a Cossack invasion could not be contained. Fear of a Russian occupation of Europe later fuelled Weber's intense interest in the first Russian revolution, about which he published two articles in 1906 on bourgeois democracy and constitutionalism in Russia (Weber 1988).

Weber did not, however, regard the prospect of a socialist revolution as an event offering the prospect of major changes in European societies. For Weber, socialist planning of the economy would require bureaucratic administration, rational legal systems, social surveillance and bureaucratic political management of a mass party. In short, a socialist transformation of society, based on the idea of a planned redistribution of wealth, would be merely a continuation and intensification of the rationalistic requirements of capitalism (Runciman 1978).

Weber's nationalistic sentiments were also evident in his Inaugural Address, with the title 'The National State and Economic Policy' (Weber 1988), on his acceptance of a professorship of economics at Freiburg University in 1894. Weber took it for granted that, while economic science can be value-free as an analytical and explanatory discipline, it has to be a national economic science in the services of a strong state as soon as it couches on questions of value. Weber thus contrasted the 'cosmopolitanism' of Smithian economics (that is Adam Smith's theory of international exchange) with his own view of sociology as a discipline which serves a national interest. Weber's professorial address has therefore to be seen against the context of British and growing American economic dominance of the world economy.

A central motif of Weberian sociology is the question of struggle in human relationships. His Inaugural Address focused unambiguously on struggle as the driving force of social history. Rejecting utilitarian ideas about the greatest happiness of the greatest number, he flatly proclaimed that 'only in a hard struggle between man and man can elbowroom be won in our earthly existence'. There is no place in this outlook for international economic co-operation, and through this centrality of struggle to his economic and sociological framework Weber embraced the idea of the state as a power-state (*Machtstaat*): International relations like all social relations can only be a struggle between states.

In 1896 Weber accepted a chair at Heidelberg, but he fell ill shortly after the death of his father in 1897 and was forced to withdraw from teaching to seek rest and cure through various convalescent vacations in Italy and Switzerland. He returned eventually to Heidelberg to work in 1902. In 1904–5 he published two articles which became the famous *The Protestant Ethic and the Spirit of Capitalism* (Weber 1930), and he was immediately plunged into controversy over its scientific validity and empirical plausibility (Weber 1978b). The debate about Weber's views on religion and capitalism has generated an enormous literature; in fact, it has proved to be one of the most enduring controversies in modern social science (Marshall 1982; Lehmann and Roth 1993). I shall return to this debate shortly, when I come to discuss Weber's relationship to Marx. It is important to note at this stage that it is unfortunate that the Protestant Ethic thesis is often discussed in isolation from Weber's equally important commentary on American religious sects. The Webers visited America in 1904 when Weber was invited to St Louis for a scientific gathering where he gave a paper on the rural community in Germany past and present. Weber was overwhelmed by New York skyscrapers, mechanized production in Chicago and the general character of mass society as indicators of the future of Western civilization (Roth 1985). It is interesting to compare Weber's sense of horrified, reluctant admiration for American capitalism with de Tocqueville's sombre view of the future of *Democracy in America* (de Tocqueville 1946) of 1835.

In his *Reflections on America* (2005) Claus Offe provides us with an instructive comparison of de Tocqueville, Weber and Adorno in their observations on American civilization. These three social theorists undertook their reflections on America under very different circumstances, motivations and consequences. De Tocqueville (and his companion Gustave de Beaumont) arrived in New York in May 1831 and stayed until February 1832, on the pretext of an official visit to study the penitentiary system in the United States. While de Tocqueville's work is frequently neglected in sociology, the sojourn of Max Weber (and his companion Ernst Troeltsch) to the United States by contrast has been a topic of considerable sociological interest, partly because of his reflections on the Protestant sects and the emergence of a fledgling democracy. Faithfully recorded by Marianne Weber in her biography of 1926, Weber travelled as far afield as Oklahoma and the Indian Territory (Rollman 1993; Scaff 2005). De Tocqueville sought to understand the French Revolution and its descent into Terror by a comparison with the successful revolution in the American War of Independence. Weber, emerging from years of psychological depression, saw a comparison between the ascetic sects of the American frontier society and the European Reformation, a comparison that resulted in 1905 in the *Protestant Ethic and the Spirit of Capitalism*. Despite these obvious differences between de Tocqueville, Adorno and Weber, Offe (2005) discovers a common theme in their work—'the precarious fate of liberty in modern capitalist societies' (p. 2)—which was expressed in terms of the 'tyranny of the majority', 'the iron cage' of dependence, and 'the administered world'.

Weber's commentary on religious sectarianism and business practice was an accurate insight into the peculiar union of secularity and religiosity in American everyday culture. Weber's essay on the American sects—'The Protestant sects and the spirit of capitalism'—appeared as part two of volume one of his collected writings on religion (*Gesammelte Aufsätze zur Religionssoziologie*), but it was excluded from Parsons' translation of the Protestant Ethic thesis. Another important feature of *From Max Weber* is the central focus which is given in general to Weber's sociology of religion, but more specifically to his essay on 'The Protestant sects and the spirit of capitalism' and his 'The social psychology of the world religions'. These two essays are an essential part of Weber's more general interest in religious rationalization as a source of modern culture, specifically economic institutions and values (Freund 1968).

In fact the analysis of the impact of religious life in shaping Western modernity resulted in a number of major studies of comparative religion which have appeared in English as *The Religion of China* (Weber 1951), *Ancient Judaism* (Weber 1952), and *The Religion of India* (Weber 1958). These studies were never fully completed; for example, Weber's comments on Islam are frustratingly brief (Huff and Schluchter 1999; Turner 1974). Nevertheless, they are essential contributions to Weber's analysis of Western rationalization (Tenbruck 1980 and 1986), but his work on the Orient has been subject to considerable criticism (Lehmann and Ouedraogo 2003; Love 2000). However, given the recent transformation of both India and China into powerful capitalist societies, Weber's sociology of Asian civilizations remains both important and relevant.

This great outpouring of Weber's genius was eventually brought to an end with the outbreak of the First World War, which Weber welcomed as 'great and wonderful', despite its ugliness, partly because it presented Germany with political choices which might transform the nation. Although Weber was patriotic and regretted that he was too old to fight, he was against a policy of territorial annexation, German settlement and colonialism. He argued for an autonomous Polish state in the east to protect Germany by offering a buffer to Russian antagonism. In 'Der verscharfte U-Boot Krieg' in 1916 (Weber 1988), he argued against the current offensive, and warned

xxii PREFACE TO THE NEW EDITION

against antagonizing America, whose entry into the war would be a disaster for Germany.

Throughout the war, Weber was especially exercised by the problems of the legacy of Bismarck, the weakness of the German middle classes, the underdevelopment of working-class leadership, the external threat of America, Britain and Russia, the stifling effect of German bureaucracy, and the inadequacies of leadership during the war (as contrasted with the bravery of the average German in the trenches). These concerns were expressed in a number of wartime publications such as in 1918 'Parlament und Regierung in neugeordneten Deutschland' (Weber 1988). These pamphlets should dispel the common notion that Weber's sociology is somewhat remote from practical political concerns.

These themes continued to dominate Weber's sociology after the war when, as professor at Vienna University, following the Russian Revolution of 1917, he gave a famous lecture to Austrian military officers on socialism (Weber 1924). He argued that unlike small-scale and traditional forms of democracy in Greece and Switzerland, modern democracy has to be an administered, and therefore a bureaucratic, democracy. The socialist mass party will in the long run become dominated by a trained administrative class, which will over time cease to be responsible and responsive to the electorate. The planned market would eventually be joined by the planned polity. Although Weber paid tribute to Karl Marx as a social thinker of the first rank, Weber saw that there would be no general collapse of capitalism and that, rather than the 'dictatorship of the proletariat', modern socialism would be the 'dictatorship of administration'.

Weber hoped that in the aftermath of the war the bourgeoisie would be forced into a position of political leadership and that it would become detached from the protective umbrella of the official culture of the administrative classes (the *Obrigkeitsstaat*). Having left Vienna to take up a position in Munich in 1919, Weber started writing about and campaigning for political changes in Germany, especially the creation of a constitutional plebiscitary presidency (Mommsen 1974). Weber was a member of the peace delegation which the German government sent to Versaille to conduct the negotiations for a permanent peace. His attitude towards the peace situation was a reflection of his general political philosophy: Tsarist Russia was the main enemy; the peace conditions were economically unacceptable, because they would destroy Germany as a strong European state; Germany should not accept war-guilt, since the war was essentially a defensive struggle against Russian domination of the eastern regions; and the German defeat was a political betrayal and not a military collapse. Consequently, Weber thought that the peace settlement which was ratified on 16th July 1919 was a disaster. He withdrew finally from politics to lecture on economic sociology at the University of Munich in 1919–20; these lectures were published posthumously (partly from student notes) as the *General Economic History* (Weber 1927). Exhausted and despairing of Germany's future, Weber fell ill and died of pneumonia on 14th June 1920.

INTERPRETING MAX WEBER

The bourgeois Marx

With the publication of Weber's essays on Protestantism and capitalism, and with their translation by Parsons into English in 1930, Weber entered the world of social science as a bourgeois answer to Marx. It was held wrongly that Weber had argued against Marx that the origins of capitalism lay in spiritual values not material causes. In fact, Weber recognized the existence of forms of capitalism in the Catholic cultures of Italy and Spain. He saw that the causes of capitalism were complex and variable: they included modern technology, rational administration, a money economy, market demand, a disciplined labour force and the free political environment which the occidental city had made possible (Holton 1985). Weber was, however, more concerned with how the 'spirit of capitalism' had combined with the this-worldly ascetic ethics of Lutheran and Calvinistic Protestantism to give western capitalism a peculiar and unique characteristic, namely its rational emphasis on calculation and predictability.

As Gerth and Mills pointed out, however, in their introductory comments on Weber's 'intellectual orientations', there were important epistemological, philosophical and methodological differences between Marxism (as it was developing in Germany) as a science of the laws of motion of the capitalist mode of production and Weber's more subtle and complex version of neo-Kantian philosophy of science. In principle, Weber opposed any notion of general laws in social history, remained sceptical even about the value of general concepts, and employed ideal types as limited, heuristic devices for specific tasks. In addition to having a strong sense of the importance of historically contingent events in social change, Weber adopted a flexible approach to the complex interaction of many causes (both material and idealist). In the case of capitalism, Weber was acutely aware of the complex 'elective affinity' between economic arrangements and religious belief, which was a fateful combination (Turner 1981). He criticized Marxists and Christians with an interest in social policy for assuming that law-like predictions about future developments were at all possible. He insisted (inconsistently in practice) on the separation of facts and values, objecting strongly to those professors who used their chairs to preach overtly or covertly specific values. To these important differences, there was an important disagreement between Marx and Weber in terms of their general approach to the question of social stratification, where Weber gave greater prominence to power relations (Holton and Turner 1989; Turner 1988). However, the relationship between Marx's primarily economic analysis of classes and Weber's political analysis of social closure is still contested by scholars (Parkin 1979).

With the revival of 'scientific Marxism' in the form of structural Marxism around the philosophers Louis Althusser, Etienne Balibar and Nicos Poulantzas, there was in the 1960s and 1970s a tendency to see Weber's sociology as an idealist, subjective and ideological reflection on capitalist social relations. By contrast, Marx was seen to have broken with common sense by developing a science of the structures of the mode of production. With the final collapse of the Soviet Union between 1989 and 1992, communist societies also changed significantly, with China and Vietnam developing economic strategies to modernize their economies on capitalist principles. Cuba may also follow in the same direction in a post-Castro era.

The idea of Weber as a critique of Marx has been abandoned in favour of stressing the importance of Weber as an economic sociologist. Towards the end of his life, Weber joined the University of Vienna and taught a course on 'Economy and Society' in the summer of 1918, becoming friendly at the time with Ludwig von Mises. Later at the University of Munich in 1919, Weber accepted a chair that was given the title 'social science, economic history and economics'. Although there is some recognition of Weber as a 'social economist',

Richard Swedberg (1998) has argued convincingly that Weber's general interest in economics has typically been ignored by commentators who focus narrowly on Weber's economic history, such as his studies of Protestantism and capitalism.

The rigid separation between Marx and Weber is therefore no longer accepted in contemporary scholarship. There is by contrast a tendency to see both Marx and Weber as critical analysts of capitalism as a version of the more general phenomenon of modernity, since both were impressed by the dynamic capacity of capitalism to liquidate all historical and traditional certainties.

The rationalization theme

Against this bifurcation of social science around Weber versus Marx, there are equally strong reasons for identifying important convergences between Marx and Weber. The argument of Gerth and Mills about the parallels between Marx and Weber was thus a useful corrective to the tendency in radical social theory to separate them in order to emphasize the notion that sociology was ideology when contrasted with the scientific basis of socialism. One important component in their presentation of Weber was the attention given to Weber's views on militarism. Modern sociology has often been criticized for its failure to develop an adequate military sociology—its neglect of the impact of warfare on social change (Giddens 1984). This accusation could not include the historical sociology of Weber. For example, Weber was particularly concerned to understand the interaction between changes in military technology, military organization and political structures. He saw the rise of modern citizenship as in part a consequence of the democratic implications of a mass infantry. Similarly, he contrasted the social impact of cavalry on the plains of Europe with the dependence of Asiatic armies on the foot-soldier. Weber has been criticized by modern historians for assuming that the emergence of state armies is an inevitable rationalization of military force and they have drawn attention to 'new wars' that are essentially conducted by mercenaries in the employ of warlords exploiting new opportunities for the global trade in drugs, guns and prostitutes (Munkler 2005).

This aspect of Weber's sociology permits one to argue that, whereas Marx was concerned to understand the monopoly of economic power in society, Weber drew attention to alternative monopolies. First, he was concerned with how the means of military violence were socially organized and distributed. Second, he looked at the institutionalism of spiritual powers in his religious sociology (Prades 1966). It was for these reasons that Weber defined the state as an institution which enjoyed a monopoly of legitimate force, and the church as an institution which sought a monopoly of spiritual power.

By arguing that Weber wanted to understand the institution of social closure (that is, how monopolies over scarce resources of wealth, spirituality and violence were constituted), we can get a better understanding of Weber's analysis of western history as the development of rationalization. By this process, Weber wanted to indicate the growing importance of rational science (instrumental rationality) in everyday life, and hence the corresponding disenchantment of the world and the erosion of religious powers. This secularization also involved the increasing dominance of the expert and professional knowledge, and the corresponding decline of charismatic authorities. These changes also required the specialization of tasks, and the growth in the division of labour. These bureaucratic changes in the organization of society were also associated with the separation of the worker from the means of production, the separation of the office worker from the means of mental production, and the alienation of the intellectual from control over the university. I have deliberately employed a Marxist terminology of alienation of workers from the means of production (both material and mental) to illustrate a convergence of Marx and Weber around the twin notions of rationalization (as disenchantment, specialization and powerlessness in the face of bureaucratic management) and alienation (as division, specialization and separation).

Both Marx and Weber responded to capitalism in the same mixture of horror and admiration. Capitalism for Marx destroyed the stagnation of traditional society and undermined what he referred to as the 'idiocy' of village and peasant life. It pushed humanity along the road of modernization, but at an enormous cost in terms of individual and collective suffering. One aspect of this suffering was alienation and dehumanization. Capitalism for Weber destroyed the securities of belief (the garden of enchantment) and disrupted the 'natural' rhythms of pre-modern means of production and consumption in the traditional household. Rationalization destroyed the authority of magical powers, but it also brought into being the machine-like regulation of bureaucracy, which ultimately challenges all systems of belief. The paradoxical outcome of rationalization was a world in which systems of meaning could no longer find any secure authority. Rational norms of authority are incompatible with charismatic and traditional powers. This relationship between alienation in Marx's analysis of capitalism and Weber's theme of rationalization as modernization was brilliantly developed in Karl Löwith's *Marx and Weber* (Löwith 1982) which was originally published in 1932 and which remains one of the most provocative and sensitive studies of the relationship between Marx and Weber. I shall return shortly to the question about rationality as Weber's central question (Hennis 1988).

Nietzsche and Weber

It is reported that in a discussion with Oswald Spengler in February 1920 Weber said that the moral stature and honesty of a present-day scholar might be measured by their attitudes towards Nietzsche and Marx (Baumgarten 1964: 554ff). It appears that Weber was especially influenced by Nietzsche from around 1892 onwards, and that the language of his Inaugural Address at Freiburg is shot through with images from Nietzsche's *Untimely Meditations* (Hennis 1988: 146–51). Again it is an indication of the sophistication of Gerth and Mills' approach to Weber that they clearly recognized Nietzsche's influence on Weber's sociology of religion and on his commentary on moral systems in terms of a theory of resentment. Although the influence of Nietzsche on Weber's sociology is now widely recognized (Fleischmann 1964; Baier 1982; Eden 1983; Hennis 1988; Stauth and Turner 1988) this Nietzschean influence was for a long time either neglected or denied. While this Nietzschean dimension to Weberian sociology is now generally accepted, the nature of that intellectual and moral relationship is still a matter of dispute.

In the Inaugural Address Weber appears to be responding to the emphasis on struggle and conflict in Nietzsche's view of the human condition. In particular, Weber's reference to the struggle for elbow-room as a motor of human history indicates Nietzsche's uncompromising view of human relations as relations of power. Thus in very general terms, it may be possible to read Weber as a 'sociologizing' of Nietzsche's notion of the will-to-power. It has been suggested often enough that Weber's ideas on charismatic leadership appear to represent a sociological version of Nietzsche's ideas about the historical functions of the Overman, who stands out against the herd-morality of the people. Furthermore, it may be that Weber's view on state-power and the problems of political leadership in the revaluation of values reflects the influence of Nietzsche (Turner 1982). It is also important to note that Nietzsche's account of the implications of the death of God significantly influenced Weber's view of the plurality of beliefs (which he described as polytheism) in his lecture on 'science as a vocation'.

These interpretations of Weber and Nietzsche are, however, ultimately unsatisfactory. The deeper impact of Nietzsche is in the area of morality, and of the possibility of a 'Science of Man' (Hennis 1988: 107ff). Weber's understanding of asceticism as simultaneously the basis of our modern civilization and as the necessary denial of our ontology (which is the psychological and culture cost of the idea of vocation in both lectures on science and politics) is a theme which was central to Nietzsche's contrast between Apollo and Dionysus. The ontology of human beings ('human nature') is thus seen to be, in some sense, out of joint with the cultural and social requirements of a modern civilization; indeed our human nature has to be suppressed by the sociological requirements of an industrial civilization. This argument was an important component of Nietzsche's philosophy, and we can also detect this influence in Weber and Freud. Although Weber publicly chose 'discipline' as some sort of solution for the life of an academic or politician, this discipline is seen to be ultimately life-denying (to use Nietzsche's terminology). It now appears that Weber's central questions involved an anthropological inquiry into human nature and into how our ontology is the product of certain 'life-orders' (Hennis 1988). Parsons' presentation of Weber as a value-free sociologist of social action is now increasingly challenged by the view that Weber's work in fact belongs to a long tradition of German philosophical anthropology. In the twentieth century, the sociology of Arnold Gehlen has been one of the most significant contributions to this German tradition (Berger and Kellner 1965).

To see Weber in this light, however, opens up a new area of inquiry. If Weber is to be viewed as a philosophical anthropologist of the life-orders which produce certain types of personality, what is Weber's relationship to the romantic wing of anti-capitalist German poets and artists who also drew upon an anthropological tradition which had its roots in Nietzsche? In specific terms, what was Weber's relationship to the cultural critics who gathered around Stefan George at Heidelberg, such as Friedrich Gundolf and Ludwig Klages? These prophetic poets occasionally assembled at Weber's famous afternoon discussions. While the ideas of the symbolist poetry of the George Circle are typically seen to be in opposition to Weber's sociology (as for example in Karl Mannheim's 'letter from Heidelberg'), Weber's notion that the ascetic life-order is ultimately destructive of Life may not be so far removed from Klages' notions about the cosmic forces of love, or the discord between consciousness and spirit in his monumental *Der Geist als Widersacher der Seele* (Klages 1929–32). In short, while Weber is often characterized as a 'liberal in despair' (Mommsen 1974), if we pursue Hennis' thesis to its logical conclusion, it also makes sense to ask, not whether Weber was a philosophical anthropologist of despair, but whether he was a conservative cultural critic of the life-orders of capitalism?

Hennis' diagnosis of Weber's texts is correct in one essential feature. To continue with the question about Weber's explanations of 'the origins of capitalism' (Giddens 1971) now appears to be a limited and out-dated exercise. Weber's own view of his work (namely to under-stand the characteristic uniqueness of our times) can probably be best appreciated as a quest after the nature of modernity. Weber's interests in rational law, administration, military technology, religious ethics and so forth can be seen in a broader context as a set of investigations into the peculiarities of modernity and in particular its fateful or even demonic properties.

Weber's attitude towards modernity was, as we have noted already, ambiguous. Like Marx, Weber believed that in capitalistic modernity 'All that is solid melts into air' (Berman 1982). Modernization disrupts the traditional order and the ideology by which traditional authorities made the world intelligible and legitimate. Modernity questions everything and measures everything against a unitary principle of rationality.

But Weber recognized that this questioning of reality by reason was ultimately self-defeating and self-destructive. Rationality began to question its own horizons, recognizing its self-limitation. How can reason be rationally justified? Are there many forms of reason? These questions had their origins in Nietzsche's probing of language, knowledge and power. As we have seen, these questions increasingly haunted Weber's sociology, finding their most condensed expression in the science as a vocation lecture.

We can now see that Weber's anthropological analysis of the life-orders that produced modern Man (in the generic sense) in the production of a rationalized social system in many respects anticipated the contemporary debate between modernists and postmodernists (Holton and Turner 1989). In particular, Weber's anxieties and uncertainties about the moral (and indeed spiritual) significance of modernity have been reproduced in our uncertainties about what sort of 'reality' might lie beyond modernity. Weber of course was at least clear in his own mind about one thing, namely that the world beyond modernity promised to be especially terrible. He once despairingly said, 'the future will be an icy night of polar darkness'. Weber's profound probing of the edges of that dark world is one reason why his sociology continues to fascinate each new generation of scholars.

CONCLUSION: GLOBAL CAPITALISM

There is now a generally accepted view that capitalism has, since the death of Weber, been radically transformed by the rise of a consumer society, the collapse of organized socialism as an alternative to capitalism, and by the globalization of society. The combined effect of these transformations of modernity has been to produce a post-Fordist social system, which is based on post-industrial means of production including the complete dependence on new information systems. Weber's rational capitalism has evolved into a 'network society' (Castells 1996). The resulting changes to social structure have been significant, such as the decline of the politics of social class, the end of ideology, the switch to consumerism over production, the rise of the global city, and the centrality of information and communication systems to modern life. Capitalist society has in short been radically transformed by globalization. There is also the view that the dominance of the secularization thesis that modernization inevitably produced the secularization of society has to be radically questioned given the obvious vitality of religion in modern societies (Taylor 2007). Many sociologists have as a result questioned the relevance of classical sociology to understanding the globalization of the social world (Urry 2000).

With the dramatic collapse of the Berlin Wall, there was an atmos-phere of euphoria in Western social philosophy, giving rise to debates about the peace dividend, the globalization of culture, the possibilities for cosmopolitanism and the end of history. In this post-communist period, Weber's pessimism appeared to be inappropriate. There was also a view that the nation state was in decline and that the growth of porous boundaries meant that sociology's focus on 'society' was increasingly obsolete. However, with the 9/11 crisis and the war on terror, there has been a renewed interest in the state, securitization and the emergence of an 'enclave society' (Turner 2007). The analysis of the demise of the state and nationalism is now held to be premature (Calhoun 2007). In global terms, the food crisis and the dramatic rise in energy costs are associated with a drift towards authoritarian politics in many societies, and Weber's analysis of Russia now looks more rather than less accurate. The crisis in the global financial system, the pressure of food and energy costs, and the emergence of new security systems all point to the continuing relevance of Weber's world view in general and his concentration on power struggles in particular. The Gerth and Mills collection therefore remains a masterly summary of Weber's political vision and the conceptual tools that Weber assembled to study the modern world.

xxxii

REFERENCES

Baehr, Peter and Wells, Gordon (eds) (2002) *The Protestant Ethic and the 'Spirit' of Capitalism and Other Writings*, Harmondsworth: Penguin.

Baier, H. (1982) 'Die Gesellschaft—ein langer Schatten des toten Gottes', *Nietzsche Studien* 10–11: 22.

Baumgarten, Eduard (1964) *Max Weber, Werk und Person*, Tübingen: Mohr.

Bendix, Rheinhard (1960) *Max Weber, An Intellectual Portrait*, London: Heinemann.

Berger, Peter L. and Kellner, Hans (1965) 'Arnold Gehlen and the theory of institutions', *Social Research* 32: 110–15.

Berman, Harold and Reid, Charles J. Jr. (2000) 'Max Weber as legal historian' in Stephen Turner (ed.) *The Cambridge Companion to Weber*, Cambridge: Cambridge University Press, pp. 223–39.

Berman, Marshall (1982) *All That is Solid Melts into Air: the experience of modernity*, London: Verso.

Brewer, John D. (2004) 'Imagining the Sociological Imagination: the biographical context of a sociological classic', *British Journal of Sociology* 55(3): 317–33.

Calhoun, Craig (2007) *Nations Matter. Culture, History and the Cosmopolitan Dream*, London and New York: Routledge.

Castells, Manuel (1996) *The Rise of the Network Society*, Oxford: Blackwell.

Eden, Robert (1983) *Political Leadership and Nihilism: a study of Weber and Nietzsche*, Tampa: University Presses of Florida.

Eliaeson, Sven (2000) 'Constitutional Caesarism: Weber's politics in their German context' in Stephen Turner (ed) *The Cambridge Companion to Weber*, Cambridge: Cambridge University Press, pp. 131–50.

Fleischmann, Eugene (1964) 'De Weber à Nietzsche', *Archives Européenes de Sociologie* 5: 190–238.

Freund, Julien (1968) *The Sociology of Max Weber*, London: Faber,

Gall, Lothar (1986) *Bismarck, the White Revolutionary, volume 2, 1871–1898*, London: Allen & Unwin.

Gerth, Hans and Mills, Charles Wright (1948) *From Max Weber: essays in sociology*, London: Routledge & Kegan Paul.

—— (1953) *Character and Social Structure: the psychology of social institutions*, New York: Harcourt Brace.

Giddens, A. (1971) *Capitalism and Modern Social Theory*, Cambridge: Cambridge University Press.

— (1984) *The Constitution of Society*, Cambridge: Polity Press.

Green, Martin (1974) *The von Richthofen Sisters. The Triumphant and the Tragic Modes of Love*, New York: Basic Books.

Hennis, Wilhelm (1988) *Max Weber: essays in reconstruction*, London: Allen & Unwin.

Hollingdale, R.J. (1973) *Nietzsche*, London: Routledge & Kegan Paul.

Holton, Robert J. (1985) *The Transition from Feudalism to Capitalism*, London: Macmillan.

Holton, Robert J. and Turner, Bryan S. (1989) *Max Weber on Economy and Society*, London: Routledge.

Honingsheim, Paul (1968) *On Max Weber*, New York: Free Press.

Huff, Toby E. and Schluchter, Wolfgang (eds) (1999) *Max Weber & Islam*, New Brunswick and London: Transaction Publishers.

Kalberg, Stephen (2002) *The Protestant Ethic and the Spirit of Capitalism*, Los Angeles: Roxbury (third Roxbury edition).

Käsler, Dirk (1988) *Max Weber, an Introduction to His Life and Work*, Cambridge: Polity Press.

Klages, Ludwig (1929–32) *Der Geist als Widersacher der Seele*, Bonn: Bouvier.

Kronman, Anthony T. (1983) *Max Weber*, London: Edward Arnold.

Lassman, Peter and Velody, Irvine (eds) (1989) *Max Weber's 'Science as a vocation'*, London: Unwin Hyman.

Lehmann, Hartmut and Roth, Guenther (eds) (1993) *Weber's Protestant Ethic. Origins, Evidence, Contexts*, Cambridge: Cambridge University Press.

Lehmann, Hartmut and Ouedraogo, Jean Martin (eds) (2003) *Max Webers Religionssoziologie in interkultureller Perspektive*, Göttingen: Vandenhoeck and Ruprecht.

Lepenies, Wolf (1985) *Die Drei Kulturen, Soziologie zwischen Literatur und Wissenschaft*, München: Carl Hanser.

Love, John (2000) 'Max Weber's Orient', in Stephen Turner (ed) *The Cambridge Companion to Weber*, Cambridge: Cambridge University Press, pp. 172–99.

Löwith, Karl (1982) *Karl Marx and Max Weber*, London: Allen & Unwin.

Marshall, Gordon (1982) *In Search of the Spirit of Capitalism*, London: Hutchinson.

Mayer, J.P. (1944) *Max Weber and German Politics: a study in political sociology*, London: Faber.

Megill, Allan (1985) *Prophets of Extremity: Nietzsche, Heidegger, Foucault, Derrida*, Berkeley: University of California Press.

Mills, C. Wright (1956) *The Power Elite*, New York: Oxford University Press.

— (1959) *The Sociological Imagination*, New York: Oxford University Press.

Mills, Kathryn with Mills, Pamela (eds) (2000) *C. Wright Mills. Letters and Autobiographical Writings*, Berkeley: University of California Press.

Mitzman, Arthur (1971) *The Iron Cage: a historical interpretation of Max Weber*, New York: The University Library.

Mommsen, Wolfgang J. (1974) *The Age of Bureaucracy: perspectives on the political sociology of Max Weber*, Oxford: Basil Blackwell.

Mommsen, Wolfgang J. and Osterhammel, Jurgen (eds) (1987) *Max Weber and his Contemporaries*, London: Allen & Unwin.

Munkler, Herfried (2005) *The New Wars*, Cambridge: Polity Press.

Offe, Claus (2005) *Reflections on America. Tocqueville, Weber and Adorno*, Cambridge: Polity.

Parkin, Frank (1979) *Marxists and Class Theory: a bourgeois critique*, London: Tavistock.

Parsons, Talcott (1947) *Max Weber. The Theory of Social and Economic Organization*, Oxford: Oxford University Press.

— (1951) *The Social System*, New York: Free Press.

— (1971) 'Value-freedom and objectivity', in Otto Stammer (ed) *Max Weber and Sociology Today*, Oxford: Basil Blackwell, pp. 27–50.

Prades, J.A. (1966) *La sociologic de la religion chez Max Weber, essai d'analyse et decritique de la methode*, Paris: Editions Nauwelaerts.

Rheinstein, Max (1954) *Max Weber on Law in Economy and Society*, Cambridge, Mass.: Harvard University Press.

Rollmann, Hans (1993) '"Meet Me in St.Louis": Troeltsch and Weber in America', in H. Lehmann and G. Roth (eds) *Weber's Protestant Ethic. Origins, Evidence, Contexts*, Cambridge : Cambridge University Press, pp. 357–83.

Roth, Guenther (1985) 'Marx and Weber on the United States Today', in R.J. Antonio and K.M. Glassman (eds) A *Weber–Marx Dialogue*, Lawrence, Kansas: University Press of Kansas, pp. 215–33.

— and Schluchter, W. (1979) *Max Weber's Vision of History, Ethics and Method*, Berkeley: University of California Press.

Runciman, W.G. (1978) *Max Weber Selections in Translation*, Cambridge; Cambridge University Press.

Scaff, Lawrence A. (2005) 'Remnants of Romanticism: Max Weber in Oklahoma and Indiana', *Journal of Classical Sociology* 5(1): 53–72.

Schapiro, Meyer (1945) 'A Note on Max Weber's Politics' *Politics* 2(2): 44–48.

Shils, Edward (1976) *Max Weber on Universities. The Power of the State and Dignity of the Academic Calling in Imperial Germany*, Chicago: University of Chicago Press.

Stauth, Georg and Turner, Bryan S. (1988) *Nietzsche's Dance. Resentment, reciprocity and resistance in social life*, Oxford: Basil Blackwell.

Swedberg, Richard (1998) *Max Weber and the Idea of Economic Sociology*, Princeton, New Jersey: Princeton University Press.

Taylor, Charles (2007) *A Secular Age*, Cambridge, Mass.: The Belknap Press of Harvard University Press.

Tenbruck, Friedrich H. (1980) 'The problem of the thematic unity in the works of Max Weber', *British Journal of Sociology*, 31: 316–51.

— (1986) 'Das Werk Max Webers. Methodologie und Sozialwissenschaften', *Kölner Zeitschrift fur Soziologie und Sozialpsychologie* 38: 13–31.

Tocqueville, Alexis de (1946) *Democracy in America*, London: Oxford University Press.

Troeltsch, Ernst (1912) *The Social Teaching of the Christian Churches*, New York: Macmillan (1931).

Turner, Bryan S. (1974) *Weber and Islam, a critical study*, London: Routledge & Kegan Paul.

— (1981) *For Max Weber: essays on the sociology of fate*, London: Routledge & Kegan Paul.

— (1982) 'Nietzsche, Weber and the devaluation of politics: the problem of state legitimacy', *Sociological Review* 30: 367–91.

— (1987) 'The rationalization of the body: reflections on modernity and discipline', in Scott Lash and Sam Whimster (eds) *Max Weber, Rationality and Modernity*, London: Allen & Unwin.

— (1988) 'Classical sociology and its legacy', *Sociological Review* 36(1): 146–57.

— (ed.) (1999) *Max Weber. Critical Responses*, London and New York: Routledge, 3 volumes.

— (2007) 'The Enclave Society: towards a sociology of immobility', *European Journal of Social Theory* 10(2): 287–303.

Turner, Stephen and Factor, Regis A. (1984) *Max Weber and the Dispute over Reason and Value: a study in philosophy, ethics and politics*, London: Routledge & Kegan Paul.

Urry, John (2000) 'Mobile sociology', *British Journal of Sociology* 51(1): 185–203.

Weber, Marianne (1926) *Max Weber. Ein Lebensbild*, Tübingen: Mohr.

— (1975) *Max Weber, a biography*, New York: John Wiley.

Weber, Max (1924) 'Socialism', in *Gesammelte Aufsätze zur Soziologie und Sozialpolitik, Tübingen*: Mohr: 492–518; and translated in W.G. Runciman (1978) *Max Weber, Selections in Translation*, Cambridge: Cambridge University Press, pp. 251–62.

— (1927) *General Economic History*, New York: Collier, 1961.

— (1930) *The Protestant Ethic and the Spirit of Capitalism*, London: Allen & Unwin.

— (1936) *Jugendbriefe*, Tübingen: Mohr.

— (1951) *The Religion of China*, New York: Macmillan.

— (1952) *Ancient Judaism*, New York: Free Press.

— (1958) *The Religion of India*, New York: Free Press.

— (1966) *The City*, New York: Free Press.

— (1978a) *Economy and Society*, Berkeley: University of California Press, 2 vols.

— (1978b) 'Anticritical Last Word on The Spirit of Capitalism', *American Journal of Sociology*, 83(5): 1105–31.

— (1988) *Gesammelte Politische Schriften*, Tübingen: Mohr.

Introduction

THE MAN AND HIS WORK

I. A Biographical View

Max Weber was born in Erfurt, Thuringia, on 21 April 1864. His father, Max Weber, Sr., a trained jurist and municipal counselor, came from a family of linen merchants and textile manufacturers of western Germany. In 1869 the Webers moved to Berlin, which was soon to become the booming capital of Bismarck's Reich. There, Weber, Sr. became a prosperous politician, active in the municipal diet of Berlin, the Prussian diet, and the new Reichstag. He belonged to the right-wing liberals led by the Hanoverian noble, Bennigsen. The family resided in Charlottenburg, then a west-end suburb of Berlin, where academic and political notables were neighbors. In his father's house young Weber came to know such men as Dilthey, Mommsen, Julian Schmidt, Sybel, Treitschke, and Friedrich Kapp.

Max Weber's mother, Helene Fallenstein Weber, was a cultured and liberal woman of Protestant faith. Various members of her Thuringian family were teachers and small officials. Her father, however, had been a well-to-do official who, on the eve of the 1848 revolution, had retired to a villa in Heidelberg. Gervinus, the eminent liberal historian and a close friend of her family, had tutored her in the several humanist subjects. Until she died, in 1919, Max Weber corresponded with her in long, intimate, and often learned letters. In Berlin Helene Weber became an overburdened *Hausfrau,* faithfully caring for the busy politician, the six children, and a constant circle of friends. Two of her children had died in infancy. The misery of the industrial classes of Berlin impressed her deeply. Her husband neither understood nor shared her religious and humanitarian concerns. He probably did not share her emotional life and certainly the two differed in their feelings about many public questions. During Max's youth and early manhood his parents' relations were increasingly estranged.

The intellectual companions of the household and the extensive travels of the family made the precocious young Weber dissatisfied with the

3

routine instruction of the schools. He was a weakly child, who suffered meningitis at the age of 4; he preferred books to sports and in early adolescence he read widely and developed intellectual interests of his own. At the age of 13 he wrote historical essays, one of which he called, 'Concerning the Course of German History, with Special Regard to the Positions of Kaiser and Pope.' Another was 'Dedicated to My Own Insignificant Ego as well as to Parents and Siblings.' At fifteen he was reading as a student reads, taking extensive notes. He seemed to have been preoccupied from an early age with the balanced and qualified statement. Criticizing the rather low tastes of his classmates, who, instead of Scott's historical novels, read contemporary trash, he was careful to add: 'Perhaps it sounds presumptuous if I maintain this position, since I am one of the youngest fellows in my class; however, this circumstance strikes one's eyes so sharply that I need not fear that I am not speaking the truth if I state it in this manner. Of course, there are always exceptions.' He appeared to be lacking also in any profound respect for his teachers. Since he was quite ready to share his knowledge with his schoolmates during examinations, they found him likeable and something of a 'phenomenon.'

Young Weber, 'a politician's son in the age of Bismarck's *Realpolitik*,' dismissed the universal literary appraisal of Cicero as bunk. In his eyes, Cicero, especially in his first Catilinarian speech, was a dilettante of phrases, a poor politician, and an irresponsible speaker. Putting himself in Cicero's shoes, he asked himself what good could these long-winded speeches accomplish? He felt Cicero ought to have 'bumped off' (*abmurksen*) Catiline and squelched the threatening conspiracy by force. After detailed arguments, he ended a letter to a cousin: 'In short, I find the speech very weak and without purpose, the whole policy vacillating with regard to its ends. I find Cicero without appropriate resolve and energy, without skill, and without the ability to bide his time.' The older correspondent, a student in Berlin University, responded by intimating that young Weber was parroting books he had read. In self-defense Weber replied sharply but with dignity:

What you have written sounds as if you believe I had copied from some book, or at least that I had rendered the substance of something I had read. After all, that is, in a nutshell, the meaning of your long lecture. You seek to bring out this point in a form as little concrete as possible because you entertain the opinion that I would mind an opinion which, so far as I myself know, is not true. Though I have summoned all knowledge of myself,

I have not been able to admit that I have let myself be swayed too much by any one book or by any phrase from the mouth of my teachers. . . To be sure . . . we younger ones profit in general from treasures that you seniors, and I consider you as one of them, have garnered. . . . I admit that probably everything indirectly stems from books, for what are books for except to enlighten and instruct man about things that are unclear to him? It is possible that I am very sensitive to books, their comments and deductions. This you can judge better than I, for in certain respects it is easier to know someone else than oneself. Yet, the content of my—perhaps completely untrue—statement does not come directly from any book. For the rest, I do not mind your criticism, as quite similar things are to be found in Mommsen, as I have only now discovered.[1]

Young Weber's mother read her son's letters without his knowledge. She was greatly concerned that she and her son were becoming intellectually estranged. It is not strange that a sincere and intelligent adolescent, aware of the difficulties between his parents and observing the characteristic ruses of a Victorian patriarchal family, learned that words and actions should not be taken at their face value. He came to feel that if one wanted to get at the truth, direct and first-hand knowledge was necessary. Thus when he was sent to 'confirmation' lessons, he learned enough Hebrew to get at the original text of the Old Testament.

Frau Weber worried about her son's religious indifference. She wrote:

The closer Max's confirmation approaches, the less can I see that he feels any of the deeper stimulating influence in this period of his development which would make him think about what he is asked to enunciate before the altar as his own conviction. The other day, when we were sitting alone, I tried to get out of him what he thinks and feels about the main questions of Christian consciousness. He seemed quite astonished that I should presuppose that the self-clarification of such questions as the belief in immortality and the Benevolence guiding our fate should result from confirmation lessons for every thinking man. I felt these things with great warmth in my innermost being—independent of any dogmatic form, they had become the most vital conviction . . . [yet] it was impossible for me to express it to my own child in such a way that it would make any impression on him.[2]

With this profound and personal piety, Helene Weber suffered under the worldliness of her external family life. Nevertheless, she lovingly resigned herself to the somewhat complacent, self-righteous, and patriarchial atmosphere created by her husband. As an adolescent, Weber had less and less of a common ground with his mother in serious mat-

ters. It was not that he was drawn to his father: the worldly atmosphere
of modern intellectual life drew Weber away from the philistinism of his
father as well as from the piety of his mother.

Although respectful, he rebelled against the authority of his elders.
Yet, rather than take part in the 'frivolous' pursuits of his classmates,
the boredom of school routine, and the intellectual insignificance of his
teachers, he withdrew into his own world. Such a boy would not submit to the impositions of his father. The thoughtless manner in which
his father used his wife did not escape the discerning eye of the seventeen-year-old boy. At one point, on a journey to Italy with his father,
he was admonished for not living up to the appropriate degree of stereotyped tourist enthusiasm. Max simply declared his intention of returning
home, at once and alone.

The confirmation motto that Weber received was: 'The Lord is the
spirit, but where the Lord's spirit is, there also is freedom.' Max Weber's
widow in her biography comments: 'Hardly any other Biblical motto
could better express the law governing this child's life.'

2

Weber's pre-university schooling came to an end in the spring of 1882.
Possessed of exceptional talent, he had had no need to 'strain.' His teachers, however, attested to his lack of routine industry and doubted his
'moral maturity.' Like many nineteenth-century thinkers, he made a
rather unfavorable impression upon his teachers. The seventeen-year-old,
stringy young man with sloping shoulders still appeared wanting in
appropriate respect for authority.

He went to Heidelberg and, following in the steps of his father, enrolled as a student of law. He also studied a variety of cultural subjects,
including history, economics, and philosophy, which at Heidelberg were
taught by eminent scholars. He accepted provisional membership in his
father's dueling fraternity, the father's influence thus bringing him into
such circles. From the mother's side, through an older cousin who was
studying theology, a son of the Strassburg historian Baumgarten, he participated in the theological and philosophical controversies of the day.

He began his daily routine at Heidelberg by rising early to attend a
lecture in logic. Then he 'fiddled around' in the dueling hall for an
hour. He sat through his lectures 'in a studious way,' went to lunch at
12:30, 'for one mark'; occasionally he had a quarter of a litre of wine or

beer with his meal. Frequently, for two hours in the early afternoon he played a 'solid game of cards.' Then he retreated to his rooms, went over his lecture notes, and read such books as Strauss' *The Old and the New Belief.* 'Sometimes in the afternoon I go with friends to the mountains and walk, and in the evening we meet again at the restaurant and have a quite good supper for 80 pfennig. I read Lotze's *Microcosm,* and we get into heated argument about it.'[3] Occasionally, invitations to the homes of professors gave him an opportunity to imitate the characteristic peculiarities of people known to the group.

During subsequent semesters, Weber joined heartily in the social life of the dueling fraternity, and he learned to hold his own in drinking bouts as well as duels. Soon his face carried the conventional dueling scar. He fell into debt and remained so during his Heidelberg years. The student and patriotic songs he learned during this period lingered in his memory throughout the course of his life. The stringy youth grew into the robust man, broad-shouldered and rather stout. When he visited his mother in Berlin, now a man with the external characteristics of Imperial Germany, his mother was shocked at his appearance and received him with a slap in the face.

Looking back upon his Heidelberg years, Weber wrote: 'The usual training for haughty aggression in the dueling fraternity and as an officer has undoubtedly had a strong influence upon me. It removed the shyness and insecurity of my adolescence.'[4]

After three semesters at Heidelberg, at the age of 19 Weber moved to Strassburg in order to serve his year in the army. Apart from dueling, he had never done any physical exercise, and the military service with its drill was difficult for him. In addition to the physical strain, he suffered greatly under the stupidity of barrack drill and the chicanery of subaltern officers. He did not like to give up his intellectual pursuits:

When I come home I usually go to bed around nine o'clock. However, I cannot fall asleep, as my eyes are not tired and the intellectual side of man is not being utilized. The feeling, which begins in the morning and increases toward the end of the day, of sinking slowly into the night of abysmal stupidity is actually the most disagreeable thing of all.[5]

Weber adjusted to this feeling by having his fill of alcohol in the evening and going through the military routine the next day in the daze of a moderate hangover. Then he felt 'that the hours fly away because nothing, not a single thought, stirs under my skull.' Although

he finally built up his endurance and met most of the physical demands
quite well, he never measured up to the gymnastic acrobatics. Once
a sergeant shouted at him, in Berlin dialect: 'Man, you look like a barrel
of beer swinging on a trapeze.' He made up for this deficiency by per-
fecting his marching endurance and his goosestep. At no time did he
cease to rebel against the

incredible waste of time required to domesticate thinking beings into machines responding to commands with automatic precision. . . One is supposed to learn patience by observing for an hour each day all sorts of senseless things which are called military education. As if, my God! after three
months of the manual of arms for hours every day and the innumerable insults of the most miserable scoundrels, one could ever be suspected of
suffering from lack of patience. The officer candidate is supposed to be deprived of the possibility of using his mind during the period of military
training.[6]

Yet Weber was quite objective; he admitted that the body works
more precisely when all thinking is eliminated. And after he received
his officer's commission, he quickly learned to see the brighter side of
army life. He was well esteemed by his superior officers, and contributed
tall stories and a keen sense of humor to the comradeship of the officers'
mess; and, as one capable of command, he won the respect of the men
under him.

The military year was over in 1884 and at the age of 20 Weber resumed his university studies in Berlin and Goettingen, where, two years
later, he took his first examination in law. But during the summer of
1885 and again in 1887 he returned to Strassburg for military exercises.
And in 1888 he participated in military maneuvers in Posen. There he
felt at close range the atmosphere of the German-Slavonic border, which
seemed to him a 'cultural' frontier. His discussion of Channing, in a letter
addressed to his mother, is characteristic of his thinking at this time.

Channing had made a deep impression upon him, but Weber could
not go along with his ethical absolutism and pacifism. 'I simply cannot
see what moral elevation will result from placing military professionals
on a footing with a gang of murderers and holding them up for public
disdain. War would not thereby gain in humaneness.' Characteristically,
Weber does not enter into a theological dispute about the Sermon on the
Mount; he keeps at a distance from Channing by locating his perspective
in the social and historical situation; he tries thereby to 'understand' and,
at the same time, he relativizes Channing's position. 'Channing obviously

has no idea of such matters [war and desertion]. He has in mind the conditions of American enlisted armies with which the predatory wars of the democratic American federal Government against Mexico etc. have been fought.'[7] The arguments indicate, *in nuce,* the position that Weber later argues, in the last section of *Politics as a Vocation* and in the discussion of religion and politics in *Religious Rejections of the World.*[8]

It is characteristic of Weber's way of life that in Strassburg his main social experience remained within his family situation. Two of his mother's sisters were married to Strassburg professors; and Weber found friendship and intellectual discourse as well as profound emotional experience in their houses. Some of the Baumgarten family were exceptionally prone to mystical and religious experiences, and young Weber participated with great sympathy in the tensions that these experiences occasioned. He became the confidant of almost everyone concerned, learning to appreciate and sympathize with their respective values. He spoke of himself as 'Ich Weltmensch' and tried to find a workable solution for the several persons involved. And for Weber this meant going beyond ethical absolutism: 'The matter does not appear to me to be so desperate if one does not ask too exclusively (as the Baumgartens, now as often, do): "Who is morally right and who is morally wrong?" But if one rather asks: "Given the existing conflict, how can I solve it with the least internal and external damage for all concerned?"'[9] Weber thus suggested a pragmatic view, a focus on the consequences of various decisions rather than on the stubborn insistence upon the introspective awareness of one's intense sincerity. His early letters and the experiences at Strassburg clearly point to his later distinction between an ethic of responsibility and an ethic of absolute ends.

Weber concluded his studies and took up service in the law courts of Berlin, in which city he lived with his parents. In the early 'eighties, he settled down, a diligent student of law, in the lecture rooms of the eminent jurists of the time. Among them, he admired Gneist, whose lectures directed his attention to current political problems. 'I find his lectures true masterpieces; really, I have wondered about his manner of directly entering questions of politics and about the way he develops strictly liberal views without becoming a propagandist, which Treitschke does become in his lectures on state and church.'[10]

Weber concentrated upon a field in which economic and legal history overlapped. He wrote his Ph.D. thesis on the history of trading companies during the Middle Ages (1889), examining hundreds of Italian and Spanish references and learning both languages in order to do so. In 1890 he passed his second examination in law. He habilitated himself in Berlin for commercial, German, and Roman law with a treatise on what Marx once called 'the secret history of the Romans,' namely, *The History of Agrarian Institutions* (1891). The modest title actually covers a sociological, economic, and cultural analysis of ancient society, a theme to which Weber repeatedly returned. He had to defend one of the finer points of his thesis against Theodor Mommsen. At the end of the inconclusive exchange, the eminent historian asserted that he knew of no better man to succeed him 'than the highly esteemed Max Weber.'

3

In the spring of 1892, a grand niece of Max Weber, Sr., came to Berlin in order to educate herself for a profession. Marianne Schnitger, the twenty-one-year-old daughter of a doctor, had attended a finishing school in the city of Hanover. Upon returning to Berlin after an earlier visit to the Weber home, she realized that she was in love with Max Weber. After some confusion, Victorian misunderstandings, and moral attempts at self-clarification, Max and Marianne announced their formal engagement. They were married in the fall of 1893.

For some six years before his marriage to Marianne, Weber had been in love with a daughter of his mother's sister in Strassburg, who, for rather long periods, was in a mental hospital. She was recovering when Weber gently broke with her. He never forgot that he had unwillingly caused suffering to this tender girl. It was perhaps an important reason for the mildness of his reactions to others who were guilty in the field of personal relations and for his general stoicism in personal affairs. In addition to this situation, another moral difficulty had stood in the way of the marriage. Perhaps because of Weber's hesitancy in approaching Marianne, a friend of his had courted her, and it was somewhat painful to Weber to cut in.

After his marriage to Marianne, Weber lived the life of a successful young scholar in Berlin. Having taken the place of Jakob Goldschmidt, a famous teacher of economics who had become ill, he was in lecture hall and seminar nineteen hours a week. He also participated in state examinations for lawyers and, in addition, imposed a heavy load of work upon himself. He was active in consultation work for government agencies, and made special studies for private reform groups, one on the stock exchange, and another on the estates in Eastern Germany.

In the fall of 1894, he accepted a full professorship in economics at Freiburg University. There he met Hugo Münsterberg, Pastor Naumann, and Wilhelm Rickert. He had an enormous load, working until very late. When Marianne urged him to get some rest, he would call out: 'If I don't work until one o'clock I can't be a professor.'

In 1895, the Webers made a trip to Scotland and the west coast of Ireland. Returning to Freiburg, Weber gave his inaugural address at the University. It was entitled, 'The National State and Economic Policy,' and was a confession of belief in imperialist *Realpolitik* and the House of Hohenzollern. It caused quite a stir. 'The brutality of my views,' he wrote, 'have caused horror. The Catholics were the most content with it, because I gave a firm kick to "Ethical Culture."'

Weber accepted a chair at Heidelberg in 1896, replacing the eminent and retired Knies, one of the heads of 'the historical school.' He thus became the colleague of former teachers, Fischer, Bekker, and others, who still stamped the intellectual and social life of Heidelberg. His circle of friends included Georg Jellinek, Paul Hensel, Karl Neumann, the art historian, and Ernst Troeltsch, the religionist, who was to become one of Weber's greatest friends and intellectual companions, and who for a time lived in the Weber household.

4

Max Weber's father died in 1897, shortly after a tense discussion in which Max heatedly defended his mother against what seemed to him autocratic impositions. Later Weber felt that his hostile outbreak against his father was a guilty act which could never be rectified.[11] During the following summer, the Webers traveled to Spain and on the return trip Weber became fevered and ill with a psychic malady. He seemed to get better when the academic year began, but towards the end of the fall semester he collapsed from tension and remorse, exhaustion and anxiety. For his essentially psychiatric condition, doctors prescribed cold water, travel, and exercise. Yet Weber continued to experience the sleeplessness of an inner tension.

For the rest of his life he suffered intermittently from severe depressions, punctuated by manic spurts of extraordinarily intense intellectual work and travel. Indeed, his way of life from this time on seems to

oscillate between neurotic collapse, travel, and work. He was held together by a profound sense of humor and an unusually fearless practice
of the Socratic maxim.

Eager to make the best of a bad situation and to comfort his wife,
Weber wrote:

> Such a disease has its compensations. It has reopened to me the human
> side of life, which mama used to miss in me. And this to an extent previously
> unknown to me. I could say, with John Gabriel Borkman, that 'an icy hand
> has let me loose.' In years past my diseased disposition expressed itself in a
> frantic grip upon scientific work, which appeared to me as a talisman. . .
> Looking back, this is quite clear. I know that sick or healthy, I shall no
> longer be the same. The need to feel crushed under the load of work is
> extinct. Now I want most of all to live out my life humanly and to see my
> love as happy as it is possible for me to make her. I do not believe that I
> shall achieve less than formerly in my inner treadmill, of course, always in
> proportion to my condition, the permanent improvement of which will in
> any case require much time and rest.[12]

He repeatedly attempted to continue his teaching. During one such
attempt his arms and back became temporarily paralyzed, yet he forced
himself to finish the semester. He felt dreadfully tired out; his head
was weary; every mental effort, especially speech, was felt to be detrimental to his entire being. In spite of occasional wrath and impatience,
he thought of his condition as part of his fate. He rejected all 'good
counsel.' Since adolescence, everything about him had been geared for
thinking. And now, every intellectual pursuit became a poison to him.
He had not developed any artistic abilities, and physical work of any
sort was distasteful. His wife attempted to persuade him to take up
some craft or hobby, but he laughed at her. For hours he sat and gazed
stupidly, picking at his finger nails, claiming that such inactivity made
him feel good. When he tried to look at his lecture notes, the words
swam in confusion before his eyes. One day, while walking in a wood,
he lost his sensory control and openly wept. A pet cat made him so angry
with its mewing that he was quite beyond himself in rage. These symptoms were present during the years 1898 and 1899. The university
authorities granted him a leave with pay. Years later, in a letter to his
friend, Karl Vossler, Weber wrote: ' "Misery teaches prayer." . . . Always? According to my personal experience, I should like to *dispute*
this statement. Of course, I agree with you that it holds very frequently,
all too frequently for man's dignity.' [13]

One fall the Webers traveled to Venice for 'a vacation.' They returned to Heidelberg and again Weber tried to resume some of his duties, but soon collapsed, more severely than ever before. At Christmas he asked to be dismissed from his position, but the University granted him a long leave of absence with a continuance of salary. 'He could not read or write, speak, walk, or sleep without pain; all mental and part of his physical functions refused to work.' [14]

Early in 1899, he entered a small mental institution and remained there alone for several weeks. A young psychopathic cousin of Weber's was brought to the institution, and during the winter, on medical advice, Weber's wife traveled with both men to Ajaccio on the island of Corsica. In the spring, they went to Rome, the ruins of which re-stimulated Weber's historical interest. He felt depressed by the presence of the psychopathic youth, who was then sent home. Several years later, this youth took his own life. Weber's letter of condolence to the parents gives us some insight into his freedom from conventional attitudes towards suicide.

He was a man [he wrote of the cousin] who, chained to an incurably diseased body, yet had developed, perhaps because of it, a sensitivity of feeling, a clarity about himself, and a deeply hidden and proud and noble height of inner deportment such as is found among few healthy people. To know and to judge this is given only to those who have seen him quite near and who have learned to love him as we have, and who, at the same time personally know what disease is. . . His future being what it was, he has done right to depart now to the unknown land and to go before you, who otherwise would have had to leave him behind on this earth, walking toward a dark fate, without counsel, and in loneliness.[15]

With such an evaluation of suicide as a last and stubborn affirmation of man's freedom, Weber takes his stand at the side of such modern Stoics as Montaigne, Hume, and Nietzsche. He was, at the same time, of the opinion that religions of salvation do not approve of 'voluntary death,' that only philosophers have hallowed it.[16]

Under the influence of the magnificent landscape of Italy and its historically grandiose scenes, Weber slowly recovered. The Webers also spent some time in Switzerland, where his mother, now 57, and his brother Alfred visited them. Shortly after his mother's visit, Max was able to resume reading, a book on art history. He commented: 'Who knows how long I can keep it up? Anything but literature in my own field.' After three and a half years of intermittently severe disease, in

1902 Weber felt able to return to Heidelberg and resume a light schedule of work. Gradually, he began to read professional journals and such books as Simmel's *Philosophy of Money*. Then, as if to make up for his years of intellectual privation, he plunged into a vast and universal literature in which art history, economics, and politics stood alongside the economic history of monastic orders.

There were, however, repeated setbacks. He was still unable fully to take up his teaching work. He asked to be dismissed from his professorship and to be made a titular professor. This request was first rejected, but at his insistence, he was made a lecturer. He had requested the right to examine Ph.D. candidates, but this was not granted. After four and a half years without production he was able to write a book review. A new phase of writing finally began, at first dealing with problems of method in the social sciences.

Weber suffered under the psychic burden of receiving money from the university without rendering adequate service. He felt that only a man at his work is a full man, and he forced himself to work. Yet after only a summer of it, he returned to Italy alone. During the year 1903, he traveled out of Germany no less than six times; he was in Italy, Holland, and Belgium. His own nervous condition, his disappointment at his own insufficiencies, frictions with the Heidelberg faculty, and the political state of the nation occasionally made him wish to turn his back on Germany forever. Yet during this year, 1903, he managed to join with Sombart in the editorship of the *Archiv für Sozialwissenschaft und Sozialpolitik,* which became perhaps the leading social science journal in Germany, until suppressed by the Nazis. This editorship provided Weber an opportunity to resume contact with a wide circle of scholars and politicians and to broaden the focus of his own work. By 1904, his productivity was in full swing again and rising steeply. He published essays on the social and economic problems of Junker estates, objectivity in the social sciences, and the first section of the *Protestant Ethic and the Spirit of Capitalism.*

Hugo Münsterberg, his colleague from Freiburg days, had helped organize a 'Congress of Arts and Science' as part of the Universal Exposition of 1904 in St. Louis. He invited Weber (along with Sombart, Troeltsch, and many others) to read a paper before the Congress.[17] By August, Weber and his wife were on the way to America.

5

Max Weber's reaction to the United States was at once enthusiastic and detached. He possessed to an eminent degree the 'virtue' which Edward Gibbon ascribes to the studious traveler abroad, that 'virtue which borders on a vice; the flexible temper which can assimilate itself to every tone of society from the court to the cottage; the happy flow of spirits which can amuse and be amused in every company and situation.'[18] Hence Weber was impatient and angry with quickly prejudiced colleagues, who, after a day and a half in New York, began to run down things in America.

He wished to enter sympathetically into the new world without surrendering his capacity for informed judgments at a later time. He was fascinated by the rush hour in lower Manhattan, which he liked to view from the middle of Brooklyn Bridge as a panorama of mass transportation and noisy motion. The skyscrapers, which he saw as 'fortresses of capital,' reminded him of 'the old pictures of the towers in Bologna and Florence.' And he contrasted these towering bulks of capitalism with the tiny homes of American college professors:

Among these masses, all individualism becomes expensive, whether it is in housing or eating. Thus, the home of Professor Hervay, of the German department in Columbia University, is surely a doll's house with tiny little rooms, with toilet and bath facilities in the same room (as is almost always the case). Parties with more than four guests are impossible (worthy of being envied!) and with all this, it takes one hour's ride to get to the center of the city. . .[19]

From New York the party journeyed to Niagara Falls. They visited a small town and then went on to Chicago, which Weber found 'incredible.' He noted well its lawlessness and violence, its sharp contrasts of gold coast and slum, the 'steam, dirt, blood, and hides' of the stockyards, the 'maddening' mixture of peoples:

the Greek shining the Yankee's shoes for five cents, the German acting as his waiter, the Irishman managing his politics, and the Italian digging his dirty ditches. With the exception of some exclusive residential districts, the whole gigantic city, more extensive than London, is like a man whose skin has been peeled off and whose entrails one sees at work.

Again and again, Weber was impressed by the extent of waste, especially the waste of human life, under American capitalism. He noticed the same conditions that the muckrakers were publicizing at the time. Thus he commented, in a letter to his mother:

After their work, the workers often have to travel for hours in order to reach their homes. The tramway company has been bankrupt for years. As usual a receiver, who has no interest in speeding up the liquidation, manages its affairs; therefore, new tram cars are not purchased. The old cars constantly break down, and about four hundred people a year are thus killed or crippled. According to the law, each death costs the company about $5,000, which is paid to the widow or heirs, and each cripple costs $10,000, paid to the casualty himself. These compensations are due so long as the company does not introduce certain precautionary measures. But they have calculated that the four hundred casualties a year cost less than would the necessary precautions. The company therefore does not introduce them.[20]

In St. Louis, Weber delivered a successful lecture on the social structure of Germany, with particular reference to rural and political problems. This was his first 'lecture' in six and a half years. Many of his colleagues were present, and according to the report of his wife, who was also present, his talk was very well received. This was gratifying to the Webers, as it seemed to indicate that he was again able to function in his profession. He traveled through the Oklahoma territory, and visited New Orleans as well as the Tuskegee Institution; he visited distant relatives in North Carolina and Virginia; and then, in fast tempo, traveled through Philadelphia, Washington, Baltimore, and Boston. In New York, he searched the library of Columbia University for materials to be used in *The Protestant Ethic.*

Of the Americans [whom we met] it was a woman, an inspector of industry, who was by far the most pre-eminent figure. One learned a great deal about the radical evil of this world from this passionate socialist. The hopelessness of social legislation in a system of state particularism, the corruption of many labor leaders who incite strikes and then have the manufacturer pay them for settling them. (I had a personal letter of introduction to such a scoundrel.) . . . and yet, [the Americans] are a wonderful people. Only the Negro question and the terrible immigration form a big, black cloud.[21]

During his travels in America Weber seems to have been most interested in labor problems, the immigrant question, problems of political management—especially of municipal government—all expressions of the 'capitalist spirit,' [22] the Indian question and its administration, the plight of the South, and the Negro problem. Of the American Negro, Weber wrote: 'I have talked to about one hundred white Southerners of all social classes and parties, and the problem of what shall become of these people [the Negroes] seems absolutely hopeless.'

He had arrived in America in September 1904; he left for Germany shortly before Christmas.*

Perhaps the United States was for Weber what England had been for previous generations of German liberals: the model of a new society. Here the Protestant sects had had their greatest scope and in their wake the secular, civic, and 'voluntary associations' had flowered. Here a political federation of states had led to a 'voluntary' union of immense contrasts.

Weber was far from the conceit of those German civil servants who prided themselves in their 'honest administration' and pointed disdainfully to the 'corrupt practices' of American politics. Friedrich Kapp, a returned German-American, had brought such attitudes home to Weber. But Weber saw things in a broader perspective. Being convinced that politics are not to be judged solely as a moral business, his attitude was rather that of Charles Sealsfield, who had, during the eighteen-thirties, unfolded an epic panorama of the birth of an empire-building nation destined to 'take its place among the mightiest nations upon the earth.' Sealsfield had asked, 'Is it not rather a necessary, absolute condition of our liberty that citizens' virtues, as well as their vices, should grow more luxuriantly because they are freely permitted to grow and increase?' Weber might have agreed, after what he saw, that 'the mouth which breathes the mephitic vapors of the Mississippi and the Red River swamps is not fit to chew raisins, that the hand which fells our gigantic trees and drains our bogs cannot put on kid gloves. Our land is the land of contrast.' [23]

The key focus of Weber's experience of America was upon the role of bureaucracy in a democracy. He saw that 'machine politics' were indispensable in modern 'mass democracy,' unless a 'leaderless democracy' and a confusion of tongues were to prevail. Machine politics, however, mean the management of politics by professionals, by the disciplined party organization and its streamlined propaganda. Such democracy may also bring to the helm the Caesarist people's tribune, whether in the role of the strong president or the city manager. And the whole process

* Some translations of Weber's letters from the United States are contained in H. W. Brann, 'Max Weber and the United States,' *Southwestern Social Science Quarterly*, June 1944, pp. 18-30.

tends towards increasing rational efficiency and therewith bureaucratic machines: party, municipal, federal.

Weber saw this machine-building, however, in a dialectic fashion: Democracy must oppose bureaucracy as a tendency towards a caste of mandarins, removed from the common people by expert training, examination certificates, and tenure of office, but: the scope of administrative functions, the end of the open frontier, and the narrowing of opportunities make the spoils system, with its public waste, irregularities, and lack of technical efficiency, increasingly impossible and undemocratic. Thus democracy has to promote what reason demands and democratic sentiment hates. In his writings, Weber repeatedly refers to those American workers who opposed civil-service reform by arguing that they preferred a set of corrupt politicians whom they could oust and despise, to a caste of expert officials who would despise them and who were irremovable. Weber was instrumental in having the German President's power strengthened as a balance of the Reichstag; this act should be understood along with his American experiences. He was, above all, impressed by the grandiose efficiency of a type of man, bred by free associations in which the individual had to prove himself before his equals, where no authoritative commands, but autonomous decision, good sense, and responsible conduct train for citizenship.

In 1918 Weber suggested in a letter to a colleague that Germany should borrow the American 'club pattern' as a means of 're-educating' Germany; for, he wrote, 'authoritarianism now fails completely, except in the form of the church.' [24] Weber thus saw the connection between voluntary associations and the personality structure of the free man. His study of the Protestant sect testifies to that. He was convinced that the automatic selection of persons, with the pressure always upon the individual to prove himself, is an infinitely deeper way for 'toughening' man than the ordering and forbidding technique of authoritarian institutions. For such authoritarianism does not reach into the innermost of those subject to its external constraint, and it leaves them incapable of self-direction once the authoritarian shell is broken by counter-violence.

6

Upon his return to Germany, Max Weber resumed his writing at Heidelberg. He finished the second part of *The Protestant Ethic,* which in a letter to Rickert he called 'Protestant asceticism as the foundation of modern vocational civilization—a sort of "spiritualist" construction of the modern economy.'[25]

The first Russian revolution redirected his scholarly work; he learned Russian, in bed before getting up each morning, in order to follow events in the Russian daily press. Then he chased 'after the events with his pen in order to pin them down as daily history.' In 1901 he published two major essays on Russia, 'The Situation of Bourgeois Democracy in Russia' and 'Russia's Transition to Sham Constitutionalism.'

Eminent social scientists, such as Schmoller and Brentano, encouraged him to resume a professorship, but Weber felt he was not capable of doing so. For a while longer, he wanted merely to write. Yet, being universally esteemed, he could not help being drawn into academic politics, judging prospective candidates for positions, or trying to open up room for various younger scholars, such as Georg Simmel and Robert Michels, to whom satisfactory careers were blocked or precluded because of anti-Semitism or prejudice against young socialist docents. The case of Robert Michels, the son of an eminent Cologne family of patrician merchants, especially enraged Weber. At the time, German universities were closed to him because he was a social democrat. Weber asserted that, 'If I compare Italian, French, and, at the moment, even Russian conditions with this condition of ours, I have to consider it a shame of a civilized nation.' Some professor maintained that in addition to political reasons for Michels' exclusion there was the further reason that Michels had not baptized his children. Upon this Weber wrote an article in the *Frankfurter Zeitung* on 'The So-called Academic Freedom,' in which he said:

> As long as such views prevail, I see no possibility of behaving as if we had such a thing as academic freedom. . . And as long as religious communities knowingly and openly allow their sacraments to be used as means for making a career, on the same level of a dueling corps or an officer's commission, they deserve the disdain about which they are so used to complaining.[26]

In 1908 he investigated the industrial psychology of his grandfather's linen factory in Westphalia. He had hoped to promote a series of such studies, and the methodological note he wrote is a causal analysis of physical and psychic factors influencing the productivity of industrial labor. In this same year, he worked out a long essay on the social structure of ancient society, published in an encyclopedia * under the modest

* *Handwörterbuch der Staatswissenschaften*, 3rd ed., vol. 1.

and somewhat misleading title, 'The Agrarian Institutions of Antiquity.'

A disciple of Freud made his appearance in the intellectual circles in Heidelberg in 1909. Conventional Victorian conceptions of marital fidelity and of morally justified jealousy were depreciated in the name of a new norm of mentally healthy living. Full of sympathy for the tragic entanglements and moral difficulties of friends, which resulted from this conduct, Weber reacted sharply against what appeared to him a confusion of valuable, though still imprecise, psychiatric insights with an ethic of vulgar pride in 'healthy nerves.' He was not willing to accept healthy nerves as an absolute end, or to calculate the moral worth of repression in terms of its cost to one's nerves. Weber thought that the therapeutic technique of Freud was a resuscitation of the oral confession, with the clinician displacing the old *directeur d'âme*. He felt that an ethic was disguised in the scientific discussion of the clinician, and that in this matter a specialized scientist, who should be concerning himself only with means, was usurping from laymen their right to make their own evaluations. Weber thus saw a 'loose' way of life draped in what he felt was a shifting clinical theory. One can easily see that he resisted a theory that is, in principle, directed against asceticism and that conceives of ends only in pragmatic terms, thus deflating the imperative claim of heroic ethics. Being personally characterized by an extremely stern conscience, Weber was often ready to forgive others but was quite rigid with himself. He believed that many of those who followed in the wake of Freud were too ready to justify what appeared to him as moral shabbiness.

It should, however, be noted that although Weber was not willing to see Freud's disciples use their theories in this personal way, he had

no doubt that Freud's ideas *can* become a source of highly significant interpretations of a whole series of cultural and historical, moral and religious phenomena. Of course, from the point of view of a cultural historian, their significance is not nearly so universal as the understandable enthusiasms of Freud and his disciples, in the joy of their discovery, would have us believe. A precondition would be the establishment of an exact typology of a scope and certainty which does not exist today, despite all assertions to the contrary, but which perhaps will exist in two to three decades.[27]

In Heidelberg, during these years from 1906 to 1910, Weber participated in intense intellectual discussions with such eminent colleagues as his brother, Alfred Weber, with Otto Klebs, Eberhard Gothein, Wilhelm Windelband, Georg Jellinek, Ernst Troeltsch, Karl Neumann, Emil Lask, Friedrich Gundolf, and Arthur Salz. During vacation times or other 'free periods,' many friends from outside Heidelberg visited the Webers. Among them were Robert Michels, Werner Sombart, the philosopher Paul Hensel, Hugo Münsterberg, Ferdinand Tönnies, Karl Vossler, and, above all, Georg Simmel. Among the younger scholars who sought Weber's stimulus were: Paul Honigsheim, Karl Löwenstein, and Georg Lukacs. These circles were not closed to the non-academic; they included a few eminent artists, such as Mina Tobler, the musician to whom Weber dedicated his study of Hinduism and Buddhism, as well as the former actress, Kläre Schmid-Romberg, and her husband, a poet, philosopher, and connoisseur of art. Karl Jaspers, a psychiatrist who was to turn philosopher and use Kierkegaard's work in his philosophy of existentialism, and H. Gruhle, a psychiatrist interested in the latest of modern art, also belonged to the circle. Three generations of intellectual and artistic elite were in active discourse at these Heidelberg meetings.

In 1908 Max Weber was active in establishing a sociological society. In a selfless manner, he carried the routine burdens of overcoming the usual difficulties of such organizations. He was decisive in setting the level of discussion at the meetings and in defining the scope of future work. He stimulated collective research enterprises, such as an investigation of voluntary associations, ranging from athletic leagues to religious sects and political parties. He proposed a methodical study of the press by questionnaires, and directed and prompted studies in industrial psychology. In addition, he assumed responsibility to the publisher Siebeck of organizing an encyclopedic series of social-science studies. This latter project was intended as a two-year job, but it continued even after his death, his own *Wirtschaft und Gesellschaft* appearing posthumously as a volume in the series.

The severity of Weber's sense of honor, his prompt chivalry, and his position as a reserve officer occasionally impelled him to engage in court actions and 'affairs of honor.' It was characteristic of him to act with great impetuosity and righteous indignation. Yet when his opponent had been morally crushed by the machinery he had set in motion, his furor cooled, and he was overcome by mercifulness and sympathy, the more so when he realized that others besides the guilty one suffered from his actions. Close friends who did not feel so strongly as Weber in such matters were inclined to consider him a querulous man who lacked a sense of measure, a Don Quixote whose actions might well boomerang. Others hailed him as Germany's foremost educator, whose moral authority raised him above the shoulders of the spineless Philistines, out only for their own careers. His Don Quixote aspect comes out clearly in a statement he made to his friend, Theodor Heuss, in 1917: 'As soon as the war has come to an end, I shall insult the Kaiser until he sues me, and then the responsible statesmen, Bülow, Tirpitz, and Bethmann-Hollweg, will be compelled to make statements under oath.' [28]

When the First World War began, Weber was 50. 'In spite of all,' it was 'a great and wonderful war,' [29] and he wanted to march at the head of his company. That his age and medical condition made this impossible was painful to him. But as a member of the reserve corps, he was commissioned as a disciplinary and economic officer, a captain, in charge of establishing and running nine hospitals in the Heidelberg area. In this position he experienced from the inside what had become a central concept in his sociology: bureaucracy. The social apparatus of which he had charge was, however, one of dilettantes, rather than of experts; and Weber worked for and witnessed its transformation into an ordered bureaucracy. From August 1914 to the fall of 1915, he served this commission, which was then dissolved in a reorganization, and Weber honorably retired. His political frustrations during the war will be discussed presently.

He went to Brussels for a short time in order to confer with Jaffé about the administration of the occupation of Belgium. Then he went to Berlin, as a self-appointed prophet of doom, to write memoranda, seek contact with political authorities, and fight the mad imperialist aspiration. In the final analysis, he debunked the conduct of the war-party as being the gamble of munition makers and agrarian capitalists. From Berlin he went to Vienna and Budapest, in the service of the government, to conduct unofficial conversations with industrialists about tariff questions.

In the fall of 1916 he was back in Heidelberg, studying the Hebrew prophets and working on various sections of *Wirtschaft und Gesellschaft*. In the summer of 1917 he vacationed at his wife's home in Westphalia, reading the poetry of Stefan George and Gundolf's book on Goethe. In the winters of 1917 and 1918, socialist-pacifist students frequented his 'open hours' on Sundays in Heidelberg. The young communist, Ernst Toller, was among them; frequently he read his poetry aloud. Later, when Toller was arrested, Weber spoke for him in the military court and effected his release, although he could not prevent the removal of the student group from the university.

In April 1918, he moved to Vienna for a summer term at the university. These were his first university lectures for nineteen years. Under the title, 'A Positive Critique of the Materialist Conception of History,' he presented his sociology of world religions and politics. His lectures became events for the university, and he had to perform them in the largest hall available, as professors, state officials, and politicians attended. Yet he experienced compulsive anxieties about these lectures, using opiates in order to induce sleep. Vienna University offered him a permanent position, but he did not accept.

In 1918 Weber shifted from Monarchist to Republican loyalties. As Meinecke said, 'We have turned from being Monarchists at heart to being Republicans by reason.' He abstained from accepting any political position in the new regime. A whole series of academic positions were offered to him: Berlin, Göttingen, Bonn, and Munich. He accepted the Munich offer, going there in the summer of 1919 as Brentano's successor. In Munich, he lived through the excitement of the Bavarian Dictatorship and its collapse. His last lectures were worked out at the request of his students and have been published as *General Economic History*. In midsummer, he fell ill, and, at a late stage of his disease, a doctor was able to diagnose his condition as deep-seated pneumonia. He died in June 1920.

7

Max Weber belonged to a generation of universal scholars, and there are definite sociological conditions for scholarship of the kind he displayed. One such condition was a gymnasium education, which, in Weber's case, equipped him in such a way that the Indo-Germanic languages were but so many dialects of one linguistic medium. (A reading knowledge of Hebrew and Russian was acquired by the way.) An intellectually stimulating family background gave him a head-start and made it possible for him to study an unusual combination of specialized subjects. When he had passed his law examination, he was at the same time a well-equipped economist, historian, and philosopher. And by virtue of having participated, through the Strassburg branch of his family, in the theological disputes of the time, he was sufficiently acquainted with the literature of theology to handle it expertly.

It is clear that the enormous amount of work Weber turned out would not have been possible without a certain type of fruitful leisure. Materially, this was made possible, at first, by his position as a scholar in a German university. The career pattern in these universities gave the German docent time for research during the years when the young American academician is overburdened with teaching. In addition, there was no pressure for rapid publication—as attested by the fact that many book-length chapters of *Wirtschaft und Gesellschaft,* written before World War I, were published after 1920. In his middle life Weber came into an inheritance that was sufficient to relieve him of serious worry about money.

The relative lack of pressure for 'practical' and immediately 'useful' knowledge, conditioned by a strongly humanist atmosphere, allowed for the pursuit of themes remote from the practical demands of the day. In the social sciences this was the more the case because the impact of Marxism almost required that the academician take up the question of capitalism as an epochal structure, rather than narrowed and 'practical' themes. In this connection the freedom of the university from local pressures was important.

Long decades of peace for Germany, from 1870 to 1914, coupled with general prosperity, had entirely changed the conditions of German scholarship. The petty bourgeois professor, harried by money matters, had been replaced by an upper-class academician with a large home and a maid. This change facilitated the establishment of an intellectual salon. It is from this position that Weber saw the residences of American university professors.

The intellectual traditions and the accumulated scholarship of Germany, especially in history, the classics, psychology, theology, comparative literature, philology, and philosophy, gave the late-nineteenth-century German scholar a pre-eminent base upon which to build his work. And the clash of two bodies of intellectual work, the conservative interpretation of ideas by academicians in the tradition of Hegel and Ranke, and the radical intellectual production of non-academic socialists, Kautsky, Bernstein, and Mehring, formed a unique and challenging intellectual tension.

A number of contradictory elements stood in tension with one another and made up the life and views of Max Weber. If, as he wrote, 'men are not open books,' we should certainly not expect to find even an easy index to his many-sided existence. To understand him, we have to grasp a series of irrational half-paradoxes.

Although he was personally irreligious—in his own words, 'religiously unmusical'—he nevertheless spent a good part of his scholarly energy in tracing the effects of religion upon human conduct and life. It may not be irrelevant in this connection to repeat that his mother and her family were deeply pious and that in his early student days Weber lived close to friends and relatives who suffered extraordinary religious and psychic states; these experiences profoundly impressed themselves upon him. That he despised the conventional 'church' Christianity goes without saying, yet he had pity and condescension for those who in political tragedy and personal despair sacrificed their intellects to the refuge of the altar.

Many of his friends considered his sincere devotion to his work, the obvious pathos and dignity of his bearing, and the forcefulness and insight of his speech as religious phenomena. Yet his work is hardly understandable without an appreciation of his disenchanted view of religious matters. His love for his mother and his genuine detachment from 'religion' prevented him from ever falling into the Promethean blasphemy of Nietzsche, the greatest atheist of the nineteenth century, which he saw, in the last analysis, as a 'painful residue of the bourgeois Philistine.' [30]

Weber was one of the last of the 'political professors' who made detached contributions to science, and, as the intellectual vanguard of the middle classes, were also leading political figures. Despite this fact, for the sake of 'objectivity' and the freedom of his students, Weber fought against 'the Treitschkes,' who used cloistered academic halls as forums of political propaganda. Although he was passionately concerned with the course of German policy, in theory he rigidly segregated his role as a professor and scientist from that of a publicist. Yet, when his friend Brentano, in Munich, asked him to accept a position, he answered that were he to accept any professorship, 'I would have to ask whether it would not be better to have someone who holds my views in Berlin at the present time as a counterweight against the absolute opportunism which now has the say there.' [31]

Throughout his life, Weber was a nationalist and believed in the mission of the *Herrenvolk*, yet at the same time he fought for individual freedom and, with analytic detachment, characterized the ideas of nationalism and racism as justificatory ideologies used by the ruling class, and their hireling publicists, to beat their impositions into weaker members of the polity. He had great esteem for the matter-of-fact conduct of labor leaders during the collapse of Germany, yet he lashed out against the doctrinal drill with which these same men domesticated the masses and trained them to believe in a future 'paradise' to be brought about by revolution. He was proud of being a Prussian officer, and yet asserted in public that the Kaiser, his commander-in-chief, was something of which all Germans should be ashamed. A Prussian officer and a member of a dueling corps, he nevertheless did not mind rooming in a Brussels hotel over which flew a red, International flag. A model of the self-conscious masculinity of Imperial Germany, he nevertheless encouraged the first woman labor official in Germany and made vital speeches to members of the woman's emancipation movement of the early twentieth century.

Weber appears to have been an eminent academic teacher, and yet his health kept him from academic lectures for almost two decades. Although a scholar, he felt out of place in the academic chair and truly at home on the political platform. In his insistence on precision and balance, his prose is full of clauses and reservations, in the most scholarly and difficult fashion. Yet at times he felt himself to be comparable to the demagogues of ancient Judea haranguing to the crowd in the street.

Among those who had dealings with him, the figure of Weber was highly controversial. At Heidelberg, many of his colleagues saw him as a difficult person, who because of demanding conscience and rigidity of honor was highly inconvenient and somewhat troublesome. Perhaps he was seen as hypochondriac. In the eyes of many friends and disciples, he appeared as an overtowering intellect. A Viennese journalist describes him in the following clichés:

Tall and fully bearded, this scholar resembles one of the German stone masons of the Renaissance period; only the eyes lack the naïveté and sensuous joy of the artist. His gaze is from the innermost, from hidden passages, and it reaches into the greatest distances. His manner of expression corresponds to the man's exterior; it is infinitely plastic. We meet here an almost Hellenic way of seeing things. The words are simply formed, and, in their quiet simplicity, they remind us of Cyclopic blocks.

A disciple in Munich, who was personally distant from Weber, worshiping him from afar, compared him to Dürer's knight: without fear or favor, taking a straight course between death and the devil. And Karl Jaspers saw him as a new type of man who had the poise to hold together in synthesis the tremendous tensions of his own self as well as the contradictions of external public life without resorting to illusions. Every day that Weber 'wasted for things political' instead of 'objectifying himself' seemed a pitiful loss to Jaspers.

In spite of the pathos of objectivity that is felt so intensely by the student of Weber's work, it nevertheless contains passages that refer to Weber's image of himself. The most obvious of these are found in his characterization of certain Hebrew prophets.[32] When the course of the war and the collapse of Germany confirmed what Weber had anticipated for two decades, and the German people alone were proclaimed guilty for all the misfortunes of the war, Weber felt that the Germans were a pariah people. During the course of his studies in ancient Judaism, in 1916 and 1917, he was profoundly moved by the analogies he saw between the situation of the ancient Hebrew peoples and modern Germany. It was not only the public and historical situation he saw as parallel; in the personality of many prophets and in their irregular and compulsive psychic states, particularly of Jeremiah, Weber saw features he felt resembled his own. When he read passages of this manuscript to his wife, she was touched in immediately seeing that this reading was an indirect analysis of himself.

Perhaps it was only in this fashion that Weber, who since childhood was incapable of directly revealing himself, could communicate his own self-image. Thus, what was most personal to him is accessible and at the same time hidden by the objectification of his work. By interpreting the prophets of disaster and doom, Weber illuminated his own personal and public experiences.

This assimilation of his image of self into a historical figure stands in a broad tradition of humanism, historicism, and romanticism so characteristic of the nineteenth century. Eminent intellectuals and even statesmen of that century often fashioned their images of themselves in the costumes of historical figures. Thus Napoleon simulated Alexander the Great; and the revolutionary republicans of the great upheavals saw themselves in terms of 'the lives of Plutarch.' In Germany, this illusionist tendency remained strong throughout the epoch of liberalism. Some of the best of German youth, among them Francis Lieber, went out to help the Greeks in their fight for liberation against the Turks. But the ragged horse trader of the Balkan mountains shattered the marble image of the ancient Greek. Historical illusions were used as a backdrop of one's life and perhaps to compensate for the banality of the Philistinism, which circumscribed the daily routine of powerless German professors with world-encompassing ideas.

If the older Weber identified himself with Jeremiah in the humanist tradition of illusion, he well knew that he was in truth no prophet. When urged by an admiring young intelligentsia to expound his faith, he rejected their pleas, asserting that such confession belongs to the circle of intimates and not the public. Only prophets, artists, and saints might bare their souls in public. For Weber, modern society is godless, and prophets as well as saints are singularly out of place. He only offered Isaiah's suggestion: 'He calleth to me out of Seir, Watchman, what of the night? Watchman, what of the night? The watchman said, The morning cometh, and also the night: if ye will enquire, enquire ye: return, come.' (21:11-12.)

8

If we are to understand Weber's biography as a whole, we must examine his tensions and his repeated psychic disturbances. Several lines of interpretation are possible; jointly or separately, they may offer an explanation.

Max Weber may have been hereditarily burdened by a constitutional affliction, which undoubtedly ran through his family line. Some evidence for this interpretation, which is the simplest one, is readily at hand. Weber's wife was a distant relative of his, and male relatives of hers ended their lives in insane asylums. Furthermore, a cousin of his entered the asylum, to which Weber himself was sent during his most severe breakdown.

If we are willing to see Weber's affliction as purely functional, we may then follow either one of two different lines of evidence: We may try to locate his personal difficulties in the private contexts of those dear to him: mother, father, loves, wife; or we may deal primarily with him in public contexts.

With reference to his personal relations, we may recall that Weber was a quiet, observant, and prematurely intelligent boy, who must have been worried under the strain of the increasingly bad relation between his father and mother. His strong sense of chivalry was, in part, a response to the patriarchal and domineering attitude of his father, who understood his wife's love as a willingness to serve and to allow herself to be exploited and controlled by him. This situation came to a climax when Weber, at the age of 31, in the presence of his mother and his wife, saw fit to hold judgment over his father: he would remorselessly break all relations with him unless he met the son's condition: the mother should visit him 'alone' without the father. We have noted that the father died only a short time after this encounter and that Weber came out of the situation with an ineffaceable sense of guilt. One may certainly infer an inordinately strong Oedipus situation.

Throughout his life, Weber maintained a full correspondence with his mother, who once referred to him as 'an older daughter.' She eagerly sought counsel with him, her first-born, rather than with her husband, in matters concerning the demeanor of her third son. One should also pay heed to what was, to be sure, a passing phase of young Weber's aspiration: his desire to become a real he-man at the university. After only three semesters, he succeeded in changing externally from a slender mother's boy to a massive, beer-drinking, duel-marked, cigar-puffing student of Imperial Germany, whom his mother greeted with a slap in the face. Clearly, this was the father's son. The two models of identification and their associated values, rooted in mother and father, never disappeared from Max Weber's inner life.

A similar tension, and subsequent source of guilt, occurred when Weber found himself estranged from an earlier love, another cousin of his, whom both his mother and his maternal aunt favored. This situation was all the more painful to him because his mother joyfully saw Marianne, his future wife, wooed by a close friend of Max. In marrying Marianne, Weber was thus beset by guilt from two sources: he was almost ready to resign his love in favor of his friend, and he was almost ready to marry a mentally burdened and unstable girl. His proposal letter to his wife, dealing with this situation, seems as much a confession of guilt as a love letter. And later letters to his wife are apologetic for sacrificing his marriage with her by allowing his energies to be used up in the 'inner treadmill' of his intellectual life.

The Webers were childless, and he did not fail to assert his virility in public by summoning others to duels in a manner which stressed his special dignity as a Prussian officer. Yet at the same time, as a writer, he was ready publicly to deflate Prussian militarism and its officer-bureaucracy for standing behind such educational institutions as the dueling corps designed to 'break in' upper-class youth to the discipline required in the career. A profound individual humanism, the 'freedom of a Christian,' and the lofty heights of his ethical demands were derived from identification with his mother.

We may shift from personal relations and the difficulties that may have arisen from them; Weber was also an intellectual involved in the political events of his day. He made matters of public concern his voluntary burden. With an extraordinary sense of responsibility, he felt intimately called to politics. Yet he had no power and no position from which his word could tip the balance of policy. And tensions arose from this fact.

Weber does not *seem* to have had much basis for his intense identification with Germany. He tore down the Junkers, the workers, as well as the spineless Philistines among the middle classes, who longed for a Caesar to protect them from the bogey of socialist labor and from the patriarchalism of the petty dynasties. When Weber traveled, his first idea was to get out of Germany. And only too frequently, with the resentment of the unsuccessful lover, he throws out angry words about turning his back forever upon what he felt to be a hopeless nation. The Kaiser, to whom he was bound by oath as a Prussian officer, was a constant object of his public contempt.

Only rarely do we get a glimpse into what nourished his love of his country and people. At the Exposition in St. Louis he viewed the German exhibition of arts, crafts, and industrial products with pride, feeling that the skill, imagination, and artistic craftsmanship of the Germans were second to none. When he mingled with itinerant socialist workers in Brussels and was told that a good proportion of the most skillful tailors in Paris and of the most skilled cobblers in London were from German Austria, he took pride in belonging to a fellowship of self-forgotten workers, who knew nothing better than devotion to the work at hand.

This attitude enables us to understand how his own ascetic drive for work was linked with his belief that the most prominent traits of the German people were the plebeian qualities of commoners and workers, lacking the social graces of the Latin courtier as well as the religiously motivated discipline and conventionality of the Anglo-Saxon gentleman. His own devotion to his work was a realization of his duty to the fellowship of Germans. At the end of November 1918, he wrote: 'One has seen all the weaknesses, but if one wishes, one may also see the fabulous capacity of work, the superbity and matter-of-factness, the capacity—not the attainment—of beautifying everyday life, in contrast to the beauty of ecstacy or of the gestures of other nations.'

Just as his relation to his father was a source of guilt, so Weber developed strong guilt feelings for living under the Kaiser:

The measure of contempt given our nation abroad (Italy, America, everywhere!), and after all deservedly so!—and this is decisive—because we tolerate this man's regime has become a factor for us of first-rate world political importance. Anyone who reads the foreign press for a few months must notice this. We are isolated because this man rules us in this fashion and because *we tolerate it and whitewash it.* No man or party who in any sense cultivates democratic, and at the same time national, political ideals should assume responsibility for this regime, the continuance of which endangers our world position more than all colonial problems of any kind.[33]

Surely Weber's life illustrates the manner in which a man's relation to political authority may be modeled upon his relation to family disciplines. One has only to add, with Rousseau, that in the family the father's love for his children compensates him for the care he extends to them; while in the State the pleasure of commanding makes up for the love which the political chief does not have for his people.[34]

II. Political Concerns

In many ways, Max Weber's life and thought are expressions of political events and concerns. His political stands, which must be understood in terms of private contexts as well as public happenings, make up a theme inextricably interwoven with Weber the man and the intellectual. For he was a political man and a political intellectual. We have noticed how the very young Weber felt that Cicero made a fool of himself in the face of a threatened political conspiracy. To judge politics and rhetoric in terms of consequences and to measure the motives of men in terms of the intended or unintended results of their actions remained a constant principle of his political thinking. In this fundamental sense, Weber the scholar always wrote from the point of view of the active politician.

His early political position was his father's National Liberalism. Under eminent leaders, this party had moved towards Bismarck during the 'eighties. In this matter, they were compromised liberals: they wished 'neither to follow nor to fight, but to influence Bismarck.' And they allowed Bismarck to fight the *Kulturkampf* against the Catholics and to suppress socialist labor. With such policies being followed, and with the several splits among the liberal and leftist camp, Bismarck could play off these parties against one another.

At the age of 20, Weber was identified with the cause of National Liberalism, but he was cautious not to commit himself definitely to any specific party. He was watchfully interested in the political process as a whole and was an eager student of the possible motives of competing leaders. But he was no 'youthful enthusiast.' It was characteristic of this detachment that when the National Liberals helped Bismarck to prolong the 'emergency law' against the socialists, Weber commented:

If one wants to justify this law one has to take the point of view, perhaps not quite incorrect, that without this emergency law a considerable restriction of many accomplishments of public life would be inevitable, namely, freedom of speech, assembly, and of association. After all, the Social Democrats, by their manner of agitation, were indeed going to compromise fundamental institutions of public life. . . However, when I think of the matter quietly, sometimes it seems to me as if equal rights for all might be preferable to everything else, and in this case the thing to do is to muzzle everybody rather than to put some in chains. The basic mistake, after all, seems to have been the Danaer present of Bismarck's Caesarism, namely, the universal franchise which was a pure murder of equal rights for all in the truest sense of the word.[1]

Weber's evaluation of Bismarck, as indicated in this passage, was not to change. He acknowledged and admired his political genius in relentless pursuit of policy of unifying Germany and in attaining for the newly created state the position of a great power. However, Weber was far from any uncritical surrender to Bismarck; he did not heroize him; indeed, he had nothing but scorn for the essentially apolitical hero worship of Bismarck that spread through the middle classes of Germany. Weber's basic criticism of Bismarck was of his intolerance of independent-minded political leaders, that he surrounded himself with docile and obedient bureaucrats. 'The horrible destruction of independent convictions which Bismarck has caused among us is, of course, the main reason, or at least one of the main reasons, for what is wrong with our condition. But, do we not bear at least the same guilt as he?'[2]

The attainment and preservation of intellectual liberty appears to have been one of Weber's highest conscious values. He rejected, without reservation, Bismarck's *Kulturkampf*, just as much as he rejected the Prussian language-policy for Germanizing the Poles and irritating the Alsatians. Yet he called the progressives 'sterile,' especially in their heads-I-win-tails-you-lose budget figuring. 'One shivers to think that these people would be called upon to take Bismarck's place.' After Kaiser William II ascended to the throne and showed his tendency towards the personal assumption of power, Weber looked to the future with profound anxieties. 'These Boulangist, Bonapartist demonstrations are undesirable, to say the least.'[3]

The first traces of Weber's shift away from the National Liberalism—which became more and more a creature of big business—and in the direction of a more progressive 'social liberalism' appears in 1887, when he was 23. At this time he seemed to feel that the state had an obligation towards the weakest social stratum, the metropolitan proletariat, which during the development of Berlin lived under the typical miserable conditions of early capitalism. This feeling of social responsibility was, after all, one of paternalism. Hence, Weber voted Conservative, though he did not join the Conservative party.

His detailed studies of the Junker economy in East Elbian, Germany, undertaken during the early 'nineties at the instigation of a reform society, which included 'Professorial socialists,' were Weber's first economic publications. They established his reputation as an expert in agrarian problems. He was trying to get at the economic and social reasons for the displacement of the German population in the east by Polish-Russian settlers. He demonstrated that the real-estate and property interests of Junker capitalism were responsible for the depopulation of the German east, an area that at one time had been a densely populated peasant land, intermixed with estates. By breaking down official census statistics into small units, Weber showed that irresistible depopulation forces went on wherever large entailed estates came into being. At the same time, the agrarian capitalists imported Polish seasonal laborers, who, by virtue of their low standards of living and exploitability, displaced the German peasant population.

Insight into this process placed Weber in political opposition to Prussia's ruling class and therewith in opposition to the class which, by virtue of a sham constitutional setup of Prussia, dominated the rest of Germany. His opposition to these landlords rested upon a belief that their interests ran counter to the interests of the nation. 'We wish to forge small peasants to the soil of the fatherland not by legal but by psychological chains. I say it openly: We wish to exploit their land-hunger in order to chain them to the homeland. And if we had to stamp a generation of men into the soil in order to guarantee the future of Germany, we would shoulder this responsibility.' [4]

In the early 'nineties, Weber argued against historical materialism by playing up the inexhaustible complexity of causal pluralism. For example, he felt, for many historical reasons, that the wages of farm hands did not follow any economic law, least of all an 'iron one.' In his 1894 lecture at Freiburg, he held that national and ethnic differences in the competitive struggle for existence were more causally important than economic and class situations. Later his political and intellectual relations with the body of Marxist knowledge were to be quite different and much more complex.

Weber's political mood when he was thirty years of age is revealed by the following passage from his inaugural lecture at Freiburg:

In the main, the fruits of all economic, social, and political endeavors of the present will benefit not living but future generations. If our work can and will have meaning, it can only attempt to provide for the future, that is, for our successors. However, no economic policy is possible on the basis of optimistic hopes for happiness. *Lasciate ogni speranza* [Man, if you enter here, leave all hopes outside] stands written over the door to the unknown future of human history. It is not a dream of peace and human happiness. The question is not how men in the future will feel, but rather who they will be. That is the question which concerns us when we think beyond the graves of our own generation. And in truth, this question lies at the root of every economic and political work. We do not strive for man's future well-being; we are eager to breed in them those traits with which we link the feeling that they constitute what is humanly great and noble in our nature. . . In the last analysis, the processes of economic development are struggles for power. Our ultimate yardstick of values is 'reasons of state,' and this is also the yardstick for our economic reflections. . .[5]

Thus, in the middle 'nineties, Weber was an imperialist, defending the power-interest of the national state as the ultimate value and using the vocabulary of social Darwinism. He warned that economic power and the call for political leadership of the nation did not always coincide. He called himself an 'economic nationalist,' measuring the various classes with the yardstick of the state's political interests. The acquisition of colonies, the saber-rattling speeches of the Kaiser, and the imperial grandeur—for these Weber had nothing but the disdain of the expert who knew that they were hopeless nonsense.

It is dangerous and, in the long run, irreconcilable with the interest of the nation if an economically sinking class holds political power in its hands. It is still more dangerous if those classes to whom economic power and therewith the claim for political authority is shifting are politically immature in their leadership of the state. Both are threatening Germany at this time and, in truth, they provide the keys to the present danger of our situation.[6]

What was this 'dangerous situation'? German foreign policy was being reoriented: Bismarck's treaty with Russia was not renewed, the opportunity for an alliance with Great Britain was not seized, and a policy of planless drifting resulted. It was covered up by braggadocio, Kaiser-bluff, and led to the political isolation of Germany. The leading strata of this nation would not orient it towards the West or towards the East. German policies were thus erratically directed against everybody and a series of defeats was cloaked in boastfulness.

It has been cogently argued that this fatal situation was the result of compromise between Western industrialism and Junker agrarianism. The National Liberals, of course, were the imperialists, the Pan-Germanists, the Anglophobes; their pride was hurt and they wanted 'to show the British' that Germans, too, could build ships. They pushed the navy program, which Tirpitz finally put over in one of the most adroit propaganda campaigns of modern history.[7] They won the Junkers' co-operation for this course by granting them protectionist tariffs in 1902 against the imports of grain from the United States and Russia. The Junkers as such did not care for the *graessliche Flotte,* and, landlubbers as they were, they did not think much of over-seas empire, with its commerce and colonies. They remained provincial, they felt politically close to Russian Czarism, and they were suspicious of the interests of Western industry in naval construction, which masqueraded as the National Task.

Both Junkers and industrialists, however, feared the mass organizations of the ascending Social Democrats, the clamor for democracy, and the attacks against the Prussian system of class suffrage. The compromise of the respective class interests of industrial National Liberals and agrarian Junker Conservatives was thus directed against the democratic and socialist Labor party. And their compromise led to the discarding of any foreign policy involving alliances with effective naval or military partners.

The political and economic compromises of the East and West led to the social fusion of Junkerdom with the new industrial stratum. It was symptomatic of these changes that Bertha Krupp, Alfred Krupp's only heir, married the nobleman, von Bohlen, an imperial career diplomat; and the Kaiser attended the wedding. The Crown also lost prestige through the scandalous exposures of the political police in the Tausch trial, the morally unsavory atmosphere of court circles exposed by Maximilian Harden in his crusade against Prince Eulenburg, the series of humiliations of the Kaiser in the foreign field, the more intense war scares, and the general armament and naval race. These were some of the events and trends that made Max Weber feel as if he were riding on 'an express train moving towards an abyss and not feeling certain whether the next switch has been set right.'

Weber was friendly with a 'radical' parson, Naumann, who flirted with socialist ideas and who under Weber's influence turned nationalist. In 1894, Parson Naumann founded a 'little magazine' to which Weber contributed.[8] For a few years, Weber was in contact with the attempts of these parsons, teachers, civil servants, artisans, and a few workers—a typical petty bourgeois circle—to organize a little party. They wished to create national unity by spreading a sense of social responsibility among bourgeois classes and training socialist labor for nationalism.[9] Max Weber's mother and Mrs. Baumgarten forwarded Naumann's campaign for a seat in the Reichstag. Although he did not lose a friendly contact, Weber soon impatiently broke his active connection with this group.

In 1897, Weber made a campaign speech in the Saar in the district of Baron von Stumm, the coal magnate, who was pressing for legislation to punish trade-union leaders in case of strikes. Although he spoke in favor of industrial capitalism, which he felt was indispensable for national power, he also believed strongly in 'individual liberty.' He had been a member of the Pan-Germanic League, but he broke with it in 1899 'in order to gain my freedom' and because 'my voice does not count in its policy.' [10]

In 1903, after the worst of his psychic collapses, he cut loose from and attacked the conservative romanticism behind which the material and political class interests of dynasty and Junkers were hidden. This was just before he left for America. After returning to Germany in 1905, his political interests were aroused by the first Russian revolution of 1905. Since he took the trouble to learn Russian, he was able to follow events in several Russian dailies. He was also in frequent conversations with the Russian political scientist, T. Kistiakovski—one of the intellectual leaders of leftist bourgeois liberalism in Russia—who worked for the revolution. The result of these studies was two exemplary essays in political sociology, which Weber published as special issues of the *Archiv*. By a sociological analysis of classes and parties in Russia, Weber—among other trains of thought—indicated that should the Czar fall, after a European war, and the extreme left come to power in another revolution, an unheard-of bureaucratization of the entire social structure of Russia might well result.

Weber's intellectual production had begun again shortly after his return from America in 1904. This was a time of political crisis for Germany, brought about in part by the speeches of the Kaiser and his excursions to Africa. By 1906 the *entente cordial* was shaping, and Germany's diplomatic isolation and decline from Bismarckian heights were obvious. The symbol of the nation, the Kaiser, had become the target of international ridicule. Weber saw the root of these difficulties in a political structure that prevented the efficient selection of responsible political leaders. He was grieved that Germany's sham constitutionalism made political careers unattractive to talented and effective men, who preferred to enter business or science.

From such views as these, Weber moved slowly towards a 'democratic' stand, though of a somewhat unique and complex nature. He did not believe in democracy as an intrinsically valuable body of ideas: 'natural law,' 'the equality of men,' their intrinsic claim to 'equal rights.' He saw democratic institutions and ideas pragmatically: not in terms of their 'inner worth' but in terms of their consequences in the selection of efficient political leaders. And he felt that in modern society such leaders must be able to build up and control a large, well-disciplined machine, in the American sense. The choice was between a leaderless democracy or a democracy run by the leaders of large-party bureaucracies.

For Weber, the universal franchise, the struggle for votes, and the freedom of organization had no value unless they resulted in powerful political leaders willing to assume responsibility rather than evade it and cover up their deeds behind court cliques and imperial bureaucrats who happened to have the Kaiser's favor.

Before Weber's critical examination, no single German stratum seemed to be satisfactory for the job at hand. Accordingly, he raised a critical voice, first of all against the head of the nation, the Kaiser, whom he scathingly derided as a dilettante covering behind divine right of kings. The structure of German party life seemed hopeless as a check on the uncontrolled power of a politically docile but technically perfected bureaucratic machine. He pierced the radical phrases of the Social Democrats as the hysterical howling of powerless party journalists drilling the masses for an intellectual goosestep, thus making them more amenable to manipulation by the bureaucracy. At the same time, the utopian comfort contained in revisionist Marxism's automatic drift into paradise appeared to substitute a harmless complacency for righteous indignation. And he thought that the Social Democrats' refusal to make any compromises with bourgeois parties and assume cabinet responsibilities was one of the factors blocking the introduction of constitutional government. Later political analyses made by Weber sprang from this desperate search for a stratum that would measure up to the political tasks of leadership in an era of imperialist rivalry.

In the fall of 1911, a militarist-minded official of a German university made a speech in which he chastised pacifist elements as 'silly' and spoke of the 'sentimentality for peace.' A general attending the beer festival that followed the speech saw fit to dub pacifists as 'men who wear trousers but have nothing in them and wish to make political eunuchs out of the people.' [11] When several professors of Freiburg defended these speeches against press attacks, Weber wrote a memorandum against what appeared to him as 'small-town stuff.' He warned that if Germany should have to go to war, 'her crowned dilettante' (the Kaiser) would interfere with the leadership of the army and ruin everything. It is interesting that Weber, a confirmed nationalist believing in force as the last argument of any policy, nevertheless submitted the following paragraph: 'To characterize a criticism of definite political ideals, no matter how high-minded, as an undermining of moral forces must call forth justified protests. In "ethics" the pacifists are undoubtedly our "betters." . . Policy making is not a moral trade, nor can it ever be.' [12] In spite of this appreciation of the ethical sincerity of such pacifists as Tolstoy, we must recall Weber's own desire for personal participation in the war.

During the war, he was against the annexation of Belgium, but this is not to say that Weber had no imperialist aspirations. He clamored for 'military bases' as far flung as Warsaw and to the north of there. And he wished the German army to occupy Liége and Namur for twenty years.

In October 1915 he wrote: 'Every victory brings us further from peace. This is the uniqueness of the situation.' He was beyond himself when Austria allowed Italy to break away from her. 'The entire statesmanship of the last twenty-five years is collapsing, and it is very poor satisfaction always to have said it. The war can now last forever.' He wrote a memorandum addressed to the Government and to members of the German Parliament, but it remained on his own desk. In it are such statements as: 'It is against German interests to force a peace of which the main result would be that the heel of the German boot in Europe stands upon everyone's toes.' [13] He saw that sheer prolongation of the war would bring world industrial supremacy to America. He was alarmed about the imperialism, which ran rampant through heavy industry and the princely houses. Desperately he wrote: 'I will learn Polish and then seek to make contacts with the Poles.' He asked the under-secretary of state for access to the official archives on Poland and to be allowed to contact Polish industrialists. Although he used a member of the Catholic Center party as a front, he was of course refused. By March 1916, Weber was disgusted with 'the whole Berlin atmosphere, in which all talented people are incapacitated by the resentful stupidity which prevails in the Reich offices.' [14]

Weber believed that the First World War was a result of a constellation of economic and political rivalries of nations. In so far as elements of 'guilt' might enter the picture, he thought that Germany was guilty of romantic and inefficient management of her affairs. He decried the aspirations of the war-party as idiotic and, from the very beginning, felt that it could only lead to disaster. He was particularly enraged by Tirpitz's naval policy, the sinking of the *Lusitania,* and the reliance upon the weapon of the submarine. He anticipated America's entrance into the war, and in February 1916 stated the following results of this development:

First, that half of our merchant marine, one-quarter in American and one-quarter in Italian harbors (!), will be confiscated and used against us; thus at once the number of British ships will be increased—a matter which these asses [of the German navy] do not calculate. Second, we shall have 500,000 American sportsmen as volunteers, brilliantly equipped, against our tired troops, a matter which these asses do not believe. Third, forty billion in cash will be available to our enemies. Fourth, three more years of war; thus, certain ruin. Fifth, Rumania, Greece, etc. against us. And all this in order that Herr von Tirpitz may show what he can do! Never has anything so stupid been thought of.[15]

In October 1916, Weber spoke in a political meeting of progressive liberals on Germany among the Great Powers of Europe. In this speech he judged policy with the yardstick of international result: the geographic position of Germany in the midst of powerful neighbors should make for a policy of sober alliances rather than a policy of boastful vanity and conquest. In Weber's view, Russia was 'the main threat.' Accordingly, he wished an understanding with England. Events in Eastern Europe brought world-historical decisions to the fore, compared to which changes in Western Europe appeared trivial. The ultimate cause of the war was Germany's late development as an industrial power-state. 'And why have we become a nation organized into a power state?' he asked.

Not for vanity, but for the sake of our responsibility to world history. The Danes, Swiss, Norwegians, and Dutch will not be held responsible by future generations, and especially not by our own descendants, for allowing, without a fight, world power to be partitioned between the decrees of Russian officials on the one hand and the conventions of Anglo-Saxon 'society'—perhaps with a dash of Latin *raison* thrown in—on the other. The division of world power ultimately means the control of the nature of future culture. Future generations will hold us responsible in these matters, and rightly so, for we are a nation of seventy and not seven millions.[16]

On 3 November 1918, the sailors at Kiel mutinied. The next day, Weber spoke in Munich on Germany's reconstruction. He was heckled by revolutionary intellectuals, among them the Russian Bolshevist Levien, as well as by veterans in the audience. Shortly afterwards a revolutionary government of workers and soldiers' councils was set up.

Max Weber was against those professors who at the moment of collapse placed the blame upon the German home front by rationalizing the collapse as 'a stab in the back.' Yet he was also against 'the revolution,' which he called 'this bloody carnival' and which he felt could only secure worse peace terms than might otherwise have been possible. At the same time, he realized that the revolution could not lead to lasting socialistic institutions.

His wife has stated that his sympathy with the struggle of the proletariat for a human and dignified existence had for decades been so great that he often pondered whether or not he should join their ranks as a party member—but always with negative conclusions. His reasoning, according to his wife, 'was that one could be an honest socialist, just like a Christian, only if one was ready to share the way of life of the unpropertied, and in any case, only if one was ready to forego a cultured existence based upon their work. Since his disease, this was impossible for Weber. His scholarship simply depended upon capital rent. Furthermore, he remained personally an "individualist."'

He accompanied the German peace delegation to Versailles as an expert. He suggested that 'the designated war criminals,' Ludendorff, Tirpitz, Capelle, Bethman, should voluntarily offer their heads to the enemy; only then, he thought, the German officer corps could again rise to glory. He wrote Ludendorff a letter to this effect, but Ludendorff curtly refused. Weber then arranged to meet Ludendorff personally and disputed with him for several hours. He reproached him with the political mistakes committed by the general staff and was in turn reproached by Ludendorff for the sins of the revolution and the new regime. Weber asked Ludendorff to offer his head to the enemy.

LUDENDORFF: How can you expect me to do anything of the sort?
WEBER: The honor of the nation can only be saved if you give yourself up.
LUDENDORFF: The nation can go jump in the lake. Such ingratitude!
WEBER: Nevertheless, you ought to render this last service.
LUDENDORFF: I hope to be able to render more important services to the nation.
WEBER: In that case, your remark is not meant so seriously. For the rest,

it is not only a matter of the German people but a matter of restoring the honor of the officer corps and of the army.

LUDENDORFF: Why don't you go and see Hindenburg? After all he was the General Field Marshal.

WEBER: Hindenburg is seventy years of age, and besides, every child knows that at the time you were Number One in Germany.

LUDENDORFF: Thank goodness.

The conversation soon drifted into politics, Ludendorff blaming Weber and the *Frankfurter Zeitung* for the 'democracy.'

WEBER: Do you believe that I think this swinish condition which we have at present is democracy?

LUDENDORFF: If you talk that way, maybe we can reach an agreement.

WEBER: But the preceding swinish condition was not a monarchy either.

LUDENDORFF: Then, what do you mean by democracy?

WEBER: In a democracy the people choose a leader in whom they trust. Then the chosen leader says, 'Now shut up and obey me.' People and party are then no longer free to interfere in his business.

LUDENDORFF: I could like such democracy.

WEBER: Later the people can sit in judgment. If the leader has made mistakes —to the gallows with him!

Weber was profoundly disappointed in Ludendorff's human stature. 'Perhaps,' he wrote, 'it is better for Germany that he does not give himself up. His personal impression would be unfavorable. The enemy would again find that the sacrifices of a war which put this type out of commission were worth their while. I now understand why the world defends itself against the attempts of men like him to place their heel upon the necks of others. If he should again mingle in politics, one will have to fight him remorselessly.' [17]

Max Weber thus looked upon German party life with disdain. It struck him as petty and as suffocating in the atmosphere of guild squabbles. In this respect, he shared the attitude of Carl Jentsch.[18]

Having absorbed the Marxist criticism of 'bourgeois democracy,' Weber turned away from conservatism, Pan-Germanism, and monarchical loyalties. He did so not because he had learned to believe in the intrinsic value of democratic constitutional government as a 'government of the people, for the people, and by the people,' but because he believed constitutional democracy was the only solution for Germany's problems at home and abroad. In April 1917, he wrote:

I would not fire a single shot and I would not buy a penny war bond if this war were anything but a national war; if it concerned the form of the state and possibly was a war for retaining this incapable monarchy and this apolitical bureaucracy. I don't give a damn for the form of the State, if only politicians were to rule the country and not such vain simpletons as William II and his like. . . For me constitutions are techniques just like any other machines. I would be just as ready to strike against parliament and for the monarch if he were a politician or if he gave promise of becoming one.[19]

Weber agitated for constitutional democracy because he hoped the Reichstag might become a balancing factor against the overwhelming weight of Prussian, and therewith German, bureaucracy and its mentality. A parliamentary competition of parties should bring political leaders of perspective and of passionate will to power. They should possess the technical know-how required for subduing the bureaucracy to their will. They should steer the bureaucracy, which for Weber made sense only as a technical means and never as a policy-making and politically responsible agency. In the best case, Weber hoped for the rise of charismatic leaders, though he felt the drift towards ever-denser and indestructible institutions in modern society narrowed the opportunity for this 'purely personal element' to be decisive in the social structure.

It is, of course, quite vain to speculate whether Weber with his Machiavellian attitude might ever have turned Nazi. To be sure, his philosophy of charisma—his skepticism and his pragmatic view of democratic sentiment—might have given him such affinities. But his humanism, his love for the underdog, his hatred of sham and lies, and his unceasing campaign against racism and anti-Semitic demagoguery would have made him at least as sharp a 'critic,' if not a sharper one, of Hitler than his brother Alfred has been.

Weber was far from following Troeltsch, who felt it necessary to speak of the 'most basic dispositions and volitional tendencies' ultimately underlying the social institutions, and ideological structures of history: 'We have no words for this and, in this case, speak of races, of plastic, historical forces, or of primeval impulses.'[20] Weber was far from this quest for a metaphysical anchorage in 'blind nature.' One may sum up Weber's dispersed and repeated disclaimers of racial arguments in the words of John Stuart Mill: 'Of all vulgar modes of escaping from the consideration of the effect of social and moral influences on the human mind, the most vulgar is that of attributing the diversities of conduct and character to inherent natural differences.'[21]

Weber, one might say, was constitutionally incapable of making 'the intellectual sacrifice' that he believed all 'faith' demands. The nightmare of faith represented by modern fascism would hardly have intrigued as passionate a servant of rational social science as Max Weber. The basic style of thought that informs his work is Western positivism, a heritage of the enlightenment. The basic volitional tendency of his thought is not, with the Ranke school, artistically to construct great tableaux of periods each of which is 'equally near to God,' but to fashion intellectual tools that would yield hindsights serviceable to foresights: *savoir pour prévoir, prévoir pour pouvoir*—this impulse of Comte's positive philosophy was basic to Weber's outlook. Even though he stemmed from the 'historical school' he had no use for any edifying attitude towards history and its uniqueness. By-passing the hostility of historians, he politely suggested an enquiry into 'lawful regularities' as an 'auxiliary' science to history. He then proceeded to write social history in the grand manner.

Urbanism, legal history, economics, music, world religions—there is hardly a field which he left untouched. He thus continued the tradition of encyclopedic scholarship of Wundt and Ratzel, of Roscher and Schmoller.

He worked through masses of data not in order to seek in the contemplation of man's historical estate a quietistic refuge for a homeless religious need, comparable to the Rousseauistic sentiment of nature, but rather in order to snatch from comparative enquiries a set of rules which would serve him in his search for political orientation in the contemporary world. That knowledge is somehow power—that is the impulse behind this quest of a powerless man for knowledge. And it is in view of this political concern that one may understand his intellectual orientations.

III. Intellectual Orientations

THE intellectual situation in Germany during Weber's lifetime was singularly unfavorable for the development of academic sociology. Historiography was largely dominated by the traditions of Hegel and Ranke, and conservative thinking was extremely potent in checking any development of theory in the social sciences. This was especially the case in economics. For in this field, the historical school discouraged systematic theory by opposing to it a massive treasure of historical detail, legal fact, and institutional description.

Liberalism, on the other hand, had been developed by an intelligentsia that was independent of any entrepreneurial middle class. Compared with the Western countries, from which the models of thought for German liberalism had been derived, everything in Germany seemed topsy-turvy. The agrarian Junkers and their following clamored for Adam Smith and free trade, that is, for free grain exports to England rather than sales to the emerging industrial cities of Germany. The liberal Friedrich List advocated protective tariffs. Bismarck and the German princes, rather than the middle classes, had geared the German people into a national state.

The liberal academic intelligentsia had scarcely recovered from the shock of 1848 and the reaction to it, when Lassalle inaugurated a Socialist party that soon turned Marxist and attracted a brilliant group of journalists and organizers, historians and sociologists. These men took pride in their detachment from national loyalties. And, in Germany, Marxism was able to establish a tradition that tried to draw into its orbit the social and political history of all ages, the interpretation of literature and philosophy, as well as the development of social and economic theory.

In 1848 the liberals had been afraid of the bearded, itinerant journeymen; under Bismarck they were afraid of Bebel and Liebknecht. Even in 1878 the doctrinaire liberal Eugen Richter advised his followers to vote for the Conservative rather than for the Social Democratic candidate, should their choice be limited to these two.[1] And ten years later, when Ferdinand Tönnies published his *Gemeinschaft und Gesellschaft,* a work rightly considered basic for modern German sociology, he made himself a hopeless outsider from 'respectable' society. For sociology smacked of socialism. Even so discerning a mind as Ludwig Bamberger spoke of the 'internal affinity of militarism and socialism.'[2] Thus the intellectual traditions of Germany were channeled into conservative, liberal, and socialist ways of thought.

German political parties, having no opportunity to wield power, remained doctrinaire parties of principled world views, each rather strictly oriented towards special classes and status groups. Agrarian conservatives were in coalition with Lutheran orthodoxy, urban merchants and bankers with liberal professional men, socialist wage workers with a low-browed intelligentsia who elaborated high-browed Marxism. The get-rich-quick atmosphere of the new industrialism, the intoxication of the parvenu with power after 1870, the Philistinism of the socially arriving burghers working their ways into dueling corps, baronial estates, and the officer corps—all this bred political apathy and fear of the upthrust of labor. And it led to a wide political accommodation to the power of the Junker.

Within this context of conflicting classes, parties, and intellectual currents, Max Weber worked out his intellectual orientations. He aimed at the comprehensiveness of a common ground. And he did so in spite of the intellectual departmentalization of sharply opposed world views. By reflecting upon some of his analytic conceptions and broad historical views, we may be able to indicate how conservative, liberal, and socialist elements of thought were assimilated, transformed, and integrated into the complex pattern of his work. As a liberal, fighting against both conservative and Marxist thought, Max Weber opened himself to certain influences from each of his opponents.

1: MARX AND WEBER

Upon taking over the editorship of the *Archiv Für Sozialwissenschaft und Sozialpolitik,* Weber proposed systematically to devote attention to the questions the Marxists had raised. Much of Weber's own work is of course informed by a skilful application of Marx's historical method. Weber, however, used this method as a 'heuristic principle.' As a view of world history, Marxism seemed to him an untenable monocausal theory and thus prejudicial to an adequate reconstruction of social and historical connections. He felt that Marx as an economist had made the same mistake that, during Weber's days, anthropology was making: raising a segmental perspective to paramount importance and reducing the multiplicity of causal factors to a single-factor theorem.

Weber does not squarely oppose historical materialism as altogether wrong; he merely takes exception to its claim of establishing a single and universal causal sequence. Apart from whether or not he 'understood' dialectical thought in his reduction of it to a causal proposition, the approach did prove eminently fruitful.

Part of Weber's own work may thus be seen as an attempt to 'round out' Marx's economic materialism by a political and military materialism. The Weberian approach to political structures closely parallels the Marxian approach to economic structures. Marx constructed economic periods and located major economic classes in them; he related the several social and political factors to the means of production. In political matters, Weber looks for the disposition over weapons and over means of administration.

Feudalism, for example, is characterized by Weber in terms of private property of the means of military violence (self-equipped armies) and in the corporate appropriation of the means of administration. The 'ruler' could not monopolize administration and warfare because he had to delegate the implements required for such a monopoly to the several privileged groupings. In time, these latter become 'owners' in their own right. This attention to the control of the material means of political power is as crucial for grasping the types of political structure as is attention to the means of production in the case of Marx for grasping economic structures.*

Whereas Marx is less careful in distinguishing between economic power and political power, Weber, as a liberal, is eager to keep these spheres clearly distinct. Thus, his criticism of most Marxist contributions is that they fail soberly to distinguish between what is strictly 'economic,' what is 'economically determined,' and what is merely 'economically relevant.' Pilgrimages to Rome are certainly relevant for the money market, but that does not make them economic enterprises. The import of religious or of political ideas for economic institutions does not

---

* See in this volume: 'Politics as a Vocation,' 'Bureaucracy,' and 'The Social Psychology of World Religions.'

thereby transform these ideas into economic factors: the question concerns their 'economic relevance.'

Having focused upon the struggle for the means of political rule, Weber sees European political history since the feudal period as an intricate parade of rulers, each attempting to appropriate the financial and military means that in feudal society were relatively dispersed. In fact, Weber formulates the very concept of the 'state' in terms of a 'monopoly' of the use of legitimate force over a given territory. The territorial aspect enters into the conception of the state in that Weber distinguishes coastal and inland states, great river states, and states of the plains. The geographical factor also seems to have a dispositional bearing in that the coastal, and hence maritime, state offers opportunities for city democracy, overseas empire; whereas the state of the plains—for example, Russia and the United States—seems to favor schematization and bureaucracy, although of course this tendency is not without exceptions.

With Marx, Weber shares an attempt to bring 'ideological' phenomena into some correlation with the 'material' interests of the economic and political orders. Weber has a keen eye for 'rationalizations,' that is, for 'fictitious superstructures,' and for incongruities between the verbal assertion and the actual intention. He fought imperial and bureaucratic bombast, and especially the phrases of the Pan-Germanists and/or revolutionary 'literati,' with a wrath comparable to Marx's campaign against Victorian cant.

The debunking technique by which ideological assertions are revealed as false cloaks for less respectable interests is obvious in Weber's attack upon the revolutionary left of 1918. Weber expressly stated at this time that Marxism is not a carriage, which one may arrest at will: he wished to extend the debunking of ideologies to include the 'proletarian interest,' and he attempted to narrow down this interest to the interests of the literati, politicians, and revolutionary guardsmen in 'the spoils of victory.' His debunking of socialist aspirations is also obvious in his reflections on imperialism. Here he obviously accepts national units as historical ultimates that can never be integrated into more comprehensive and harmonious wholes. At best there will be strong socialist nation-states energetically exploiting weaker states. The concept of the nation and of national interest is thus the limit of Weber's political outlook and at the same time constitutes his ultimate value. Yet it is characteristic of his restless analysis that he breaks down 'national sentiment' into a composite of various communal sentiments and attitudes.

In addition to this attention to 'interests' and 'ideologies,' Weber's sociology is related to Marx's thought in the common attempt to grasp the interrelations on all institutional orders making up a social structure. In Weber's work, military and religious, political and juridical institutional systems are functionally related to the economic order in a variety of ways. Yet, the political judgments and evaluations involved differ entirely from those of Marx. For Marx, the modern economy is basically irrational; this irrationality of capitalism results from a contradiction between the rational technological advances of the productive forces and the fetters of private property, private profit, and unmanaged market competition. The system is characterized by an 'anarchy of production.'

For Weber, on the other hand, modern capitalism is not 'irrational'; indeed, its institutions appear to him as the very embodiment of rationality. As a type of bureaucracy, the large corporation is rivaled only by the state bureaucracy in promoting rational efficiency, continuity of operation, speed, precision, and calculation of results. And all this goes on within institutions that are rationally managed, and in which combined and specialized functions occupy the center of attention. The whole structure is dynamic, and by its anonymity compels modern man to become a specialized expert, a 'professional' man qualified for the accomplishment of a special career within pre-scheduled channels. Man is thus prepared for his absorption in the clattering process of the bureaucratic machinery.

The concept of rational bureaucracy is played off against the Marxist concept of the class struggle. As is the case with 'economic materialism,' so with 'class struggle': Weber does not deny class struggles and their part in history, but he does not see them as the central dynamic. Nor does he deny the possibility of a socialization of the means of production. He merely relegates this demand to a far distant future and disputes any hope of 'socialism for our time.' He does not see anything attractive in socialism. In his eyes, socialism would merely complete in the economic order what had already happened in the sphere of political means. The feudal estates had been expropriated of their political means and had been displaced by the salaried officialdom of the modern bureaucratic state. The state had 'nationalized' the possession of arms and of administrative means. Socialization of the means of production would merely subject an as yet relatively autonomous economic life to the bureaucratic management of the state. The state would indeed become total, and Weber, hating bureaucracy as a shackle upon the liberal individual, felt that socialism would thus lead to a further serfdom. 'For the time being,' he wrote, 'the dictatorship of the official and not that of the worker is on the march.' [3]

Weber thus saw himself as holding paradoxical opinions. He could not but recognize the inevitability of bureaucratic management in public administration, in large capitalist enterprises, and in politically efficient party machines. During the war he personally scolded the stupidity of the Berlin bureaucrats, yet in his classic account of bureaucracy he is very far from John Stuart Mill's verdict against 'pedantocracy.' On the contrary, for Weber nothing is more efficient and more precise than bureaucratic management. Again in his pride in bureaucracy, 'in spite of all,' one may discern an attitude comparable to Marx's admiration for the achievements of bourgeois capitalism in wiping out feudal survivals, the 'idiocy' of rural life, and various spooks of the mind.

Marx's emphasis upon the wage worker as being 'separated' from the means of production becomes, in Weber's perspective, merely one special case of a universal trend. The modern soldier is equally 'separated' from the means of violence; the scientist from the means of enquiry, and the civil servant from the means of administration. Weber thus tries to relativize Marx's work by placing it into a more generalized context and showing that Marx's conclusions rest upon observations drawn from a dramatized 'special case,' which is better seen as one case in a broad series of similar cases. The series as a whole exemplifies the comprehensive underlying trend of bureaucratization. Socialist class struggles are merely a vehicle implementing this trend.

Weber thus identifies bureaucracy with rationality, and the process of rationalization with mechanism, depersonalization, and oppressive routine. Rationality, in this context, is seen as adverse to personal freedom. Accordingly, Weber is a nostalgic liberal, feeling himself on the defensive. He deplores the type of man that the mechanization and the routine of bureaucracy selects and forms. The narrowed professional, publicly certified and examined, and ready for tenure and career. His craving for security is balanced by his moderate ambitions and he is rewarded by the honor of official status. This type of man Weber deplored as a petty routine creature, lacking in heroism, human spontaneity, and inventiveness: 'The Puritan willed to be the vocational man that we have to be.'

2: BUREAUCRACY AND CHARISMA: A PHILOSOPHY OF HISTORY

The principle of rationalization is the most general element in Weber's philosophy of history. For the rise and fall of institutional structures, the ups and downs of classes, parties, and rulers implement the general drift of secular rationalization. In thinking of the change of human attitudes and mentalities that this process occasions, Weber liked to quote Friedrich Schiller's phrase, the 'disenchantment of the world.' The extent and direction of 'rationalization' is thus measured negatively in terms of the degree to which magical elements of thought are displaced, or positively by the extent to which ideas gain in systematic coherence and naturalistic consistency.

The urge towards such a comprehensive and meaningful interpretation of the universe is ascribed to groups of intellectuals, to religious prophets and teachers, to sages and philosophers, to jurists and experimental artists, and finally, to the empirical scientist. 'Rationalization,' socially and historically differentiated, thus comes to have a variety of meanings. In this connection Weber makes a masterful contribution to what has come to be known as the 'sociology of knowledge.' *

Weber's view of 'disenchantment' embodies an element of liberalism and of the enlightenment philosophy that construed man's history as a unilinear 'progress' towards moral perfection (sublimation), or towards cumulative technological rationalization. Yet his skeptical aversion to any 'philosophical' element in empirical science precluded any explicit constructions of historical time in terms of 'cycles' or 'unilinear' evolution. 'Thus far the continuum of European culture development has known neither completed cyclical movements nor an unambiguously oriented "unilinear development." ' [4] We nevertheless feel justified in holding that a unilinear construction is clearly implied in Weber's idea of the bureaucratic trend. Even so 'inward' and apparently subjective an area of experience as that of music lends itself to a sociological treatment under Weber's concept of 'rationalization.' The fixation of clang patterns, by a more concise notation and the establishment of the well-tempered scale; 'harmonious' tonal music and the standardization of the quartet of wood winds and string instruments as the core of the symphony orchestra. These are seen as progressive 'rationalizations.' The

* We have included one chapter from Weber's study of China for the sake of acquainting the reader with this aspect of his work.

musical systems of Asia, of preliterate Indian tribes, of Antiquity, and of the Middle East are compared in regard to their scope and degree of 'rationalization.' The same comparative focus is of course used in the account of religious systems, as may be seen in the typological sketch contained in 'The Social Psychology of World Religions.'

This process of rationalization is punctured, however, by certain discontinuities of history. Hardened institutional fabrics may thus disintegrate and routine forms of life prove insufficient for mastering a growing state of tension, stress, or suffering. It is in such crises that Weber introduces a balancing conception for bureaucracy: the concept of 'charisma.'

Weber borrowed this concept from Rudolf Sohm, the Strassburg church historian and jurist. Charisma, meaning literally 'gift of grace,' is used by Weber to characterize self-appointed leaders who are followed by those who are in distress and who need to follow the leader because they believe him to be extraordinarily qualified. The founders of world religions and the prophets as well as military and political heroes are the archetypes of the charismatic leader. Miracles and revelations, heroic feats of valor and baffling success are characteristic marks of their stature. Failure is their ruin.

Although Weber is aware of the fact that social dynamics result from many social forces, he nevertheless places great emphasis upon the rise of charismatic leaders. Their movements are enthusiastic, and in such extraordinary enthusiasms class and status barriers sometimes give way to fraternization and exuberant community sentiments.[5] Charismatic heroes and prophets are thus viewed as truly revolutionary forces in history.[6]

Bureaucracy and other institutions, especially those of the household, are seen as routines of workaday life; charisma is opposed to all institutional routines, those of tradition and those subject to rational management. This holds for the economic order: Weber characterizes conquistadores and robber barons as charismatic figures. When used in a strictly technical manner, the concept of charisma is free of all evaluations. Stefan George as well as Jeremiah, Napoleon as well as Jesus Christ, a raving berserk warrior of Arabia as well as the founder of Mormonism—all these are typified as charismatic leaders, for they have in common the fact that people obey them because of faith in their personally extraordinary qualities.

A genuinely charismatic situation is direct and inter-personal. In the contrast of the everyday life of institutions with the personalized and spontaneous nature of charismatic leadership, one may readily discern the heritage of liberalism that has always confronted similar dichotomies: mass *versus* personality, the 'routine' *versus* the 'creative' entrepreneur, the conventions of ordinary people *versus* the inner freedom of the pioneering and exceptional man, institutional rules *versus* the spontaneous individual, the drudgery and boredom of ordinary existence *versus* the imaginative flight of the genius. In spite of the careful nominalism of his method, Weber's conception of the charismatic leader is a continuation of a 'philosophy of history' which, after Carlyle's *Heroes and Hero Worship,* influenced a great deal of nineteenth-century history writing. In such an emphasis, the monumentalized individual becomes the sovereign of history.

Weber's conception of the charismatic leader is in continuity with the concept of 'genius' as it was applied since the Renaissance to artistic and intellectual leaders. Within the confines of 'moral' history, W. E. H. Lecky broadened the conception in such a way as to apply it to leaders of human conduct rather than merely to creators of symbols. Not only men of ideas but ideal men thus came into focus, as the following passage indicates:

There arise from time to time men who bear to the moral condition of their age much the same relations as men of genius bear to its intellectual condition. They anticipate the moral standard of a later age, cast abroad conceptions of disinterested virtue, of philanthropy, or of self-denial that seem to have no relation to the spirit of their time, inculcate duties and suggest motives of action that appear to most men altogether chimerical. Yet the magnetism of their perfections tells powerfully upon their contemporaries. An enthusiasm is kindled, a group of adherents is formed, and many are emancipated from the moral condition of their age. Yet the full effects of such a movement are but transient. The first enthusiasm dies away, surrounding circumstances resume their ascendency, the pure faith is materialised, encrusted with conceptions that are alien to its nature, dislocated, and distorted, till its first features have almost disappeared. The moral teaching, being unsuited to the time, becomes inoperative until its appropriate civilisation has dawned; or at most it faintly and imperfectly filters through an accumulation of dogmas, and thus accelerates in some measure the arrival of the condition it requires.[7]

It is clear that Lecky was interested in the genius as an extraordinary man who transcends the bounds of everyday routines; and in this, his

statement foreshadows one of the key theories of Weber: the routinization of charisma.

Like Lecky, Weber sees the genuine charismatic situation quickly give
way to incipient institutions, which emerge from the cooling off of extraordinary states of devotion and fervor. As the original doctrines are
democratized, they are intellectually adjusted to the needs of that stratum
which becomes the primary carrier of the leader's message. If these ideas
are not adaptable in this way, then, regardless of their intrinsic merit,
either their message will fail to influence the conduct of everyday life
or those whom they do influence will remain enclosed in a special way
of life and alien to the larger social body. The religions of India, according to Weber, have very often ended up as the doctrines of such aristocracies of salvation.*

Emphasis upon the 'sovereignty of the charismatic man' does not
minimize the mechanics of institutions; on the contrary, by tracing out
the routinization of charisma, Weber is able to assign a heavy causal
weight to institutional routines. Thus he retains a social determinism
by emphasizing charisma's routinization. His handling of this problem
testifies to his constant endeavor to maintain a causal pluralism and to
bring the economic order into the balance.

In general, Weber's construction of historical dynamics in terms of
charisma and routinization is an attempt to answer the paradox of
unintended consequences. For the charisma of the first hour may incite
the followers of a warrior hero or prophet to forsake expediency for ultimate values. But during the routinization of charisma, the material interests of an increased following are the compelling factor.

A charismatic movement may be routinized into traditionalism or into
bureaucratization. Which course is taken does not depend primarily
upon the subjective intentions of the followers or of the leader; it is
dependent upon the institutional framework of the movement, and especially upon the economic order. 'The routinization of charisma, in quite
essential respects, is identical with adjustment to the conditions of the
economy, that is, to the continuously effective routines of workaday life.
In this, the economy leads and is not led.' [8] Just as in this particular context a leading role is given to the economy, so does the very title of his
key work, *Economics and Society,* bespeak an appreciation of the determining weight of the economic bases.

* See chapter xi, 'The Social Psychology of World Religions.'

The 'philosophical' element in Weber's construction of history is this antinomic balance of charismatic movements (leaders and ideas) with rational routinization (enduring institutions and material interests). Man's spontaneity and freedom are placed on the side of heroic enthusiasm, and thus there is an aristocratic emphasis upon elites ('virtuosos'!). This emphasis is intimately associated with Weber's attitude towards modern democracy, which we have already indicated.

Yet Weber sees in the concept of 'personality' a much-abused notion referring to a profoundly irrational center of creativity, a center before which analytical inquiry comes to a halt. And he combats this poeticized and romantic element.[9] For his conceptual nominalism and his pragmatic outlook are opposed to all reification of 'unanalyzed' processes. The ultimate unit of analysis for him is the understandable motivations of the single individual. His concepts are analytical tools with which he reconstructs various mechanisms. They are not descriptive categories, with which one tries to 'taste' the color and grasp the surface image of the 'spirit of the times.' They are not concepts that contemplate the supposed substances of great men and epochs. In fact, despite Weber's emphasis on charisma, he is not likely to focus on 'the great figures of history.' Napoleon, Calvin and Cromwell, Washington and Lincoln appear in his texts only in passing. He tries to grasp what is retained of their work in the institutional orders and continuities of history. Not Julius Caesar, but Caesarism; not Calvin, but Calvinism is Weber's concern. In order to understand this fully, we have to understand his conceptual tools: the constructed type, the typological series, the comparative method.

3: Methods of Social Science

Weber's methodological reflections are clearly indebted to the philosophy of the enlightenment. His point of departure and the ultimate unit of his analysis is the individual person:

Interpretative sociology considers the individual [*Einzelindividuum*] and his action as the basic unit, as its 'atom'—if the disputable comparison for once may be permitted. In this approach, the individual is also the upper limit and the sole carrier of meaningful conduct. . . In general, for sociology, such concepts as 'state,' 'association,' 'feudalism,' and the like, designate certain categories of human interaction. Hence it is the task of sociology to reduce these concepts to 'understandable' action, that is, without exception, to the actions of participating individual men.[10]

The 'Robinson-Crusoe approach' of the classical economists and the rationalist philosophers of the contract is echoed in this emphasis upon the individual. But within Weber's thought such emphasis stands in opposition to the tradition of Hegel and Ranke.

This latter tradition attempts to 'interpret' the individual person, institution, act, or style of work by seeing it as a 'document,' 'manifestation,' or an 'expression' of a larger morphological unit that underlies particular data. 'Interpretation' thus consists in understanding the union of the more comprehensive totality with its part. The aspect partakes of the quality of the whole. Thus Sombart, writing a book on *The Jews and Economic Life,* tries to show the contribution and the paramount significance of Jewry for the rise and workings of modern capitalism by 'understanding' Jewry and capitalism as partaking of the same 'spirit.' This mode of 'understanding' the particular by seeing it as a document of an underlying whole is rooted in German romantic and conservative thought —a style that was elaborated in great detail and with surprising subtlety and fruitfulness by Wilhelm Dilthey.

Max Weber incorporated the problem of understanding in his sociological approach, which, as he was prone to emphasize, was one type of sociology among other possibilities. He therefore called his perspective 'interpretative' or 'understanding' sociology. It is characteristic of his rational and positivist position that he transformed the concept of understanding. 'Understanding' remained for him, however, a unique approach of the moral or cultural sciences, which deals with man rather than with other animals or with lifeless nature. Man can 'understand" or attempt to 'understand' his own intentions through introspection, and he may interpret the motives of other men's conduct in terms of their professed or ascribed intentions.

Weber distinguishes different 'types' of motivated actions. Characteristically he rated as the most 'understandable' type those actions which are in the nature of rational expediencies, and of which the conduct of the 'economic man' is a prime example.

Less 'rational' actions are typed by Weber in terms of the pursuit of 'absolute ends,' as flowing from affectual sentiments, or as 'traditional.' Since absolute ends are to be taken as 'given' data by the sociologist, an action may be rational with reference to the means employed, but 'irrational' with respect to the ends pursued. 'Affectual' action, which flows purely from sentiment, is a less rational type of conduct. And finally, approaching the 'instinctual' level, there is 'traditional' conduct: unreflective and habitual, this type is sanctified because it 'has always been done' and is therefore deemed appropriate. These types of 'actions' are construed operationally in terms of a scale of rationality and irrationality. A typological device rather than a 'psychology' of motivations is thus described. This nominalist approach, with its emphasis upon the rational relations of ends and means as the most 'understandable' type of conduct, distinguishes Weber's work from conservative thought and its documentary 'understanding' by assimilating the singularity of an object into a spiritualized whole. Yet, by emphasizing the understandability of human conduct, as opposed to the mere causal explanation of 'social facts' as in natural science, Weber draws the line between his interpretative sociology and the 'physique sociale' in the tradition of Condorcet, which Comte called *sociologie*[11] and Durkheim worked out in such an eminent manner. It has correctly been observed that the basic types of social structure that Weber uses—'society,' 'association,' and 'community'—correspond closely with his 'types of action'—the 'rationally expedient,' the 'affective,' and the 'traditionalist.'[12]

Were one to accept Weber's methodological reflections on his own work at their face value, one would not find a systematic justification for his analysis of such phenomena as stratification or capitalism. Taken literally, the 'method of understanding' would hardly allow for Weber's use of structural explanations; for this type of explanation attempts to account for the motivation of systems of action by their functions as going concerns rather than by the subjective intentions of the individuals who act them out.

According to Weber's method of understanding, we should expect him to adhere to a subjective theory of stratification, but he does not do so. Similarly, one may point to Weber's refutation of a widespread German stereotype of America as a nation of 'atomized individuals': 'In the past and up to the very present, it has been a characteristic precisely of the specifically American *democracy* that it did *not* constitute a formless sand heap of individuals but rather a buzzing complex of strictly exclusive, yet voluntary, *associations*.' * Again, Weber sees the drift towards Athenian democracy as determined by a change in military organization: Democracy emerged when the older army of Hoplites gave way to Navalism. Similar structural explanations are displayed in the manner in which he links the spread of bureaucracies with the task of

* See pp. 307 ff., this volume.

administering large inland empires, such as Rome and China, Russia and the United States.

In using the structural principle of explanation, Weber comes quite close to the analytical procedure of Marxist thought, which, in a 'despiritualized' way, makes use of the originally Hegelian and conservative way of thinking.

In his methodological emphasis upon understanding the individual as the ultimate unit of explanation, Weber is polemical against this organicist thought of conservatism as well as the Marxist use of objective meanings of social action irrespective of the awareness of the actor.

Like Hegel and Adam Smith, Marx ascribed meanings to the process of social interactions. Adam Smith's 'unseen hand' and Hegel's 'ruse of the idea' appear in Marx's system as an objective logic of dynamic institutions that work themselves out behind the backs of the actors. In so far as men know not what they do, they realize the blind forces of society. Although these forces are the work of men, they simply remain, in Veblen's term, 'opaque.' Thus Marx measures the subjective notions of the actors of the system against the objective meaning as revealed by scientific study. And in the comparison and typical incongruity between what men think they do and the objective social functions of their acts, Marx locates the ideological nature of the subject's 'false consciousness.'

In his writings on method, Weber rejects the assumption of any 'objective meaning.' He wished to restrict the understanding and interpretation of meaning to the subjective intentions of the actor. Yet, in his actual work, he is no less aware than is Marx of the paradoxical fact that the results of interactions are by no means always identical with what the actor intended to do. Thus the Puritan wished to serve God, but he helped to bring about modern capitalism. The point is also shown in the following passage concerning capitalism and the individual:

This masterless slavery in which capitalism enmeshes the worker or the debtor is only debatable ethically as an institution. In principle, the personal conduct of those who participate, on either the side of the rulers or of the ruled, is not morally debatable, as such conduct is essentially prescribed by objective situations. If they do not conform, they are threatened by economic bankruptcy which would, in every respect, be useless.[13]

One might easily accumulate statements from Weber's work that would reinforce this point, as the translations in the present volume make clear. It is understandable that Weber felt it equally wrong to consider his work as an idealist interpretation of history as it was to consider it as a case of historical materialism.

The nominalism of Weber's method may be understood in terms of his attempt to avoid a philosophical emphasis upon either material or ideal factors, or upon either structural or individual principles of explanation. His attachment to Western positivist thought is shown in his scorn for any 'philosophical' or 'metaphysical' elements in the social sciences. He wants to give these sciences the same matter-of-fact approach with which the natural sciences approach nature.

A quantitative method goes hand in hand with such a conception and stands in opposition to a perspective in which all phenomena are seen as qualitatively unique entities. For Weber, historical and social uniqueness results from specific combinations of general factors, which when isolated are quantifiable. Thus the 'same' elements may be seen in a series of other unique combinations. '. . . Of course, in the last analysis, all qualitative contrasts in reality can somehow be comprehended as purely quantitative differences made up of combinations of various single factors.'[14] He does not say that quality can be 'reduced' to quantity; indeed, as a nominalist, he is quite sensitive to the qualitative uniqueness of cultural reality and to the qualitative differences resulting from quantitative changes. For instance: 'From our special point of view, where the increased fear of the world has led to a flight from occupational pursuits in the private economy, pietism not only turns into something differing in degree but into an element differing in quality.'[15]

The much-discussed 'ideal type,' a key term in Weber's methodological discussion, refers to the construction of certain elements of reality into a logically precise conception. The term 'ideal' has nothing to do with evaluations of any sort. For analytical purposes, one may construct ideal types of prostitution as well as of religious leaders. The term does not mean that either prophets or harlots are exemplary or should be imitated as representatives of an ideal way of life.

By using this term, Weber did not mean to introduce a new conceptual tool. He merely intended to bring to full awareness what social scientists and historians had been doing when they used words like 'the economic man,' 'feudalism,' 'Gothic *versus* Romanesque architecture,' or 'kingship.' He felt that social scientists had the choice of using logically controlled and unambiguous conceptions, which are thus more removed from historical reality, or of using less precise concepts, which are more closely geared to the empirical world. Weber's interest in world-wide comparisons led him to consider extreme and 'pure cases.' These cases became 'crucial instances' and controlled the level of abstraction that he used in connection with any particular problem. The real meat of history would usually fall in between such extreme types; hence Weber would approximate the multiplicity of specific historical situations by bringing various type concepts to bear upon the specific case under his focus.

The quantitative approach to unique cultural constellations and the conception of ideal types are intimately linked with the comparative method. This method implies that two constellations are comparable in terms of some feature common to them both. A statement of such common features implies the use of general concepts. The manner in which Weber construes the world religions as variant interpretations of 'senseless suffering' displays his technique of arranging 'cases' on a typological scale.* The same technique is at work in his typology of capitalism, built along a scale of different avenues for profit-opportunities. As general concepts, ideal types are tools with which Weber prepares the descriptive materials of world history for comparative analysis. These types vary in scope and in the level of their abstraction. When Weber characterizes 'democracy' as 'a minimization of power,' he has the broadest formulation, and the least specific historically. Several techniques of minimizing power, such as short terms of office, checks and balances, the referendum, and so on, are possible in particular historical cases. These cases are worked into sub-types of democracy. By incorporating selected historical features into the general conception of democracy, he is able to restrict this general type and approximate historical cases more closely.

His concern with specific historical problems and his interest in a comparative sociology of a generalizing nature are thus related; the difference between them is one of emphasis. By the use of a battery of ideal types, he builds up a conception of a particular historical case. In his comparative studies, he uses the same ideal type conceptions, but he uses history as a storehouse of examples for these concepts. In short, the respective research interest—in elaborating a concept or in constructing a historical object—determines his procedure.

In any case, Weber is concerned with using generalized conceptions in order to understand society as subject to lawful regularities. For such

* See chapter xi, 'The Social Psychology of World Religions.'

regularities are necessary in order to satisfy an interest in causation. To understand a sequence of regular events causally, one must examine comparable conditions. Thus, in an attempt to validate his causal analysis of religion and capitalism in the Occident, Weber examined many other civilizations. Although capitalist beginnings could be observed in these other civilizations, capitalism in the Western sense did not emerge. Weber wished to find those factors in other civilizations which blocked the emergence of capitalism, even though there were many favorable conditions present for its emergence. By such a comparative analysis of causal sequences, Weber tried to find not only the necessary but the sufficient conditions of capitalism. Only in the Occident, particularly where inner-worldly asceticism produced a specific personality type, were the sufficient conditions present. In his pluralism, he naturally did not consider this type of personality the only factor involved in the origin of capitalism; he merely wished to have it included among the conditions of capitalism.

4: The Sociology of Ideas and Interests

The discussion of bureaucratic institutions and personal leaders, of workaday routines and extraordinariness, is paralleled by Weber's conception of the relations between ideas and interests. Both Marx and Nietzsche had contributed to a theory of the function and content of ideas; both of them shifted the traditional emphasis upon the content of ideas to an emphasis upon the pragmatic connection of ideas with their results. They developed techniques for interpreting ideas in terms of their intended or actual service rather than in terms of their face value.

Marx viewed ideas in terms of their public function in the struggles of classes and parties. Nietzsche approached ideas in terms of their psychological service to the individual thinker, or at least when he did speak of the public context, his sociological tools were so crude that only the psychological mechanisms were fruitfully brought out in his analysis. If for Marx ideas of practical import became ideologies as weapons in the struggles of groups, for Nietzsche they turned into the rationalizations of individuals, or at best of 'masters and slaves.' Marx commented that ideas become material forces as soon as they take hold of the masses; he linked the historical vitality of ideas to their role in justifying economic interests. Nietzsche modified Matthew's statement, 'He who humbles himself shall be raised,' into 'He who humbles himself wants to be raised.' Thus he ascribed volitions to the speaker which lay beneath the content of his ideas. ' "I did that," says my memory, "I could not have done that," says my pride and remains inexorable. Eventually—the memory yields.' [16]

Weber attempts to incorporate the points of view both of Marx and of Nietzsche in his discussion: With Marx, he shares the sociological approach to ideas: they are powerless in history unless they are fused with material interests: And with Nietzsche, he is deeply concerned with the importance of ideas for psychic reactions.*

Yet, in contrast to both Nietzsche and Marx, Weber refuses to conceive of ideas as being 'mere' reflections of psychic or social interests. All spheres—intellectual, psychic, political, economic, religious—to some extent follow developments of their own. Where Marx and Nietzsche are quick to see a correspondence between ideas and interests, Weber is also eager to state possible tensions between ideas and interests, between one sphere and another, or between internal states and external demands. Thus, in analyzing Hebrew prophecy, he seeks to balance psychological and historical influences:

In any case, one can hardly assume that an unambiguous psychic determination of 'political hypochondria' has been the source of the prophets' stand. The prophecy of doom has to be deduced, to a large extent, from the psychical disposition of the prophets, as determined by constitutional endowments and personal experiences. Yet, it is no less certain that the historical destinies of Israel have indeed given the prophecies of doom their place in religious development. And this is so, not only in the sense that tradition has of course preserved those oracles of the prophets that were fulfilled, which have appeared to be fulfilled, or whose advent could still be expected. The increasingly unshatterable prestige of prophecy in general has rested upon those few cases that were terribly impressive for the prophet's contemporaries, and in which the prophets by their success were unexpectedly in the right.[17]

The decisive conception by which Weber relates ideas and interests is that of 'elective affinity,' rather than 'correspondence,' 'reflection,' or 'expression.' For Marx, ideas 'express' interests; thus, the hidden God of the Puritans expresses the irrationality and anonymity of the market. For Nietzsche, asceticist Christianity 'reflects' the resentment of the slaves, who thus 'express' their 'revolt in morals.' For Weber, there is hardly ever a close connection between the interests or the social origin

* A brief discussion of Nietzsche's theory of resentment will be found in chapter XI, 'Social Psychology of World Religions,' and chapter VII, 'Class, Status, Party.'

of the speaker or of his following with the content of the idea during its inception. The ancient Hebrew prophets, the leaders of the Reformation, or the revolutionary vanguard of modern class movements were not necessarily recruited from the strata which in due course became the prime bearers of their respective ideas. Only during the process of routinization do the followers 'elect' those features of the idea with which they have an 'affinity,' a 'point of coincidence' or 'convergence.'

There is no pre-established correspondence between the content of an idea and the interests of those who follow from the first hour. But, in time, ideas are discredited in the face of history unless they point in the direction of conduct that various interests promote. Ideas, selected and reinterpreted from the original doctrine, do gain an affinity with the interests of certain members of special strata; if they do not gain such an affinity, they are abandoned. Thus by distinguishing the phases of the personal and charismatic origin of ideas and their routinization and social impact, Weber is able to take into account a number of complications, which are reflected in changing shades of meaning. Both the ideas and their publics are seen as independent; by a selective process elements in both find their affinities.

Throughout his life, Max Weber was engaged in a fruitful battle with historical materialism. In his last course of lectures in Munich at the time of the Revolution, he presented his course under the title, 'A Positive Critique of Historical Materialism.' Yet there is a definite drift of emphasis in his intellectual biography towards Marx.

When writing the *Protestant Ethic,* Weber was eager to emphasize the autonomous role of ideas in the origin of modern capitalism—though not, of course, in the sense of Hegel. He felt that modern capitalism in its beginnings required a certain type of personality. This personality type, in turn, was psychologically construed as a result of belief in a set of ideas that unwittingly resulted in the development of those specific personality traits useful in capitalist conduct. Thus in giving 'a spiritualist construction' of the background of modern capitalism, Weber begins with religious conceptions. In his last essays, however, he begins his analysis of China, for instance, with chapters on the economic basis. The more embittered Weber became with German politics, the more he came to appreciate the weight of material interests in the success of ideas, however lofty in content and intention they might be. Thus during the war he wrote: 'Not ideas, but material and ideal interests directly govern man's conduct. Yet very frequently the "world images" which have been created by "ideas" have, like switchmen, determined the tracks along which action has been pushed by the dynamic of interests.'[18]

Such passages remind one of the mechanical metaphors of Marx, with his revolutions as the 'locomotives of history,' or of Trotsky with his 'ideological switchmen.'[19] Mechanical imagery of this sort seems to stand opposite the organic metaphors of growth and development favored by more conservative writers. Where images of organic nature are utilized they are not images of gradualism and vegetative growth, but of incubation and birth.

In Weber's handling of specific ideas, one may discern different levels of sociological interpretation at work. In a sweeping way, he locates entire 'world images' as symbol constructions associated with the social conditions of specific strata. Thus he sees a connection between the religious conception of a quietistic and passive Being and the mystic states and contemplative techniques of genteel and literary intellectuals, especially in India and China. He tries to establish an intimate relation between the nature of a predominant psychological state, the structure of an act of perception, and the meaning of an object. All three aspects, in turn, are facilitated by and have an affinity to the social-historical situation of the intellectuals within the social structure. This historical structure, by itself, does not determine the direction in which the strata of intellectuals may elaborate their conceptions; rather it permits or blocks the attempt, characteristic of intellectuals, to tackle the senselessness of suffering and of the world. In the Occident, intellectuals also experimented in the direction of mystic contemplation; but such endeavors, according to Weber, were repeatedly frustrated. A more volitional and active search for meaning became predominant in the Occident.

The active interests of Occidental intellectuals in mastering political events have been connected with the volitional and anthropomorphic image of a wrathful yet benign God. The main stream of Christianity is thus seen in continuity with Hebrew prophecy. The prophets of ancient Judaism are characterized as active demagogues, who by the power of the word aimed at a mastery of the course of historical events. The priesthood was not strong enough to suppress effectively such self-appointed religious demagogues.

Weber, in his sociology of knowledge, was not, however, exclusively concerned with such world images. He also concerned himself with many particular ideologies, which he saw as notions that justify and motivate materially interested strata.

Here are some examples: The acceptance of the religious propaganda of the Crusades is linked to the imperialist aspirations of feudal lords, who were interested in securing fiefs for their progeny. Other strata, of course, displayed other motives. The emergence and diffusion of the mendicant monk order, or Franciscans, is linked to the interests of secular power leaders in exploiting their skill as unpaid teachers, or as urban demagogues who during crises were able to tame urban masses. Whether or not these mendicant monks would have survived against the opposition of the Pope and the priesthood without having had these skills is an open question. The same situation applies to the Jesuit order, after the Pope outlawed them and Frederick the Great gave them asylum in Prussia. The advocacy of the intrinsic value of a particular language is often associated with the material interests of publishers in nationalism. The commands of modern bureaucracies assume the form of 'general rules' rather than of 'particular decrees,' as may be seen in connection with their general rationalizing tendency. When Weber deals with political problems, he seems to use this mode of interpreting ideas as simple justifications. When he handles religious problems, he is more likely to emphasize the concept of 'elective affinity.'

5: SOCIAL STRUCTURES AND TYPES OF CAPITALISM

The pragmatic view of ideas, which Max Weber shares with Karl Marx and John Dewey, is associated with a refutation of the Hegelian tradition. Weber thus rejects such conceptions as 'national character' and 'folk spirit,' which have permeated German historiography and which, in conservative thinking, have served as tools of interpretation. He construes social dynamics in terms of a pluralistic analysis of factors, which may be isolated and gauged in terms of their respective causal weights. He does this by comparative analyses of comparable units, which are found in different cultural settings.

This does not mean that he has no total conceptions of social structures. On the contrary, the more Weber comes to an analysis of the contemporary era, the more ready he is to speak of capitalism as a unit. The unit is seen as a configuration of institutions, which by the logic of their own requirements increasingly narrow the range of effective choices open to men.

For Weber, a unit, such as capitalism, is not an undifferentiated whole to be equated with 'an acquisitive instinct' or with 'pecuniary society.' Rather it is seen, as Marx and Sorel saw it, as a scale of types, each of which has peculiar institutional features. The further back Weber goes historically, the more he is willing to see capitalism as one feature of a historical situation; the more he approaches modern industrial capitalism, the more willing he is to see capitalism as a pervasive and unifying affair. High capitalism absorbs other institutions into its own image, and numerous institutional crisscrosses give way to a set of parallel forces heading in the same direction. This direction is towards the rationalization of all spheres of life. In such an increasingly unilinear construction of history, one may discern a sublimated conception of the liberal notion of 'progress.'

In conformity with liberal thinking, which is interested in separating politics and economics, Weber distinguishes between two basic types of capitalism: 'political capitalism' and 'modern industrial' or 'bourgeois capitalism.' * Capitalism, of course, can only emerge when at least the beginnings of a money-economy exists.

In *political capitalism,* opportunities for profit are dependent upon the preparation for and the exploitation of warfare, conquest, and the prerogative power of political administration. Within this type are imperialist, colonial, adventure or booty, and fiscal. In addition, with a view of locating the peculiar marginal situation of trading groups, Weber speaks of *pariah* capitalism. This concept is applied to Occidental Jewry from later Antiquity to the present, and to the Parsees in India. Although functionally indispensable, for reasons of ethnic and religious background, such strata are socially segregated and reduced to a pariah status. By *imperialist* capitalism, Weber refers to a situation in which profit interests are either the pacemakers or the beneficiaries of political expansion. The greatest examples are the Roman and the British Empires, and the competitive imperialism of the present epoch. *Colonial* capitalism, intimately connected with political imperialism, refers to those capitalisms which profit from the commercial exploitation of political prerogatives over conquered territories. Such prerogatives include politically guaranteed trading monopolies, shipping privileges, the politi-

* 'In my opinion Sombart has, in important respects, quite adequately characterized what should be understood by the early capitalist epoch. There are no "definitive" historical concepts. I do not share the vanity of contemporary authors who conduct themselves in the face of a terminology used by some one else as if it were his toothbrush.' *Archiv für Sozialwissenschaft und Sozialpolitik,* 1906, p. 348.

cally determined acquisition and exploitation of land, as well as compulsory labor. *Adventure* capitalism refers to charismatically led raids on foreign countries for the sake of treasure. Such treasures may be extracted from temples, tombs, mines, or the chests of conquered princes, or they may be raised as levies on the ornaments and jewelry of the population. The heroic period of the conquest of the Western Hemisphere by the Spaniards, the overseas enterprises of the Italian city-states during the Middle Ages, the Hanseatic League, and the merchant adventurers of England are pre-eminent historical examples. Whereas adventure capitalism emphasizes the discontinuous and charismatic nature of these operations, the term *booty* capitalism emphasizes the objectives sought.

In certain contexts, Weber is eager to distinguish the extraordinary capitalist from the routine activities of the workaday enterpriser; in the former case he speaks of charismatic capitalists as 'economic supermen.' Such figures have occurred in many historical contexts: in the new empire of ancient Egypt, in ancient China, India, in western Antiquity, in the waning of the Middle Ages, as well as in nineteenth-century America. The Fuggers and Rockefeller, Mellon, and Cecil Rhodes are examples. The difference between such charismatic capitalists and 'sober bourgeois' capitalists has been overlooked quite frequently in controversies over the problem of the Protestant ethic and its causal relevance for the rise of 'modern capitalism.'[20]

Fiscal capitalism, as used by Weber, refers to certain profit opportunities that accrue from the exploitation of political prerogatives. The most important phenomenon of this type is the farming out of tax collection to private enterprisers, as was the rule in ancient Rome and the *ancien régime* in France. The leasing of the sale of indulgences to Italian merchants as compensations for their loans to the Vatican; the entrepreneurial organization of military and naval forces by condottieri; the leasing of the right to coin money to private enterprisers, such as Jacob Fugger, are further examples.

These analytical types of capitalism serve to emphasize different aspects of historical situations that are themselves quite fluid. The uniqueness of *modern industrial capitalism* consists in the fact that a specific *production* establishment emerges and is enlarged at the expense of precapitalist production units. This production establishment has its legal, political, and ideological preconditions, but it is nevertheless historically unique. It is based on the organization of formally free labor and the fixed plant. The owner of the plant operates at his own risk and produces commodities for anonymous and competitive markets. His operations are usually controlled rationally by a constant balancing of costs and returns. All elements, including his own entrepreneurial services, are brought to book as items in the balance of his accounts.

Like Marx, Weber insists upon locating the basic institutional unit of modern capitalism in production rather than in commerce or finance. A system of capitalism grows from these units of production. This system undergoes various historical phases; its highest stage is characterized by the separation of ownership and management and the financing of corporations by sales to the public of shares in the possible returns from future operations. For this late stage of capitalism, Weber accepts Sombart's term, 'High Capitalism.'

Unlike Marx, however, Weber is not interested in investigating the problems of capitalist dynamics. The problem of the business cycle and the capitalist crises, which were so essential for Marx's characterization of capitalism as 'an anarchy of production,' have little part in Weber's analysis. This omission is of consequence for Weber's conception of rationality in modern society. For Marx, the rational elements of society were the means which served, yet which increasingly contradicted, unmastered and irrational elements. For Weber, capitalism is the highest form of rational operations; yet it is implemented by two irrationalities: the remains of an originally religiously anchored attitude: the irrational calling and drive for continuous work; and modern socialism, seen as the 'utopia' of those who cannot stand up under what seems to them the senseless injustice of an economic order which makes them dependent upon propertied entrepreneurs. Being keenly aware of the institutional pressures of modern capitalism, Weber, at this point, is ready to make use of the category of social totalities as 'going concerns.' Once in the saddle, for instance, capitalism no longer needs religious motives.

In sociological theory, a 'subjective' theory of the stratification of capitalism has often been opposed to an 'objective' one. The classic English economists, prominently Ricardo, as well as Marx represented the objective theory, defining 'class' in terms of typically recurrent incomes: rent, profit, wage. Accordingly, for them, landlord, entrepreneur, and worker make up the class structure. It does not matter whether these agents conceive of themselves as Britons, highlanders, or what not; their class positions are strictly located by their place and function within the objective economic order. Marx, adhering to this tradition, added a historical aspect by emphasizing the specifically modern nature of bourgeois and proletarian classes.

Subjective theories of class, on the other hand, have placed great emphasis upon the psychic traits of 'class members.' Those holding this subjective theory have been eager to speak of the 'fourth estate' as emerging side by side with the older estates. Conceptions of respectability and of social honor, descriptive elements of political and religious opinions, and sentiments connected with local and regional ways of life displace the strict theoretical approach of the economists. It was left to Moeller van den Bruck, author of *The Third Reich,* to carry the subjective theory of classes to absurdity: 'He is a proletariat who wants to think of himself as one. The proletarian consciousness makes man a proletariat, not the machine, not the mechanization of labor, not wage-dependency on the capitalist mode of production.' [21]

Max Weber is not ready to let man overcome hard economic fate by such acrobatics of will power. Class situations are determined by the relations of the market; in the last analysis, they go back to the differences between the propertied and the non-propertied. He thus shares with the objective school the emphasis upon the economic order and the strict distinction between objectively characterized positions and a variety of shifting and subjective attitudes that *may* be related to such positions.

In locating the class problem in the market and in the streams of income and property, Weber points towards production and its modern unit, the capitalist enterprise. He is prepared to give full credit to Marx for his insight into the historical nature of the modern class structure. Only when subjective opinions can be attributed to men in an objective class situation does Weber speak of 'class-consciousness'; and when he focuses upon problems of 'conventions,' 'styles of life,' of occupational attitudes, he prefers to speak of prestige or of 'status groups.' These latter problems, of course, point towards consumption, which, to be sure, depends upon income derived from production or from property, but which goes beyond this sphere. By making this sharp distinction between *class* and *status,* and by differentiating between types of classes and types of status groups, Weber is able to refine the problems of stratification to an extent which thus far has not been surpassed.*

* See chapter VII, 'Class, Status, Party,' for his analysis.

6: Conditions of Freedom and the Image of Man

The habit of the modern political intelligentsia of cloaking the aspirations of their parties under historical necessity, and of advancing such constructions with the pathos of 'iron necessity,' is characteristic of conservatism as well as Marxism. In both cases the concept of freedom follows Hegel's 'Fata nolentem trahunt, volentem ducunt' (The fates drag the one who does not will; they lead the one who does). On the political right, the pre-eminent prophet of doom was Oswald Spengler, whose morphological construction of culture cycles Weber criticized as arbitrary intuitions exploiting historical literature for non-scientific ends.

Weber's liberal heritage and urge prevented him from taking a determinist position. He felt that freedom consists not in realizing alleged historical necessities but rather in making deliberate choices between open alternatives. The future is a field for strategy rather than a mere repetition or unfolding of the past. Yet the possibilities of the future are not infinite, nor are they clay in the hands of the wilful man.

Weber saw social life as a polytheism of values in combat with one another, and choices were possible among these values.* The decision-making, morally responsible individual is, of course, a specifically modern and Occidental type of personality. This man can be more than a mere cog in his occupational groove. If he is responsible, he will have to make informed decisions. To Weber, sociological knowledge is of a kind that the complexity of modern civilization requires of one who would take intelligent stands on public issues. Such responsible decisions are equally remote from the emotional fanaticism of followers of demagogues as from the cynical sophistication of the snob or the blasé smugness of the Philistine.

As he was not willing to see bureaucrats as harbingers of freedom, Weber felt that the field of responsible freedom was shrinking. He saw himself, in this connection, as an old-fashioned liberal, unafraid of being on the defensive or of swimming against the stream. The following passage, which we reproduce at length, may illustrate Weber's fears as well as his assertion of the conditions of modern freedom. It was written in 1906.

* See chapter v, 'Science as a Vocation,' and chapter xiii, 'Religious Rejections of the World.'

The opportunities for democracy and indi/idualism would look very bad today were we to rely upon the lawful effects of material interests for their development. For the development of material interests points, as distinctly as possible, in the opposite direction: in the American 'benevolent feudalism,' in the so-called 'welfare institutions' of Germany, in the Russian factory constitution . . . everywhere the house is ready-made for a new servitude. It only waits for the tempo of technical economic 'progress' to slow down and for rent to triumph over profit. The latter victory, joined with the exhaustion of the remaining free soil and free market, will make the masses 'docile.' Then man will move into the house of servitude. At the same time, the increasing complexity of the economy, the partial governmentalization of economic activities, the territorial expansion of the population—these processes create ever-new work for the clerks, an ever-new specialization of functions, and expert vocational training and administration. All this means caste.

Those American workers who were against the 'Civil Service Reform' knew what they were about. They wished to be governed by parvenus of doubtful morals rather than by a certified caste of mandarins. But their protest was in vain.

In the face of all this, those who constantly fear that in the world of the future too much democracy and individualism may exist and too little authority, aristocracy, esteem for office, or such like, may calm down. Only too much provision has been made to see to it that the trees of democratic individualism do not shoot into the sky. According to all experience, history relentlessly gives rebirth to aristocracies and authorities; and those who deem it necessary for themselves, or for 'the people,' may cling to them. If only material conditions and interest-constellations directly or indirectly created by them mattered, then every sober reflection would convince us that all economic weathercocks point in the direction of increasing servitude.

It is utterly ridiculous to see any connection between the high capitalism of today—as it is now being imported into Russia and as it exists in America—with democracy or with freedom in any sense of these words. Yet this capitalism is an unavoidable result of our economic development. The question is: how are freedom and democracy in the long run at all possible under the domination of highly developed capitalism? Freedom and democracy are only possible where the resolute will of a nation not to allow itself to be ruled like sheep is permanently alive. We are 'individualists' and partisans of 'democratic' institutions 'against the stream' of material constellations. He who wishes to be the weathercock of an evolutionary trend should give up these old-fashioned ideals as soon as possible. The historical origin of modern freedom has had certain unique preconditions which will never repeat themselves. Let us enumerate the most important of these:

First, the overseas expansions. In the armies of Cromwell, in the French

constituent assembly, in our whole economic life even today this breeze from
across the ocean is felt . . . but there is no new continent aᵗ our disposal.
Irresistibly the point of gravity of the population of Western civilization advances toward the great inland areas of the North American continent on
the one side and of Russia on the other. This happened once before, in late
antiquity. The monotonous plains of Russia and the United States facilitate
schematism.

Second, the uniqueness of the economic and social structure of the early
capitalist epoch in western Europe.

Third, the conquest of life by science, 'the self-realization of the spirit.'
The rational construction of institutional life, doubtless after having destroyed innumerable 'values,' today, at least in principle, has done its work.
In the wake of the standardization of production, it has made the external
way of life uniform. Under present conditions of business, the impact of such
standardization is universal. Today, science itself no longer creates universal
personalities.

Finally, certain conceptions of ideal values, grown out of a world of definite religious ideas, have stamped the ethical peculiarity and cultural values
of modern man. They have done so by working with numerous political constellations, themselves quite unique, and with the material preconditions of
early capitalism. One need merely ask whether any material development or
even any development of the high capitalism of today could maintain or create
again these unique historical conditions of freedom and democracy in order
to know the answer. No shadow of probability speaks for the fact that
economic 'socialization' as such must harbor in its lap either the development
of inwardly 'free' personalities of 'altruistic' ideals.[22]

The defensive pessimism for the future of freedom, which is displayed
in this passage and which is a major theme of Weber's work, is rein-
forced by the fate he sees for charisma in the modern world. Although
he gives a quite nominalist definition of charisma, it is clear that the
concept serves him as a metaphysical vehicle of man's freedom in history.
That freedom, as carried by charisma, is doomed is evident by his nostalgic remark concerning the French Revolution. After tracing and classifying modern liberties, Weber indicates that such liberties find their ultimate justification in the concept of the natural law of reason; and then:
'The charismatic glorification of "reason" found its characteristic expression in Robespierre's apotheosis. This is the last form which charisma
has assumed in its long road of varied and rich destinies.'[23] Weber's
concern with freedom was not only historical; it influenced his image
of contemporary man as an individual.

He conceived of individual man as a composite of general characteristics derived from social institutions; the individual as an actor of social
roles. However, this holds only for men in so far as they do not
transcend the routines of everyday institutions. The concept of charisma
serves to underline Weber's view that all men everywhere are not to be
comprehended merely as social products.

Just as for George H. Mead the 'I' is ordinarily in tension with the social
roles derived from the expectations of others, so for Weber the potentially
charismatic quality of man stands in tension with the external demands
of institutional life. For Mead, the tension between the I and the role-
demands is resolved in the creative response of the genius. For Weber,
the response of the charismatic leader to distress unifies external demands
and internal urges. In a broad sense, one may say that externality is
identified with constraint and charisma with freedom. Weber's conception of human freedom thus partakes of the humanist tradition of
liberalism which is concerned with the freedom of the individual to
create free institutions. Having incorporated the Marxist critique of capitalism, he sees the economic system as a compulsive apparatus rather
than as the locus of freedom.

For Weber, capitalism is the embodiment of rational impersonality;
the quest for freedom is identified with irrational sentiment and privacy.
Freedom is at best a tarrying for loving companionship and for the ca-
thartic experience of art as a this-worldly escape from institutional
routines. It is the privilege of the propertied and educated: it is freedom
without equality.

In this conception of freedom as a historically developed phenomena,
now on the defensive against both capitalism and bureaucracy, Weber
represents humanist and cultural liberalism rather than economic liberalism. The humanist tradition in which Schiller wrote that 'Der Mensch
ist freigeschaffen, ist frei, und würd' er in ketten geboren' is evidenced in
Weber's concern with the decline of the cultivated man as a well-rounded
personality in favor of the technical expert, who, from the human point
of view, is crippled.* Weber's own work is a realization of his self-image
as a cultivated man concerned with all things human. And the decline of
the humanist and the ascendancy of the expert is another documentation
for Weber of the diminished chances for freedom.

In terms of these two types of men, Weber sees modern civilization
as unique in world history. Past civilizations produced various types of

* See chapter VIII, 'Bureaucracy.'

humanist elites: in China, the mandarin, a stratum of gentlemanly literati; in antiquity, a leisured stratum of athletic and cultured men; in England, the modern conventional gentlemen, a result of compromises between 'merry old England' and middle-class Puritanism consummated in the masculine club; in Latin civilizations, the French cavalier and the Italian *cortegiano,* compromises between court nobilities and urban patricians, consummated in the salon of the lady. Such cultivated types are now unfit for the management of economic and political affairs; they are being displaced by the specialist bureaucrat and the professional politician. Weber gave little weight to followers of artistic and literary cult leaders, who must belong to or depend upon circles of rentiers, or else serve the literary fashions promoted by shrewd publishers.

In contrast to the liberalism of Kant and Fichte, and some modern American educators, Max Weber saw education and the social production of personalities as dependent upon politics and economics. His pessimism about political and economic freedom is thus supplemented by his pessimism about the realms of art, cultivation, and the personality types possible for contemporary man.

Part I

SCIENCE AND POLITICS

IV. Politics as a Vocation

THIS lecture, which I give at your request, will necessarily disappoint you in a number of ways. You will naturally expect me to take a position on actual problems of the day. But that will be the case only in a purely formal way and toward the end, when I shall raise certain questions concerning the significance of political action in the whole way of life. In today's lecture, all questions that refer to what policy and what content one should give one's political activity must be eliminated. For such questions have nothing to do with the general question of what politics as a vocation means and what it can mean. Now to our subject matter.

What do we understand by politics? The concept is extremely broad and comprises any kind of *independent* leadership in action. One speaks of the currency policy of the banks, of the discounting policy of the Reichsbank, of the strike policy of a trade union; one may speak of the educational policy of a municipality or a township, of the policy of the president of a voluntary association, and, finally, even of the policy of a prudent wife who seeks to guide her husband. Tonight, our reflections are, of course, not based upon such a broad concept. We wish to understand by politics only the leadership, or the influencing of the leadership, of a *political* association, hence today, of a *state*.

But what is a 'political' association from the sociological point of view? What is a 'state'? Sociologically, the state cannot be defined in terms of its ends. There is scarcely any task that some political association has not taken in hand, and there is no task that one could say has always been exclusive and peculiar to those associations which are designated as political ones: today the state, or historically, those associations which have been the predecessors of the modern state. Ultimately, one can define

'Politik als Beruf,' *Gesammelte Politische Schriften* (Muenchen, 1921), pp. 396-450. Originally a speech at Munich University, 1918, published in 1919 by Duncker & Humblodt, Munich.

the modern state sociologically only in terms of the specific *means* peculiar to it, as to every political association, namely, the use of physical force.

'Every state is founded on force,' said Trotsky at Brest-Litovsk. That is indeed right. If no social institutions existed which knew the use of violence, then the concept of 'state' would be eliminated, and a condition would emerge that could be designated as 'anarchy,' in the specific sense of this word. Of course, force is certainly not the normal or the only means of the state—nobody says that—but force is a means specific to the state. Today the relation between the state and violence is an especially intimate one. In the past, the most varied institutions—beginning with the sib—have known the use of physical force as quite normal. Today, however, we have to say that a state is a human community that (successfully) claims the *monopoly of the legitimate use of physical force* within a given territory. Note that 'territory' is one of the characteristics of the state. Specifically, at the present time, the right to use physical force is ascribed to other institutions or to individuals only to the extent to which the state permits it. The state is considered the sole source of the 'right' to use violence. Hence, 'politics' for us means striving to share power or striving to influence the distribution of power, either among states or among groups within a state.

This corresponds essentially to ordinary usage. When a question is said to be a 'political' question, when a cabinet minister or an official is said to be a 'political' official, or when a decision is said to be 'politically' determined, what is always meant is that interests in the distribution, maintenance, or transfer of power are decisive for answering the questions and determining the decision or the official's sphere of activity. He who is active in politics strives for power either as a means in serving other aims, ideal or egoistic, or as 'power for power's sake,' that is, in order to enjoy the prestige-feeling that power gives.

Like the political institutions historically preceding it, the state is a relation of men dominating men, a relation supported by means of legitimate (i.e. considered to be legitimate) violence. If the state is to exist, the dominated must obey the authority claimed by the powers that be. When and why do men obey? Upon what inner justifications and upon what external means does this domination rest?

To begin with, in principle, there are three inner justifications, hence basic *legitimations* of domination.

First, the authority of the 'eternal yesterday,' i.e. of the mores sanctified through the unimaginably ancient recognition and habitual orientation to conform. This is 'traditional' domination exercised by the patriarch and the patrimonial prince of yore.

There is the authority of the extraordinary and personal *gift of grace* (charisma), the absolutely personal devotion and personal confidence in revelation, heroism, or other qualities of individual leadership. This is 'charismatic' domination, as exercised by the prophet or—in the field of politics—by the elected war lord, the plebiscitarian ruler, the great demagogue, or the political party leader.

Finally, there is domination by virtue of 'legality,' by virtue of the belief in the validity of legal statute and functional 'competence' based on rationally created *rules*. In this case, obedience is expected in discharging statutory obligations. This is domination as exercised by the modern 'servant of the state' and by all those bearers of power who in this respect resemble him.

It is understood that, in reality, obedience is determined by highly robust motives of fear and hope—fear of the vengeance of magical powers or of the power-holder, hope for reward in this world or in the beyond—and besides all this, by interests of the most varied sort. Of this we shall speak presently. However, in asking for the 'legitimations' of this obedience, one meets with these three 'pure' types: 'traditional,' 'charismatic,' and 'legal.'

These conceptions of legitimacy and their inner justifications are of very great significance for the structure of domination. To be sure, the pure types are rarely found in reality. But today we cannot deal with the highly complex variants, transitions, and combinations of these pure types, which problems belong to 'political science.' Here we are interested above all in the second of these types: domination by virtue of the devotion of those who obey the purely personal 'charisma' of the 'leader.' For this is the root of the idea of a *calling* in its highest expression.

Devotion to the charisma of the prophet, or the leader in war, or to the great demagogue in the *ecclesia* or in parliament, means that the leader is personally recognized as the innerly 'called' leader of men. Men do not obey him by virtue of tradition or statute, but because they believe in him. If he is more than a narrow and vain upstart of the moment, the leader lives for his cause and 'strives for his work.'[1] The devotion of his disciples, his followers, his personal party friends is oriented to his person and to its qualities.

Charismatic leadership has emerged in all places and in all historical epochs. Most importantly in the past, it has emerged in the two figures of the magician and the prophet on the one hand, and in the elected war lord, the gang leader and *condotierre* on the other hand. *Political* leadership in the form of the free 'demagogue' who grew from the soil of the city state is of greater concern to us; like the city state, the demagogue is peculiar to the Occident and especially to Mediterranean culture. Furthermore, political leadership in the form of the parliamentary 'party leader' has grown on the soil of the constitutional state, which is also indigenous only to the Occident.

These politicians by virtue of a 'calling,' in the most genuine sense of the word, are of course nowhere the only decisive figures in the cross-currents of the political struggle for power. The sort of auxiliary means that are at their disposal is also highly decisive. How do the politically dominant powers manage to maintain their domination? The question pertains to any kind of domination, hence also to political domination in all its forms, traditional as well as legal and charismatic.

Organized domination, which calls for continuous administration, requires that human conduct be conditioned to obedience towards those masters who claim to be the bearers of legitimate power. On the other hand, by virtue of this obedience, organized domination requires the control of those material goods which in a given case are necessary for the use of physical violence. Thus, organized domination requires control of the personal executive staff and the material implements of administration.

The administrative staff, which externally represents the organization of political domination, is, of course, like any other organization, bound by obedience to the power-holder and not alone by the concept of legitimacy, of which we have just spoken. There are two other means, both of which appeal to personal interests: material reward and social honor. The fiefs of vassals, the prebends of patrimonial officials, the salaries of modern civil servants, the honor of knights, the privileges of estates, and the honor of the civil servant comprise their respective wages. The fear of losing them is the final and decisive basis for solidarity between the executive staff and the power-holder. There is honor and booty for the followers in war; for the demagogue's following, there are 'spoils'—that is, exploitation of the dominated through the monopolization of office—and there are politically determined profits and premiums of vanity. All of these rewards are also derived from the domination exercised by a charismatic leader.

To maintain a dominion by force, certain material goods are required, just as with an economic organization. All states may be classified according to whether they rest on the principle that the staff of men themselves *own* the administrative means, or whether the staff is 'separated' from these means of administration. This distinction holds in the same sense in which today we say that the salaried employee and the proletarian in the capitalistic enterprise are 'separated' from the material means of production. The power-holder must be able to count on the obedience of the staff members, officials, or whoever else they may be. The administrative means may consist of money, building, war material, vehicles, horses, or whatnot. The question is whether or not the power-holder himself directs and organizes the administration while delegating executive power to personal servants, hired officials, or personal favorites and confidants, who are non-owners, i.e. who do not use the material means of administration in their own right but are directed by the lord. The distinction runs through all administrative organizations of the past.

These political associations in which the material means of administration are autonomously controlled, wholly or partly, by the dependent administrative staff may be called associations organized in *'estates.'* The vassal in the feudal association, for instance, paid out of his own pocket for the administration and judicature of the district enfeoffed to him. He supplied his own equipment and provisions for war, and his subvassals did likewise. Of course, this had consequences for the lord's position of power, which only rested upon a relation of personal faith and upon the fact that the legitimacy of his possession of the fief and the social honor of the vassal were derived from the overlord.

However, everywhere, reaching back to the earliest political formations, we also find the lord himself directing the administration. He seeks to take the administration into his own hands by having men personally dependent upon him: slaves, household officials, attendants, personal 'favorites,' and prebendaries enfeoffed in kind or in money from his magazines. He seeks to defray the expenses from his own pocket, from the revenues of his patrimonium; and he seeks to create an army which is dependent upon him personally because it is equipped and provisioned out of his granaries, magazines, and armories. In the association of 'estates,' the lord rules with the aid of an autonomous 'aristocracy' and hence shares his domination with it; the lord who personally administers is supported either by members of his household or by plebeians. These are propertyless strata having no social honor of their own; materially, they are completely chained to him and are not backed up by any competing power of their own. All forms of patriarchal and patrimonial domination, Sultanist despotism, and bureaucratic states belong to this latter type. The bureaucratic state order is especially important; in its most rational development, it is precisely characteristic of the modern state.

Everywhere the development of the modern state is initiated through the action of the prince. He paves the way for the expropriation of the autonomous and 'private' bearers of executive power who stand beside him, of those who in their own right possess the means of administration, warfare, and financial organization, as well as politically usable goods of all sorts. The whole process is a complete parallel to the development of the capitalist enterprise through gradual expropriation of the independent producers. In the end, the modern state controls the total means of political organization, which actually come together under a single head. No single official personally owns the money he pays out, or the buildings, stores, tools, and war machines he controls. In the contemporary 'state'—and this is essential for the concept of state—the 'separation' of the administrative staff, of the administrative officials, and of the workers from the material means of administrative organization is completed. Here the most modern development begins, and we see with our own eyes the attempt to inaugurate the expropriation of this expropriator of the political means, and therewith of political power.

The revolution [of Germany, 1918] has accomplished, at least in so far as leaders have taken the place of the statutory authorities, this much: the leaders, through usurpation or election, have attained control over the political staff and the apparatus of material goods; and they deduce their legitimacy—no matter with what right—from the will of the governed. Whether the leaders, on the basis of this at least apparent success, can rightfully entertain the hope of also carrying through the expropriation within the capitalist enterprises is a different question. The direction of capitalist enterprises, despite far-reaching analogies, follows quite different laws than those of political administration.

Today we do not take a stand on this question. I state only the purely *conceptual* aspect for our consideration: the modern state is a compulsory association which organizes domination. It has been successful in seeking to monopolize the legitimate use of physical force as a means of domination within a territory. To this end the state has combined the material means of organization in the hands of its leaders, and it has expropriated all autonomous functionaries of estates who formerly controlled these means in their own right. The state has taken their positions and now stands in the top place.

During this process of political expropriation, which has occurred with varying success in all countries on earth, 'professional politicians' in another sense have emerged. They arose first in the service of a prince. They have been men who, unlike the charismatic leader, have not wished to be lords themselves, but who have entered the *service* of political lords. In the struggle of expropriation, they placed themselves at the princes' disposal and by managing the princes' politics they earned, on the one hand, a living and, on the other hand, an ideal content of life. Again, it is *only* in the Occident that we find this kind of professional politician in the service of powers other than the princes. In the past, they have been the most important power instrument of the prince and his instrument of political expropriation.

Before discussing 'professional politicians' in detail, let us clarify in all its aspects the state of affairs their existence presents. Politics, just as economic pursuits, may be a man's avocation or his vocation. One may engage in politics, and hence seek to influence the distribution of power within and between political structures, as an 'occasional' politician. We are all 'occasional' politicians when we cast our ballot or consummate a similar expression of intention, such as applauding or protesting in a 'political' meeting, or delivering a 'political' speech, etc. The whole relation of many people to politics is restricted to this. Politics as an avocation is today practiced by all those party agents and heads of voluntary political associations who, as a rule, are politically active only in case of need and for whom politics is, neither materially nor ideally, 'their life' in the first place. The same holds for those members of state counsels and similar deliberative bodies that function only when summoned. It also holds for rather broad strata of our members of parliament who are politically active only during sessions. In the past, such strata were found especially among the estates. Proprietors of military implements in their own right, or proprietors of goods important for the administration, or proprietors of personal prerogatives may be called 'estates.' A large portion of them were far from giving their lives wholly, or merely preferentially, or more than occasionally, to the service of politics. Rather, they exploited their prerogatives in the interest of gaining rent or even profits; and they became active in the service of political associations only when the overlord of their status-equals especially demanded it. It was not different in the case of some of the auxiliary forces which the prince drew into the struggle for the creation of a political organization to be exclusively at his disposal. This was the nature of the *Räte von Haus aus* [councilors] and, still further back, of a considerable part of the councilors assembling in the 'Curia' and other deliberating bodies of the princes. But these merely occasional auxiliary forces engaging in politics on the side were naturally not sufficient for the prince. Of necessity, the prince sought to create a staff of helpers dedicated wholly and exclusively to serving him, hence making this their major vocation. The structure of the emerging dynastic political organization, and not only this but the whole articulation of the culture, depended to a considerable degree upon the question of where the prince recruited agents.

A staff was also necessary for those political associations whose members constituted themselves politically as (so-called) 'free' communes under the complete abolition or the far-going restriction of princely power.

They were 'free' not in the sense of freedom from domination by force, but in the sense that princely power legitimized by tradition (mostly religiously sanctified) as the exclusive source of all authority was absent. These communities have their historical home in the Occident. Their nucleus was the city as a body politic, the form in which the city first emerged in the Mediterranean culture area. In all these cases, what did the politicians who made politics their major vocation look like?

There are two ways of making politics one's vocation: Either one lives 'for' politics or one lives 'off' politics. By no means is this contrast an exclusive one. The rule is, rather, that man does both, at least in thought, and certainly he also does both in practice. He who lives 'for' politics makes politics his life, in an internal sense. Either he enjoys the naked possession of the power he exerts, or he nourishes his inner balance and self-feeling by the consciousness that his life has *meaning* in the service of a 'cause.' In this internal sense, every sincere man who lives for a cause also lives off this cause. The distinction hence refers to a much more substantial aspect of the matter, namely, to the economic. He who strives to make politics a permanent *source of income* lives 'off' politics as a vocation, whereas he who does not do this lives 'for' politics. Under the dominance of the private property order, some—if you wish—

very trivial preconditions must exist in order for a person to be able to live 'for' politics in this economic sense. Under normal conditions, the politician must be economically independent of the income politics can bring him. This means, quite simply, that the politician must be wealthy or must have a personal position in life which yields a sufficient income.

This is the case, at least in normal circumstances. The war lord's following is just as little concerned about the conditions of a normal economy as is the street crowd following of the revolutionary hero. Both live off booty, plunder, confiscations, contributions, and the imposition of worthless and compulsory means of tender, which in essence amounts to the same thing. But necessarily, these are extraordinary phenomena. In everyday economic life, only some wealth serves the purpose of making a man economically independent. Yet this alone does not suffice. The professional politician must also be economically 'dispensable,' that is, his income must not depend upon the fact that he constantly and personally places his ability and thinking entirely, or at least by far predominantly, in the service of economic acquisition. In the most unconditional way, the rentier is dispensable in this sense. Hence, he is a man who receives completely unearned income. He may be the territorial lord of the past or the large landowner and aristocrat of the present who receives ground rent. In Antiquity and the Middle Ages they who received slave or serf rents or in modern times rents from shares or bonds or similar sources—these are rentiers.

Neither the worker nor—and this has to be noted well—the entrepreneur, especially the modern, large-scale entrepreneur, is economically dispensable in this sense. For it is precisely the entrepreneur who is tied to his enterprise and is therefore *not* dispensable. This holds for the entrepreneur in industry far more than for the entrepreneur in agriculture, considering the seasonal character of agriculture. In the main, it is very difficult for the enterpreneur to be represented in his enterprise by someone else, even temporarily. He is as little dispensable as is the medical doctor, and the more eminent and busy he is the less dispensable he is. For purely organizational reasons, it is easier for the lawyer to be dispensable; and therefore the lawyer has played an incomparably greater, and often even a dominant, role as a professional politician. We shall not continue in this classification; rather let us clarify some of its ramifications.

The leadership of a state or of a party by men who (in the economic sense of the word) live exclusively for politics and not off politics means necessarily a 'plutocratic' recruitment of the leading political strata. To be sure, this does not mean that such plutocratic leadership signifies at the same time that the politically dominant strata will not also seek to live 'off' politics, and hence that the dominant stratum will not usually exploit their political domination in their own economic interest. All that is unquestionable, of course. There has never been such a stratum that has not somehow lived 'off' politics. Only this is meant: that the professional politician need not seek remuneration directly for his political work, whereas every politician without means must absolutely claim this. On the other hand, we do not mean to say that the propertyless politician will pursue private economic advantages through politics, exclusively, or even predominantly. Nor do we mean that he will not think, in the first place, of 'the subject matter.' Nothing would be more incorrect. According to all experience, a care for the economic 'security' of his existence is consciously or unconsciously a cardinal point in the whole life orientation of the wealthy man. A quite reckless and unreserved political idealism is found if not exclusively at least predominantly among those strata who by virtue of their propertylessness stand entirely outside of the strata who are interested in maintaining the economic order of a given society. This holds especially for extraordinary and hence revolutionary epochs. A non-plutocratic recruitment of interested politicians, of leadership and following, is geared to the self-understood precondition that regular and reliable income will accrue to those who manage politics.

Either politics can be conducted 'honorifically' and then, as one usually says, by 'independent,' that is, by wealthy, men, and especially by rentiers. Or, political leadership is made accessible to propertyless men who must then be rewarded. The professional politician who lives 'off' politics may be a pure 'prebendary' or a salaried 'official.' Then the politician receives either income from fees and perquisites for specific services—tips and bribes are only an irregular and formally illegal variant of this category of income—or a fixed income in kind, a money salary, or both. He may assume the character of an 'entrepreneur,' like the *condottiere* or the holder of a farmed-out or purchased office, or like the American boss who considers his costs a capital investment which he brings to fruition through exploitation of his influence. Again, he may receive a fixed wage, like a journalist, a party secretary, a modern cabinet minister, or a political official. Feudal fiefs, land grants, and prebends of all sorts have been typical, in the past. With the development of the

money economy, perquisites and prebends especially are the typical rewards for the following of princes, victorious conquerors, or successful
party chiefs. For loyal services today, party leaders give offices of all sorts
—in parties, newspapers, co-operative societies, health insurance, municipalities, as well as in the state. *All* party struggles are struggles for the
patronage of office, as well as struggles for objective goals.

In Germany, all struggles between the proponents of local and of
central government are focused upon the question of which powers shall
control the patronage of office, whether they are of Berlin, Munich,
Karlsruhe, or Dresden. Setbacks in participating in offices are felt more
severely by parties than is action against their objective goals. In France,
a turnover of prefects because of party politics has always been considered a greater transformation and has always caused a greater uproar
than a modification in the government's program—the latter almost having the significance of mere verbiage. Some parties, especially those in
America since the disappearance of the old conflicts concerning the interpretation of the constitution, have become pure patronage parties hand-
ing out jobs and changing their material program according to the chances
of grabbing votes.

In Spain, up to recent years, the two great parties, in a conventionally
fixed manner, took turns in office by means of 'elections,' fabricated from
above, in order to provide their followers with offices. In the Spanish
colonial territories, in the so-called 'elections,' as well as in the so-called
'revolutions,' what was at stake was always the state bread-basket from
which the victors wished to be fed.

In Switzerland, the parties peacefully divided the offices among themselves proportionately, and some of our 'revolutionary' constitutional
drafts, for instance the first draft of the Badenian constitution, sought
to extend this system to ministerial positions. Thus, the state and state
offices were considered as pure institutions for the provision of spoilsmen.

Above all, the Catholic Center party was enthusiastically for this draft.
In Badenia, the party, as part of the party platform, made the distribution
of offices proportional to confessions and hence without regard to achievement. This tendency becomes stronger for all parties when the number
of offices increase as a result of general bureaucratization and when the
demand for offices increases because they represent specifically secure
livelihoods. For their followings, the parties become more and more a
means to the end of being provided for in this manner.

The development of modern officialdom into a highly qualified, professional labor force, specialized in expertness through long years of preparatory training, stands opposed to all thes. arrangements. Modern bureaucracy in the interest of integrity has developed a high sense of status honor; without this sense the danger of an awful corruption and a vulgar Philistinism threatens fatally. And without such integrity, even the purely technical functions of the state apparatus would be endangered. The significance of the state apparatus for the economy has been steadily rising, especially with increasing socialization, and its significance will be further augmented.

In the United States, amateur administration through booty politicians in accordance with the outcome of presidential elections resulted in the exchange of hundreds of thousands of officials, even down to the mail carrier. The administration knew nothing of the professional civil-servant-for-life, but this amateur administration has long since been punctured by the Civil Service Reform. Purely technical, irrefrageable needs of the administration have determined this development.

In Europe, expert officialdom, based on the division of labor, has emerged in a gradual development of half a thousand years. The Italian cities and seigniories were the beginning, among the monarchies, and the states of the Norman conquerors. But the decisive step was taken in connection with the administration of the finances of the prince. With the administrative reforms of Emperor Max, it can be seen how hard it was for the officials to depose successfully of the prince in this field, even under the pressure of extreme emergency and of Turkish rule. The sphere of finance could afford least of all a ruler's dilettantism—a ruler who at that time was still above all a knight. The development of war technique called forth the expert and specialized officer; the differentiation of legal procedure called forth the trained jurist. In these three areas—finance, war, and law—expert officialdom in the more advanced states was definitely triumphant during the sixteenth century. With the ascendancy of princely absolutism over the estates, there was simultaneously a gradual abdication of the prince's autocratic rule in favor of an expert officialdom. These very officials had only facilitated the prince's victory over the estates.

The development of the 'leading politicians' was realized along with the ascendancy of the specially trained officialdom, even if in far less noticeable transitions. Of course, such really decisive advisers of the princes have existed at all times and all over the world. In the Orient, the need for relieving the Sultan as far as possible from personal responsibility for the success of the government has created the typical figure of the 'Grand Vizier.' In the Occident, influenced above all by the reports of the Venetian legates, diplomacy first became a *consciously* cultivated art in the age of Charles V, in Machiavelli's time. The reports of the Venetian legates were read with passionate zeal in expert diplomatic circles. The adepts of this art, who were in the main educated humanistically, treated one another as trained initiates, similar to the humanist Chinese statesmen in the last period of the warring states. The necessity of a formally unified guidance of the whole policy, including that of home affairs, by a leading statesman finally and compellingly arose only through constitutional development. Of course, individual personalities, such as advisers of the princes, or rather, in fact, leaders, had again and again existed before then. But the organization of administrative agencies even in the most advanced states first proceeded along other avenues. Top collegial administrative agencies had emerged. In theory, and to a gradually decreasing extent in fact, they met under the personal chairmanship of the prince who rendered the decision. This collegial system led to memoranda, counter-memoranda, and reasoned votes of the majority and the minority. In addition to the official and highest authorities, the prince surrounded himself with purely personal confidants—the 'cabinet'—and through them rendered his decisions, after considering the resolutions of the state counsel, or whatever else the highest state agency was called. The prince, coming more and more into the position of a dilettante, sought to extricate himself from the unavoidably increasing weight of the expertly trained officials through the collegial system and the cabinet. He sought to retain the highest leadership in his own hands. This latent struggle between expert officialdom and autocratic rule existed everywhere. Only in the face of parliaments and the power aspirations of party leaders did the situation change. Very different conditions led to the externally identical result, though to be sure with certain differences. Wherever the dynasties retained actual power in their hands—as was especially the case in Germany—the interests of the prince were joined with those of officialdom *against* parliament and its claims for power. The officials were also interested in having leading positions, that is, ministerial positions, occupied by their own ranks, thus making these positions an object of the official career. The monarch, on his part, was interested in being able to appoint the ministers from the ranks of devoted officials according to his own discretion. Both parties, however, were interested in seeing the political leadership confront parliament in a unified and solidary fashion, and hence in seeing the collegial system replaced by a single cabinet head. Furthermore, in order to be removed in a purely formal way from the struggle of parties and from party attacks, the monarch needed a single personality to cover him and to assume responsibility, that is, to answer to parliament and to negotiate with the parties. All these interests worked together and in the same direction: a minister emerged to direct the officialdom in a unified way.

Where parliament gained supremacy over the monarch—as in England —the development of parliamentary power worked even more strongly in the direction of a unification of the state apparatus. In England, the 'cabinet,' with the single head of Parliament as its 'leader,' developed as a committee of the party which at the time controlled the majority. This party power was ignored by official law but, in fact, it alone was politically decisive. The official collegial bodies as such were not organs of the actual ruling power, the party, and hence could not be the bearers of real government. The ruling party required an ever-ready organization composed *only* of its actually leading men, who would confidentially discuss matters in order to maintain power within and be capable of engaging in grand politics outside. The cabinet is simply this organization. However, in relation to the public, especially the parliamentary public, the party needed a leader responsible for all decisions—the cabinet head. The English system has been taken over on the Continent in the form of parliamentary ministries. In America alone, and in the democracies influenced by America, a quite heterogeneous system was placed into opposition with this system. The American system placed the directly and popularly elected leader of the victorious party at the head of the apparatus of officials appointed by him and bound him to the consent of 'parliament' only in budgetary and legislative matters.

The development of politics into an organization which demanded training in the struggle for power, and in the methods of this struggle as developed by modern party policies, determined the separation of public functionaries into two categories, which, however, are by no means rigidly but nevertheless distinctly separated. These categories are 'administrative' officials on the one hand, and 'political' officials on the other. The 'political' officials, in the genuine sense of the word, can regularly and externally be recognized by the fact that they can be transferred any time at will, that they can be dismissed, or at least temporarily withdrawn. They are like the French prefects and the comparable officials of other countries, and this is in sharp contrast to the 'independence' of officials with judicial functions. In England, officials who, according to fixed convention, retire from office when there is a change in the parliamentary majority, and hence a change in the cabinet, belong to this category. There are usually among them some whose competence includes the management of the general 'inner administration.' The political element consists, above all, in the task of maintaining 'law and order' in the country, hence maintaining the existing power relations. In Prussia these officials, in accordance with Puttkamer's decree and in order to avoid censure, were obliged to 'represent the policy of the government.' And, like the prefects in France, they were used as an official apparatus for influencing elections. Most of the 'political' officials of the German system—in contrast to other countries—were equally qualified in so far as access to these offices required a university education, special examinations, and special preparatory service. In Germany, only the heads of the political apparatus, the ministers, lack this specific characteristic of modern civil service. Even under the old regime, one could be the Prussian minister of education without ever having attended an institution of higher learning; whereas one could become *Vortragender Rat*,[2] in principle, only on the basis of a prescribed examination. The specialist and trained *Dezernent*[8] and *Vortragender Rat* were of course infinitely better informed about the real technical problems of the division than was their respective chief—for instance, under Althoff in the Prussian ministry of education. In England it was not different. Consequently, in all routine demands the divisional head was more powerful than the minister, which was not without reason. The minister was simply the representative of the political power constellation; he had to represent these powerful political staffs and he had to take measure of the proposals of his subordinate expert officials or give them directive orders of a political nature.

After all, things in a private economic enterprise are quite similar: the real 'sovereign,' the assembled shareholders, is just as little influential in the business management as is a 'people' ruled by expert officials. And the personages who decide the policy of the enterprise, the bank-controlled 'directorate,' give only directive economic orders and select persons for the management without themselves being capable of technically directing the enterprise. Thus the present structure of the revolutionary state signifies nothing new in principle. It places power over the administration into the hands of absolute dilettantes, who, by virtue of their control of the machine-guns, would like to use expert officials only as executive heads and hands. The difficulties of the present system lie elsewhere than here, but today these difficulties shall not concern us. We shall, rather, ask for the typical peculiarity of the professional politicians, of the 'leaders' as well as their followings. Their nature has changed and today varies greatly from one case to another.

We have seen that in the past 'professional politicians' developed through the struggle of the princes with the estates and that they served the princes. Let us briefly review the major types of these professional politicians.

Confronting the estates, the prince found support in politically exploitable strata outside of the order of the estates. Among the latter, there was, first, the clergy in Western and Eastern India, in Buddhist China and Japan, and in Lamaist Mongolia, just as in the Christian territories of the Middle Ages. The clergy were technically useful because they were literate. The importation of Brahmins, Buddhist priests, Lamas, and the employment of bishops and priests as political counselors, occurred with an eye to obtaining administrative forces who could read and write and who could be used in the struggle of the emperor, prince, or Khan against the aristocracy. Unlike the vassal who confronted his overlord, the cleric, especially the celibate cleric, stood outside the machinery of normal political and economic interests and was not tempted by the struggle for political power, for himself or for his descendants. By virtue of his own status, the cleric was 'separated' from the managerial implements of princely administration.

The humanistically educated literati comprised a second such stratum. There was a time when one learned to produce Latin speeches and Greek verses in order to become a political adviser to a prince and, above all things, to become a memorialist. This was the time of the first flowering of the humanist schools and of the princely foundations of professorships for 'poetics.' This was for us a transitory epoch, which has had a quite persistent influence upon our educational system, yet no deeper results politically. In East Asia, it has been different. The Chinese mandarin is, or rather originally was, what the humanist of our Renaissance period approximately was: a literator humanistically trained and tested in the language monuments of the remote past. When you read the diaries of Li Hung Chang you will find that he is most proud of having composed poems and of being a good calligrapher. This stratum, with its conventions developed and modeled after Chinese Antiquity, has determined the whole destiny of China; and perhaps our fate would have been similar if the humanists in their time had had the slightest chance of gaining a similar influence.

The third stratum was the court nobility. After the princes had succeeded in expropriating political power from the nobility as an estate, they drew the nobles to the court and used them in their political and diplomatic service. The transformation of our educational system in the seventeenth century was partly determined by the fact that court nobles as professional politicians displaced the humanist literati and entered the service of the princes.

The fourth category was a specifically English institution. A patrician stratum developed there which was comprised of the petty nobility and the urban rentiers; technically they are called the 'gentry.' The English gentry represents a stratum that the prince originally attracted in order to counter the barons. The prince placed the stratum in possession of the offices of 'self-government,' and later he himself became increasingly dependent upon them. The gentry maintained the possession of all offices of local administration by taking them over without compensation in the interest of their own social power. The gentry has saved England from the bureaucratization which has been the fate of all continental states.

A fifth stratum, the university-trained jurist, is peculiar to the Occident, especially to the European continent, and has been of decisive significance for the Continent's whole political structure. The tremendous after-effect of Roman law, as transformed by the late Roman bureaucratic state, stands out in nothing more clearly than the fact that everywhere the revolution of political management in the direction of the evolving rational state has been borne by trained jurists. This also occurred in England, although there the great national guilds of jurists hindered the reception of Roman law. There is no analogy to this process to be found in any area of the world.

All beginnings of rational juristic thinking in the Indian Mimamsa School and all further cultivation of the ancient juristic thinking in Islam have been unable to prevent the idea of rational law from being overgrown by theological forms of thought. Above all, legal trial procedure has not been fully rationalized in the cases of India and of Islamism. Such rationalization has been brought about on the Continent only through the borrowing of ancient Roman jurisprudence by the Italian jurists. Roman jurisprudence is the product of a political structure arising from the city state to world domination—a product of quite unique nature. The *usus modernus* of the late medieval pandect jurists and canonists was blended with theories of natural law, which were born from juristic and Christian thought and which were later secularized. This juristic rationalism has had its great representatives among the Italian Podesta, the French crown jurists (who created the formal means for the undermining of the rule of seigneurs by royal power), among the canonists and the theologians of the ecclesiastic councils (thinking in terms of natural law), among the court jurists and academic judges of the continental princes, among the Netherland teachers of natural law and the monarchomachists, among the English crown and parliamentary jurists, among the *noblesse de robe* of the French Parliament, and finally, among the lawyers of the age of the French Revolution.

Without this juristic rationalism, the rise of the absolute state is just as little imaginable as is the Revolution. If you look through the remonstrances of the French Pàrliaments or through the cahiers of the French Estates-General from the sixteenth century to the year 1789, you will find everywhere the spirit of the jurists. And if you go over the occupational composition of the members of the French Assembly, you will find there—although the members of the Assembly were elected through equal franchise—a single proletarian, very few bourgeois enter-prisers, but jurists of all sorts, *en masse*. Without them, the specific mentality that inspired these radical intellectuals and their projects would be quite inconceivable. Since the French Revolution, the modern lawyer and modern democracy absolutely belong together. And lawyers, in our sense of an independent status group, also exist only in the Occident. They have developed since the Middle Ages from the *Fürsprech* of the formalistic Germanic legal procedure under the impact of the rationalization of the trial.

The significance of the lawyer in Occidental politics since the rise of parties is not accidental. The management of politics through parties simply means management through interest groups. We shall soon see what that means. The craft of the trained lawyer is to plead effectively the cause of interested clients. In this, the lawyer is superior to any 'official,' as the superiority of enemy propaganda [Allied propaganda 1914-18] could teach us. Certainly he can advocate and win a cause supported by logically weak arguments and one which, in this sense, is a 'weak' cause. Yet he wins it because technically he makes a 'strong case' for it. But only the lawyer successfully pleads a cause that can be supported by logically strong arguments, thus handling a 'good' cause 'well.' All too often the civil servant as a politician turns a cause that is good in every sense into a 'weak' cause, through technically 'weak' pleading. This is what we have had to experience. To an outstanding degree, politics today is in fact conducted in public by means of the spoken or written word. To weigh the effect of the word properly falls within the range of the lawyer's tasks; but not at all into that of the civil servant. The latter is no demagogue, nor is it his purpose to be one. If he nevertheless tries to become a demagogue, he usually becomes a very poor one.

According to his proper vocation, the genuine official—and this is decisive for the evaluation of our former regime—will not engage in politics. Rather, he should engage in impartial 'administration.' This also holds for the so-called 'political' administrator, at least officially, in so far as the *raison d'état,* that is, the vital interests of the ruling order, are not in question. *Sine ira et studio,* 'without scorn and bias,' he shall administer his office. Hence, he shall not do precisely what the politician, the leader as well as his following, must always and necessarily do, namely, *fight.*

To take a stand, to be passionate—*ira et studium*—is the politician's element, and above all the element of the political *leader*. His conduct is subject to quite a different, indeed, exactly the opposite, principle of responsibility from that of the civil servant. The honor of the civil servant is vested in his ability to execute conscientiously the order of the superior authorities, exactly as if the order agreed with his own conviction. This holds even if the order appears wrong to him and if, despite the civil servant's remonstrances, the authority insists on the order. Without this moral discipline and self-denial, in the highest sense, the whole apparatus would fall to pieces. The honor of the political leader, of the leading statesman, however, lies precisely in an exclusive *personal* responsibility for what he does, a responsibility he cannot and must not reject or transfer. It is in the nature of officials of high moral standing to be poor politicians, and above all, in the political sense of the word, to be irresponsible politicians. In this sense, they are politicians of low moral standing, such as we unfortunately have had again and again in leading positions. This is what we have called *Beamtenherrschaft* [civil-service rule], and truly no spot soils the honor of our officialdom if we reveal what is politically wrong with the system from the standpoint of success. But let us return once more to the types of political figures.

Since the time of the constitutional state, and definitely since democracy has been established, the 'demagogue' has been the typical political leader in the Occident. The distasteful flavor of the word must not make us forget that not Cleon but Pericles was the first to bear the name of demagogue. In contrast to the offices of ancient democracy that were filled by lot, Pericles led the sovereign *Ecclesia* of the demos of Athens as a supreme strategist holding the only elective office or without holding any office at all. Modern demagoguery also makes use of oratory, even to a tremendous extent, if one considers the election speeches a modern candidate has to deliver. But the use of the printed word is more enduring. The political publicist, and above all the journalist, is nowadays the most important representative of the demagogic species.

Within the limits of this lecture, it is quite impossible even to sketch the sociology of modern political journalism, which in every respect constitutes a chapter in itself. Certainly, only a few things concerning it are in place here. In common with all demagogues and, by the way, with the lawyer (and the artist), the journalist shares the fate of lacking a fixed social classification. At least, this is the case on the Continent, in contrast to the English, and, by the way, also to former conditions in Prussia. The journalist belongs to a sort of pariah caste, which is always estimated by 'society' in terms of its ethically lowest representative. Hence, the strangest notions about journalists and their work are abroad. Not everybody realizes that a really good journalistic accomplishment requires at least as much 'genius'[4] as any scholarly accomplishment, especially because of the necessity of producing at once and 'on order,' and because of the necessity of being effective, to be sure, under quite different conditions of production. It is almost never acknowledged that the responsibility of the journalist is far greater, and that the sense of responsibility of every honorable journalist is, on the average, not a bit lower than that of the scholar, but rather, as the war has shown, higher. This is because, in the very nature of the case, irresponsible journalistic accomplishments and their often terrible effects are remembered.

Nobody believes that the discretion of any able journalist ranks above the average of other people, and yet that is the case. The quite incomparably graver temptations, and the other conditions that accompany journalistic work at the present time, produce those results which have conditioned the public to regard the press with a mixture of disdain and pitiful cowardice. Today we cannot discuss what is to be done. Here we are interested in the question of the occupational destiny of the political journalist and of his chance to attain a position of political leadership. Thus far, the journalist has had favorable chances only in the Social Democratic party. Within the party, editorial positions have been predominantly in the nature of official positions, but editorial positions have not been the basis for positions of leadership.

In the bourgeois parties, on the whole, the chances for ascent to political power along this avenue have rather become worse, as compared with those of the previous generation. Naturally every politician of consequence has needed influence over the press and hence has needed relations with the press. But that party leaders would emerge from the ranks of the press has been an absolute exception and one should not have expected it. The reason for this lies in the strongly increased 'indispensability' of the journalist, above all, of the propertyless and hence professionally bound journalist, an indispensability which is determined by the tremendously increased intensity and tempo of journalistic operations. The necessity of gaining one's livelihood by the writing of daily or at least weekly articles is like lead on the feet of the politicians. I know of cases in which natural leaders have been permanently paralyzed in their ascent to power, externally and above all internally, by this compulsion. The relations of the press to the ruling powers in the state and in the parties, under the old regime [of the Kaiser], were as detrimental as they could be to the level of journalism; but that is a chapter in itself. These conditions were different in the countries of our opponents [the Allies]. But there also, and for all modern states, apparently the journalist worker gains less and less as the capitalist lord of the press, of the sort of 'Lord' Northcliffe, for instance, gains more and more political influence.

Thus far, however, our great capitalist newspaper concerns, which attained control, especially over the 'chain newspapers,' with 'want ads,' have been regularly and typically the breeders of political indifference. For no profits could be made in an independent policy; especially no profitable benevolence of the politically dominant powers could be obtained. The advertising business is also the avenue along which, during the war, the attempt was made to influence the press politically in a grand style—an attempt which apparently it is regarded as desirable to continue now. Although one may expect the great papers to escape this pressure, the situation of the small ones will be far more difficult. In any case, for the time being, the journalist career is not among us, a normal avenue for the ascent of political leaders, whatever attraction journalism may otherwise have and whatever measure of influence, range of activity, and especially political responsibility it may yield. One has to wait and see. Perhaps journalism does not have this function any longer, or perhaps journalism does not yet have it. Whether the renunciation of the principle of anonymity would mean a change in this is difficult to say. Some journalists—not all—believe in dropping principled anonymity. What we have experienced during the war in the German press, and in the 'management' of newspapers by especially hired personages and talented writers who always expressly figured under their names, has unfortunately shown, in some of the better known cases, that an increased awareness of responsibility is not so certain to be bred as might be believed. Some of the papers were, without regard to party, precisely the notoriously worst boulevard sheets; by dropping anonymity they strove for and attained greater sales. The publishers as well as the journalists of sensationalism have gained fortunes but certainly not honor. Nothing is here being said against the principle of promoting sales; the question is indeed an intricate one, and the phenomenon of irresponsible sensationalism does not hold in general. But thus far, sensationalism has not been the road to genuine leadership or to the responsible management of politics. How conditions will further develop remains to be seen. Yet the journalist career remains under all circumstances one of the most important avenues of professional political activity. It is not a road for everybody, least of all for weak characters, especially for people who can maintain their inner balance only with a secure status position. If the life of a young scholar is a gamble, still he is walled in by firm status conventions, which prevent him from slipping. But the journalist's life is an absolute gamble in every respect and under conditions that test one's inner security in a way that scarcely occurs in any other situation. The often bitter experiences in occupational life are perhaps not even the worst. The inner demands that are directed precisely at the successful journalist are especially difficult. It is, indeed, no small matter to frequent the salons of the powerful on this earth on a seemingly equal footing and often to be flattered by all because one is feared, yet knowing all the time that having hardly closed the door the host has perhaps to justify before his guests his association with the 'scavengers from the press.' Moreover, it is no small matter that one must express oneself promptly and convincingly about this and that, on all conceivable problems of life—whatever the 'market' happens to demand—and this without becoming absolutely shallow and above all without losing one's dignity by baring oneself, a thing which has merciless results. It is not astonishing that there are many journalists who have become human failures and worthless men. Rather, it is astonishing that, despite all this, this very stratum includes such a great number of valuable and quite genuine men, a fact that outsiders would not so easily guess.

If the journalist as a type of professional politician harks back to a rather considerable past, the figure of the party official belongs only to the development of the last decades and, in part, only to recent years. In order to comprehend the position of this figure in historical evolution, we shall have to turn to a consideration of parties and party organizations.

In all political associations which are somehow extensive, that is, associations going beyond the sphere and range of the tasks of small rural districts where power-holders are periodically elected, political organization is necessarily managed by men interested in the management of politics. This is to say that a relatively small number of men are primarily interested in political life and hence interested in sharing political power. They provide themselves with a following through free recruitment, present themselves or their protégés as candidates for election, collect the financial means, and go out for vote-grabbing. It is unimaginable how in large associations elections could function at all without this managerial pattern. In practice this means the division of the citizens with the right to vote into politically active and politically passive elements. This difference is based on voluntary attitudes, hence it cannot be abolished through measures like obligatory voting, or 'occupational status group' representation, or similar measures that are expressly or actually directed against this state of affairs and the rule of professional politicians. The active leadership and their freely recruited following are the necessary elements in the life of any party. The following, and through it the passive electorate, are necessary for the election of the leader. But the structure of parties varies. For instance, the 'parties' of the medieval cities, such as those of the Guelfs and the Ghibellines, were purely personal followings. If one considers various things about these medieval parties, one is reminded of Bolshevism and its Soviets. Consider the *Statuta della perta Guelfa,* the confiscations of the Nobili's estates—which originally meant all those families who lived a chivalrous life and who thus qualified for fiefs—consider the exclusion from office-holding and the denial of the right to vote, the inter-local party committees, the strictly military organizations and the premiums for informers. Then consider Bolshevism with its strictly sieved military and, in Russia especially, informer organizations, the disarmament and denial of the political rights of the 'bourgeois,' that is, of the entrepreneur, trader, rentier, clergyman, descendants of the dynasty, police agents, as well as the confiscation policy.

This analogy is still more striking when one considers that, on the one hand, the military organization of the medieval party constituted a pure army of knights organized on the basis of the registered feudal estates and that nobles occupied almost all leading positions, and, on the other hand, that the Soviets have preserved, or rather reintroduced, the highly paid enterpriser, the group wage, the Taylor system, military and workshop discipline, and a search for foreign capital. Hence, in a word, the Soviets have had to accept again absolutely *all* the things that Bolshevism had been fighting as bourgeois class institutions. They have had to do this in order to keep the state and the economy going at all. Moreover, the Soviets have reinstituted the agents of the former Ochrana [Tsarist Secret Police] as the main instrument of their state power. But here we do not have to deal with such organizations for violence, but rather with professional politicians who strive for power through sober and 'peaceful' party campaigns in the market of election votes.

Parties, in the sense usual with us, were at first, for instance in England, pure followings of the aristocracy. If, for any reason whatever, a peer changed his party, everybody dependent upon him likewise changed. Up to the Reform Bill [of 1832], the great noble families and, last but not least, the king controlled the patronage of an immense number of election boroughs. Close to these aristocratic parties were the parties of notables, which develop everywhere with the rising power of the bourgeois. Under the spiritual leadership of the typical intellectual strata of the Occident, the propertied and cultured circles differentiated themselves into parties and followed them. These parties were formed partly according to class interest, partly according to family traditions, and partly for ideological reasons. Clergymen, teachers, professors, lawyers, doctors, apothecaries, prosperous farmers, manufacturers—in England the whole stratum that considered itself as belonging to the class of gentlemen—formed, at first, occasional associations at most local political clubs. In times of unrest the petty bourgeoisie raised its voice, and once in a while the proletariat, if leaders arose who, however, as a rule did not stem from their midst. In this phase, parties organized as permanent associations between localities do not yet exist in the open country. Only the parliamentary delegates create the cohesion; and the local notables are decisive for the selection of candidates. The election programs originate partly in the election appeals of the candidates and partly in the meetings of the notables; or, they originate as resolutions of the parliamentary party. Leadership of the clubs is an avocation and an honorific pursuit, as demanded by the occasion.

Where clubs are absent (as is mostly the case), the quite formless management of politics in normal times lies in the hands of the few people constantly interested in it. Only the journalist is a paid professional politician; only the management of the newspaper is a continuous political organization. Besides the newspaper, there is only the parliamentary session. The parliamentary delegates and the parliamentary party leaders know to which local notables one turns if a political action seems desirable. But permanent associations of the parties exist only in the large cities with moderate contributions of the members and periodical conferences and public meetings where the delegate gives account of the parliamentary activities. The party is alive only during election periods.

The members of parliament are interested in the possibility of inter-local electoral compromises, in vigorous and unified programs endorsed by broad circles and in a unified agitation throughout the country. In general these interests form the driving force of a party organization which becomes more and more strict. In principle, however, the nature of a party apparatus as an association of notables remains unchanged. This is so, even though a network of local party affiliations and agents is spread over the whole country, including middle-sized cities. A member of the parliamentary party acts as the leader of the central party office and maintains constant correspondence with the local organizations. Outside of the central bureau, paid officials are still absent; thoroughly 'respectable' people head the local organizations for the sake of the deference which they enjoy anyway. They form the extra-parliamentary 'notables' who exert influence alongside the stratum of political notables who happen to sit in parliament. However, the party correspondence, edited by the party, increasingly provides intellectual nourishment for the press and for the local meetings. Regular contributions of the members become indispensable; a part of these must cover the expenses of headquarters.

Not so long ago most of the German party organizations were still in this stage of development. In France, the first stage of party development was, at least in part, still predominant, and the organization of the members of parliament was quite unstable. In the open country, we find a small number of local notables and programs drafted by the candidates or set up for them by their patrons in specific campaigns for office. To be sure, these platforms constitute more or less local adaptations to the resolutions and programs of the members of parliament. This system was only partially punctured. The number of full-time professional politicians was small, consisting in the main of the elected deputies, the few employees of headquarters, and the journalists. In France, the system has also included those job hunters who held 'political office' or, at the moment, strove for one. Politics was formally and by far predominantly an avocation. The number of delegates qualifying for ministerial office was also very restricted and, because of their position as notables, so was the number of election candidates.

However, the number of those who indirectly had a stake in the management of politics, especially a material one, was very large. For, all administrative measures of a ministerial department, and especially all decisions in matters of personnel, were made partly with a view to their influence upon electoral chances. The realization of each and every kind of wish was sought through the local delegate's mediation. For better or for worse the minister had to lend his ear to this delegate, especially if the delegate belonged to the minister's majority. Hence everybody strove for such influence. The single deputy controlled the patronage of office and, in general, any kind of patronage in his election district. In order to be re-elected the deputy, in turn, maintained connections with the local notables.

Now then, the most modern forms of party organizations stand in sharp contrast to this idyllic state in which circles of notables and, above all, members of parliament rule. These modern forms are the children of democracy, of mass franchise, of the necessity to woo and organize the masses, and develop the utmost unity of direction and the strictest discipline. The rule of notables and guidance by members of parliament ceases. 'Professional' politicians *outside* the parliaments take the organization in hand. They do so either as 'entrepreneurs'—the American boss and the English election agent are, in fact, such entrepreneurs—or as officials with a fixed salary. Formally, a fargoing democratization takes place. The parliamentary party no longer creates the authoritative programs, and the local notables no longer decide the selection of candidates. Rather assemblies of the organized party members select the candidates and delegate members to the assemblies of a higher order. Possibly there are several such conventions leading up to the national convention of the party. Naturally power actually rests in the hands of those who, within the organization, handle the work *continuously*. Otherwise, power rests in the hands of those on whom the organization in its processes depends financially or personally—for instance, on the Maecenases or the directors of powerful political clubs of interested persons (Tammany Hall). It is decisive that this whole apparatus of people—characteristically called a 'machine' in Anglo-Saxon countries—or rather those who direct the machine, keep the members of the parliament in check. They are in a position to impose their will to a rather far-reaching extent, and that is of special significance for the selection of the party leader. The man whom the machine follows now becomes the leader, even over the head of the parliamentary party. In other words, the creation of such machines signifies the advent of *plebiscitarian* democracy.

The party following, above all the party official and party entrepreneur, naturally expect personal compensation from the victory of their leader—that is, offices or other advantages. It is decisive that they expect such advantages from their leader and not merely from the individual member of parliament. They expect that the demagogic effect of the leader's *personality* during the election fight of the party will increase votes and mandates and thereby power, and, thereby, as far as possible, will extend opportunities to their followers to find the compensation for which they hope. Ideally, one of their mainsprings is the satisfaction of working with loyal personal devotion for a man, and not merely for an abstract program of a party consisting of mediocrities. In this respect, the 'charismatic' element of all leadership is at work in the party system.

In very different degrees this system made headway, although it was in constant, latent struggle with local notables and the members of parliament who wrangled for influence. This was the case in the bourgeois parties, first, in the United States, and, then, in the Social Democratic party, especially of Germany. Constant setbacks occur as soon as no generally recognized leader exists, and, even when he is found, concessions of all sorts must be made to the vanity and the personal interest of the party notables. The machine may also be brought under the domination of the party officials in whose hands the regular business rests. According to the view of some Social Democratic circles, their party had succumbed to this 'bureaucratization.' But 'officials' submit relatively easily to a leader's personality if it has a strong demagogic appeal. The material and the ideal interests of the officials are intimately connected with the effects of party power which are expected from the leader's appeal, and besides, inwardly it is *per se* more satisfying to work for a leader. The ascent of leaders is far more difficult where the notables, along with the officials, control the party, as is usually the case in the bourgeois parties. For ideally the notables make 'their way of life' out of the petty chairmanships or committee memberships they hold. Resentment against the demagogue as a *homo novus,* the conviction of the superiority of political party 'experience' (which, as a matter of fact, actually is of considerable importance), and the ideological concern for the crumbling of the old party traditions—these factors determine the conduct of the notables. They can count on all the traditionalist elements within the party. Above all, the rural but also the petty bourgeois voter looks for the name of the notable familiar to him. He distrusts the man who is unknown to him. However, once this man has become successful, he clings to him the more unwaveringly. Let us now consider, by some major examples, the struggle of the two structural forms —of the notables and of the party—and especially let us consider the ascendancy of the plebiscitarian form as described by Ostrogorsky.

First England: there until 1868 the party organization was almost purely an organization of notables. The Tories in the country found support, for instance, from the Anglican parson, and from the schoolmaster, and above all from the large landlords of the respective county. The Whigs found support mostly from such people as the nonconformist preacher (when there was one), the postmaster, the blacksmith, the tailor, the ropemaker—that is, from such artisans who could disseminate political influence because they could chat with people most frequently. In the city the parties differed, partly according to economics, partly according to religion, and partly simply according to the party opinions handed down in the families. But always the notables were the pillars of the political organization.

Above all these arrangements stood Parliament, the parties with the cabinet, and the 'leader,' who was the chairman of the council of ministers or the leader of the opposition. This leader had beside him the 'whip'—the most important professional politician of the party organization. Patronage of office was vested in the hands of the 'whip'; thus the job hunter had to turn to him and he arranged an understanding with the deputies of the individual election boroughs. A stratum of professional politicians gradually began to develop in the boroughs. At first the locally recruited agents were not paid; they occupied approximately the same position as our *Vertrauensmänner*.[5] However, along with them, a capitalist entrepreneurial type developed in the boroughs. This was the 'election agent,' whose existence was unavoidable under England's modern legislation which guaranteed fair elections.

This legislation aimed at controlling the campaign costs of elections and sought to check the power of money by making it obligatory for the candidate to state the costs of his campaign. For in England, the candidate, besides straining his voice—far more so than was formerly the case with us [in Germany]—enjoyed stretching his purse. The election agent made the candidate pay a lump sum, which usually meant a good deal for the agent. In the distribution of power in Parliament and the country between the 'leader' and the party notables, the leader in England used to hold a very eminent position. This position was based on the compelling fact of making possible a grand, and thereby steady, political strategy. Nevertheless the influence of the parliamentary party and of party notables was still considerable.

That is about what the old party organization looked like. It was half an affair of notables and half an entrepreneurial organization with salaried employees. Since 1868, however, the 'caucus' system developed, first for local elections in Birmingham, then all over the country. A nonconformist parson and along with him Joseph Chamberlain brought this system to life. The occasion for this development was the democratization of the franchise. In order to win the masses it became necessary to call into being a tremendous apparatus of apparently democratic associations. An electoral association had to be formed in every city district to help keep the organization incessantly in motion and to bureaucratize everything rigidly. Hence, hired and paid officials of the local electoral committees increased numerically; and, on the whole, perhaps 10 per cent of the voters were organized in these local committees. The elected party managers had the right to co-opt others and were the formal bearers of party politics. The driving force was the local circle, which was, above all, composed of those interested in municipal politics—from which the fattest material opportunities always spring. These local circles were also first to call upon the world of finance. This newly emerging machine, which was no longer led by members of Parliament, very soon had to struggle with the previous power-holders, above all, with the 'whip.' Being supported by locally interested persons, the machine came out of the fight so victoriously that the whip had to submit and compromise with the machine. The result was a centralization of all power in the hands of the few and, ultimately, of the one person who stood at the top of the party. The whole system had arisen in the Liberal party in connection with Gladstone's ascent to power. What brought this machine to such swift triumph over the notables was the fascination of Gladstone's 'grand' demagogy, the firm belief of the masses in the ethical substance of his policy, and, above all, their belief in the ethical character of his personality. It soon became obvious that a Caesarist plebiscitarian element in politics—the dictator of the battlefield of elections—had appeared on the plain. In 1877 the caucus became active for the first time in national elections, and with brilliant success, for the result was Disraeli's fall at the height of his great achievements. In 1866, the machine was already so completely oriented to the charismatic personality that when the question of home rule was raised the whole apparatus from top to bottom did not question whether it actually stood on Gladstone's ground; it simply, on his word, fell in line with him: they said, Gladstone right or wrong, we follow him. And thus the machine deserted its own creator, Chamberlain.

Such machinery requires a considerable personnel. In England there are about 2,000 persons who live directly off party politics. To be sure, those who are active in politics purely as job seekers or as interested persons are far more numerous, especially in municipal politics. In addition to economic opportunities, for the useful caucus politician, there are the opportunities to satisfy his vanity. To become 'J.P.' or even 'M.P.' is, of course, in line with the greatest (and normal) ambition; and such people, who are of demonstrably good breeding, that is, 'gentlemen,' attain their goal. The highest goal is, of course, a peerage, especially for the great financial Maecenases. About 50 per cent of the finances of the party depend on contributions of donors who remained anonymous.

Now then, what has been the effect of this whole system? Nowadays the members of Parliament, with the exception of the few cabinet members (and a few insurgents), are normally nothing better than well-disciplined 'yes' men. With us, in the Reichstag, one used at least to take care of one's private correspondence on his desk, thus indicating that one was active in the weal of the country. Such gestures are not demanded in England; the member of Parliament must only vote, not commit party treason. He must appear when the whips call him, and do what the cabinet or the leader of the opposition orders. The caucus machine in the open country is almost completely unprincipled if a strong leader exists who has the machine absolutely in hand. Therewith the plebiscitarian dictator actually stands above Parliament. He brings the masses behind him by means of the machine and the members of Parliament are for him merely political spoilsmen enrolled in his following.

How does the selection of these strong leaders take place? First, in terms of what ability are they selected? Next to the qualities of will—decisive all over the world—naturally the force of demagogic speech is above all decisive. Its character has changed since the time speakers like Cobden addressed themselves to the intellect, and Gladstone who mastered the technique of apparently 'letting sober facts speak for themselves.' At the present time often purely emotional means are used—the means the Salvation Army also exploits in order to set the masses in motion. One may call the existing state of affairs a 'dictatorship resting on the exploitation of mass emotionality.' Yet, the highly developed system of committee work in the English Parliament makes it possible and compelling for every politician who counts on a share in leadership to co-operate in committee work. All important ministers of recent decades have this very real and effective work-training as a background. The practice of committee reports and public criticism of these deliberations is a condition for training, for really selecting leaders and eliminating mere demagogues.

Thus it is in England. The caucus system there, however, has been a weak form, compared with the American party organization, which brought the plebiscitarian principle to an especially early and an especially pure expression.

According to Washington's idea, America was to be a commonwealth administered by 'gentlemen.' In his time, in America, a gentleman was also a landlord, or a man with a college education—this was the case at first. In the beginning, when parties began to organize, the members of the House of Representatives claimed to be leaders, just as in England at the time when notables ruled. The party organization was quite loose and continued to be until 1824. In some communities, where modern development first took place, the party machine was in the making even before the eighteen-twenties. But when Andrew Jackson was first elected President—the election of the western farmers' candidate—the old traditions were overthrown. Formal party leadership by leading members of Congress came to an end soon after 1840, when the great parliamentarians, Calhoun and Webster, retired from political life because Congress had lost almost all of its power to the party machine in the open country. That the plebiscitarian 'machine' has developed so early in America is due to the fact that there, and there alone, the executive—this is what mattered—the chief of office-patronage, was a President elected by plebiscite. By virtue of the 'separation of powers' he was almost independent of parliament in his conduct of office. Hence, as the price of victory, the true booty object of the office-prebend was held out precisely at the presidential election. Through Andrew Jackson the 'spoils system' was quite systematically raised to a principle and the conclusions were drawn.

What does this spoils system, the turning over of federal offices to the following of the victorious candidate, mean for the party formations of today? It means that quite unprincipled parties oppose one another; they are purely organizations of job hunters drafting their changing platforms according to the chances of vote-grabbing, changing their colors to a degree which, despite all analogies, is not yet to be found elsewhere. The parties are simply and absolutely fashioned for the election campaign that is most important for office patronage: the fight for the presidency and for the governorships of the separate states. Platforms and candidates are selected at the national conventions of the parties without intervention by congressmen. Hence they emerge from party conventions, the delegates of which are formally, very democratically elected. These delegates are determined by meetings of other delegates, who, in turn, owe their mandate to the 'primaries,' the assembling of the direct voters of the party. In the primaries the delegates are already elected in the name of the candidate for the nation's leadership. Within the parties the most embittered fight rages about the question of 'nomination.' After all, 300,000 to 400,000 official appointments lie in the hands of the President, appointments which are executed by him only with the approval of the senators from the separate states. Hence the senators are powerful politicians. By comparison, however, the House of Representatives is, politically, quite impotent, because patronage of office is removed from it and because the cabinet members, simply assistants to the President, can conduct office apart from the confidence or lack of confidence of the people. The President, who is legitimatized by the people, confronts everybody, even Congress; this is a result of 'the separation of powers.'

In America, the spoils system, supported in this fashion, has been technically possible because American culture with its youth could afford purely dilettante management. With 300,000 to 400,000 such party men who have no qualifications to their credit other than the fact of having performed good services for their party, this state of affairs of course could not exist without enormous evils. A corruption and wastefulness second to none could be tolerated only by a country with as yet unlimited economic opportunities.

Now then, the boss is the figure who appears in the picture of this system of the plebiscitarian party machine. Who is the boss? He is a political capitalist entrepreneur who on his own account and at his own risk provides votes. He may have established his first relations as a lawyer or a saloonkeeper or as a proprietor of similar establishments, or perhaps as a creditor. From here he spins his threads out until he is able to 'control' a certain number of votes. When he has come this far he establishes contact with the neighboring bosses, and through zeal, skill, and above all discretion, he attracts the attention of those who have already further advanced in the career, and then he climbs. The boss is indispensable to the organization of the party and the organization is centralized in his hands. He substantially provides the financial means. How does he get them? Well, partly by the contributions of the members, and especially by taxing the salaries of those officials who came into office through him and his party. Furthermore, there are bribes and tips. He who wishes to trespass with impunity one of the many laws needs the boss's connivance and must pay for it; or else he will get into trouble. But this alone is not enough to accumulate the necessary capital for political enterprises. The boss is indispensable as the direct recipient of the money of great financial magnates, who would not entrust their money for election purposes to a paid party official, or to anyone else giving public account of his affairs. The boss, with his judicious discretion in financial matters, is the natural man for those capitalist circles who finance the election. The typical boss is an absolutely sober man. He does not seek social honor; the 'professional' is despised in 'respectable society.' He seeks power alone, power as a source of money, but also power for power's sake. In contrast to the English leader, the American boss works in the dark. He is not heard speaking in public; he suggests to the speakers what they must say in expedient fashion. He himself, however, keeps silent. As a rule he accepts no office, except that of senator. For, since the senators, by virtue of the Constitution, participate in office patronage, the leading bosses often sit in person in this body. The distribution of offices is carried out, in the first place, according to services done for the party. But, also, auctioning offices on financial bids often occurs and there are certain rates for individual offices; hence, a system of selling offices exists which, after all, has often been known also to the monarchies, the church-state included, of the seventeenth and eighteenth centuries.

The boss has no firm political 'principles'; he is completely unprincipled in attitude and asks merely: What will capture votes? Frequently he is a rather poorly educated man. But as a rule he leads an inoffensive and correct private life. In his political morals, however, he naturally adjusts to the average ethical standards of political conduct, as a great many of us also may have done during the hoarding period in the field of economic ethics.[6] That as a 'professional' politician the boss is socially despised does not worry him. That he personally does not attain high federal offices, and does not wish to do so, has the frequent advantage that extra-party intellects, thus notables, may come into candidacy when the bosses believe they will have great appeal value at the polls. Hence the same old party notables do not run again and again, as is the case in Germany. Thus the structure of these unprincipled parties with their socially despised power-holders has aided able men to attain the presidency —men who with us never would have come to the top. To be sure, the bosses resist an outsider who might jeopardize their sources of money and power. Yet in the competitive struggle to win the favor of the voters, the bosses frequently have had to condescend and accept candidates known to be opponents of corruption.

Thus there exists a strong capitalist party machine, strictly and thoroughly organized from top to bottom, and supported by clubs of extraordinary stability. These clubs, such as Tammany Hall, are like Knight orders. They seek profits solely through political control, especially of the municipal government, which is the most important object of booty. This structure of party life was made possible by the high degree of democracy in the United States—a 'New Country.' This connection, in turn, is the basis for the fact that the system is gradually dying out. America can no longer be governed only by dilettantes. Scarcely fifteen years ago, when American workers were asked why they allowed themselves to be governed by politicians whom they admitted they despised, the answer was: 'We prefer having people in office whom we can spit upon, rather than a caste of officials who spit upon us, as is the case with you.' This was the old point of view of American 'democracy.' Even then, the socialists had entirely different ideas and now the situation is no longer bearable. The dilettante administration does not suffice and the Civil Service Reform establishes an ever-increasing number of positions for life with pension rights. The reform works out in such a way that university-trained officials, just as incorruptible and quite as capable as our officials, get into office. Even now about 100,000 offices have ceased being objects of booty to be turned over after elections. Rather, the offices qualify their holders for pensions, and are based upon tested qualifications. The spoils system will thus gradually recede into the background and the nature of party leadership is then likely to be transformed also—but as yet, we do not know in what way.

In Germany, until now, the decisive conditions of political management have been in essence as follows:

First, the parliaments have been impotent. The result has been that no man with the qualities of a leader would enter Parliament permanently. If one wished to enter Parliament, what could one achieve there? When a chancellery position was open, one could tell the administrative chief: 'I have a very able man in my election district who would be suitable; take him.' And he would have concurred with pleasure; but that was about all that a German member of Parliament could do to satisfy his instincts for power—if he possessed any.

To this must be added the tremendous importance of the trained expert officialdom in Germany. This factor determined the impotence of Parliament. Our officialdom was second to none in the world. This importance of the officialdom was accompanied by the fact that the officials claimed not only official positions but also cabinet positions for themselves. In the Bavarian state legislature, when the introduction of parliamentary government was debated last year, it was said that if members of the legislature were to be placed in cabinet positions talented people would no longer seek official careers. Moreover, the civil-service administration systematically escaped such control as is signified by the English committee discussions. The administration thus made it impossible for parliaments—with a few exceptions—to train really useful administrative chiefs from their own ranks.

A third factor is that in Germany, in contrast to America, we have had parties with principled political views who have maintained that their members, at least subjectively, represented bona-fide *Weltanschauungen*. Now then, the two most important of these parties, the Catholic Centre Party and the Social Democratic party, have, from their inceptions, been minority parties and have meant to be minority parties. The leading circles of the Centre party in the Reich have never concealed their opposition to parliamentarian democracy, because of fear of remaining in the minority and thus facing great difficulties in placing their job hunters in office as they have done by exerting pressure on the government. The Social Democratic party was a principled minority party and a handicap to the introduction of parliamentary government because the party did not wish to stain itself by participating in the existing bourgeois political order. The fact that both parties dissociated themselves from the parliamentary system made parliamentary government impossible.

Considering all this, what then became of the professional politicians in Germany? They have had no power, no responsibility, and could play only a rather subordinate role as notables. In consequence, they have been animated anew by the guild instincts, which are typical everywhere. It has been impossible for a man who was not of their hue to climb high in the circle of those notables who made their petty positions their lives. I could mention many names from every party, the Social Democratic party, of course, not excepted, that spell tragedies of political careers because the persons had leadership qualities, and precisely because of these qualities were not tolerated by the notables. All our parties have taken this course of development and have become guilds of notables. Bebel, for instance, was still a leader through temperament and purity of character, however modest his intellect. The fact that he was a martyr, that he never betrayed confidence in the eyes of the masses, resulted in his having the masses absolutely behind him. There was no power in the party that could have seriously challenged him. Such leadership came to an end, after his death, and the rule of officials began. Trade-union officials, party secretaries, and journalists came to the top. The instincts of officialdom dominated the party—a highly respectable officialdom, of rare respectability one may say, compared to conditions in other countries, especially the often corruptible trade-union officials in America. But the results of control by officialdom, which we discussed above, also began in the party.

Since the eighteen-eighties the bourgeois parties have completely become guilds of notables. To be sure, occasionally the parties had to draw on extra-party intellects for advertising purposes, so that they could say, 'We have such and such names.' So far as possible, they avoided letting these names run for election; only when it was unavoidable and the person insisted could he run for election. The same spirit prevailed in Parliament. Our parliamentary parties were and are guilds. Every speech delivered from the floor of the Reichstag is thoroughly censored in the party before it is delivered. This is obvious from their unheard-of boredom. Only he who is summoned to speak can have the word. One can hardly conceive of a stronger contrast to the English, and also—for quite opposite reasons—the French usage.

Now, in consequence of the enormous collapse, which is customarily called the Revolution, perhaps a transformation is under way. Perhaps—but not for certain. In the beginning there were new kinds of party apparatuses emerging. First, there were amateur apparatuses. They are especially often represented by students of the various universities, who tell a man to whom they ascribe leadership qualities: we want to do the necessary work for you; carry it out. Secondly, there are apparatuses of businessmen. It happened that men to whom leadership qualities were ascribed were approached by people willing to take over the propaganda, at fixed rates for every vote. If you were to ask me honestly which of these two apparatuses I think the more reliable, from the purely technical-political point of view, I believe I would prefer the latter. But both apparatuses were fast-emerging bubbles, which swiftly vanished again. The existing apparatuses transformed themselves, but they continued to work. The phenomena are only symptoms of the fact that new apparatuses would come about if there were only leaders. But even the technical peculiarity of proportionate representation precluded their ascendancy. Only a few dictators of the street crowds arose and fell again. And only the following of a mob dictatorship is organized in a strictly disciplined fashion: whence the power of these vanishing minorities.

Let us assume that all this were to change; then, after what has been said above, it has to be clearly realized that the plebiscitarian leadership of parties entails the 'soullessness' of the following, their intellectual proletarianization, one might say. In order to be a useful apparatus, a machine in the American sense—undisturbed either by the vanity of notables or pretensions to independent views—the following of such a leader must obey him blindly. Lincoln's election was possible only through this character of party organization, and with Gladstone, as mentioned before, the same happened in the caucus. This is simply the price paid for guidance by leaders. However, there is only the choice between leadership democracy with a 'machine' and leaderless democracy, namely, the rule of professional politicians without a calling, without the inner charismatic qualities that make a leader, and this means what the party insurgents in the situation usually designate as 'the rule of the clique.' For the time being, we in Germany have only the latter. For the future, the permanence of this situation, at least in the Reich, is primarily facilitated by the fact that the *Bundesrat*[7] will rise again and will of necessity restrict the power of the Reichstag and therewith its significance as a selective agency of leaders. Moreover, in its present form, proportional representation is a typical phenomenon of leaderless democracy. This is the case not only because it facilitates the horse-trading of the notables for placement on the ticket, but also because in the future it will give organized interest groups the possibility of compelling parties to include their officials in the list of candidates, thus creating an unpolitical Parliament in which genuine leadership finds no place. Only the President of the Reich could become the safety-valve of the demand for leadership if he were elected in a plebiscitarian way and not by Parliament. Leadership on the basis of proved work could emerge and selection could take place, especially if, in great municipalities, the plebiscitarian city-manager were to appear on the scene with the right to organize his bureaus independently. Such is the case in the U.S.A. whenever one wishes to tackle corruption seriously. It requires a party organization fashioned for such elections. But the very petty-bourgeois hostility of all parties to leaders, the Social Democratic party certainly included, leaves the future formation of parties and all these chances still completely in the dark.

Therefore, today, one cannot yet see in any way how the management of politics as a 'vocation' will shape itself. Even less can one see along what avenue opportunities are opening to which political talents can be put for satisfactory political tasks. He who by his material circumstances is compelled to live 'off' politics will almost always have to consider the alternative positions of the journalist or the party official as the typical direct avenues. Or, he must consider a position as representative of interest groups—such as a trade union, a chamber of commerce, a farm bureau,[8] a craft association,[9] a labor board, an employer's association, et cetera, or else a suitable municipal position. Nothing more than this can be said about this external aspect: in common with the journalist, the party official bears the odium of being *déclassé*. 'Wage writer' or 'wage speaker' will unfortunately always resound in his ears, even though the words remain unexpressed. He who is inwardly defenseless and unable to find the proper answer for himself had better stay away from this career. For in any case, besides grave temptations, it is an avenue that may constantly lead to disappointments. Now then, what inner enjoyments can this career offer and what personal conditions are presupposed for one who enters this avenue?

Well, first of all the career of politics grants a feeling of power. The knowledge of influencing men, of participating in power over them, and above all, the feeling of holding in one's hands a nerve fiber of historically important events can elevate the professional politician above everyday routine even when he is placed in formally modest positions. But now the question for him is: Through what qualities can I hope to do justice to this power (however narrowly circumscribed it may be in the individual case)? How can he hope to do justice to the responsibility that power imposes upon him? With this we enter the field of ethical questions, for that is where the problem belongs: What kind of a man must one be if he is to be allowed to put his hand on the wheel of history?

One can say that three pre-eminent qualities are decisive for the politician: passion, a feeling of responsibility, and a sense of proportion.

This means passion in the sense of *matter-of-factness*, of passionate devotion to a 'cause,' to the god or demon who is its overlord. It is not passion in the sense of that inner bearing which my late friend, Georg Simmel, used to designate as 'sterile excitation,' and which was peculiar especially to a certain type of Russian intellectual (by no means all of them!). It is an excitation that plays so great a part with our intellectuals in this carnival we decorate with the proud name of 'revolution.' It is a 'romanticism of the intellectually interesting,' running into emptiness devoid of all feeling of objective responsibility.

To be sure, mere passion, however genuinely felt, is not enough. It does not make a politician, unless passion as devotion to a 'cause' also makes responsibility to this cause the guiding star of action. And for this, a sense of proportion is needed. This is the decisive psychological quality of the politician: his ability to let realities work upon him with inner concentration and calmness. Hence his *distance* to things and men. 'Lack of distance' *per se* is one of the deadly sins of every politician. It is one of those qualities the breeding of which will condemn the progeny of our intellectuals to political incapacity. For the problem is simply how can warm passion and a cool sense of proportion be forged together in one and the same soul? Politics is made with the head, not with other parts of the body or soul. And yet devotion to politics, if it is not to be frivolous intellectual play but rather genuinely human conduct, can be born and nourished from passion alone. However, that firm taming of the soul, which distinguishes the passionate politician and differentiates him from the 'sterilely excited' and mere political dilettante, is possible only through habituation to detachment in every sense of the word. The 'strength' of a political 'personality' means, in the first place, the possession of these qualities of passion, responsibility, and proportion.

Therefore, daily and hourly, the politician inwardly has to overcome a quite trivial and all-too-human enemy: a quite vulgar vanity, the deadly enemy of all matter-of-fact devotion to a cause, and of all distance, in this case, of distance towards one's self.

Vanity is a very widespread quality and perhaps nobody is entirely free from it. In academic and scholarly circles, vanity is a sort of occupational disease, but precisely with the scholar, vanity—however disagreeably it may express itself—is relatively harmless; in the sense that as a rule it does not disturb scientific enterprise. With the politician the case is quite different. He works with the striving for power as an unavoidable means. Therefore, 'power instinct,' as is usually said, belongs indeed to his normal qualities. The sin against the lofty spirit of his vocation, however, begins where this striving for power ceases to be *objective* and becomes purely personal self-intoxication, instead of exclusively entering the service of 'the cause.' For ultimately there are only two kinds of deadly sins in the field of politics: lack of objectivity and—often but not always identical with it—irresponsibility. Vanity, the need personally to stand in the foreground as clearly as possible, strongly tempts the politician to commit one or both of these sins. This is more truly the case as the demagogue is compelled to count upon 'effect.' He therefore is constantly in danger of becoming an actor as well as taking lightly the responsibility for the outcome of his actions and of being concerned merely with the 'impression' he makes. His lack of objectivity tempts him to strive for the glamorous semblance of power rather than for actual power. His irresponsibility, however, suggests that he enjoy power merely for power's sake without a substantive purpose. Although, or rather just because, power is the unavoidable means, and striving for power is one of the driving forces of all politics, there is no more harmful distortion of political force than the parvenu-like braggart with power, and the vain self-reflection in the feeling of power, and in general every worship of power *per se*. The mere 'power politician' may get strong effects, but actually his work leads nowhere and is senseless. (Among us, too, an ardently promoted cult seeks to glorify him.) In this, the critics of 'power politics' are absolutely right. From the sudden inner collapse of typical representatives of this mentality, we can see what inner weakness and impotence hides behind this boastful but entirely empty gesture. It is a product of a shoddy and superficially blasé attitude towards the meaning of human conduct; and it has no relation whatsoever to the knowledge of tragedy with which all action, but especially political action, is truly interwoven.

The final result of political action often, no, even regularly, stands in completely inadequate and often even paradoxical relation to its original meaning. This is fundamental to all history, a point not to be proved in detail here. But because of this fact, the serving of a cause must not be absent if action is to have inner strength. Exactly what the cause, in the service of which the politician strives for power and uses power, looks like is a matter of faith. The politician may serve national, humanitarian, social, ethical, cultural, worldly, or religious ends. The politician may be sustained by a strong belief in 'progress'— no matter in which sense—or he may coolly reject this kind of belief. He may claim to stand in the service of an 'idea' or, rejecting this in principle, he may want to serve external ends of everyday life. However, some kind of faith must always exist. Otherwise, it is absolutely true that the curse of the creature's worthlessness overshadows even the externally strongest political successes.

With the statement above we are already engaged in discussing the last problem that concerns us tonight: the *ethos* of politics as a 'cause.' What calling can politics fulfil quite independently of its goals within the total ethical economy of human conduct—which is, so to speak, the ethical locus where politics is at home? Here, to be sure, ultimate *Weltanschauungen* clash, world views among which in the end one has to make a choice. Let us resolutely tackle this problem, which recently has been opened again, in my view in a very wrong way.

But first, let us free ourselves from a quite trivial falsification: namely, that ethics may first appear in a morally highly compromised role. Let us consider examples. Rarely will you find that a man whose love turns from one woman to another feels no need to legitimate this before himself by saying: she was not worthy of my love, or, she has disappointed me, or whatever other like 'reasons' exist. This is an attitude that, with a profound lack of chivalry, adds a fancied 'legitimacy' to the plain fact that he no longer loves her and that the woman has to bear it. By virtue of this 'legitimation,' the man claims a right for himself and besides causing the misfortune seeks to put her in the wrong. The successful amatory competitor proceeds exactly in the same way: namely, the opponent must be less worthy, otherwise he would not have lost out.

It is no different, of course, if after a victorious war the victor in undignified self-righteousness claims, 'I have won because I was right.' Or, if somebody under the frightfulness of war collapses psychologically, and instead of simply saying it was just too much, he feels the need of legitimizing his war weariness to himself by substituting the feeling, 'I could not bear it because I had to fight for a morally bad cause.' And likewise with the defeated in war. Instead of searching like old women for the 'guilty one' after the war—in a situation in which the structure of society produced the war—everyone with a manly and controlled attitude would tell the enemy, 'We lost the war. You have won it. That is now all over. Now let us discuss what conclusions must be drawn according to the *objective* interests that came into play and what is the main thing in view of the responsibility towards the *future* which above all burdens the victor.' Anything else is undignified and will become a boomerang. A nation forgives if its interests have been damaged, but no nation forgives if its honor has been offended, especially by a bigoted self-righteousness. Every new document that comes to light after decades revives the undignified lamentations, the hatred and scorn, instead of allowing the war at its end to be buried, at least morally. This is possible only through objectivity and chivalry and above all only through dignity. But never is it possible through an 'ethic,' which in truth signifies a lack of dignity on both sides. Instead of being concerned about what the politician is interested in, the future and the responsibility towards the future, this ethic is concerned about politically sterile questions of past guilt, which are not to be settled politically. To act in this way is politically guilty, if such guilt exists at all. And it overlooks the unavoidable falsification of the whole problem, through very material interests: namely, the victor's interest in the greatest possible moral and material gain; the hopes of the defeated to trade in advantages through confessions of guilt. If anything is 'vulgar,' then, this is, and it is the result of this fashion of exploiting 'ethics' as a means of 'being in the right.'

Now then, what relations do ethics and politics actually have? Have the two nothing whatever to do with one another, as has occasionally been said? Or, is the reverse true: that the ethic of political conduct is identical with that of any other conduct? Occasionally an exclusive choice has been believed to exist between the two propositions—either the one or the other proposition must be correct. But is it true that any ethic of the world could establish commandments of identical content for erotic, business, familial, and official relations; for the relations to one's wife, to the greengrocer, the son, the competitor, the friend, the defend-ant? Should it really matter so little for the ethical demands on politics that politics operates with very special means, namely, power backed up by *violence?* Do we not see that the Bolshevik and the Spartacist ideolo-gists bring about exactly the same results as any militaristic dictator just because they use this political means? In what but the persons of the power-holders and their dilettantism does the rule of the workers' and soldiers' councils differ from the rule of any power-holder of the old regime? In what way does the polemic of most representatives of the presumably new ethic differ from that of the opponents which they criticized, or the ethic of any other demagogues? In their noble intention, people will say. Good! But it is the means about which we speak here, and the adversaries, in complete subjective sincerity, claim, in the very same way, that their ultimate intentions are of lofty character. 'All they that take the sword shall perish with the sword' and fighting is every-where fighting. Hence, the ethic of the Sermon on the Mount.

By the Sermon on the Mount, we mean the absolute ethic of the gospel, which is a more serious matter than those who are fond of quoting these commandments today believe. This ethic is no joking matter. The same holds for this ethic as has been said of causality in science: it is not a cab, which one can have stopped at one's pleasure; it is all or nothing. This is precisely the meaning of the gospel, if trivialities are not to result. Hence, for instance, it was said of the wealthy young man, 'He went away sorrowful: for he had great possessions.' The evange-list commandment, however, is unconditional and unambiguous: give what thou hast—absolutely everything. The politician will say that this is a socially senseless imposition as long as it is not carried out every-where. Thus the politician upholds taxation, confiscatory taxation, out-right confiscation; in a word, compulsion and regulation for all. The ethical commandment, however, is not at all concerned about that, and this unconcern is its essence. Or, take the example, 'turn the other cheek': This command is unconditional and does not question the source of the other's authority to strike. Except for a saint it is an ethic of indignity. This is it: one must be saintly in everything; at least in inten-tion, one must live like Jesus, the apostles, St. Francis, and their like. *Then* this ethic makes sense and expresses a kind of dignity; otherwise it does not. For if it is said, in line with the acosmic ethic of love, 'Resist not him that is evil with force,' for the politician the reverse proposition holds, 'thou *shalt* resist evil by force,' or else you are responsible for the evil winning out. He who wishes to follow the ethic of the gospel should abstain from strikes, for strikes mean compulsion; he may join the company unions. Above all things, he should not talk of 'revolution.' After all, the ethic of the gospel does not wish to teach that civil war is the only legitimate war. The pacifist who follows the gospel will refuse to bear arms or will throw them down; in Germany this was the recommended ethical duty to end the war and therewith all wars. The politician would say the only sure means to discredit the war for all foreseeable time would have been a *status quo* peace. Then the nations would have questioned, what was this war for? And then the war would have been argued *ad absurdum*, which is now impossible. For the victors, at least for part of them, the war will have been politically profitable. And the responsibility for this rests on behavior that made all resistance impossible for us. Now, as a result of the ethics of absolutism, when the period of exhaustion will have passed, *the peace will be discredited, not the war.*

Finally, let us consider the duty of truthfulness. For the absolute ethic it holds unconditionally. Hence the conclusion was reached to publish all documents, especially those placing blame on one's own country. On the basis of these one-sided publications the confessions of guilt followed —and they were one-sided, unconditional, and without regard to consequences. The politician will find that as a result truth will not be furthered but certainly obscured through abuse and unleashing of passion; only an all-round methodical investigation by non-partisans could bear fruit; any other procedure may have consequences for a nation that cannot be remedied for decades. But the absolute ethic just does not *ask* for 'consequences.' That is the decisive point.

We must be clear about the fact that all ethically oriented conduct may be guided by one of two fundamentally differing and irreconcilably opposed maxims: conduct can be oriented to an 'ethic of ultimate ends' or to an 'ethic of responsibility.' This is not to say that an ethic of ultimate ends is identical with irresponsibility, or that an ethic of responsibility is identical with unprincipled opportunism. Naturally nobody says that. However, there is an abysmal contrast between conduct that follows the maxim of an ethic of ultimate ends—that is, in religious terms, 'The Christian does rightly and leaves the results with the Lord'—and conduct that follows the maxim of an ethic of responsibility, in which case one has to give an account of the foreseeable results of one's action.

You may demonstrate to a convinced syndicalist, believing in an ethic of ultimate ends, that his action will result in increasing the opportunities of reaction, in increasing the oppression of his class, and obstructing its ascent—and you will not make the slightest impression upon him. If an action of good intent leads to bad results, then, in the actor's eyes, not he but the world, or the stupidity of other men, or God's will who made them thus, is responsible for the evil. However a man who believes in an ethic of responsibility takes account of precisely the average deficiences of people; as Fichte has correctly said, he does not even have the right to presuppose their goodness and perfection. He does not feel in a position to burden others with the results of his own actions so far as he was able to foresee them; he will say: these results are ascribed to my action. The believer in an ethic of ultimate ends feels 'responsible' only for seeing to it that the flame of pure intentions is not quelched: for example, the flame of protesting against the injustice of the social order. To rekindle the flame ever anew is the purpose of his quite irrational deeds, judged in view of their possible success. They are acts that can and shall have only exemplary value.

But even herewith the problem is not yet exhausted. No ethics in the world can dodge the fact that in numerous instances the attainment of 'good' ends is bound to the fact that one must be willing to pay the price of using morally dubious means or at least dangerous ones—and facing the possibility or even the probability of evil ramifications. From no ethics in the world can it be concluded when and to what extent the ethically good purpose 'justifies' the ethically dangerous means and ramifications.

The decisive means for politics is violence. You may see the extent of the tension between means and ends, when viewed ethically, from the following: as is generally known, even during the war the revolutionary socialists (Zimmerwald faction) professed a principle that one might strikingly formulate: 'If we face the choice either of some more years of war and then revolution, or peace now and no revolution, we choose— some more years of war!' Upon the further question: 'What can this revolution bring about?' every scientifically trained socialist would have had the answer: One cannot speak of a transition to an economy that in our sense could be called socialist; a bourgeois economy will re-emerge, merely stripped of the feudal elements and the dynastic vestiges. For this very modest result, they are willing to face 'some more years of war.' One may well say that even with a very robust socialist conviction one might reject a purpose that demands such means. With Bolshevism and Spartacism, and, in general, with any kind of revolutionary socialism, it is precisely the same thing. It is of course utterly ridiculous if the power politicians of the old regime are morally denounced for their use of the same means, however justified the rejection of their *aims* may be.

The ethic of ultimate ends apparently must go to pieces on the problem of the justification of means by ends. As a matter of fact, logically it has only the possibility of rejecting all action that employs morally dangerous means—in theory! In the world of realities, as a rule, we encounter the ever-renewed experience that the adherent of an ethic of ultimate ends suddenly turns into a chiliastic prophet. Those, for example, who have just preached 'love against violence' now call for the use of force for the *last* violent deed, which would then lead to a state of affairs in which *all* violence is annihilated. In the same manner, our officers told the soldiers before every offensive: 'This will be the last one; this one will bring victory and therewith peace.' The proponent of an ethic of absolute ends cannot stand up under the ethical irrationality of the world. He is a cosmic-ethical 'rationalist.' Those of you who know Dostoievski will remember the scene of the 'Grand Inquisitor,' where the problem is poignantly unfolded. If one makes any concessions at all to the principle that the end justifies the means, it is not possible to bring an ethic of ultimate ends and an ethic of responsibility under one roof or to decree ethically which end should justify which means.

My colleague, Mr. F. W. Förster, whom personally I highly esteem for his undoubted sincerity, but whom I reject unreservedly as a politician, believes it is possible to get around this difficulty by the simple thesis: 'from good comes only good; but from evil only evil follows.' In that case this whole complex of questions would not exist. But it is rather astonishing that such a thesis could come to light two thousand five hundred years after the Upanishads. Not only the whole course of world history, but every frank examination of everyday experience points to the very opposite. The development of religions all over the world is determined by the fact that the opposite is true. The age-old problem of theodicy consists of the very question of how it is that a power which is said to be at once omnipotent and kind could have created such an irrational world of undeserved suffering, unpunished injustice, and hopeless stupidity. Either this power is not omnipotent or not kind, or, entirely different principles of compensation and reward govern our life—principles we may interpret metaphysically, or even principles that forever escape our comprehension.

This problem—the experience of the irrationality of the world—has been the driving force of all religious evolution. The Indian doctrine of karma, Persian dualism, the doctrine of original sin, predestination and the *deus absconditus,* all these have grown out of this experience. Also the early Christians knew full well the world is governed by demons and that he who lets himself in for politics, that is, for power and force as means, contracts with diabolical powers and for his action it is *not* true that good can follow only from good and evil only from evil, but that often the opposite is true. Anyone who fails to see this is, indeed, a political infant.

We are placed into various life-spheres, each of which is governed by different laws. Religious ethics have settled with this fact in different ways. Hellenic polytheism made sacrifices to Aphrodite and Hera alike, to Dionysus and to Apollo, and knew these gods were frequently in conflict with one another. The Hindu order of life made each of the different occupations an object of a specific ethical code, a Dharma, and forever segregated one from the other as castes, thereby placing them into a fixed hierarchy of rank. For the man born into it, there was no escape from it, lest he be twice-born in another life. The occupations were thus placed at varying distances from the highest religious goods of salvation. In this way, the caste order allowed for the possibility of fashioning the Dharma of each single caste, from those of the ascetics and Brahmins to those of the rogues and harlots, in accordance with the immanent and autonomous laws of their respective occupations. War and politics were also included. You will find war integrated into the totality of life-spheres in the *Bhagavad-Gita,* in the conversation between Krishna and Arduna. 'Do what must be done,' i.e. do that work which, according to the Dharma of the warrior caste and its rules, is obligatory and which, according to the purpose of the war, is objectively necessary. Hinduism believes that such conduct does not damage religious salvation but, rather, promotes it. When he faced the hero's death, the Indian warrior was always sure of Indra's heaven, just as was the Teuton warrior of Valhalla. The Indian hero would have despised Nirvana just as much as the Teuton would have sneered at the Christian paradise with its angels' choirs. This specialization of ethics allowed for the Indian ethic's quite unbroken treatment of politics by following politics' own laws and even radically enhancing this royal art.

A really radical 'Machiavellianism,' in the popular sense of this word, is classically represented in Indian literature, in the *Kautaliya Arthasastra* (long before Christ, allegedly dating from Chandragupฺa's time). In contrast with this document Machiavelli's *Principe* is harmless. As is known in Catholic ethics—to which otherwise Professor Förster stands close—the *consilia evangelica* are a special ethic for those endowed with the charisma of a holy life. There stands the monk who must not shed blood or strive for gain, and beside him stand the pious knight and the burgher, who are allowed to do so, the one to shed blood, the other to pursue gain. The gradation of ethics and its organic integration into the doctrine of salvation is less consistent than in India. According to the presuppositions of Christian faith, this could and had to be the case. The wickedness of the world stemming from original sin allowed with relative ease the integration of violence into ethics as a disciplinary means against sin and against the heretics who endangered the soul. However, the demands of the Sermon on the Mount, an acosmic ethic of ultimate ends, implied a natural law of absolute imperatives based upon religion. These absolute imperatives retained their revolutionizing force and they came upon the scene with elemental vigor during almost all periods of social upheaval. They produced especially the radical pacifist sects, one of which in Pennsylvania experimented in establishing a polity that renounced violence towards the outside. This experiment took a tragic course, inasmuch as with the outbreak of the War of Independence the Quakers could not stand up arms-in-hand for their ideals, which were those of the war.

Normally, Protestantism, however, absolutely legitimated the state as a divine institution and hence violence as a means. Protestantism, especially, legitimated the authoritarian state. Luther relieved the individual of the ethical responsibility for war and transferred it to the authorities. To obey the authorities in matters other than those of faith could never constitute guilt. Calvinism in turn knew principled violence as a means of defending the faith; thus Calvinism knew the crusade, which was for Islam an element of life from the beginning. One sees that it is by no means a modern disbelief born from the hero worship of the Renaissance which poses the problem of political ethics. All religions have wrestled with it, with highly differing success, and after what has been said it could not be otherwise. It is the specific means of legitimate violence as such in the hand of human associations which determines the peculiarity of all ethical problems of politics.

Whosoever contracts with violent means for whatever ends—and every politician does—is exposed to its specific consequences. This holds espe-

cially for the crusader, religious and revolutionary alike. Let us confi-
dently take the present as an example. He who wants to establish absolute justice on earth by force requires a following, a human 'machine.'
He must hold out the necessary internal and external premiums, heavenly
or worldly reward, to this 'machine' or else the machine will not function. Under the conditions of the modern class struggle, the internal
premiums consist of the satisfying of hatred and the craving for revenge; above all, resentment and the need for pseudo-ethical self-righteousness: the opponents must be slandered and accused of heresy. The
external rewards are adventure, victory, booty, power, and spoils. The
leader and his success are completely dependent upon the functioning of
his machine and hence not on his own motives. Therefore he also depends upon whether or not the premiums can be *permanently* granted
to the following, that is, to the Red Guard, the informers, the agitators,
whom he needs. What he actually attains under the conditions of his
work is therefore not in his hand, but is prescribed to him by the following's motives, which, if viewed ethically, are predominantly base. The
following can be harnessed only so long as an honest belief in his person
and his cause inspires at least part of the following, probably never on
earth even the majority. This belief, even when subjectively sincere, is in
a very great number of cases really no more than an ethical 'legitimation'
of cravings for revenge, power, booty, and spoils. We shall not be de-
ceived about this by verbiage; the materialist interpretation of history is
no cab to be taken at will; it does not stop short of the promoters of
revolutions. Emotional revolutionism is followed by the traditionalist
routine of everyday life; the crusading leader and the faith itself fade
away, or, what is even more effective, the faith becomes part of the conventional phraseology of political Philistines and banausic technicians.
This development is especially rapid with struggles of faith because they
are usually led or inspired by genuine leaders, that is, prophets of revolution. For here, as with every leader's machine, one of the conditions for
success is the depersonalization and routinization, in short, the psychic
proletarianization, in the interests of discipline. After coming to power the
following of a crusader usually degenerates very easily into a quite common stratum of spoilsmen.

Whoever wants to engage in politics at all, and especially in politics
as a vocation, has to realize these ethical paradoxes. He must know that
he is responsible for what may become of himself under the impact of
these paradoxes. I repeat, he lets himself in for the diabolic forces lurking

in all violence. The great *virtuosi* of acosmic love of humanity and goodness, whether stemming from Nazareth or Assisi or from Indian royal
castles, have not operated with the political means of violence. Their
kingdom was 'not of this world' and yet they worked and still work
in this world. The figures of Platon Karatajev and the saints of Dostoievski still remain their most adequate reconstructions. He who seeks
the salvation of the soul, of his own and of others, should not seek
it along the avenue of politics, for the quite different tasks of politics
can only be solved by violence. The genius or demon of politics lives in
an inner tension with the god of love, as well as with the Christian God
as expressed by the church. This tension can at any time lead to an
irreconcilable conflict. Men knew this even in the times of church rule.
Time and again the papal interdict was placed upon Florence and at
the time it meant a far more robust power for men and their salvation
of soul than (to speak with Fichte) the 'cool approbation' of the Kantian
ethical judgment. The burghers, however, fought the church-state. And
it is with reference to such situations that Machiavelli in a beautiful
passage, if I am not mistaken, of the *History of Florence,* has one of his
heroes praise those citizens who deemed the greatness of their native
city higher than the salvation of their souls.

If one says 'the future of socialism' or 'international peace,' instead of
native city or 'fatherland' (which at present may be a dubious value
to some), then you face the problem as it stands now. Everything that
is striven for through political action operating with violent means and
following an ethic of responsibility endangers the 'salvation of the soul.'
If, however, one chases after the ultimate good in a war of beliefs, following a pure ethic of absolute ends, then the goals may be damaged
and discredited for generations, because responsibility for *consequences*
is lacking, and two diabolic forces which enter the play remain unknown to the actor. These are inexorable and produce consequences for
his action and even for his inner self, to which he must helplessly submit, unless he perceives them. The sentence: 'The devil is old; grow old
to understand him!' does not refer to age in terms of chronological years.
I have never permitted myself to lose out in a discussion through a
reference to a date registered on a birth certificate; but the mere fact
that someone is twenty years of age and that I am over fifty is no
cause for me to think that this alone is an achievement before which I am
overawed. Age is not decisive; what is decisive is the trained relentless-

ness in viewing the realities of life, and the ability to face such realities and to measure up to them inwardly.

Surely, politics is made with the head, but it is certainly not made with the head alone. In this the proponents of an ethic of ultimate ends are right. One cannot prescribe to anyone whether he should follow an ethic of absolute ends or an ethic of responsibility, or when the one and when the other. One can say only this much: If in these times, which, in your opinion, are not times of 'sterile' excitation—excitation is not, after all, genuine passion—if now suddenly the *Weltanschauungs-*politicians crop up *en masse* and pass the watchword, 'The world is stupid and base, not I,' 'The responsibility for the consequences does not fall upon me but upon the others whom I serve and whose stupidity or baseness I shall eradicate,' then I declare frankly that I would first inquire into the degree of inner poise backing this ethic of ultimate ends. I am under the impression that in nine out of ten cases I deal with windbags who do not fully realize what they take upon themselves but who intoxicate themselves with romantic sensations. From a human point of view this is not very interesting to me, nor does it move me profoundly. However, it is immensely moving when a *mature* man—no matter whether old or young in years—is aware of a responsibility for the consequences of his conduct and really feels such responsibility with heart and soul. He then acts by following an ethic of responsibility and somewhere he reaches the point where he says: 'Here I stand; I can do no other.' That is something genuinely human and moving. And every one of us who is not spiritually dead must realize the possibility of finding himself at some time in that position. In so far as this is true, an ethic of ultimate ends and an ethic of responsibility are not absolute contrasts but rather supplements, which only in unison constitute a genuine man—a man who *can* have the 'calling for politics.'

Now then, ladies and gentlemen, let us debate this matter once more ten years from now. Unfortunately, for a whole series of reasons, I fear that by then the period of reaction will have long since broken over us. It is very probable that little of what many of you, and (I candidly confess) I too, have wished and hoped for will be fulfilled; little—perhaps not exactly nothing, but what to us at least seems little. This will not crush me, but surely it is an inner burden to realize it. Then, I wish I could see what has become of those of you who now feel yourselves to be genuinely 'principled' politicians and who share in the intoxication signified by this revolution. It would be nice if matters turned out in such a way that Shakespeare's Sonnet 102 should hold true:

> Our love was new, and then but in the spring,
> When I was wont to greet it with my lays;
> As Philomel in summer's front doth sing,
> And stops her pipe in growth of riper days.

But such is not the case. Not summer's bloom lies ahead of us, but rather a polar night of icy darkness and hardness, no matter which group may triumph externally now. Where there is nothing, not only the Kaiser but also the proletarian has lost his rights. When this night shall have slowly receded, who of those for whom spring apparently has bloomed so luxuriously will be alive? And what will have become of all of you by then? Will you be bitter or banausic? Will you simply and dully accept world and occupation? Or will the third and by no means the least frequent possibility be your lot: mystic flight from reality for those who are gifted for it, or—as is both frequent and unpleasant—for those who belabor themselves to follow this fashion? In every one of such cases, I shall draw the conclusion that they have not measured up to their own doings. They have not measured up to the world as it really is in its everyday routine. Objectively and actually, they have not experienced the vocation for politics in its deepest meaning, which they thought they had. They would have done better in simply cultivating plain brotherliness in personal relations. And for the rest—they should have gone soberly about their daily work.

Politics is a strong and slow boring of hard boards. It takes both passion and perspective. Certainly all historical experience confirms the truth —that man would not have attained the possible unless time and again he had reached out for the impossible. But to do that a man must be a leader, and not only a leader but a hero as well, in a very sober sense of the word. And even those who are neither leaders nor heroes must arm themselves with that steadfastness of heart which can brave even the crumbling of all hopes. This is necessary right now, or else men will not be able to attain even that which is possible today. Only he has the calling for politics who is sure that he shall not crumble when the world from his point of view is too stupid or too base for what he wants to offer. Only he who in the face of all this can say 'In spite of all!' has the calling for politics.

V. Science as a Vocation

You wish me to speak about 'Science as a Vocation.' Now, we political economists have a pedantic custom, which I should like to follow, of always beginning with the external conditions. In this case, we begin with the question: What are the conditions of science as a vocation in the material sense of the term? Today this question means, practically and essentially: What are the prospects of a graduate student who is resolved to dedicate himself professionally to science in university life? In order to understand the peculiarity of German conditions it is expedient to proceed by comparison and to realize the conditions abroad. In this respect, the United States stands in the sharpest contrast with Germany, so we shall focus upon that country.

Everybody knows that in Germany the career of the young man who is dedicated to science normally begins with the position of *Privatdozent.* After having conversed with and received the consent of the respective specialists, he takes up residence on the basis of a book and, usually, a rather formal examination before the faculty of the university. Then he gives a course of lectures without receiving any salary other than the lecture fees of his students. It is up to him to determine, within his *venia legendi,* the topics upon which he lectures.

In the United States the academic career usually begins in quite a different manner, namely, by employment as an 'assistant.' This is similar to the great institutes of the natural science and medical faculties in Germany, where usually only a fraction of the assistants try to habilitate themselves as *Privatdozenten* and often only later in their career.

Practically, this contrast means that the career of the academic man in Germany is generally based upon plutocratic prerequisites. For it is extremely hazardous for a young scholar without funds to expose himself

'Wissenschaft als Beruf,' *Gesammelte Aufsaetze zur Wissenschaftslehre* (Tübingen, 1922), pp. 524-55. Originally a speech at Munich University, 1918, published in 1919 by Duncker & Humblodt, Munich.

to the conditions of the academic career. He must be able to endure this condition for at least a number of years without knowing whether he will have the opportunity to move into a position which pays well enough for maintenance.

In the United States, where the bureaucratic system exists, the young academic man is paid from the very beginning. To be sure, his salary is modest; usually it is hardly as much as the wages of a semi-skilled laborer. Yet he begins with a seemingly secure position, for he draws a fixed salary. As a rule, however, notice may be given to him just as with German assistants, and frequently he definitely has to face this should he not come up to expectations.

These expectations are such that the young academic in America must draw large crowds of students. This cannot happen to a German docent; once one has him, one cannot get rid of him. To be sure, he cannot raise any 'claims.' But he has the understandable notion that after years of work he has a sort of moral right to expect some consideration. He also expects—and this is often quite important—that one have some regard for him when the question of the possible habilitation of other *Privatdozenten* comes up.

Whether, in principle, one should habilitate every scholar who is qualified or whether one should consider enrollments, and hence give the existing staff a monopoly to teach—that is an awkward dilemma. It is associated with the dual aspect of the academic profession, which we shall discuss presently. In general, one decides in favor of the second alternative. But this increases the danger that the respective full professor, however conscientious he is, will prefer his own disciples. If I may speak of my personal attitude, I must say I have followed the principle that a scholar promoted by me must legitimize and habilitate himself with *somebody else* at another university. But the result has been that one of my best disciples has been turned down at another university because nobody there *believed* this to be the reason.

A further difference between Germany and the United States is that in Germany the *Privatdozent* generally teaches fewer courses than he wishes. According to his formal right, he can give any course in his field. But to do so would be considered an improper lack of consideration for the older docents. As a rule, the full professor gives the 'big' courses and the docent confines himself to secondary ones. The advantage of these arrangements is that during his youth the academic man is free to do scientific work, although this restriction of the opportunity to teach is somewhat involuntary.

In America, the arrangement is different in principle. Precisely during the early years of his career the assistant is absolutely overburdened just because he is paid. In a department of German, for instance, the full professor will give a three-hour course on Goethe and that is enough, whereas the young assistant is happy if, besides the drill in the German language, his twelve weekly teaching hours include assignments of, say, Uhland. The officials prescribe the curriculum, and in this the assistant is just as dependent as the institute assistant in Germany.

Of late we can observe distinctly that the German universities in the broad fields of science develop in the direction of the American system. The large institutes of medicine or natural science are 'state capitalist' enterprises, which cannot be managed without very considerable funds. Here we encounter the same condition that is found wherever capitalist enterprise comes into operation: the 'separation of the worker from his means of production.' The worker, that is, the assistant, is dependent upon the implements that the state puts at his disposal; hence he is just as dependent upon the head of the institute as is the employee in a factory upon the management. For, subjectively and in good faith, the director believes that this institute is 'his,' and he manages its affairs. Thus the assistant's position is often as precarious as is that of any 'quasi-proletarian' existence and just as precarious as the position of the assistant in the American university.

In very important respects German university life is being Americanized, as is German life in general. This development, I am convinced, will engulf those disciplines in which the craftsman personally owns the tools, essentially the library, as is still the case to a large extent in my own field. This development corresponds entirely to what happened to the artisan of the past and it is now fully under way.

As with all capitalist and at the same time bureaucratized enterprises, there are indubitable advantages in all this. But the 'spirit' that rules in these affairs is different from the historical atmosphere of the German university. An extraordinarily wide gulf, externally and internally, exists between the chief of these large, capitalist, university enterprises and the usual full professor of the old style. This contrast also holds for the inner attitude, a matter that I shall not go into here. Inwardly as well as externally, the old university constitution has become fictitious. What has remained and what has been essentially increased is a factor peculiar to the university career: the question whether or not such a *Privatdozent,* and still more an assistant, will ever succeed in moving into the position of a full professor or even become the head of an institute. That is simply a hazard. Certainly, chance does not rule alone, but it rules to an unusually high degree. I know of hardly any career on earth where chance plays such a role. I may say so all the more since I personally owe it to some mere accidents that during my very early years I was appointed to a full professorship in a discipline in which men of my generation undoubtedly had achieved more that I had. And, indeed, I fancy, on the basis of this experience, that I have a sharp eye for the undeserved fate of the many whom accident has cast in the opposite direction and who within this selective apparatus in spite of all their ability do not attain the positions that are due them.

The fact that hazard rather than ability plays so large a role is not alone or even predominantly owing to the 'human, all too human' factors, which naturally occur in the process of academic selection as in any other selection. It would be unfair to hold the personal inferiority of faculty members or educational ministries responsible for the fact that so many mediocrities undoubtedly play an eminent role at the universities. The predominance of mediocrity is rather due to the laws of human co-operation, especially of the co-operation of several bodies, and, in this case, co-operation of the faculties who recommend and of the ministries of education.

A counterpart are the events at the papal elections, which can be traced over many centuries and which are the most important controllable examples of a selection of the same nature as the academic selection. The cardinal who is said to be the 'favorite' only rarely has a chance to win out. The rule is rather that the Number Two cardinal or the Number Three wins out. The same holds for the President of the United States. Only exceptionally does the first-rate and most prominent man get the nomination of the convention. Mostly the Number Two and often the Number Three men are nominated and later run for election. The Americans have already formed technical sociological terms for these categories, and it would be quite interesting to enquire into the laws of selection by a collective will by studying these examples, but we shall not do so here. Yet these laws also hold for the collegiate bodies of German universities, and one must not be surprised at the frequent mistakes that are made, but rather at the number of *correct* appointments, the proportion of which, in spite of all, is very considerable. Only where parliaments, as in some countries, or monarchs, as in Germany thus far (both work out in the same way), or revolutionary power-holders, as in Germany now, intervene for political reasons in academic selections, can one be certain that convenient mediocrities or strainers will have the opportunities all to themselves.

No university teacher likes to be reminded of discussions of appointments, for they are seldom agreeable. And yet I may say that in the numerous cases known to me there was, without exception, the good will to allow purely objective reasons to be decisive.

One must be clear about another thing: that the decision over academic fates is so largely a 'hazard' is not merely because of the insufficiency of the selection by the collective formation of will. Every young man who feels called to scholarship has to realize clearly that the task before him has a double aspect. He must qualify not only as a scholar but also as a teacher. And the two do not at all coincide. One can be a pre-eminent scholar and at the same time an abominably poor teacher. May I remind you of the teaching of men like Helmholtz or Ranke; and they are not by any chance rare exceptions.

Now, matters are such that German universities, especially the small universities, are engaged in a most ridiculous competition for enrollments. The landlords of rooming houses in university cities celebrate the advent of the thousandth student by a festival, and they would love to celebrate Number Two Thousand by a torchlight procession. The interest in fees—and one should openly admit it—is affected by appointments in the neighboring fields that 'draw crowds.' And quite apart from this, the number of students enrolled is a test of qualification, which may be grasped in terms of numbers, whereas the qualification for scholarship is imponderable and, precisely with audacious innovators, often debatable—that is only natural. Almost everybody thus is affected by the suggestion of the immeasurable blessing and value of large enrollments. To say of a docent that he is a poor teacher is usually to pronounce an academic sentence of death, even if he is the foremost scholar in the world. And the question whether he is a good or a poor teacher is answered by the enrollments with which the students condescendingly honor him.

It is a fact that whether or not the students flock to a teacher is determined in large measure, larger than one would believe possible, by purely external things: temperament and even the inflection of his voice. After rather extensive experience and sober reflection, I have a deep distrust of courses that draw crowds, however unavoidable they may be Democracy should be used only where it is in place. Scientific training, as we are held to practice it in accordance with the tradition of German universities, is the affair of an intellectual aristocracy, and we should not hide this from ourselves. To be sure, it is true that to present scientific problems in such a manner that an untutored but receptive mind can understand them and—what for us is alone decisive—can come to think about them independently is perhaps the most difficult pedagogical task of all. But whether this task is or is not realized is not decided by enrollment figures. And—to return to our theme—this very art is a personal gift and by no means coincides with the scientific qualifications of the scholar.

In contrast to France, Germany has no corporate body of 'immortals' in science. According to German tradition, the universities shall do justice to the demands both of research and of instruction. Whether the abilities for both are found together in a man is a matter of absolute chance. Hence academic life is a mad hazard. If the young scholar asks for my advice with regard to habilitation, the responsibility of encouraging him can hardly be borne. If he is a Jew, of course one says *lasciate ogni speranza*. But one must ask every other man: Do you in all conscience believe that you can stand seeing mediocrity after mediocrity, year after year, climb beyond you, without becoming embittered and without coming to grief? Naturally, one always receives the answer: 'Of course, I live only for my "calling."' Yet, I have found that only a few men could endure this situation without coming to grief.

This much I deem necessary to say about the external conditions of the academic man's vocation. But I believe that actually you wish to hear of something else, namely, of the *inward* calling for science. In our time, the internal situation, in contrast to the organization of science as a vocation, is first of all conditioned by the facts that science has entered a phase of specialization previously unknown and that this will forever remain the case. Not only externally, but inwardly, matters stand at a point where the individual can acquire the sure consciousness of achieving something truly perfect in the field of science only in case he is a strict specialist.

All work that overlaps neighboring fields, such as we occasionally undertake and which the sociologists must necessarily undertake again and again, is burdened with the resigned realization that at best one provides the specialist with useful questions upon which he would not so easily hit from his own specialized point of view. One's own work must inevitably remain highly imperfect. Only by strict specialization can the scientific worker become fully conscious, for once and perhaps never again in his lifetime, that he has achieved something that will endure. A really definitive and good accomplishment is today always a specialized accomplishment. And whoever lacks the capacity to put on blinders, so to speak, and to come up to the idea that the fate of his soul depends upon whether or not he makes the correct conjecture at this passage of this manuscript may as well stay away from science. He will never have what one may call the 'personal experience' of science. Without this strange intoxication, ridiculed by every outsider; without this passion, this 'thousands of years must pass before you enter into life and thousands more wait in silence'—according to whether or not you succeed in making this conjecture; without this, you have *no* calling for science and you should do something else. For nothing is worthy of man as man unless he can pursue it with passionate devotion.

Yet it is a fact that no amount of such enthusiasm, however sincere and profound it may be, can compel a problem to yield scientific results. Certainly enthusiasm is a prerequisite of the 'inspiration' which is decisive. Nowadays in circles of youth there is a widespread notion that science has become a problem in calculation, fabricated in laboratories or statistical filing systems just as 'in a factory,' a calculation involving only the cool intellect and not one's 'heart and soul.' First of all one must say that such comments lack all clarity about what goes on in a factory or in a laboratory. In both some idea has to occur to someone's mind, and it has to be a correct idea, if one is to accomplish anything worthwhile. And such intuition cannot be forced. It has nothing to do with any cold calculation. Certainly calculation is also an indispensable prerequisite. No sociologist, for instance, should think himself too good, even in his old age, to make tens of thousands of quite trivial computations in his head and perhaps for months at a time. One cannot with impunity try to transfer this task entirely to mechanical assistants if one wishes to figure something, even though the final result is often small indeed. But if no 'idea' occurs to his mind about the direction of his computations and, during his computations, about the bearing of the emergent single results, then even this small result will not be yielded.

Normally such an 'idea' is prepared only on the soil of very hard work, but certainly this is not always the case. Scientifically, a dilettante's idea may have the very same or even a greater bearing for science than that of a specialist. Many of our very best hypotheses and insights are due precisely to dilettantes. The dilettante differs from the expert, as Helmholtz has said of Robert Mayer, only in that he lacks a firm and reliable work procedure. Consequently he is usually not in the position to control, to estimate, or to exploit the idea in its bearings. The idea is not a substitute for work; and work, in turn, cannot substitute for or compel an idea, just as little as enthusiasm can. Both, enthusiasm and work, and above all both of them *jointly,* can entice the idea.

Ideas occur to us when they please, not when it pleases us. The best ideas do indeed occur to one's mind in the way in which Ihering describes it: when smoking a cigar on the sofa; or as Helmholtz states of himself with scientific exactitude: when taking a walk on a slowly ascending street; or in a similar way. In any case, ideas come when we do not expect them, and not when we are brooding and searching at our desks. Yet ideas would certainly not come to mind had we not brooded at our desks and searched for answers with passionate devotion.

However this may be, the scientific worker has to take into his bargain the risk that enters into all scientific work: Does an 'idea' occur or does it not? He may be an excellent worker and yet never have had any valuable idea of his own. It is a grave error to believe that this is so only in science, and that things for instance in a business office are different from a laboratory. A merchant or a big industrialist without 'business imagination,' that is, without ideas or ideal intuitions, will for all his life remain a man who would better have remained a clerk or a technical official. He will never be truly creative in organization. Inspiration in the field of science by no means plays any greater role, as academic conceit fancies, than it does in the field of mastering problems of practical life by a modern entrepreneur. On the other hand, and this also is often misconstrued, inspiration plays no less a role in science than it does in the realm of art. It is a childish notion to think that a mathematician attains any scientifically valuable results by sitting at his desk with a ruler, calculating machines or other mechanical means. The mathematical imagination of a Weierstrass is naturally quite differently oriented in meaning and result than is the imagination of an artist, and differs basically in quality. But the psychological processes do not differ. Both are frenzy (in the sense of Plato's 'mania') and 'inspiration.'

Now, whether we have scientific inspiration depends upon destinies that are hidden from us, and besides upon 'gifts.' Last but not least, because of this indubitable truth, a very understandable attitude has

become popular, especially among youth, and has put them in the service of idols whose cult today occupies a broad place on all street corners
and in all periodicals. These idols are 'personality' and 'personal experience.' Both are intimately connected, the notion prevails that the
latter constitutes the former and belongs to it. People belabor themselves
in trying to 'experience' life—for that befits a personality, conscious of
its rank and station. And if we do not succeed in 'experiencing' life, we
must at least pretend to have this gift of grace. Formerly we called this
'experience,' in plain German, 'sensation'; and I believe that we then
had a more adequate idea of what personality is and what it signifies.

Ladies and gentlemen. In the field of science only he who is devoted
solely to the work at hand has 'personality.' And this holds not only
for the field of science; we know of no great artist who has ever done
anything but serve his work and only his work. As far as his art is
concerned, even with a personality of Goethe's rank, it has been detrimental to take the liberty of trying to make his 'life' into a work of art.
And even if one doubts this, one has to be a Goethe in order to dare
permit oneself such liberty. Everybody will admit at least this much:
that even with a man like Goethe, who appears once in a thousand years,
this liberty did not go unpaid for. In politics matters are not different,
but we shall not discuss that today. In the field of science, however, the
man who makes himself the impresario of the subject to which he
should be devoted, and steps upon the stage and seeks to legitimate himself through 'experience,' asking: How can I prove that I am something
other than a mere 'specialist' and how can I manage to say something
in form or in content that nobody else has ever said?—such a man is no
'personality.' Today such conduct is a crowd phenomenon, and it always makes a petty impression and debases the one who is thus concerned. Instead of this, an inner devotion to the task, and that alone,
should lift the scientist to the height and dignity of the subject he pretends to serve. And in this it is not different with the artist.

In contrast with these preconditions which scientific work shares with
art, science has a fate that profoundly distinguishes it from artistic work.
Scientific work is chained to the course of progress; whereas in the realm
of art there is no progress in the same sense. It is not true that the
work of art of a period that has worked out new technical means, or,
for instance, the laws of perspective, stands therefore artistically higher
than a work of art devoid of all knowledge of those means and laws—
if its form does justice to the material, that is, if its object has been

chosen and formed so that it could be artistically mastered without applying those conditions and means. A work of art which is genuine 'fulfilment' is never surpassed; it will never be antiquated. Individuals may differ in appreciating the personal significance of works of art, but no one will ever be able to say of such a work that it is 'outstripped by another work which is also 'fulfilment.'

In science, each of us knows that what he has accomplished will be antiquated in ten, twenty, fifty years. That is the fate to which science is subjected; it is the very *meaning* of scientific work, to which it is devoted in a quite specific sense, as compared with other spheres of culture for which in general the same holds. Every scientific 'fulfilment' raises new 'questions'; it *asks* to be 'surpassed' and outdated. Whoever wishes to serve science has to resign himself to this fact. Scientific works certainly can last as 'gratifications' because of their artistic quality, or they may remain important as a means of training. Yet they will be surpassed scientifically—let that be repeated—for it is our common fate and, more, our common goal. We cannot work without hoping that others will advance further than we have. In principle, this progress goes on *ad infinitum*. And with this we come to inquire into the *meaning* of science. For, after all, it is not self-evident that something subordinate to such a law is sensible and meaningful in itself. Why does one engage in doing something that in reality never comes, and never can come, to an end?

One does it, first, for purely practical, in the broader sense of the word, for technical, purposes: in order to be able to orient our practical activities to the expectations that scientific experience places at our disposal. Good. Yet this has meaning only to practitioners. What is the attitude of the academic man towards his vocation—that is, if he is at all in quest of such a personal attitude? He maintains that he engages in 'science for science's sake' and not merely because others, by exploiting science, bring about commercial or technical success and can better feed, dress, illuminate, and govern. But what does he who allows himself to be integrated into this specialized organization, running on *ad infinitum,* hope to accomplish that is significant in these productions that are always destined to be outdated? This question requires a few general considerations.

Scientific progress is a fraction, the most important fraction, of the process of intellectualization which we have been undergoing for thousands of years and which nowadays is usually judged in such an extremely negative way. Let us first clarify what this intellectualist rationalization, created by science and by scientifically oriented technology, means practically.

Does it mean that we, today, for instance, everyone sitting in this hall, have a greater knowledge of the conditions of life under which we exist than has an American Indian or a Hottentot? Hardly. Unless he is a physicist, one who rides on the streetcar has no idea how the car happened to get into motion. And he does not need to know. He is satisfied that he may 'count' on the behavior of the streetcar, and he orients his conduct according to this expectation; but he knows nothing about what it takes to produce such a car so that it can move. The savage knows incomparably more about his tools. When we spend money today I bet that even if there are colleagues of political economy here in the hall, almost every one of them will hold a different answer in readiness to the question: How does it happen that one can buy something for money—sometimes more and sometimes less? The savage knows what he does in order to get his daily food and which institutions serve him in this pursuit. The increasing intellectualization and rationalization do *not,* therefore, indicate an increased and general knowledge of the conditions under which one lives.

It means something else, namely, the knowledge or belief that if one but wished one *could* learn it at any time. Hence, it means that principally there are no mysterious incalculable forces that come into play, but rather that one can, in principle, master all things by calculation. This means that the world is disenchanted. One need no longer have recourse to magical means in order to master or implore the spirits, as did the savage, for whom such mysterious powers existed. Technical means and calculations perform the service. This above all is what intellectualization means.

Now, this process of disenchantment, which has continued to exist in Occidental culture for millennia, and, in general, this 'progress,' to which science belongs as a link and motive force, do they have any meanings that go beyond the purely practical and technical? You will find this question raised in the most principled form in the works of Leo Tolstoi. He came to raise the question in a peculiar way. All his broodings increasingly revolved around the problem of whether or not death is a meaningful phenomenon. And his answer was: for civilized man death has no meaning. It has none because the individual life of civilized man, placed into an infinite 'progress,' according to its own imminent meaning should never come to an end; for there is always a further step ahead of one who stands in the march of progress. And no man who comes to die stands upon the peak which lies in infinity. Abraham, or some peasant of the past, died 'old and satiated with life' because he stood in the organic cycle of life; because his life, in terms of its meaning and on the eve of his days, had given to him what life had to offer; because for him there remained no puzzles he might wish to solve; and therefore he could have had 'enough' of life. Whereas civilized man, placed in the midst of the continuous enrichment of culture by ideas, knowledge, and problems, may become 'tired of life' but not 'satiated with life.' He catches only the most minute part of what the life of the spirit brings forth ever anew, and what he seizes is always something provisional and not definitive, and therefore death for him is a meaningless occurrence. And because death is meaningless, civilized life as such is meaningless; by its very 'progressiveness' it gives death the imprint of meaninglessness. Throughout his late novels one meets with this thought as the keynote of the Tolstoyan art.

What stand should one take? Has 'progress' as such a recognizable meaning that goes beyond the technical, so that to serve it is a meaningful vocation? The question must be raised. But this is no longer merely the question of man's calling *for* science, hence, the problem of what science as a vocation means to its devoted disciples. To raise this question is to ask for the vocation of science within the total life of humanity. What is the value of science?

Here the contrast between the past and the present is tremendous. You will recall the wonderful image at the beginning of the seventh book of Plato's *Republic:* those enchained cavemen whose faces are turned toward the stone wall before them. Behind them lies the source of the light which they cannot see. They are concerned only with the shadowy images that this light throws upon the wall, and they seek to fathom their interrelations. Finally one of them succeeds in shattering his fetters, turns around, and sees the sun. Blinded, he gropes about and stammers of what he saw. The others say he is raving. But gradually he learns to behold the light, and then his task is to descend to the cavemen and to lead them to the light. He is the philosopher; the sun, however, is the truth of science, which alone seizes not upon illusions and shadows but upon the true being.

Well, who today views science in such a manner? Today youth feels rather the reverse: the intellectual constructions of science constitute an unreal realm of artificial abstractions, which with their bony hands seek to grasp the blood-and-the-sap of true life without ever catching up with it. But here in life, in what for Plato was the play of shadows on the walls of the cave, genuine reality is pulsating; and the rest are derivatives of life, lifeless ghosts, and nothing else. How did this change come about?

Plato's passionate enthusiasm in *The Republic* must, in the last analysis, be explained by the fact that for the first time the *concept*, one of the great tools of all scientific knowledge, had been consciously discovered. Socrates had discovered it in its bearing. He was not the only man in the world to discover it. In India one finds the beginnings of a logic that is quite similar to that of Aristotle's. But nowhere else do we find this realization of the significance of the concept. In Greece, for the first time, appeared a handy means by which one could put the logical screws upon somebody so that he could not come out without admitting either that he knew nothing or that this and nothing else was truth, the *eternal* truth that never would vanish as the doings of the blind men vanish. That was the tremendous experience which dawned upon the disciples of Socrates. And from this it seemed to follow that if one only found the right concept of the beautiful, the good, or, for instance, of bravery, of the soul—or whatever—that then one could also grasp its true being. And this, in turn, seemed to open the way for knowing and for teaching how to act rightly in life and, above all, how to act as a citizen of the state; for this question was everything to the Hellenic man, whose thinking was political throughout. And for these reasons one engaged in science.

The second great tool of scientific work, the rational experiment, made its appearance at the side of this discovery of the Hellenic spirit during the Renaissance period. The experiment is a means of reliably controlling experience. Without it, present-day empirical science would be impossible. There were experiments earlier; for instance, in India physiological experiments were made in the service of ascetic yoga technique; in Hellenic antiquity, mathematical experiments were made for purposes of war technology; and in the Middle Ages, for purposes of mining. But to raise the experiment to a principle of research was the achievement of the Renaissance. They were the great innovators in *art*, who were the pioneers of experiment. Leonardo and his like and, above all, the sixteenth-century experimenters in music with their experimental pianos were characteristic. From these circles the experiment entered science, especially through Galileo, and it entered theory through Bacon; and then it was taken over by the various exact disciplines of the continental universities, first of all those of Italy and then those of the Netherlands.

What did science mean to these men who stood at the threshold of modern times? To artistic experimenters of the type of Leonardo and the musical innovators, science meant the path to *true* art, and that meant for them the path to true *nature*. Art was to be raised to the rank of a science, and this meant at the same time and above all to raise the artist to the rank of the doctor, socially and with reference to the meaning of his life. This is the ambition on which, for instance, Leonardo's sketch book was based. And today? 'Science as the way to nature' would sound like blasphemy to youth. Today, youth proclaims the opposite: redemption from the intellectualism of science in order to return to one's own nature and therewith to nature in general. Science as a way to art? Here no criticism is even needed.

But during the period of the rise of the exact sciences one expected a great deal more. If you recall Swammerdam's statement, 'Here I bring you the proof of God's providence in the anatomy of a louse,' you will see what the scientific worker, influenced (indirectly) by Protestantism and Puritanism, conceived to be his task: to show the path to God. People no longer found this path among the philosophers, with their concepts and deductions. All pietist theology of the time, above all Spener, knew that God was not to be found along the road by which the Middle Ages had sought him. God is hidden, His ways are not our ways, His thoughts are not our thoughts. In the exact sciences, however, where one could physically grasp His works, one hoped to come upon the traces of what He planned for the world. And today? Who—aside from certain big children who are indeed found in the natural sciences—still believes that the findings of astronomy, biology, physics, or chemistry could teach us anything about the *meaning* of the world? If there is any such 'meaning,' along what road could one come upon its tracks? If these natural sciences lead to anything in this way, they are apt to make the belief that there is such a thing as the 'meaning' of the universe die out at its very roots.

And finally, science as a way 'to God'? Science, this specifically irreligious power? That science today is irreligious no one will doubt in his innermost being, even if he will not admit it to himself. Redemption from the rationalism and intellectualism of science is the fundamental presupposition of living in union with the divine. This, or something similar in meaning, is one of the fundamental watchwords one hears among German youth, whose feelings are attuned to religion or who crave religious experiences. They crave not only religious experience but experience as such. The only thing that is strange is the method that is now followed: the spheres of the irrational, the only spheres that intellectualism has not yet touched, are now raised into consciousness and put under its lens. For in practice this is where the modern intellectualist form of romantic irrationalism leads. This method of emancipation from intellectualism may well bring about the very opposite of what those who take to it conceive as its goal.

After Nietzsche's devastating criticism of those 'last men' who 'invented happiness,' I may leave aside altogether the naive optimism in which science—that is, the technique of mastering life which rests upon science—has been celebrated as the way to happiness. Who believes in this?—aside from a few big children in university chairs or editorial offices. Let us resume our argument.

Under these internal presuppositions, what is the meaning of science as a vocation, now after all these former illusions, the 'way to true being,' the 'way to true art,' the 'way to true nature,' the 'way to true God,' the 'way to true happiness,' have been dispelled? Tolstoi has given the simplest answer, with the words: 'Science is meaningless because it gives no answer to our question, the only question important for us: "What shall we do and how shall we live?"' That science does not give an answer to this is indisputable. The only question that remains is the sense in which science gives 'no' answer, and whether or not science might yet be of some use to the one who puts the question correctly.

Today one usually speaks of science as 'free from presuppositions.' Is there such a thing? It depends upon what one understands thereby. All scientific work presupposes that the rules of logic and method are valid; these are the general foundations of our orientation in the world; and, at least for our special question, these presuppositions are the least problematic aspect of science. Science further presupposes that what is yielded by scientific work is important in the sense that it is 'worth being known.' In this, obviously, are contained all our problems. For this presupposition cannot be proved by scientific means. It can only be *interpreted* with reference to its ultimate meaning, which we must reject or accept according to our ultimate position towards life.

Furthermore, the nature of the relationship of scientific work and its presuppositions varies widely according to their structure. The natural sciences, for instance, physics, chemistry, and astronomy, presuppose as self-evident that it is worth while to know the ultimate laws of cosmic events as far as science can construe them. This is the case not only because with such knowledge one can attain technical results but for its own sake, if the quest for such knowledge is to be a 'vocation.' Yet this presupposition can by no means be proved. And still less can it be proved that the existence of the world which these sciences describe is worth while, that it has any 'meaning,' or that it makes sense to live in such a world. Science does not ask for the answers to such questions.

Consider modern medicine, a practical technology which is highly developed scientifically. The general 'presupposition' of the medical enterprise is stated trivially in the assertion that medical science has the task of maintaining life as such and of diminishing suffering as such to the greatest possible degree. Yet this is problematical. By his means the medical man preserves the life of the mortally ill man, even if the patient implores us to relieve him of life, even if his relatives, to whom his life is worthless and to whom the costs of maintaining his worthless life grow unbearable, grant his redemption from suffering. Perhaps a poor lunatic is involved, whose relatives, whether they admit it or not, wish and must wish for his death. Yet the presuppositions of medicine, and the penal code, prevent the physician from relinquishing his therapeutic efforts. Whether life is worth while living and when—this question is not asked by medicine. Natural science gives us an answer to the question of what we must do if we wish to master life technically. It leaves quite aside, or assumes for its purposes, whether we should and do wish to master life technically and whether it ultimately makes sense to do so.

Consider a discipline such as aesthetics. The fact that there are works of art is given for aesthetics. It seeks to find out under what conditions this fact exists, but it does not raise the question whether or not the realm of art is perhaps a realm of diabolical grandeur, a realm of this world, and therefore, in its core, hostile to God and, in its innermost and aristocratic spirit, hostile to the brotherhood of man. Hence, aesthetics does not ask whether there *should* be works of art.

Consider jurisprudence. It establishes what is valid according to the rules of juristic thought, which is partly bound by logically compelling and partly by conventionally given schemata. Juridical thought holds when certain legal rules and certain methods of interpretations are recognized as binding. Whether there should be law and whether one should establish just these rules—such questions jurisprudence does not answer.

It can only state: If one wishes this result, according to the norms of our legal thought, this legal rule is the appropriate means of attaining it.

Consider the historical and cultural sciences. They teach us how to understand and interpret political, artistic, literary, and social phenomena in terms of their origins. But they give us no answer to the question, whether the existence of these·cultural phenomena have been and are *worth while*. And they do not answer the further question, whether it is worth the effort required to know them. They presuppose that there is an interest in partaking, through this procedure, of the community of 'civilized men.' But they cannot prove 'scientifically' that this is the case; and that they presuppose this interest by no means proves that it goes without saying. In fact it is not at all self-evident.

Finally, let us consider the disciplines close to me: sociology, history, economics, political science, and those types of cultural philosophy that make it their task to interpret these sciences. It is said, and I agree, that politics is out of place in the lecture-room. It does not belong there on the part of the students. If, for instance, in the lecture-room of my former colleague Dietrich Schäfer in Berlin, pacifist students were to surround his desk and make an uproar, I should deplore it just as much as I should deplore the uproar which anti-pacifist students are said to have made against Professor Förster, whose views in many ways are as remote as could be from mine. Neither does politics, however, belong in the lecture-room on the part of the docents, and when the docent is scientifically concerned with politics, it belongs there least of all.

To take a practical political stand is one thing, and to analyze political structures and party positions is another. When speaking in a political meeting about democracy, one does not hide one's personal standpoint; indeed, to come out clearly and take a stand is one's damned duty. The words one uses in such a meeting are not means of scientific analysis but means of canvassing votes and winning over others. They are not plow-shares to loosen the soil of contemplative thought; they are swords against the enemies: such words are weapons. It would be an outrage, however, to use words in this fashion in a lecture or in the lecture-room. If, for instance, 'democracy' is under discussion, one considers its various forms, analyzes them in the way they function, determines what results for the conditions of life the one form has as compared with the other. Then one confronts the forms of democracy with non-democratic forms of political order and endeavors to come to a position where the student may find the point from which, in terms of his ultimate ideals, he can take a stand. But the true teacher will beware of imposing from the platform any political position upon the student, whether it is expressed or suggested. 'To let the facts speak for themselves' is the most unfair way of putting over a political position to the student.

Why should we abstain from doing this? I state in advance that some highly esteemed colleagues are of the opinion that it is not possible to carry through this self-restraint and that, even if it were possible, it would be a whim to avoid declaring oneself. Now one cannot demonstrate scientifically what the duty of an academic teacher is. One can only demand of the teacher that he have the intellectual integrity to see that it is one thing to state facts, to determine mathematical or logical relations or the internal structure of cultural values, while it is another thing to answer questions of the *value* of culture and its individual contents and the question of how one should act in the cultural community and in political associations. These are quite heterogeneous problems. If he asks further why he should not deal with both types of problems in the lecture-room, the answer is: because the prophet and the demagogue do not belong on the academic platform.

To the prophet and the demagogue, it is said: 'Go your ways out into the streets and speak openly to the world,' that is, speak where criticism is possible. In the lecture-room we stand opposite our audience, and it has to remain silent. I deem it irresponsible to exploit the circumstance that for the sake of their career the students have to attend a teacher's course while there is nobody present to oppose him with criticism. The task of the teacher is to serve the students with his knowledge and scientific experience and not to imprint upon them his personal political views. It is certainly possible that the individual teacher will not entirely succeed in eliminating his personal sympathies. He is then exposed to the sharpest criticism in the forum of his own conscience. And this deficiency does not prove anything; other errors are also possible, for instance, erroneous statements of fact, and yet they prove nothing against the duty of searching for the truth. I also reject this in the very interest of science. I am ready to prove from the works of our historians that whenever the man of science introduces his personal value judgment, a full understanding of the facts *ceases*. But this goes beyond tonight's topic and would require lengthy elucidation.

I ask only: How should a devout Catholic, on the one hand, and a Freemason, on the other, in a course on the forms of church and state or on religious history ever be brought to evaluate these subjects alike?

This is out of the question. And yet the academic teacher must desire and must demand of himself to serve the one as well as the other by his knowledge and methods. Now you will rightly say that the devout Catholic will never accept the view of the factors operative in bringing about Christianity which a teacher who is free of his dogmatic presuppositions presents to him. Certainly! The difference, however, lies in the following: Science 'free from presuppositions,' in the sense of a rejection of religious bonds, does not know of the 'miracle' and the 'revelation.' If it did, science would be unfaithful to its own 'presuppositions.' The believer knows both, miracle and revelation. And science 'free from presuppositions' expects from him no less—and no more—than acknowledgment that *if* the process can be explained without those supernatural interventions, which an empirical explanation has to eliminate as causal factors, the process has to be explained the way science attempts to do. And the believer can do this without being disloyal to his faith.

But has the contribution of science no meaning at all for a man who does not care to know facts as such and to whom only the practical standpoint matters? Perhaps science nevertheless contributes something.

The primary task of a useful teacher is to teach his students to recognize 'inconvenient' facts—I mean facts that are inconvenient for their party opinions. And for every party opinion there are facts that are extremely inconvenient, for my own opinion no less than for others. I believe the teacher accomplishes more than a mere intellectual task if he compels his audience to accustom itself to the existence of such facts. I would be so immodest as even to apply the expression 'moral achievement,' though perhaps this may sound too grandiose for something that should go without saying.

Thus far I have spoken only of practical reasons for avoiding the imposition of a personal point of view. But these are not the only reasons. The impossibility of 'scientifically' pleading for practical and interested stands—except in discussing the means for a firmly given and presupposed end—rests upon reasons that lie far deeper.

'Scientific' pleading is meaningless in principle because the various value spheres of the world stand in irreconcilable conflict with each other. The elder Mill, whose philosophy I will not praise otherwise, was on this point right when he said: If one proceeds from pure experience, one arrives at polytheism. This is shallow in formulation and sounds paradoxical, and yet there is truth in it. If anything, we realize again today that something can be sacred not only in spite of its not being beautiful, but rather because and in so far as it is not beautiful. You will find this documented in the fifty-third chapter of the book of Isaiah and in the twenty-first Psalm. And, since Nietzsche, we realize that something can be beautiful, not only in spite of the aspect in which it is not good, but rather in that very aspect. You will find this expressed earlier in the *Fleurs du mal,* as Baudelaire named his volume of poems. It is commonplace to observe that something may be true although it is not beautiful and not holy and not good. Indeed it may be true in precisely those aspects. But all these are only the most elementary cases of the struggle that the gods of the various orders and values are engaged in. I do not know how one might wish to decide 'scientifically' the value of French and German culture; for here, too, different gods struggle with one another, now and for all times to come.

We live as did the ancients when their world was not yet disenchanted of its gods and demons, only we live in a different sense. As Hellenic man at times sacrificed to Aphrodite and at other times to Apollo, and, above all, as everybody sacrificed to the gods of his city, so do we still nowadays, only the bearing of man has been disenchanted and denuded of its mystical but inwardly genuine plasticity. Fate, and certainly not 'science,' holds sway over these gods and their struggles. One can only understand what the godhead is for the one order or for the other, or better, what godhead is in the one or in the other order. With this understanding, however, the matter has reached its limit so far as it can be discussed in a lecture-room and by a professor. Yet the great and vital problem that is contained therein is, of course, very far from being concluded. But forces other than university chairs have their say in this matter.

What man will take upon himself the attempt to 'refute scientifically' the ethic of the Sermon on the Mount? For instance, the sentence, 'resist no evil,' or the image of turning the other cheek? And yet it is clear, in mundane perspective, that this is an ethic of undignified conduct; one has to choose between the religious dignity which this ethic confers and the dignity of manly conduct which preaches something quite different; 'resist evil—lest you be co-responsible for an overpowering evil.' According to our ultimate standpoint, the one is the devil and the other the God, and the individual has to decide which is God for him and which is the devil. And so it goes throughout all the orders of life.

The grandiose rationalism of an ethical and methodical conduct of life which flows from every religious prophecy has dethroned this polytheism in favor of the 'one thing that is needful.' Faced with the realities of outer and inner life, Christianity has deemed it necessary to make those compromises and relative judgments, which we all know from its history. Today the routines of everyday life challenge religion. Many old gods ascend from their graves; they are disenchanted and hence take the form of impersonal forces. They strive to gain power over our lives and again they resume their eternal struggle with one another. What is hard for modern man, and especially for the younger generation, is to measure up to *workaday* existence. The ubiquitous chase for 'experience' stems from this weakness; for it is weakness not to be able to countenance the stern seriousness of our fateful times.

Our civilization destines us to realize more clearly these struggles again, after our eyes have been blinded for a thousand years—blinded by the allegedly or presumably exclusive orientation towards the grandiose moral fervor of Christian ethics.

But enough of these questions which lead far away. Those of our youth are in error who react to all this by saying, 'Yes, but we happen to come to lectures in order to experience something more than mere analyses and statements of fact.' The error is that they seek in the professor something different from what stands before them. They crave a leader and not a teacher. But we are placed upon the platform solely as teachers. And these are two different things, as one can readily see. Permit me to take you once more to America, because there one can often observe such matters in their most massive and original shape.

The American boy learns unspeakably less than the German boy. In spite of an incredible number of examinations, his school life has not had the significance of turning him into an absolute creature of examinations, such as the German. For in America, bureaucracy, which presupposes the examination diploma as a ticket of admission to the realm of office prebends, is only in its beginnings. The young American has no respect for anything or anybody, for tradition or for public office— unless it is for the personal achievement of individual men. This is what the American calls 'democracy.' This is the meaning of democracy, however distorted its intent may in reality be, and this intent is what matters here. The American's conception of the teacher who faces him is: he sells me his knowledge and his methods for my father's money, just as the greengrocer sells my mother cabbage. And that is all. To be sure, if the teacher happens to be a football coach, then, in this field, he is a leader. But if he is not this (or something similar in a different field of sports), he is simply a teacher and nothing more. And no young American would think of having the teacher sell him a *Weltanschauung* or a code of conduct. Now, when formulated in this manner, we should reject this. But the question is whether there is not a grain of salt contained in this feeling, which I have deliberately stated in extreme with some exaggeration.

Fellow students! You come to our lectures and demand from us the qualities of leadership, and you fail to realize in advance that of a hundred professors at least ninety-nine do not and must not claim to be football masters in the vital problems of life, or even to be 'leaders' in matters of conduct. Please, consider that a man's value does not depend on whether or not he has leadership qualities. And in any case, the qualities that make a man an excellent scholar and academic teacher are not the qualities that make him a leader to give directions in practical life or, more specifically, in politics. It is pure accident if a teacher also possesses this quality, and it is a critical situation if every teacher on the platform feels himself confronted with the students' expectation that the teacher should claim this quality. It is still more critical if it is left to every academic teacher to set himself up as a leader in the lecture-room. For those who most frequently think of themselves as leaders often qualify least as leaders. But irrespective of whether they are or are not, the platform situation simply offers no possibility of *proving* themselves to be leaders. The professor who feels called upon to act as a counselor of youth and enjoys their trust may prove himself a man in personal human relations with them. And if he feels called upon to intervene in the struggles of world views and party opinions, he may do so outside, in the market place, in the press, in meetings, in associations, wherever he wishes. But after all, it is somewhat too convenient to demonstrate one's courage in taking a stand where the audience and possible opponents are condemned to silence.

Finally, you will put the question: 'If this is so, what then does science actually and positively contribute to practical and personal "life"?' Therewith we are back again at the problem of science as a 'vocation.'

First, of course, science contributes to the technology of controlling life by calculating external objects as well as man's activities. Well, you will say, that, after all, amounts to no more than the greengrocer of the American boy. I fully agree.

Second, science can contribute something that the greengrocer cannot: methods of thinking, the tools and the training for thought. Perhaps you will say: well, that is no vegetable, but it amounts to no more than the means for procuring vegetables. Well and good, let us leave it at that for today.

Fortunately, however, the contribution of science does not reach its limit with this. We are in a position to help you to a third objective: to gain *clarity*. Of course, it is presupposed that we ourselves possess clarity. As far as this is the case, we can make clear to you the following:

In practice, you can take this or that position when concerned with a problem of value—for simplicity's sake, please think of social phenomena as examples. *If* you take such and such a stand, then, according to scientific experience, you have to use such and such a *means* in order to carry out your conviction practically. Now, these means are perhaps such that you believe you must reject them. Then you simply must choose between the end and the inevitable means. Does the end 'justify' the means? Or does it not? The teacher can confront you with the necessity of this choice. He cannot do more, so long as he wishes to remain a teacher and not to become a demagogue. He can, of course, also tell you that if you want such and such an end, then you must take into the bargain the subsidiary consequences which according to all experience will occur. Again we find ourselves in the same situation as before. These are still problems that can also emerge for the technician, who in numerous instances has to make decisions according to the principle of the lesser evil or of the relatively best. Only to him one thing, the main thing, is usually given, namely, the end. But as soon as truly 'ultimate' problems are at stake for us this is not the case. With this, at long last, we come to the final service that science as such can render to the aim of clarity, and at the same time we come to the limits of science.

Besides we can and we should state: In terms of its meaning, such and such a practical stand can be derived with inner consistency, and hence integrity, from this or that ultimate *weltanschauliche* position. Perhaps it can only be derived from one such fundamental position, or maybe from several, but it cannot be derived from these or those other positions. Figuratively speaking, you serve this god and you offend the other god when you decide to adhere to this position. And if you remain faithful to yourself, you will necessarily come to certain final conclusions that subjectively make sense. This much, in principle at least, can be accomplished. Philosophy, as a special discipline, and the essentially philosophical discussions of principles in the other sciences attempt to achieve this. Thus, if we are competent in our pursuit (which must be presupposed here) we can force the individual, or at least we can help him, to give himself an *account of the ultimate meaning of his own conduct*. This appears to me as not so trifling a thing to do, even for one's own personal life. Again, I am tempted to say of a teacher who succeeds in this: he stands in the service of 'moral' forces; he fulfils the duty of bringing about self-clarification and a sense of responsibility. And I believe he will be the more able to accomplish this, the more conscientiously he avoids the desire personally to impose upon or suggest to his audience his own stand.

This proposition, which I present here, always takes its point of departure from the one fundamental fact, that so long as life remains immanent and is interpreted in its own terms, it knows only of an unceasing struggle of these gods with one another. Or speaking directly, the ultimately possible attitudes toward life are irreconcilable, and hence their struggle can never be brought to a final conclusion. Thus it is necessary to make a decisive choice. Whether, under such conditions, science is a worth while 'vocation' for somebody, and whether science itself has an objectively valuable 'vocation' are again value judgments about which nothing can be said in the lecture-room. To affirm the value of science is a presupposition for teaching there. I personally by my very work answer in the affirmative, and I also do so from precisely the standpoint that hates intellectualism as the worst devil, as youth does today, or usually only fancies it does. In that case the word holds for these youths: 'Mind you, the devil is old; grow old to understand him.' This does not mean age in the sense of the birth certificate. It means that if one wishes to settle with this devil, one must not take to flight before him as so many like to do nowadays. First of all, one has to see the devil's ways to the end in order to realize his power and his limitations.

Science today is a 'vocation' organized in special disciplines in the service of self-clarification and knowledge of interrelated facts. It is not the gift of grace of seers and prophets dispensing sacred values and revelations, nor does it partake of the contemplation of sages and philosophers about the meaning of the universe. This, to be sure, is the inescapable condition of our historical situation. We cannot evade it so long as we remain true to ourselves. And if Tolstoi's question recurs to you: as science does not, who is to answer the question: 'What shall we do, and, how shall we arrange our lives?' or, in the words used here tonight: 'Which of the warring gods should we serve? Or should we serve perhaps an entirely different god, and who is he?' then one can say that only a prophet or a savior can give the answers. If there is no such man, or if his message is no longer believed in, then you will certainly not compel him to appear on this earth by having thousands of professors, as privileged hirelings of the state, attempt as petty prophets in their lecture-rooms to take over his role. All they will accomplish is to show that they are unaware of the decisive state of affairs: the prophet for whom so many of our younger generation yearn simply does not exist. But this knowledge in its forceful significance has never become vital for them. The inward interest of a truly religiously 'musical' man can never be served by veiling to him and to others the fundamental fact that he is destined to live in a godless and prophetless time by giving him the *ersatz* of armchair prophecy. The integrity of his religious organ, it seems to me, must rebel against this.

Now you will be inclined to say: Which stand does one take towards the factual existence of 'theology' and its claims to be a 'science'? Let us not flinch and evade the answer. To be sure, 'theology' and 'dogmas' do not exist universally, but neither do they exist for Christianity alone. Rather (going backward in time), they exist in highly developed form also in Islam, in Manicheanism, in Gnosticism, in Orphism, in Parsism, in Buddhism, in the Hindu sects, in Taoism, and in the Upanishads, and, of course, in Judaism. To be sure their systematic development varies greatly. It is no accident that Occidental Christianity —in contrast to the theological possessions of Jewry—has expanded and elaborated theology more systematically, or strives to do so. In the Occident the development of theology has had by far the greatest historical significance. This is the product of the Hellenic spirit, and all theology of the West goes back to it, as (obviously) all theology of the East goes back to Indian thought. All theology represents an intellectual *rationalization* of the possession of sacred values. No science is absolutely free from presuppositions, and no science can prove its fundamental value to the man who rejects these presuppositions. Every theology, however, adds a few specific presuppositions for its work and thus for the justification of its existence. Their meaning and scope vary. Every theology, including for instance Hinduist theology, presupposes that the world must have a *meaning,* and the question is how to interpret this meaning so that it is intellectually conceivable.

It is the same as with Kant's epistemology. He took for his point of departure the presupposition: 'Scientific truth exists and it is valid,' and then asked: 'Under which presuppositions of thought is truth possible and meaningful?' The modern aestheticians (actually or expressly, as for instance, G. v. Lukacs) proceed from the presupposition that 'works of art exist,' and then ask: 'How is their existence meaningful and possible?'

As a rule, theologies, however, do not content themselves with this (essentially religious and philosophical) presupposition. They regularly proceed from the further presupposition that certain 'revelations' are facts relevant for salvation and as such make possible a meaningful conduct of life. Hence, these revelations must be believed in. Moreover, theologies presuppose that certain subjective states and acts possess the quality of holiness, that is, they constitute a way of life, or at least elements of one, that is religiously meaningful. Then the question of theology is: How can these presuppositions, which must simply be accepted be meaningfully interpreted in a view of the universe? For theology, these presuppositions as such lie beyond the limits of 'science.' They do not represent 'knowledge,' in the usual sense, but rather a 'possession.' Whoever does not 'possess' faith, or the other holy states, cannot have theology as a substitute for them, least of all any other science. On the contrary, in every 'positive' theology, the devout reaches the point where the Augustinian sentence holds: *credo non quod, sed quia absurdum est.*

The capacity for the accomplishment of religious virtuosos—the 'intellectual sacrifice'—is the decisive characteristic of the positively religious man. That this is so is shown by the fact that in spite (or rather in consequence) of theology (which unveils it) the tension between the value-spheres of 'science' and the sphere of 'the holy' is unbridgeable. Legitimately, only the disciple offers the 'intellectual sacrifice' to the prophet, the believer to the church. Never as yet has a new prophecy emerged (and I repeat here deliberately this image which has offended some) by way of the need of some modern intellectuals to furnish their souls with, so to speak, guaranteed genuine antiques. In doing so, they happen to remember that religion has belonged among such antiques, and of all things religion is what they do not possess. By way of substitute, however, they play at decorating a sort of domestic chapel with small sacred images from all over the world, or they produce surrogates through all sorts of psychic experiences to which they ascribe the dignity of mystic holiness, which they peddle in the book market. This is plain humbug or self-deception. It is, however, no humbug but rather something very sincere and genuine if some of the youth groups who during recent years have quietly grown together give their human community the interpretation of a religious, cosmic, or mystical relation, although occasionally perhaps such interpretation rests on misunderstanding of self. True as it is that every act of genuine brotherliness may be linked with the awareness that it contributes something imperishable to a super-personal realm, it seems to me dubious whether the dignity of purely human and communal relations is enhanced by these religious interpretations. But that is no longer our theme.

The fate of our times is characterized by rationalization and intellectualization and, above all, by the 'disenchantment of the world.' Precisely the ultimate and most sublime values have retreated from public life either into the transcendental realm of mystic life or into the brotherliness of direct and personal human relations. It is not accidental that our greatest art is intimate and not monumental, nor is it accidental that today only within the smallest and intimate circles, in personal human situations, in *pianissimo,* that something is pulsating that corresponds to the prophetic *pneuma,* which in former times swept through the great communities like a firebrand, welding them together. If we attempt to force and to 'invent' a monumental style in art, such miserable monstrosities are produced as the many monuments of the last twenty years. If one tries intellectually to construe new religions without a new and genuine prophecy, then, in an inner sense, something similar will result, but with still worse effects. And academic prophecy, finally, will create only fanatical sects but never a genuine community.

To the person who cannot bear the fate of the times like a man, one must say: may he rather return silently, without the usual publicity build-up of renegades, but simply and plainly. The arms of the old churches are opened widely and compassionately for him. After all, they do not make it hard for him. One way or another he has to bring his 'intellectual sacrifice'—that is inevitable. If he can really do it, we shall not rebuke him. For such an intellectual sacrifice in favor of an unconditional religious devotion is ethically quite a different matter than the evasion of the plain duty of intellectual integrity, which sets in if one lacks the courage to clarify one's own ultimate standpoint and rather facilitates this duty by feeble relative judgments. In my eyes, such religious return stands higher than the academic prophecy, which does not clearly realize that in the lecture-rooms of the university no other virtue holds but plain intellectual integrity. Integrity, however, compels us to state that for the many who today tarry for new prophets and saviors, the situation is the same as resounds in the beautiful Edomite watchman's song of the period of exile that has been included among Isaiah's oracles:

He calleth to me out of Seir, Watchman, what of the night? The watchman said, The morning cometh, and also the night: if ye will enquire, enquire ye: return, come.

The people to whom this was said has enquired and tarried for more than two millennia, and we are shaken when we realize its fate. From this we want to draw the lesson that nothing is gained by yearning and tarrying alone, and we shall act differently. We shall set to work and meet the 'demands of the day,' in human relations as well as in our vocation. This, however, is plain and simple, if each finds and obeys the demon who holds the fibers of his very life.

Part II

POWER

VI. Structures of Power

1: The Prestige and Power of the 'Great Powers'

ALL political structures use force, but they differ in the manner in which and the extent to which they use or threaten to use it against other political organizations. These differences play a specific role in determining the form and destiny of political communities. Not all political structures are equally 'expansive.' They do not all strive for an outward expansion of their power, or keep their force in readiness for acquiring political power over other territories and communities by incorporating them or making them dependent. Hence, as structures of power, political organizations vary in the extent to which they are turned outward.

The political structure of Switzerland is 'neutralized' through a collective guarantee of the Great Powers. For various reasons, Switzerland is not very strongly desired as an object for incorporation. Mutual jealousies existing among neighboring communities of equal strength protect it from this fate. Switzerland, as well as Norway, is less threatened than is the Netherlands, which possesses colonies; and the Netherlands is less threatened than Belgium, for the latter's colonial possessions are especially exposed, as is Belgium herself in case of war between her powerful neighbors. Sweden too is quite exposed.

The attitude of political structures towards the outside may be more 'isolationist' or more 'expansive.' And such attitudes change. The power of political structures has a specific internal dynamic. On the basis of this power, the members may pretend to a special 'prestige,' and their pretensions may influence the external conduct of the power structures.

Wirtschaft und Gesellschaft (Tübingen, 1922 edition), part III, chap. 3, pp. 619-30; and *Gesammelte Aufsaetze zur Soziologie und Sozialpolitik* (Tübingen, 1924), pp. 484-6. *Wirtschaft und Gesellschaft* appeared posthumously (1921) as part of the Grundriss für Sozialokonomik, handled by J. C. B. Mohr (P. Siebeck), Tübingen. Weber worked on the descriptive parts of *Wirtschaft und Gesellschaft* from 1910, and most of the chapters were essentially written before 1914.

Experience teaches that claims to prestige have always played into the origin of wars. Their part is difficult to gauge; it cannot be determined in general, but it is very obvious. The realm of 'honor,' which is comparable to the 'status order' within a social structure, pertains also to the interrelations of political structures.

Feudal lords, like modern officers or bureaucrats, are the natural and primary exponents of this desire for power-oriented prestige for one's own political structure. Power for their political community means power for themselves, as well as the prestige based on this power.

For the bureaucrat and the officer, an expansion of power, however, means more office positions, more sinecures, and better opportunities for promotion. (This last may be the case even for the officer in a lost war.) For the feudal vassal, expansion of power means the acquisition of new objects for infeudation and more provisions for his progeny. In his speech promoting the crusades, Pope Urban focused attention on these opportunities and not, as has been said, on 'overpopulation.'

Besides and beyond these direct economic interests, which naturally exist everywhere among strata living off the exercise of political power, the striving for prestige pertains to all specific power structures and hence to all political structures. This striving is not identical simply with 'national pride'—of this, more later—and it is not identical with the mere pride in the excellent qualities, actual or presumed, of one's own political community or in the mere possession of such a polity. Such pride can be highly developed, as is the case among the Swiss and the Norwegians, yet it may actually be strictly isolationist and free from pretension to political prestige.

The prestige of power, as such, means in practice the glory of power over other communities; it means the expansion of power, though not always by way of incorporation or subjection. The big political communities are the natural exponents of such pretensions to prestige.

Every political structure naturally prefers to have weak rather than strong neighbors. Furthermore, as every big political community is a potential aspirant to prestige and a potential threat to all its neighbors, the big political community, simply because it is big and strong, is latently and constantly endangered. Finally, by virtue of an unavoidable 'dynamic of power,' wherever claims to prestige flame up—and this normally results from an acute political danger to peace—they challenge and call forth the competition of all other possible bearers of prestige. The history of the last decade,[1] especially the relations between Germany and France, shows the prominent effect of this irrational element in all political foreign relations. The sentiment of prestige is able to strengthen the ardent belief in the actual existence of one's own might, for this belief is important for positive self-assurance in case of conflict. Therefore, all those having vested interests in the political structure tend systematically to cultivate this prestige sentiment. Nowadays one usually refers to those polities that appear to be the bearers of power prestige as the 'Great Powers.'

Among a plurality of co-existing polities, some, the Great Powers, usually ascribe to themselves and usurp an interest in political and economic processes over a wide orbit. Today such orbits encompass the whole surface of the planet.

During Hellenic Antiquity, the 'King,' that is, the Persian king, despite his defeat, was the most widely recognized Great Power. Sparta turned to him in order to impose, with his sanction, the King's Peace (Peace of Antalcidas) upon the Hellenic world. Later on, before the establishment of an empire, the Roman polity assumed such a role.

For general reasons of 'power dynamics' *per se,* the Great Powers are very often expansive powers; that is, they are associations aiming at expanding the territories of their respective political communities by the use or the threat of force or by both. Great Powers, however, are not necessarily and not always oriented towards expansion. Their attitude in this respect often changes, and in these changes economic factors play a weighty part.

For a time British policy, for instance, quite deliberately renunciated further political expansion. It renounced even the retention of colonies by means of force in favor of a 'little England' policy, resting upon an isolationist limitation and a reliance on an economic primacy held to be unshakable. Influential representatives of the Roman rule by notables would have liked to carry through a similar program of a 'little Rome' after the Punic Wars, to restrict Roman political subjection to Italy and the neighboring islands.

The Spartan aristocrats, so far as they were able, quite deliberately limited their political expansion for the sake of isolation. They restricted themselves to the smashing of all other political structures that endangered their power and prestige. They favored the particularism of city states. Usually, in such cases, and in many similar ones, the ruling groups of notables (the Roman nobility of office, the English and other liberal notables, the Spartan overlords) harbor more or less distinct fears lest an 'Imperator,' that is, a charismatic war lord, emerge. A tendency towards centralization of power goes very readily with a chronically conquering 'imperialism,' and the war lord might gain the ascendancy at the expense of the power of the ruling notables.

Like the Romans, the British, after a short time, were forced out of their policy of self-restraint and pressed into political expansion. This occurred, in part, through capitalist interests in expansion.

2: THE ECONOMIC FOUNDATIONS OF 'IMPERIALISM'

One might be inclined to believe that the formation as well as the expansion of Great Power structures is always and primarily determined economically. The assumption that trade, especially if it is intensive and if it already exists in an area, is the normal prerequisite and the reason for its political unification might readily be generalized. In individual cases this assumption does actually hold. The example of the *Zollverein* [2] lies close at hand, and there are numerous others. Closer attention, however, very often reveals that this coincidence is not a necessary one, and that the causal nexus by no means always points in a single direction.

Germany, for instance, has been made into a unified economic territory only through custom frontiers at her borders, which, in their course, were determined in a purely political manner. If the inhabitants of a territory seek to sell their products primarily in their own market, we may speak of an economically unified territory. Were all custom barriers eliminated, the economically determined market for the Eastern German cereal surplus, poor in gluten, would not be Western Germany but rather England. The economically determined market of the mining products and the heavy iron goods of Western Germany is by no means Eastern Germany; and Western Germany is not, in the main, the economically determined supplier of the industrial products for Eastern Germany. Above all, the interior lines of communications (railroads) of Germany would not be—and, in part, are not now—economically determined routes for transporting heavy goods between east and west. Eastern Germany, however, would be the economic location for strong industries, the economically determined market and hinterland for which would be the whole of Western Russia. Such industries are now [3] cut off by Russian custom barriers and have been moved to Poland, directly behind the Russian custom frontier. Through this development, as is known, the political *Anschluss* of the Russian Poles to the Russian imperial idea, which seemed to be politically out of the question, has been brought into the realm of possibility. Thus, in this case, purely economically determined market relations have a politically unifying effect.

Germany, however, has been politically united against the economic determinants as such. It is not unusual for the frontiers of a polity to conflict with the mere geographically given location of industries; the political frontiers may encompass an area that, in terms of economic factors, strives to separate from it. In such situations, tensions between economic interests nearly always arise. However, if the political bond is once created, it is very often, yet not always, so incomparably stronger that under otherwise favorable conditions (e.g. the existence of a common language) nobody would even think of political separation because of such economic tensions. This applies, for instance, to Germany.

The formation of great states does not always follow the routes of export trade, although nowadays we are inclined to see things in this imperialist way. As a rule, the 'continental' imperialism—European, Russian, and American—just like the 'overseas imperialism' of the British and of those modeled after it, follow the tracks of previously existing capitalist interests, especially in foreign areas that are politically weak. And of course, at least for the formation of great overseas dominions of the past—in the overseas empires of Athens, Carthage, and Rome—export trade played its decisive part.

Yet, even in these state organizations of Antiquity other economic interests were at least of equal and often of far greater importance than were commercial profits: ground rents, farmed-out taxes, office fees, and similar gains were especially desired. In foreign trade, in turn, the interest in selling within foreign territories definitely receded into the background as a motive for expansion. In the age of modern capitalism the interest in exporting to foreign territories is dominant, but in the ancient states the interest was rather in the possession of territories from which goods (raw materials) could be *imported*.

Among the great states that have formed on the inland plains, the exchange of goods played no regular or decisive part. The trading of goods was most relevant for the river-border states of the Orient, especially for Egypt; that is, for states that in this respect were similar to overseas states. The 'empire' of the Mongols, however, certainly did not rest on any intensive trade in goods. There, the mobility of the ruling stratum of horsemen made up for the lack of material means of communication and made centralized administration possible. Neither the Chinese, nor the Persian, nor the Roman Empire after its transition from a coastal to a continental empire, originated and maintained itself on the basis of a pre-existing and a particularly intensive inland traffic in goods or highly developed means of communication. The continental expansion of Rome was undoubtedly very strongly, though not exclusively, determined by capitalist interests; and these interests were above all the interests of tax-farmers, office hunters, and land speculators. They were not, in the first place, the interests of groups pursuing a particularly intensive trade in goods.

The expansion of Persia was not in any way served by capitalist interest groups. Such groups did not exist there as motivating forces or as pace-makers, and just as little did they serve the founders of the Chinese Empire or the founders of the Carolingian Monarchy.

Of course, even in these cases, the economic importance of trade was not altogether absent; yet other motives have played their part in every political overland expansion of the past, including the Crusades. These motives have included the interest in higher princely incomes, in prebends, fiefs, offices, and social honors for the vassals, knights, officers, officials, the younger sons of hereditary officeholders, and so on. The interests of trading seaports have not, of course, been so decisive as has overland expansion, although they were important as additional factors playing their secondary parts. The First Crusade was mainly an overland campaign.

By no means has trade always pointed the way for political expansion. The causal nexus has very often been the reverse. Among the empires named above, those which had an administration technically able to establish at least overland means of communication did so for administrative purposes. In principle, this has often been the exclusive purpose, regardless of whether or not the means of communication were advantageous for existing or future trading needs.

Under present-day conditions, Russia may well be considered a polity whose means of communication (railroads today) have been primarily determined not economically but rather politically. The Austrian southern railroad, however, is another example. (Its shares are still called 'lombards,' a term loaded with political reminiscences.) And there is hardly a polity without 'strategic railroads.' Nevertheless, great achievements of this kind have been made with the concomitant expectation of a traffic guaranteeing long-run profitableness. It was no different in the past: it cannot be proved that the ancient Roman military highroads served a commercial purpose; and it certainly was not the case for the Persian and Roman mail posts, which served exclusively political purposes. In spite of this, however, the development of trade in the past has of course been the normal result of political unification. Political unification first placed trade upon an assured and guaranteed legal basis. Even this rule, however, is not without exceptions. For, besides depending on pacification and formal guarantees of law enforcement, the development of trade has been bound to certain economic conditions (especially the development of capitalism).

The evolution of capitalism may be strangled by the manner in which a unified political structure is administered. This was the case, for instance, in the late Roman Empire. Here a unified structure took the place of a league of city states; it was based upon a strong subsistence agrarian economy. This increasingly made for liturgies as the way of raising the means for the army and the administration; and these directly suffocated capitalism.

Yet, if trade in itself is by no means the decisive factor in political expansion, the economic structure in general does co-determine the extent and manner of political expansion. Besides women, cattle, and slaves, scarce land is one of the original and foremost objects of forceful acquisition. For conquering peasant communities, the natural way is to take the land directly and to wipe out its settled population.

The Teutonic people's movement has, on the whole, taken this course only to a moderate degree. As a compact mass, this movement probably went somewhat beyond the present linguistic frontiers, but only in scattered zones. How far a 'land scarcity,' caused by overpopulation, contributed, how far the political pressure of other tribes, or simply good opportunities, must be left open. In any case, some of the individual groups who went out for conquest over a long period of time reserved their claims to the arable land back home, in case they should return. The land of foreign territories has been politically incorporated in more or less violent fashion.

Since land is important for the way in which the victor will exploit his rights, it also plays an important role for other economic structures. As Franz Oppenheimer again and again has rightly emphasized, ground rent is frequently the product of violent political subjection. Given a subsistence economy and a feudal structure this subjection means, of course, that the peasantry of the incorporated area will not be wiped out but rather will be spared and made tributary to the conqueror, who becomes the landlord. This has happened wherever the army was no longer a *Volksheerbann* composed of self-equipped freemen, or yet a mercenary or bureaucratic mass army, but rather an army of self-equipped knights, as was the case with the Persians, the Arabs, the Turks, the Normans, and the Occidental feudal vassals in general.

The interest in ground rent has also meant a great deal for plutocratic trading communities engaged in conquest. As commercial profits were preferably invested in land and in indebted bondsmen, the normal aim of warfare, even in Antiquity, was to gain fertile land fit to yield ground rent. The Lelantine War,[4] which marked a sort of epoch in early Hellenic history, was almost wholly carried on at sea and among trading cities. But the original object of dispute between the leading patricians of Chalcis and Eretria, besides tributes of various sorts, was the fertile Lelantine plain. One of the most important privileges that the Attic Maritime League evidently offered to the *demos* of the ruling city was to break up the land monopoly of the subject cities. The Athenians were to receive the right to acquire and mortgage land anywhere.

The establishment of *commercium* among cities allied to Rome meant in practice the same thing. Also, the overseas interests of the mass of Italics settled throughout the Roman sphere of influence certainly represented, at least in part, land interests of an essentially capitalist nature, as we know them from the Verrinic speeches.

⁎ During its expansion, the capitalist interest in land may come into conflict with the land interest of the peasantry. Under a policy of expansion, such a conflict has played its part in the struggles between the Roman estates in the long epoch ending with the Gracchi. The big holders of money, cattle, and men naturally wished the newly gained land to be dealt with as public land for lease (*ager publicus*). As long as the regions were not too remote, the peasants demanded that the land be partitioned in order to provide for their progeny. The compromises between these two interests are distinctly reflected in tradition, although the details are certainly not very reliable.

Rome's overseas expansion, as far as it was economically determined, shows features that have since recurred in basic outline again and again and which still recur today. These features occurred in Rome in pronounced fashion and in gigantic dimensions, for the first time in history. However fluid the transitions to other types may be, these 'Roman' features are peculiar to a specific type of capitalist relations, or rather, they provide the conditions for the existence of this specific type, which we wish to call imperialist capitalism.

These features are rooted in the capitalist interests of tax-farmers, of state creditors, of suppliers to the state, of overseas traders privileged by the state, and of colonial capitalists. The profit opportunities of all these groups rest upon the direct exploitation of executive powers, that is, of political power directed towards expansion.

By forcibly enslaving the inhabitants, or at least tying them to the soil (*glebae adscriptio*) and exploiting them as plantation labor, the acquisition of overseas colonies brings tremendous opportunities for profit for capitalist interest-groups. The Carthaginians seem to have been the first to have arranged such an organization on a large scale; the Spaniards in South America, the English in the Southern States of the Union, and the Dutch in Indonesia were the last to do it in the grand manner. The acquisition of overseas colonies also facilitates the forceful monopolization of trade with these colonies and possibly with other areas. Wherever the administrative apparatus of the polity is not suited for the collection of taxes from the newly occupied territories—of this, later—the taxes give opportunities for profit to capitalist tax-farmers.

The material implements of war may be part of the equipment provided by the army itself, as is the case in pure feudalism. But if these implements are furnished by the polity, rather than by the army, then expansion through war and the procurement of armaments to prepare for war represent by far the most profitable occasion for the raising of loans on the largest scale. The profit opportunities of capitalist state creditors then increase. Even during the Second Punic War capitalist state creditors prescribed their own conditions to the Roman polity.

Where the ultimate state creditors are a mass stratum of state rentiers (bondholders), such credits provide profit opportunities for bond-issuing banks, as is characteristic of our day. The interests of those who supply the materials of war point in the same direction. In all this, economic forces interested in the emergence of military conflagrations *per se,* no matter what be the outcome for their own community, are called into life.

Aristophanes distinguished between industries interested in war and industries interested in peace, although, as is evident from his enumeration, the center of gravity in his time was still the self-equipped army. The individual citizen gave orders to artisans such as the sword-maker and the armourer. But even then the large private commercial storehouses, often designated as 'factories,' were above all stores of armaments.

Today the polity as such is almost the sole agent to order war material and the engines of war. This enhances the capitalist nature of the process. Banks, which finance war loans, and today large sections of heavy industry are *quand même* economically interested in warfare; the direct suppliers of armour plates and guns are not the only ones so interested. A lost war, as well as a successful war, brings increased business to these banks and industries.

The partners within a polity are politically and economically interested in the existence of large home factories for war engines. This interest compels them to allow these factories to provide the whole world with their products, political opponents included.

The extent to which the interests of imperialist capitalism are counterbalanced depends above all on the profitableness of imperialism as compared with the capitalist interests of pacifist orientation, in so far as purely capitalist motives here play a direct part. And this in turn is closely connected with the extent to which economic needs are satisfied by a private or a collective economy. The relation between the two is highly decisive for the nature of expansive economic tendencies backed up by political communities.

In general and at all times, imperialist capitalism, especially colonial booty capitalism based on direct force and compulsory labor, has offered by far the greatest opportunities for profit. They have been greater by far than those normally open to industrial enterprises which worked for exports and which oriented themselves to peaceful trade with members of other polities. Therefore, imperialist capitalism has always existed wherever to any relevant degree the polity *per se,* or its subdivisions (municipalities), has engaged in a public collective economy for satisfying demands. The stronger such collective economy has been, the more important imperialist capitalism has been.

Increasing opportunities for profit abroad emerge again today, especially in territories that are 'opened up' politically and economically, that is, brought into the specifically modern forms of public and private 'enterprise.' These opportunities spring from 'public commissions' of arms; from railroad and other construction tasks carried out by the polity or by builders endowed with monopoly rights; from monopolist organizations for the collection of levies for trade and industry; from monopolist concessions; and from government loans.

Such opportunities for profits may be more important and may be gained at the expense of profits from the usual private trade. The more that public, collective enterprises gain in economic importance as a general form of supplying needs, the more this preponderance increases. This tendency is directly paralleled by the tendency of politically backed economic expansion and competition among individual polities whose partners control investment capital. They aim at securing for themselves such monopolies and shares in public commissions. And the importance of the mere 'open door' for the private importation of goods recedes into the background.

The safest way of guaranteeing these monopolized profit opportunities to the members of one's own polity is to occupy it or at least to subject the foreign political power in the form of a 'protectorate' or some such arrangement. Therefore, this 'imperialist' tendency increasingly displaces the 'pacifist' tendency of expansion, which aims merely at 'freedom of trade.' The latter gained the upper hand only so long as the organization of supply by private capitalism shifted the optimum of capitalist profit opportunities towards pacifist trade and not towards monopolist trade, or at least trade not monopolized by political power.

The universal revival of 'imperialist' capitalism, which has always been the normal form in which capitalist interests have influenced politics, and the revival of political drives for expansion are thus not accidental. For the predictable future, the prognosis will have to be made in their favor.

This situation would hardly change fundamentally if for a moment we were to make the mental experiment of assuming the individual polities to be somehow 'state-socialist' communities, that is, associations supplying a maximum amount of their needs through a collective economy. All political associations of such a collective economy would seek to buy as cheaply as possible indispensable goods not produced on their own territory (cotton in Germany, for instance) from communities that have natural monopolies which these communities would seek to exploit. It is probable that force would be used where it would lead easily to favorable conditions of exchange; the weaker party would thereby be obliged to pay tribute, if not formally then at least actually. For the rest, one cannot see why the strong state-socialist communities should disdain to squeeze tribute out of the weaker communities for their own partners where they could do so, just as happened everywhere during early history.

Economically, in a polity without state-socialism the 'mass' of partners need be as little interested in pacifism as is any single stratum.

The Attic *demos*—and not they alone—lived economically off war. War brought them soldiers' pay and, in case of victory, tribute from the subjects. This tribute was actually distributed among the full citizens in the hardly veiled form of attendance-fees at popular assemblies, court hearings, and public festivities. Here, every full citizen could directly grasp the interest in imperialist policy and power. Nowadays, the yields flowing from abroad to the partners of a polity, including those of imperialist origin and those actually representing 'tribute,' do not result in a constellation of interests so comprehensible to the masses. For under the present economic order, the tribute to 'creditor nations' assumes the form of interest payments on debts or of capital profits transferred from abroad to the propertied strata of the 'creditor nation.' Were one to think these tributes cancelled for countries like England, France, and Germany, it would mean a very palpable decline of purchasing power for home products. This would influence the labor market of the respective workers in an unfavorable manner.

In spite of this, labor in creditor nations is of strongly pacifist mind and on the whole shows no interest whatsoever in the continuation and compulsory collection of such tributes from foreign debtor communities that are in arrears. Nor does labor show an interest in forcibly participating in the exploitation of foreign colonial territories and in sharing public commissions. If this is the case, it is a natural outcome of the immediate class situation, on the one hand, and, on the other, of the internal social and political situation of communities in a capitalist era. Those entitled to tribute belong to the opponent class, who dominate the community. Every successful imperialist policy of coercing the outside normally—or at least at first—also strengthens the domestic 'prestige' and therewith the power and influence of those classes, status groups, and parties, under whose leadership the success has been attained.

In addition to the sources determined by the social and political constellation, there are economic sources of pacifist sympathy among the masses, especially among the proletariat. Every investment of capital in the production of war engines and war material creates job and income opportunities; every administrative agency may become a factor directly contributing to prosperity in a particular case and, even more so, indirectly contributing to prosperity by increasing demand and fostering the intensity of business enterprise. This may become a source of enhanced confidence in the economic opportunities of the participating industries, which may lead to a speculative boom.

The administration, however, withdraws capital from alternate uses and makes it more difficult to satisfy demands in other fields. Above all, the means of war are raised by way of levies, which the ruling strata, by virtue of their social and political power, usually know how to transfer to the masses, quite apart from the limits set to the regimentation of property for 'mercantilist' considerations.

Countries little burdened by military expenses (the United States) and especially the small countries (Switzerland, for example) often experience a stronger economic expansion than do other Powers. Moreover, occasionally small countries are more readily admitted to the economic exploitation of foreign countries because they do not arouse the fear that political intervention might follow economic intrusion.

Experience shows that the pacifist interests of petty bourgeois and proletarian strata very often and very easily fail. This is partly because of the easier accessibility of all unorganized 'masses' to emotional influences and partly because of the indefinite notion (which they entertain) of some unexpected opportunity somehow arising through war. Specific interests, like the hope entertained in overpopulated countries of acquiring territories for emigration, are, of course, also important in this connection. Another contributing cause is the fact that the 'masses,' in contrast to other interest-groups, subjectively risk a smaller stake in the game. In case of a lost war, the 'monarch' has to fear for his throne, republican power-holders and groups having vested interests in a 'republican constitution' have to fear the victorious 'general.' The majority of the propertied bourgeoisie have to fear economic loss from the brakes' being placed upon 'business as usual.' Under certain circumstances, should disorganization follow defeat, the ruling stratum of notables has to fear a violent shift in power in favor of the propertyless. The 'masses' as such, at least in their subjective conception and in the extreme case, have nothing concrete to lose but their lives. The valuation and effect of this danger strongly fluctuates in their own minds. On the whole, it can easily be reduced to zero through emotional influence.

3: THE NATION

The fervor of this emotional influence does not, in the main, have an economic origin. It is based upon sentiments of prestige, which often extend deep down to the petty bourgeois masses of political structures rich in the historical attainment of power-positions. The attachment to all this political prestige may fuse with a specific belief in responsibilty towards succeeding generations. The great power structures *per se* are then held to have a responsibility of their own for the way in which power and prestige are distributed between their own and foreign polities. It goes without saying that all those groups who hold the power to steer common conduct within a polity will most strongly instill themselves with this ideal fervor of power prestige. They remain the specific and most reliable bearers of the idea of the state as an imperialist power structure demanding unqualified devotion.

In addition to the direct and material imperialist interests, discussed above, there are partly indirect and material and partly ideological interests of strata that are in various ways intellectually privileged within a polity and, indeed, privileged by its very existence. They comprise especially all those who think of themselves as being the specific 'partners' of a specific 'culture' diffused among the members of the polity. Under the influence of these circles, the naked prestige of 'power' is unavoidably transformed into other special forms of prestige and especially into the idea of the 'nation.'

If the concept of 'nation' can in any way be defined unambiguously, it certainly cannot be stated in terms of empirical qualities common to those who count as members of the nation. In the sense of those using the term at a given time, the concept undoubtedly means, above all, that one may exact from certain groups of men a specific sentiment of solidarity in the face of other groups. Thus, the concept belongs in the sphere of values. Yet, there is no agreement on how these groups should be delimited or about what concerted action should result from such solidarity.

In ordinary language, 'nation' is, first of all, not identical with the 'people of a state,' that is, with the membership of a given polity. Numerous polities comprise groups among whom the independence of their 'nation' is emphatically asserted in the face of the other groups; or, on the other hand, they comprise parts of a group whose members declare this group to be one homogeneous 'nation' (Austria before 1918, for example). Furthermore, a 'nation' is not identical with a community speaking the same language; that this by no means always suffices is indicated by the Serbs and Croats, the North Americans, the Irish, and the English. On the contrary, a common language does not seem to be absolutely necessary to a 'nation.' In official documents, besides 'Swiss People' one also finds the phrase 'Swiss Nation.' And some language groups do not think of themselves as a separate 'nation,' for example, at least until recently, the white Russians. The pretension, however, to be considered a special 'nation' is regularly associated with a common language as a culture value of the masses; this is predominantly the case in the classic country of language conflicts, Austria, and equally so in Russia and in eastern Prussia. But this linkage of the common language and 'nation' is of varying intensity; for instance, it is very low in the United States as well as in Canada.

'National' solidarity among men speaking the same language may be just as well rejected as accepted. Solidarity, instead, may be linked with differences in the other great 'culture value of the masses,' namely, a religious creed, as is the case with the Serbs and Croats. National solidarity may be connected with differing social structure and mores and hence with 'ethnic' elements, as is the case with the German Swiss and the Alsatians in the face of the Germans of the Reich, or with the Irish facing the British. Yet above all, national solidarity may be linked to memories of a common political destiny with other nations, among the Alsatians with the French since the revolutionary war which represents their common heroic age, just as among the Baltic Barons with the Russians whose political destiny they helped to steer.

It goes without saying that 'national' affiliation need not be based upon common blood. Indeed, everywhere the especially radical 'nationalists' are often of foreign descent. Furthermore, although a specific common anthropological type is not irrelevant to nationality, it is neither sufficient nor a prerequisite to found a nation. Nevertheless, the idea of the 'nation' is apt to include the notions of common descent and of an essential, though frequently indefinite, homogeneity. The nation has these notions in common with the sentiment of solidarity of ethnic communities, which is also nourished from various sources. But the sentiment of ethnic solidarity does not by itself make a 'nation.' Undoubtedly, even the white Russians in the face of the Great Russians have always had a sentiment of ethnic solidarity, yet even at the present time they would hardly claim to qualify as a separate 'nation.' The Poles of Upper Silesia, until recently, had hardly any feeling of solidarity with the 'Polish Nation.' They felt themselves to be a separate ethnic group in the face of the Germans, but for the rest they were Prussian subjects and nothing else.

Whether the Jews may be called a 'nation' is an old problem. The mass of the Russian Jews, the assimilating West-European-American Jews, the Zionists—these would in the main give a negative answer. In any case, their answers would vary in nature and extent. In particular, the question would be answered very differently by the peoples of their environment, for example, by the Russians on the one side and by the Americans on the other—or at least by those Americans who at the present time still maintain American and Jewish nature to be essentially similar, as an American President has asserted in an official document.

Those German-speaking Alsatians who refuse to belong to the German 'nation' and who cultivate the memory of political union with France do not thereby consider themselves simply as members of the French 'nation.' The Negroes of the United States, at least at present, consider themselves members of the American 'nation,' but they will hardly ever be so considered by the Southern Whites.

Only fifteen years ago, men knowing the Far East, still denied that the Chinese qualified as a 'nation'; they held them to be only a 'race.' Yet today, not only the Chinese political leaders but also the very same observers would judge differently. Thus it seems that a group of people under certain conditions may attain the quality of a nation through specific behavior, or they may claim this quality as an 'attainment'—and within short spans of time at that.

There are, on the other hand, social groups that profess indifference to, and even directly relinquish, any evaluational adherence to a single nation. At the present time, certain leading strata of the class movement of the modern proletariat consider such indifference and relinquishment to be an accomplishment. Their argument meets with varying success, depending upon political and linguistic affiliations and also upon different strata of the proletariat; on the whole, their success is rather diminishing at the present time.

An unbroken scale of quite varied and highly changeable attitudes toward the idea of the 'nation' is to be found among social strata and also within single groups to whom language usage ascribes the quality of 'nations.' The scale extends from emphatic affirmation to emphatic negation and finally complete indifference, as may be characteristic of the citizens of Luxembourg and of nationally 'unawakened' peoples. Feudal strata, strata of officials, entrepreneurial bourgeois strata of various categories, strata of 'intellectuals' do not have homogeneous or historically constant attitudes towards the idea.

The reasons for the belief that one represents a nation vary greatly, just as does the empirical conduct that actually results from affiliation or lack of it with a nation. The 'national sentiments' of the German, the Englishman, the North American, the Spaniard, the Frenchman, or the Russian do not function in an identical manner. Thus, to take only the simplest illustration, national sentiment is variously related to political associations, and the 'idea' of the nation may become antagonistic to the empirical scope of given political associations. This antagonism may lead to quite different results.

Certainly the Italians in the Austrian state-association would fight Italian troops only if coerced into doing so. Large portions of the German Austrians would today fight against Germany only with the greatest reluctance; they could not be relied upon. The German Americans, however, even those valuing their 'nationality' most highly, would fight against Germany, not gladly, yet, given the occasion, unconditionally. The Poles in the German State would fight readily against a Russian Polish army but hardly against an autonomous Polish army. The Austrian Serbs would fight against Serbia with very mixed feelings and only in the hope of attaining common autonomy. The Russian Poles would fight more reliably against a German than against an Austrian army.

It is a well-known historical fact that within the same nation the intensity of solidarity felt toward the outside is changeable and varies greatly in strength. On the whole, this sentiment has grown even where internal conflicts of interest have not diminished. Only sixty years ago the *Kreuzzeitung*[5] still appealed to the intervention of the emperor of Russia in internal German affairs; today, in spite of increased class antagonism, this would be difficult to imagine.

In any case, the differences in national sentiment are both significant and fluid and, as is the case in all other fields, fundamentally different answers are given to the question: What conclusions are a group of people willing to draw from the 'national sentiment' found among them? No matter how emphatic and subjectively sincere a pathos may be formed among them, what sort of specific joint action are they ready to develop? The extent to which in the diaspora a convention is adhered to as a 'national' trait varies just as much as does the importance of common conventions for the belief in the existence of a separate 'nation.' In the face of these value concepts of the 'idea of the nation,' which empirically are entirely ambiguous, a sociological typology would have to analyze all sorts of community sentiments of solidarity in their genetic conditions and in their consequences for the concerted action of the participants. This cannot here be attempted.

Instead, we shall have to look a little closer into the fact that the idea of the nation for its advocates stands in very intimate relation to 'prestige' interests. The earliest and most energetic manifestations of the idea, in some form, even though it may have been veiled, have contained the legend of a providential 'mission.' Those to whom the representatives of the idea zealously turned were expected to shoulder this mission. Another element of the early idea was the notion that this mission was facilitated solely through the very cultivation of the peculiarity of the group set off as a nation. Therewith, in so far as its self-justification is sought in the value of its content, this mission can consistently be thought of only as a specific 'culture' mission. The significance of the 'nation' is usually anchored in the superiority, or at least the irreplaceability, of the culture values that are to be preserved and developed only through the cultivation of the peculiarity of the group. It therefore goes without saying that the intellectuals, as we have in a preliminary fashion called them, are to a specific degree predestined to propagate the 'national idea,' just as those who wield power in the polity provoke the idea of the state.

By 'intellectuals' we understand a group of men who by virtue of their peculiarity have special access to certain achievements considered to be 'culture values,' and who therefore usurp the leadership of a 'culture community.'[6]

* * *

In so far as there is at all a common object lying behind the obviously ambiguous term 'nation,' it is apparently located in the field of politics. One might well define the concept of nation in the following way: a nation is a community of sentiment which would adequately manifest itself in a state of its own; hence, a nation is a community which normally tends to produce a state of its own.

The causal components that lead to the emergence of a national sentiment in this sense may vary greatly. If we for once disregard religious belief—which has not yet played its last role in this matter, especially among Serbs and Croats—then common purely political destinies have first to be considered. Under certain conditions, otherwise heterogeneous peoples can be melted together through common destinies. The reason for the Alsatians' not feeling themselves as belonging to the German nation has to be sought in their memories. Their political destiny has taken its course outside the German sphere for too long; their heroes are the heroes of French history. If the custodian of the Kolmar museum wants to show you which among his treasures he cherishes most, he takes you away from Grünewald's altar to a room filled with tricolors, *pompier,* and other helmets and souvenirs of a seemingly most insignificant nature; they are from a time that to him is a heroic age.

An existing state organization whose heroic age is not felt as such by the masses can nevertheless be decisive for a powerful sentiment of solidarity, in spite of the greatest internal antagonisms. The state is valued as the agency that guarantees security, and this is above all the case in times of external danger, when sentiments of national solidarity flare up, at least intermittently. Thus we have seen how the elements of the Austrian state, which apparently strove to separate without regard for consequences, united during the so-called Nibelung danger.[7] It was not only the officials and officers, who were interested in the state as such, who could be relied upon, but also the masses of the army.

The conditions of a further component, namely, the influence of race, is especially complex. Here we had better disregard entirely the mystic effects of a community of blood, in the sense in which the racial fanaticists use the phrase. The differences among anthropological types are but one factor of closure, social attraction, and repulsion. They stand with equal right beside differences acquired through tradition. There are characteristic differences in these matters. Every Yankee accepts the civilized quarter-breed or octoroon Indian as a member of the nation; he may himself claim to have Indian blood. But he behaves quite differently toward the Negro, and he does so especially when the Negro adopts the same way of life as he and therewith develops the same social aspirations. How can we explain this fact?

Aesthetic aversions may come into play. The 'odor of Negroes,' however, of which so many fables are told, is, according to my experience, not to be discovered. Black wet-nurses, black coachmen riding shoulder to shoulder with the lady steering the cabriolet, and above all, several million mixed bloods are all too clear proof against the allegedly natural repulsion between these races. This aversion is social in nature, and I have heard but one plausible explanation for it: the Negroes have been slaves; the Indians have not.

Of those cultural elements that represent the most important positive basis for the formation of national sentiment everywhere, a common language takes first place. But even a common language is not entirely indispensable nor sufficient by itself. One may state that there was a specific Swiss national sentiment in spite of the lack of common language; and, in spite of a common language, the Irish have no common national sentiment with the British. The importance of language is necessarily increasing along with the democratization of state, society, and culture. For the masses a common language plays a more decisive economic part than it does for the propertied strata of feudal or bourgeois stamp. For these latter, at least in the language areas of an identical culture, usually speak the foreign language, whereas the petty bourgeois and the proletarian in a foreign language area are much more dependent upon cohesion with those speaking the same language. Above all, the language, and that means the literature based upon it, is the first and for the time being the only cultural value at all accessible to the masses who ascend toward participation in culture. The enjoyment of art requires a far greater degree of education, and art has a far more aristocratic nature than has literature. This is precisely the case in literature's greatest achievements. It is for this reason that the notion held in Austria that democratization must soften the language conflicts was so utopian. The facts have, in the meanwhile, thoroughly disproved such notions. Common cultural values can provide a unifying national bond. But for this the objective quality of the cultural values does not matter at all, and therefore one must not conceive of the 'nation' as a 'culture community.'

Newspapers, which certainly do not assemble what is most sublime in literary culture, cement the masses most strongly. Concerning the actual social conditions that make for the rise of a unified literary language and for a literature in the vernacular, which is something else, all research is now only in its beginnings. For the case of France, one may refer to the essays of my esteemed friend Vossler.

I should like to point to only one typical supporter of this development, because it is one seldom recognized as such, namely, women. They contributed specifically to the formation of national sentiment linked to language. An erotic lyric addressed to a woman can hardly be written in a foreign language, because then it would be unintelligible to the addressee. The courtly and chivalrous lyric was neither singular, nor always the first literature to displace Latin by the national language, as happened in France, Italy, Germany, or to displace Chinese, as happened in Japan. Nevertheless, the courtly lyric has frequently and permanently done so, and has sublimated national languages into literary languages. I cannot here describe how after this initial displacement the importance of the vernacular steadily progressed under the influence of the broadening administrative tasks of state and church, hence as the language of administration and of the sermon. I may, however, add one more word about the economic determination of modern language conflicts.

Today quite considerable pecuniary and capitalist interests are anchored in the maintenance and cultivation of the popular language: the interests of the publishers, editors, authors, and the contributors to books and periodicals and, above all, to newspapers. Once Polish and Latvian newspapers existed, the language fight conducted by governments or ruling strata of another language community had become as good as hopeless, for reasons of state are powerless against these forces. And to the interests in profits of the capitalist another material interest of great weight has to be added: the bilingual candidates in competing for office throw their bilingualism into the balance and seek to lay claim upon as large an area of patronage as possible. This occurred among the Czechs in Austria with their surplus of intellectual proletariat bred *en masse*. The tendency as such is old.

The conciliar, and at the same time nationalist, reaction against the universalism of the papacy in the waning Middle Ages had its origin, to a great extent, in the interests of the intellectuals who wished to see the prebends of their own country reserved for themselves and not occupied by strangers *via* Rome. After all, the name *natio* as a legal concept for an organized community is found first at the universities and at the reform councils of the church. At that time, however, the linkage to the national language *per se* was lacking; this linkage, for the reasons stated, is specifically modern.

If one believes that it is at all expedient to distinguish national sentiment as something homogeneous and specifically set apart, one can do so only by referring to a tendency toward an autonomous state. And one must be clearly aware of the fact that sentiments of solidarity, very heterogeneous in both their nature and their origin, are comprised within national sentiments.

VII. Class, Status, Party

LAW exists when there is a probability that an order will be upheld by a specific staff of men who will use physical or psychical compulsion with the intention of obtaining conformity with the order, or of inflicting sanctions for infringement of it.* The structure of every legal order directly influences the distribution of power, economic or otherwise, within its respective community. This is true of all legal orders and not only that of the state. In general, we understand by 'power' the chance of a man or of a number of men to realize their own will in a communal action even against the resistance of others who are participating in the action.

'Economically conditioned' power is not, of course, identical with 'power' as such. On the contrary, the emergence of economic power may be the consequence of power existing on other grounds. Man does not strive for power only in order to enrich himself economically. Power, including economic power, may be valued 'for its own sake.' Very frequently the striving for power is also conditioned by the social 'honor' it entails. Not all power, however, entails social honor: The typical American Boss, as well as the typical big speculator, deliberately relinquishes social honor. Quite generally, 'mere economic' power, and especially 'naked' money power, is by no means a recognized basis of social honor. Nor is power the only basis of social honor. Indeed, social honor, or prestige, may even be the basis of political or economic power, and very frequently has been. Power, as well as honor, may be guaranteed by the legal order, but, at least normally, it is not their primary source. The

* *Wirtschaft und Gesellschaft,* part III, chap. 4, pp. 631-40. The first sentence in paragraph one and the several definitions in this chapter which are in brackets do not appear in the original text. They have been taken from other contexts of *Wirtschaft und Gesellschaft.*

legal order is rather an additional factor that enhances the chance to hold power or honor; but it cannot always secure them.

The way in which social honor is distributed in a community between typical groups participating in this distribution we may call the 'social order.' The social order and the economic order are, of course, similarly related to the 'legal order.' However, the social and the economic order are not identical. The economic order is for us merely the way in which economic goods and services are distributed and used. The social order is of course conditioned by the economic order to a high degree, and in its turn reacts upon it.

Now: 'classes,' 'status groups,' and 'parties' are phenomena of the distribution of power within a community.

2: Determination of Class-Situation by Market-Situation

In our terminology, 'classes' are not communities; they merely represent possible, and frequent, bases for communal action. We may speak of a 'class' when (1) a number of people have in common a specific causal component of their life chances, in so far as (2) this component is represented exclusively by economic interests in the possession of goods and opportunities for income, and (3) is represented under the conditions of the commodity or labor markets. [These points refer to 'class situation,' which we may express more briefly as the typical chance for a supply of goods, external living conditions, and personal life experiences, in so far as this chance is determined by the amount and kind of power, or lack of such, to dispose of goods or skills for the sake of income in a given economic order. The term 'class' refers to any group of people that is found in the same class situation.]

It is the most elemental economic fact that the way in which the disposition over material property is distributed among a plurality of people, meeting competitively in the market for the purpose of exchange, in itself creates specific life chances. According to the law of marginal utility this mode of distribution excludes the non-owners from competing for highly valued goods; it favors the owners and, in fact, gives to them a monopoly to acquire such goods. Other things being equal, this mode of distribution monopolizes the opportunities for profitable deals for all those who, provided with goods, do not necessarily have to exchange them. It increases, at least generally, their power in price wars with those who, being propertyless, have nothing to offer but their services in native form or goods in a form constituted through their own labor, and who above all are compelled to get rid of these products in order barely to subsist. This mode of distribution gives to the propertied a monopoly on the possibility of transferring property from the sphere of use as a 'fortune,' to the sphere of 'capital goods'; that is, it gives them the entrepreneurial function and all chances to share directly or indirectly in returns on capital. All this holds true within the area in which pure market conditions prevail. 'Property' and 'lack of property' are, therefore, the basic categories of all class situations. It does not matter whether these two categories become effective in price wars or in competitive struggles.

Within these categories, however, class situations are further differentiated: on the one hand, according to the kind of property that is usable for returns; and, on the other hand, according to the kind of services that can be offered in the market. Ownership of domestic buildings; productive establishments; warehouses; stores; agriculturally usable land, large and small holdings—quantitative differences with possibly qualitative consequences—; ownership of mines; cattle; men (slaves); disposition over mobile instruments of production, or capital goods of all sorts, especially money or objects that can be exchanged for money easily and at any time; disposition over products of one's own labor or of others' labor differing according to their various distances from consumability; disposition over transferable monopolies of any kind—all these distinctions differentiate the class situations of the propertied just as does the 'meaning' which they can and do give to the utilization of property, especially to property which has money equivalence. Accordingly, the propertied, for instance, may belong to the class of rentiers or to the class of entrepreneurs.

Those who have no property but who offer services are differentiated just as much according to their kinds of services as according to the way in which they make use of these services, in a continuous or discontinuous relation to a recipient. But always this is the generic connotation of the concept of class: that the kind of chance in the *market* is the decisive moment which presents a common condition for the individual's fate. 'Class situation' is, in this sense, ultimately 'market situation.' The effect of naked possession *per se,* which among cattle breeders gives the non-owning slave or serf into the power of the cattle owner, is only a forerunner of real 'class' formation. However, in the cattle loan and in the naked severity of the law of debts in such communities, for the first time mere 'possession' as such emerges as decisive for the fate of the individual. This is very much in contrast to the agricultural communities based on labor. The creditor-debtor relation becomes the basis of 'class situations' only in those cities where a 'credit market,' however primitive, with rates of interest increasing according to the extent of dearth and a factual monopolization of credits, is developed by a plutocracy. Therewith 'class struggles' begin.

Those men whose fate is not determined by the chance of using goods or services for themselves on the market, e.g. slaves, are not, however, a 'class' in the technical sense of the term. They are, rather, a 'status group.'

3: COMMUNAL ACTION FLOWING FROM CLASS INTEREST

According to our terminology, the factor that creates 'class' is unambiguously economic interest, and indeed, only those interests involved in the existence of the 'market.' Nevertheless, the concept of 'class-interest' is an ambiguous one: even as an empirical concept it is ambiguous as soon as one understands by it something other than the factual direction of interests following with a certain probability from the class situation for a certain 'average' of those people subjected to the class situation. The class situation and other circumstances remaining the same, the direction in which the individual worker, for instance, is likely to pursue his interests may vary widely, according to whether he is constitutionally qualified for the task at hand to a high, to an average, or to a low degree. In the same way, the direction of interests may vary according to whether or not a *communal* action of a larger or smaller portion of those commonly affected by the 'class situation,' or even an association among them, e.g. a 'trade union,' has grown out of the class situation from which the individual may or may not expect promising results. [Communal action refers to that action which is oriented to the feeling of the actors that they belong together. Societal action, on the other hand, is oriented to a rationally motivated adjustment of interests.] The rise of societal or even of communal action from a common class situation is by no means a universal phenomenon.

The class situation may be restricted in its effects to the generation of essentially *similar* reactions, that is to say, within our terminology, of 'mass actions.' However, it may not have even this result. Furthermore, often merely an amorphous communal action emerges. For example, the 'murmuring' of the workers known in ancient oriental ethics: the moral disapproval of the work-master's conduct, which in its practical significance was probably equivalent to an increasingly typical phenomenon of precisely the latest industrial development, namely, the 'slow down' (the deliberate limiting of work effort) of laborers by virtue of tacit agreement. The degree in which 'communal action' and possibly 'societal action,' emerges from the 'mass actions' of the members of a class is linked to general cultural conditions, especially to those of an intellectual sort. It is also linked to the extent of the contrasts that have already evolved, and is especially linked to the *transparency* of the connections between the causes and the consequences of the 'class situation.' For however different life chances may be, this fact in itself, according to all experience, by no means gives birth to 'class action' (communal action by the members of a class). The fact of being conditioned and the results of the class situation must be distinctly recognizable. For only then the contrast of life chances can be felt not as an absolutely given fact to be accepted, but as a resultant from either (1) the given distribution of property, or (2) the structure of the concrete economic order. It is only then that people may react against the class structure not only through acts of an intermittent and irrational protest, but in the form of rational association. There have been 'class situations' of the first category (1), of a specifically naked and transparent sort, in the urban centers of Antiquity and during the Middle Ages; especially then, when great fortunes were accumulated by factually monopolized trading in industrial products of these localities or in foodstuffs. Furthermore, under certain circumstances, in the rural economy of the most diverse periods, when agriculture was increasingly exploited in a profit-making manner. The most important historical example of the second category (2) is the class situation of the modern 'proletariat.'

4: Types of 'Class Struggle'

Thus every class may be the carrier of any one of the possibly innumerable forms of 'class action,' but this is not necessarily so. In any case, a class does not in itself constitute a community. To treat 'class' conceptually as having the same value as 'community' leads to distortion. That men in the same class situation regularly react in mass actions to such tangible situations as economic ones in the direction of those interests that are most adequate to their average number is an important and after all simple fact for the understanding of historical events. Above all, this fact must not lead to that kind of pseudo-scientific operation with the concepts of 'class' and 'class interests' so frequently found these days, and which has found its most classic expression in the statement of a talented author, that the individual may be in error concerning his interests but that the 'class' is 'infallible' about its interests. Yet, if classes as such are not communities, nevertheless class situations emerge only on the basis of communalization. The communal action that brings forth class situations, however, is not basically action between members of the identical class; it is an action between members of different classes. Communal actions that directly determine the class situation of the worker and the entrepreneur are: the labor market, the commodities market, and the capitalistic enterprise. But, in its turn, the existence of a capitalistic enterprise presupposes that a very specific communal action exists and that it is specifically structured to protect the possession of goods *per se,* and especially the power of individuals to dispose, in principle freely, over the means of production. The existence of a capitalistic enterprise is preconditioned by a specific kind of 'legal order.' Each kind of class situation, and above all when it rests upon the power of property *per se,* will become most clearly efficacious when all other determinants of reciprocal relations are, as far as possible, eliminated in their significance. It is in this way that the utilization of the power of property in the market obtains its most sovereign importance.

Now 'status groups' hinder the strict carrying through of the sheer market principle. In the present context they are of interest to us only from this one point of view. Before we briefly consider them, note that not much of a general nature can be said about the more specific kinds of antagonism between 'classes' (in our meaning of the term). The great shift, which has been going on continuously in the past, and up to our times, may be summarized. although at the cost of some precision: the struggle in which class situations are effective has progressively shifted from consumption credit toward, first, competitive struggles in the commodity market and, then, toward price wars on the labor market. The 'class struggles' of antiquity—to the extent that they were genuine class struggles and not struggles between status groups—were initially carried on by indebted peasants, and perhaps also by artisans threatened by debt bondage and struggling against urban creditors. For debt bondage is the normal result of the differentiation of wealth in commercial cities, especially in seaport cities. A similar situation has existed among cattle breeders. Debt relationships as such produced class action up to the time of Cataline. Along with this, and with an increase in provision of grain for the city by transporting it from the. outside, the struggle over the means of sustenance emerged. It centered in the first place around the provision of bread and the determination of the price of bread. It lasted throughout antiquity and the entire Middle Ages. The propertyless as such flocked together against those who actually and supposedly were interested in the dearth of bread. This fight spread until it involved all those commodities essential to the way of life and to handicraft production. There were only incipient discussions of wage disputes in antiquity and in the Middle Ages. But they have been slowly increasing up into modern times. In the earlier periods they were completely secondary to slave rebellions as well as to fights in the commodity market.

The propertyless of antiquity and of the Middle Ages protested against monopolies, pre-emption, forestalling, and the withholding of goods from the market in order to raise prices. Today the central issue is the determination of the price of labor.

This transition is represented by the fight for access to the market and for the determination of the price of products. Such fights went on between merchants and workers in the putting-out system of domestic handicraft during the transition to modern times. Since it is quite a general phenomenon we must mention here that the class antagonisms that are conditioned through the market situation are usually most bitter between those who actually and directly participate as opponents in price wars. It is not the rentier, the share-holder, and the banker who suffer the ill will of the worker, but almost exclusively the manufacturer and the business executives who are the direct opponents of workers in price wars. This is so in spite of the fact that it is precisely the cash boxes of the rentier, the share-holder, and the banker into which the more or less 'unearned' gains flow, rather than into the pockets of the manufacturers or of the business executives. This simple state of affairs has very frequently been decisive for the role the class situation has played in the formation of political parties. For example, it has made possible the varieties of patriarchal socialism and the frequent attempts—formerly, at least—of threatened status groups to form alliances with the proletariat against the 'bourgeoisie.'

5: Status Honor

In contrast to classes, *status groups* are normally communities. They are, however, often of an amorphous kind. In contrast to the purely economically determined 'class situation' we wish to designate as 'status situation' every typical component of the life fate of men that is determined by a specific, positive or negative, social estimation of *honor*. This honor may be connected with any quality shared by a plurality, and, of course, it can be knit to a class situation: class distinctions are linked in the most varied ways with status distinctions. Property as such is not always recognized as a status qualification, but in the long run it is, and with extraordinary regularity. In the subsistence economy of the organized neighborhood, very often the richest man is simply the chieftain. However, this often means only an honorific preference. For example, in the so-called pure modern 'democracy,' that is, one devoid of any expressly ordered status privileges for individuals, it may be that only the families coming under approximately the same tax class dance with one another. This example is reported of certain smaller Swiss cities. But status honor need not necessarily be linked with a 'class situation.' On the contrary, it normally stands in sharp opposition to the pretensions of sheer property.

Both propertied and propertyless people can belong to the same status group, and frequently they do with very tangible consequences. This 'equality' of social esteem may, however, in the long run become quite precarious. The 'equality' of status among the American 'gentlemen,' for instance, is expressed by the fact that outside the subordination determined by the different functions of 'business,' it would be considered strictly repugnant—wherever the old tradition still prevails—if even the richest 'chief,' while playing billiards or cards in his club in the evening, would not treat his 'clerk' as in every sense fully his equal in birthright. It would be repugnant if the American 'chief' would bestow upon his 'clerk' the condescending 'benevolence' marking a distinction of 'position,' which the German chief can never dissever from his attitude. This is one of the most important reasons why in America the German 'clubby-ness' has never been able to attain the attraction that the American clubs have.

6: Guarantees of Status Stratification

In content, status honor is normally expressed by the fact that above all else a specific *style of life* can be expected from all those who wish to belong to the circle. Linked with this expectation are restrictions on 'social' intercourse (that is, intercourse which is not subservient to economic or any other of business's 'functional' purposes). These restrictions may confine normal marriages to within the status circle and may lead to complete endogamous closure. As soon as there is not a mere individual and socially irrelevant imitation of another style of life, but an agreed-upon communal action of this closing character, the 'status' development is under way.

In its characteristic form, stratification by 'status groups' on the basis of conventional styles of life evolves at the present time in the United States out of the traditional democracy. For example, only the resident of a certain street ('the street') is considered as belonging to 'society,' is qualified for social intercourse, and is visited and invited. Above all, this differentiation evolves in such a way as to make for strict submission to the fashion that is dominant at a given time in society. This submission to fashion also exists among men in America to a degree unknown in Germany. Such submission is considered to be an indication of the fact that a given man *pretends* to qualify as a gentleman. This submission decides, at least *prima facie,* that he will be treated as such. And this recognition becomes just as important for his employment chances in 'swank' establishments, and above all, for social intercourse and marriage with 'esteemed' families, as the qualification for dueling among Germans in the Kaiser's day. As for the rest: certain families resident for a long time, and, of course, correspondingly wealthy, e.g. 'F. F. V., i.e. First Families of Virginia,' or the actual or alleged descendants of the 'Indian Princess' Pocahontas, of the Pilgrim fathers, or of the Knickerbockers, the members of almost inaccessible sects and all sorts of circles setting themselves apart by means of any other characteristics and badges . . . all these elements usurp 'status' honor. The development of status is essentially a question of stratification resting upon usurpation. Such usurpation is the normal origin of almost all status honor. But the road from this purely conventional situation to legal privilege, positive or negative, is easily traveled as soon as a certain stratification of the social order has in fact been 'lived in' and has achieved stability by virtue of a stable distribution of economic power.

7: 'Ethnic' Segregation and 'Caste'

Where the consequences have been realized to their full extent, the status group evolves into a closed 'caste.' Status distinctions are then guaranteed not merely by conventions and laws, but also by *rituals.* This occurs in such a way that every physical contact with a member of any caste that is considered to be 'lower' by the members of a 'higher' caste is considered as making for a ritualistic impurity and to be a stigma which must be expiated by a religious act. Individual castes develop quite distinct cults and gods.

In general, however, the status structure reaches such extreme consequences only where there are underlying differences which are held to be 'ethnic.' The 'caste' is, indeed, the normal form in which ethnic communities usually live side by side in a 'societalized' manner. These ethnic communities believe in blood relationship and exclude exogamous marriage and social intercourse. Such a caste situation is part of the phenomenon of 'pariah' peoples and is found all over the world. These people form communities, acquire specific occupational traditions of handicrafts or of other arts, and cultivate a belief in their ethnic community. They live in a 'diaspora' strictly segregated from all personal intercourse, except that of an unavoidable sort, and their situation is legally precarious. Yet, by virtue of their economic indispensability, they are tolerated, indeed, frequently privileged, and they live in interspersed political communities. The Jews are the most impressive historical example.

A 'status' segregation grown into a 'caste' differs in its structure from a mere 'ethnic' segregation: the caste structure transforms the horizontal and unconnected coexistences of ethnically segregated groups into a vertical social system of super- and subordination. Correctly formulated: a comprehensive societalization integrates the ethnically divided communities into specific political and communal action. In their consequences they differ precisely in this way: ethnic coexistences condition a mutual repulsion and disdain but allow each ethnic community to consider its own honor as the highest one; the caste structure brings about a social subordination and an acknowledgment of 'more honor' in favor of the privileged caste and status groups. This is due to the fact that in the caste structure ethnic distinctions as such have become 'functional' distinctions within the political societalization (warriors, priests, artisans that are politically important for war and for building, and so on). But even pariah people who are most despised are usually apt to continue cultivating in some manner that which is equally peculiar to ethnic and to status communities: the belief in their own specific 'honor.' This is the case with the Jews.

Only with the negatively privileged status groups does the 'sense of dignity' take a specific deviation. A sense of dignity is the precipitation in individuals of social honor and of conventional demands which a positively privileged status group raises for the deportment of its members. The sense of dignity that characterizes positively privileged status groups is naturally related to their 'being' which does not transcend itself, that is, it is to their 'beauty and excellence' (καλο-κἀγαϑια). Their kingdom is 'of this world.' They live for the present and by exploiting their great past. The sense of dignity of the negatively privileged strata naturally refers to a future lying beyond the present, whether it is of this life or of another. In other words, it must be nurtured by the belief in a providential 'mission' and by a belief in a specific honor before God. The 'chosen people's' dignity is nurtured by a belief either that in the beyond 'the last will be the first,' or that in this life a Messiah will appear to bring forth into the light of the world which has cast them out the hidden honor of the pariah people. This simple state of affairs, and not the 'resentment' which is so strongly emphasized in Nietzsche's much admired construction in the *Genealogy of Morals,* is the source of the religiosity cultivated by pariah status groups. In passing, we may note that resentment may be accurately applied only to a limited extent; for one of Nietzsche's main examples, Buddhism, it is not at all applicable.

Incidentally, the development of status groups from ethnic segregations is by no means the normal phenomenon. On the contrary, since objective 'racial differences' are by no means basic to every subjective sentiment of an ethnic community, the ultimately racial foundation of status structure is rightly and absolutely a question of the concrete individual case. Very frequently a status group is instrumental in the production of a thoroughbred anthropological type. Certainly a status group is to a high degree effective in producing extreme types, for they select personally qualified individuals (e.g. the Knighthood selects those who are fit for warfare, physically and psychically). But selection is far from being the only, or the predominant, way in which status groups are formed: Political membership or class situation has at all times been at least as frequently decisive. And today the class situation is by far the predominant factor, for of course the possibility of a style of life expected for members of a status group is usually conditioned economically.

8: STATUS PRIVILEGES

For all practical purposes, stratification by status goes hand in hand with a monopolization of ideal and material goods or opportunities, in a manner we have come to know as typical. Besides the specific status honor, which always rests upon distance and exclusiveness, we find all sorts of material monopolies. Such honorific preferences may consist of the privilege of wearing special costumes, of eating special dishes taboo to others, of carrying arms—which is most obvious in its consequences—the right to pursue certain non-professional dilettante artistic practices, e.g. to play certain musical instruments. Of course, material monopolies provide the most effective motives for the exclusiveness of a status group; although, in themselves, they are rarely sufficient, almost always they come into play to some extent. Within a status circle there is the question of intermarriage: the interest of the families in the monopolization of potential bridegrooms is at least of equal importance and is parallel to the interest in the monopolization of daughters. The daughters of the circle must be provided for. With an increased inclosure of the status group, the conventional preferential opportunities for special employment grow into a legal monopoly of special offices for the members. Certain goods become objects for monopolization by status groups. In the typical fashion these include 'entailed estates' and frequently also the possessions of serfs or bondsmen and, finally, special trades. This monopolization occurs positively when the status group is exclusively entitled to own and to manage them; and negatively when, in order to maintain its specific way of life, the status group must *not* own and manage them.

The decisive role of a 'style of life' in status 'honor' means that status groups are the specific bearers of all 'conventions.' In whatever way it may be manifest, all 'stylization' of life either originates in status groups or is at least conserved by them. Even if the principles of status conventions differ greatly, they reveal certain typical traits, especially among those strata which are most privileged. Quite generally, among privileged status groups there is a status disqualification that operates against the performance of common physical labor. This disqualification is now 'setting in' in America against the old tradition of esteem for labor. Very frequently every rational economic pursuit, and especially 'entrepreneurial activity,' is looked upon as a disqualification of status. Artistic and literary activity is also considered as degrading work as soon as it is exploited for income, or at least when it is connected with hard physical exertion. An example is the sculptor working like a mason in his dusty smock as over against the painter in his salon-like 'studio' and those forms of musical practice that are acceptable to the status group.

9: Economic Conditions and Effects of Status Stratification

The frequent disqualification of the gainfully employed as such is a direct result of the principle of status stratification peculiar to the social order, and of course, of this principle's opposition to a distribution of power which is regulated exclusively through the market. These two factors operate along with various individual ones, which will be touched upon below.

We have seen above that the market and its processes 'knows no personal distinctions': 'functional' interests dominate it. It knows nothing of 'honor.' The status order means precisely the reverse, viz.: stratification in terms of 'honor' and of styles of life peculiar to status groups as such. If mere economic acquisition and naked economic power still bearing the stigma of its extra-status origin could bestow upon anyone who has won it the same honor as those who are interested in status by virtue of style of life claim for themselves, the status order would be threatened at its very root. This is the more so as, given equality of status honor, property *per se* represents an addition even if it is not overtly acknowledged to be such. Yet if such economic acquisition and power gave the agent any honor at all, his wealth would result in his attaining more honor than those who successfully claim honor by virtue of style of life. Therefore all groups having interests in the status order react with special sharpness precisely against the pretensions of purely economic acquisition. In most cases they react the more vigorously the more they feel themselves threatened. Calderon's respectful treatment of the peasant, for instance, as opposed to Shakespeare's simultaneous and ostensible disdain of the *canaille* illustrates the different way in which a firmly structured status order reacts as compared with a status order that has become economically precarious. This is an example of a state of affairs that recurs everywhere. Precisely because of the rigorous reactions against the claims of property *per se,* the 'parvenu' is never accepted, personally and without reservation, by the privileged status groups, no matter how completely his style of life has been adjusted to theirs. They will only accept his descendants who have been educated in the conventions of their status group and who have never besmirched its honor by their own economic labor.

As to the general *effect* of the status order, only one consequence can be stated, but it is a very important one: the hindrance of the free development of the market occurs first for those goods which status groups directly withheld from free exchange by monopolization. This monopolization may be effected either legally or conventionally. For example, in many Hellenic cities during the epoch of status groups, and also originally in Rome, the inherited estate (as is shown by the old formula for indiction against spendthrifts) was monopolized just as were the estates of knights, peasants, priests, and especially the clientele of the craft and merchant guilds. The market is restricted, and the power of naked property *per se,* which gives its stamp to 'class formation,' is pushed into the background. The results of this process can be most varied. Of course, they do not necessarily weaken the contrasts in the economic situation. Frequently they strengthen these contrasts, and in any case, where stratification by status permeates a community as strongly as was the case in all political communities of antiquity and of the Middle Ages, one can never speak of a genuinely free market competition as we understand it today. There are wider effects than this direct exclusion of special goods from the market. From the contrariety between the status order and the purely economic order mentioned above, it follows that in most instances the notion of honor peculiar to status absolutely abhors that which is essential to the market: higgling. Honor abhors higgling among peers and occasionally it taboos higgling for the members of a status group in general. Therefore, everywhere some status groups, and usually the most influential, consider almost any kind of overt participation in economic acquisition as absolutely stigmatizing.

With some over-simplification, one might thus say that 'classes' are stratified according to their relations to the production and acquisition of goods; whereas 'status groups' are stratified according to the principles of their *consumption* of goods as represented by special 'styles of life.'

An 'occupational group' is also a status group. For normally, it successfully claims social honor only by virtue of the special style of life which may be determined by it. The differences between classes and status groups frequently overlap. It is precisely those status communities most strictly segregated in terms of honor (viz. the Indian castes) who today show, although within very rigid limits, a relatively high degree of indifference to pecuniary income. However, the Brahmins seek such income in many different ways.

As to the general economic conditions making for the predominance of stratification by 'status,' only very little can be said. When the bases of the acquisition and distribution of goods are relatively stable, stratification by status is favored. Every technological repercussion and economic transformation threatens stratification by status and pushes the class situation into the foreground. Epochs and countries in which the naked class situation is of predominant significance are regularly the periods of technical and economic transformations. And every slowing down of the shifting of economic stratifications leads, in due course, to the growth of status structures and makes for a resuscitation of the important role of social honor.

10: Parties

Whereas the genuine place of classes' is within the economic order, the place of 'status groups' is within the social order, that is, within the sphere of the distribution of 'honor.' From within these spheres, classes and status groups influence one another and they influence the legal order and are in turn influenced by it. But 'parties' live in a house of 'power.'

Their action is oriented toward the acquisition of social 'power,' that is to say, toward influencing a communal action no matter what its content may be. In principle, parties may exist in a social 'club' as well as in a 'state.' As over against the actions of classes and status groups, for which this is not necessarily the case, the communal actions of 'parties' always mean a societalization. For party actions are always directed toward a goal which is striven for in planned manner. This goal may be a 'cause' (the party may aim at realizing a program for ideal or material purposes), or the goal may be 'personal' (sinecures, power, and from these, honor for the leader and the followers of the party). Usually the party action aims at all these simultaneously. Parties are, therefore, only possible within communities that are societalized, that is, which have some rational order and a staff of persons available who are ready to enforce it. For parties aim precisely at influencing this staff, and if possible, to recruit it from party followers.

In any individual case, parties may represent interests determined through 'class situation' or 'status situation,' and they may recruit their following respectively from one or the other. But they need be neither purely 'class' nor purely 'status' parties. In most cases they are partly class parties and partly status parties, but sometimes they are neither. They may represent ephemeral or enduring structures. Their means of attaining power may be quite varied, ranging from naked violence of any sort to canvassing for votes with coarse or subtle means: money, social influence, the force of speech, suggestion, clumsy hoax, and so on to the rougher or more artful tactics of obstruction in parliamentary bodies.

The sociological structure of parties differs in a basic way according to the kind of communal action which they struggle to influence. Parties also differ according to whether or not the community is stratified by status or by classes. Above all else, they vary according to the structure of domination within the community. For their leaders normally deal with the conquest of a community. They are, in the general concept which is maintained here, not only products of specially modern forms of domination. We shall also designate as parties the ancient and medieval 'parties,' despite the fact that their structure differs basically from the structure of modern parties. By virtue of these structural differences of domination it is impossible to say anything about the structure of parties without discussing the structural forms of social domination *per se*. Parties, which are always structures struggling for domination, are very frequently organized in a very strict 'authoritarian' fashion. . .

Concerning 'classes,' 'status groups,' and 'parties,' it must be said in general that they necessarily presuppose a comprehensive societalization, and especially a political framework of communal action, within which they operate. This does not mean that parties would be confined by the frontiers of any individual political community. On the contrary, at all times it has been the order of the day that the societalization (even when it aims at the use of military force in common) reaches beyond the frontiers of politics. This has been the case in the solidarity of interests among the Oligarchs and among the democrats in Hellas, among the Guelfs and among Ghibellines in the Middle Ages, and within the Calvinist party during the period of religious struggles. It has been the case up to the solidarity of the landlords (international congress of agrarian landlords), and has continued among princes (holy alliance, Karlsbad decrees), socialist workers, conservatives (the longing of Prussian conservatives for Russian intervention in 1850). But their aim is not necessarily the establishment of new international political, i.e. *territorial,* dominion. In the main they aim to influence the existing dominion.*

* The posthumously published text breaks off here. We omit an incomplete sketch of types of 'warrior estates.'

VIII. Bureaucracy

I: CHARACTERISTICS OF BUREAUCRACY

MODERN officialdom functions in the following specific manner:

I. There is the principle of fixed and official jurisdictional areas, which are generally ordered by rules, that is, by laws or administrative regulations.

1. The regular activities required for the purposes of the bureaucratically governed structure are distributed in a fixed way as official duties.

2. The authority to give the commands required for the discharge of these duties is distributed in a stable way and is strictly delimited by rules concerning the coercive means, physical, sacerdotal, or otherwise, which may be placed at the disposal of officials.

3. Methodical provision is made for the regular and continuous fulfilment of these duties and for the execution of the corresponding rights; only persons who have the generally regulated qualifications to serve are employed.

In public and lawful government these three elements constitute 'bureaucratic authority.' In private economic domination, they constitute bureaucratic 'management.' Bureaucracy, thus understood, is fully developed in political and ecclesiastical communities only in the modern state, and, in the private economy, only in the most advanced institutions of capitalism. Permanent and public office authority, with fixed jurisdiction, is not the historical rule but rather the exception. This is so even in large political structures such as those of the ancient Orient, the Germanic and Mongolian empires of conquest, or of many feudal structures of state. In all these cases, the ruler executes the most important measures through personal trustees, table-companions, or court-servants. Their

Wirtschaft und Gesellschaft, part III, chap. 6, pp. 650-78.

196

commissions and authority are not precisely delimited and are temporarily called into being for each case.

II. The principles of office hierarchy and of levels of graded authority mean a firmly ordered system of super- and subordination in which there is a supervision of the lower offices by the higher ones. Such a system offers the governed the possibility of appealing the decision of a lower office to its higher authority, in a definitely regulated manner. With the full development of the bureaucratic type, the office hierarchy is monocratically organized. The principle of hierarchical office authority is found in all bureaucratic structures: in state and ecclesiastical structures as well as in large party organizations and private enterprises. It does not matter for the character of bureaucracy whether its authority is called 'private' or 'public.'

When the principle of jurisdictional 'competency' is fully carried through, hierarchical subordination—at least in public office—does not mean that the 'higher' authority is simply authorized to take over the business of the 'lower.' Indeed, the opposite is the rule. Once established and having fulfilled its task, an office tends to continue in existence and be held by another incumbent.

III. The management of the modern office is based upon written documents ('the files'), which are preserved in their original or draught form. There is, therefore, a staff of subaltern officials and scribes of all sorts. The body of officials actively engaged in a 'public' office, along with the respective apparatus of material implements and the files, make up a 'bureau.' In private enterprise, 'the bureau' is often called 'the office.'

In principle, the modern organization of the civil service separates the bureau from the private domicile of the official, and, in general, bureaucracy segregates official activity as something distinct from the sphere of private life. Public monies and equipment are divorced from the private property of the official. This condition is everywhere the product of a long development. Nowadays, it is found in public as well as in private enterprises; in the latter, the principle extends even to the leading entrepreneur. In principle, the executive office is separated from the household, business from private correspondence, and business assets from private fortunes. The more consistently the modern type of business management has been carried through the more are these separations the case. The beginnings of this process are to be found as early as the Middle Ages.

It is the peculiarity of the modern entrepreneur that he conducts himself as the 'first official' of his enterprise, in the very same way in which the ruler of a specifically modern bureaucratic state spoke of himself as 'the first servant' of the state.[1] The idea that the bureau activities of the state are intrinsically different in character from the management of private economic offices is a continental European notion and, by way of contrast, is totally foreign to the American way.

IV. Office management, at least all specialized office management—and such management is distinctly modern—usually presupposes thorough and expert training. This increasingly holds for the modern executive and employee of private enterprises, in the same manner as it holds for the state official.

V. When the office is fully developed, official activity demands the full working capacity of the official, irrespective of the fact that his obligatory time in the bureau may be firmly delimited. In the normal case, this is only the product of a long development, in the public as well as in the private office. Formerly, in all cases, the normal state of affairs was reversed: official business was discharged as a secondary activity.

VI. The management of the office follows general rules, which are more or less stable, more or less exhaustive, and which can be learned. Knowledge of these rules represents a special technical learning which the officials possess. It involves jurisprudence, or administrative or business management.

The reduction of modern office management to rules is deeply embedded in its very nature. The theory of modern public administration, for instance, assumes that the authority to order certain matters by decree—which has been legally granted to public authorities—does not entitle the bureau to regulate the matter by commands given for each case, but only to regulate the matter abstractly. This stands in extreme contrast to the regulation of all relationships through individual privileges and bestowals of favor, which is absolutely dominant in patrimonialism, at least in so far as such relationships are not fixed by sacred tradition.

2: The Position of the Official

All this results in the following for the internal and external position of the official:

I. Office holding is a 'vocation.' This is shown, first, in the requirement of a firmly prescribed course of training, which demands the entire

capacity for work for a long period of time, and in the generally prescribed and special examinations which are prerequisites of employment.
Furthermore, the position of the official is in the nature of a duty. This
determines the internal structure of his relations, in the following manner: Legally and actually, office holding is not considered a source to be
exploited for rents or emoluments, as was normally the case during the
Middle Ages and frequently up to the threshold of recent times. Nor is
office holding considered a usual exchange of services for equivalents,
as is the case with free labor contracts. Entrance into an office, including
one in the private economy, is considered an acceptance of a specific obligation of faithful management in return for a secure existence. It is decisive for the specific nature of modern loyalty to an office that, in the
pure type, it does not establish a relationship to a *person,* like the vassal's
or disciple's faith in feudal or in patrimonial relations of authority. Modern loyalty is devoted to impersonal and functional purposes. Behind the
functional purposes, of course, 'ideas of culture-values' usually stand.
These are *ersatz* for the earthly or supra-mundane personal master:
ideas such as 'state,' 'church,' 'community,' 'party,' or 'enterprise' are
thought of as being realized in a community; they provide an ideological
halo for the master.

The political official—at least in the fully developed modern state—is
not considered the personal servant of a ruler. Today, the bishop, the
priest, and the preacher are in fact no longer, as in early Christian times,
holders of purely personal charisma. The supra-mundane and sacred
values which they offer are given to everybody who seems to be worthy
of them and who asks for them. In former times, such leaders acted
upon the personal command of their master; in principle, they were responsible only to him. Nowadays, in spite of the partial survival of the
old theory, such religious leaders are officials in the service of a functional purpose, which in the present-day 'church' has become routinized
and, in turn, ideologically hallowed.

II. The personal position of the official is patterned in the following
way:

1. Whether he is in a private office or a public bureau, the modern
official always strives and usually enjoys a distinct *social esteem* as compared with the governed. His social position is guaranteed by the pre-
scriptive rules of rank order and, for the political official, by special
definitions of the criminal code against 'insults of officials' and 'contempt' of state and church authorities.

The actual social position of the official is normally highest where, as in old civilized countries, the following conditions prevail: a strong demand for administration by trained experts; a strong and stable social differentiation, where the official predominantly derives from socially and economically privileged strata because of the social distribution of power; or where the costliness of the required training and status conventions are binding upon him. The possession of educational certificates—to be discussed elsewhere [2]—are usually linked with qualification for office. Naturally, such certificates or patents enhance the 'status element' in the social position of the official. For the rest this status factor in individual cases is explicitly and impassively acknowledged; for example, in the prescription that the acceptance or rejection of an aspirant to an official career depends upon the consent ('election') of the members of the official body. This is the case in the German army with the officer corps. Similar phenomena, which promote this guild-like closure of officialdom, are typically found in patrimonial and, particularly, in prebendal officialdoms of the past. The desire to resurrect such phenomena in changed forms is by no means infrequent among modern bureaucrats. For instance, they have played a role among the demands of the quite proletarian and expert officials (the *tretyj* element) during the Russian revolution.

Usually the social esteem of the officials as such is especially low where the demand for expert administration and the dominance of status conventions are weak. This is especially the case in the United States; it is often the case in new settlements by virtue of their wide fields for profit-making and the great instability of their social stratification.

2. The pure type of bureaucratic official is *appointed* by a superior authority. An official elected by the governed is not a purely bureaucratic figure. Of course, the formal existence of an election does not by itself mean that no appointment hides behind the election—in the state, especially, appointment by party chiefs. Whether or not this is the case does not depend upon legal statutes but upon the way in which the party mechanism functions. Once firmly organized, the parties can turn a formally free election into the mere acclamation of a candidate designated by the party chief. As a rule, however, a formally free election is turned into a fight, conducted according to definite rules, for votes in favor of one of two designated candidates.

In all circumstances, the designation of officials by means of an election among the governed modifies the strictness of hierarchical subordination. In principle, an official who is so elected has an autonomous position opposite the superordinate official. The elected official does not derive his position 'from above' but 'from below,' or at least not from a superior authority of the official hierarchy but from powerful party men ('bosses'), who also determine his further career. The career of the elected official is not, or at least not primarily, dependent upon his chief in the administration. The official who is not elected but appointed by a chief normally functions more exactly, from a technical point of view, because, all other circumstances being equal, it is more likely that purely functional points of consideration and qualities will determine his selection and career. As laymen, the governed can become acquainted with the extent to which a candidate is expertly qualified for office only in terms of experience, and hence only after his service. Moreover, in every sort of selection of officials by election, parties quite naturally give decisive weight not to expert considerations but to the services a follower renders to the party boss. This holds for all kinds of procurement of officials by elections, for the designation of formally free, elected officials by party bosses when they determine the slate of candidates, or the free appointment by a chief who has himself been elected. The contrast, however, is relative: substantially similar conditions hold where legitimate monarchs and their subordinates appoint officials, except that the influence of the followings are then less controllable.

Where the demand for administration by trained experts is considerable, and the party followings have to recognize an intellectually developed, educated, and freely moving 'public opinion,' the use of unqualified officials falls back upon the party in power at the next election. Naturally, this is more likely to happen when the officials are appointed by the chief. The demand for a trained administration now exists in the United States, but in the large cities, where immigrant votes are 'corraled,' there is, of course, no educated public opinion. Therefore, popular elections of the administrative chief and also of his subordinate officials usually endanger the expert qualification of the official as well as the precise functioning of the bureaucratic mechanism. It also weakens the dependence of the officials upon the hierarchy. This holds at least for the large administrative bodies that are difficult to supervise. The superior qualification and integrity of federal judges, appointed by the President, as over against elected judges in the United States is well known, although both types of officials have been selected primarily in terms of party considerations. The great changes in American metropolitan administrations demanded by reformers have proceeded essentially from elected mayors working with an apparatus of officials who were appointed by them. These reforms have thus come about in a 'Caesarist' fashion. Viewed technically, as an organized form of authority, the efficiency of 'Caesarism,' which often grows out of democracy, rests in general upon the position of the 'Caesar' as a free trustee of the masses (of the army or of the citizenry), who is unfettered by tradition. The 'Caesar' is thus the unrestrained master of a body of highly qualified military officers and officials whom he selects freely and personally without regard to tradition or to any other considerations. This 'rule of the personal genius,' however, stands in contradiction to the formally 'democratic' principle of a universally elected officialdom.

3. Normally, the position of the official is held for life, at least in public bureaucracies; and this is increasingly the case for all similar structures. As a factual rule, *tenure for life* is presupposed, even where the giving of notice or periodic reappointment occurs. In contrast to the worker in a private enterprise, the official normally holds tenure. Legal or actual life-tenure, however, is not recognized as the official's right to the possession of office, as was the case with many structures of authority in the past. Where legal guarantees against arbitrary dismissal or transfer are developed, they merely serve to guarantee a strictly objective discharge of specific office duties free from all personal considerations. In Germany, this is the case for all juridical and, increasingly, for all administrative officials.

Within the bureaucracy, therefore, the measure of 'independence,' legally guaranteed by tenure, is not always a source of increased status for the official whose position is thus secured. Indeed, often the reverse holds, especially in old cultures and communities that are highly differentiated. In such communities, the stricter the subordination under the arbitrary rule of the master, the more it guarantees the maintenance of the conventional seigneurial style of living for the official. Because of the very absence of these legal guarantees of tenure, the conventional esteem for the official may rise in the same way as, during the Middle Ages, the esteem of the nobility of office [3] rose at the expense of esteem for the freemen, and as the king's judge surpassed that of the people's judge. In Germany, the military officer or the administrative official can be removed from office at any time, or at least far more readily than the 'independent judge,' who never pays with loss of his office for even the grossest offense against the 'code of honor' or against social conventions of the salon. For this very reason, if other things are equal, in the eyes of the master stratum the judge is considered less qualified for social intercourse than are officers and administrative officials, whose greater dependence on the master is a greater guarantee of their conformity with status conventions. Of course, the average official strives for a civil-service law, which would materially secure his old age and provide increased guarantees against his arbitrary removal from office. This striving, however, has its limits. A very strong development of the 'right to the office' naturally makes it more difficult to staff them with regard to technical efficiency, for such a development decreases the career-opportunities of ambitious candidates for office. This makes for the fact that officials, on the whole, do not feel their dependency upon those at the top. This lack of a feeling of dependency, however, rests primarily upon the inclination to depend upon one's equals rather than upon the socially inferior and governed strata. The present conservative movement among the Badenia clergy, occasioned by the anxiety of a presumably threatening separation of church and state, has been expressly determined by the desire not to be turned 'from a master into a servant of the parish.' [4]

4. The official receives the regular *pecuniary* compensation of a normally fixed *salary* and the old age security provided by a pension. The salary is not measured like a wage in terms of work done, but according to 'status,' that is, according to the kind of function (the 'rank') and, in addition, possibly, according to the length of service. The relatively great security of the official's income, as well as the rewards of social esteem, make the office a sought-after position, especially in countries which no longer provide opportunities for colonial profits. In such countries, this situation permits relatively low salaries for officials.

5. The official is set for a *'career'* within the hierarchical order of the public service. He moves from the lower, less important, and lower paid to the higher positions. The average official naturally desires a mechanical fixing of the conditions of promotion: if not of the offices, at least of the salary levels. He wants these conditions fixed in terms of 'seniority,' or possibly according to grades achieved in a developed system of expert examinations. Here and there, such examinations actually form a character *indelebilis* of the official and have lifelong effects on his career. To this is joined the desire to qualify the right to office and the increasing tendency toward status group closure and economic security. All of this makes for a tendency to consider the offices as 'prebends' of those who are

qualified by educational certificates. The necessity of taking general personal and intellectual qualifications into consideration, irrespective of the often subaltern character of the educational certificate, has led to a condition in which the highest political offices, especially the positions of 'ministers,' are principally filled without reference to such certificates.

3: The Presuppositions and Causes of Bureaucracy

The social and economic presuppositions of the modern structure of the office are as follows:

The development of the *money economy,* in so far as a pecuniary compensation of the officials is concerned, is a presupposition of bureaucracy. Today it not only prevails but is predominant. This fact is of very great importance for the whole bearing of bureaucracy, yet by itself it is by no means decisive for the existence of bureaucracy.

Historical examples of rather distinctly developed and quantitatively large bureaucracies are: (a) Egypt, during the period of the new Empire which, however, contained strong patrimonial elements; (b) the later Roman Principate, and especially the Diocletian monarchy and the Byzantine polity which developed out of it and yet retained strong feudal and patrimonial elements; (c) the Roman Catholic Church, increasingly so since the end of the thirteenth century; (d) China, from the time of Shi Hwangti until the present, but with strong patrimonial and prebendal elements; (e) in ever purer forms, the modern European states and, increasingly, all public corporations since the time of princely absolutism; (f) the large modern capitalist enterprise, the more so as it becomes greater and more complicated.

To a very great extent, partly even predominantly, cases (a) to (d) have rested upon compensation of the officials in kind. Yet they have displayed many other traits and effects characteristic of bureaucracy. The historical model of all later bureaucracies—the new Empire of Egypt—is at the same time one of the most grandiose examples of an organized subsistence economy. Yet this coincidence of bureaucracy and subsistence economy is understandable in view of the quite unique conditions that existed in Egypt. And the reservations—and they are quite considerable—which one must make in classifying this Egyptian structure as a bureaucracy are conditioned by the subsistence economy. A certain measure of a developed money economy is the normal precondition for the unchanged and continued existence, if not for the establishment, of pure bureaucratic administrations.

According to historical experience, without a money economy the bureaucratic structure can hardly avoid undergoing substantial internal changes, or indeed, turning into another type of structure. The allocation of fixed income in kind, from the magazines of the lord or from his current intake, to the officials easily means a first step toward appropriation of the sources of taxation and their exploitation as private property. This kind of allocation has been the rule in Egypt and China for thousands of years and played an important part in the later Roman monarchy as well as elsewhere. The income in kind has protected the official against the often sharp fluctuations in the purchasing power of money. Whenever the lord's prerogatives have relaxed, the taxes in kind, as a rule, have been irregular. In this case, the official has direct recourse to the tributaries of his bailiwick, whether or not he is authorized. Close at hand is the idea of securing the official against such oscillations by mortgaging or transferring the levies and therewith the power to tax, or by leasing profitable lands of the lord to the official for his own use. Every central authority which is not strictly organized is tempted to take this course either voluntarily or because the officials compel it to do so. The official may satisfy himself with the use of these levies or loans up to the level of his salary claim and then hand over the surplus. This implies strong temptation and therefore yields results chiefly unsatisfactory to the lord. Another process involves fixing the official's salary: This often occurred in the early history of German officialdom; and it happened on the largest scale in all Eastern Satrap administrations: the official hands over a stipulated amount and retains the surplus.

In such cases the official is economically in a position rather similar to that of the entrepreneurial tax-farmer. Indeed, office-farming including even the leasing of offices to the highest bidder is regularly found. On the soil of a private economy, the transformation of the statutes of villenage into tenancy relations is one of the most important among numerous examples. By tenancy arrangements the lord can transfer the trouble of changing his income-in-kind into money-income to the office tenant or to the official who is to be given a fixed sum. This was plainly the case with some Oriental regents in Antiquity. And above all, the farming out of public collection of taxes in lieu of the lord's own management of taxgathering served this purpose. From this procedure there develops the possibility for the lord to progress in the ordering of his finances into a systematic budget. This is a very important advance, for it means that a fixed estimate of the income, and correspondingly of the expenses, can take the place of a hand-to-mouth living from incalculable incomes in kind, a condition typical of all the early states of public households. On the other hand, in systematizing his budget in this way, the lord renounces the control and full exploitation of his capacity to tax for his own use. According to the measure of freedom left to the official, to the office, or to the tax-farmer, the lasting capacity to pay taxes is endangered by inconsiderate exploitation. For, unlike the political overlord, the capitalist is not in the same way permanently interested in the subject's ability to pay.

The lord seeks to safeguard himself against this loss of control by regulations. The mode of tax-farming or the transfer of taxes can thus vary widely, according to the distribution of power between the lord and the tenant. Either the tenant's interest in the free exploitation of capacity to pay taxes or the lord's interest in the permanence of this capacity prevails. The nature of the tax-farming system rests essentially upon the joint or the opposing influence of these motives: the elimination of oscillations in the yields, the possibility of a budget, the safeguarding of the subjects' capacity to pay by protecting them against uneconomical exploitation, and a state control of the tax-farmer's yields for the sake of appropriating the maximum possible. In the Ptolemaic empire, as in Hellas and in Rome, the tax-farmer was still a private capitalist. The raising of taxes, however, was bureaucratically executed and controlled by the Ptolemaic state. The tenant's profit consisted in only a share of the respective surplus over and above the tax-farmer's fee, which was, in fact, only a guarantee. The tax-farmer's risk consisted in the possibility of yields that were lower than this sum.

The purely economic conception of the office as a source of the official's private income can also lead to the direct purchase of offices. This occurs when the lord finds himself in a position in which he requires not only a current income but money capital—for instance, for warfare or for debt payments. The purchase of office as a regular institution has existed in modern states, in the church state as well as in that of France and England; it has existed in the cases of sinecures as well as of very serious offices; and, in the case of officers' commissions, it lagged over until the early nineteenth century. In individual cases, the economic meaning of such a purchase of office can be altered so that the purchasing sum is partly or wholly in the nature of bail deposited for faithful service, but this has not been the rule.

Every sort of assignment of usufructs, tributes and services which are due to the lord himself or to the official for personal exploitation, always means a surrender of the pure type of bureaucratic organization. The official in such positions has a personal right to the possession of his office. This is the case to a still higher degree when official duty and compensation are interrelated in such a way that the official does not transfer to the lord any yields gained from the objects left to him, but handles these objects for his private ends and in turn renders to the lord services of a personal or a military, political, or ecclesiastical character.

We wish to speak of *'prebends'* and of a 'prebendal' organization of office, wherever the lord assigns to the official rent payments for life, payments which are somehow fixed to objects or which are essentially *economic* usufruct from lands or other sources. They must be compensations for the fulfilment of actual or fictitious office duties; they are goods permanently set aside for the economic assurance of the office.

The transition from such prebendal organization of office to salaried officialdom is quite fluid. Very often the economic endowment of priesthoods has been 'prebendal,' as in Antiquity and the Middle Ages, and even up to the modern period. But in almost all periods the same form has been found in other areas. In Chinese sacerdotal law, the prebendal character of all offices forced the mourning official to resign his office. For during the ritual mourning period for the father or other household authorities abstention from the enjoyment of possessions was prescribed. Originally this prescription was aimed at avoiding the ill-will of the deceased master of the house, for the house belonged to this master and the office was considered purely as a prebend, a source for rent.

When not only economic rights but also lordly prerogatives are leased for personal execution with the stipulation of *personal* services to the lord, a further step away from salaried bureaucracy is taken. These leased prerogatives vary; for instance, with the political official, they may be in the nature of landlordism or in the nature of office authority. In both instances, and certainly in the latter, the specific nature of bureaucratic organization is completely destroyed and we enter the organizational realm of *feudal* dominion. All kinds of assignments of services and usufructs in kind as endowments for officials tend to loosen the bureaucratic mechanism, and especially to weaken hierarchic subordination. This subordination is most strictly developed in the discipline of modern officialdom. A precision similar to the precision of the con tractually employed official of the modern Occident can only be attained —at least under very energetic leadership—where the subjection of the officials to the lord is personally absolute, where slaves, or employees treated like slaves, are used for administration.

The Egyptian officials were slaves of the Pharaoh, if not legally, at least in fact. The Roman latifundia owners liked to commission slaves with the direct management of money matters, because of the possibility of subjecting them to torture. In China, similar results have been sought by the prodigial use of the bamboo as a disciplinary instrument. The chances, however, for such direct means of coercion to function with *steadiness* are extremely unfavorable. According to experience, the relative optimum for the success and maintenance of a strict mechanization of the bureaucratic apparatus is offered by a secured money salary connected with the opportunity of a career that is not dependent upon mere accident and arbitrariness. Strict discipline and control, which at the same time has consideration for the official's sense of honor, and the development of prestige sentiments of the status group, as well as the possibility of public criticism, work in the direction of strict mechanization. With all this, the bureaucratic apparatus functions more assuredly than does any legal enslavement of functionaries. A strong status sentiment among officials not only agrees with the official's readiness to subordinate himself to the chief without any will of his own, but—just as is the case with the officer—status sentiments are the consequence of such subordination, for internally they balance the official's self-feeling. The purely impersonal character of office work, with its principled separation of the private sphere of the official from that of the office, facilitates the official's integration into the given functional conditions of a fixed mechanism based upon discipline.

Even though the full development of a money economy is not an indispensable precondition for bureaucratization, bureaucracy as a permanent structure is knit to the one presupposition of a constant income for maintaining it. Where such an income cannot be derived from private profits, as is the case with the bureaucratic organization of large modern enterprises, or from fixed land rents, as with the manor, a stable system of *taxation* is the precondition for the permanent existence of bureaucratic administration. For well-known and general reasons, only a fully developed money economy offers a secure basis for such a taxation system. The degree of administrative bureaucratization in urban communities with fully developed money economies has not infrequently been relatively greater in the contemporary far larger states of plains. Yet as soon as these plain states have been able to develop orderly systems of tribute, bureaucracy has developed more comprehensively than in city states. Whenever the size of the city states has remained confined to moderate limits, the tendency for a plutocratic and collegial administration by notables has corresponded most adequately to their structure.

4: The Quantitative Development of Administrative Tasks

The proper soil for the bureaucratization of an administration has always been the specific developments of administrative tasks. We shall first discuss the quantitative extension of such tasks. In the field of politics, the great state and the mass party are the classic soil for bureaucratization.

This does not mean that every historically known and genuine formation of great states has brought about a bureaucratic administration. The permanence of a once-existing great state, or the homogeneity of a culture borne by such a state, has not always been attached to a bureaucratic structure of state. However, both of these features have held to a great extent, for instance, in the Chinese empire. The numerous great Negro empires, and similar formations, have had only an ephemerical existence primarily because they have lacked an apparatus of officials. And the unity of the Carolingian empire disintegrated when its organization of officials disintegrated. This organization, however, was predominantly patrimonial rather than bureaucratic in nature. From a purely temporal view, however, the empire of the Caliphs and its predecessors on Asiatic soil have lasted for considerable periods of time, and their organization of office was essentially patrimonial and prebendal. Also, the Holy Roman Empire lasted for a long time in spite of the almost complete absence of bureaucracy. All these realms have represented a cultural unity of at least approximately the same strength as is usually created by bureaucratic polities.

The ancient Roman Empire disintegrated internally in spite of increasing bureaucratization and even during its very execution. This was because of the way the tax burdens were distributed by the bureaucratic state, which favored the subsistence economy. Viewed with regard to the intensity of their purely *political* unities, the temporal existences of the empires of the Caliphs, Carolingian and other medieval emperors were essentially unstable, nominal, and cohesive conglomerates. On the whole, the capacity for political action steadily diminished, and the relatively great unity of *culture* flowed from ecclesiastic structures that were in part strictly unified and, in the Occidental Middle Ages, increasingly bureaucratic in character. The unity of their cultures resulted partly from the far-going homogeneity of their social structures, which in turn was the aftermath and transformation of their former political unity. Both are phenomena of the traditional stereotyping of culture, which favors an unstable equilibrium. Both of these factors proved so strong a foundation that even grandiose attempts at expansion, such as the Crusades, could be undertaken in spite of the lack of intensive political unity; they were, one might say, performed as 'private undertakings.' The failure of the Crusades and their often irrational political course, however, is associated with the absence of a unified and intensive state power to back them up. And there is no doubt that the nuclei of intensive 'modern' states in the Middle Ages developed concomitantly with bureaucratic structures. Furthermore, in the end these quite bureaucratic political structures undoubtedly shattered the social conglomerates, which rested essentially upon unstable equilibriums.

The disintegration of the Roman Empire was partly conditioned by the very bureaucratization of its army and official apparatus. This bureaucratization could only be realized by carrying through at the same time a method of taxation which by its distribution of burdens was bound to lead to relative increase in the importance of a subsistence economy. Individual factors of this sort always enter the picture. Also the 'intensity' of the external and the internal state activities play their part. Quite apart from the relation between the state influence upon culture and the degree of bureaucratization, it may be said that 'normally'—though not without exception—the vigor to expand is directly related to the degree of bureaucratization. For two of the most expansive polities, the Roman Empire and the British world empire, during their most expansive periods, rested upon bureaucratic foundations only to a small extent. The Norman state in England carried through a strict organization on the basis of a feudal hierarchy. To a large extent, it received its unity and its push through the bureaucratization of the royal exchequer, which, in comparison to other political structures of the feudal period, was extremely strict. Later on, the English state did not share in the continental development towards bureaucratization, but remained an administration of notables. Just as in the republican administration of Rome, this English rule by notables was a result of the relative absence of a continental character, as well as of absolutely unique preconditions, which at the present time are disappearing. The dispensability of the large standing armies, which a continental state with equally expansive tendencies requires for its land frontiers, is among these special preconditions. In Rome, bureaucratization advanced with the transition from a coastal to a continental ring of frontiers. For the rest, in the domination structure of Rome, the strictly military character of the magistrate authorities—in the Roman manner unknown to any other people—made up for the lack of a bureaucratic apparatus with its technical efficiency,[5] its precision and unity of administrative functions, especially outside the city limits. The continuity of administration was safeguarded by the unique position of the Senate. In Rome, as in England, one presupposition for this dispensability of bureaucracy which should not be forgotten was that the state authorities increasingly 'minimized' the scope of their functions at home. They restricted their functions to what was absolutely demanded for direct 'reasons of state.'

At the beginning of the modern period, all the prerogatives of the continental states accumulated in the hands of those princes who most relentlessly took the course of administrative bureaucratization. It is obvious that technically the great modern state is absolutely dependent upon a bureaucratic basis. The larger the state, and the more it is or the more it becomes a great power state, the more unconditionally is this the case.

The United States still bears the character of a polity which, at least in the technical sense, is not fully bureaucratized. But the greater the zones of friction with the outside and the more urgent the needs for administrative unity at home become, the more this character is inevitably and gradually giving way formally to the bureaucratic structure. Moreover, the partly unbureaucratic form of the state structure of the United States is materially balanced by the more strictly bureaucratic structures of those formations which, in truth, dominate politically, namely, the parties under the leadership of professionals or experts in organization and election tactics. The increasingly bureaucratic organization of all genuine mass parties offers the most striking example of the role of sheer quantity as a leverage for the bureaucratization of a social structure. In Germany, above all, the Social Democratic party, and abroad both of the 'historical' American parties are bureaucratic in the greatest possible degree.

5: Qualitative Changes of Administrative Tasks

Bureaucratization is occasioned more by intensive and qualitative enlargement and internal deployment of the scope of administrative tasks than by their extensive and quantitative increase. But the direction bureaucratization takes and the reasons that occasion it vary widely.

In Egypt, the oldest country of bureaucratic state administration, the public and collective regulation of waterways for the whole country and from the top could not be avoided because of technical economic factors. This regulation created the mechanism of scribes and officials. Once established, this mechanism, even in early times, found its second realm of business in the extraordinary construction activities which were organized militarily. As mentioned before, the bureaucratic tendency has chiefly been influenced by needs arising from the creation of standing armies as determined by power politics and by the development of public finance connected with the military establishment. In the modern state, the increasing demands for administration rest on the increasing complexity of civilization and push towards bureaucratization.

Very considerable expansions, especially overseas, have, of course, been managed by states ruled by notables (Rome, England, Venice), as will become evident in the appropriate context. Yet the 'intensity' of the administration, that is, the transfer of as many tasks as possible to the organization of the state proper for continuous management and discharge, has been only slightly developed among the great states ruled by notables, especially Rome and England, if we compare them with bureaucratic polities.

Both in notable and bureaucratic administrations the *structure* of state power has influenced culture very strongly. But it has done so relatively slightly in the form of management and control by the state. This holds from justice down to education. The growing demands on culture, in turn, are determined, though to a varying extent, by the growing wealth of the most influential strata in the state. To this extent increasing bureaucratization is a function of the increasing possession of goods used for consumption, and of an increasingly sophisticated technique of fashioning external life—a technique which corresponds to the opportunities provided by such wealth. This reacts upon the standard of living and makes for an increasing subjective indispensability of organized, collective, inter-local, and thus bureaucratic, provision for the most varied wants, which previously were either unknown, or were satisfied locally or by a private economy.

Among purely political factors, the increasing demand of a society, accustomed to absolute pacification, for order and protection ('police') in all fields exerts an especially persevering influence in the direction of bureaucratization. A steady road leads from modifications of the blood feud, sacerdotally, or by means of arbitration, to the present position of the policeman as the 'representative of God on earth.' The former means placed the guarantees for the individual's rights and security squarely upon the members of his sib, who are obligated to assist him with oath and vengeance. Among other factors, primarily the manifold tasks of the so-called 'policy of social welfare' operate in the direction of bureaucratization, for these tasks are, in part, saddled upon the state by interest groups and, in part, the state usurps them, either for reasons of power policy or for ideological motives. Of course, these tasks are to a large extent economically determined.

Among essentially technical factors, the specifically modern means of communication enter the picture as pacemakers of bureaucratization. Public land and water-ways, railroads, the telegraph, et cetera—they must, in part, necessarily be administered in a public and collective way; in part, such administration is technically expedient. In this respect, the contemporary means of communication frequently play a role similar to that of the canals of Mesopotamia and the regulation of the Nile in the ancient Orient. The degree to which the means of communication have been developed is a condition of decisive importance for the possibility of bureaucratic administration, although it is not the only decisive condition. Certainly in Egypt, bureaucratic centralization, on the basis of an almost pure subsistence economy, could never have reached the actual degree which it did without the natural trade route of the Nile. In order to promote bureaucratic centralization in modern Persia, the telegraph officials were officially commissioned with reporting all occurrences in the provinces to the Shah, over the heads of the local authorities. In addition, everyone received the right to remonstrate directly by telegraph. The modern Occidental state can be administered the way it actually is only because the state controls the telegraph network and has the mails and railroads at its disposal.

Railroads, in turn, are intimately connected with the development of an inter-local traffic of mass goods. This traffic is among the causal factors in the formation of the modern state. As we have already seen, this does not hold unconditionally for the past.

6: TECHNICAL ADVANTAGES OF BUREAUCRATIC ORGANIZATION

The decisive reason for the advance of bureaucratic organization has always been its purely technical superiority over any other form of organization. The fully developed bureaucratic mechanism compares with other organizations exactly as does the machine with the non-mechanical modes of production.

Precision, speed, unambiguity, knowledge of the files, continuity, discretion, unity, strict subordination, reduction of friction and of material and personal costs—these are raised to the optimum point in the strictly bureaucratic administration, and especially in its monocratic form. As compared with all collegiate, honorific, and avocational forms of administration, trained bureaucracy is superior on all these points. And as far as complicated tasks are concerned, paid bureaucratic work is not only more precise but, in the last analysis, it is often cheaper than even formally unremunerated honorific service.

Honorific arrangements make administrative work an avocation and, for this reason alone, honorific service normally functions more slowly; being less bound to schemata and being more formless. Hence it is less precise and less unified than bureaucratic work because it is less dependent upon superiors and because the establishment and exploitation of the apparatus of subordinate officials and filing services are almost unavoidably less economical. Honorific service is less continuous than bureaucratic and frequently quite expensive. This is especially the case if one thinks not only of the money costs to the public treasury—costs which bureaucratic administration, in comparison with administration by notables, usually substantially increases—but also of the frequent economic losses of the governed caused by delays and lack of precision. The possibility of administration by notables normally and permanently exists only where official management can be satisfactorily discharged as an avocation. With the qualitative increase of tasks the administration has to face, administration by notables reaches its limits—today, even in England. Work organized by collegiate bodies causes friction and delay and requires compromises between colliding interests and views. The administration, therefore, runs less precisely and is more independent of superiors; hence, it is less unified and slower. All advances of the Prussian administrative organization have been and will in the future be advances of the bureaucratic, and especially of the monocratic, principle.

Today, it is primarily the capitalist market economy which demands that the official business of the administration be discharged precisely, unambiguously, continuously, and with as much speed as possible. Normally, the very large, modern capitalist enterprises are themselves unequalled models of strict bureaucratic organization. Business management throughout rests on increasing precision, steadiness, and, above all, the speed of operations. This, in turn, is determined by the peculiar nature of the modern means of communication, including, among other things, the news service of the press. The extraordinary increase in the speed by which public announcements, as well as economic and political facts, are transmitted exerts a steady and sharp pressure in the direction of speeding up the tempo of administrative reaction towards various situations. The optimum of such reaction time is normally attained only by a strictly bureaucratic organization.*

Bureaucratization offers above all the optimum possibility for carrying through the principle of specializing administrative functions according to purely objective considerations. Individual performances are allocated to functionaries who have specialized training and who by constant practice learn more and more. The 'objective' discharge of business primarily means a discharge of business according to *calculable rules* and 'without regard for persons.'

'Without regard for persons' is also the watchword of the 'market' and, in general, of all pursuits of naked economic interests. A consistent execution of bureaucratic domination means the leveling of status 'honor.' Hence, if the principle of the free-market is not at the same time restricted, it means the universal domination of the 'class situation.' That this consequence of bureaucratic domination has not set in everywhere, parallel to the extent of bureaucratization, is due to the differences among possible principles by which polities may meet their demands.

The second element mentioned, 'calculable rules,' also is of paramount importance for modern bureaucracy. The peculiarity of modern culture, and specifically of its technical and economic basis, demands this very 'calculability' of results. When fully developed, bureaucracy also stands, in a specific sense, under the principle of *sine ira ac studio*. Its specific

---

* Here we cannot discuss in detail how the bureaucratic apparatus may, and actually does, produce definite obstacles to the discharge of business in a manner suitable for the single case.

nature, which is welcomed by capitalism, develops the more perfectly the more the bureaucracy is 'dehumanized,' the more completely it succeeds in eliminating from official business love, hatred, and all purely personal, irrational, and emotional elements which escape calculation. This is the specific nature of bureaucracy and it is appraised as its special virtue.

The more complicated and specialized modern culture becomes, the more its external supporting apparatus demands the personally detached and strictly 'objective' *expert,* in lieu of the master of older social structures, who was moved by personal sympathy and favor, by grace and gratitude. Bureaucracy offers the attitudes demanded by the external apparatus of modern culture in the most favorable combination. As a rule, only bureaucracy has established the foundation for the administration of a rational law conceptually systematized on the basis of such enactments as the latter Roman imperial period first created with a high degree of technical perfection. During the Middle Ages, this law was received along with the bureaucratization of legal administration, that is to say, with the displacement of the old trial procedure which was bound to tradition or to irrational presuppositions, by the rationally trained and specialized expert.

7: BUREAUCRACY AND LAW

The 'rational' interpretation of law on the basis of strictly formal conceptions stands opposite the kind of adjudication that is primarily bound to sacred traditions. The single case that cannot be unambiguously decided by tradition is either settled by concrete 'revelation' (oracle, prophetic dicta, or ordeal—that is, by 'charismatic' justice) or—and only these cases interest us here—by informal judgments rendered in terms of concrete ethical or other practical valuations. This is 'Kadi-justice,' as R. Schmidt has fittingly called it. Or, formal judgments are rendered, though not by subsumption under rational concepts, but by drawing on 'analogies' and by depending upon and interpreting concrete 'precedents.' This is 'empirical justice.'

Kadi-justice knows no reasoned judgment whatever. Nor does empirical justice of the pure type give any reasons which in our sense could be called rational. The concrete valuational character of Kadi-justice can advance to a prophetic break with all tradition. Empirical justice, on the other hand, can be sublimated and rationalized into a 'technology.' All non-bureaucratic forms of domination display a peculiar coexistence: on the one hand, there is a sphere of strict traditionalism, and, on the other, a sphere of free arbitrariness and lordly grace. Therefore, combinations and transitional forms between these two principles are very frequent; they will be discussed in another context.

Even today in England, as Mendelssohn has demonstrated, a broad substratum of justice is actually Kadi-justice to an extent that is hardly conceivable on the Continent. The justice of German juries which preclude a statement of the reasons for their verdict often functions in practice in the same way as this English justice. In general, one has to beware of believing that 'democratic' principles of justice are identical with 'rational' adjudication (in the sense of formal rationality). Indeed, the contrary holds, as will be shown in another context. The English and American adjudication of the highest courts is still to a great extent empirical; and especially is it adjudication by precedents. In England, the reason for the failure of all efforts at a rational codification of law, as well as the failure to borrow Roman law, was due to the successful resistance against such rationalization offered by the great and centrally organized lawyers' guilds. These guilds formed a monopolistic stratum of notables from whose midst the judges of the high courts of the realm were recruited. They retained in their hands juristic training as an empirical and highly developed technology, and they successfully fought all moves towards rational law that threatened their social and material position. Such moves came especially from the ecclesiastical courts and, for a time, also from the universities.

The fight of the common law advocates against the Roman and ecclesiastical law and the power of the church in general was to a considerable degree economically caused by the lawyer's interest in fees; this is distinctly evidenced by the way in which the king intervened in this struggle. But the power position of the lawyers, who emerged victoriously from this struggle, was conditioned by political centralization. In Germany, primarily for political reasons, a socially powerful estate of notables was lacking. There was no estate which, like the English lawyers, could have been the carriers of a national administration of law, which could have raised national law to the level of a technology with regulated apprenticeship, and which could have offered resistance to the intrusion of the technically superior training of jurists in Roman law.

That fact that Roman law was substantively better adjusted to the needs of emerging capitalism did not decide its victory on the Continent.

All legal institutions specific for modern capitalism are alien to Roman law and are medieval in origin. What was decisive was the rational form of Roman law and, above all, the technical necessity to place the trial procedure in the hands of rationally trained experts, which meant men trained in the universities and learned in Roman law. This training was necessary because the increasing complexity of practical legal cases and the increasingly rationalized economy demanded a rational procedure of evidence rather than the ascertainment of true facts by concrete revelation or sacerdotal guarantee, which, of course, are the ubiquitous and primeval means of proof. This legal situation was also determined to a large extent by structural changes in the economy. This factor, however, was efficacious everywhere, including England, where the royal power introduced the rational procedure of evidence for the sake of the merchants. The predominant reasons for the differences, which still exist, in the development of substantive law in England and Germany do not rest upon this economic factor. As is already obvious, these differences have sprung from the lawfully autonomous development of the respective structures of domination.

In England centralized justice and notable rule have been associated; in Germany, at the same time, there is bureaucratization and an absence of political centralization. England, which in modern times was the first and most highly developed capitalist country, thereby retained a less rational and less bureaucratic judicature. Capitalism in England, however, could quite easily come to terms with this, especially because the nature of the court constitution and of the trial procedure up to the modern period amounted in effect to a far-going denial of justice to the economically weak groups. This fact exerted a profound influence upon the distribution of landholdings in England by favoring the accumulation and immobilization of landed wealth. The length and expense of real estate transfers, determined by the economic interests of the lawyers, also worked in the same direction.

During the time of the Republic, Roman law represented a unique mixture of rational and empirical elements, and even of elements of Kadi-justice. The appointment of a jury as such, and the *praetor's actiones in factum,* which at first undoubtedly occurred 'from one given case to another,' contained an element of Kadi-justice. The bailing system of Roman justice and all that grew out of it, including even a part of the classic jurists' practice of responses, bore an 'empirical' character. The decisive turn of juridical thought toward rational thinking was first prepared by the technical nature of the instruction for trial procedure at the hands of the praetorian edict's formula, which were geared to legal conceptions. Today, under the dominance of the principle of substantiation, the presentation of facts is decisive, no matter from what legal point of view they may make the complaint seem justified. A similar compulsion to bring out the scope of the concepts unambiguously and formally is now lacking; but such a compulsion was produced by the technical culture of Roman law at its very height. Technical factors of trial procedure thus played their part in the development of rational law, factors which resulted only indirectly from the structure of the state. The rationalization of Roman law into a closed system of concepts to be scientifically handled was brought to perfection only during the period when the polity itself underwent bureaucratization. This rational and systematic quality sets off Roman law sharply from all law produced by the Orient or by Hellenic Greece.

The rabbinic responses of the *Talmud* is a typical example of empirical justice that is not rational but 'rationalist,' and at the same time strictly *fettered* by tradition. Every prophetic verdict is in the end pure Kadi-justice, *unfettered* by tradition, and follows the schema: 'It is written . . . but I say unto you.' The more strongly the religious nature of the Kadi's (or a similar judge's) position is emphasized, the more freely the judgment of the single case prevails and the less it is encumbered by rules within that sphere of its operation which is not fettered by sacred tradition. For a generation after the occupation of Tunisia by the French, for instance, a very tangible handicap for capitalism remained in that the ecclesiastic court (the *Chara*) decided over land holdings by 'free discretion,' as the Europeans put it. We shall become acquainted with the sociological foundation of these older types of justice when we discuss the structures of domination in another context.

It is perfectly true that 'matter-of-factness' and 'expertness' are not necessarily identical with the rule of general and abstract norms. Indeed, this does not even hold in the case of the modern administration of justice. In principle, the idea of 'a law without gaps' is, of course, vigorously disputed. The conception of the modern judge as an automaton into which the files and the costs are thrown in order that it may spill forth the verdict at the bottom along with the reasons, read mechanically from codified paragraphs—this conception is angrily rejected, perhaps because a certain approximation to this type is implied by a consistent bureaucratization of justice. In the field of court procedure there are areas in which the bureaucratic judge is directly held to 'individualizing' procedures by the legislator.

For the field of administrative activity proper, that is, for all state activities that fall outside the field of law creation and court procedure, one is accustomed to claiming the freedom and paramountcy of individual circumstances. General norms are held to play primarily a negative role as barriers to the official's positive and 'creative' activity, which should never be regulated. The bearing of this thesis may be disregarded here. Yet the point that this 'freely' creative administration (and possibly judicature) does not constitute a realm of *free,* arbitrary action, of mercy, and of *personally* motivated favor and valuation, as we shall find to be the case among pre-bureaucratic forms, is a very decisive point. The rule and the rational estimation of 'objective' purposes, as well as devotion to them, always exist as a norm of conduct. In the field of executive administration, especially where the 'creative' arbitrariness of the official is most strongly built up, the specifically modern and strictly 'objective' idea of 'reasons of state' is upheld as the supreme and ultimate guiding star of the official's behavior.

Of course, and above all, the sure instincts of the bureaucracy for the conditions of maintaining its power in its own state (and through it, in opposition to other states) are inseparably fused with the canonization of the abstract and 'objective' idea of 'reasons of state.' In the last analysis, the power interests of the bureaucracy only give a concretely exploitable content to this by no means unambiguous ideal; and, in dubious cases, power interests tip the balance. We cannot discuss this further here. The only decisive point for us is that in principle a system of rationally debatable 'reasons' stands behind every act of bureaucratic administration, that is, either subsumption under norms or a weighing of ends and means.

The position of all 'democratic' currents, in the sense of currents that would minimize 'authority,' is necessarily ambiguous. 'Equality before the law' and the demand for legal guarantees against arbitrariness demand a formal and rational 'objectivity' of administration, as opposed to the personally free discretion flowing from the 'grace' of the old patrimonial domination. If, however, an 'ethos'—not to speak of instincts— takes hold of the masses on some individual question, it postulates *substantive* justice oriented toward some concrete instance and person; and such an 'ethos' will unavoidably collide with the formalism and the rule-bound and cool 'matter-of-factness' of bureaucratic administration. For this reason, the ethos must emotionally reject what reason demands.

The propertyless masses especially are not served by a formal 'equality before the law' and a 'calculable' adjudication and administration, as demanded by 'bourgeois' interests. Naturally, in their eyes justice and administration should serve to compensate for their economic and social life-opportunities in the face of the propertied classes. Justice and administration can fulfil this function only if they assume an informal character to a far-reaching extent. It must be informal because it is substantively 'ethical' ('Kadi-justice'). Every sort of 'popular justice'—which usually does not ask for reasons and norms—as well as every sort of intensive influence on the administration by so-called public opinion, crosses the rational course of justice and administration just as strongly, and under certain conditions far more so, as the 'star chamber' proceedings of an 'absolute' ruler has been able to do. In this connection, that is, under the conditions of mass democracy, public opinion is communal conduct born of irrational 'sentiments.' Normally it is staged or directed by party leaders and the press.

8: The Concentration of the Means of Administration

The bureaucratic structure goes hand in hand with the concentration of the material means of management in the hands of the master. This concentration occurs, for instance, in a well-known and typical fashion, in the development of big capitalist enterprises, which find their essential characteristics in this process. A corresponding process occurs in public organizations.

The bureaucratically led army of the Pharaohs, the army during the later period of the Roman republic and the principate, and, above all, the army of the modern military state are characterized by the fact that their equipment and provisions are supplied from the magazines of the war lord. This is in contrast to the folk armies of agricultural tribes, the armed citizenry of ancient cities, the militias of early medieval cities, and all feudal armies; for these, the self-equipment and the self-provisioning of those obliged to fight was normal.

War in our time is a war of machines. And this makes magazines technically necessary, just as the dominance of the machine in industry promotes the concentration of the means of production and management. In the main, however, the bureaucratic armies of the past, equipped and provisioned by the lord, have risen when social and economic development has absolutely or relatively diminished the stratum of citizens who were economically able to equip themselves, so that their number was no longer sufficient for putting the required armies in the field. They were reduced at least relatively, that is, in relation to the range of power claimed for the polity. Only the bureaucratic army structure allowed for the development of the professional standing armies which are necessary for the constant pacification of large states of the plains, as well as for warfare against far-distant enemies, especially enemies overseas. Specifically, military discipline and technical training can be normally and fully developed, at least to its modern high level, only in the bureaucratic army.

Historically, the bureaucratization of the army has everywhere been realized along with the transfer of army service from the propertied to the propertyless. Until this transfer occurs, military service is an honorific privilege of propertied men. Such a transfer was made to the native-born unpropertied, for instance, in the armies of the generals of the late Roman republic and the empire, as well as in modern armies up to the nineteenth century. The burden of service has also been transferred to strangers, as in the mercenary armies of all ages. This process typically goes hand in hand with the general increase in material and intellectual culture. The following reason has also played its part everywhere: the increasing density of population, and therewith the intensity and strain of economic work, makes for an increasing 'indispensability' of the acquisitive strata [6] for purposes of war. Leaving aside periods of strong ideological fervor, the propertied strata of sophisticated and especially of urban culture as a rule are little fitted and also little inclined to do the coarse war work of the common soldier. Other circumstances being equal, the propertied strata of the open country are at least usually better qualified and more strongly inclined to become professional officers. This difference between the urban and the rural propertied is balanced only where the increasing possibility of mechanized warfare requires the leaders to qualify as 'technicians.'

The bureaucratization of organized warfare may be carried through in the form of private capitalist enterprise, just like any other business. Indeed, the procurement of armies and their administration by private capitalists has been the rule in mercenary armies, especially those of the Occident up to the turn of the eighteenth century. During the Thirty Years' War, in Brandenburg the soldier was still the predominant owner of the material implements of his business. He owned his weapons, horses, and dress, although the state, in the role, as it were, of the merchant of the 'putting-out system,' did supply him to some extent. Later on, in the standing army of Prussia, the chief of the company owned the material means of warfare, and only since the peace of Tilsit has the concentration of the means of warfare in the hands of the state definitely come about. Only with this concentration was the introduction of uniforms generally carried through. Before then, the introduction of uniforms had been left to a great extent to the arbitrary discretion of the regimental officer, with the exception of individual categories of troops to whom the king had 'bestowed' certain uniforms, first, in 1620, to the royal bodyguard, then, under Frederick II, repeatedly.

Such terms as 'regiment' and 'battalion' usually had quite different meanings in the eighteenth century from the meanings they have today. Only the battalion was a tactical unit (today both are); the 'regiment' was then a managerial unit of an economic organization established by the colonel's position as an 'entrepreneur.' 'Official' maritime ventures (like the Genoese *maonae*) and army procurement belong to private capitalism's first giant enterprises of far-going bureaucratic character. In this respect, the 'nationalization' of these enterprises by the state has its modern parallel in the nationalization of the railroads, which have been controlled by the state from their beginnings.

In the same way as with army organizations, the bureaucratization of administration goes hand in hand with the concentration of the means of organization in other spheres. The old administration by satraps and regents, as well as administration by farmers of office, purchasers of office, and, most of all, administration by feudal vassals, decentralize the material means of administration. The local demand of the province and the cost of the army and of subaltern officials are regularly paid for in advance from local income, and only the surplus reaches the central treasure. The enfeoffed official administers entirely by payment out of his own pocket. The bureaucratic state, however, puts its whole administrative expense on the budget and equips the lower authorities with the current means of expenditure, the use of which the state regulates and controls. This has the same meaning for the 'economics' of the administration as for the large centralized capitalist enterprise.

In the field of scientific research and instruction, the bureaucratization of the always existing research institutes of the universities is a function of the increasing demand for material means of management. Liebig's laboratory at Giessen University was the first example of big enterprise in this field. Through the concentration of such means in the hands of the privileged head of the institute, the mass of researchers and docents are separated from their 'means of production,' in the same way as capitalist enterprise has separated the workers from theirs.

In spite of its indubitable technical superiority, bureaucracy has everywhere been a relatively late development. A number of obstacles have contributed to this, and only under certain social and political conditions have they definitely receded into the background.

9: THE LEVELING OF SOCIAL DIFFERENCES

Bureaucratic organization has usually come into power on the basis of a leveling of economic and social differences. This leveling has been at least relative, and has concerned the significance of social and economic differences for the assumption of administrative functions.

Bureaucracy inevitably accompanies modern *mass democracy* in contrast to the democratic self-government of small homogeneous units. This results from the characteristic principle of bureaucracy: the abstract regularity of the execution of authority, which is a result of the demand for 'equality before the law' in the personal and functional sense—hence, of the horror of 'privilege,' and the principled rejection of doing business 'from case to case.' Such regularity also follows from the social preconditions of the origin of bureaucracies. The non-bureaucratic administration of any large social structure rests in some way upon the fact that existing social, material, or honorific preferences and ranks are connected with administrative functions and duties. This usually means that a direct or indirect economic exploitation or a 'social' exploitation of position, which every sort of administrative activity gives to its bearers, is equivalent to the assumption of administrative functions.

Bureaucratization and democratization within the administration of the state therefore signify and increase the cash expenditures of the public treasury. And this is the case in spite of the fact that bureaucratic administration is usually more 'economical' in character than other forms of administration. Until recent times—at least from the point of view of the treasury—the cheapest way of satisfying the need for administration was to leave almost the entire local administration and lower judicature to the landlords of Eastern Prussia. The same fact applies to the administration of sheriffs in England. Mass democracy makes a clean sweep of the feudal, patrimonial, and—at least in intent—the pluto-cratic privileges in administration. Unavoidably it puts paid professional labor in place of the historically inherited avocational administration by notables.

This not only applies to structures of the state. For it is no accident that in their own organizations, the democratic mass parties have com-pletely broken with traditional notable rule based upon personal rela-tionships and personal esteem. Yet such personal structures frequently continue among the old conservative as well as the old liberal parties. Democratic mass parties are bureaucratically organized under the lead-ership of party officials, professional party and trade union secretaries, et cetera. In Germany, for instance, this has happened in the Social Democratic party and in the agrarian mass-movement; and in England, for the first time, in the caucus democracy of Gladstone-Chamberlain, which was originally organized in Birmingham and since the 1870's has spread. In the United States, both parties since Jackson's administration have developed bureaucratically. In France, however, attempts to organ-ize disciplined political parties on the basis of an election system that would compel bureaucratic organization have repeatedly failed. The resistance of local circles of notables against the ultimately unavoidable bureaucratization of the parties, which would encompass the entire coun-try and break their influence, could not be overcome. Every advance of the simple election techniques, for instance the system of proportional elec-tions, which calculates with figures, means a strict and inter-local bureau-cratic organization of the parties and therewith an increasing domina-tion of party bureaucracy and discipline, as well as the elimination of the local circles of notables—at least this holds for great states.

The progress of bureaucratization in the state administration itself is a parallel phenomenon of democracy, as is quite obvious in France, North America, and now in England. Of course one must always re-member that the term 'democratization' can be misleading. The *demos* itself, in the sense of an inarticulate mass, never 'governs' larger associa-tions; rather, it is governed, and its existence only changes the way in which the executive leaders are selected and the measure of influence which the *demos,* or better, which social circles from its midst are able to exert upon the content and the direction of administrative activities by supplementing what is called 'public opinion.' 'Democratization,' in the sense here intended, does not necessarily mean an increasingly active share of the governed in the authority of the social structure. This may be a result of democratization, but it is not necessarily the case.

We must expressly recall at this point that the political concept of democracy, deduced from the 'equal rights' of the governed, includes these postulates: (1) prevention of the development of a closed status group of officials in the interest of a universal accessibility of office, and (2) minimization of the authority of officialdom in the interest of expanding[7] the sphere of influence of 'public opinion' as far as practicable. Hence, wherever possible, political democracy strives to shorten the term of office by election and recall and by not binding the candidate to a special expertness. Thereby democracy inevitably comes into conflict with the bureaucratic tendencies which, by its fight against notable rule, democracy has produced. The generally loose term 'democratization' cannot be used here, in so far as it is understood to mean the minimization of the civil servants' ruling power in favor of the greatest possible 'direct' rule of the *demos,* which in practice means the respective party leaders of the *demos*. The most decisive thing here—indeed it is rather exclusively so—is the *leveling of the governed* in opposition to the ruling and bureaucratically articulated group, which in its turn may occupy a quite autocratic position, both in fact and in form.

In Russia, the destruction of the position of the old landed nobility through the regulation of the Mjeshtshitelstvo (rank order) and the permeation of the old nobility by an office nobility were characteristic transitional phenomena in the development of bureaucracy. In China, the estimation of rank and the qualification for office according to the number of examinations passed mean something similar, but they have had consequences which, in theory at least, are still sharper. In France, the Revolution and still more Bonapartism have made the bureaucracy all-powerful. In the Catholic Church, first the feudal and then all independent local intermediary powers were eliminated. This was begun by Gregory VII and continued through the Council of Trent, the Vatican Council, and it was completed by the edicts of Pius X. The transformation of these local powers into pure functionaries of the central authority were connected with the constant increase in the factual significance of the formally quite dependent chaplains, a process which above all was based on the political party organization of Catholicism. Hence this process meant an advance of bureaucracy and at the same time of 'passive democratization,' as it were, that is, the leveling of the governed. The substitution of the bureaucratic army for the self-equipped army of notables is everywhere a process of 'passive' democratization, in the sense in which every establishment of an absolute military monarchy in the place of a feudal state or of a republic of notables is. This has held, in principle, even for the development of the state in Egypt in spite of all the peculiarities involved. Under the Roman principate the bureaucratization of the provincial administration in the field of tax collection, for instance, went hand in hand with the elimination of the plutocracy of a capitalist class, which, under the Republic, had been all-powerful. Ancient capitalism itself was finally eliminated with this stroke.

It is obvious that almost always economic conditions of some sort play their part in such 'democratizing' developments. Very frequently we meet with the influence of an economically determined origin of new classes, whether plutocratic, petty bourgeois, or proletarian in character. Such classes may call on the aid of, or they may only call to life or recall to life, a political power, no matter whether it is of legitimate or of Caesarist stamp. They may do so in order to attain economic or social advantages by political assistance. On the other hand, there are equally possible and historically documented cases in which initiative came 'from on high' and was of a purely political nature and drew advantages from political constellations, especially in foreign affairs. Such leadership exploited economic and social antagonisms as well as class interests merely as a means for their own purpose of gaining purely political power. For this reason, political authority has thrown the antagonistic classes out of their almost always unstable equilibrium and called their latent interest conflicts into battle. It seems hardly possible to give a general statement of this.

The extent and direction of the course along which economic influences have moved, as well as the nature in which political power relations exert influence, vary widely. In Hellenic Antiquity, the transition to disciplined combat by Hoplites, and in Athens, the increasing importance of the navy laid the foundation for the conquest of political power by the strata on whose shoulders the military burden rested. In Rome, however, the same development shook the rule of the office nobility only temporarily and seemingly. Although the modern mass army has everywhere been a means of breaking the power of notables, by itself it has in no way served as a leverage for active, but rather for merely passive, democratization. One contributing factor, however, has been the fact that the ancient citizen army rested economically upon self-equipment, whereas the modern army rests upon the bureaucratic procurement of requirements.

The advance of the bureaucratic structure rests upon 'technical' superiority. This fact leads here, as in the whole field of technique, to the following: the advance has been realized most slowly where older structural forms have been technically well developed and functionally adjusted to the requirements at hand. This was the case, for instance, in the administration of notables in England and hence England was the slowest of all countries to succumb to bureaucratization or, indeed, is still only partly in the process of doing so. The same general phenomenon exists when highly developed systems of gaslight or of steam railroads with large and fixed capital offer stronger obstacles to electrification than in completely new areas which are opened up for electrification.

10: The Permanent Character of the Bureaucratic Machine

Once it is fully established, bureaucracy is among those social structures which are the hardest to destroy. Bureaucracy is *the* means of carrying 'community action' over into rationally ordered 'societal action.' Therefore, as an instrument for 'societalizing' relations of power, bureaucracy has been and is a power instrument of the first order—for the one who controls the bureaucratic apparatus.

Under otherwise equal conditions, a 'societal action,' which is methodically ordered and led, is superior to every resistance of 'mass' or even of 'communal action.' And where the bureaucratization of administration has been completely carried through, a form of power relation is established that is practically unshatterable.

The individual bureaucrat cannot squirm out of the apparatus in which he is harnessed. In contrast to the honorific or avocational 'notable,' the professional bureaucrat is chained to his activity by his entire material and ideal existence. In the great majority of cases, he is only a single cog in an ever-moving mechanism which prescribes to him an essentially fixed route of march. The official is entrusted with specialized tasks and normally the mechanism cannot be put into motion or arrested by him, but only from the very top. The individual bureaucrat is thus forged to the community of all the functionaries who are integrated into the mechanism. They have a common interest in seeing that the mechanism continues its functions and that the societally exercised authority carries on.

The ruled, for their part, cannot dispense with or replace the bureaucratic apparatus of authority once it exists. For this bureaucracy rests upon expert training, a functional specialization of work, and an attitude set for habitual and virtuoso-like mastery of single yet methodically integrated functions. If the official stops working, or if his work is forcefully interrupted, chaos results, and it is difficult to improvise replacements from among the governed who are fit to master such chaos. This holds for public administration as well as for private economic management. More and more the material fate of the masses depends upon the steady and correct functioning of the increasingly bureaucratic organizations of private capitalism. The idea of eliminating these organizations becomes more and more utopian.

The discipline of officialdom refers to the attitude-set of the official for precise obedience within his *habitual* activity, in public as well as in private organizations. This discipline increasingly becomes the basis of all order, however great the practical importance of administration on the basis of the filed documents may be. The naive idea of Bakuninism of destroying the basis of 'acquired rights' and 'domination' by destroying public documents overlooks the settled orientation of *man* for keeping to the habitual rules and regulations that continue to exist independently of the documents. Every reorganization of beaten or dissolved troops, as well as the restoration of administrative orders destroyed by revolt, panic, or other catastrophes, is realized by appealing to the trained orientation of obedient compliance to such orders. Such compliance has been conditioned into the officials, on the one hand, and, on the other hand, into the governed. If such an appeal is successful it brings, as it were, the disturbed mechanism into gear again.

The objective indispensability of the once-existing apparatus, with its peculiar, 'impersonal' character, means that the mechanism—in contrast to feudal orders based upon personal piety—is easily made to work for anybody who knows how to gain control over it. A rationally ordered system of officials continues to function smoothly after the enemy has occupied the area; he merely needs to change the top officials. This body of officials continues to operate because it is to the vital interest of everyone concerned, including above all the enemy.

During the course of his long years in power, Bismarck brought his ministerial colleagues into unconditional bureaucratic dependence by eliminating all independent statesmen. Upon his retirement, he saw to his surprise that they continued to manage their offices unconcerned and undismayed, as if he had not been the master mind and creator of these creatures, but rather as if some single figure had been exchanged for some other figure in the bureaucratic machine. With all the changes of masters in France since the time of the First Empire, the power machine has remained essentially the same. Such a machine makes 'revolution,' in the sense of the forceful creation of entirely new formations of authority, technically more and more impossible, especially when the apparatus controls the modern means of communication (telegraph, et cetera) and also by virtue of its internal rationalized structure. In classic fashion, France has demonstrated how this process has substituted *coups d'état* for 'revolutions': all successful transformations in France have amounted to *coups d'état*.

11: ECONOMIC AND SOCIAL CONSEQUENCES OF BUREAUCRACY

It is clear that the bureaucratic organization of a social structure, and especially of a political one, can and regularly does have far-reaching economic consequences. But what sort of consequences? Of course in any individual case it depends upon the distribution of economic and social power, and especially upon the sphere that is occupied by the emerging bureaucratic mechanism. The consequences of bureaucracy depend therefore upon the direction which the powers using the apparatus give to it. And very frequently a crypto-plutocratic distribution of power has been the result.

In England, but especially in the United States, party donors regularly stand behind the bureaucratic party organizations. They have financed these parties and have been able to influence them to a large extent. The breweries in England, the so-called 'heavy industry,' and in Germany the Hansa League with their voting funds are well enough known as political donors to parties. In modern times bureaucratization and social leveling within political, and particularly within state organizations in connection with the destruction of feudal and local privileges, have very frequently benefited the interests of capitalism. Often bureaucratization has been carried out in direct alliance with capitalist interests, for example, the great historical alliance of the power of the absolute prince with capitalist interests. In general, a legal leveling and destruction of firmly established local structures ruled by notables has usually made for a wider range of capitalist activity. Yet one may expect as an effect of bureaucratization, a policy that meets the petty bourgeois interest in a secured traditional 'subsistence,' or even a state socialist policy that strangles opportunities for private profit. This has occurred in several cases of historical and far-reaching importance, specifically during antiquity; it is undoubtedly to be expected as a future development. Perhaps it will occur in Germany.

The very different effects of political organizations which were, at least in principle, quite similar—in Egypt under the Pharaohs and in Hellenic and Roman times—show the very different economic significances of bureaucratization which are possible according to the direction of other factors. The mere fact of bureaucratic organization does not unambiguously tell us about the concrete direction of its economic effects, which are always in some manner present. At least it does not tell us as much as can be told about its relatively leveling effect socially. In this respect, one has to remember that bureaucracy as such is a precision instrument which can put itself at the disposal of quite varied—purely political as well as purely economic, or any other sort—of interests in domination. Therefore, the measure of its parallelism with democratization must not be exaggerated, however typical it may be. Under certain conditions, strata of feudal lords have also put bureaucracy into their service. There is also the possibility—and often it has become a fact, for instance, in the Roman principate and in some forms of absolutist state structures—that a bureaucratization of administration is deliberately connected with the formation of *estates,* or is entangled with them by the force of the existing groupings of social power. The express reservation of offices for certain status groups is very frequent, and actual reservations are even more frequent. The democratization of society in its totality, and in the *modern* sense of the term, whether actual or perhaps merely formal, is an especially favorable basis of bureaucratization, but by no means the only possible one. After all, bureaucracy strives merely to level those powers that stand in its way and in those areas that, in the individual case, it seeks to occupy. We must remember this fact—which we have encountered several times and which we shall have to discuss repeatedly: that 'democracy' as such is opposed to the 'rule' of bureaucracy, in spite and perhaps because of its unavoidable yet unintended promotion of bureaucratization. Under certain conditions, democracy creates obvious ruptures and blockages to bureaucratic organization.

Hence, in every individual historical case, one must observe in what special direction bureaucratization has developed.

12: The Power Position of Bureaucracy

Everywhere the modern state is undergoing bureaucratization. But whether the *power* of bureaucracy within the polity is universally increasing must here remain an open question.

The fact that bureaucratic organization is technically the most highly developed means of power in the hands of the man who controls it does not determine the weight that bureaucracy as such is capable of having in a particular social structure. The ever-increasing 'indispensability' of the officialdom, swollen to millions, is no more decisive for this question than is the view of some representatives of the proletarian movement that the economic indispensability of the proletarians is decisive for the measure of their social and political power position. If 'indispensability' were decisive, then where slave labor prevailed and where freemen usually abhor work as a dishonor, the 'indispensable' slaves ought to have held the positions of power, for they were at least as indispensable as officials and proletarians are today. Whether the power of bureaucracy as such increases cannot be decided *a priori* from such reasons. The drawing in of economic interest groups or other non-official experts, or the drawing in of non-expert lay representatives, the establishment of local, inter-local, or central parliamentary or other representative bodies, or of occupational associations—these *seem* to run directly against the bureaucratic tendency. How far this appearance is the truth must be discussed in another chapter rather than in this purely formal and typological discussion. In general, only the following can be said here:

Under normal conditions, the power position of a fully developed bureaucracy is always overtowering. The 'political master' finds himself in the position of the 'dilettante' who stands opposite the 'expert,' facing the trained official who stands within the management of administration. This holds whether the 'master' whom the bureaucracy serves is a 'people,' equipped with the weapons of 'legislative initiative,' the 'referendum,' and the right to remove officials, or a parliament, elected on a more aristocratic or more 'democratic' basis and equipped with the right to vote a lack of confidence, or with the actual authority to vote it. It holds whether the master is an aristocratic, collegiate body, legally or actually based on self-recruitment, or whether he is a popularly elected president, a hereditary and 'absolute' or a 'constitutional' monarch.

Every bureaucracy seeks to increase the superiority of the professionally informed by keeping their knowledge and intentions secret. Bureaucratic administration always tends to be an administration of 'secret sessions': in so far as it can, it hides its knowledge and action from criticism. Prussian church authorities now threaten to use disciplinary measures against pastors who make reprimands or other admonitory measures in any way accessible to third parties. They do this because the pastor, in making such criticism available, is 'guilty' of facilitating a possible criticism of the church authorities. The treasury officials of the Persian shah have made a secret doctrine of their budgetary art and even use secret script. The official statistics of Prussia, in general, make public only what cannot do any harm to the intentions of the power-wielding bureaucracy. The tendency toward secrecy in certain administrative fields follows their material nature: everywhere that the power interests of the domination structure toward *the outside* are at stake, whether it is an economic competitor of a private enterprise, or a foreign, potentially hostile polity, we find secrecy. If it is to be successful, the management of diplomacy can only be publicly controlled to a very limited extent. The military administration must insist on the concealment of its most important measures; with the increasing significance of purely technical aspects, this is all the more the case. Political parties do not proceed differently, in spite of all the ostensible publicity of Catholic congresses and party conventions. With the increasing bureaucratization of party organizations, this secrecy will prevail even more. Commercial policy, in Germany for instance, brings about a concealment of production statistics. Every fighting posture of a social structure toward the outside tends to buttress the position of the group in power.

The pure interest of the bureaucracy in power, however, is efficacious far beyond those areas where purely functional interests make for secrecy. The concept of the 'official secret' is the specific invention of bureaucracy, and nothing is so fanatically defended by the bureaucracy as this attitude, which cannot be substantially justified beyond these specifically qualified areas. In facing a parliament, the bureaucracy, out of a sure power instinct, fights every attempt of the parliament to gain knowledge by means of its own experts or from interest groups. The so-called right of parliamentary investigation is one of the means by which parliament seeks such knowledge. Bureaucracy naturally welcomes a poorly informed and hence a powerless parliament—at least in so far as ignorance somehow agrees with the bureaucracy's interests.

The absolute monarch is powerless opposite the superior knowledge of the bureaucratic expert—in a certain sense more powerless than any other political head. All the scornful decrees of Frederick the Great concerning the 'abolition of serfdom' were derailed, as it were, in the course of their realization because the official mechanism simply ignored them as the occasional ideas of a dilettante. When a constitutional king agrees with a socially important part of the governed, he very frequently exerts a greater influence upon the course of administration than does the absolute monarch. The constitutional king can control these experts better because of what is, at least relatively, the public character of criticism, whereas the absolute monarch is dependent for information solely upon the bureaucracy. The Russian czar of the old regime was seldom able to accomplish permanently anything that displeased his bureaucracy and hurt the power interests of the bureaucrats. His ministerial departments, placed directly under him as the autocrat, represented a conglomerate of satrapies, as was correctly noted by Leroy-Beaulieu. These satrapies constantly fought against one another by all the means of personal intrigue, and, especially, they bombarded one another with voluminous 'memorials,' in the face of which, the monarch, as a dilettante, was helpless.

With the transition to constitutional government, the concentration of the power of the central bureaucracy in one head became unavoidable. Officialdom was placed under a monocratic head, the prime minister, through whose hands everything had to go before it got to the monarch. This put the latter, to a large extent, under the tutelage of the chief of the bureaucracy. Wilhelm II, in his well-known conflict with Bismarck, fought against this principle, but he had to withdraw his attack very soon. Under the rule of expert knowledge, the actual influence of the monarch can attain steadiness only by a continuous communication with the bureaucratic chiefs; this intercourse must be methodically planned and directed by the head of the bureaucracy.

At the same time, constitutionalism binds the bureaucracy and the ruler into a community of interests against the desires of party chiefs for power in the parliamentary bodies. And if he cannot find support in parliament the constitutional monarch is powerless against the bureaucracy. The desertion of the 'Great of the Reich,' the Prussian ministers and top officials of the Reich in November 1918, brought a monarch into approximately the same situation as existed in the feudal state in 1056. However, this is an exception, for, on the whole, the power position of a monarch opposite bureaucratic officials is far stronger than it was in any feudal state or in the 'stereotyped' patrimonial state. This is because of the constant presence of aspirants for promotion, with whom the monarch can easily replace inconvenient and independent officials. Other circumstances being equal, only economically independent officials, that is, officials who belong to the propertied strata, can permit themselves to risk the loss of their offices. Today as always, the recruitment of officials from among propertyless strata increases the power of the rulers. Only officials who belong to a socially influential stratum, whom the monarch believes he must take into account as personal supporters, like the so-called *Kanalrebellen* in Prussia,[8] can permanently and completely paralyse the substance of his will.

Only the expert knowledge of private economic interest groups in the field of 'business' is superior to the expert knowledge of the bureaucracy. This is so because the exact knowledge of facts in their field is vital to the economic existence of businessmen. Errors in official statistics do not have direct economic consequences for the guilty official, but errors in the calculation of a capitalist enterprise are paid for by losses, perhaps by its existence. The 'secret,' as a means of power, is, after all, more safely hidden in the books of an enterpriser than it is in the files of public authorities. For this reason alone authorities are held within narrow barriers when they seek to influence economic life in the capitalist epoch. Very frequently the measures of the state in the field of capitalism take unforeseen and unintended courses, or they are made illusory by the superior expert knowledge of interest groups.

13: Stages in the Development of Bureaucracy

More and more the specialized knowledge of the expert became the foundation for the power position of the officeholder. Hence an early concern of the ruler was how to exploit the special knowledge of experts without having to abdicate in their favor but preserve his dominant position. With the qualitative extension of administrative tasks and therewith the indispensability of expert knowledge, it typically happens that the lord no longer is satisfied by occasional consultation with individual and proved confidants or even with an assembly of such men called together intermittently and in difficult situations. The lord begins to surround himself with *collegiate* bodies who deliberate and resolve in continuous session.* The *Räte von Haus aus* [9] is a characteristic transitional phenomenon in this development.

The position of such collegiate bodies naturally varies according to whether they become the highest administrative authority, or whether a central and monocratic authority, or several such authorities stand at their side. In addition, a great deal depends upon their procedure. When the collegiate type is fully developed, such bodies, in principle or in fiction, meet with the lord in the chair and all important matters are elucidated from all points of view in the papers of the respective experts and their assistants and by the reasoned votes of the other members. The matter is then settled by a resolution, which the lord will sanction or reject by an edict. This kind of collegiate body is the typical form in which the ruler, who increasingly turns into a 'dilettante,' at the same time exploits expert knowledge and—what frequently remains unnoticed —seeks to fend off the overpowering weight of expert knowledge and to maintain his dominant position in the face of experts. He keeps one expert in check by others and by such cumbersome procedures he seeks personally to gain a comprehensive picture as well as the certainty that nobody prompts him to arbitrary decisions. Often the prince expects to assure himself a maximum of personal influence less from personally presiding over the collegiate bodies than from having written memoranda submitted to him. Frederick William I of Prussia actually exerted a very considerable influence on the administration, but he almost never attended the collegiately organized sessions of the cabinet ministers! He rendered his decisions on written presentations by means of marginal comments or edicts. These decisions were delivered to the ministers by the *Feldjaeger* of the *Cabinett,* after consultation with those servants who belonged to the cabinet and were personnally attached to the king.

The hatred of the bureaucratic departments turns against the cabinet just as the distrust of the subjects turns against the bureaucrats in case of failure. The cabinet in Russia, as well as in Prussia and in other states, thus developed into a personal fortress in which the ruler, so to

* *Conseil d'Etat*, Privy Council, *Generaldirektorium*, *Cabinett*, *Divan*, *Tsung-li Yamen*, *Wai-wu pu*, etc.

speak, sought refuge in the face of expert knowledge and the impersonal and functional routinization of administration.

By the collegiate principle the ruler furthermore tries to fashion a sort of synthesis of *specialized experts* into a collective unit. His success in doing this cannot be ascertained in general. The phenomenon itself, however, is common to very different forms of state, from the patrimonial and feudal to the early bureaucratic, and it is especially typical for early princely absolutism. The collegiate principle has proved itself to be one of the strongest educative means for 'matter-of-factness' in administration. It has also made possible the drawing in of socially influential private persons and thus to combine in some measure the authority of notables and the practical knowledge of private enterprisers with the specialized expertness of professional bureaucrats. The collegiate bodies were one of the first institutions to allow the development of the modern concept of 'public authorities,' in the sense of enduring structures independent of the person.

As long as an expert knowledge of administrative affairs was the exclusive product of a long empirical practice, and administrative norms were not regulations but elements of tradition, the council of *elders*— in a manner typical often with priests, 'elder statesmen,' and notables participating—was the adequate form for collegiate authorities, which in the beginning merely gave advice to the ruler. But as such bodies continued to exist in the face of changing rulers, they often usurped actual power. The Roman Senate and the Venetian Council, as well as the Athenian *Areopag* until its downfall and replacement by the rule of the *demagogos* acted in this manner. We must of course sharply distinguish such authorities from the corporate bodies under discussion here.

In spite of manifold transitions, collegiate bodies, as a type, emerge on the basis of the rational specialization of functions and the rule of expert knowledge. On the other hand, they must be distinguished from advisory bodies selected from among private and *interested* circles, which are frequently found in the modern state and whose nucleus is not formed of officials or of former officials. These collegiate bodies must also be distinguished sociologically from the boards of control found in the bureaucratic structures of the modern private economy (economic corporations). This distinction must be made in spite of the fact that such corporate bodies not infrequently complete themselves by drawing in notables from among disinterested circles for the sake of their expert knowledge or in order to exploit them for representation and advertising. Normally, such bodies do not unite holders of special expert knowledge but rather the decisive representatives of paramount economic interest groups, especially the bank creditors of the enterprise—and such men by no means hold merely advisory positions. They have at least a controlling voice, and very often they occupy an actually dominant position. They are to be compared (not without some distortion) to the assemblies of the great independent holders of feudal fiefs and offices and other socially powerful interest groups of patrimonial or feudal polities. Occasionally, however, these have been the precursors of the 'councilors' who have emerged in consequence of an increased intensity of administration. And even more frequently they have been precursors of corporations of legally privileged estates.

With great regularity the bureaucratic collegiate principle has been transferred from the central authority to the most varied lower authorities. Within locally closed, and especially within urban units, collegiate administration is the original form of the rule of notables, as was indicated at the beginning of this discussion. Originally it worked through elected, later on, usually, or at least in part, through co-opted 'councilors,' collegiate bodies of 'magistrates,' *decuriones,* and 'jurors.' Such bodies are a normal element of organized 'self-government,' that is, the management of administrative affairs by local interest groups under the control of the bureaucratic authorities of the state. The above-mentioned examples of the Venetian Council and even more so of the Roman Senate represent transfers of notable rule to great overseas empires. Normally such a rule of notables is rooted in local political associations. Within the bureaucratic state, collegiate administration disappears as soon as progress in the means of communication and the increasing technical demands of administration necessitate quick and unambiguous decisions, and as soon as the dominant motives for full bureaucratization and monocracy, which we discussed above, push to the fore. Collegiate administration disappears when from the point of view of the ruler's interests a strictly unified administrative leadership appears to be more important than thoroughness in the preparation of administrative decisions. This is the case as soon as parliamentary institutions develop and —usually at the same time—as criticism from the outside and publicity increase.

Under these modern conditions the thoroughly rationalized system of departmental ministers and prefects, as in France, offers significant opportunities for pushing the old forms into the background. Probably the system is supplemented by the calling in of interest groups as advisory bodies recruited from among the economically and socially most influential strata. This practice, which I have mentioned above, is increasingly frequent and gradually may well be ordered more formally.

This latter development seeks especially to put the concrete experience of interest groups into the service of a rational administration of expertly trained officials. It will certainly be important in the future and it further increases the power of bureaucracy. It is known that Bismarck sought to realize the plan of a 'national economic council' as a means of power against parliament. Bismarck, who would never have given the Reichstag the right of investigation in the sense of the British Parliament, reproached the majority, who rejected his proposal, by stating that in the interest of parliamentary power the majority sought to protect officialdom from becoming 'too prudent.' Discussion of the position of organized interest groups within the administration, which may be in the offing, does not belong in this context.

Only with the bureaucratization of the state and of law in general can one see a definite possibility of separating sharply and conceptually an 'objective' legal order from the 'subjective rights' of the individual which it guarantees; of separating 'public' law from 'private' law. Public law regulates the interrelationships of public authorities and their relationships with the 'subjects'; private law regulates the relationships of the governed individuals among themselves. This conceptual separation presupposes the conceptual separation of the 'state,' as an abstract bearer of sovereign prerogatives and the creator of 'legal norms,' from all personal 'authorizations' of individuals. These conceptual forms are necessarily remote from the nature of pre-bureaucratic, and especially from patrimonial and feudal, structures of authority. This conceptual separation of private and public was first conceived and realized in urban communities; for as soon as their officeholders were secured by periodic *elections,* the individual power-holder, even if he was in the highest position, was obviously no longer identical with the man who possessed authority 'in his own right.' Yet it was left to the complete depersonalization of administrative management by bureaucracy and the rational systematization of law to realize the separation of public and private fully and in principle.

14: THE 'RATIONALIZATION' OF EDUCATION AND TRAINING

We cannot here analyze the far-reaching and general cultural effects that the advance of the rational bureaucratic structure of domination, as such, develops quite independently of the areas in which it takes hold. Naturally, bureaucracy promotes a 'rationalist' way of life, but the concept of rationalism allows for widely differing contents. Quite generally, one can only say that the bureaucratization of all domination very strongly furthers the development of 'rational matter-of-factness' and the personality type of the professional expert. This has far-reaching ramifications, but only one important element of the process can be briefly indicated here: its effect upon the nature of training and education.

Educational institutions on the European continent, especially the institutions of higher learning—the universities, as well as technical academies, business colleges, gymnasiums, and other middle schools—are dominated and influenced by the need for the kind of 'education' that produces a system of special examinations and the trained expertness that is increasingly indispensable for modern bureaucracy.

The 'special examination,' in the present sense, was and is found also outside of bureaucratic structures proper; thus, today it is found in the 'free' professions of medicine and law and in the guild-organized trades. Expert examinations are neither indispensable to nor concomitant phenomena of bureaucratization. The French, English, and American bureaucracies have for a long time foregone such examinations entirely or to a large extent, for training and service in party organizations have made up for them.

'Democracy' also takes an ambivalent stand in the face of specialized examinations, as it does in the face of all the phenomena of bureaucracy —although democracy itself promotes these developments. Special examinations, on the one hand, mean or appear to mean a 'selection' of those who qualify from all social strata rather than a rule by notables. On the other hand, democracy fears that a merit system and educational certificates will result in a privileged 'caste.' Hence, democracy fights against the special-examination system.

The special examination is found even in pre-bureaucratic or semi-bureaucratic epochs. Indeed, the regular and earliest locus of special examinations is among prebendally organized dominions. Expectancies of prebends, first of church prebends—as in the Islamite Orient and in the Occidental Middle Ages—then, as was especially the case in China, secular prebends, are the typical prizes for which people study and are examined. These examinations, however, have in truth only a partially specialized and expert character.

The modern development of full bureaucratization brings the system of rational, specialized, and expert examinations irresistibly to the fore. The civil-service reform gradually imports expert training and specialized examinations into the United States. In all other countries this system also advances, stemming from its main breeding place, Germany. The increasing bureaucratization of administration enhances the importance of the specialized examination in England. In China, the attempt to replace the semi-patrimonial and ancient bureaucracy by a modern bureaucracy brought the expert examination; it took the place of a former and quite differently structured system of examinations. The bureaucratization of capitalism, with its demand for expertly trained technicians, clerks, et cetera, carries such examinations all over the world. Above all, the development is greatly furthered by the social prestige of the educational certificates acquired through such specialized examinations. This is all the more the case as the educational patent is turned to economic advantage. Today, the certificate of education becomes what the test for ancestors has been in the past, at least where the nobility has remained powerful: a prerequisite for equality of birth, a qualification for a canonship, and for state office.

The development of the diploma from universities, and business and engineering colleges, and the universal clamor for the creation of educational certificates in all fields make for the formation of a privileged stratum in bureaus and in offices. Such certificates support their holders' claims for intermarriages with notable families (in business offices people naturally hope for preferment with regard to the chief's daughter), claims to be admitted into the circles that adhere to 'codes of honor,' claims for a 'respectable' remuneration rather than remuneration for work done, claims for assured advancement and old-age insurance, and, above all, claims to monopolize socially and economically advantageous positions. When we hear from all sides the demand for an introduction of regular curricula and special examinations, the reason behind it is, of course, not a suddenly awakened 'thirst for education' but the desire for restricting the supply for these positions and their monopolization by the owners of educational certificates. Today, the 'examination' is the uni-

versal means of this monopolization, and therefore examinations irresistibly advance. As the education prerequisite to the acquisition of the
educational certificate requires considerable expense and a period of
waiting for full remuneration, this striving means a setback for talent
(charisma) in favor of property. For the 'intellectual' costs of educational
certificates are always low, and with the increasing volume of such
certificates, their intellectual costs do not increase, but rather decrease.

The requirement of a chivalrous style of life in the old qualification
for fiefs in Germany is replaced by the necessity of participating in its
present rudimental form as represented by the dueling corps of the
universities which also distribute the educational certificates. In Anglo-
Saxon countries, athletic and social clubs fulfil the same function. The
bureaucracy, on the other hand, strives everywhere for a 'right to the
office' by the establishment of a regular disciplinary procedure and by
removal of the completely arbitrary disposition of the 'chief' over the
subordinate official. The bureaucracy seeks to secure the official position,
the orderly advancement, and the provision for old age. In this, the
bureaucracy is supported by the 'democratic' sentiment of the governed,
which demands that domination be minimized. Those who hold this
attitude believe themselves able to discern a weakening of the master's
prerogatives in every weakening of the arbitrary disposition of the master over the officials. To this extent, bureaucracy, both in business offices
and in public service, is a carrier of a specific 'status' development, as
have been the quite differently structured officeholders of the past. We
have already pointed out that these status characteristics are usually also
exploited, and that by their nature they contribute to the technical usefulness of the bureaucracy in fulfilling its specific tasks.

'Democracy' reacts precisely against the unavoidable 'status' character
of bureaucracy. Democracy seeks to put the election of officials for short
terms in the place of appointed officials; it seeks to substitute the removal
of officials by election for a regulated procedure of discipline. Thus,
democracy seeks to replace the arbitrary disposition of the hierarchically
superordinate 'master' by the equally arbitrary disposition of the governed and the party chiefs dominating them.

Social prestige based upon the advantage of special education and
training as such is by no means specific to bureaucracy. On the contrary!
But educational prestige in other structures of domination rests upon
substantially different foundations.

Expressed in slogan-like fashion, the 'cultivated man,' rather than the 'specialist,' has been the end sought by education and has formed the basis of social esteem in such various systems as the feudal, theocratic, and patrimonial structures of dominion: in the English notable administration, in the old Chinese patrimonial bureaucracy, as well as under the rule of demagogues in the so-called Hellenic democracy.

The term 'cultivated man' is used here in a completely value-neutral sense; it is understood to mean solely that the goal of education consists in the quality of a man's bearing in life which was *considered* 'cultivated,' rather than in a specialized training for expertness. The 'cultivated' personality formed the educational ideal, which was stamped by the structure of domination and by the social condition for membership in the ruling stratum. Such education aimed at a chivalrous or an ascetic type; or, at a literary type, as in China; a gymnastic-humanist type, as in Hellas; or it aimed at a conventional type, as in the case of the Anglo-Saxon gentleman. The qualification of the ruling stratum as such rested upon the possession of 'more' cultural quality (in the absolutely changeable, value-neutral sense in which we use the term here), rather than upon 'more' expert knowledge. Special military, theological, and juridical ability was of course intensely practiced; but the point of gravity in Hellenic, in medieval, as well as in Chinese education, has rested upon educational elements that were entirely different from what was 'useful' in one's specialty.

Behind all the present discussions of the foundations of the educational system, the struggle of the 'specialist type of man' against the older type of 'cultivated man' is hidden at some decisive point. This fight is determined by the irresistibly expanding bureaucratization of all public and private relations of authority and by the ever-increasing importance of expert and specialized knowledge. This fight intrudes into all intimate cultural questions.

During its advance, bureaucratic organization has had to overcome those essentially negative obstacles that have stood in the way of the leveling process necessary for bureaucracy. In addition, administrative structures based on different principles intersect with bureaucratic organizations. Since these have been touched upon above, only some especially important structural *principles* will be briefly discussed here in a very simplified schema. We would be led too far afield were we to discuss all the actually existing types. We shall proceed by asking the following questions:

1. How far are administrative structures subject to economic determina-

tion? Or, how far are opportunities for development created by other circumstances, for instance, the purely political? Or, finally, how far are developments created by an 'autonomous' logic that is solely of the technical structure as such?

2. We shall ask whether or not these structural principles, in turn, release specific economic effects, and if so, what effects. In doing this, one of course from the beginning has to keep his eye on the fluidity and the overlapping transitions of all these organizational principles. Their 'pure' types, after all, are to be considered merely as border cases which are especially valuable and indispensable for analysis. Historical realities, which almost always appear in mixed forms, have moved and still move between such pure types.

The bureaucratic structure is everywhere a late product of development. The further back we trace our steps, the more typical is the absence of bureaucracy and officialdom in the structure of domination. Bureaucracy has a 'rational' character: rules, means, ends, and matter-of-factness dominate its bearing. Everywhere its origin and its diffusion have therefore had 'revolutionary' results, in a special sense, which has still to be discussed. This is the same influence which the advance of *rationalism* in general has had. The march of bureaucracy has destroyed structures of domination which had no rational character, in the special sense of the term. Hence, we may ask: What were these structures? *

---

* In chapters following the present one in *Wirtschaft und Gesellschaft*, Weber discusses Patriarchialism, Patrimonialism, Feudalism, and Charismatic Authority. Chapter IX of the present volume presents a short discussion of charismatic authority. For comments on the other concepts, see the end of Chapter XI. For the way in which Weber analyzes a specific bureaucracy in terms of intersecting structural principles, see Chapter XVII.

IX. The Sociology of Charismatic Authority

1: The General Character of Charisma

Bureaucratic and patriarchal structures are antagonistic in many ways, yet they have in common a most important peculiarity: permanence. In this respect they are both institutions of daily routine. Patriarchal power especially is rooted in the provisioning of recurrent and normal needs of the workaday life. Patriarchal authority thus has its original locus in the economy, that is, in those branches of the economy that can be satisfied by means of normal routine. The patriarch is the 'natural leader' of the daily routine. And in this respect, the bureaucratic structure is only the counter-image of patriarchalism transposed into rationality. As a permanent structure with a system of rational rules, bureaucracy is fashioned to meet calculable and recurrent needs by means of a normal routine.

The provisioning of all demands that go beyond those of everyday routine has had, in principle, an entirely heterogeneous, namely, a *charismatic,* foundation; the further back we look in history, the more we find this to be the case. This means that the 'natural' leaders—in times of psychic, physical, economic, ethical, religious, political distress—have been neither officeholders nor incumbents of an 'occupation' in the present sense of the word, that is, men who have acquired expert knowledge and who serve for remuneration. The natural leaders in distress have been holders of specific gifts of the body and spirit; and these gifts have been believed to be supernatural, not accessible to everybody. The concept of 'charisma' is here used in a completely 'value-neutral' sense.

The capacity of the Irish culture hero, Cuchulain, or of the Homeric Achilles for heroic frenzy is a manic seizure, just as is that of the Arabian berserk who bites his shield like a mad dog—biting around until he darts off in raving bloodthirstiness. For a long time it has been maintained that the seizure of the berserk is artificially produced through

Wirtschaft und Gesellschaft, part iii, chap. 9, pp. 753-7.

245

acute poisoning. In Byzantium, a number of 'blond beasts,' disposed to such seizures, were kept about, just as war elephants were formerly kept. Shamanist ecstasy is linked to constitutional epilepsy, the possession and the testing of which represents a charismatic qualification. Hence neither is 'edifying' to our minds. They are just as little edifying to us as is the kind of 'revelation,' for instance, of the Sacred Book of the Mormons, which, at least from an evaluative standpoint, perhaps would have to be called a 'hoax.' But sociology is not concerned with such questions. In the faith of their followers, the chief of the Mormons has proved himself to be charismatically qualified, as have 'heroes' and 'sorcerers.' All of them have practiced their arts and ruled by virtue of this gift (charisma) and, where the idea of God has already been clearly conceived, by virtue of the divine mission lying therein. This holds for doctors and prophets, just as for judges and military leaders, or for leaders of big hunting expeditions.

It is to his credit that Rudolf Sohm brought out the sociological peculiarity of this category of domination-structure for a historically important special case, namely, the historical development of the authority of the early Christian church. Sohm performed this task with logical consistency, and hence, by necessity, he was one-sided from a purely historical point of view. In principle, however, the very same state of affairs recurs universally, although often it is most clearly developed in the field of religion.

In contrast to any kind of bureaucratic organization of offices, the charismatic structure knows nothing of a form or of an ordered procedure of appointment or dismissal. It knows no regulated 'career,' 'advancement,' 'salary,' or regulated and expert training of the holder of charisma or of his aids. It knows no agency of control or appeal, no local bailiwicks or exclusive functional jurisdictions; nor does it embrace permanent institutions like our bureaucratic 'departments,' which are independent of persons and of purely personal charisma.

Charisma knows only inner determination and inner restraint. The holder of charisma seizes the task that is adequate for him and demands obedience and a following by virtue of his mission. His success determines whether he finds them. His charismatic claim breaks down if his mission is not recognized by those to whom he feels he has been sent. If they recognize him, he is their master—so long as he knows how to maintain recognition through 'proving' himself. But he does not derive his 'right' from their will, in the manner of an election. Rather, the reverse holds: it is the *duty* of those to whom he addresses his mission to recognize him as their charismatically qualified leader.

In Chinese theory, the emperor's prerogatives are made dependent upon the recognition of the people. But this does not mean recognition of the sovereignty of the people any more than did the prophet's necessity of getting recognition from the believers in the early Christian community. The Chinese theory, rather, characterizes the charismatic nature of the *monarch's position,* which adheres to his *personal* qualification and to his *proved* worth.

Charisma can be, and of course regularly is, qualitatively particularized. This is an internal rather than an external affair, and results in the qualitative barrier of the charisma holder's mission and power. In meaning and in content the mission may be addressed to a group of men who are delimited locally, ethnically, socially, politically, occupationally, or in some other way. If the mission is thus addressed to a limited group of men, as is the rule, it finds its limits within their circle.

In its economic sub-structure, as in everything else, charismatic domination is the very opposite of bureaucratic domination. If bureaucratic domination depends upon regular income, and hence at least *a potiori* on a money economy and money taxes, charisma lives in, though not off, this world. This has to be properly understood. Frequently charisma quite deliberately shuns the possession of money and of pecuniary income *per se,* as did Saint Francis and many of his like; but this is of course not the rule. Even a pirate genius may exercise a 'charismatic' domination, in the value-neutral sense intended here. Charismatic political heroes seek booty and, above all, gold. But charisma, and this is decisive, always rejects as undignified any pecuniary gain that is methodical and rational. In general, charisma rejects all rational economic conduct.

The sharp contrast between charisma and any 'patriarchal' structure that rests upon the ordered base of the 'household' lies in this rejection of rational economic conduct. In its 'pure' form, charisma is never a source of private gain for its holders in the sense of economic exploitation by the making of a deal. Nor is it a source of income in the form of pecuniary compensation, and just as little does it involve an orderly taxation for the material requirements of its mission. If the mission is one of peace, individual patrons provide the necessary means for charismatic structures; or those to whom the charisma is addressed provide honorific gifts, donations, or other voluntary contributions. In the case of charismatic warrior heroes, booty represents one of the ends as well as the material means of the mission. 'Pure' charisma is contrary to all patriarchal domination (in the sense of the term used here). It is the opposite of all ordered economy. It is the very force that disregards economy. This also holds, indeed precisely, where the charismatic leader is after the acquisition of goods, as is the case with the charismatic warrior hero. Charisma can do this because by its very nature it is not an 'institutional' and permanent structure, but rather, where its 'pure' type is at work, it is the very opposite of the institutionally permanent.

In order to do justice to their mission, the holders of charisma, the master as well as his disciples and followers, must stand outside the ties of this world, outside of routine occupations, as well as outside the routine obligations of family life. The statutes of the Jesuit order preclude the acceptance of church offices; the members of orders are forbidden to own property or, according to the original rule of St. Francis, the order as such is forbidden to do so. The priest and the knight of an order have to live in celibacy, and numerous holders of a prophetic or artistic charisma are actually single. All this is indicative of the unavoidable separation from this world of those who partake ('κλῆρος') of charisma. In these respects, the economic conditions of participation in charisma may have an (apparently) antagonistic appearance, depending upon the type of charisma—artistic or religious, for instance—and the way of life flowing from its meaning. Modern charismatic movements of artistic origin represent 'independents without gainful employment' (in everyday language, rentiers). Normally such persons are the best qualified to follow a charismatic leader. This is just as logically consistent as was the medieval friar's vow of poverty, which demanded the very opposite.

2: Foundations and Instability of Charismatic Authority

By its very nature, the existence of charismatic authority is specifically unstable. The holder may forego his charisma; he may feel 'forsaken by his God,' as Jesus did on the cross; he may prove to his followers that 'virtue is gone out of him.' It is then that his mission is extinguished, and hope waits and searches for a new holder of charisma. The charismatic holder is deserted by his following, however, (only) because pure charisma does not know any 'legitimacy' other than that flowing from personal strength, that is, one which is constantly being proved. The charismatic hero does not deduce his authority from codes and statutes, as is the case with the jurisdiction of office; nor does he deduce his authority from traditional custom or feudal vows of faith, as is the case with patrimonial power.

The charismatic leader gains and maintains authority solely by proving his strength in life. If he wants to be a prophet, he must perform miracles; if he wants to be a war lord, he must perform heroic deeds. Above all, however, his divine mission must 'prove' itself in that those who faithfully surrender to him must fare well. If they do not fare well, he is obviously not the master sent by the gods.

This very serious meaning of genuine charisma evidently stands in radical contrast to the convenient pretensions of present rulers to a 'divine right of kings,' with its reference to the 'inscrutable' will of the Lord, 'to whom alone the monarch is responsible.' The genuinely charismatic ruler is responsible precisely to those whom he rules. He is responsible for but one thing, that he personally and actually be the God-willed master.

During these last decades we have witnessed how the Chinese monarch impeaches himself before all the people because of his sins and insufficiencies if his administration does not succeed in warding off some distress from the governed, whether it is inundations or unsuccessful wars. Thus does a ruler whose power, even in vestiges and theoretically, is genuinely charismatic deport himself. And if even this penitence does not reconcile the deities, the charismatic emperor faces dispossession and death, which often enough is consummated as a propitiatory sacrifice.

Meng-tse's (Mencius') thesis that the people's voice is 'God's voice' (according to him the *only* way in which God speaks!) has a very specific meaning: if the people cease to recognize the ruler, it is expressly stated that he simply becomes a private citizen; and if he then wishes to be more, he becomes a usurper deserving of punishment. The state of affairs that corresponds to these phrases, which sound highly revolutionary, recurs under primitive conditions without any such pathos. The charismatic character adheres to almost all primitive authorities with the exception of domestic power in the narrowest sense, and the chieftain is often enough simply deserted if success does not remain faithful to him.

The subjects may extend a more active or passive 'recognition' to the personal mission of the charismatic master. His power rests upon this purely factual recognition and springs from faithful devotion. It is devotion to the extraordinary and unheard-of, to what is strange to all rule and tradition and which therefore is viewed as divine. It is a devotion born of distress and enthusiasm.

Genuine charismatic domination therefore knows of no abstract legal codes and statutes and of no 'formal' way of adjudication. Its 'objective' law emanates concretely from the highly personal experience of heavenly grace and from the god-like strength of the hero. Charismatic domination means a rejection of all ties to any external order in favor of the exclusive glorification of the genuine mentality of the prophet and hero. Hence, its attitude is revolutionary and transvalues everything; it makes a sovereign break with all traditional or rational norms: 'It is written, but I say unto you.'

The specifically charismatic form of settling disputes is by way of the prophet's revelation, by way of the oracle, or by way of 'Solomonic' arbitration by a charismatically qualified sage. This arbitration is determined by means of strictly concrete and individual evaluations, which, however, claim absolute validity. Here lies the proper locus of 'Kadi-justice' in the proverbial—not the historical—sense of the phrase. In its actual historical appearance the jurisdiction of the Islamic Kadi is, of course, bound to sacred tradition and is often a highly formalistic interpretation.

Only where these intellectual tools fail does jurisdiction rise to an unfettered individual act valuing the particular case; but then it does indeed. Genuinely charismatic justice always acts in this manner. In its pure form it is the polar opposite of formal and traditional bonds, and it is just as free in the face of the sanctity of tradition as it is in the face of any rationalist deductions from abstract concepts.

This is not the place to discuss how the reference to the *aegum et bonum* in the Roman administration of justice and the original meaning of English 'equity' are related to charismatic justice in general and to the theocratic Kadi-justice of Islamism in particular.[1] Both the *aegum et bonum* and 'equity' are partly the products of a strongly rationalized administration of justice and partly the product of abstract conceptions of natural law. In any case the *ex bona fide* contains a reference to the 'mores' of business life and thus retains just as little of a genuine irrational justice as does, for instance, the German judge's 'free discretion.'

Any kind of ordeal as a means of evidence is, of course, a derivative of charismatic justice. But the ordeal displaces the personal authority of the holder of charisma by a mechanism of rules for formally ascertaining the divine will. This falls in the sphere of the 'routinization' of charisma, with which we shall deal below.

3: CHARISMATIC KINGSHIP

In the evolution of political charisma, kingship represents a particularly important case in the historical development of the charismatic legitimization of institutions. The king is everywhere primarily a war lord, and kingship evolves from charismatic heroism.

In the form it displays in the history of civilized peoples, kingship is not the oldest evolutionary form of 'political' domination. By 'political' domination is meant a power that reaches beyond and which is, in principle, distinct from domestic authority. It is distinct because, in the first place, it is not devoted to leading the peaceful struggle of man with nature; it is, rather, devoted to leading in the violent conflict of one human community with another.

The predecessors of kingship were the holders of all those charismatic powers that guaranteed to remedy extraordinary external and internal distress, or guaranteed the success of extraordinary ventures. The chieftain of early history, the predecessor of kingship, is still a dual figure. On the one hand, he is the patriarchal head of the family or sib, and on the other, he is the charismatic leader of the hunt and war, the sorcerer, the rainmaker, the medicine man—and thus the priest and the doctor— and finally, the arbiter. Often, yet not always, such charismatic functions are split into as many special holders of charisma. Rather frequently the chieftain of the hunt and of war stands beside the chieftain of peace, who has essentially economic functions. In contrast to the latter, the chieftain of war acquires his charisma by proving his heroism to a voluntary following in successful raids leading to victory and booty. Even the royal Assyrian inscriptions enumerate booties of the hunt and cedars from Lebanon—dragged along for building purposes—alongside figures on the slain enemies and the size of the walls of conquered cities, which are covered with skins peeled off the enemies.

The charismatic position (among primitives) is thus acquired without regard to position in the sibs or domestic communities and without any rules whatsoever. This dualism of charisma and everyday routine is very frequently found among the American Indians, for instance, among the Confederacy of the Iroquois, as well as in Africa and elsewhere.

Where war and the big game hunt are absent, the charismatic chieftain —the 'war lord' as we wish to call him, in contrast to the chieftain of peace—is absent as well. In peacetime, especially if elemental calamities, particularly drought and diseases, are frequent, a charismatic sorcerer may have an essentially similar power in his hands. He is a priestly lord. The charisma of the war lord may or may not be unstable in nature according to whether or not he proves himself and whether or not there is any need for a war lord. He becomes a permanent figure when warfare becomes a chronic state of affairs. It is a mere terminological question whether one wishes to let kingship, and with it the state, begin only when strangers are affiliated with and integrated into the community as subjects. For our purposes it will be expedient to continue delimiting the term 'state' far more narrowly.

The existence of the war lord as a regular figure certainly does not depend upon a tribal rule over subjects of other tribes or upon individual slaves. His existence depends solely upon a chronic state of war and upon a comprehensive organization set for warfare. On the other hand, the development of kingship into a regular royal administration does emerge only at the stage when a following of royal professional warriors rules over the working or paying masses; at least, that is often the case. The forceful subjection of strange tribes, however, is not an absolutely indispensable link in this development. Internal class stratification may bring about the very same social differentiation: the charismatic following of warriors develops into a ruling caste. But in every case, princely power and those groups having interests vested in it—that is, the war lord's following—strive for legitimacy as soon as the rule has become stable. They crave for a characteristic which would define the charismatically qualified ruler.[2]

X. The Meaning of Discipline

It is the fate of charisma, whenever it comes into the permanent institutions of a community, to give way to powers of tradition or of rational socialization. This waning of charisma generally indicates the diminishing importance of individual action. And of all those powers that lessen the importance of individual action, the most irresistible is *rational discipline*.

The force of discipline not only eradicates personal charisma but also stratification by status groups; at least one of its results is the rational transformation of status stratification.

The content of discipline is nothing but the consistently rationalized, methodically trained and exact execution of the received order, in which all personal criticism is unconditionally suspended and the actor is unswervingly and exclusively set for carrying out the command. In addition, this conduct under orders is uniform. Its quality as the communal action af a *mass* organization conditions the specific effects of such uniformity. Those who obey are not necessarily a simultaneously obedient or an especially large mass, nor are they necessarily united in a specific locality. What is decisive for discipline is that the obedience of a plurality of men is rationally uniform.

Discipline as such is certainly not hostile to charisma or to status group honor. On the contrary, status groups that are attempting to rule over large territories or large organizations—the Venetian aristocratic counselors, the Spartans, the Jesuits in Paraguay, or a modern officer corps with a prince at its head—can maintain their alertness and their superiority over their subjects only by means of a very strict discipline. This discipline is enforced within their own group, for the blind obedience of subjects can be secured only by training them exclusively for submission under the disciplinary code. The cultivation of a stereotyped prestige and style of life of a status group, only for reasons of discipline, will have a

'Legitimacy,' *Wirtschaft und Gesellschaft,* part iii, chap. 5, pp. 642-9.

strongly conscious and rationally intended character. This factor effects all culture in any way influenced by these status communities; we shall not discuss these effects here. A charismatic hero may make use of discipline in the same way; indeed, he must do so if he wishes to expand his sphere of domination. Thus Napoleon created a strict disciplinary organization for France, which is still effective today.

Discipline in general, like its most rational offspring, bureaucracy, is impersonal. Unfailingly neutral, it places itself at the disposal of every power that claims its service and knows how to promote it. This does not prevent bureaucracy from being intrinsically alien and opposed to charisma, as well as to honor, especially of a feudal sort. The berserk with maniac seizures of frenzy and the feudal knight who measures swords with an equal adversary in order to gain personal honor are equally alien to discipline. The berserk is alien to it because his action is irrational; the knight because his subjective attitude lacks matter-of-factness. In place of individual hero-ecstasy or piety, of spirited enthusiasm or devotion to a leader as a person, of the cult of 'honor,' or the exercise of personal ability as an 'art'—discipline substitutes habituation to routinized skill. In so far as discipline appeals to firm motives of an 'ethical' character, it presupposes a 'sense of duty' and 'conscientiousness.' ('Men of Conscience' *versus* 'Men of Honor,' in Cromwell's terms.)

The masses are uniformly conditioned and trained for discipline in order that their optimum of physical and psychic power in attack may be rationally calculated. Enthusiasm and unreserved devotion may, of course, have a place in discipline; every modern conduct of war weighs, frequently above everything else, precisely the 'moral' elements of a troop's endurance. Military leadership uses emotional means of all sorts —just as the most sophisticated techniques of religious discipline, the *exercitia spiritualia* of Ignatius Loyola, do in their way. In combat, military leadership seeks to influence followers through 'inspiration' and, even more, to train them in 'emphatic understanding' of the leader's will. The sociologically decisive points, however, are, first, that everything, and especially these 'imponderable' and irrational emotional factors, are rationally calculated—in principle, at least, in the same manner as one calculates the yields of coal and iron deposits. Secondly, devotion, in its purposefulness and according to its normal content, is of an objective character. It is devotion to a common 'cause,' to a rationally intended 'success'; it does not mean devotion to a person as such—however 'personally' tinged it may be in the concrete instance of a fascinating leader.

The case is different only when the prerogatives of a slaveholder create a situation of discipline—on a plantation or in a slave army of the ancient Orient, on galleys manned by slaves or among prisoners in Antiquity and the Middle Ages. Indeed, the individual cannot escape from such a mechanized organization, for routinized training puts him in his place and compels him to 'travel along.' Those who are enlisted in the ranks are forcibly integrated into the whole. This integration is a strong element in the efficacy of all discipline, and especially in every war conducted in a disciplined fashion. It is the only efficacious element and—as *caput mortuum*—it always remains after the 'ethical' qualities of duty and conscientiousness have failed.

1: THE ORIGINS OF DISCIPLINE IN WAR

The conflict between discipline and individual charisma has been full of vicissitudes. It has its classic seat in the development of the structure of warfare, in which sphere the conflict is, of course, to some extent determined by the technique of warfare. The kind of weapons—pike, sword, bow—are not necessarily decisive; for all of them allow disciplined as well as individual combat. At the beginning of the known history of the Near East and of the Occident, however, the importation of the horse and probably, to some uncertain degree, the beginning of the predominance of iron for tools have played parts which have been epoch-making in every way.

The horse brought the war chariot and with it the hero driving into combat and possibly fighting from his chariot. The hero has been dominant in the warfare of the Oriental, Indian, and ancient Chinese kings, as well as throughout Occidental societies, including the Celtic. In Ireland 'hero combat' prevailed until late times. Horseback riding came after the war chariot, but persisted longer. From such horseback riding the 'knight' emerged—the Persian, as well as the Thessalian, Athenian, Roman, Celtic, and Germanic. The footman, who certainly played some part earlier in the development of discipline, receded in importance for quite some time.

The substitution of iron side-arms for bronze javelins was probably among the factors that again pushed development in the opposite direction, toward discipline. Yet, just as in the Middle Ages gun powder can scarcely be said to have brought about the transition from undisciplined to disciplined fighting, so iron, as such, did not bring about the change—for long-range and knightly weapons were made of iron.

It was the discipline of the Hellenic and Roman Hoplites[1] which brought about the change. Even Homer, as an oft-quoted passage indicates, knew of the beginnings of discipline with its prohibition of fighting out of line. For Rome, the important turning-point is symbolized by the legend of the execution of the consul's son, who, in accordance with the ancient fashion of heroes, had slain the opposing war lord in individual combat. At first, the well-trained army of the Spartan professional soldier, the holy Lochos[2] of the Boeotians, the well-trained *sarissa*-equipped[3] phalanx of the Macedonians, and then the tactic of the highly trained, more mobile maniple[4] of the Romans, gained supremacy over the Persian knight, the militias of the Hellenic and Italic citizenry, and the people's armies of the Barbarians. In the early period of the Hellenic Hoplites, incipient attempts were made to exclude long range weapons by 'international law' as unchivalrous, just as during the Middle Ages there were attempts to forbid the cross-bow.

The kind of weapon has been the result and not the cause of discipline. Exclusive use of the infantry tactic of close combat during antiquity brought about the decay of cavalry, and in Rome the 'census of knights' became practically equivalent to exemption from military service.

At the close of the Middle Ages it was the massed force of the Swiss, with its parallel and ensuing developments, which first broke the monopoly of knighthood to wage war. And even then, the Swiss still allowed the Halberdiers[5] to break forth from the main force for hero combat, after the main force had advanced in closed formation—the pike-men occupying the outside positions. At first these massed forces of the Swiss only succeeded in dispersing the knights. And in the battles of the sixteenth and seventeenth centuries, cavalry, as such, increasingly disciplined, still played a completely decisive role. Without cavalry it was still impossible to wage offensive wars and actually to overpower the enemy, as the course of the English Civil War demonstrated.

It was discipline and not gun powder which initiated the transformation. The Dutch army under Maurice of the House of Orange was one of the first modern disciplined armies. It was shorn of all status privileges; and thus, for example, the previously effective refusal of the mercenaries to do rampart work (*opera servitia*) became ineffective. Cromwell's victories—despite the fierce bravery of the Cavaliers—were due to sober and rational Puritan discipline. His 'Ironsides'—the 'men of conscience'—trotted forward in firmly closed formation, at the same time calmly firing, and then, thrusting, brought about a successful attack. The major contrast lies in the fact that after the attack they remained in closed formation or immediately re-aligned themselves. It was this disciplined cavalry attack which was technically superior to the Cavaliers' ardor. For it was the habit of the Cavaliers to gallop enthusiastically into the attack and then, without discipline, to disperse, either to plunder the camp of the enemy or prematurely and individually to pursue single opponents in order to capture them for ransom. All successes were forfeited by such habits, as was typically and often the case in Antiquity and the Middle Ages (for example, at Tagliacozzo). Gun powder and all the war techniques associated with it became significant only with the existence of discipline—and to the full extent only with the use of war machinery, which presupposes discipline.

The economic bases upon which army organizations have been founded are not the only agent determining the development of discipline, yet they have been of considerable importance. The discipline of well-trained armies and the major or minor role they have played in warfare reacted still more, and with more lasting effects, upon the political and social order. This influence, however, has been ambiguous. Discipline, as the basis of warfare, gave birth to patriarchal kingship among the Zulus, where the monarch is constitutionally limited by the power of the army leaders (like the Spartan Ephors).[6] Similarly, discipline gave birth to the Hellenic polis with its gymnasiums.

When infantry drill is perfected to the point of virtuosity (Sparta), the polis has an inevitably 'aristocratic' structure. When cities are based upon naval discipline, they have 'democratic' structures (Athens). Discipline gave rise to Swiss 'democracy,' which is quite different in nature. It involved a dominance (in Hellenic terms) over metics as well as territorial helots, during the time when Swiss mercenaries enlisted in foreign armies. The rule of the Roman particiate, of the Egyptian, Assyrian, and finally of the modern European bureaucratic state organizations—all have their origin in discipline.

War discipline may go hand in hand with totally different economic conditions, as these examples show. However, discipline has always affected the structure of the state, the economy, and possibly the family. For in the past a fully disciplined army has necessarily been a professional army, and therefore the basic problem has always been how to provide for the sustenance of the warriors.

The primeval way of creating trained troops—ever ready to strike, and allowing themselves to be disciplined—was *warrior communism,* which we have already mentioned. It may take the form of the bachelor house as a kind of barracks or casino of the professional warriors; in this form it is spread over the largest part of the earth. Or, it may follow the pattern of the communist community of the Ligurian pirates, or of the Spartan syssitia organized according to the 'picnic' principle; or it may follow Caliph Omar's organization, or the religious knight orders of the Middle Ages. The warrior community may constitute, as we have noticed above, either a completely autonomous society closed against the outside, or, as is the rule, it may be incorporated into a political association whose territory is fixed by boundaries. As a part of such a corporate group, the warrior community may decisively determine its order. Thus, the recruitment of the warrior community is linked to the order of the corporate group. But this linkage is largely relative. Even the Spartans, for example, did not insist upon a strict 'purity of blood.' Military education was decisive for membership in its warrior community.

Under warrior communism, the existence of the warrior is the perfect counterpart to the existence of the monk, whose garrisoned and communist life in the monastery also serves the purpose of disciplining him in the service of his master in the hereafter (and possibly also resulting in service to a this-worldly master). The dissociation from the family and from all private economic interests also occurs outside the celibate knight orders, which were created in direct analogy to the monk orders.

When the institution of the bachelor house is fully developed, familial relations are often completely excluded. The inmates of the house purchase or capture girls, or they claim that the girls of the subject community be at their disposal so long as they have not been sold in marriage. The children of the Ariloi—the ruling estate in Melanesia—are killed. Men can join enduring sexual communities with a separate economy only after having completed their 'service' in the bachelor house—often only at an advanced age. Stratification according to age groups, which with some peoples is also important for the regulation of sexual relationship; the alleged survivals from primitive 'endogenous sexual promiscuity'; the alleged survivals of a supposedly 'primeval right' of all comrades to all girls not yet appropriated by an individual; as well as 'marriage by capture'—allegedly the earliest form of marriage; and, above all, the 'matriarchate'—all of these might be in most cases survivals of such military organizations as we are discussing. These military organizations split the life of the warrior from the household and family, and,

THE MEANING OF DISCIPLINE 259

under conditions of chronic warfare, such organizations have been widely diffused.

Almost everywhere the communistic warrior community may be the *caput mortuum* of the followers of charismatic war lords. Such a following has usually been societalized into a chronic institution and, once existing in peacetime, has led to the decline of warrior chieftainship. Yet under favorable conditions, the warrior chief may well rise to absolute lordship over the disciplined warrior formations. Accordingly, the *oikos,* as the basis of a military structure, offers an extreme contrast to this communism of warriors who live on accumulated stores, as well as contributions of the women, of those unfit to bear arms, and possibly of serfs. The patrimonial army is sustained and equipped from the stores of a commanding overlord. It was known especially in Egypt, but its fragments are widely dispersed in military organizations of different natures, and they form the bases of princely despotisms.

The reverse phenomenon, the emancipation of the warrior community from the unlimited power of the overlord, as evidenced in Sparta through the institution of the Ephors, has proceeded only so far as the interest in discipline has permitted. In the polis, therefore, the weakening of the king's power—which meant the weakening of discipline—prevailed only in peace and in the homeland (*domi* in contrast to *militiae,* according to the technical terms of Roman administrative law). The Spartan king's prerogatives approached the zero point only in peacetime. In the interests of discipline, the king was omnipotent in the field.

An all-around weakening of discipline usually accompanies any kind of decentralized military establishment—whether it is of prebendal or of feudal type. This weakening of discipline may vary greatly in degree. The well-trained Spartan army, the δχλῆροι [7] of the other Hellenic and Macedonian and of several Oriental military establishments, the Turkish quasi-prebendal fiefs, and finally the feudal fiefs of the Japanese and Occidental Middle Ages—all of these were phases of economic decentralization, usually going hand in hand with the weakening of discipline and the rising importance of individual heroism.

From the disciplinary aspect, just as from the economic, the feudal lord and vassal represents an extreme contrast to the patrimonial or bureaucratic soldier. And the disciplinary aspect is a consequence of the economic aspect. The feudal vassal and lord not only cares for his own equipment and provisions, directs his own baggage-train, but he summons and leads sub-vassals who, in turn, also equip themselves.

Discipline has grown on the basis of an increased concentration of the means of warfare in the hands of the war lord. This has been achieved by having a condottiere recruit mercenary armies, in part or wholly, in the manner of a private capitalist. Such an arrangement was dominant in the late Middle Ages and the beginning of the modern era. It was followed by the raising and equipping of standing armies by means of political authority and a collective economy. We shall not describe here in detail the increasing rationalization of procurement for the armies. It began with Maurice of the House of Orange, proceeded to Wallenstein, Gustav Adolf, Cromwell, the armies of the French, of Frederick the Great, and of Maria Theresa; it passed through a transition from the professional army to the people's army of the French Revolution, and from the disciplining of the people's army by Napoleon into a partly professional army. Finally universal conscription was introduced during the nineteenth century. The whole development meant, in effect, the clearly increasing importance of discipline and, just as clearly, the consistent execution of the economic process through which a public and collective economy was substituted for private capitalism as the basis for military organization.

Whether the exclusive dominance of universal conscription will be the last word in the age of machine warfare remains to be seen. The shooting records of the British navy, for instance, seem to be affected by ensembling gun crews of professional soldiers, which allows for their continuation as a team through the years. The belief in the technical superiority of the professional soldier for certain categories of troops is almost sure to gain in influence, especially if the process of shortening the term of service—stagnating in Europe at the moment—should continue. In several officers' circles, this view is already esoterically held. The introduction of a three-year period of compulsory service by the French army (1913) was motivated here and there by the slogan of 'professional army'—a somewhat inappropriate slogan, since all differentiation of the troops into categories was absent. These still ambiguous possibilities, and also their possible political consequences, are not to be discussed here. In any case, none of them will alter the exclusive importance of mass discipline. What has concerned us here has been to show that the separation of the warrior from the means of warfare, and the concentration of the means of warfare in the hands of the war lord have everywhere been one of the typical bases of mass discipline. And this has been the case whether the process of separation and of concentration was executed in the form of oikos, capitalist enterprise, or bureau-cratic organization.

2: THE DISCIPLINE OF LARGE-SCALE ECONOMIC ORGANIZATIONS

The discipline of the army gives birth to all discipline. The large-scale economic organization is the second great agency which trains men for discipline. No direct historical and transitional organizations link the Pharaonic workshops and construction work (however little detail about their organization is known) with the Carthaginian Roman plantation, the mines of the late Middle Ages, the slave plantation of colonial economies, and finally the modern factory. However, all of these have in common the one element of discipline.

The slaves of the ancient plantations slept in barracks, living without family and without property. Only the managers—especially the *villicus*—had individual domiciles, somewhat comparable to the lieutenant's domi-cile or the residence of a manager of a modern, large-scale agricultural enterprise. The *villicus* alone usually had quasi-property (*peculium,* i.e. originally property in cattle) and quasi-marriage (*contubernium*). In the morning the work-slaves lined up in 'squads' (in *decuriae*) and were led to work by overseers (*monitores*); their personal equipment (to use a barrack term) was stored away and handed out according to need. And hospitals and prison cells were not absent. The discipline of the manor of the Middle Ages and the modern era was considerably less strict because it was traditionally stereotyped, and therefore it somewhat limited the lord's power.

No special proof is necessary to show that military discipline is the ideal model for the modern capitalist factory, as it was for the ancient plantation. In contrast to the plantation, organizational discipline in the factory is founded upon a completely rational basis. With the help of appropriate methods of measurement, the optimum profitability of the individual worker is calculated like that of any material means of pro-duction. On the basis of this calculation, the American system of 'scien-tific management' enjoys the greatest triumphs in the rational condition-ing and training of work performances. The final consequences are drawn from the mechanization and discipline of the plant, and the psycho-physical apparatus of man is completely adjusted to the demands of the outer world, the tools, the machines—in short, to an individual 'function.' The individual is shorn of his natural rhythm as determined by the structure of his organism; his psycho-physical apparatus is atuned to a new rhythm through a methodical specialization of separately functioning muscles, and an optimal economy of forces is established corresponding to the conditions of work. This whole process of rationalization, in the factory as elsewhere, and especially in the bureaucratic state machine, parallels the centralization of the material implements of organization in the discretionary power of the overlord.

The ever-widening grasp of discipline irresistibly proceeds with the rationalization of the supply of economic and political demands. This universal phenomenon increasingly restricts the importance of charisma and of individually differentiated conduct.

3: DISCIPLINE AND CHARISMA

Charisma, as a creative power, recedes in the face of domination, which hardens into lasting institutions, and becomes efficacious only in short-lived mass emotions of incalculable effects, as on elections and similar occasions. Nevertheless charisma remains a highly important element of the social structure, although of course in a greatly changed sense.

We must now return to the economic factors, already mentioned above, which predominantly determine the routinization of charisma: the need of social strata, privileged through existing political, social, and economic orders, to have their social and economic positions 'legitimized.' They wish to see their positions transformed from purely factual power relations into a cosmos of acquired rights, and to know that they are thus sanctified. These interests comprise by far the strongest motive for the conservation of charismatic elements of an objectified nature within the structure of domination. Genuine charisma is absolutely opposed to this objectified form. It does not appeal to an enacted or traditional order, nor does it base its claims upon acquired rights. Genuine charisma rests upon the legitimation of personal heroism or personal revelation. Yet precisely this quality of charisma as an extraordinary, supernatural, divine power transforms it, after its routinization, into a suitable source for the legitimate acquisition of sovereign power by the successors of the charismatic hero. Routinized charisma thus continues to work in favor of all those whose power and possession is guaranteed by that sovereign power, and who thus depend upon the continued existence of such power.

The forms in which a ruler's charismatic legitimation may express itself vary according to the relation of the original charismatic power-holder with the supernatural powers. If the ruler's legitimation cannot be determined, according to unambiguous rules, through hereditary charisma, he is in need of legitimation through some other charismatic power. Normally, this can only be hierocratic power. This holds expressly for the sovereign who represents a divine incarnation, and who thus possesses the highest 'personal charisma.' Unless it is supported and proved by personal deeds, his claim of charisma requires the acknowledgment of professional experts in divinity. Incarnated monarchs are indeed exposed to the peculiar process of interment by close court officials and priests, who are materially and ideally interested in legitimacy. This seclusion may proceed to a permanent palace arrest and even to killing upon maturity, lest the god have occasion to compromise divinity or to free himself from tutelage. Yet generally, according to the genuine view as well as in practice, the weight of responsibility which the charismatic ruler must carry before his subjects works very definitely in the direction of the need for his tutelage.

It is because of their high charismatic qualifications that such rulers as the Oriental Caliph, Sultan, and Shah urgently need, even nowadays (1913), a single personality to assume responsibility for governmental actions, especially for failures and unpopular actions. This is the basis for the traditional and specific position of the 'Grand Vizier' in all those realms. The attempt to abolish and replace the office of the Grand Vizier by bureaucratic departments under ministers with the Shah's personal chairmanship failed in Persia during the last generation. This change would have placed the Shah in the role of a leader of the administration, personally responsible for all its abuses and for all the sufferings of the people. This role not only would have continuously jeopardized him, but would have shaken the belief in his very 'charismatic' legitimacy. The office of Grand Vizier with its responsibilities had to be restored in order to protect the Shah and his charisma.

The Grand Vizier is the Oriental counterpart of the position of the responsible prime minister of the Occident, especially in parliamentary states. The formula, *le roi règne mais il ne gouverne pas,* and the theory that, in the interest of the dignity of his position, the king must not 'figure without ministerial decorations,' or, that he must abstain entirely from intervening in the normal administration directed by bureaucratic experts and specialists, or that he must abstain from administration in favor of the political party leaders occupying ministerial positions—all these theories correspond entirely to the enshrinement of the deified, patrimonial sovereign by the experts in tradition and ceremony: priests, court officers, and high dignitaries. In all these cases the sociological nature of charisma plays just as great a part as that of court officials or party leaders and their followings. Despite his lack of parliamentary power, the constitutional monarch is preserved, and above all, his mere existence and his charisma guarantee the *legitimacy* of the existing social and property order, since decisions are carried out 'in his name.' Besides, all those interested in the social order must fear for the belief in 'legality' lest it be shaken by doubts of its legitimacy.

A president elected according to fixed rules can formally legitimize the governmental actions of the respective victorious party as 'lawful,' just as well as a parliamentary monarch. But the monarch, in addition to such legitimation, can perform a function which an elected president can not fulfil: a parliamentary monarch formally delimits the politicians' quest for power, because the highest position in the state is occupied once and for all. From a political point of view this essentially negative function, associated with the mere existence of a king enthroned according to fixed rules, is of the greatest practical importance. Formulated positively it means, for the archetype of the species, that the king cannot gain an actual share in political power by prerogative (kingdom of prerogative). He can share power only by virtue of outstanding personal ability or social influence (kingdom of influence). Yet he is in position to exert this influence in spite of all parliamentary government, as events and personalities of recent times have shown.

'Parliamentary' kingship in England means a selective admission to actual power for that monarch who qualifies as a statesman. But a misstep at home or in foreign affairs, or the raising of pretensions that do not correspond with his personal abilities and prestige, may cost him his crown. Thus English parliamentary kingship is formed in a more genuinely charismatic fashion than kingships on the Continent. On the Continent, mere birth-right equally endows the fool and the political genius with the pretensions of a sovereign.

Part III

RELIGION

XI. The Social Psychology of the World Religions

By 'world religions,' we understand the five religions or religiously determined systems of life-regulation which have known how to gather multitudes of confessors around them. The term is used here in a completely value-neutral sense. The Confucian, Hinduist, Buddhist, Christian, and Islamist religious ethics all belong to the category of world religion. A sixth religion, Judaism, will also be dealt with. It is included because it contains historical preconditions decisive for understanding Christianity and Islamism, and because of its historic and autonomous significance for the development of the modern economic ethic of the Occident—a significance, partly real and partly alleged, which has been discussed several times recently. References to other religions will be made only when they are indispensable for historical connections.[1]

What is meant by the 'economic ethic' of a religion will become increasingly clear during the course of our presentation. This term does not bring into focus the ethical theories of theological compendia; for however important such compendia may be under certain circumstances, they merely serve as tools of knowledge. The term 'economic ethic' points to the practical impulses for action which are founded in the psychological and pragmatic contexts of religions. The following presentation may be sketchy, but it will make obvious how complicated the structures and how many-sided the conditions of a concrete economic ethic usually are. Furthermore, it will show that externally similar forms of economic organization may agree with very different economic ethics

'Die Wirtschaftsethik der Weltreligionen,' *Gesammelte Aufsaetze zur Religionssoziologie* (Tübingen, 1922-3), vol. I, pp. 237-68. This is a translation of the Introduction to a series of studies which Weber published as articles in the *Archiv für Sozialforschung* under the title 'Die Wirtschaftsethik der Weltreligionen' (The Economic Ethic of the World Religions). The Introduction and the first parts on Confucianism and Taoism were written in 1913. They were not published until September 1915, in the 41st volume of the *Archiv.*

and, according to the unique character of their economic ethics, how such forms of economic organization may produce very different historical results. An economic ethic is not a simple 'function' of a form of economic organization; and just as little does the reverse hold, namely, that economic ethics unambiguously stamp the form of the economic organization.

No economic ethic has ever been determined solely by religion. In the face of man's attitudes towards the world—as determined by religious or other (in our sense) 'inner' factors—an economic ethic has, of course, a high measure of autonomy. Given factors of economic geography and history determine this measure of autonomy in the highest degree. The religious determination of life-conduct, however, is also one—note this—only one, of the determinants of the economic ethic. Of course, the religiously determined way of life is itself profoundly influenced by economic and political factors operating within given geographical, political, social, and national boundaries. We should lose ourselves in these discussions if we tried to demonstrate these dependencies in all their singularities. Here we can only attempt to peel off the directive elements in the life-conduct of those social *strata* which have most strongly influenced the practical ethic of their respective religions. These elements have stamped the most characteristic features upon practical ethics, the features that distinguish one ethic from others; *and,* at the same time, they have been important for the respective economic ethics.

By no means must we focus upon only one stratum. Those strata which are decisive in stamping the characteristic features of an economic ethic may change in the course of history. And the influence of a single stratum is never an exclusive one. Nevertheless, as a rule one may determine the strata whose styles of life have been at least predominantly decisive for certain religions. Here are some examples, if one may anticipate:

Confucianism was the status ethic of prebendaries, of men with literary educations who were characterized by a secular rationalism. If one did not belong to this *cultured* stratum he did not count. The religious (or if one wishes, irreligious) status ethic of this stratum has determined the Chinese way of life far beyond the stratum itself.

Earlier Hinduism was borne by a hereditary caste of cultured literati, who, being remote from any office, functioned as a kind of ritualist and spiritual advisers for individuals and communities. They formed a stable center for the orientation of the status stratification, and they placed their stamp upon the social order. Only Brahmans, *educated* in the Veda, formed, as bearers of tradition, the fully recognized religious status group. And only later a non-Brahman status group of ascetics emerged by the side of the Brahmans and competed with them. Still later, during the Indian Middle Ages, Hinduism entered the plain. It represented the ardent[2] sacramental religiosity of the savior, and was borne by the lower strata with their plebeian mystagogues.

Buddhism was propagated by strictly contemplative, mendicant monks, who rejected the world and, having no homes, migrated. Only these were full members of the religious community; all others remained religious laymen of inferior value: objects, not subjects, of religiosity.

During its first period, Islamism was a religion of world-conquering warriors, a knight order of disciplined crusaders. They lacked only the sexual asceticism of their Christian copies of the age of the Crusades. But during the Islamic Middle Ages, contemplative and mystical Sufism[3] attained at least an equal standing under the leadership of plebeian technicians of orgiastics. The brotherhoods of the petty bourgeoisie grew out of Sufism in a manner similar to the Christian Tertiarians, except they were far more universally developed.

Since the Exile, Judaism has been the religion of a civic 'pariah people.' We shall in time become acquainted with the precise meaning of the term. During the Middle Ages Judaism fell under the leadership of a stratum of intellectuals who were trained in literature and ritual, a peculiarity of Judaism. This stratum has represented an increasingly quasi-proletarian and rationalist petty-bourgeois intelligentsia.

Christianity, finally, began its course as a doctrine of itinerant artisan journeymen. During all periods of its mighty external and internal development it has been a quite specifically urban, and above all a civic, religion. This was true during Antiquity, during the Middle Ages, and in Puritanism. The city of the Occident, unique among all other cities of the world—and citizenship, in the sense in which it has emerged only in the Occident—has been the major theatre for Christianity. This holds for the pneumatic piety of the ancient religious community, for the mendicant monk orders of the high Middle Ages, and for the [Protestant] sects of the reformation up to pietism and methodism.

It is not our thesis that the specific nature of a religion is a simple 'function' of the social situation of the stratum which appears as its characteristic bearer, or that it represents the stratum's 'ideology,' or that it is a 'reflection' of a stratum's material or ideal interest-situation. On the contrary, a more basic misunderstanding of the standpoint of these discussions would hardly be possible.

However incisive the social influences, economically and politically determined, may have been upon a religious ethic in a particular case, it receives its stamp primarily from religious sources, and, first of all, from the content of its annunciation and its promise. Frequently the very next generation reinterprets these annunciations and promises in a fundamental fashion. Such reinterpretations adjust the revelations to the needs of the religious community. If this occurs, then it is at least usual that religious doctrines are adjusted to *religious needs*. Other spheres of interest could have only a secondary influence; often, however, such influence is very obvious and sometimes it is decisive.

For every religion we shall find that a change in the socially decisive strata has usually been of profound importance. On the other hand, the type of a religion, once stamped, has usually exerted a rather far-reaching influence upon the life-conduct of very heterogeneous strata. In various ways people have sought to interpret the connection between religious ethics and interest-situations in such a way that the former appear as mere 'functions' of the latter. Such interpretation occurs in so-called historical materialism—which we shall not here discuss—as well as in a purely psychological sense.

A quite general and abstract class-determination of religious ethics might be deduced from the theory of 'resentment,' known since Friedrich Nietzsche's brilliant essay and since then spiritedly treated by psychologists. As is known, this theory regards the moral glorification of mercy and brotherliness as a 'slave revolt in morals' among those who are disadvantaged, either in their natural endowments or in their opportunities as determined by life-fate. The ethic of 'duty' is thus considered a product of 'repressed' sentiments for vengeance on the part of banausic men who 'displace' their sentiments because they are powerless, and condemned to work and to money-making. They resent the way of life of the lordly stratum who live free of duties. A very simple solution of the most important problems in the typology of religious ethics would obviously result if this were the case. However fortunate and fruitful the disclosure of the psychological significance of resentment as such has been, great caution is necessary in estimating its bearing for social ethics.

Later we shall have to discuss the motives that have determined the different forms of ethical 'rationalization' of life conduct, *per se*. In the main, these have had nothing whatsoever to do with resentment. But that the evaluation of *suffering* in religious ethics has been subject to a typical change is beyond doubt. If properly understood, this change carries a certain justification for the theory first worked out by Nietzsche. The primeval attitude towards suffering has been thrown into relief most drastically during the religious festivities of the community, especially in the treatment of those haunted by disease or other cases of obstinate misfortune. Men, permanently suffering, mourning, diseased, or otherwise unfortunate, were, according to the nature of their suffering, believed either to be possessed by a demon or burdened with the wrath of a god whom they had insulted. To tolerate such men in the midst of the cultic community could result in disadvantages for it. In any case, they were not allowed to participate in cultic feasts and sacrifices, for the gods did not enjoy the sight of them and could be incited to wrath by it. The sacrificial feasts were occasions for rejoicing—even in Jerusalem during times of siege.

In treating suffering as a symptom of odiousness in the eyes of the gods and as a sign of secret guilt, religion has psychologically met a very general need. The fortunate is seldom satisfied with the fact of being fortunate. Beyond this, he needs to know that he has a *right* to his good fortune. He wants to be convinced that he 'deserves' it, and above all, that he deserves it in comparison with others. He wishes to be allowed the belief that the less fortunate also merely experience his due. Good fortune thus wants to be 'legitimate' fortune.

If the general term 'fortune' covers all the 'good' of honor, power, possession, and pleasure, it is the most general formula for the service of legitimation, which religion has had to accomplish for the external and the inner interests of all ruling men, the propertied, the victorious, and the healthy. In short, religion provides the theodicy of good fortune for those who are fortunate. This theodicy is anchored in highly robust ('pharisaical') needs of man and is therefore easily understood, even if sufficient attention is often not paid to its effects.

In contrast, the way in which this negative evaluation of suffering has led to its religious glorification is more complicated. Numerous forms of chastisement and of abstinences from normal diet and sleep, as well as from sexual intercourse, awaken, or at least facilitate, the charisma of ecstatic, visionary, hysterical, in short, of all extraordinary states that are evaluated as 'holy.' Their production therefore forms the object of magical asceticism. The prestige of these chastisements has resulted from

the notion that certain kinds of suffering and abnormal states provoked
through chastisement are avenues to the attainment of superhuman,
that is magical, powers. The ancient prescriptions of taboo and abstinences in the interest of cultic purity, which follow from a belief in
demons, has worked in the same direction. The development of cults of
'redemption' has been added to these prescriptions, abstinences, and interests. In principle, these cults have occupied an independent and new
position in the face of individual suffering. The primeval cult, and above
all, the cult of the political associations, have left all individual interests
out of consideration. The tribal and local god, the gods of the city and
of the empire, have taken care only of interests that have concerned the
collectivity as a whole. They have been concerned with rain and with
sunshine, with the booty of the hunt and with victory over enemies.
Thus, in the community cult, the collectivity as such turned to its god.
The individual, in order to avoid or remove evils that concerned himself—above all, sickness—has not turned to the cult of the community,
but as an individual he has approached the sorcerer as the oldest personal and 'spiritual adviser.' The prestige of particular magicians, and
of those spirits or divinities in whose names they have performed their
miracles, has brought them patronage, irrespective of local or of tribal
affiliation. Under favorable conditions this has led to the formation of a
religious 'community,' which has been independent of ethnic associations.
Some, though not all, 'mysteries' have taken this course. They have
promised the salvation of individuals *qua* individuals from sickness,
poverty, and from all sorts of distress and danger. Thus the magician
has transformed himself into the mystagogue; that is, hereditary
dynasties of mystagogues or organizations of trained personnel under a
head determined in accordance with some sort of rules have developed.
This head has either been recognized as the incarnation of a superhuman
being or merely as a prophet, that is, as the mouthpiece and agent of his
god. Collective religious arrangements for individual 'suffering' *per se,*
and for 'salvation' from it, have originated in this fashion.

The annunciation and the promise of religion have naturally been
addressed to the masses of those who were in need of salvation. They
and their interests have moved into the center of the professional organization for the 'cure of the soul,' which, indeed, only therewith originated.
The typical service of magicians and priests becomes the determination
of the factors to be blamed for suffering, that is, the confession of 'sins.'
At first, these sins were offenses against ritual commandments. The

magician and priest also give counsel for behavior fit to remove the suffering. The material and ideal interests of magicians and priests could thereby actually and increasingly enter the service of specifically *plebeian* motives. A further step along this course was signified when, under the pressure of typical and ever-recurrent distress, the religiosity of a 're-deemer' evolved. This religiosity presupposed the myth of a savior, hence (at least relatively) of a *rational* view of the world. Again, suffering became the most important topic. The primitive mythology of nature frequently offered a point of departure for this religiosity. The spirits who governed the coming and going of vegetation and the paths of celestial bodies important for the seasons of the year became the pre-ferred carriers of the myths of the suffering, dying, and resurrecting god to needful men. The resurrected god guaranteed the return of good fortune in this world or the security of happiness in the world beyond. Or, a popularized figure from heroic sagas—like Krishna in India—is embellished with the myths of childhood, love, and struggle; and such figures became the object of an ardent cult of the savior. Among people under political pressure, like the Israelites, the title of 'savior' (Moshuach name) was originally attached to the saviors from political distress, as transmitted by hero sagas (Gideon, Jephthah). The 'Messianic' promises were determined by these sagas. With this people, and in this clear-cut fashion only among them and under other very particular conditions, the suffering of a people's *community,* rather than the suffering of an indi-vidual, became the object of hope for religious salvation. The rule was that the savior bore an individual and universal character at the same time that he was ready to guarantee salvation for the *individual* and to every individual who would turn to him.

The figure of the savior has been of varying stamp. In the late form of Zoroastrianism with its numerous abstractions, a purely constructed figure assumed the role of the mediator and savior in the economy of salvation. The reverse has also occurred: a historical person, legitimized through miracles and visionary reappearances, ascends to the rank of savior. Purely historical factors have been decisive for the realization of these very different possibilities. Almost always, however, some kind of theodicy of suffering has originated from the hope for salvation.

The promises of the religions of salvation at first remained tied to ritualist rather than to ethical preconditions. Thus, for instance, both the worldly and the other worldly advantages of the Eleusinian mysteries were tied to ritual purity and to attendance at the Eleusinian mass. When law gained in significance, these special deities played an increasing role, and the task of protecting the traditional order, of punishing the unjust and rewarding the righteous, was transferred to them as guardians of juridical procedure.

Where religious development was decisively influenced by a prophecy, naturally 'sin' was no longer a mere magical offense. Above all, it was a sign of disbelief in the prophet and in his commandments. Sin figured as the basic cause of all sorts of misfortunes.

The prophet has not regularly been a descendant or a representative of depressed classes. The reverse, as we shall see, has almost always been the rule. Neither has the content of the prophet's doctrine been derived preponderantly from the intellectual horizon of the depressed classes. As a rule, however, the oppressed, or at least those threatened by distress, were in need of a redeemer and prophet; the fortunate, the propertied, the ruling strata were not in such need. Therefore, in the great majority of cases, a prophetically announced religion of redemption has had its permanent locus among the less-favored social strata. Among these, such religiosity has either been a substitute for, or a rational supplement to, magic.

Wherever the promises of the prophet or the redeemer have not sufficiently met the needs of the socially less-favored strata, a secondary salvation religion of the masses has regularly developed beneath the official doctrine. The rational conception of the world is contained in germ within the myth of the redeemer. A rational theodicy of misfortune has, therefore, as a rule, been a development of this conception of the world. At the same time, this rational view of the world has often furnished suffering as such with a 'plus' sign, which was originally quite foreign to it.

Suffering, voluntarily created through mortification, changed its meaning with the development of ethical divinities who punish and reward. Originally, the magical coercion of spirits by the formula of prayer was increased through mortification as a source of charismatic states. Such coercion was preserved in mortification by prayer as well as in cultic prescriptions of abstinence. This has remained the case, even after the magical formula for coercing spirits became a supplication to be heard by a deity. Penances were added as a means of cooling the wrath of deities by repentance, and of avoiding through self-punishment the sanctions that have been incurred. The numerous abstinences were originally attached to the mourning for the dead (with special clarity in China) in order to turn away their jealousy and wrath. These abstinences were easily transferred to relations with the appropriate divinities; they made self-mortification, and finally, unintentional deprivation as such, appear more pleasing to the gods than the naive enjoyment of the goods of this earth. Such enjoyment, indeed, made the pleasure-seeking man less accessible to the influence of the prophet or the priest.

The force of all these individual factors was tremendously enhanced under certain conditions.

The need for an ethical interpretation of the 'meaning' of the distribution of fortunes among men increased with the growing rationality of conceptions of the world. As the religious and ethical reflections upon the world were increasingly rationalized and primitive, and magical notions were eliminated, the theodicy of suffering encountered increasing difficulties. Individually 'undeserved' woe was all too frequent; not 'good' but 'bad' men succeeded—even when 'good' and 'bad' were measured by the yardstick of the master stratum and not by that of a 'slave morality.'

One can explain suffering and injustice by referring to individual sin committed in a former life (the migration of souls), to the guilt of ancestors, which is avenged down to the third and fourth generation, or—the most principled—to the wickedness of all creatures *per se*. As compensatory promises, one can refer to hopes of the individual for a better life in the future in this world (transmigration of souls) or to hopes for the successors (Messianic realm), or to a better life in the hereafter (paradise).

The metaphysical conception of God and of the world, which the ineradicable demand for a theodicy called forth, could produce only a few systems of ideas on the whole—as we shall see, only three. These three gave rationally satisfactory answers to the questioning for the basis of the incongruity between destiny and merit: the Indian doctrine of Kharma, Zoroastrian dualism, and the predestination decree of the *deus abscondidus*. These solutions are rationally closed; in pure form, they are found only as exceptions.

The rational need for a theodicy of suffering and of dying has had extremely strong effects. As a matter of fact, this need has molded important traits of such religions as Hinduism, Zoroastrism, and Judaism, and, to a certain extent, Paulinian and later Christianity. Even as late as 1906, a mere minority among a rather considerable number of proletarians gave as reasons for their disbelief in Christianity conclusions derived

from modern theories of natural sciences. The majority, however, referred to the 'injustice' of the order of this world—to be sure, essentially
because they believed in a revolutionary compensation in this world.

The theodicy of suffering can be colored by resentment. But the need
of compensation for the insufficiency of one's fate in this world has not,
as a rule, had resentment as a basic and decisive color. Certainly, the
need for vengeance has had a special affinity with the belief that the
unjust are well off in this world only because hell is reserved for them
later. Eternal bliss is reserved for the pious; occasional sins, which, after
all, the pious also commit, ought therefore to be expiated in this world.
Yet one can readily be convinced that even this way of thinking, which
occasionally appears, is not always determined by resentment, and that
it is by no means always the product of socially oppressed strata. We
shall see that there have been only a few examples of religion to which
resentment contributed essential features. Among these examples only one
is a fully developed case. All that can be said is that resentment *could* be,
and often and everywhere has been, significant as one factor, among
others, in influencing the religiously determined rationalism of socially
disadvantaged strata. It has gained such significance, in highly diverse
and often minute degrees, in accordance with the nature of the promises
held out by different religions.

In any case, it would be quite wrong to attempt to deduce 'asceticism'
in general from these sources. The distrust of wealth and power, which
as a rule exists in genuine religions of salvation, has had its natural basis
primarily in the experience of redeemers, prophets, and priests. They
understood that those strata which were 'satiated' and favored in this
world had only a small urge to be saved, regardless of the kind of salvation offered. Hence, these master strata have been less 'devout' in the
sense of salvation religions. The development of a rational religious ethic
has had positive and primary roots in the inner conditions of those social
strata which were less socially valued.

Strata in solid possession of social honor and power usually tend to
fashion their status-legend in such a way as to claim a special and intrinsic quality of their own, usually a quality of blood; their sense of
dignity feeds on their actual or alleged being. The sense of dignity of
socially repressed strata or of strata whose status is negatively (or at least
not positively) valued is nourished most easily on the belief that a special
'mission' is entrusted to them; their worth is guaranteed or constituted
by an *ethical imperative,* or by their own functional *achievement.* Their

value is thus moved into something beyond themselves, into a 'task' placed before them by God. One source of the ideal power of ethical prophecies among socially disadvantaged strata lies in this fact. Resentment has not been required as a leverage; the rational interest in material and ideal compensations as such has been perfectly sufficient.

There can be no doubt that prophets and priests through intentional or unintentional propaganda have taken the resentment of the masses into their service. But this is by no means always the case. This essentially negative force of resentment, so far as is known, has never been the source of those essentially metaphysical conceptions which have lent uniqueness to every salvation religion. Moreover, in general, the nature of a religious promise has by no means necessarily or even predominantly been the mere mouthpiece of a class interest, either of an external or internal nature.

By themselves, the masses, as we shall see, have everywhere remained engulfed in the massive and archaic growth of magic—unless a prophecy that holds out specific promises has swept them into a religious movement of an ethical character. For the rest, the specific nature of the great religious and ethical systems has been determined by social conditions of a far more particular nature than by the mere contrast of ruling and ruled strata.

In order to avoid repetition, some further comments about these relationships may be stated in advance. For the empirical student, the sacred values, differing among themselves, are by no means only, nor even preferably, to be interpreted as 'other-worldly.' This is so quite apart from the fact that not every religion, nor every world religion, knows of a 'beyond' as a locus of definite promises. At first the sacred values of primitive as well as of cultured, prophetic or non-prophetic, religions were quite solid goods of this world. With the only partial exception of Christianity and a few other specifically ascetic creeds, they have consisted of health, a long life, and wealth. These were offered by the promises of the Chinese, Vedic, Zoroastrian, ancient Hebrew, and Islamite religions; and in the same manner by the Phoenician, Egyptian, Babylonian, and ancient Germanic religions, as well as by the promises of Hinduism and Buddhism for the devout laymen. Only the religious virtuoso, the ascetic, the monk, the Sufi, the Dervish strove for sacred values, which were 'other-worldly' as compared with such solid goods of this world, as health, wealth, and long life. And these other-worldly sacred values were by no means only values of the *beyond*. This was not the case even where it was understood to be so by the participants. Psychologically considered, man in quest of salvation has been primarily preoccupied by attitudes of the here and now. The puritan *certitudo salutis,* the permanent state of grace that rests in the feeling of 'having proved oneself,' was psychologically the only concrete object among the sacred values of this ascetic religion. The Buddhist monk, certain to enter Nirvana, seeks the sentiment of a cosmic love; the devout Hindu seeks either Bhakti (fervent love in the possession of God) or apathetic ecstasy. The Chlyst with his radjeny, as well as the dancing Dervish, strives for orgiastic ecstasy. Others seek to be possessed by God and to possess God, to be a bridegroom of the Virgin Mary, or to be the bride of the Savior. The Jesuit's cult of the heart of Jesus, quietistic edification, the pietists' tender love for the child Jesus and its 'running sore,'[4] the sexual and semi-sexual orgies at the wooing of Krishna, the sophisticated cultic dinners of the Vallabhacharis, the gnostic onanist cult activities, the various forms of the *unio mystica,* and the contemplative submersion in the All-one—these states undoubtedly have been sought, first of all, for the sake of such emotional value as they directly offered the devout. In this respect, they have in fact been absolutely equal to the religious and alcoholic intoxication of the Dionysian or the soma cult; to totemic meat-orgies, the cannibalistic feasts, the ancient and religiously consecrated use of hashish, opium, and nicotine; and, in general, to all sorts of magical intoxication. They have been considered specifically consecrated and divine because of their psychic extraordinariness and because of the intrinsic value of the respective states conditioned by them. Even the most primitive orgy has not entirely lacked a meaningful interpretation, although only the rationalized religions have imputed a metaphysical meaning into such specifically religious actions, in addition to the direct appropriation of sacred values. Rationalized religions have thus sublimated the orgy into the 'sacrament.' The orgy, however, has had a pure animist and magical character; it has contained only small or, indeed, no beginnings of the universalist, cosmic pragmatism of the holy. And such pragmatism is peculiar to all religious rationalism.

Yet even after such a sublimation of orgy into sacrament has occurred, the fact remains, of course, that for the devout the sacred value, first and above all, has been a psychological state in the *here and now.* Primarily this state consists in the emotional attitude *per se,* which was directly called forth by the specifically religious (or magical) act, by methodical asceticism, or by contemplation.

As extraordinary attitudes, religious states can be only transient in character and in external appearance. Originally this, of course, was everywhere the case. The only way of distinguishing between 'religious' and 'profane' states is by referring to the extraordinary character of the religious states. A special state, attained by religious means, can be striven for as a 'holy state' which is, meant to take possession of the entire man and of his lasting fate. The transition from a passing to a permanent holy state has been fluid.

The two highest conceptions of sublimated religious doctrines of salvation are 'rebirth' and 'redemption.' Rebirth, a primeval magical value, has meant the acquisition of a new soul by means of an orgiastic act or through methodically planned asceticism. Man transitorily acquired a new soul in ecstasy; but by means of magical asceticism, he could seek to gain it permanently. The youth who wished to enter the community of warriors as a hero, or to participate in its magical dances or orgies, or who wished to commune with the divinities in cultic feasts, had to have a new soul. The heroic and magical asceticism, the initiation rites of youths, and the sacramental customs of rebirth at important phases of private and collective life are thus quite ancient. The means used in these activities varied, as did their ends: that is, the answers to the question, 'For what should I be reborn?'

The various religious or magical states that have given their psychological stamp to religions may be systematized according to very different points of view. Here we shall not attempt such a systematization. In connection with what we have said, we merely wish to indicate quite generally the following.

The kind of empirical state of bliss or experience of rebirth that is sought after as the supreme value by a religion has obviously and necessarily varied according to the character of the stratum which was foremost in adopting it. The chivalrous warrior class, peasants, business classes, and intellectuals with literary education have naturally pursued different religious tendencies. As will become evident, these tendencies have not by themselves determined the psychological character of religion; they have, however, exerted a very lasting influence upon it. The contrast between warrior and peasant classes, and intellectual and business classes, is of special importance. Of these groups, the intellectuals have always been the exponents of a rationalism which in their case has been relatively theoretical. The business classes (merchants and artisans) have been at least possible exponents of rationalism of a more practical sort. Rational-

ism of either kind has borne very different stamps, but has always exerted
a great influence upon the religious attitude.

Above all, the peculiarity of the intellectual strata in this matter has
been in the past of the greatest importance for religion. At the present
time, it matters little in the development of a religion whether or not
modern intellectuals feel the need of enjoying a 'religious' state as an
'experience,' in addition to all sorts of other sensations, in order to decorate their internal and stylish furnishings with paraphernalia guaranteed
to be genuine and old. A religious revival has never sprung from such a
source. In the past, it was the work of the intellectuals to sublimate the
possession of sacred values into a belief in 'redemption.' The conception
of the idea of redemption, as such, is very old, if one understands by it a
liberation from distress, hunger, drought, sickness, and ultimately from
suffering and death. Yet redemption attained a specific significance only
where it expressed a systematic and rationalized 'image of the world' and
represented a stand in the face of the world. For the meaning as well as
the intended and actual psychological quality of redemption has depended upon such a world image and such a stand. Not ideas, but
material and ideal interests, directly govern men's conduct. Yet very frequently the 'world images' that have been created by 'ideas' have, like
switchmen, determined the tracks along which action has been pushed
by the dynamic of interest. 'From what' and 'for what' one wished to
be redeemed and, let us not forget, 'could be' redeemed, depended upon
one's image of the world.

There have been very different possibilities in this connection: One could
wish to be saved from political and social servitude and lifted into a
Messianic realm in the future of this world; or one could wish to be saved
from being defiled by ritual impurity and hope for the pure beauty of
psychic and bodily existence. One could wish to escape being incarcerated
in an impure body and hope for a purely spiritual existence. One could wish
to be saved from the eternal and senseless play of human passions and desires and hope for the quietude of the pure beholding of the divine. One
could wish to be saved from radical evil and the servitude of sin and hope
for the eternal and free benevolence in the lap of a fatherly god. One could
wish to be saved from peonage under the astrologically conceived determination of stellar constellations and long for the dignity of freedom and partaking of the substance of the hidden deity. One could wish to be redeemed
from the barriers to the finite, which express themselves in suffering, misery
and death, and the threatening punishment of hell, and hope for an eternal

bliss in an earthly or paradisical future existence. One could wish to be saved from the cycle of rebirths with their inexorable compensations for the deeds of the times past and hope for eternal rest. One could wish to be saved from senseless brooding and events and long for the dreamless sleep. Many more varieties of belief have, of course, existed. Behind them always lies a stand towards something in the actual world which is experienced as specifically 'senseless.' Thus, the demand has been implied: that the world order in its totality is, could, and should somehow be a meaningful 'cosmos.' This quest, the core of genuine religious rationalism, has been borne precisely by strata of intellectuals. The avenues, the results, and the efficacy of this metaphysical need for a meaningful cosmos have varied widely. Nevertheless, some general comments may be made.

The general result of the modern form of thoroughly rationalizing the conception of the world and of the way of life, theoretically and practically, in a purposive manner, has been that religion has been shifted into the realm of the irrational. This has been the more the case the further the purposive type of rationalization has progressed, if one takes the standpoint of an intellectual articulation of an image of the world. This shift of religion into the irrational realm has occurred for several reasons. On the one hand, the calculation of consistent rationalism has not easily come out even with nothing left over. In music, the Pythagorean 'comma' resisted complete rationalization oriented to tonal physics. The various great systems of music of all peoples and ages have differed in the manner in which they have either covered up or bypassed this inescapable irrationality or, on the other hand, put irrationality into the service of the richness of tonalities. The same has seemed to happen to the theoretical conception of the world, only far more so; and above all, it has seemed to happen to the rationalization of practical life. The various great ways of leading a rational and methodical life have been characterized by irrational presuppositions, which have been accepted simply as 'given' and which have been incorporated into such ways of life. What these presuppositions have been is historically and socially determined, at least to a very large extent, through the peculiarity of those strata that have been the carriers of the ways of life during its formative and decisive period. The *interest* situation of these strata, as determined socially and psychologically, has made for their peculiarity, as we here understand it.

Furthermore, the irrational elements in the rationalization of reality have been the *loci* to which the irrepressible quest of intellectualism for the possession of supernatural values has been compelled to retreat. That is the more so the more denuded of irrationality the world appears to be. The unity of the primitive image of the world, in which everything was concrete magic, has tended to split into rational cognition and mastery of nature, on the one hand, and into 'mystic' experiences, on the other. The inexpressible contents of such experiences remain the only possible 'beyond,' added to the mechanism of a world robbed of gods. In fact, the beyond remains an incorporeal and metaphysical realm in which individuals intimately possess the holy. Where this conclusion has been drawn without any residue, the individual can pursue his quest for salvation only as an individual. This phenomenon appears in some form, with progressive intellectualist rationalism, wherever men have ventured to rationalize the image of the world as being a cosmos governed by impersonal rules. Naturally it has occurred most strongly among religions and religious ethics which have been quite strongly determined by genteel strata of intellectuals devoted to the purely cognitive comprehension of the world and of its 'meaning.' This was the case with Asiatic and, above all, Indian world religions. For all of them, contemplation became the supreme and ultimate religious value accessible to man. Contemplation offered them entrance into the profound and blissful tranquillity and immobility of the All-one. All other forms of religious states, however, have been at best considered a relatively valuable *Ersatz* for contemplation. This has had far-reaching consequences for the relation of religion to life, including economic life, as we shall repeatedly see. Such consequences flow from the general character of 'mystic' experiences, in the contemplative sense, and from the psychological preconditions of the search for them.

The situation in which strata decisive for the development of a religion were active in practical life has been entirely different. Where they were chivalrous warrior heroes, political officials, economically acquisitive classes, or, finally, where an organized hierocracy dominated religion, the results were different than where genteel intellectuals were decisive.

The rationalism of hierocracy grew out of the professional preoccupation with cult and myth or—to a far higher degree—out of the cure of souls, that is, the confession of sin and counsel to sinners. Everywhere hierocracy has sought to monopolize the administration of religious values. They have also sought to bring and to temper the bestowal of religious goods into the form of 'sacramental' or 'corporate grace,' which could be ritually bestowed only by the priesthood and could not be attained by the individual. The individual's quest for salvation or the quest of free communities by means of contemplation, orgies, or asceticism, has been considered highly suspect and has had to be regulated ritually and, above all, controlled hierocratically. From the standpoint of the interests of the priesthood in power, this is only natural.

Every body of *political* officials, on the other hand, has been suspicious of all sorts of individual pursuits of salvation and of the free formation of communities as sources of emancipation from domestication at the hands of the institution of the state. Political officials have distrusted the competing priestly corporation of grace and, above all, at bottom they have despised the very quest for these impractical values lying beyond utilitarian and worldly ends. For all political bureaucracies, religious duties have ultimately been simply official or social obligations of the citizenry and of status groups. Ritual has corresponded to rules and regulations, and, therefore, wherever a bureaucracy has determined its nature, religion has assumed a ritualist character.

It is also usual for a stratum of *chivalrous* warriors to pursue absolutely worldly interests and to be remote from all 'mysticism.' Such strata, however, have lacked—and this is characteristic of heroism in general—the desire as well as the capacity for a rational mastery of reality. The irrationality of 'fate' and, under certain conditions, the idea of a vague and deterministically conceived 'destiny' (the Homeric *Moira*) has stood above and behind the divinities and demons who were conceived of as passionate and strong heroes, measuring out assistance and hostility, glory and booty, or death to the human heroes.

Peasants have been inclined towards magic. Their whole economic existence has been specifically bound to nature and has made them dependent upon elemental forces. They readily believe in a compelling sorcery directed against spirits who rule over or through natural forces, or they believe in simply buying divine benevolence. Only tremendous transformations of life-orientation have succeeded in tearing them away from this universal and primeval form of religiosity. Such transformations have been derived either from other strata or from mighty prophets, who, through the power of miracles, legitimize themselves as sorcerers. Orgiastic and ecstatic states of 'possession,' produced by means of toxics or by the dance, are strange to the status honor of knights because they are considered undignified. Among the peasants, however, such states have taken the place that 'mysticism' holds among the intellectuals.

Finally, we may consider the strata that in the western European sense are called 'civic,' as well as those which elsewhere correspond to them: artisans, traders, enterprisers engaged in cottage industry, and their derivatives existing only in the modern Occident. Apparently these strata have been the most ambiguous with regard to the religious stands open to them. And this is especially important to us.

Among these 'civic' strata the following religious phenomena have had especially strong roots: the institutional and sacramental grace of the Roman church in the medieval cities—the pillars of the popes; the mystagogic and sacramental grace in the ancient cities and in India; the orgiastic and contemplative Sufi, and Dervish religion of the Middle Eastern Orient; the Taoist magic; the Buddhist contemplation; the ritualist appropriation of grace under the direction of souls by mystagogues in Asia; all the forms of love for a savior; the beliefs in redemption the world over, from the cult of Krishna to the cult of Christ; the rational ritualism of the law and the sermon of the synagogue denuded of all magic among Jewry; the pneumatic and ancient as well as the asceticist medieval sects; the grace of predestination and the ethical regeneration of the Puritan and the Methodist; as well as all sorts of individual pursuits of salvation. All of these have been more firmly rooted among 'civic' strata than among any other.

Of course, the religions of all strata are certainly far from being unambiguously dependent upon the character of the strata we have presented as having special affinities with them. Yet, at first sight, civic strata appear, in this respect and on the whole, to lend themselves to a more varied determination. Yet it is precisely among these strata that elective affinities for special types of religion stand out. The tendency towards a *practical* rationalism in conduct is common to all civic strata; it is conditioned by the nature of their way of life, which is greatly detached from economic bonds to nature. Their whole existence has been based upon technological or economic calculations and upon the mastery of nature and of man, however primitive the means at their disposal. The technique of living handed down among them may, of course, be frozen in traditionalism, as has occurred repeatedly and everywhere. But precisely for these, there has always existed the possibility—even though in greatly varying measure—of letting an *ethical* and rational regulation of life arise. This may occur by the linkage of such an ethic to the tendency of technological and economic rationalism. Such regulation has not always been able to make headway against traditions which, in the main, were magically stereotyped. But where prophecy has provided a religious basis, this basis could be one of two fundamental types of prophecy which we shall repeatedly discuss: 'exemplary' prophecy, and 'emissary' prophecy.

Exemplary prophecy points out the path to salvation by exemplary living, usually by a contemplative and apathetic-ecstatic life. The emissary type of prophecy addresses its *demands* to the world in the name of a god. Naturally these demands are ethical; and they are often of an active ascetic character.

It is quite understandable that the more weighty the civic strata as such have been, and the more they have been torn from bonds of taboo and from divisions into sibs and castes, the more favorable has been the soil for religions that call for action in this world. Under these conditions, the preferred religious attitude could become the attitude of active asceticism, of God-willed *action* nourished by the sentiment of being God's 'tool,' rather than the possession of the deity or the inward and contemplative surrender to God, which has appeared as the supreme value to religions influenced by strata of genteel intellectuals. In the Occident the attitude of active asceticism has repeatedly retained supremacy over contemplative mysticism and orgiastic or apathetic ecstasy, even though these latter types have been well known in the Occident. Active asceticism, however, has not been confined to civic strata. Such an unambiguous social determination has not in any way existed. The prophecy of Zoroaster was directed at the nobility and the peasantry; the prophecy of Islam was directed to warriors. These prophecies, like the Israelite and the early Christian prophecy and preaching, have had an active character, which stands in contrast with the propaganda of Buddhism, Taoism, Neo-Pythagorism, Gnosticism, and Sufism. Certain specific conclusions of emissary prophecies, however, have been drawn precisely on 'civic' grounds.

In the missionary prophecy the devout have not experienced themselves as vessels of the divine but rather as instruments of a god. This emissary prophecy has had a profound elective affinity to a special conception of God: the conception of a supra-mundane, personal, wrathful, forgiving, loving, demanding, punishing Lord of Creation. Such a conception stands in contrast to the supreme being of exemplary prophecy. As a rule, though by no means without exception, the supreme being of an exemplary prophecy is an impersonal being because, as a static state, he is accessible only by means of contemplation. The conception of an active God, held by emissary prophecy, has dominated the Iranian and Mid-Eastern religions and those Occidental religions which are derived from them. The conception of a supreme and static being, held by exemplary prophecy, has come to dominate Indian and Chinese religiosity.

These differences are not primitive in nature. On the contrary, they have come into existence only by means of a far-reaching sublimation of primitive conceptions of animist spirits and of heroic deities which are everywhere similar in nature. Certainly the connection of conceptions of God with religious states, which are evaluated and desired as sacred values, have also been strongly influential in this process of sublimation. These religious states have simply been interpreted in the direction of a different conception of God, according to whether the holy states, evaluated as supreme, were contemplative mystic experiences or apathetic ecstasy, or whether they were the orgiastic possession of god, or visionary inspirations and 'commands.'

At the present time, it is widely held that one should consider emotional content as primary, with thoughts being merely its secondary expression. Of course, this point of view is to a great extent justified. From such a standpoint one might be inclined to consider the primacy of 'psychological' as over against 'rational' connections as the only decisive causal nexus, hence to view these rational connections as *mere* interpretations of the psychological ones. This, however, would be going much too far, according to factual evidence. A whole series of purely historical motives have determined the development toward the supramundane or the immanent conception of God. These conceptions, in turn, have decisively influenced the way in which experiences of salvation have been articulated. This definitely holds for the conception of the supra-mundane God, as we shall see again and again. If even Meister Eckhart occasionally and expressly placed Martha above Mary, he did so ultimately because he could not realize the pantheist experience of God, which is peculiar to the mystic, without entirely sacrificing all the decisive elements of Occidental belief in God and creation.

The rational elements of a religion, its 'doctrine,' also have an autonomy: for instance, the Indian doctrine of Kharma, the Calvinist belief in predestination, the Lutheran justification through faith, and the Catholic doctrine of sacrament. The rational religious pragmatism of salvation, flowing from the nature of the images of God and of the world, have under certain conditions had far-reaching results for the fashioning of a practical way of life.

These comments presuppose that the nature of the desired sacred values has been strongly influenced by the nature of the external interest-situation and the corresponding way of life of the ruling strata and thus by the social stratification itself. But the reverse also holds: wherever the direction of the whole way of life has been methodically rationalized, it has been profoundly determined by the ultimate values toward which this rationalization has been directed. These values and positions were thus *religiously* determined. Certainly they have not always, or exclusively, been decisive; however, they have been decisive in so far as an *ethical* rationalization held sway, at least so far as its influence reached. As a rule, these religious values have been also, and frequently absolutely, decisive.

One factor has been very important in determining the nature of the mutual inter-relations between external and internal interest-situations. The 'supreme' sacred values, which are promised by religion and have been discussed above, have not necessarily been the most universal ones. Not everybody had entree to Nirvana, to the contemplative union with the divine, the orgiastic or the ascetic possession of God. In a weakened form, the transposition of persons into religious states of frenzy or into the trance may become the object of a universal cult of the people. But even in this form such psychic states have not been elements of everyday life.

The empirical fact, important for us, that men are *differently qualified* in a religious way stands at the beginning of the history of religion. This fact had been dogmatized in the sharpest rationalist form in the 'particularism of grace,' embodied in the doctrine of predestination by the Calvinists. The sacred values that have been most cherished, the ecstatic and visionary capacities of shamans, sorcerers, ascetics, and pneumatics of all sorts, could not be attained by everyone. The possession of such faculties is a 'charisma,' which, to be sure, might be awakened in some but not in all. It follows from this that all intensive religiosity has a tendency toward a sort of *status stratification,* in accordance with differences in the charismatic qualifications. 'Heroic' or 'virtuoso' religiosity [5] is opposed to mass religiosity. By 'mass' we understand those who are religiously 'unmusical; we do not, of course, mean those who occupy an inferior position in the secular status order. In this sense, the status carriers of a virtuoso religion have been the leagues of sorcerers and sacred dancers; the religious status group of the Indian Sramana and of the early Christian 'ascetics,' who were expressly recognized in the congregation as a special 'estate'; the Paulinian, and still more the Gnostic, 'pneumatics,' the pietist *ecclesiola;* all genuine 'sects'—that is, sociologically speaking, associations that accept oniy religiously qualified persons in their midst; and finally, monk communities all over the world.

Now, every hierocratic and official authority of a 'church'—that is, a community organized by officials into an institution which bestows gifts of grace—fights principally against all virtuoso-religion and against its autonomous development. For the church, being the holder of institutionalized grace, seeks to organize the religiosity of the masses and to put its own officially monopolized and mediated sacred values in the place of the autonomous and religious status qualifications of the religious virtuosos. By its nature, that is, according to the interest-situation of its officeholders, the church must be 'democratic' in the sense of making the sacred values generally accessible. This means that the church stands for a universalism of grace and for the ethical sufficiency of all those who are enrolled under its institutional authority. Sociologically, the process of leveling constitutes a complete parallel with the political struggles of the bureaucracy against the political privileges of the aristocratic estates. As with hierocracy, every full-grown political bureaucracy is necessarily and in a quite similar sense 'democratic'—namely, in the sense of leveling and of fighting against status privileges that compete with its power.

The most varied compromises have resulted from this struggle between officialdoms and the virtuosos. These struggles have not always been official but they have always existed at least covertly. Thus, the religiosity of the Ulema [6] stood against the religiosity of the Dervishes; the early Christian bishops against the pneumatics and heroist sectaries as well as against the power of The Key of asceticist charisma; the Lutheran preacher's office and the Anglican and priestly church stood against asceticism in general; the Russian state church was opposed to the sects; and the official management of the Confucian cult stood against Buddhist, Taoist, and sectarian pursuits of salvation of all sorts. The religious virtuosos saw themselves compelled to adjust their demands to the possibilities of the religiosity of everyday life in order to gain and to maintain ideal and material mass-patronage. The nature of their concessions have naturally been of primary significance for the way in which they have religiously influenced everyday life. In almost all Oriental religions, the virtuosos allowed the masses to remain stuck in magical tradition. Thus, the influence of religious virtuosos has been infinitely smaller than was the case where religion has undertaken ethically and generally to rationalize everyday life. This has been the case even when religion has aimed precisely at the masses and has cancelled however many of its ideal demands. Besides the relations between the religiosity of the virtuosos and the religion of the masses, which finally resulted from this struggle, the peculiar nature of the concrete religiosity of the virtuosos has been of decisive importance for the development of the way of life of the masses. This virtuoso religiosity has therefore also been important for the economic ethic of the respective religion. The religion of the virtuoso has been the genuinely 'exemplary' and practical religion. According to the way of life his religion prescribed to the virtuoso, there have been various possibilities of establishing a rational ethic of everyday life. The relation of virtuoso religion to *workaday life* in the locus of the economy has varied, especially according to the peculiarity of the sacred values desired by such religions.

Wherever the sacred values and the redemptory means of a virtuoso religion bore a contemplative or orgiastic-ecstatic character, there has been no bridge between religion and the practical action of the workaday world. In such cases, the economy and all other action in the world has been considered religiously inferior, and no psychological motives for worldly action could be derived from the attitude cherished as the supreme value. In their innermost beings, contemplative and ecstatic religions have been rather specifically hostile to economic life. Mystic, orgiastic, and ecstatic experiences are extraordinary psychic states; they lead away from everyday life and from all expedient conduct. Such experiences are, therefore, deemed to be 'holy.' With such religions, a deep abyss separates the way of life of the laymen from that of the community of virtuosos. The rule of the status groups of religious virtuosos over the religious community readily shifts into a magical anthropolatry; the virtuoso is directly worshipped as a Saint, or at least laymen buy his blessing and his magical powers as a means of promoting mundane success or religious salvation. As the peasant was to the landlord, so the layman was to the Buddhist and Jainist bhikshu: [7] ultimately, mere sources of tribute. Such tribute allowed the virtuosos to live entirely for religious salvation without themselves performing profane work, which always would endanger their salvation. Yet the conduct of the layman could still undergo a certain ethical regulation, for the virtuoso was the layman's spiritual adviser, his father confessor and *directeur de l'âme*. Hence, the virtuoso frequently exercises a powerful influence over the religiously 'unmusical' laymen; this influence might not be in the direction of his (the virtuoso's) own religious way of life; it might be an influence in merely ceremonious, ritualist, and conventional particulars. For action in this world remained in principle religiously insignificant; and compared with the desire for the religious end, action lay in the very opposite direction.

In the end, the charisma of the pure 'mystic' serves only himself. The charisma of the genuine magician serves others.

Things have been quite different where the religiously qualified virtuosos have combined into an ascetic sect, striving to mould life in this world according to the will of a god. To be sure, two things were necessary before this could happen in a genuine way. First, the supreme and sacred value must not be of a contemplative nature; it must not consist of a union with a supra-mundane being who, in contrast to the world, lasts forever; nor in a *unia mystica* to be grasped orgiastically or apathetic-ecstatically. For these ways always lie apart from everyday life and beyond the real world and lead away from it. Second, such a religion must, so far as possible, have given up the purely magical or sacramental character of the *means* of grace. For these means always devalue action in this world as, at best, merely relative in their religious significance, and they link the decision about salvation to the success of processes which are *not* of a rational everyday nature.

When religious virtuosos have combined into an active asceticist sect, two aims are completely attained: the disenchantment of the world and the blockage of the path to salvation by a flight from the world. The path to salvation is turned away from a contemplative 'flight from the world' and towards an active ascetic 'work in this world.' If one disregards the small rationalist sects, such as are found all over the world, this has been attained only in the great church and sect organizations of Occidental and asceticist Protestantism. The quite distinct and the purely historically determined destinies of Occidental religions have co-operated in this matter. Partly, the social environment exerted an influence, above all, the environment of the stratum that was decisive for the development of such religion. Partly, however—and just as strongly—the intrinsic character of Christianity exerted an influence: the supra-mundane God and the specificity of the means and paths of salvation as determined historically, first by Israelite prophecy and the thora doctrine.[8]

The religious virtuoso can be placed in the world as the instrument of a God and cut off from all magical means of salvation. At the same time, it is imperative for the virtuoso that he 'prove' himself before God, as being called *solely* through the ethical quality of his conduct in this world. This actually means that he 'prove' himself to himself as well. No matter how much the 'world' as such is religiously devalued and rejected as being creatural and a vessel of sin, yet psychologically the world is all the more affirmed as the theatre of God-willed activity in one's worldly 'calling.' For this inner-worldly asceticism rejects the world in the sense that it despises and taboos the values of dignity and beauty, of the beautiful frenzy and the dream, purely secular power, and the purely worldly pride of the hero. Asceticism outlawed these values as competitors of the kingdom of God. Yet precisely because of this rejection, asceticism did not fly from the world, as did contemplation. Instead, asceticism has wished to rationalize the world ethically in accordance with God's commandments. It has therefore remained oriented towards the world in a more specific and thoroughgoing sense than did the naive 'affirmation of the world' of unbroken humanity, for instance, in Antiquity and in lay-Catholicism. In inner-worldly asceticism, the grace and the chosen state of the religiously qualified man prove themselves in everyday life. To be sure, they do so not in the everyday life as it is given, but in methodical and rationalized routine-activities of workaday life in the service of the Lord. Rationally raised into a vocation, everyday conduct becomes the locus for proving one's state of grace. The Occidental sects of the religious virtuosos have fermented the methodical rationalization of conduct, including economic conduct. These sects have not constituted valves for the longing to escape from the senselessness of work in this world, as did the Asiatic communities of the ecstatics: contemplative, orgiastic, or apathetic.

The most varied transitions and combinations are found between the polar opposites of 'exemplary' and 'emissary' prophecy. Neither religions nor men are open books. They have been historical rather than logical or even psychological constructions without contradiction. Often they have borne within themselves a series of motives, each of which, if separately and consistently followed through, would have stood in the way of the others or run against them head-on. In religious matters 'consistency' has been the exception and not the rule. The ways and means of salvation are also psychologically ambiguous. The search for God of the early Christian monk as well as of the Quaker contained very strong contemplative elements. Yet the total content of their religions and, above all, their supra-mundane God of creation and their way of making sure of their states of grace again and again directed them to the course of action. On the other hand, the Buddhist monk was also active, but his activities were withdrawn from any consistent rationalization *in this world;* his quest for salvation was ultimately oriented to the flight from the 'wheel' of the rebirths. The sectarians and other brotherhoods of the Occidental Middle Ages spearheaded the religious penetration of everyday life. They found their counter-image in the brotherhoods of Islam, which were even more widely developed. The stratum typical of such brotherhoods in the Occident and in Islam were identical: petty bourgeois and especially artisans. Yet the spirit of their respective religions were very different. Viewed externally, numerous Hinduist religious communities appear to be 'sects' just as do those of the Occident. The sacred value, however, and the manner in which values were mediated pointed in radically different directions.

We shall not accumulate more examples here, as we wish to consider the great religions separately. In no respect can one simply integrate various world religions into a chain of types, each of them signifying a new 'stage.' All the great religions are historical individualities of a highly complex nature; taken all together, they exhaust only a few of the possible combinations that could conceivably be formed from the the very numerous individual factors to be considered in such historical combinations.

Thus, the following presentations do not in any way constitute a systematic 'typology' of religion. On the other hand, they do not constitute a purely historical work. They are 'typological' in the sense that they consider what is typically important in the historical realizations of the religious ethics. This is important for the connection of religions with the great contrasts of the *economic* mentalities. Other aspects will be neglected; these presentations do not claim to offer a well-rounded picture of world religions. Those features peculiar to the individual religions, in contrast to other religions, but which at the same time are important for our interest, must be brought out strongly. A presentation that disregards these special accents of importance would often have to tone down the special features in which we are interested. Such a balanced presentation would almost always have to add other features and occasionally would have to give greater emphasis to the fact that, of course, all qualitative contrasts in reality, in the last resort, can somehow be comprehended as purely quantitative differences in the combinations of single factors. However, it would be extremely unfruitful to emphasize and repeat here what goes without saying.

The features of religions that are important for economic ethics shall interest us primarily from a definite point of view: we shall be interested in the way in which they are related to economic rationalism. More precisely, we mean the economic rationalism of the type which, since the sixteenth and seventeenth centuries, has come to dominate the Occident as part of the particular rationalization of civic life, and which has become familiar in this part of the world.

We have to remind ourselves in advance that 'rationalism' may mean very different things. It means one thing if we think of the kind of rationalization the systematic thinker performs on the image of the world: an increasing theoretical mastery of reality by means of increasingly precise and abstract concepts. Rationalism means another thing if we think of the methodical attainment of a definitely given and practical end by means of an increasingly precise calculation of adequate means. These types of rationalism are very different, in spite of the fact that ultimately they belong inseparately together. Similar types may be distinguished even within the intellectual comprehension of reality; for instance, the differences between English Physics and Continental Physics has been traced back to such a type difference within the comprehension of reality. The rationalization of life conduct with which we have to deal here can assume unusually varied forms.

In the sense of the absence of all metaphysics and almost all residues of religious anchorage, Confucianism is rationalist to such a far-going extent that it stands at the extreme boundary of what one might possibly call a 'religious' ethic. At the same time, Confucianism is more rationalist and sober, in the sense of the absence and the rejection of all non-utilitarian yardsticks, than any other ethical system, with the possible exception of J. Bentham's. Yet Confucianism, in spite of constantly actual and apparent analogies, nevertheless differs extraordinarily from Bentham's as well as from all other Occidental types of practical rationalism. The supreme artistic ideal of the Renaissance was 'rational' in the sense of a belief in a valid 'canon,' and the view of life of the Renaissance was rational in the sense of rejecting traditionalist bonds and of having faith in the power of the *naturalis ratio*. This type of rationalism prevailed in spite of certain elements of Platonizing mysticism.

'Rational' may also mean a 'systematic arrangement.'[9] In this sense, the following methods are rational: methods of mortificatory or of magical asceticism, of contemplation in its most consistent forms—for instance, in *yoga*—or in the manipulations of the prayer machines of later Buddhism.

In general, all kinds of practical ethics that are systematically and unambiguously oriented to fixed goals of salvation are 'rational,' partly in the same sense as formal method is rational, and partly in the sense that they distinguish between 'valid' norms and what is empirically given. These types of rationalization processes are of interest to us in the following presentations. It would be senseless to try to anticipate the typologies of these presentations here, for they aim to make a contribution to such typology.

In order to make this attempt, the author must take the liberty of being 'unhistorical,' in the sense that the ethics of individual religions are presented systematically and essentially in greater unity than has ever been the case in the flux of their actual development. Rich contrasts which have been alive in individual religions, as well as incipient developments and ramifications, must be left aside; and the features that to the author are important must often be presented in greater logical consistency and less historical development than was actually the case. If it were done arbitrarily, this simplification would be a historical 'falsification.' This, however, is not the case, at least not intentionally. The author has always underscored those features in the total picture of a religion which have been decisive for the fashioning of the *practical* way of life, as well as those which distinguish one religion from another.[10]

Finally, before going into the subject matter, some remarks by way of explaining terminological peculiarities which frequently recur in the presentation may be advanced.[11]

When fully developed, religious associations and communities belong to a type of corporate authority. They represent 'hierocratic' associations, that is, their power to rule is supported by their monopoly in the bestowal or denial of sacred values.

All ruling powers, profane and religious, political and apolitical, may be considered as variations of, or approximations to, certain pure types. These types are constructed by searching for the basis of *legitimacy*, which the ruling power claims. Our modern 'associations,' above all the political ones, are of the type of 'legal' authority. That is, the legitimacy of the power-holder to give commands rests upon rules that are rationally established by enactment, by agreement, or by imposition. The legitimation for establishing these rules rests, in turn, upon a rationally enacted or interpreted 'constitution.' Orders are given in the name of the impersonal norm, rather than in the name of a personal authority; and even the giving of a command constitutes obedience toward a norm rather than an arbitrary freedom, favor, or privilege.

The 'official' is the holder of the power to command; he never exercises this power in his own right; he holds it as a trustee of the impersonal and 'compulsory institution.'[12] This institution is made up of the specific patterns of life of a plurality of men, definite or indefinite, yet specified according to rules. Their joint pattern of life is normatively governed by statutory regulations.

The 'area of jurisdiction' is a functionally delimited realm of possible objects for command and thus delimits the sphere of the official's legitimate power. A hierarchy of superiors, to which officials may appeal and complain in an order of rank, stands opposite the citizen or member of the association. Today this situation also holds for the hierocratic association that is the church. The pastor or priest has his definitely limited 'jurisdiction,' which is fixed by rules. This also holds for the supreme head of the church. The present concept of [papal] 'infallibility' is a jurisdictional concept. Its inner meaning differs from that which preceded it, even up to the time of Innocent III.

The separation of the 'private sphere' from the 'official sphere' (in the case of infallibility: the *ex cathedra* definition) is carried through in the church in the same way as in political, or other, officialdoms. The legal separation of the official from the means of administration (either in natural or in pecuniary form) is carried through in the sphere of political and hierocratic associations in the same way as is the separation of the worker from the means of production in capitalist economy: it runs fully parallel to them.

No matter how many beginnings may be found in the remote past, in its full development all this is specifically modern. The past has known other bases for authority, bases which, incidentally, extend as survivals into the present. Here we wish merely to outline these bases of authority in a terminological way.

1. In the following discussions the term 'charisma' shall be understood to refer to an *extraordinary* quality of a person, regardless of whether this quality is actual, alleged, or presumed. 'Charismatic authority,' hence, shall refer to a rule over men, whether predominantly external or predominantly internal, to which the governed submit because of their belief in the extraordinary quality of the specific *person*. The magical

sorcerer, the prophet, the leader of hunting and booty expeditions, the warrior chieftain, the so-called 'Caesarist' ruler, and, under certain conditions, the personal head of a party are such types of rulers for their disciples, followings, enlisted troops, parties, et cetera. The legitimacy of their rule rests on the belief in and the devotion to the extraordinary, which is valued because it goes beyond the normal human qualities, and which was originally valued as supernatural. The legitimacy of charismatic rule thus rests upon the belief in magical powers, revelations and hero worship. The source of these beliefs is the 'proving' of the charismatic quality through miracles, through victories and other successes, that is, through the welfare of the governed. Such beliefs and the claimed authority resting on them therefore disappear, or threaten to disappear, as soon as proof is lacking and as soon as the charismatically qualified person appears to be devoid of his magical power or forsaken by his god. Charismatic rule is not managed according to general norms, either traditional or rational, but, in principle, according to concrete revelations and inspirations, and in this sense, charismatic authority is 'irrational.' It is 'revolutionary' in the sense of not being bound to the existing order: 'It is written—but I say unto you . . . !'

2. 'Traditionalism' in the following discussions shall refer to the psychic attitude-set for the habitual workaday and to the belief in the everyday routine as an inviolable norm of conduct. Domination that rests upon this basis, that is, upon piety for what actually, allegedly, or presumably has always existed, will be called 'traditionalist authority.'

Patriarchalism is by far the most important type of domination the legitimacy of which rests upon tradition. Patriarchalism means the authority of the father, the husband, the senior of the house, the sib elder over the members of the household and sib; the rule of the master and patron over bondsmen, serfs, freed men; of the lord over the domestic servants and household officials; of the prince over house- and court-officials, nobles of office, clients, vassals; of the patrimonial lord and sovereign prince (*Landesvater*) over the 'subjects.'

It is characteristic of patriarchical and of patrimonial authority, which represents a variety of the former, that the system of inviolable norms is considered sacred; an infraction of them would result in magical or religious evils. Side by side with this system there is a realm of free arbitrariness and favor of the lord, who in principle judges only in terms of 'personal,' not 'functional,' relations. In this sense, traditionalist authority is irrational.

3. Throughout early history, charismatic authority, which rests upon a belief in the sanctity or the value of the extraordinary, and traditionalist (patriarchical) domination, which rests upon a belief in the sanctity of everyday routines, divided the most important authoritative relations between them. The bearers of charisma, the oracles of prophets, or the edicts of charismatic war lords alone could integrate 'new' laws into the circle of what was upheld by tradition. Just as revelation and the sword were the two extraordinary powers, so were they the two typical innovators. In typical fashion, however, both succumbed to routinization as soon as their work was done.

With the death of the prophet or the war lord the question of successorship arises. This question can be solved by *Kürung,* which was originally not an 'election' but a selection in terms of charismatic qualification; or the question can be solved by the sacramental substantiation of charisma, the successor being designated by consecration, as is the case in hierocratic or apostolic succession; or the belief in the charismatic qualification of the charismatic leader's sib can lead to a belief in hereditary charisma, as represented by hereditary kingship and hereditary hierocracy. With these routinizations, *rules* in some form always come to govern. The prince or the hierocrat no longer rules by virtue of purely personal qualities, but by virtue of acquired or inherited qualities, or because he has been legitimized by an act of charismatic election. The process of routinization, and thus traditionalization, has set in.

Perhaps it is even more important that when the organization of authority becomes permanent, the staff supporting the charismatic ruler becomes routinized. The ruler's disciples, apostles, and followers became priests, feudal vassals and, above all, officials. The original charismatic community lived communistically off donations, alms, and the booty of war: they were thus specifically alienated from the economic order. The community was transformed into a stratum of aids to the ruler and depended upon him for maintenance through the usufruct of land, office fees, income in kind, salaries, and hence, through prebends. The staff derived its legitimate power in greatly varying stages of appropriation, infeudation, conferment, and appointment. As a rule, this meant that princely prerogatives became *patrimonial* in nature. Patrimonialism can also develop from pure patriarchalism through the disintegration of the patriarchical master's strict authority. By virtue of conferment, the prebendary or the vassal has as a rule had a personal *right* to the office bestowed upon him. Like the artisan who possessed the economic means of production, the prebendary possessed the means of administration. He had to bear the costs of administration out of his office fees or other income, or he passed on to the lord only part of the taxes gathered from the subjects, retaining the rest. In the extreme case he could bequeath and alienate his office like other possession. We wish to speak of *status* patrimonialism when the development by appropriation of prerogatory power has reached this stage, without regard to whether it developed from charismatic or patriarchical beginnings.

The development, however, has seldom stopped at this stage. We always meet with a *struggle* between the political or hierocratic lord and the owners or usurpers of prerogatives, which they have appropriated as status groups. The ruler attempts to expropriate the estates, and the estates attempt to expropriate the ruler. The more the ruler succeeds in attaching to himself a staff of officials who depend solely on him and whose interests are linked to his, the more this struggle is decided in favor of the ruler and the more the privilege-holding estates are gradually expropriated. In this connection, the prince acquires administrative means of his own and he keeps them firmly in his own hands. Thus we find political rulers in the Occident, and progressively from Innocent III to Johann XXII, also hierocratic rulers who have finances of their own, as well as secular rulers who have magazines and arsenals of their own for the provisioning of the army and the officials.

The *character* of the stratum of officials upon whose support the ruler has relied in the struggle for the expropriation of status prerogatives has varied greatly in history. In Asia and in the Occident during the early Middle Ages they were typically clerics; during the Oriental Middle Ages they were typically slaves and clients; for the Roman Principate, freed slaves to a limited extent were typical; humanist literati were typical for China; and finally, jurists have been typical for the modern Occident, in ecclesiastical as well as in political associations.

The triumph of princely power and the expropriation of particular prerogatives has everywhere signified at least the possibility, and often the actual introduction, of a rational administration. As we shall see, however, this rationalization has varied greatly in extent and meaning. One must, above all, distinguish between the *substantive* rationalization of administration and of judiciary by a patrimonial prince, and the *formal* rationalization carried out by trained jurists. The former bestows utilitarian and social ethical blessings upon his subjects, in the manner of the master of a large house upon the members of his household. The trained jurists have carried out the rule of general laws applying to all 'citizens of the state.' However fluid the difference has been—for instance, in Babylon or Byzantium, in the Sicily of the Hohenstaufen, or the England of the Stuarts, or the France of the Bourbons—in the final analysis, the difference between substantive and formal rationality has persisted. And, in the main, it has been the work of *jurists* to give birth to the modern Occidental 'state' as well as to the Occidental 'churches.' We shall not discuss at this point the source of their strength, the substantive ideas, and the technical means for this work.

With the triumph of *formalist* juristic rationalism, the legal type of domination appeared in the Occident at the side of the transmitted types of domination. Bureaucratic rule was not and is not the only variety of legal authority, but it is the purest. The modern state and municipal official, the modern Catholic priest and chaplain, the officials and employees of modern banks and of large capitalist enterprises represent, as we have already mentioned, the most important types of this structure of domination.

The following characteristic must be considered decisive for our terminology: in legal authority, submission does not rest upon the belief and devotion to charismatically gifted persons, like prophets and heroes, or upon sacred tradition, or upon piety toward a personal lord and master who is defined by an ordered tradition, or upon piety toward the possible incumbents of office fiefs and office prebends who are legitimized in their own right through privilege and conferment. Rather, submission under legal authority is based upon an *impersonal* bond to the generally defined and functional 'duty of office.' The official duty—like the corresponding right to exercise authority: the 'jurisdictional competency'—is fixed by *rationally established* norms, by enactments, decrees, and regulations, in such a manner that the legitimacy of the authority becomes the legality of the general rule, which is purposely thought out, enacted, and announced with formal correctness.

The differences between the types of authority we have sketched pertain to all particulars of their social structure and of their economic significance. Only a systematic presentation could demonstrate how far the distinctions and terminology chosen here are expedient. Here we may emphasize merely that by approaching in this way, we do not claim to use the only possible approach nor do we claim that all empirical structures of domination must correspond to one of these 'pure' types. On the contrary, the great majority of empirical cases represent a combination or a state of transition among several such pure types. We shall be compelled again and again to form expressions like 'patrimonial bureaucracy' in order to make the point that the characteristic traits of the respective phenomenon belong in part to the rational form of domination, whereas other traits belong to a traditionalist form of domination, in this case to that of estates. We also recognize highly important forms that have been universally diffused throughout history, such as the feudal structure of domination. Important aspects of these structures, however, cannot be classified smoothly under any one of the three forms we have distinguished. They can be understood only as combinations involving several concepts, in this case the concepts of 'status group' and 'status honor.' There are also forms that have to be understood partly in terms of principles other than those of 'domination,' partly in terms of peculiar variations of the concept of charisma. Examples are: the functionaries of *pure* democracy with rotations of honorific offices and similar forms, on the one hand, and plebiscitarian domination, on the other hand, or certain forms of notable rule that are special forms of traditional domination. Such forms, however, have certainly belonged to the most important ferments for the delivery of political rationalism. By the terminology suggested here, we do not wish to force schematically the infinite and multifarious historical life, but simply to create concepts useful for special purposes and for orientation.

The same qualifications hold for a final terminological distinction. We understand by 'status' situation the probability of certain social groups' receiving positive or negative social *honor*. The chances of attaining social honor are primarily determined by differences in the *styles of life* of these groups, hence chiefly by differences of *education*. Referring to the preceding terminology of forms of authority, we may say that, secondarily, social honor very frequently and typically is associated with the respective stratum's legally guaranteed and monopolized claim to sovereign rights or to income and profit opportunities of a certain kind. Thus, if all these characteristics are found, which, of course, is not always the case, a 'status group' is a group societalized through its special styles of life, its conventional and specific notions of honor, and the economic opportunities it legally monopolizes. A status group is always somehow societalized, but it is not always organized into an association. *Commercium,* in the sense of 'social intercourse,' and *connubium* among groups are the typical characteristics of the *mutual esteem* among status equals; their absence signifies status differences.

By 'class situation,' in contrast, we shall understand the opportunities to gain sustenance and income that are primarily determined by typical, *economically* relevant, situations; property of a certain kind, or acquired skill in the execution of services that are in demand, is decisive for income opportunities. 'Class situation' also comprises the ensuing general and typical living conditions, for instance, the necessity of complying with the discipline of a capitalist proprietor's workshop.

A 'status situation' can be the cause as well as the result of a 'class situation,' but it need be neither. Class situations, in turn, can be primarily *determined by markets,* by the labor market and the commodity market. The specific and typical cases of class situation today are ones determined by markets. But such is not necessarily the case: class situations of landlord and small peasant may depend upon market relations only in a negligible way. In their differing situations, the various categories of 'rentiers' depend on the market in greatly varying senses and extents, according to whether they derive their rents as landlords, slaveholders, or as owners of bonds and effects.

One must therefore distinguish between 'propertied classes' and primarily market-determined 'income classes.' Present-day society is predominantly stratified in classes, and to an especially high degree in income classes. But in the special *status* prestige of the 'educated' strata, our society contains a very tangible element of stratification by status. Externally, this status factor is most obviously represented by economic monopolies and the preferential social opportunities of the holders of degrees.

In the past the significance of stratification by status was far more decisive, above all, for the economic structure of the societies. For, on the one hand, status stratification influences the economic structure by barriers or regulations of consumption, and by status monopolies which from the point of view of economic rationality are irrational, and on the other hand, status stratification influences the economy very strongly through the bearing of the status *conventions* of the respective ruling strata who set the example. These conventions may be in the nature of *ritualist* stereotyped forms, which to a large extent has been the case with the status stratification of Asia.

XII. The Protestant Sects and the Spirit of Capitalism[1]

For some time in the United States a principled 'separation of state and church' has existed. This separation is carried through so strictly that there is not even an official census of denominations, for it would be considered against the law for the state even to ask the citizen for his denomination. We shall not here discuss the practical importance of this principle of the relation between religious organizations and the state.* We are interested, rather, in the fact that scarcely two and a half decades ago the number of 'persons without church affiliation' in the U.S.A. was estimated to be only about 6 per cent;[2] and this despite the absence of all those highly effective premiums which most of the European states then placed upon affiliation with certain privileged churches and despite the immense immigration to the U.S.A.

It should be realized, in addition, that church affiliation in the U.S.A. brings with it incomparably higher financial burdens, especially for the poor, than anywhere in Germany. Published family budgets prove this, and I have personally known of many burdened cases in a congregation in a city on Lake Erie, which was almost entirely composed of German immigrant lumberjacks. Their regular contributions for religious purposes amounted to almost $80 annually, being paid out of an average annual income of about $1,000. Everyone knows that even a small fraction of this financial burden in Germany would lead to a mass exodus from the church. But quite apart from that, nobody who visited the United States fifteen or twenty years ago, that is, before the recent Europeanization of the country began, could overlook the very intense church-mindedness which then prevailed in all regions not yet flooded

'Die Protestantischen Sekten und der Geist des Kapitalismus,' *Gesammelte Aufsaetze zur Religionssoziologie*, vol. I, pp. 207-36.

* The principle is often only theoretical; note the importance of the Catholic vote, as well as subsidies to confessional schools.

by European immigrants.* Every old travel book reveals that formerly church-mindedness in America went unquestioned, as compared with recent decades, and was even far stronger. Here we are especially interested in one aspect of this situation.

Hardly a generation ago when businessmen were establishing themselves and making new social contacts, they encountered the question: 'To what church do you belong?' This was asked unobtrusively and in a manner that seemed to be apropos, but evidently it was never asked accidentally. Even in Brooklyn, New York's twin city, this older tradition was retained to a strong degree, and the more so in communities less exposed to the influence of immigration. This question reminds one of the typical Scotch *table d'hôte,* where a quarter of a century ago the continental European on Sundays almost always had to face the situation of a lady's asking, 'What service did you attend today?' Or, if the Continental, as the oldest guest, should happen to be seated at the head of the table, the waiter when serving the soup would ask him: 'Sir, the prayer, please.' In Portree (Skye) on one beautiful Sunday I faced this typical question and did not know any better way out than to remark: 'I am a member of the *Badische Landeskirche* and could not find a chapel of my church in Portree.' The ladies were pleased and satisfied with the answer. 'Oh, he doesn't attend any service except that of his own denomination!'

If one looked more closely at the matter in the United States, one could easily see that the question of religious affiliation was almost always posed in social life and in business life which depended on permanent and credit relations. However, as mentioned above, the American authorities never posed the question. Why?

First, a few personal observations [from 1904] may serve as illustrations. On a long railroad journey through what was then Indian territory, the author, sitting next to a traveling salesman of 'undertaker's hardware' (iron letters for tombstones), casually mentioned the still impressively strong church-mindedness. Thereupon the salesman remarked, 'Sir, for my part everybody may believe or not believe as he pleases; but if I saw a farmer or a businessman not belonging to any church at all, I wouldn't trust him with fifty cents. Why pay me, if he doesn't believe in anything?' Now that was a somewhat vague motivation.

* The opening by prayer of not only every session of the U. S. Supreme Court but also of every Party Convention has been aǹ annoying ceremonial for quite some time.

The matter became somewhat clearer from the story of a German-born nose-and-throat specialist, who had established himself in a large city on the Ohio River and who told me of the visit of his first patient. Upon the doctor's request, he lay down upon the couch to be examined with the [aid of a] nose reflector. The patient sat up once and remarked with dignity and emphasis, 'Sir, I am a member of the —— Baptist Church in —— Street.' Puzzled about what meaning this circumstance might have for the disease of the nose and its treatment, the doctor discreetly inquired about the matter from an American colleague. The colleague smilingly informed him that the patient's statement of his church membership was merely to say: 'Don't worry about the fees.' But *why* should it mean precisely that? Perhaps this will become still clearer from a third happening.

On a beautiful clear Sunday afternoon early in October I attended a baptism ceremony of a Baptist congregation. I was in the company of some relatives who were farmers in the backwoods some miles out of M. [a county seat] in North Carolina. The baptism was to take place in a pool fed by a brook which descended from the Blue Ridge Mountains, visible in the distance. It was cold and it had been freezing during the night. Masses of farmers' families were standing all around the slopes of the hills; they had come, some from great distances, some from the neighborhood, in their light two-wheeled buggies.

The preacher in a black suit stood waist deep in the pond. After preparations of various sorts, about ten persons of both sexes in their Sunday-best stepped into the pond, one after another. They avowed their faith and then were immersed completely—the women in the preacher's arms. They came up, shaking and shivering in their wet clothes, stepped out of the pond, and everybody 'congratulated' them. They were quickly wrapped in thick blankets and then they drove home. One of my relatives commented that 'faith' provides unfailing protection against sneezes. Another relative stood beside me and, being unchurchly in accordance with German traditions, he looked on, spitting disdainfully over his shoulder. He spoke to one of those baptised, 'Hello, Bill, wasn't the water pretty cool?' and received the very earnest reply, 'Jeff, I thought of some pretty hot place (Hell!), and so I didn't mind the cool water.' During the immersion of one of the young men, my relative was startled.

'Look at him,' he said. 'I told you so!'

When I asked him after the ceremony, 'Why did you anticipate the baptism of that man?' he answered, 'Because he wants to open a bank in M.'

'Are there so many Baptists around that he can make a living?'

'Not at all, but once being baptised he will get the patronage of the whole region and he will outcompete everybody.'

Further questions of 'why' and 'by what means' led to the following conclusion: Admission to the local Baptist congregation follows only upon the most careful 'probation' and after closest inquiries into conduct going back to early childhood (Disorderly conduct? Frequenting taverns? Dance? Theatre? Card Playing? Untimely meeting of liability? Other Frivolities?) The congregation still adhered strictly to the religious tradition.

Admission to the congregation is recognized as an absolute guarantee of the moral qualities of a gentleman, especially of those qualities required in business matters. Baptism secures to the individual the deposits of the whole region and unlimited credit without any competition. He is a 'made man.' Further observation confirmed that these, or at least very similar phenomena, recur in the most varied regions. In general, *only* those men had success in business who belonged to Methodist or Baptist or other *sects* or sectlike conventicles. When a sect member moved to a different place, or if he was a traveling salesman, he carried the certificate of his congregation with him; and thereby he found not only easy contact with sect members but, above all, he found credit everywhere. If he got into economic straits through no fault of his own, the sect arranged his affairs, gave guarantees to the creditors, and helped him in every way, often according to the Biblical principle, *mutuum date nihil inde sperantes.* (Luke vi:35)

The expectation of the creditors that his sect, for the sake of their prestige, would not allow creditors to suffer losses on behalf of a sect member was not, however, decisive for his opportunities. What was decisive was the fact that a fairly reputable sect would only accept for membership one whose 'conduct' made him appear to be morally *qualified* beyond doubt.

It is crucial that sect membership meant a certificate of moral qualification and especially of business morals for the individual. This stands in contrast to membership in a 'church' into which one is 'born' and which lets grace shine over the righteous and the unrighteous alike. Indeed, a church is a corporation which organizes grace and administers religious gifts of grace, like an endowed foundation. Affiliation with the church is, in principle, obligatory and hence proves nothing with regard to the member's qualities. A sect, however, is a voluntary association of only those who, according to the principle, are religiously and morally qualified. If one finds voluntary reception of his membership, by virtue of religious *probation,* he joins the sect voluntarily.

It is, of course, an established fact that this selection has often been very strongly counteracted, precisely in America, through the proselyting of souls by competing sects, which, in part, was strongly determined by the material interests of the preachers. Hence, cartels for the restriction of proselyting have frequently existed among the competing denominations. Such cartels were formed, for instance, in order to exclude the easy wedding of a person who had been divorced for reasons which, from a religious point of view, were considered insufficient. Religious organizations that facilitated remarriage had great attraction. Some Baptist communities are said at times to have been lax in this respect, whereas the Catholic as well as the Lutheran (Missouri) churches were praised for their strict correctness. This correctness, however, allegedly reduced the membership of both churches.

Expulsion from one's sect for moral offenses has meant, economically, loss of credit and, socially, being declassed.

Numerous observations during the following months confirmed not only that church-mindedness *per se,* although still (1904) rather important, was rapidly dying out; but the particularly important trait, mentioned above, was definitely confirmed. In metropolitan areas I was spontaneously told, in several cases, that a speculator in undeveloped real estate would regularly erect a church building, often an extremely modest one; then he would hire a candidate from one of the various theological seminaries, pay him $500 to $600, and hold out to him a splendid position as a preacher for life if he would gather a congregation and thus preach the building terrain 'full.' Deteriorated churchlike structures which marked failures were shown to me. For the most part, however, the preachers were said to be successful. Neighborly contact, Sunday School, and so on, were said to be indispensable to the newcomer, but above all association with 'morally' reliable neighbors.

Competition among sects is strong, among other things, through the kind of material and spiritual offerings at evening teas of the congregations. Among genteel churches also, musical presentations contribute to this competition. (A tenor in Trinity Church, Boston, who allegedly had to sing on Sundays *only,* at that time received $8,000.) Despite this sharp competition, the sects often maintained fairly good mutual relations. For instance, in the service of the Methodist church which I attended, the Baptist ceremony of the baptism, which I mentioned above, was recommended as a spectacle to edify everybody. In the main, the congregations refused entirely to listen to the preaching of 'dogma' and to confessional distinctions. 'Ethics' alone could be offered. In those instances where I listened to sermons for the middle classes, the typical bourgeois morality, respectable and solid, to be sure, and of the most homely and sober kind, was preached. But the sermons were delivered with obvious inner conviction; the preacher was often moved.

Today the kind of denomination [to which one belongs] is rather irrelevant. It does not matter whether one be Freemason,* Christian Scientist, Adventist, Quaker, or what not. What is decisive is that one be admitted to membership by 'ballot,' after an *examination* and an ethical *probation* in the sense of the virtues which are at a premium for the inner-worldly asceticism of protestantism and hence, for the ancient puritan tradition. Then, the same effect could be observed.

Closer scrutiny revealed the steady progress of the characteristic process of 'secularization,' to which in modern times all phenomena that originated in religious conceptions succumb. Not only religious associations, hence sects, had this effect on American life. Sects exercised this influence, rather, in a steadily decreasing proportion. If one paid some attention it was striking to observe (even fifteen years ago) that surprisingly many men among the American middle classes (always outside of the quite modern metropolitan areas and the immigration centers) were wearing a little badge (of varying color) in the buttonhole, which reminded one very closely of the rosette of the French Legion of Honor.

When asked what it meant, people regularly mentioned an association with a sometimes adventurous and fantastic name. And it became obvious that its significance and purpose consisted in the following: Almost always the association functioned as a burial insurance, besides offering

---

* An assistant of Semitic languages in an eastern university told me that he regretted not having become 'master of the chair,' for then he would go back into business. When asked what good that would do the answer was: As a traveling salesman or seller he could present himself in a role famous for respectability. He could beat any competition and would be worth his weight in gold.

greatly varied services. But often, and especially in those areas least touched by modern disintegration, the association offered the member the (ethical) claim for brotherly help on the part of every brother who had the means. If he faced an economic emergency for which he himself was not to be blamed, he could make this claim. And in several instances that came to my notice at the time, this claim again followed the very principle, *mutuum date nihil inde sperantes,* or at least a very low rate of interest prevailed. Apparently, such claims were willingly recognized by the members of the brotherhood. Furthermore—and this is the main point in this instance—membership was again acquired through balloting after investigation and a determination of moral worth. And hence the badge in the buttonhole meant, 'I am a gentleman patented after investigation and probation and guaranteed by my membership.' Again, this meant, in business life above all, tested *credit worthiness.* One could observe that business opportunities were often decisively influenced by such legitimation.

All these phenomena, which seemed to be rather rapidly disintegrating —at least the religious organizations—were essentially confined to the middle classes. Some cultured Americans often dismissed these facts briefly and with a certain angry disdain as 'humbug' or backwardness, or they even denied them; many of them actually did not know anything about them, as was affirmed to me by William James. Yet these survivals were still alive in many different fields, and sometimes in forms which appeared to be grotesque.

These associations were especially the typical vehicles of social ascent into the circle of the entrepreneurial middle class. They served to diffuse and to maintain the bourgeois capitalist business ethos among the broad strata of the middle classes (the farmers included).

As is well known, not a few (one may well say the majority of the older generation) of the American 'promoters,' 'captains of industry,' of the multi-millionaires and trust magnates belonged formally to sects, especially to the Baptists. However, in the nature of the case, these persons were often affiliated for merely conventional reasons, as in Germany, and only in order to legitimate themselves in personal and social life—not in order to legitimate themselves as businessmen; during the age of the Puritans, such 'economic supermen' did not require such a crutch, and *their* 'religiosity' was, of course, often of a more than dubious sincerity. The middle classes, above all the strata ascending with and out of the middle classes, were the bearers of that specific religious orientation which one must, indeed, beware viewing among them as only opportunistically determined.* Yet one must never overlook that without the universal diffusion of these qualities and principles of a methodical way of life, qualities which were maintained through these religious communities, capitalism today, even in America, would not be what it is. In the history of any economic area on earth there is no epoch, [except] those quite rigid in feudalism or patrimonialism, in which capitalist figures of the kind of Pierpont Morgan, Rockefeller, Jay Gould, *et al.* were absent. Only the technical *means* which they used for the acquisition of wealth have changed (of course!). *They* stood and they stand 'beyond good and evil.' But, however high one may otherwise evaluate their importance for economic transformation, they have never been decisive in determining what economic mentality was to dominate a given epoch and a given area. Above all, they were not the creators and they were not to become the bearers of the specifically Occidental bourgeois mentality.

This is not the place to discuss in detail the political and social importance of the religious sects and the numerous similarly exclusive associations and clubs in America which are based upon recruitment by ballot. The entire life of a typical Yankee of the last generation led through a series of such exclusive associations, beginning with the Boys' Club in school, proceeding to the Athletic Club or the Greek Letter Society or to another student club of some nature, then onward to one of the numerous notable clubs of businessmen and the bourgeoisie, or finally to the clubs of the metropolitan plutocracy. To gain admission was identical to a ticket of ascent, especially with a certificate before the forum of one's self-feeling; to gain admission meant to have 'proved' oneself. A student in college who was not admitted to *any* club (or quasi-society) whatsoever was usually a sort of pariah. (Suicides because of failure to be admitted have come to my notice.) A businessman, clerk, technician, or doctor who had the same fate usually was of questionable ability to serve. Today, numerous clubs of this sort are bearers

* 'Hypocrisy' and conventional opportunism in these matters were hardly stronger developed in America than in Germany where, after all, an officer or civil servant 'without religious affiliation or preference' was also an impossibility. And a Berlin ('Aryan!') Lord Mayor was not confirmed officially because he failed to have one of his children baptised. Only the direction in which conventional 'hypocrisy' moved differed: official careers in Germany, business opportunities in the United States.

of those tendencies leading toward aristocratic status groups which characterize contemporary American development. These status groups develop alongside of and, what has to be well noted, partly in contrast to the naked plutocracy.

In America mere 'money' in itself also purchases power, but not social honor. Of course, it is a means of acquiring social prestige. It is the same in Germany and everywhere else; except in Germany the appropriate avenue to social honor led from the purchase of a feudal estate to the foundation of an entailed estate, and acquisition of titular nobility, which in turn facilitated the reception of the *grandchildren* in aristocratic 'society.' In America, the old tradition respected the self-made man more than the heir, and the avenue to social honor consisted in affiliation with a genteel fraternity in a distinguished college, formerly with a distinguished sect (for instance, Presbyterian, in whose churches in New York one could find soft cushions and fans in the pews). At the present time, affiliation with a distinguished club is essential above all else. In addition, the kind of home is important (in 'the street' which in middle-sized cities is almost never lacking) and the kind of dress and sport. Only recently descent from the Pilgrim fathers, from Pocahontas and other Indian ladies, et cetera has become important. This is not the place for a more detailed treatment. There are masses of translating bureaus and agencies of all sorts concerned with reconstructing the pedigrees of the plutocracy. All these phenomena, often highly grotesque, belong in the broad field of the Europeanization of American 'society.'

In the past and up to the very present, it has been a characteristic precisely of the specifically American democracy that it did *not* constitute a formless sand heap of individuals, but rather a buzzing complex of strictly exclusive, yet voluntary associations. Not so long ago these associations still did not recognize the prestige of birth and *inherited* wealth, of the office and educational diploma; at least they recognized these things to such a low degree as has only very rarely been the case in the rest of the world. Yet, even so, these associations were far from accepting anybody with open arms as an equal. To be sure, fifteen years ago an American farmer would not have led his guest past a plowing farmhand (American born!) in the field without making his guest 'shake hands' with the worker after formally introducing them.

Formerly, in a typical American club nobody would remember that the two members, for instance, who play billiards once stood in the relation of boss and clerk. Here equality of gentlemen prevailed absolutely.* To be sure, the American worker's wife accompanying the trade unionist to lunch had completely accommodated herself in dress and behavior, in a somewhat plainer and more awkward fashion, to the bourgeois lady's model.

He who wished to be fully recognized in this democracy, in whatever position, had not only to conform to the conventions of bourgeois society, the very strict men's fashions included, but as a rule he had to be able to show that he had succeeded in gaining admission by ballot to one of the sects, clubs, or fraternal societies, no matter *what* kind, were it only recognized as sufficiently legitimate. And he had to maintain himself in the society by proving himself to be a gentleman. The parallel in Germany consists in the importance of the *Couleur* † and the commission of an officer of the reserve for *commercium* and *connubium,* and the great status significance of qualifying to give satisfaction by duel. The thing is the same, but the direction and material consequence characteristically differ.

He who did not succeed in joining was no gentleman; he who despised doing so, as was usual among Germans, ‡ had to take the hard road, and especially so in business life.

However, as mentioned above, we shall not here analyze the social significance of these conditions, which are undergoing a profound transformation. First, we are interested in the fact that the modern position of the secular clubs and societies with recruitment by ballot is largely the product of a process of *secularization.* Their position is derived from the far more exclusive importance of the prototype of these voluntary associations, to wit, the sects. They stem, indeed, from the sects in the homeland of genuine Yankeedom, the North Atlantic states. Let us recall, first, that the universal and equal franchise within American democracy (of the Whites! for Negroes and all mixtures have, even today, no *de facto* franchise) and likewise the 'separation of state and church' are only achievements of the recent past, beginning essentially with the nineteenth century. Let us remember that during the colonial

* This was not always the case in the German-American clubs. When asking young German merchants in New York (with the best Hanseatic names) why they all strove to be admitted to an American club instead of the very nicely furnished German one, they answered that their (German-American) bosses would play billiards with them occasionally, however not without making them realize that they (the bosses) thought themselves to be 'very nice' in doing so.

† Student fraternity, comparable to a 'Greek letter society.'

‡ But note above. Entry into an American club (in school or later) is always the decisive moment for the loss of German nationality.

period in the central areas of New England, especially in Massachusetts, full citizenship status in the church congregation was the precondition for full citizenship in the state (besides some other prerequisites). The religious congregation indeed determined admission or non-admission to political citizenship status.[3]

The decision was made according to whether or not the person had *proved* his religious qualification through conduct, in the broadest meaning of the word, as was the case among all Puritan sects. The Quakers in Pennsylvania were not in any lesser way masters of that state until some time before the War of Independence. This was actually the case, though *formally* they were not the only full political citizens. They were political masters only by virtue of extensive gerrymandering.

The tremendous social significance of admission to full enjoyment of the rights of the sectarian congregation, especially the privilege of being admitted to the *Lord's Supper,* worked among the sects in the direction of breeding that ascetist professional ethic which was adequate to modern capitalism during the period of its origin. It can be demonstrated that everywhere, including Europe, the religiosity of the ascetist sects has for several centuries worked in the same way as has been illustrated by the personal experiences mentioned above for [the case of] America.

When focusing on the religious background [4] of these Protestant sects, we find in their literary documents, especially among those of the Quakers and Baptists up to and throughout the seventeenth century, again and again jubilation over the fact that the sinful 'children of the world' distrust one another in business but that they have confidence in the religiously determined righteousness of the pious.[5]

Hence, they give credit and deposit their money only with the pious, and they make purchases in their stores because there, and there alone, they are given honest and *fixed prices*. As is known, the Baptists have always claimed to have first raised this price policy to a principle. In addition to the Baptists, the Quakers raise the claim, as the following quotation shows, to which Mr. Eduard Bernstein drew my attention at the time:

But it was not only in matters which related to the law of the land where the primitive members held their words and engagements sacred. This trait was remarked to be true of them in their concerns of trade. On their first appearance as a society, they suffered as tradesmen because others, displeased with the peculiarity of their manners, withdrew their custom from their shops. But in a little time the great outcry against them was that they got the trade of the country into their hands. This outcry arose in part from a strict exemption of all commercial agreements between them and others and *because they never asked two prices for the commodities they sold.*[6]

The view that the gods bless with riches the man who pleases them, through sacrifice or through his kind of conduct, was indeed diffused all over the world. However, the Protestant sects consciously brought this idea into connection with this *kind* of religious conduct, according to the principle of early capitalism: 'Honesty is the best policy.' This connection is found, although not quite exclusively, among these Protestant sects, but with characteristic continuity and consistency it is found *only* among them.

The whole typically bourgeois ethic was from the beginning common to all aceticist sects and conventicles and it is identical with the ethic practiced by the sects in America up to the very present. The Methodists, for example, held to be forbidden:

(1) to make words when buying and selling ('haggling')
(2) to trade with commodities before the custom tariff has been paid on them
(3) to charge rates of interest higher than the law of the country permits
(4) 'to gather treasures on earth' (meaning the transformation of investment capital into 'funded wealth'
(5) to borrow without being sure of one's ability to pay back the debt
(6) luxuries of all sorts

But it is not only this ethic, already discussed in detail,* which goes back to the early beginnings of asceticist sects. Above all, the social premiums, the means of discipline, and, in general, the whole organizational basis of Protestant sectarianism with all its ramifications reach back to those beginnings. The survivals in contemporary America are the derivatives of a religious regulation of life which once worked with penetrating efficiency. Let us, in a brief survey, clarify the nature of these sects and the mode and direction of their operation.

Within Protestantism the principle of the 'believer's church' first emerged distinctly among the Baptists in Zürich in 1523-4.[7] This principle restricted the congregation to 'true' Christians; hence, it meant a voluntary association of really sanctified people segregated from the

* In *The Protestant Ethic and the Spirit of Capitalism.*

world. Thomas Münzer had rejected infant baptism; but he did not take the next step, which demanded repeated baptism of adults baptized as children (anabaptism). Following Thomas Münzer, the Zürich Baptists in 1525 introduced adult baptism (possibly including anabaptism). Migrant journeymen-artisans were the main bearers of the Baptist movement. After each suppression they carried it to new areas. Here we shall not discuss in detail the individual forms of this voluntarist inner-worldly asceticism of the Old Baptists, the Mennonites, the Baptists, the Quakers, nor shall we again describe how every asceticist denomination, Calvinism [8] and Methodism included, were again and again constrained into the same path.

This resulted either in the conventicle of the exemplary Christians *within* the church (Pietism), or else the community of religious 'full citizens,' legitimated as faultless, became masters *over* the church. The rest of the members merely belonged as a passive status group, as minor Christians subject to discipline (Independents).

In Protestantism the external and internal conflict of the two structural principles—of the 'church' as a compulsory association for the administration of grace, and of the 'sect' as a voluntary association of religiously qualified persons—runs through the centuries from Zwingli to Kuyper and Stöcker. Here we merely wish to consider those consequences of the voluntarist principle which are practically important in their influence upon conduct. In addition, we recall merely that the decisive idea of keeping the Lord's Supper pure, and therefore excluding unsanctified persons, led also to a way of treating church discipline among those denominations which failed to form sects. It was especially the predestinarian Puritans who, in effect, approached the discipline of the sects.[9]

The central social significance of the Lord's Supper for the Christian communities is evidenced in this. For the sects themselves, the idea of the purity of the sacramental communion was decisive at the very time of their origin.[10] Immediately the first consistent voluntarist, Browne, in his 'Treatise of Reformation without tarying for anie' (presumably 1582), emphasized the compulsion to hold communion at the Lord's Supper with 'wicked men' as the main reason for rejecting Episcopalianism and Presbyterianism.[11] The Presbyterian church struggled in vain to settle the problem. Already under Elizabeth (Wandworth Conference) this was the decisive point.*

* The English Presbyterians under Elizabeth wished to recognize the 39 articles of the Church of England (with reservations concerning articles 34 to 36, which are here of no interest).

The question of *who* might exclude a person from the Lord's Supper played an ever-recurrent role in the Parliament of the English Revolution. At first (1645) ministers and elders, that is, laymen, were to decide these matters freely. Parliament attempted to determine those cases in which exclusion should be permissible. All other cases were to be made dependent on the consent of Parliament. This meant 'Erastianism,' against which the Westminster Assembly protested sharply.

The Independent party excelled in that it admitted only persons with tickets to communion, besides the local residents recognized to be in good standing. Members from outside congregations received tickets only upon recommendation by qualified members. The certificates of qualification (letters of recommendation), which were issued in case of removal to another place or in case of travel, also occur in the seventeenth century.[12] *Within* the official church, Baxter's conventicles (associations), which in 1657 were introduced in sixteen counties, were to be established as a kind of voluntary censorship bureau. These would assist the minister in determining the qualification and exclusion of scandalous persons from the Lord's Supper.[13] The 'five dissenting brethren' of the Westminster Assembly—upper-class refugees who had lived in Holland—had already aimed at similar ends when they proposed to permit voluntaristic congregations to exist *beside* the parish and also to grant them the right to vote for delegates to the synod. The entire church history of New England is filled with struggles over such questions: who was to be admitted to the sacraments (or, for instance, as a godfather), whether the children of non-admitted persons could be baptized,* under what clauses the latter could be admitted, and similar questions. The difficulty was that not only was the worthy person allowed to receive the Lord's Supper, but he *had* to receive it.[14] Hence, if the believer doubted his own worth and decided to stay away from the Lord's Supper, the decision did not remove his sin.[15] The congregation, on the other hand, was jointly responsible to the Lord for keeping unworthy and especially reprobated persons[16] away from communion, for purity's sake. Thus the congregation was jointly and especially responsible for the administration of the sacrament by a worthy minister in a state of grace. Therewith, the primordial problems of church constitution were resurrected. In vain Baxter's compromise proposal attempted to mediate by suggesting that at least in case of an emergency the sacrament should be received from an unworthy minister, thus from one whose conduct was questionable.[17]

* Even the Brownist petition to King James of 1603 protested against this.

The ancient Donatist principle of personal charisma stood in hard and unmitigated opposition to the principle of the church as an institution administering grace,[18] as in the time of early Christianity. The principle of instituted grace was radically established in the Catholic Church through the priest's *character indelebilis,* but it also dominated the official churches of the Reformation. The uncompromising radicalism of the Independentist world of ideas rested upon the religious responsibility of the congregation as a whole. This held for the worthiness of the ministers as well as for the brethren admitted to communion. And that is how things still stand in principle.

As is known, the Kuyper schism in Holland during recent decades had far-reaching political ramifications. It originated in the following manner: Against the claims of the Synodal church government of the Herformde Kerk der Nederlanden, the elders of a church in Amsterdam, hence *laymen,* with the later prime minister Kuyper (who was also a plain lay elder) at the helm, refused to acknowledge the confirmation certificates of preachers of outside congregations as sufficient for admission to communion if from their standpoint such outside preachers were unworthy or unbelieving.[19] In substance, this was precisely the antagonism between Presbyterians and Independents during the sixteenth century; for consequences of the greatest importance emerged from the joint responsibility of the congregation. Next to the voluntarist principle, that is, free admission of the qualified, and of the qualified alone, as members of the congregation, we find the principle of the sovereignty of the local sacramental *community.* Only the local religious community, by virtue of personal acquaintance and investigation, could judge whether a member were qualified. But a church government of an inter-local association could not do so, however freely elected such church government might be. The local congregation could discriminate only if the number of members were restricted. Hence, in principle, only relatively small congregations were appropriate.[20]

Where the communities were too large for this, either conventicles were formed, as in Pietism, or the members were organized in groups, which, in turn, were the bearers of church discipline, as in Methodism.[21]

The extraordinarily strict moral discipline [22] of the self-governing congregation constituted the third principle. This was unavoidable because of the interest in the purity of the sacramental community (or, as among the Quakers, the interest in the purity of the community of prayer). The discipline of the asceticist sect was, in fact, far more rigorous than the discipline of any church. In this respect, the sect resembles the monastic order. The sect discipline is also analogous to monastic discipline in that it established the principle of the novitiate.* In contrast to the principles of the official Protestant churches, persons expelled because of moral offenses were often denied all intercourse with the members of the congregation. The sect thus invoked an absolute boycott against them, which included business life. Occasionally the sect avoided any relation with non-brethren except in cases of absolute necessity.[23] And the sect placed disciplinary power predominantly into the hands of laymen. No spiritual authority could assume the community's joint responsibility before God. The weight of the lay elders was very great even among the Presbyterians. However, the Independents, and even more, the Baptists signified a struggle against the domination of the congregation by theologians.[24] In exact correspondence this struggle led naturally to the clericalization of the lay members, who now took over the functions of moral control through self-government, admonition, and possible excommunication.[25] The domination of laymen in the church found its expression, in part, in the quest for freedom of the layman to preach (liberty of prophesying).[26] In legitimizing this demand, reference was made to the conditions of the early Christian community. This demand was not only very shocking to the Lutheran idea of the pastoral office but also to the Presbyterian idea of God's order. The domination of laymen, in part, found its expression in an opposition to any professional theologian and preacher. Only charisma, neither training nor office, should be recognized. †

The Quakers have adhered to the principle that in the religious assembly anyone could speak, but he alone should speak who was moved by the spirit. Hence no professional minister exists at all. To be sure, today this is, in all probability, nowhere radically effected. The official 'legend' is that members who, in the experience of the congregation, are especially accessible to the spirit during service are seated upon a special bench opposite the congregation. In profound silence the people wait for the spirit to take possession of one of them (or of some other member of the congregation). But during service in a Pennsylvania college, unfortunately and against my hopes, the spirit did not take hold of the

---

* In all probability among all sects there existed a period of probation. Among the Methodists, for example, it lasted for six months.

† Already Smyth in Amsterdam demanded that when preaching the regenerate must not even have the Bible in front of him.

plainly and beautifully costumed old lady who was seated on the bench and whose charisma was so highly praised. Instead, undoubtedly by agreement, the spirit took hold of a brave college librarian who gave a very learned lecture on the concept of the 'saint.'

To be sure, other sects have not drawn such radical conclusions, or at least not for good. However, either the minister is not active principally as a 'hireling,'[27] holding only honorific position, or else he serves for voluntary honorific donations.* Again his ministerial service may be a secondary occupation and only for the refunding of his expenses; † or he can be dismissed at any time; or a sort of missionary organization prevails with itinerant preachers [28] working only once in a while in the same 'circuit,' as is the case with Methodism.[29] Where the office (in the traditional sense) and hence the theological qualification were maintained,[30] such skill was considered as a mere technical and specialist prerequisite. However, the really decisive quality was the charisma of the state of grace, and the authorities were geared to discern it.

Authorities, like Cromwell's triers (local bodies for the handling of certificates of religious qualification) and the ejectors (ministerial disciplinary office), ‡ had to examine the fitness of the ministers to serve. The charismatic character of authority is seen to have been preserved in the same way in which the charismatic character of the membership in the community itself was preserved. Just as Cromwell's army of Saints allowed only religiously qualified persons to pass the Lord's Supper to them, so Cromwell's soldiers refused to go into battle under an officer who did not belong to his sacramental community of the religiously qualified.[31]

Internally, among the sect members, the spirit of early Christian brotherliness prevailed, at least among the early Baptists and derived denominations; or at least brotherliness was demanded.[32] Among some sects it was considered taboo to call on the law courts. § In case of need, mutual aid was obligatory.[33] Naturally, *business* dealings with non-

---

* The latter was demanded for all preachers in the Agreement of the People of 1 May 1649.

† Thus the local preachers of the Methodists.

‡ Thus, in accordance with the proposal of 1652 and essentially also in accordance with the church constitution of 1654.

§ The Methodists have often attempted to sanction the appeal to the secular judge by expulsion. On the other hand, in several cases, they have established authorities upon which one could call if debtors did not pay promptly.

members were not interdicted (except occasionally among wholly radical communities).

Yet it was self-understood that one preferred the brethren.* From the very beginning, one finds the system of certificates (concerning membership and conduct),[34] which were given to members who moved to another place. The charities of the Quakers were so highly developed that in consequence of the burdens incurred their inclination to propagandize was finally crippled. The cohesiveness of the congregations was so great that, with good reason, it is said to be one of the factors determining New England settlements. In contrast to the South, New England settlements were generally compact and, from the beginning, strongly urban in character. †

It is obvious that in all these points the modern functions of American sects and sectlike associations, as described in the beginning of this essay, are revealed as straight derivatives, rudiments, and survivals of those conditions which once prevailed in all asceticist sects and conventicles. Today they are decaying. Testimony for the sectarian's immensely exclusive 'pride in caste' has existed from the very beginning. ‡

Now, what part of this whole development was and is actually decisive for our problem? Excommunication in the Middle Ages also had political and civic consequences. Formally this was even harsher than where sect freedom existed. Moreover, in the Middle Ages only Christians could be full citizens. During the Middle Ages it was also possible to proceed through the disciplinary powers of the church against a bishop who would not pay his debts, and, as Aloys Schulte has beautifully shown, this possibility gave the bishop a credit rating over and above a secular prince. Likewise, the fact that a Prussian Lieutenant was subject to discharge if he was incapable of paying off debts provided a higher credit rating for him. And the same held for the German fraternity student. Oral confession and the disciplinary power of the church during the Middle Ages also provided the means to enforce church discipline effectively. Finally, to secure a legal claim, the opportunity provided by the oath was exploited to secure excommunication of the debtor.

* With the Methodists this is expressly prescribed.

† Doyle in his work which we have repeatedly cited ascribes the industrial character of New England, in contrast to the agrarian colonies, to this factor.

‡ Cf., for example, Doyle's comments about the status conditions in New England, where the families bearing old religious literary tradition, not the 'propertied classes,' formed the aristocracy.

In all these cases, however, the forms of behavior that were favored or tabooed through such conditions and means differed totally from those which Protestant asceticism bred or suppressed. With the lieutenant, for instance, or the fraternity student, and probably with the bishop as well, the enhanced credit rating certainly did not rest upon the breeding of personal qualities suitable for *business;* and following up this remark directly: even though the effects in all three cases were intended to have the same direction, they were worked out in quite different ways. The medieval, like the Lutheran church discipline, first, was vested in the hands of the ministerial officeholder; secondly, this discipline worked —as far as it was effective at all—through authoritarian means; and, thirdly, it punished and placed premiums upon concrete individual acts.

The church discipline of the Puritans and of the sects was vested, first, at least in part and often wholly, in the hands of laymen. Secondly, it worked through the necessity of one's having to hold one's own; and, thirdly, it bred or, if one wishes, selected qualities. The last point is the most important one.

The member of the sect (or conventicle) had to have qualities of a certain kind in order to enter the community circle. Being endowed with these qualities was important for the development of rational modern capitalism, as has been shown in the first essay.* In order to hold his own in this circle, the member had to *prove* repeatedly that he was endowed with these qualities. They were constantly and continuously bred in him. For, like his bliss in the beyond, his whole social existence in the here and now depended upon his 'proving' himself. The Catholic confession of sins was, to repeat, by comparison a means of *relieving* the person from the tremendous internal pressure under which the sect member in his conduct was constantly held. How certain orthodox and heterodox religious communities of the Middle Ages have been forerunners of the ascetic denominations of Protestantism shall not here and now be discussed.

According to all experience there is no stronger means of breeding traits than through the necessity of holding one's own in the circle of one's associates. The continuous and unobtrusive ethical discipline of the sects was, therefore, related to authoritarian church discipline as rational breeding and selection are related to ordering and forbidding.

In this as in almost every other respect, the Puritan sects are the most specific bearers of the inner-worldly form of asceticism. Moreover, they

* *The Protestant Ethic and the Spirit of Capitalism.*

are the most consistent and, in a certain sense, the only consistent antithesis to the universalist Catholic Church—a compulsory organization for the administration of grace. The Puritan sects put the most powerful individual interest of social self-esteem in the service of this breeding of traits. Hence *individual* motives and personal self-interests were also placed in the service of maintaining and propagating the 'bourgeois' Puritan ethic, with all its ramifications. This is absolutely decisive for its penetrating and for its powerful effect.

To repeat, it is not the ethical *doctrine* of a religion, but that form of ethical conduct upon which *premiums* are placed that matters.[35] Such premiums operate through the form and the condition of the respective goods of salvation. And such conduct constitutes 'one's' specific 'ethos' in the sociological sense of the word. For Puritanism, that conduct was a certain methodical, rational way of life which—given certain conditions— paved the way for the 'spirit' of modern capitalism. The premiums were placed upon 'proving' oneself before God in the sense of attaining salvation—which is found in *all* Puritan denominations—and 'proving' oneself before men in the sense of socially holding one's own within the Puritan sects. Both aspects were mutually supplementary and operated in the same direction: they helped to deliver the 'spirit' of modern capitalism, its specific *ethos:* the ethos of the modern *bourgeois middle classes.*

The ascetic conventicles and sects formed one of the most important historical foundations of modern 'individualism.' Their radical break away from patriarchal and authoritarian bondage,[36] as well as *their* way of interpreting the statement that one owes more obedience to God than to man, was especially important.

Finally, in order to understand the nature of these ethical effects, a comparative remark is required. In the *guilds* of the Middle Ages there was frequently a control of the general ethical standard of the members similar to that exercised by the discipline of the ascetic Protestant sects.[37] But the unavoidable difference in the effects of guild and of sect upon the economic conduct of the individual is obvious.

The guild united members of the same occupation; hence it united *competitors.* It did so in order to limit competition as well as the rational striving for profit which operated through competition. The guild trained for 'civic' virtues and, in a certain sense, was the bearer of bourgeois 'rationalism' (a point which will not be discussed here in detail). The guild accomplished this through a 'subsistence policy' and through tra-

ditionalism. In so far as guild regulation of the economy gained effectiveness, its practical results are well known.

The sects, on the other hand, united men through the selection and
the breeding of ethically qualified *fellow believers*. Their membership
was not based upon apprenticeship or upon the family relations of technically qualified members of an occupation. The sect controlled and
regulated the members' conduct *exclusively* in the sense of formal
righteousness and methodical asceticism. It was devoid of the purpose
of a material subsistence policy which handicapped an expansion of the
rational striving for profit. The capitalist success of a guild member
undermined the spirit of the guild—as happened in England and France
—and hence capitalist success was shunned. But the capitalist success of
a sect brother, if legally attained, was proof of his worth and of his state
of grace, and it raised the prestige and the propaganda chances of the
sect. Such success was therefore welcome, as the several statements quoted
above show. The organization of free labor in guilds, in their Occidental
medieval form, has certainly—very much against their intention—not
only been a handicap but also a precondition for the capitalist organization of labor, which was, perhaps, indispensable.[38] But the guild, of
course, could not give birth to the modern bourgeois capitalist *ethos*.
Only the methodical way of life of the ascetic sects could legitimate and
put a halo around the economic 'individualist' impulses of the modern
capitalist ethos.

XIII. Religious Rejections of the World and Their Directions

In strongest contrast to the case of China, Indian religiosity, which we are about to consider, is the cradle of those religious ethics which have abnegated the world, theoretically, practically, and to the greatest extent. It is also in India that the 'technique' which corresponds to such abnegation has been most highly developed. Monkhood, as well as the typical ascetic and contemplative manipulations, were not only first but also most consistently developed in India. And it was perhaps from India that this rationalization set out on its historical way throughout the world at large.

1: Motives for the Rejection of the World: the Meaning of Their Rational Construction

Before turning to this religiosity it may be expedient to clarify briefly, in a schematic and theoretical way, the motives from which religious ethics of world abnegation have originated, and the directions they have taken. In this way we may clarify their possible 'meaning.'

The constructed scheme, of course, only serves the purpose of offering an ideal typical means of orientation. It does not teach a philosophy of its own. The theoretically constructed types of conflicting 'life orders' are merely intended to show that at certain points such and such internal conflicts are possible and 'adequate.' They are not intended to show that there is no standpoint from which the conflicts could not be held to be resolved in a higher synthesis. As will readily be seen, the individual spheres of value are prepared with a rational consistency which is rarely found in reality. But they *can* appear thus in reality and in historically

From 'Zwischenbetrachtung,' *Gesammelte Aufsaetze zur Religionssoziologie,* vol. i, pp. 436-73. This essay was published in November 1915 in the *Archiv.*

important ways, and they have. Such constructions make it possible to determine the typological locus of a historical phenomenon. They enable us to see if, in particular traits or in their total character, the phenomena approximate one of our constructions: to determine the degree of approximation of the historical phenomenon to the theoretically constructed type. To this extent, the construction is merely a technical aid which facilitates a more lucid arrangement and terminology. Yet, under certain conditions, a construction might mean more. For the rationality, in the sense of logical or teleological 'consistency,' of an intellectual-theoretical or practical-ethical attitude has and always has had power over man, however limited and unstable this power is and always has been in the face of other forces of historical life.

Religious interpretations of the world and ethics of religions created by intellectuals and meant to be rational have been strongly exposed to the imperative of consistency. The effect of the *ratio,* especially of a teleological deduction of practical postulates, is in some way, and often very strongly, noticeable among all religious ethics. This holds however little the religious interpretations of the world in the individual case have complied with the demand for consistency, and however much they might integrate points of view into their ethical postulates which could *not* be rationally deduced. Thus, for substantive reasons, we may hope to facilitate the presentation of an otherwise immensely multifarious subject matter by expediently constructed rational types. To do this we must prepare and emphasize the internally most 'consistent' forms of practical conduct that can be deduced from fixed and given presuppositions.

Above all, such an essay in the sociology of religion necessarily aims at contributing to the typology and sociology of rationalism. This essay therefore proceeds from the most rational forms reality *can* assume; it attempts to find out how far certain rational conclusions, which can be established theoretically, have been drawn in reality. And perhaps we will find out why not.

2: TYPOLOGY OF ASCETICISM AND OF MYSTICISM

The great importance of the conception of the supra-mundane God and Creator for religious ethics has been touched upon.* This conception has been especially important for the active and asceticist direction of the

* Cf. chapter xi.

quest for salvation. It has not been so important for the contemplative and mystical quest, which has an internal affinity with the depersonalization and immanence of the divine power. However, this intimate connection, which E. Troeltsch has repeatedly and rightly stressed, between the conception of a supra-mundane God and active asceticism is not absolute; the supra-mundane God has not, as such, determined the direction of Occidental asceticism, as will be seen from the following reflections. The Christian Trinity, with its incarnate Savior and the saints, represented a conception of God which fundamentally was rather less supra-mundane than was the God of Jewry, especially of later Jewry, or the Allah of Islamism.

Jewry developed mysticism, but it developed hardly any asceticism of the Occidental type. And early Islamism directly repudiated asceticism. The peculiarity of Dervish religiosity stemmed from quite different sources than from the relation to a supra-mundane God and Creator. It stemmed from mystic, ecstatic sources and in its inner essence it was remote from Occidental asceticism. Important though it was, the conception of a supra-mundane God, in spite of its affinity to emissary prophecy and active asceticism, obviously did not operate alone but always in conjunction with other circumstances. The nature of religious promises and the paths of salvation which they determined were paramount among these circumstances. This matter has to be discussed in connection with particular cases.

We have had repeatedly to use the terms 'asceticism' and 'mysticism' as polar concepts. In order to elucidate this terminology we shall here further differentiate these terms.

In our introductory comments * we contrasted, as abnegations of the world, the active asceticism that is a God-willed *action* of the devout who are God's tools, and, on the other hand, the contemplative *possession* of the holy, as found in mysticism. Mysticism intends a state of 'possession,' not action, and the individual is not a tool but a 'vessel' of the divine. Action in the world must thus appear as endangering the absolutely irrational and other-worldly religious state. Active asceticism operates within the world; rationally active asceticism, in mastering the world, seeks to tame what is creatural and wicked through work in a worldly 'vocation' (inner-worldly asceticism). Such asceticism contrasts radically with mysticism, if the latter draws the full conclusion of fleeing from the world (contemplative flight from the world).

* Cf. chapter XI.

The contrast is tempered, however, if active asceticism confines itself to keeping down and to overcoming creatural wickedness in the actor's own nature. For then it enhances the concentration on the firmly established God-willed and active redemptory accomplishments to the point of avoiding any action in the orders of the world (asceticist flight from the world). Thereby active asceticism in external bearing comes close to contemplative flight from the world.

The contrast between asceticism and mysticism is also tempered if the contemplative mystic does not draw the conclusion that he should flee from the world, but, like the inner-worldly asceticist, remain in the orders of the world (inner-worldly mysticism).

In both cases the contrast can actually disappear in practice and some combination of both forms of the quest for salvation may occur. But the contrast may continue to exist even under the veil of external similarity. For the true mystic the principle continues to hold: the creature must be silent so that God may speak. He 'is' in the world and externally 'accommodates' to its orders, but only in order to gain a certainty of his state of grace in opposition to the world by resisting the temptation to take the ways of the world seriously. As we can see with Lao-tse, the typical attitude of the mystic is one of a specifically broken humility, a minimization of action, a sort of religious incognito existence in the world. He proves himself *against* the world, against his action in the world. Inner-worldly asceticism, on the contrary, proves itself *through* action. To the inner-worldly asceticist the conduct of the mystic is an indolent enjoyment of self; to the mystic the conduct of the (inner-worldly active) asceticist is an entanglement in the godless ways of the world combined with complacent self-righteousness. With that 'blissful bigotry,' usually ascribed to the typical Puritan, inner-worldly asceticism executes the positive and divine resolutions whose ultimate meaning remains concealed. Asceticism executes these resolutions as given in the God-ordained rational orders of the creatural. To the mystic, on the contrary, what matters for his salvation is only the grasping of the ultimate and completely irrational meaning through mystic experience. The forms in which both ways of conduct flee from the world can be distinguished by similar confrontations. But we reserve the discussion of these for monographic presentation.

3: DIRECTIONS OF THE ABNEGATION OF THE WORLD

We shall now consider in detail the tensions existing between religion and the world. We shall proceed from the reflections of the introduction,* but we shall now give them a somewhat different turn.

We have said that these modes of behavior, once developed into a methodical way of life, formed the nucleus of asceticism as well as of mysticism, and that they originally grew out of magical presuppositions. Magical practices were engaged in, either for the sake of awakening charismatic qualities or for the sake of preventing evil charms. The first case has, of course, been more important for historical developments. For even at the threshold of its appearance, asceticism showed its Janus-face: on the one hand, abnegation of the world, and on the other, mastery of the world by virtue of the magical powers obtained by abnegation.

The magician has been the historical precursor of the prophet, of the exemplary as well as of the emissary prophet and savior. As a rule the prophet and the savior have legitimized themselves through the possession of a magical charisma. With them, however, this has been merely a means of securing recognition and followers for the exemplary significance, the mission, or the savior quality of their personalities. For the substance of the prophecy or of the savior's commandment is to direct a way of life to the pursuit of a sacred value. Thus understood, the prophecy or commandment means, at least relatively, to systematize and rationalize the way of life, either in particular points or totally. The latter has been the rule with all true 'religions of salvation,' that is, with all religions that hold out deliverance from suffering to their adherents. This is more likely to be the case the more sublimated, the more inward, and the more principled the essence of suffering is conceived. For then it is important to put the follower into a *permanent* state which makes him inwardly safe against suffering. Formulated abstractly, the rational aim of redemption religion has been to secure for the saved a holy state, and thereby a habitude that assures salvation. This takes the place of an acute and extraordinary, and thus a holy, state which is transitorily attained by means of orgies, asceticism, or contemplation.

Now if a religious community emerges in the wake of a prophecy or of the propaganda of a savior, the control of regular conduct first falls into the hands of the charismatically qualified successors, pupils, disci-

* Cf. chapter XI.

ples of the prophet or of the savior. Later, under certain very regularly recurrent conditions, which we shall not deal with here, this task falls into the hands of a priestly, hereditary, or official hierocracy. Yet, as a rule, the prophet or the savior personally has stood in opposition to the traditional hierocratic powers of magicians or of priests. He has set his personal charisma against their dignity consecrated by tradition in order to break their power or force them to his service.

In the aforementioned discussion, we have taken for granted and presupposed that a large and, for the historical development, an especially important fraction of all cases of prophetic and redemptory religions have lived not only in an acute but in a permanent state of tension in relation to the world and its orders. This goes without saying, according to the terminology used here. The more the religions have been true religions of salvation, the greater has this tension been. This follows from the meaning of salvation and from the substance of the prophetic teachings as soon as these develop into an ethic. The tension has also been the greater, the more rational in principle the ethic has been, and the more it has been oriented to *inward* sacred values as means of salvation. In common language, this means that the tension has been the greater the more religion has been sublimated from ritualism and towards 'religious absolutism.' Indeed, the further the rationalization and sublimation of the external and internal possession of—in the widest sense—'things worldly' has progressed, the stronger has the tension on the part of religion become. For the rationalization and the conscious sublimation of man's relations to the various spheres of values, external and internal, as well as religious and secular, have then pressed towards making conscious the *internal and lawful autonomy* of the individual spheres; thereby letting them drift into those tensions which remain hidden to the originally naïve relation with the external world. This results quite generally from the development of inner- and other-worldly values towards rationality, towards conscious endeavor, and towards sublimation by *knowledge*. This consequence is very important for the history of religion. In order to elucidate the typical phenomena which recur in connection with greatly varying religious ethics, we shall consider a series of these values.

Wherever prophecies of salvation have created religious communities, the first power with which they have come into conflict has been the natural sib. The sib has had to fear devaluation by the prophecy. Those who cannot be hostile to members of the household, to father and to mother, cannot be disciples of Jesus. 'I came not to send peace, but a sword' (Matthew x, 34) was said in this connection, and, it should be noted, solely in this connection. The preponderant majority of all religions have, of course, regulated the inner-worldly bonds of piety. Yet the more comprehensive and the more inward the aim of salvation has been, the more it has been taken for granted that the faithful should ultimately stand closer to the savior, the prophet, the priest, the father confessor, the brother in the faith than to natural relations and to the matrimonial community.

Prophecy has created a new social community, particularly where it became a soteriological religion of congregations. Thereby the relationships of the sib and of matrimony have been, at least relatively, devalued. The magical ties and exclusiveness of the sibs have been shattered, and within the new community the prophetic religion has developed a religious ethic of brotherliness. This ethic has simply taken over the original principles of social and ethical conduct which the 'association of neighbors' had offered, whether it was the community of villagers, members of the sib, the guild, or of partners in seafaring, hunting, and warring expeditions. These communities have known two elemental principles: first, the dualism of in-group and out-group morality; second, for in-group morality, simple reciprocity: 'As you do unto me I shall do unto you.' From these principles the following have resulted for economic life: For in-group morality the principled obligation to give brotherly support in distress has existed. The wealthy and the noble were obliged to loan, free of charge, goods for the use of the propertyless, to give credit free of interest, and to extend liberal hospitality and support. Men were obliged to render services upon the request of their neighbors, and likewise, on the lord's estate, without compensation other than mere sustenance. All this followed the principle: your want of today may be mine of tomorrow. This principle was not, of course, rationally weighed, but it played its part in sentiment. Accordingly, higgling in exchange and loan situations, as well as permanent enslavement resulting, for instance, from debts, were confined to out-group morality and applied only to outsiders.

The religiosity of the congregation transferred this ancient economic ethic of neighborliness to the relations among brethren of the faith. What had previously been the obligations of the noble and the wealthy became the fundamental imperatives of all ethically rationalized religions of the world: to aid widows and orphans in distress, to care for the sick and impoverished brother of the faith, and to give alms. The giving of alms was especially required of the rich, for the holy minstrels and magicians as well as the ascetics were economically dependent upon the rich.

The principle that constituted the communal relations among the salvation prophecies was the suffering common to all believers. And this was the case whether the suffering actually existed or was a constant threat, whether it was external or internal. The more imperatives that issued from the ethic of reciprocity among neighbors were raised, the more rational the conception of salvation became, and the more it was sublimated into an ethic of absolute ends. Externally, such commands rose to a communism of loving brethren; internally they rose to the attitude of *caritas,* love for the sufferer *per se,* for one's neighbor, for man, and finally for the enemy. The barrier to the bond of faith and the existence of hatred in the face of a world conceived to be the locus of undeserved suffering seem to have resulted from the same imperfections and depravities of empirical reality that originally caused the suffering. Above all, the peculiar euphoria of all types of sublimated religious ecstasy operated psychologically in the same general direction. From being 'moved' and edified to feeling direct communion with God, ecstasies have always inclined men towards the flowing out into an objectless acosmism of love. In religions of salvation, the profound and quiet bliss of all heroes of acosmic benevolence has always been fused with a charitable realization of the natural imperfections of all human doings, including one's own. The psychological tone as well as the rational, ethical interpretation of this inner attitude can vary widely. But its ethical demand has always lain in the direction of a universalist brotherhood, which goes beyond all barriers of societal associations, often including that of one's own faith.

The religion of brotherliness has always clashed with the orders and values of this world, and the more consistently its demands have been carried through, the sharper the clash has been. The split has usually become wider the more the values of the world have been rationalized and sublimated in terms of their own laws. And that is what matters here.

4: The Economic Sphere

The tension between brotherly religion and the world has been most obvious in the economic sphere.

All the primeval magical or mystagogic ways of influencing spirits and deities have pursued special interests. They have striven for wealth, as well as long life, health, honor, progeny and, possibly, the improvement of one's fate in the hereafter. The Eleusian mysteries promised all this, just as did the Phoenician and Vedic religions, the Chinese folk-religion, ancient Judaism, and ancient Islam; and it was the promise held out to the pious Hindu and Buddhist laymen. The sublimated religions of salvation, however, have been increasingly tense in their relationships with rationalized economies.

A rational economy is a functional organization oriented to money-prices which originate in the interest-struggles of men in the *market*. Calculation is not possible without estimation in money prices and hence without market struggles. Money is the most abstract and 'impersonal' element that exists in human life. The more the world of the modern capitalist economy follows its own immanent laws, the less accessible it is to any imaginable relationship with a religious ethic of brotherliness. The more rational, and thus impersonal, capitalism becomes, the more is this the case. In the past it was possible to regulate ethically the personal relations between master and slave precisely because they were personal relations. But it is not possible to regulate—at least not in the same sense or with the same success—the relations between the shifting holders of mortgages and the shifting debtors of the banks that issue these mortgages: for in this case, no personal bonds of any sort exist. If one nevertheless tried to do so, the results would be the same as those we have come to know from China, namely, stifling formal rationality. For in China, formal rationality and substantive rationality were in conflict.

As we have seen, the religions of salvation have had a tendency to depersonalize and objectify love in the unique sense of acosmism. Yet these same religions have watched with profound suspicion the deployment of economic forces which, in a different sense, have likewise been impersonal, and because of this they have been specifically opposed to brotherliness.

The Catholic *Deo placere non potest* has always been the characteristic attitude of salvation religions towards the profit economy; with all rational methods of salvation the warnings against attachment to money and goods have pushed to the height of tabooing goods and money. The dependence of religious communities themselves, and of their propaganda and maintenance, upon economic means, and their accommodation to cultural needs and the everyday interests of the masses, have compelled them to enter compromises of which the history of the interdiction of interests is but one example. Yet, ultimately no genuine religion of salvation has overcome the tension between their religiosity and a rational economy.

Externally, the ethic of religious virtuosos has touched this tense relation in the most radical fashion: by rejecting the possession of economic goods. The ascetic monk has fled from the world by denying himself individual property; his existence has rested entirely upon his own work; and, above all, his needs have been correspondingly restricted to what was absolutely indispensable. The paradox of all rational asceticism, which in an identical manner has made monks in all ages stumble, is that rational asceticism itself has created the very wealth it rejected. Temples and monasteries have everywhere become the very *loci* of rational economies.

Contemplative seclusion as a principle has only been able to establish the rule that the propertyless monk must enjoy only what nature and men voluntarily offer: berries, roots, and free alms. Labor was something which distracted the monk from concentration upon the contemplated value of salvation. Yet even contemplative seclusion has made its compromises by establishing districts for begging, as in India.

There have been only two consistent avenues for escaping the tension between religion and the economic world in a principled and *inward* manner: First, the paradox of the Puritan ethic of 'vocation.' As a religion of virtuosos, Puritanism renounced the universalism of love, and rationally routinized all work in this world into serving God's will and testing one's state of grace. God's will in its ultimate meaning was quite incomprehensible, yet it was the only positive will that could be known. In this respect, Puritanism accepted the routinization of the economic cosmos, which, with the whole world, it devalued as creatural and depraved. This state of affairs appeared as God-willed, and as material and given for fulfilling one's duty. In the last resort, this meant in principle to renounce salvation as a goal attainable by man, that is, by everybody. It meant to renounce salvation in favor of the groundless and always only particularized grace. In truth, this standpoint of un-brotherliness was no longer a genuine 'religion of salvation.' A genuine religion of salvation can exaggerate brotherliness to the height of the mystic's acosmism of love.

Mysticism is the other consistent avenue by which the tension between economics and religion has been escaped. This way is represented quite purely in the mystic's 'benevolence,' which does not at all enquire into the man to whom and for whom it sacrifices. Ultimately, mysticism is not interested in his person. Once and for all, the benevolent mystic gives his shirt when he is asked for his coat, by anybody who accidentally happens to come his way—and merely because he happens to come his way. Mysticism is a unique escape from this world in the form of an objectless devotion to anybody, not for man's sake but purely for devotion's sake, or, in Baudelaire's words, for the sake of 'the soul's sacred prostitution.'

5: THE POLITICAL SPHERE

The consistent brotherly ethic of salvation religions has come into an equally sharp tension with the *political* orders of the world. This problem did not exist for magic religiosity or for the religion of functional deities. The ancient god of war as well as the god who guaranteed the legal order were functional deities who protected the undoubted values of everyday routine. The gods of locality, tribe, and polity were only concerned with the interests of their respective associations. They had to fight other gods like themselves, just as their communities fought, and they had to prove their divine powers in this very struggle.

The problem only arose when these barriers of locality, tribe, and polity were shattered by universalist religions, by a religion with a unified God of the entire world. And the problem arose in full strength only when this God was a God of 'love.' The problem of tensions with the political order emerged for redemption religions out of the basic demand for brotherliness. And in politics, as in economics, the more rational the political order became the sharper the problems of these tensions became.

The bureaucratic state apparatus, and the rational *homo politicus* integrated into the state, manage affairs, including the punishment of evil, when they discharge business in the most ideal sense, according to the rational rules of the state order. In this, the political man acts just like the economic man, in a matter-of-fact manner 'without regard to the person,' *sine ira et studio,* without hate and therefore without love. By virtue of its depersonalization, the bureaucratic state, in important points, is less accessible to substantive moralization than were the patriarchal orders of the past, however many appearances may point to the contrary. The patriarchal orders of the past were based upon personal obligations of piety, and the patriarchal rulers considered the merit of the concrete, single case precisely with 'regard to the person.' In the final analysis, in spite of all 'social welfare policies,' the whole course of the state's inner political functions, of justice and administration, is repeatedly and unavoidably regulated by the objective pragmatism of 'reasons of state.' The state's absolute end is to safeguard (or to change) the external and internal distribution of power; ultimately, this end must seem meaningless to any universalist religion of salvation. This fact has held and still holds, even more so, for foreign policy. It is absolutely essential for every political association to appeal to the naked violence of coercive means in the face of outsiders as well as in the face of internal enemies. It is only this very appeal to violence that constitutes a political association in our terminology. The state is an association that claims the monopoly of the *legitimate use of violence,* and cannot be defined in any other manner.

The Sermon on the Mount says 'resist no evil.' In opposition, the state asserts: 'You *shall* help right to triumph by the use of *force,* otherwise you too may be responsible for injustice.' Where this factor is absent, the 'state' is also absent; the 'anarchism' of the pacifist will have then come to life. According to the inescapable pragmatism of all action, however, force and the threat of force unavoidably breed more force. 'Reasons of state' thus follow their own external and internal laws. The very success of force, or of the threat of force, depends ultimately upon power relations and not on ethical 'right,' even were one to believe it possible to discover objective criteria for such 'right.'

In contrast to naive, primitive heroism, it is typical of the rational state systems for groups or rulers to line up for violent conflict, all quite sincerely believing themselves to be 'in the right.' To any consistent religious rationalization, this must seem only an aping of ethics. Moreover, to draw the Lord's name into such violent political conflict must be viewed as a taking of His name in vain. In the face of this, the cleaner and only honest way may appear to be the complete elimination of ethics from political reasoning. The more matter-of-fact and calculating politics is, and the freer of passionate feelings, of wrath, and of love it becomes, the more it must appear to an ethic of brotherliness to be estranged from brotherliness.

The mutual strangeness of religion and politics, when they are both completely rationalized, is all the more the case because, in contrast to economics, politics may come into direct competition with religious ethics at decisive points. As the consummated threat of violence among modern polities, war creates a pathos and a sentiment of community. War thereby makes for an unconditionally devoted and sacrificial community among the combatants and releases an active mass compassion and love for those who are in need. And, as a mass phenomenon, these feelings break down all the naturally given barriers of association. In general, religions can show comparable achievements only in heroic communities professing an ethic of brotherliness.

Moreover, war does something to the warrior which, in its concrete meaning, is unique: it makes him experience a consecrated meaning of death which is characteristic only of death in war. The community of the army standing in the field today feels itself—as in the times of the war lords 'following'—to be a community unto death, and the greatest of its kind. Death on the field of battle differs from death that is only man's common lot. Since death is a fate that comes to everyone, nobody can ever say why it comes precisely to him and why it comes just when it does. As the values of culture increasingly unfold and are sublimated to immeasurable heights, such ordinary death marks an end where only a beginning seems to make sense. Death on the field of battle differs from this merely unavoidable dying in that in war, and in this massiveness *only* in war, the individual can *believe* that he knows he is dying 'for' something. The why and the wherefore of his facing death can, as a rule, be so indubitable to him that the problem of the 'meaning' of death does not even occur to him. At least there may be no presuppositions for the emergence of the problem in its universal significance, which is the form in which religions of salvation are impelled to be concerned with the meaning of death. Only those who perish 'in their callings' are in the same situation as the soldier who faces death on the battlefield.

This location of death within a series of meaningful and consecrated events ultimately lies at the base of all endeavors to support the autonomous dignity of the polity resting on force. Yet the way in which death can be conceived as meaningful in such endeavors points in directions that differ radically from the direction in which the theodicy of death in a religion of brotherliness may point. The brotherliness of a group of men bound together in war must appear devalued in such brotherly religions. It must be seen as a mere reflection of the technically sophisticated brutality of the struggle. And the inner-worldly consecration of death in war must appear as a glorification of fratricide. The very extraordinary quality of brotherliness of war, and of death in war, is shared with sacred charisma and the experience of the communion with God, and this fact raises the competition between the brotherliness of religion and of the warrior community to its extreme height. As in economics, the only two consistent solutions of this tension are those of puritanism and of mysticism.

Puritanism, with its particularism of grace and vocational asceticism, believes in the fixed and revealed commandments of a God who is otherwise quite incomprehensible. It interprets God's will to mean that these commandments should be imposed upon the creatural world by the means of this world, namely, violence—for the world is subject to violence and ethical barbarism. And this means at least barriers which resist the obligation of brotherliness in the interest of God's 'cause.'

On the other hand, there is the solution of the mystic's radical antipolitical attitude, his quest for redemption with its acosmic benevolence and brotherliness. With its 'resist no evil' and with its maxim 'then turn the other cheek,' mysticism is necessarily vulgar and lacking in dignity in the eyes of every self-assured worldly ethic of heroism. It withdraws from the pragma of violence which no political action can escape.

All other solutions to the tensions of politics and religion are full of compromises or of presuppositions which must necessarily appear dishonest or inacceptable to the genuine ethic of brotherliness. Some of these solutions are nevertheless interesting in principle and as types.

Every organization of salvation by a compulsory and universalist *institution* of grace feels responsible before God for the souls of everyone, or at least of all the men entrusted to it. Such an institution will therefore feel entitled, and in duty bound, to oppose with ruthless force any danger through misguidance in faith. It feels bound to promote the diffusion of its saving means of grace.

When salvation aristocracies are charged by the command of their God to tame the world of sin, for His glory, they give birth to the 'crusader.' Such was the case in Calvinism and, in a different form, in Islamism. At the same time, however, salvation aristocracies separate 'holy' or 'just' wars from other, purely secular, and therefore profoundly devalued, wars. The just war is engaged in for the sake of executing God's commandment, or for the sake of faith, which in some sense always means a war of religion. Therefore, salvation aristocracies reject the compulsion to participate in those wars of the political authorities which are not clearly established as holy wars corresponding to God's will, that is, wars not affirmed by one's own conscience. The victorious army of Cromwell's Saints acted in this way when it took a stand against compulsory military service. Salvation aristocracies prefer mercenary armies to compulsory war service. In case men violate God's will, especially on behalf of the faith, the faithful draw conclusions in favor of an active religious revolution, by virtue of the sentence that one should obey God rather than man.

Churchly Lutheranism, for instance, has taken the very opposite stand. It has rejected the crusade and the right to active resistance against any secular coercion in matters of faith; it has considered such coercion an arbitrary wilfulness, which entangles salvation in the pragmatism of violence. In this field Lutheranism has known only passive resistance. It has, however, accepted obedience to secular authority as unobjectionable, even when this authority has given the order for war, because the responsibility for war is on the secular authority and not on the individual and because the ethical autonomy of the secular authority, in contrast to the inwardly universalist (Catholic) institution of grace, was recognized. The insertion of mystic religiosity peculiar to Luther's personal Christianity stopped short of drawing the full conclusions in this matter.

The religious virtuosos' genuinely mystic and charismatic search for salvation has naturally and everywhere been apolitical or anti-political in nature. Such quests for salvation have readily recognized the autonomy of the temporal order, but they have done so only in order to infer consistently its radically diabolic character, or at least to take that standpoint of absolute indifference in the face of the world which has been expressed in the sentence: 'Render unto Caesar the things which are Caesar's' (for what is the relevance of these things for salvation?).

The widely varying empirical stands which historical religions have taken in the face of political action have been determined by the entanglement of religious organizations in power interests and in struggles for power, by the always unavoidable collapse of even the highest states of tension with the world in favor of compromises and relativities, by the usefulness and the use of religious organizations for the political taming of the masses and, especially, by the need of the powers-that-be for the religious consecration of their legitimacy. As we may see from history, almost all the platforms of religious organizations have been religiously relative so far as sacred values, ethical rationality, and lawful autonomy are concerned. In practice, the most important type of these relative forms has been the 'organic' social ethics. This type has been diffused in many forms and its conception of vocational work has been, in principle, the most important contrast to the idea of 'calling,' as found in inner-worldly asceticism.

Organic social ethics, where religiously sub-structured, stands on the soil of 'brotherliness,' but, in contrast to mystic and acosmic love, is dominated by a cosmic, rational demand for brotherliness. Its point of departure is the experience of the inequality of religious charisma. The very fact that the holy should be accessible only to some and not to all is unbearable to organic social ethics. It therefore attempts to synthesize this inequality of charismatic qualifications with secular stratification by status, into a cosmos of God-ordained services which are specialized in function. Certain tasks are given to every individual and every group according to their personal charisma and their social and economic position as determined by fate. As a rule, these tasks stand in the service of the realization of a condition which, in spite of its compromise nature, is pleasing to God. This condition is interpreted as being at the same time utilitarian, social, and providential. In the face of the wickedness of the world, such a condition facilitates at least a relative taming of sin and of suffering; the preservation and salvation of as many souls as possible for the kingdom of God is thereby facilitated. We shall soon learn of a theodicy of far greater pathos, which the Indian doctrine of Kharma has imparted to the organic doctrine of society from the standpoint of re- demptory pragmatism oriented solely to the interests of the individual. Without this very special linkage, every organic social ethic unavoidably represents an accommodation to the interests of the privileged strata of this world. At least that is the view of the radical, mystical ethic of reli- gious brotherliness. From the standpoint of inner-worldly asceticism, the organic ethic lacks the inward drive for an ethical and thorough ration- alization of individual life. In such matters, it has no premium for the rational and methodical patterning of personal life in the interest of the individual's own salvation.

The organic pragmatism of salvation must consider the redemptory aristocracy of inner-worldly asceticism, with its rational depersonalization of life orders, as the hardest form of lovelessness and lack of brotherliness. It must consider the redemptory pragmatism of mysticism as a sublimated and, in truth, unbrotherly indulgence of the mystic's own charisma. The mystic's unmethodical and planless acosmism of love is viewed as a mere selfish means in the search for the mystic's own salvation. Both inner-worldly asceticism and mysticism ultimately condemn the social world to absolute meaninglessness, or at least they hold that God's aims concerning the social world are utterly incomprehensible. The rationalism of religious and organic doctrines of society cannot stand up under this idea; for it seeks to comprehend the world as an at least relatively rational cosmos in spite of all its wickedness; the world is held to bear at least traces of the divine plan of salvation. For the absolute charisma of virtuoso religiosity, this relativization is indeed objectionable and estranged from the holy.

As economic and rational political actions follow laws of their own, so every other rational action within the world remains inescapably bound to worldly conditions. These conditions are remote from brotherliness and must serve as means or as ends of rational action. Hence all rational action somehow comes to stand in tension with the ethic of brotherliness, and carries within itself a profound tension. For there seems to exist no means of deciding even the very first question: Where, in the individual case, can the ethical value of an act be determined? In terms of success, or in terms of some intrinsic value of the act *per se?* The question is whether and to what extent the responsibility of the actor for the results sanctifies the means, or whether the value of the actor's intention justifies him in rejecting the responsibility for the outcome, whether to pass on the results of the act to God or to the wickedness and foolishness of the world which are permitted by God. The absolutist sublimation of religious ethic will incline men towards the latter alternative: 'The Christian does right and leaves success to God.' In this, however, the actor's own conduct when it is really consistent, and not the lawful autonomy of the world, is condemned as irrational in its effects.* In the face of this, a sublimated and thoroughgoing search for salvation may lead to an acosmism increasing to the point where it rejects purposive-rational action *per se,* and hence, all action in terms of means-ends relations, for it considers them tied to worldly things and thus estranged from God. We shall see how this has occurred with

---

* Theoretically this is most consistently carried through in the *Bhagavad-Gita,* as we shall see.

varying consistency, from the Biblical parable of the lilies in the field to the more principled formulations, for instance, of Buddhism.

The organic ethic of society is everywhere an eminently conservative power and hostile to revolution. Under certain conditions, however, revolutionary consequences may follow from a genuine virtuoso religiosity. Naturally, this occurs only when the pragmatism of force, calling forth more force and leading merely to changes in personnel, or at best to changes in methods of ruling by force, is not recognized as a permanent quality of the creaturely. According to the coloration of the virtuoso religion, its revolutionary turn may in principle assume two forms. One form springs from inner-worldly asceticism, wherever this asceticism is capable of opposing an absolute and divine 'natural law' to the creaturally, wicked, and empirical orders of the world. It then becomes a religious duty to realize this divine natural law, according to the sentence that one must obey God rather than men, which in some sense holds for all rational religions. The genuine Puritan revolutions, whose counterparts can be found elsewhere, are typical. This attitude absolutely corresponds to the obligation to crusade.

It is a different matter with the mystic. The psychological turn from possession of God to possession by God is always possible and with the mystic it is consummated. This is meaningful and possible when eschatological expectations of an immediate beginning and of the millennium of acosmic brotherliness are flaming up, hence, when the belief is dropped that an everlasting tension exists between the world and the irrational metaphysical realm of salvation. The mystic then turns into a savior and prophet. The commands, however, which he enunciates have no rational character. As products of his charisma, they are revelations of a concrete sort and the radical rejection of the world easily turns into radical *anomism*. The commands of the world do not hold for the man who is assured in his obsession with God: 'πάντα μοι εξεστιν.' All chiliasm, up to the revolution of the Anabaptists, rested somehow upon this substructure. For him who 'possesses God' and is thereby saved, the manner of action is without significance for salvation. We shall find that similar states hold in the case of the Indian djivanmukhti.

6: THE ESTHETIC SPHERE

The religious ethic of brotherliness stands in dynamic tension with any purposive-rational conduct that follows its own laws. In no less degree, this tension occurs between the religious ethic and 'this-worldly' life-forces, whose character is essentially non-rational or basically anti-rational. Above all, there is tension between the ethic of religious brotherliness and the spheres of esthetic and erotic life.

Magical religiosity stands in a most intimate relation to the esthetic sphere. Since its beginnings, religion has been an inexhaustible fountain of opportunities for artistic creation, on the one hand, and of stylizing through traditionalization, on the other. This is shown in a variety of objects and processes: in idols, icons, and other religious artifacts; in the stereotyping of magically proved forms, which is a first step in the overcoming of naturalism by a fixation of 'style'; in music as a means of ecstasy, exorcism, or apotropaic magic; in sorcerers as holy singers and dancers; in magically proved and therefore magically stereotyped tone relations—the earliest preparatory stages in the development of tonal systems; in the magically proved dance-step as one of the sources of rhythm and as an ecstasy technique; in temples and churches as the largest of all buildings, with the architectural task becoming stereotyped (and thus style-forming) as a consequence of purposes which are established once for all, and with the structural forms becoming stereotyped through magical efficacy; in paraments and church implements of all kinds which have served as objects of applied art. All these processes and objects have been displayed in connection with the churches' and temples' wealth flowing from religious zeal.

For the religious ethic of brotherliness, just as for *a priori* ethical rigorism,[1] art as a carrier of magical effects is not only devalued but even suspect. The sublimation of the religious ethic and the quest for salvation, on the one hand, and the evolution of the inherent logic of art, on the other, have tended to form an increasingly tense relation. All sublimated religions of salvation have focused upon the meaning alone, not upon the form, of the things and actions relevant for salvation. Salvation religions have devalued form as contingent, as something creaturely and distracting from meaning. On the part of art, however, the naive relation to the religious ethic of brotherliness can remain unbroken or can be repeatedly restored as long and as often as the conscious interest of the recipient of art is naively attached to the content and not to the form as such. The relationship between a religious ethic and art will remain harmonious as far as art is concerned for so long as the creative artist experiences his work as resulting either from a charisma of 'ability' (originally magic) or from spontaneous play.

The development of intellectualism and the rationalization of life change this situation. For under these conditions, art becomes a cosmos of more and more consciously grasped independent values which exist in their own right. Art takes over the function of a this-worldly salvation, no matter how this may be interpreted. It provides a *salvation* from the routines of everyday life, and especially from the increasing pressures of theoretical and practical rationalism.

With this claim to a redemptory function, art begins to compete directly with salvation religion. Every rational religious ethic must turn against this inner-worldly, irrational salvation. For in religion's eyes, such salvation is a realm of irresponsible indulgence and secret lovelessness. As a matter of fact, the refusal of modern men to assume responsibility for moral judgments tends to transform judgments of moral intent into judgments of taste ('in poor taste' instead of 'reprehensible'). The inaccessibility of appeal from esthetic judgments excludes discussion. This shift from the moral to the esthetic evaluation of conduct is a common characteristic of intellectualist epochs; it results partly from subjectivist needs and partly from the fear of appearing narrow-minded in a traditionalist and Philistine way.

The ethical norm and its 'universal validity' create a community, at least in so far as an individual might reject the act of another on moral grounds and yet still face it and participate in the common life. Knowing his own creaturely weakness, the individual places himself under the common norm. In contrast with this ethical attitude, the escape from the necessity of taking a stand on rational, ethical grounds by resorting to esthetic evaluations *may* very well be regarded by salvation religion as a very base form of unbrotherliness. To the creative artist, however, as well as to the esthetically excited and receptive mind, the ethical norm as such may easily appear as a coercion of their genuine creativeness and innermost selves.

The most irrational form of religious behavior, the mystic experience, is in its innermost being not only alien but hostile to all form. Form is unfortunate and inexpressible to the mystic because he believes precisely in the experience of exploding all forms, and hopes by this to be absorbed into the 'All-oneness' which lies beyond any kind of determination and form. For him the indubitable psychological affinity of profoundly shaking experiences in art and religion can only be a symptom of the diabolical nature of art. Especially music, the most 'inward' of all the arts, can appear in its purest form of instrumental music as an irresponsible *Ersatz* for primary religious experience. The internal logic of instrumental music as a realm not living 'within' appears as a deceptive pretension to religious experience. The well-known stand of the Council of Trent may in part have stemmed from this sentiment. Art becomes an 'idolatry,' a competing power, and a deceptive bedazzlement; and the images and the allegory of religious subjects appear as blasphemy.

In empirical, historical reality, this psychological affinity between art and religion has led to ever-renewed alliances, which have been quite significant for the evolution of art. The great majority of religions have in some manner entered such alliances. The more they wished to be universalist mass religions and were thus directed to emotional propaganda and mass appeals, the more systematic were their alliances with art. But all genuine virtuoso religions have remained very coy when confronting art, as a consequence of the inner structure of the contradiction between religion and art. This holds true for virtuoso religiosity in its active asceticist bent as well as in its mystical turn. The more religion has emphasized either the supra-worldliness of its God or the other-worldliness of salvation, the more harshly has art been refuted.

7: The Erotic Sphere

The brotherly ethic of salvation religion is in profound tension with the greatest irrational force of life: sexual love. The more sublimated sexuality is, and the more principled and relentlessly consistent the salvation ethic of brotherhood is, the sharper is the tension between sex and religion.

Originally the relation of sex and religion was very intimate. Sexual intercourse was very frequently part of magic orgiasticism or was an unintended result of orgiastic excitement. The foundation of the Skoptsy (Castrators) sect in Russia evolved from an attempt to do away with the sexual result of the orgiastic dance (radjeny) of the *Chlyst,* which was evaluated as sinful. Sacred harlotry has had nothing whatsoever to do with an alleged 'primitive promiscuity'; it has usually been a survival of magical orgiasticism in which every ecstasy was considered 'holy.' And profane heterosexual, as well as homosexual, prostitution is very ancient and often rather sophisticated. (The training of tribades occurs among so-called *aborigines.*)

The transition from such prostitution to legally constituted marriage is full of all sorts of intermediary forms. Conceptions of marriage as an economic arrangement for providing security for the wife and legal inheritance for the child; as an institution which is important (because of the death sacrifices of the descendants) for destiny in the beyond; and as important for the begetting of children—these conceptions of marriage are pre-prophetic and universal. They therefore have had nothing to do with asceticism as such. And sexual life, *per se,* has had its ghosts and gods as has every other function.

A certain tension between religion and sex came to the fore only with the temporary cultic chastity of priests. This rather ancient chastity may well have been determined by the fact that from the point of view of the strictly stereotyped ritual of the regulated community cult, sexuality was readily considered to be specifically dominated by demons. Furthermore, it was no accident that subsequently the prophetic religions, as well as the priest-controlled life orders, have, almost without significant exception, regulated sexual intercourse in favor of *marriage.* The contrast of all rational regulation of life with magical orgiasticism and all sorts of irrational frenzies is expressed in this fact.

The tension of religion and sex has been augmented by evolutionary factors on both sides. On the side of sexuality the tension has led through sublimation into 'eroticism,' and therewith into a consciously cultivated, and hence, a non-routinized sphere. Sex has been non-routinized not solely or necessarily in the sense of being estranged from conventions, for eroticism is a contrast to the sober naturalism of the peasant. And it was precisely eroticism which the conventions of knighthood usually made the object of regulation. These conventions, however, characteristically regulated eroticism by veiling the natural and organic basis of sexuality.

The extraordinary quality of eroticism has consisted precisely in a gradual turning away from the naive naturalism of sex. The reason and significance of this evolution, however, involve the universal rationalization and intellectualization of culture. We wish to present, in a few sketches, the phases of this development. We shall proceed with examples from the Occident.

The total being of man has now been alienated from the organic cycle of peasant life; life has been increasingly enriched in cultural content, whether this content is evaluated as intellectually or otherwise supraindividual. All this has worked, through the estrangement of life-value from that which is merely naturally given, toward a further enhancement of the special position of eroticism. Eroticism was raised into the sphere of conscious enjoyment (in the most sublime sense of the term). Nevertheless, indeed because of this elevation, eroticism appeared to be like a gate into the most irrational and thereby real kernel of life, as compared with the mechanisms of rationalization. The degree and the manner in which a value-emphasis was thus placed upon eroticism as such has varied enormously throughout history.

To the unrestrained feelings of a warriordom, the possession of and the fight for women has ranked about equally with the fight for treasure and the conquest of power. At the time of pre-classic Hellenism, in the period of knighthood romance, an erotic disappointment could be considered by Archilochos as a significant experience of lasting relevance, and the capture of a woman could be considered the incomparable incident of a heroic war.

The tragedians knew sexual love as a genuine power of destiny, and their lore incorporated lingering echoes of the myths. On the whole, however, a woman, Sappho, remained unequalled by man in the capacity for erotic feeling. The classic Hellenic period, the period of the Hoplite army, conceived of erotic matters in a relatively and unusually sober manner. As all their self-revelations prove, these men were even more sober than the educated stratum of the Chinese. Yet it is not true that this period did not know the deadly earnestness of sexual love. Rather, the contrary was characteristic of Hellenic love. We should remind ourselves—despite Aspasia—of Pericles' speech and finally of the well-known statement of Demosthenes.

To the exclusively masculine character of this epoch of 'democracy,' the treatment of erotic experience with women as 'life-fate'—to speak in our vocabulary—would have appeared as almost sophomoric and sentimental. The 'comrade,' the boy, was the object demanded with all the ceremony of love, and this fact stood precisely in the center of Hellenic culture. Thus, with all its magnificence, Plato's eros is nevertheless a strongly tempered feeling. The beauty of Bacchian passion as such was not an official component of this relation.

The possibility of problems and of tragedy of a principled character came about in the erotical sphere, at first, through certain demands for responsibility, which, in the Occident, stem from Christianity. However, the value-accentuation of the erotic sensation as such evolved primarily and before all else under the cultural conditioning of feudal notions of honor. This happened by a carrying over of the symbols of knightly vassalship into the erotically sublimated sexual relation. Eroticism was

given a value-accent most frequently when, during the fusion of vassalship and erotic relations, there occurred a combination with crypto-erotic
religiosity, or directly with asceticism as during the Middle Ages. The
troubadour love of the Christian Middle Ages is known to have been an
erotic service of vassals. It was not oriented towards girls, but exclusively
towards the wives of other men; it involved (in theory!) abstentious
love nights and a casuistic code of duties. Therewith began the 'probation' of the man, not before his equals but in the face of the erotic
interest of the 'lady.'

The conception of the 'lady' was constituted solely and precisely by
virtue of her judging function. The masculinity of Hellenism is in
strict contrast to this relation of the vassal to the 'lady.'

A further enhancement of the 'specifically sensational character of
eroticism developed with the transition from the conventions of the
Renaissance to the increasingly non-military intellectualism of salon culture. Despite the great differences between the conventions of Antiquity
and the Renaissance, the latter were essentially masculine and agonistic;
in this respect, they were closely related to antiquity. This was due to the
fact that by the time of the Cortegiano and of Shakespeare, the Renaissance conventions had cast off the asceticism of Christian knighthood.

Salon culture rested upon the conviction that inter-sexual conversation
is valuable as a creative power. The overt or latent erotic sensation and
the agonistic probation of the cavalier before the lady became an indispensable means of stimulating this conversation. Since the *Lettres Portu-
gaises,* the actual love problems of women became a specific intellectual
market value, and feminine love correspondence became 'literature.'

The last accentuation of the erotical sphere occurred in terms of intellectualist cultures. It occurred where this sphere collided with the
unavoidably ascetic trait of the vocational specialist type of man. Under
this tension between the erotic sphere and rational everyday life, specifically extramarital sexual life, which had been removed from everyday
affairs, could appear as the only tie which still linked man with the
natural fountain of all life. For man had now been completely emancipated from the cycle of the old, simple, and organic existence of the
peasant.

A tremendous value emphasis on the specific sensation of an inner-
worldly salvation from rationalization thus resulted. A joyous triumph
over rationality corresponded in its radicalism with the unavoidable and
equally radical rejection by an ethics of any kind of other- or supra-

worldly salvation. For such ethics, the triumph of the spirit over the body should find its climax precisely here, and sexual life could even gain the character of the only and the ineradicable connection with animality. But this tension between an inner-worldly and an other-worldly salvation from rationality must be sharpest and most unavoidable precisely where the sexual sphere is systematically prepared for a highly valued erotic sensation. This sensation reinterprets and glorifies all the pure animality of the relation, whereas the religion of salvation assumes the character of a religion of love, brotherhood, and neighborly love.

Under these conditions, the erotic relation seems to offer the unsurpassable peak of the fulfilment of the request for love in the direct fusion of the souls of one to the other. This boundless giving of oneself is as radical as possible in its opposition to all functionality, rationality, and generality. It is displayed here as the unique meaning which one creature in his irrationality has for another, and only for this specific other. However, from the point of view of eroticism, this meaning, and with it the value-content of the relation itself, rests upon the possibility of a communion which is felt as a complete unification, as a fading of the 'thou.' It is so overpowering that it is interpreted 'symbolically': as a sacrament. The lover realizes himself to be rooted in the kernel of the truly living, which is eternally inaccessible to any rational endeavor. He knows himself to be freed from the cold skeleton hands of rational orders, just as completely as from the banality of everyday routine. This consciousness of the lover rests upon the ineffaceability and inexhaustibleness of his own experience. The experience is by no means communicable and in this respect it is equivalent to the 'having' of the mystic. This is not only due to the intensity of the lover's experience, but to the immediacy of the possessed reality. Knowing 'life itself' joined to him, the lover stands opposite what is for him the objectless experiences of the mystic, as if he were facing the fading light of an unreal sphere.

As the knowing love of the mature man stands to the passionate enthusiasm of the youth, so stands the deadly earnestness of this eroticism of intellectualism to chivalrous love. In contrast to chivalrous love, this mature love of intellectualism reaffirms the natural quality of the sexual sphere, but it does so consciously, as an embodied creative power.

A principled ethic of religious brotherhood is radically and antagonistically opposed to all this. From the point of view of such an ethic, this inner, earthly sensation of salvation by mature love competes in the sharpest possible way with the devotion of a supra-mundane God, with the devotion of an ethically rational order of God, or with the devotion of a mystical bursting of individuation, which alone appear 'genuine' to the ethic of brotherhood.

Certain psychological interrelations of both spheres sharpen the tension between religion and sex. The highest eroticism stands psychologically and physiologically in a mutually substitutive relation with certain sublimated forms of heroic piety. In opposition to the rational, active asceticism which rejects the sexual as irrational, and which is felt by eroticism to be a powerful and deadly enemy, this substitutive relationship is oriented especially to the mystic's union with God. From this relation there follows the constant threat of a deadly sophisticated revenge of animality, or of an unmediated slipping from the mystic realm of God into the realm of the All-Too-Human. This psychological affinity naturally increases the antagonism of inner meanings between eroticism and religion.

From the point of view of any religious ethic of brotherhood, the erotic relation must remain attached, in a certain sophisticated measure, to brutality. The more sublimated it is, the more brutal. Unavoidably, it is considered to be a relation of conflict. This conflict is not only, or even predominantly, jealousy and the will to possession, excluding third ones. It is far more the most intimate coercion of the soul of the less brutal partner. This coercion exists because it is never noticed by the partners themselves. Pretending to be the most humane devotion, it is a sophisticated enjoyment of oneself in the other. No consummated erotic communion will know itself to be founded in any way other than through a mysterious *destination* for one another: *fate,* in this highest sense of the word. Thereby, it will know itself to be 'legitimized' (in an entirely amoral sense).

But, for salvation religion, this 'fate' is nothing but the purely fortuitous flaming up of passion. The thus established pathological obsession, idiosyncrasy, and shifting of perspectives and of every objective justice must appear to salvation religion as the most complete denial of all brotherly love and of bondage to God. The euphoria of the happy lover is felt to be 'goodness'; it has a friendly urge to poeticize all the world with happy features or to bewitch all the world in a naive enthusiasm for the diffusion of happiness. And always it meets with the cool mockery of the genuinely religiously founded and radical ethic of brotherhood. The psychologically most thorough portions of Tolstoi's early work may be cited in this connection.* In the eyes of this ethic, the most sublimated eroticism is the counter-pole of all religiously oriented brotherliness, in these aspects: it must necessarily be exclusive in its inner core; it must be subjective in the highest imaginable sense; and it must be absolutely incommunicable.

All this, of course, is quite apart from the fact that the passionate character of eroticism as such appears to the religion of brotherhood as an undignified loss of self-control and as the loss of orientation towards either the rationality and wisdom of norms willed by God or the mystic 'having' of godliness. However, for eroticism, genuine 'passion' *per se* constitutes the type of *beauty,* and its rejection is blasphemy.

For psychological reasons and in accordance with its meaning, the erotic frenzy stands in unison only with the orgiastic and charismatic form of religiosity. This form is, however, in a special sense, inner-worldly. The acknowledgment of the *act* of marriage, of the *copula carnalis,* as a 'sacrament' of the Catholic Church is a concession to this sentiment. Eroticism enters easily into an unconscious and unstable relation of surrogateship or fusion with other-worldly and extraordinary mysticism. This occurs with very sharp inner tension between eroticism and mysticism. It occurs because they are psychologically substitutive. Out of this fusion the collapse into orgiasticism follows very readily.

Inner-worldly and rational asceticism (vocational asceticism) can accept only the rationally regulated marriage. This type of marriage is accepted as one of the divine ordinations given to man as a creature who is hopelessly wretched by virtue of his 'concupiscence.' Within this divine order it is given to man to live according to the rational purposes laid down by it and only according to them: to procreate and to rear children, and mutually to further one another in the state of grace. This inner-worldly rational asceticism must reject every sophistication of the sexual into eroticism as idolatry of the worst kind. In its turn, this asceticism gathers the primal, naturalist, and *un*sublimated sexuality of the peasant into a rational order of man as creature. All elements of 'passion,' however, are then considered as residues of the Fall. According to Luther, God, in order to prevent worse, peeks at and is lenient with these elements of passion. The other-worldly rational asceticism (active

* Especially in *War and Peace.* The position of the religion of salvation is fixed fairly clearly with Ascvagosha. Incidentally, Nietzsche's well-known analyses in the *Will to Power* are in substance completely in unison with this, despite—indeed precisely because of—the clearly recognized transvaluation of values.

asceticism of the monk) also rejects these passionate elements, and with them all sexuality, as a diabolic power endangering salvation. The ethic of the Quakers (as it is displayed in William Penn's letters to his wife) may well have achieved a genuinely humane interpretation of the inner and religious values of marriage. In this respect the Quaker ethic went beyond the rather gross Lutheran interpretation of the meaning of marriage.

From a purely inner-worldly point of view, only the linkage of marriage with the thought of ethical responsibility for one another—hence a category heterogeneous to the purely erotic sphere—can carry the sentiment that something unique and supreme might be embodied in marriage; that it might be the transformation of the feeling of a love which is conscious of responsibility throughout all the nuances of the organic life process, 'up to the pianissimo of old age,' and a mutual granting of oneself to another and the becoming indebted to each other (in Goethe's sense). Rarely does life grant such value in pure form. He to whom it is given may speak of fate's fortune and grace—not of his own 'merit.'

8: THE INTELLECTUAL SPHERE

The rejection of all naive surrender to the most intensive ways of experiencing existence, artistic and erotical, is as such only a negative attitude. But it is obvious that such rejection could increase the force with which energies flow into rational achievement, both the ethical as well as the purely intellectual. It must be noted, however, that the self-conscious tension of religion is greatest and most principled where religion faces the sphere of intellectual knowledge.

There is a unity in the realm of magic and in the purely magical image of the world, as we have noted in the case of Chinese thought. A far-going and mutual recognition is also possible between religion and purely metaphysical speculation, although as a rule this speculation easily leads to skepticism. Religion, therefore, frequently considers purely empirical research, including that of natural science, as more reconcilable to religious interests than it does philosophy. This is the case above all in ascetic Protestantism.

The tension between religion and intellectual knowledge definitely comes to the fore wherever rational, empirical knowledge has consistently worked through to the disenchantment of the world and its transformation into a causal mechanism. For then science encounters the claims of the ethical postulate that the world is a God-ordained, and hence somehow *meaningfully* and ethically oriented, cosmos. In principle, the empirical as well as the mathematically oriented view of the world develops refutations of every intellectual approach which in any way asks for a 'meaning' of inner-worldly occurrences. Every increase of rationalism in empirical science increasingly pushes religion from the rational into the irrational realm; but only today does religion become *the* irrational or anti-rational supra-human power. The extent of consciousness or of consistency in the experience of this contrast, however, varies widely. Athanasius won out with his formula—completely absurd when viewed rationally—in his struggle against the majority of the Hellenic philosophers of the time; it does not seem inconceivable, as has been said, that among other reasons he really wanted to compel them expressly to make the intellectual sacrifice and to fix a limit to rational discussion. Soon afterwards, however, the Trinity itself was rationally argued and discussed.

Because of this apparently irreconcilable tension, prophetic as well as priestly religions have repeatedly stood in intimate relation with rational intellectualism. The less magic or merely contemplative mysticism and the more 'doctrine' a religion contains, the greater is its need of rational apologetics. The sorcerers everywhere have been the typical keepers of myths and heroic sagas, because they have participated in educating and training young warriors in order to awaken them for heroic ecstasy and heroic regeneration. From them the priesthood, as the only agents capable of conserving tradition, took over the training of youth in the law and often also in purely administrative technologies, and, above all, in writing and in calculus. The more religion became book-religion and doctrine, the more literary it became and the more efficacious it was in provoking rational lay-thinking, freed of priestly control. From the thinking laymen, however, emerged the prophets, who were hostile to priests; as well as the mystics, who searched salvation independently of priests and sectarians; and finally the skeptics and philosophers, who were hostile to faith.

A rationalization of priestly apologetics reacted against all of these developments. Anti-religious skepticism, *per se,* was represented in China, in Egypt, in the Vedas, in post-exilic Jewish literature. In principle, it was just as it is today; almost no new arguments have been added. Therefore, the central question of power for the priesthood became the monopolization of the education of youth.

With the increasing rationalization of political administration, the power of the priesthood could increase. In the early times of Egypt and Babylon, the priesthood alone procured the scribes for the state. It was the same for the medieval prince when administration based on documents began. Of the great systems of pedagogy, only Confucianism and that of Mediterranean Antiquity have known how to escape the power of priesthood. The former succeeded by virtue of its powerful state bureaucracy the latter through the absolute lack of bureaucratic administration. With the elimination of priests from education, priestly religion itself was eliminated in these cases. With these exceptions, however, the priesthoods have regularly furnished and controlled the personnel of schools.

It has not only been these genuinely priestly interests that have made for ever-renewed connections between religion and intellectualism. It has also been the inward compulsion of the rational character of religious ethics and the specifically intellectualist quest for salvation. In effect, every religion in its psychological and intellectual sub-structure and in its practical conclusions has taken a different stand towards intellectualism, without however allowing the ultimate inward tension to disappear. For the tension rests on the unavoidable disparity among ultimate forms of images of the world.

There is absolutely no 'unbroken' religion working as a vital force which is not compelled at *some* point to demand the *credo non quod, sed quia absurdum*—the 'sacrifice of the intellect.'

It is hardly necessary and it would be impossible to treat in detail the stages of the tension between religion and intellectual knowledge. Redemptory religion defends itself against the attack of the self-sufficient intellect. It does so, of course, in the most principled fashion, by raising the claim that religious knowledge moves in a different sphere and that the nature and meaning of religious knowledge is entirely different from the accomplishments of the intellect. Religion claims to offer an ultimate stand toward the world by virtue of a direct grasp of the world's 'meaning.' It does not claim to offer intellectual knowledge concerning what is or what should be. It claims to unlock the meaning of the world not by means of the intellect but by virtue of a charisma of illumination. This charisma is said to be imparted only to those who make use of the respective technique and free themselves from the misleading and deceptive surrogates which are given out as knowledge by the confused impressions of the senses and the empty abstractions of the intellect. Religion believes that these are in truth irrelevant for salvation. By freeing himself from them, a religious man is said to make himself ready for the reception of the all-important grasp of the meaning of the world and of his own existence. In all the endeavors of philosophy to make this ultimate meaning, and the (practical) stand which follows from grasping, demonstrable redemptory religion will see nothing but the intellect's desire to escape its own lawful autonomy. The same view is held of philosophical attempts to gain any intuitive knowledge, which, although concerned with the 'being' of things, has a dignity which principally differs from that of religious knowledge. Above all, religion sees all this as a specific product of the very rationalism that intellectualism, by these endeavors, would very much like to escape.

Salvation religion, however, viewed from its own position, is to be blamed for equally inconsistent trespasses as soon as it surrenders the unassailable incommunicability of mystic experiences. If it is consistent, such religion can only have the means of bringing mystic experiences about as *events;* it has no means of adequately communicating and demonstrating them. Every attempt to influence the world must entice mystical religion to run this danger, as soon as the attempt assumes the character of propaganda. The same holds for every attempt to interpret the meaning of the universe rationally, but nevertheless the attempt has been made again and again.

Religious postulates can come into conflict with the 'world' from differing points of view, and the point of view involved is always of the greatest importance for the direction and for the way in which *salvation* will be striven for. At all times and in all places, the need for salvation—consciously cultivated as the substance of religiosity—has resulted from the endeavor of a systematic and practical rationalization of life's realities. To be sure, this connection has been maintained with varying degrees of transparency: on this level, all religions have demanded as a specific presupposition that the course of the world be somehow *meaningful,* at least in so far as it touches upon the interests of men. As we have seen, this claim naturally emerged first as the customary problem of unjust suffering, and hence as the postulate of a just compensation for the unequal distribution of individual happiness in the world. From here, the claim has tended to progress step by step towards an ever-increasing devaluation of the world. For the more intensely rational thought has seized upon the problem of a just and retributive compensation, the less an entirely inner-worldly solution could seem possible, and the less an other-worldly solution could appear probable or even meaningful.

In so far as appearances show, the actual course of the world has been little concerned with this postulate of compensation. The ethically unmotivated inequality in the distribution of happiness and misery, for which a compensation has seemed conceivable, has remained irrational; and so has the brute fact that suffering exists. For the universal diffusion of suffering could only be replaced by another and still more irrational problem, the question of the origin of sin, which, according to the teaching of prophets and priests, is to explain suffering as a punishment or as a means of discipline. A world created for the committing of sin must appear still less ethically perfect than a world condemned to suffering. In any case, the absolute imperfection of this world has been firmly established as an ethical postulate. And the futility of worldly things has seemed to be meaningful and justified only in terms of this imperfection. Such justification, however, could appear suitable for devaluating the world even further. For it was not only, or even primarily, the worthless which proved to be transitory. The fact that death and ruin, with their leveling effects, overtake good men and good works, as well as evil ones, could appear to be a depreciation of precisely the supreme values of this world—once the idea of a perpetual duration of time, of an eternal God, and an eternal order had been conceived. In the face of this, values —and precisely the most highly cherished values—have been hallowed as being 'timelessly' valid. Hence, the significance of their realization in 'culture' has been stated to be independent of the temporal duration of their concretion. Thereupon the ethical rejection of the empirical world could be further intensified. For at this point onto the religious horizon could enter a train of thoughts of far greater significance than were the imperfection and futility of worldly things, because these ideas were fit to indict precisely the 'cultural values' which usually rank highest.

These values have borne the stigma of a deadly sin, of an unavoidable and specific burden of guilt. They have proved to be bound to the charisma of the mind or of taste. Their cultivation has seemed inevitably to presuppose modes of existence which run counter to the demand for brotherliness and which could only be adapted to this demand by self-deception. The barriers of education and of esthetic cultivation are the most intimate and the most insuperable of all status differences. Religious guilt could now appear not only as an occasional concomitant, but as an integral part of all culture, of all conduct in a civilized world, and finally, of all structured life in general. And thereby the ultimate values which this world offered have seemed burdened with the greatest guilt.

Wherever the external order of the social community has turned into the culture community of the state it obviously could be maintained only by brutal force, which was concerned with justice only nominally and occasionally and in any case only so far as reasons of state have permitted. This force has inevitably bred new deeds of violence against external and internal enemies; in addition, it has bred dishonest pretexts for such deeds. Hence it has signified an overt, or what must appear worse, a pharisaically veiled, absence of love. The routinized economic cosmos, and thus the rationally highest form of the provision of material goods which is indispensable for all worldly culture, has been a structure to which the absence of love is attached from the very root. All forms of activity in the structured world has appeared to be entangled in the same guilt.

Veiled and sublimated brutality, idiosyncrasy hostile to brotherliness, as well as illusionist shifts of a just sense of proportion have inevitably accompanied sexual love. The more powerfully the forces of sexual love are deployed the less they are noticed by the participants, and the more veiled they are in a Pharisaic way. Ethical religiosity has appealed to rational knowledge, which has followed its own autonomous and inner-worldly norms. It has fashioned a cosmos of truths which no longer had anything to do with the systematic postulates of a rational religious ethic; with the result that the world as a cosmos must satisfy the demands of a religious ethic or evince some 'meaning.' On the contrary, rational knowledge has had to reject this claim in principle. The cosmos of natural causality and the postulated cosmos of ethical, compensatory causality have stood in irreconcilable opposition.

Science has created this cosmos of natural causality and has seemed unable to answer with certainty the question of its own ultimate presuppositions. Nevertheless science, in the name of 'intellectual integrity,' has come forward with the claim of representing the only possible form of a reasoned view of the world. The intellect, like all culture values, has created an aristocracy based on the possession of rational culture and independent of all personal ethical qualities of man. The aristocracy of intellect is hence an unbrotherly aristocracy. Worldly man has regarded this possession of culture as the highest good. In addition to the burden of ethical guilt, however, something has adhered to this cultural value which was bound to depreciate it with still greater finality, namely, senselessness—if this cultural value is to be judged in terms of its own standards.

The purely inner-worldly perfection of self of a man of culture, hence the ultimate value to which 'culture' has seemed to be reducible, is meaningless for religious thought. This follows for religious thought from the obvious meaninglessness of death, meaningless precisely when viewed from the inner-worldly standpoint. And under the very conditions of 'culture,' senseless death has seemed only to put the decisive stamp upon the senselessness of life itself.

The peasant, like Abraham, could die 'satiated with life.' The feudal landlord and the warrior hero could do likewise. For both fulfilled a cycle of their existence beyond which they did not reach. Each in his way could attain an inner-worldly perfection as a result of the naive unambiguity of the substance of his life. But the 'cultivated' man who strives for self-perfection, in the sense of acquiring or creating 'cultural values,' cannot do this. He can become 'weary of life' but he cannot become 'satiated with life' in the sense of completing a cycle. For the perfectibility of the man of culture in principle progresses indefinitely, as do the cultural values. And the segment which the individual and passive recipient or the active co-builder can comprise in the course of a finite life becomes the more trifling the more differentiated and multiplied the cultural values and the goals for self-perfection become. Hence the harnessing of man into this external and internal cosmos of culture can offer the less likelihood that an individual would absorb either culture as a whole or what in any sense is 'essential' in culture. Moreover there exists no definitive criterion for judging the latter. It thus becomes less and less likely that 'culture' and the striving for culture can have any inner-worldly meaning for the individual.

The 'culture' of the individual certainly does not consist of the *quantity* of 'cultural values' which he amasses; it consists of an articulated *selection* of culture values. But there is no guarantee that this selection has reached an end that would be meaningful to him precisely at the 'accidental' time of his death. He might even turn his back to life with an air of distinction: 'I have enough—life has offered (or denied) all that made living worthwhile for *me*.' This proud attitude to the religion of salvation must appear as a disdainful blasphemy of the God-ordained ways of life and destinies. No redemption religion positively *approves* of 'death by one's own hand,' that is, a death which has been hallowed only by philosophies.

Viewed in this way, all 'culture' appears as man's emancipation from the organically prescribed cycle of natural life. For this very reason culture's every step forward seems condemned to lead to an ever more devastating senselessness. The advancement of cultural values, however, seems to become a senseless hustle in the service of worthless, moreover self-contradictory, and mutually antagonistic ends. The advancement of cultural values appears the more meaningless the more it is made a holy task, a 'calling.'

Culture becomes ever more senseless as a locus of imperfection, of injustice, of suffering, of sin, of futility. For it is necessarily burdened with guilt, and its deployment and differentiation thus necessarily become ever more meaningless. Viewed from a purely ethical point of view, the world has to appear fragmentary and devalued in all those instances when judged in the light of the religious postulate of a divine 'meaning' of existence. This devaluation results from the conflict between the rational claim and reality, between the rational ethic and the partly rational, and partly irrational values. With every construction of the specific nature of each special sphere existing in the world, this conflict has seemed to come to the fore ever more sharply and more insolubly. The need for 'salvation' responds to this devaluation by becoming more other-worldly, more alienated from all structured forms of life, and, in exact parallel, by confining itself to the specific religious essence. This reaction is the stronger the more systematic the thinking about the 'meaning' of the universe becomes, the more the external organization of the world is rationalized, and the more the conscious experience of the world's irrational content is sublimated. And not only theoretical thought, disenchanting the world, led to this course, but also the very attempt of religious ethics practically and ethically to rationalize the world.

The specific intellectual and mystical attempts at salvation in the face of these tensions succumb in the end to the world dominion of unbrotherliness. On the one hand, their charisma is *not* accessible to everybody. Hence, in intent, mystical salvation definitely means aristocracy; it is an aristocratic religiosity of redemption. And, in the midst of a culture that is rationally organized for a vocational workaday life, there is hardly any room for the cultivation of acosmic brotherliness, unless it is among strata who are economically carefree. Under the technical and social conditions of rational culture, an imitation of the life of Buddha, Jesus, or Francis seems condemned to failure for purely external reasons.

9: The Three Forms of Theodicy

The individual redemption ethics of the past which have rejected the world have applied their rejection of the world at very different points of this purely rationally constructed scale. This has depended upon numerous concrete circumstances which cannot be ascertained by a theoretical typology. Besides these circumstances, a rational element has played its part, namely, the structure of a special *theodicy*. The metaphysical need responded to the awareness of existing and unbridgeable tensions, and through theodicy it tried to find a common meaning in spite of all.

Among the three types of theodicy we have already * designated as alone consistent, *dualism* could well serve this need. Dualism maintains that always the powers of light and truth, purity and goodness coexist and conflict with the powers of darkness and falsehood, impurity and evil. In the last analysis this dualism is only a direct systematization of the magical pluralism of the spirits with their division of good (useful) and evil (harmful) spirits which represent the preliminary stages of the antagonism between deities and demons.

Zoroastrism was the prophetic religiousness which realized this conception most consistently. Here dualism set out with the magical contrast between 'clean' and 'unclean.' All virtues and vices were integrated into this contrast. It involved renouncing the omnipotence of a god whose power was indeed limited by the existence of a great antagonist. The contemporary followers (the Parsees) have actually given up this belief because they could not endure this limitation of divine power. In the most consistent eschatology, the world of purity and the world of impurity, from the mixture of which the fragmentary empirical world emanated, separated again and again into two unrelated realms. The more modern eschatological hope, however, makes the god of purity and benevolence triumph, just as Christianity makes the Savior triumph over the devil. This less consistent form of dualism is the popular, worldwide conception of heaven and hell, which restores God's sovereignty over the evil spirit who is His creature, and thereby believes that divine omnipotence is saved. But, willy-nilly, it must then, overtly or covertly, sacrifice some of the divine love. For if omniscience is maintained, the creation of a power of radical evil and the admission of sin, especially

* Cf. chapter XI, pp. 275 ff. of this volume.

in communion with the enternity of hell's punishments for one of God's own and finite creatures and for finite sins, simply does not correspond to divine love. In that case, only a renunciation of benevolence is consistent.

The belief in *predestination* realizes this renunciation, in fact and with full consistency. Man's acknowledged incapacity to scrutinize the ways of God means that he renounces in a loveless clarity man's accessibility to any meaning of the world. This renunciation brought all problems of this sort to an end. Outside of the circle of eminent virtuosos the belief in this consistency has not been permanently endured. This was the case because the belief in predestination—in contrast to the belief in the irrational power of 'fate'—demands the assumption of a providential, and hence a somehow rational, destination of the condemned, not only to doom but to evil, while demanding the 'punishment' of the condemned and therewith the application of an ethical category.

We have dealt with the significance of the belief in predestination [elsewhere].[2] We shall deal with Zoroastrian dualism later, and only briefly—because the number of the believers is small. It might be omitted entirely were it not for the influence of the Persian ideas of final judgment, as well as of the doctrine of demons and angels, upon late Judaism. Because of such influences, Zoroastrism is of considerable historical significance.

The third form of theodicy which we are going to discuss was peculiar to the religiosity of Indian intellectuals. It stands out by virtue of its consistency as well as by its extraordinary metaphysical achievement: It unites virtuoso-like self-redemption by man's own effort with universal accessibility of salvation, the strictest rejection of the world with organic social ethics, and contemplation as the paramount path to salvation with an inner-worldly vocational ethic.

Part IV

SOCIAL STRUCTURES

XIV. Capitalism and Rural Society in Germany

Of all communities, the social constitution of rural districts are the most individual and the most closely connected with particular historical developments. It would not be reasonable to speak collectively of the rural conditions of Russia, Ireland, Sicily, Hungary, and the Black Belt. Even if I confine myself to districts with developed capitalistic cultures, it is scarcely possible to treat the subject from one common point of view. For a rural society, separate from the urban social community, does not exist at the present time in a great part of the modern civilized world. It no longer exists in England, except, perhaps, in the thoughts of dreamers. The constant proprietor of the soil, the landlord, is not an agriculturist but a lessor; and the temporary owner of the estate, the tenant or lessee, is an entrepreneur, a capitalist like any other. The laborers are partly seasonal and migrating; the rest are journeymen of exactly the same class as other proletarians; they are joined together for a certain time and then are scattered again. If there is a specific rural social problem it is only this: Whether and how the rural community or society, which no longer exists, can arise again so as to be strong and enduring.

In the United States, at least in the vast cereal-producing areas, what might be called 'rural society' does not now exist. The old New England town, the Mexican village, and the old slave plantation do not determine the physiognomy of the country any longer. The peculiar conditions of the first settlements in the primeval forests and on the prairies have disappeared. The American farmer is an entrepreneur like any other. Certainly there are numerous farmers' problems, chiefly of a technical character or pertaining to transportation, which have played their role in politics and have been excellently discussed by American scholars.

Adapted from a translation by C. W. Seidenadel, 'The Relations of the Rural Community to other Branches of Social Science,' *Congress of Arts and Science, Universal Exposition, St. Louis* (Boston and New York: Houghton-Mifflin, 1906), vol. VII, pp. 725-46.

But no specific rural social problem exists as yet in America, indeed no such problem has existed since the abolition of slavery and the solution of the question of settling and disposing of the immense area which was in the hands of the Union. The present difficult social problems of the South, in the rural districts also, are essentially ethnic and not economic. One cannot establish a theory of rural community as a characteristic social formation on the basis of questions concerning irrigation, railroad tariff, homestead laws, et cetera, however important these matters may be. This may change in the future. But if anything is characteristic of the rural conditions of the great wheat-producing states of America, it is—to speak in general terms—the absolute economic individualism of the farmer, the quality of the farmer as a mere businessman.

Probably it will be fruitful to explain briefly in what respects and for what reasons all this is different on the European Continent. The difference is caused by the specific effects of capitalism in old civilized countries with dense populations.

If a nation such as Germany supports its inhabitants, whose number is only a little smaller than the white population of the United States, in a space smaller in size than the state of Texas; if it has founded and is determined to maintain its political position and the importance of its culture for the world upon this narrow, limited basis—then the manner in which the land is distributed becomes of determining importance for the differentiation of the society and for all economic and political conditions of the country. Because of the close congestion of the inhabitants and the lower valuation of the raw labor force, the possibility of quickly acquiring estates which have not been inherited is limited. Thus social differentiation is necessarily fixed—a fate which the United States also approaches. This fate increases the power of historical tradition, which is naturally great in agricultural production.

The importance of technical revolutions in agricultural production is diminished by the so-called 'law of decreasing productivity of the land,' by the stronger natural limits and conditions of production, and by the more constant limitation of the quality and quantity of the means of production. In spite of technical progress, rural production can be revolutionized least by a purely rational division and combination of labor, by acceleration of the turnover of capital, and by substituting inorganic raw materials and mechanical means of production for organic raw materials and labor forces. The power of tradition inevitably predominates in agriculture; it creates and maintains types of rural population on the European Continent which do not exist in a new country, such as the United States; to these types belongs, first of all, the European peasant.

The European peasant is totally different from the farmer of England or of America. The English farmer today is sometimes quite a remarkable entrepreneur and producer for the market; almost always he has rented his estate. The American farmer is an agriculturist who has usually acquired, by purchase or by being the first settler, the land as his own property; but sometimes he rents it. In America the farmer produces for the market. The market is older than the producer in America. The European peasant of the old type was a man who, in most instances, inherited the land and who produced primarily for his own wants. In Europe the market is younger than the producer. Of course, for many years the peasant sold his surplus products and, though he spun and wove, he could not satisfy his needs by his own work. The past two thousand years did not train the peasant to produce in order to gain profit.

Until the time of the French Revolution, the European peasant was only considered a means for supporting certain ruling classes. His first duty was to provide, as cheaply as possible, the neighboring town with food. As far as possible, the city prohibited rural trade and the exportation of cereals as long as its own citizens were not provided. Matters remained in this condition until the end of the eighteenth century. The artificial maintenance of the cities at the expense of the country was also a principle followed by the princes, who wanted to have money in their respective countries and large intakes of taxes. Moreover by his services and by his payment of taxes, the peasant was doomed to support the landlord, who possessed the higher ownership of the land and quite often the right to the peasant's body as well. This remained the case until the revolutions of 1789 and 1848. The peasant's duties included the payment of taxes on his estate to the political lord. The knight was exempt from this. The peasant also had to supply the armies with recruits, from which the cities were exempt. These conditions remained in force until tax-privileges were abolished and service in the army became compulsory for everyone, in the nineteenth century. Finally, the peasant was dependent upon the productive community into which the half-communist settlement had placed him two thousand years ago. He could not manage as he wanted, but as the primeval rotation of crops prescribed, a condition which continued to exist until these half-communist bonds were dissolved. Yet even after the abolition of all this legal dependency, the peasant could not become a rationally producing small agriculturist as, for instance, is the case with the American farmer.

Numerous relics of the ancient communist conditions of forest, water, pasture, and even arable land, which firmly united the peasants and tied them to the inherited form of husbandry, survived their liberation. The village, with the characteristic contrasts to the individual settlements of American farmers, also survived. To these relics of the past, which America has never known, certain factors are nowadays added. America will one day also experience the effects of such factors—the effects of modern capitalism under the conditions of completely settled old civilized countries. In Europe limited territory causes a specific social estimation of the ownership of land, and the tendency to retain it, by bequest, in the family. The superabundance of the labor force diminishes the desire to save labor by the use of machines. By virtue of migration into cities and foreign countries, the labor force in Europe has become limited and dear. On the other hand, the high price of the land, caused by continual purchases and hereditary divisions, diminishes the capital of the buyer. It is not now possible to gain a possible fortune by agriculture in Europe. And the time in which this will be possible in the United States is approaching its limit. We must not forget that the boiling heat of modern capitalistic culture is connected with heedless consumption of natural resources, for which there are no substitutes. It is difficult to determine how long the present supply of coal and ore will last. The utilization of new farm lands will soon have reached an end in America; in Europe it no longer exists. The agriculturist can never hope to gain more than a modest equivalent for his work as a husbandman. He is, in Europe, and also to a great extent in this country, excluded from participating in the great opportunities open to speculative business talent.

The strong blast of modern capitalistic competition rushes against a conservative opposing current in agriculture, and it is exactly rising capitalism which increases this counter-current in old civilized countries. The use of the land as a capital investment, and the sinking rate of interest in connection with the traditional social evaluation of rural lands, push up the price of land to such a height that it is always paid partly *au fonds perdu,* that is to say, as *entrée,* as an entrance fee into this social stratum. Thus by increasing the capital required for agricultural operations, capitalism causes an increase in the number of renters of land who are idle. In these ways, peculiar contrasting effects of capitalism are produced, and these contrasting effects by themselves make the open countryside of Europe appear to support a separate 'rural society.' Under the conditions of old civilized countries, the differences caused by capitalism assume the character of a cultural contest. Two social tendencies resting upon entirely heterogeneous bases thus wrestle with each other.

The old economic order asked: How can I give, on this piece of land, work and sustenance to the greatest possible number of men? Capitalism asks: From this given piece of land how can I produce as many crops as possible for the market with as few men as possible? From the technical economic point of view of capitalism, the old rural settlements of the country are, therefore, considered overpopulated. Capitalism extracts produce from the land, from the mines, foundries, and machine industries. The thousands of years of the past struggle against the invasion of the capitalistic spirit.

This struggle assumes, at least in part, the form of a peaceful transformation. In certain points of agricultural production, the small peasant, if he knows how to free himself from the fetters of tradition, is able to adapt to the conditions of the new husbandry. The rising rate of rent in the vicinity of the cities, the rising prices for meat, dairy products, and garden vegetables, as well as the intensive care of young cattle possible for the self-employed small farmer, and the higher expenses involved in hiring men—these factors usually afford very favorable opportunities to the small farmer who works without hired help near wealthy centers of industry. This is the case wherever the process of production is developed in the direction of increasing intensity of labor, rather than of capital.

The former peasant is thus transformed into a laborer who owns his means of production, as we may observe in France and in southwestern Germany. He maintains his independence because of the intensity and the high quality of his work, which is increased by his private interest in it and his adaptability of it to the demands of the local market. These factors give him an economic superiority, which continues, even where agriculture on a large scale could technically predominate.

The great success of the formation of co-operatives among the small farmers of the Continent must be ascribed to these peculiar advantages which, in certain branches of production, the responsible small agriculturist possesses as over against the hired laborer of the large farmer. These co-operatives have proved the most influential means of the peasants' education for husbandry. Through them new communities of husbandry are created, which bind the peasants together and direct their way of economic thinking and feeling away from the purely individualistic form which the economic struggle for existence in industry assumes under the pressure of competition. This, again, is only possible because of the great importance of the natural conditions of production in agriculture—its being bound to place, time, and organic means of work—and the social visibility of all farming operations which weaken the effectiveness of competition among farmers.

Wherever the conditions of a specific economic superiority of small farming do not exist, because the qualitative importance of self-responsible work is replaced by the importance of capital, there the old peasant struggles for his existence as a hireling of capital. It is the high social valuation of the landowner that makes him a subject of capital and ties him psychologically to the clod. Given the stronger economic and social differentiation of an old civilized country, the loss of his estate means degradation for the peasant. The peasant's struggle for existence often becomes an economic selection in favor of the most frugal, which means, of those most lacking in culture. For the pressure of agricultural competition is not felt by those who use their products for their own consumption and not as articles of trade; they sell only a few of their products and hence they can buy only a few other products. Sometimes a partial retrogression into subsistence farming occurs. Only with the French 'system of two children' can the peasant maintain himself for generations as a small proprietor of the inherited land. The obstacles that the peasant who wants to become a modern agriculturist meets urge the separation of ownership from management. The landlord may either keep his capital in operation or withdraw it. In some areas the government tries to create a balance between property and lease. But on account of the high valuation of the land, the peasant can neither remain a peasant nor become a capitalist landlord.

It is not yet possible to speak of a real 'contest' between capitalism and the power of historical influence, in this case of a growing conflict between capital and ownership of the land. It is partly a process of selection, and partly one of depravation. Quite different conditions prevail not only where an unorganized multitude of peasants are powerless in the chains of the financial powers of the cities, but where there is an aristocratic stratum above the peasants which struggles not only for its economic existence but also for the social standing which for centuries has been granted it. This is the case especially where such an aristocracy is not tied to the country by purely financial interests, as is the English landlord, or only by the interests of recreation and sport, but where its representatives are involved as agriculturists in the economic conflict and are closely connected with the country. The dissolving effects of capitalism are then increased. Because ownership of the land gives social position, the prices of the large estates rise high above the value of their productivity. Of the landlord, Byron asked: 'Why did God in his wrath create him?' The answer is: 'Rents! Rents! Rents!' And, in fact, rents are the economic basis of all aristocracies which need a gentlemanly unearned income for their existence. But precisely because the Prussian 'Junker' despises the urban possession of money, capitalism makes a debtor of him. A strong, growing tension between city and country results from this. The conflict between capitalism and tradition is now tinged politically, for, if economic and political power definitely passes into the hands of the urban capitalist, the question arises whether the small rural centers of political intelligence, with their peculiarly tinged social culture, shall decay, and the cities, as the only carriers of political, social, and esthetic culture, shall occupy the entire field of the combat. This question is identical with the question whether people who have been able to live for politics and the state, for example, the old, economically independent land aristocracy, shall be replaced by the exclusive domination of professional politicians who must live off politics and the state.

In the United States this question has been decided, at any rate for the present, by one of the bloodiest wars of modern times, which ended with the destruction of the aristocratic, social, and political centers of the rural districts. Even in America, with its democratic traditions handed down by Puritanism as an everlasting heirloom, the victory over the planters' aristocracy was difficult and was gained with great political and social sacrifices. But in countries with old civilizations, matters are much more complicated. For there the struggle between the power of historical notions and the pressure of capitalist interests summon certain social forces to battle as adversaries of bourgeois capitalism. In the United States such forces were partly unknown, or stood partly on the side of the North. A few remarks concerning this may be made here.

In the countries of old civilization and limited possibilities for economic expansion, money-making and its representatives necessarily play a considerably smaller social role than in a country that is still new.

The importance of the stratum of state officials is and must be much greater in Europe than in the United States. The much more complicated social organization makes a host of specially trained officials, employed for life, indispensable in Europe. In the United States only a much smaller number of them will exist, even after the movement of civil-service reform shall have attained all its aims. The jurist and administrative official in Germany, in spite of his shorter and more intensive education in preparation for the university, is about thirty-five years old when his time of preparation and his unsalaried activity is completed and he obtains a salaried office. Therefore, he can come only from wealthy circles; he is trained to unsalaried or low-salaried service and can find his reward for service only in the high social standing of his vocation.. A character is thus stamped on him which is far from the interests of money-makers and which places him on the side of the adversaries of their dominion. If, in old civilized countries such as Germany, the necessity of a strong army arises in order to maintain independence, this means, for political institutions, the support of an hereditary dynasty.

The resolute follower of democratic institutions—as I am—cannot wish to remove the dynasty where it has been preserved. For in military states, if it is not the only historically indorsed form in which the Caesarian domination of military parvenus can be averted, it is still the best. France is continually menaced by such domination; dynasties are personally interested in the preservation of rights and of a legal government. Hereditary monarchy—one may judge about it theoretically as one wishes—warrants to a state, which is forced to be a military state, the greatest freedom of the citizens—as great as it can be in a monarchy—and so long as the dynasty does not become degenerated, it will have the political support of the majority of the nation. The English Parliament knew very well why it offered Cromwell the crown, and Cromwell's army knew equally well why it prevented him from accepting it. Such an hereditary, privileged dynasty has a natural affinity with the holders of other social privileges.

The church belongs to the conservative forces in European countries; first, the Roman Catholic Church, which, in Europe, even on account of the multitude of its followers, is a power of quite different importance and character than it possesses in Anglo-Saxon countries; but also the Lutheran Church. Both of these churches support the peasant, with his conservative way of life, against the dominion of urban rationalist culture. The rural co-operative movement stands, to a great extent, under the guidance of clergymen, who are the only ones capable of leadership in the rural districts. Ecclesiastic, political, and economic points of view are here intermingled. In Belgium, the rural co-operatives are a means of the clerical party in their conflict against the socialists; the latter are supported by the consumers' unions and trade unions. In Italy, almost nobody finds credit with certain co-operatives unless he presents his confessional certificate. Likewise, a landed aristocracy finds strong backing in the church, although the Catholic Church is, in social regards, more democratic nowadays than formerly. The church is pleased with patriarchal labor relations because contrary to the purely commercial relations which capitalism creates, they are of a personal human character. The church holds the sentiment that the relation between a lord and a serf, rather than the bare commercial conditions created by the labor market, can be developed and penetrated ethically. Deep, historically conditioned contrasts, which have always separated Catholicism and Lutheranism from Calvinism, strengthen this anti-capitalistic attitude of the European churches.

Finally, in an old civilized country, the 'aristocracy of education,' as it likes to be called, is a definite stratum of the population without personal interests in economics; hence it views the triumphal procession of capitalism more skeptically and criticizes more sharply than can naturally and justly be the case in a country such as the United States.

As soon as intellectual and esthetic education has become a profession, its representatives are bound by an inner affinity to all the carriers of ancient social culture, because for them, as for their prototypes, their profession cannot and must not be a source of heedless gain. They look distrustfully upon the abolition of traditional conditions of the community and upon the annihilation of all the innumerable ethical and esthetic values which cling to these traditions. They doubt if the dominion of capital would give better, more lasting guaranties to personal liberty and to the development of intellectual, esthetic, and social culture which they represent than the aristocracy of the past has given. They want to be ruled only by persons whose social culture they consider equivalent to their own; therefore, they prefer the rule of the economically independent aristocracy to the rule of the professional politician. Thus, it happens nowadays in the civilized countries—a peculiar and, in more than one respect, a serious fact—that the representatives of the highest interests of culture turn their eyes back, and, with deep antipathy standing opposed to the inevitable development of capitalism, refuse to co-operate in rearing the structure of the future. Moreover, the disciplined masses of workingmen created by capitalism are naturally inclined to unite in a class party, if new districts for settlement are no longer available, and if the workingman is conscious of being forced to remain inevitably a proletarian as long as he lives, which is bound to come about sooner or later also in this country, or has already come about. The progress of capitalism is not hemmed in by this; the workingman's chances to gain political power are insignificant. Yet they weaken the political power of the bourgeois and strengthen the power of the bourgeois' aristocratic adversaries. The downfall of German bourgeois liberalism is based upon the joint effectiveness of these motives.

Thus, in old countries, where a rural community, aristocratically differentiated, exists, a complex of social and political problems arises. An American finds it difficult to understand the importance of agrarian questions on the European continent, especially in Germany, even in German politics. He will arrive at entirely wrong conclusions if he does not keep before his eyes these great complexes. A peculiar combination of motives is effective in these old countries and explains the deviation of European from American conditions. Besides the necessity for strong military preparedness, there are essentially two factors: *First,* something which never existed in the greater part of America, which may be designated as 'backwardness,' that is, the influence of a gradually disappearing older form of rural society. The second set of circumstances which have not yet become effective in America, but to which this country—so elated by every million of increased population and by every rise of the valuation of the land—will unavoidably be exposed exactly as Europe has been, is the density of population, the high value of the land, the stronger differentiation of occupations, and the peculiar conditions resulting therefrom. Under all these conditions, the rural community of old civilized countries faces capitalism which is joined with the influence of great political and social powers only known to old countries. Even today under these circumstances, capitalism produces effects in Europe which can be produced in America only in the future.

In consequence of all those influences, European capitalism, at least on the Continent, has a peculiar authoritarian stamp, which contrasts with the citizen's equality of rights and which is usually distinctly felt by Americans. These authoritarian tendencies, and the anti-capitalist sentiments of all those elements of continental society of which I have spoken, find their social backing in the conflict between the landed aristocracy and the urban citizenry. Under the influence of capitalism, the landed aristocracy undergoes a serious inner transformation, which completely alters the character the aristocracy inherited from the past. I should like to show how this has taken place in the past and how it continues to be carried on in the present, using the example of Germany.

There are sharp contrasts in the rural social structure of Germany that no one traveling in the country fails to observe: towards the west and the south, the rural settlement grows denser, the small farmers predominate more, and the culture becomes more dispersed and various. The farther towards the east, especially the northeast one goes, the more extended are the fields of cereals, sugar beets, and potatoes, the more an extensive cultivation prevails, and the more a large rural class of propertyless farm hands stands in opposition to the landowning aristocracy. This difference is of great importance.

The class of the rural landowners of Germany, consisting particularly of noblemen residing in the region east of the Elbe, are the political rulers of the leading German state. The Prussian House of Lords represents this class, and the right of election by classes also gives them a determining position in the Prussian House of Representatives. These Junkers imprint their character upon the officer corps, as well as upon the Prussian officials and upon German diplomacy, which is almost exclusively in the hands of noblemen. The German student adopts their style of life in the fraternities in the universities. The civilian 'officer of the reserve'—a growing part of all the more highly educated Germans belong to this rank—also bears their imprint. Their political sympathies and antipathies explain many of the most important presuppositions of German foreign policies. Their obstructionism impedes the progress of the laboring-class; the manufacturers alone would never be sufficiently strong to oppose the workingmen under the democratic rights of electing representatives to the German Reichstag. The Junkers are the props of a protectionism which industry alone would never have been able to accomplish. They support orthodoxy in the state church. The foreigner sees only the exterior side of Germany and has neither the time nor opportunity to enter into the essence of German culture. Whatever survivals of authoritarian conditions surprise him, and cause the erroneous opinions circulated in foreign countries concerning Germany, result directly or indirectly from the influence of these upper classes; and many of the most important contrasts of our internal politics are based upon this difference between the rural social structures of the east and the west. Since this difference has not always existed, the question arises: How can it be explained historically?

Five centuries ago landlordism dominated the social structure of the rural districts. However various the conditions of the peasant's dependency which arose from this might have been, and however complicated the structure of rural society was, in one point harmony prevailed in the thirteenth and fourteenth centuries: the usually extensive possessions of the feudal lord were nowhere—not even in the east—connected with extensive cultivation. Though the landlord cultivated a part of his estate, the cultivated portion was only a little larger than the cultivated fields of the peasants. By far the greater part of the lord's income depended upon the taxes the peasants contributed. One of the most important questions of German social history is how the present strong contrast has arisen from this comparative uniformity.

Exclusive landlordship was dissolved at the beginning of the nineteenth century, partly because of the French Revolution, or because of the ideas disseminated by it, and partly because of the Revolution of 1848. The division of rights of ownership of land between landlords and peasants was abolished, the duties and taxes of the peasants were removed. The brilliant investigations of Professor G. F. Knapp and his school have shown how decisive, for the kind of agrarian constitution which originated then and still exists, was the question: How was the estate divided between the former landlords and the peasants after the manorial community had been dissolved? In the west and south for the most part, the land came into the hands of the peasants (or remained in their hands). But in the east a very large part fell into the hands of the former masters of the peasant, the feudal lords, who established extensive cultivation with free laborers. But this was only the consequence of the fact that the uniformity of the agrarian society had disappeared before the emancipation of the peasants. The difference between the west and the east was confirmed but not created by this process. In its main points the difference had existed since the sixteenth century, and meanwhile had constantly grown. Landlordship had undergone internal changes before the dissolution of the manor.

Everywhere, in the east and in the west, the endeavor of the landlords to increase their intakes was the motivating factor. This desire had sprung up with the invasion of capitalism, the growing wealth of the city dwellers, and the growing opportunity of selling agricultural products. Some of the transformations effected in the west and south date back to the thirteenth century, in the east to the fifteenth century. The landlords pursued their aim in characteristic fashion. In the south and west they remained landlords [*Grundherren*], that is, they increased the rates of rent, interest, and the taxes of the peasants, but they did not themselves engage in cultivating the land. In the east they became lords [*Gutsherren*], who cultivated their lands; they appropriated parts of the peasants' land (the enclosures) and thus procuring a large estate for themselves, became agriculturists, using the peasants as serfs to till their own soil. Extensive cultivation existed in the east—only to a smaller extent, and with the labor of serfs—even before the emancipation of the peasants; but not in the west. Now, what has caused this difference?

When this question is discussed, vast weight is laid upon the conduct of political power; indeed, this power was greatly interested in the formation of the agrarian society. Since the knight was exempted from paying taxes, the peasant was the only one in the country who paid them. When standing armies were established, the peasants furnished the recruits. This, in connection with certain points of view of commercialism, induced the rising territorial state to forbid the enclosures by edicts, that is, the appropriation of the peasants' land by the lords, and hence to protect the existing peasants' holdings. The stronger the ruler of the country was, the better he succeeded; the mightier the noble was, the less he succeeded. According to this the differences of the agrarian structure in the east were based, to a great extent, upon these conditions of power. But in the west and south we find that, in spite of the greatest weakness of a good many states and of the indubitable possibility of appropriating peasants' land, the landlords do not even attempt to do so. They show no tendency at all to deprive the peasant, to establish an extensive cultivation and become agriculturists themselves. Neither could the important development of the peasants' rights to the soil have been the decisive reason. In the east great numbers of peasants who originally had very good titles to the land have disappeared; in the west those with the least favorable titles have been preserved, because the landlords did not want to remove them.

The devisive question is therefore: How did it happen that the landlord of the German south and west, although he had ample opportunity to appropriate the peasants' land, did not do so, whereas the eastern landlord deprived the peasants of their land in spite of the resistance of the power of the state? This question can be put in a different form.

When the western landlord renounced the appropriation of the peasants' land, he did not renounce its utilization as a source of income. The difference between east and west in this connection is merely that the western landlord used the peasants as taxpayers, while the eastern landlord, by becoming a cultivator, began to use the peasants as a laboring force. Therefore, the question must be asked: Why one thing in the east, and another in the west?

As with most historical developments, it is rather improbable that a single reason can be assigned as the exclusive cause of this different conduct of the landlords; for in this case we should chance upon it in documentary sources. Therefore, a long series of single causative factors have been adduced as explanation, especially by Professor von Below in a classical investigation in his work, *Territorium und Stadt*. The task can only be that of widening the points of view, especially by economical considerations. Let us see in what points the conditions of the eastern and the western landlord differed when they each endeavored to extort from their peasants more than the traditional taxes.

The establishment of extensive operations was facilitated, for the eastern landlords, by the fact that their landlordship as well as the patrimonialization of the public authorities had grown gradually on the soil of ancient liberty of the people. The east, on the other hand, was a territory of colonization. The patriarchal Slavonic social structure was invaded by German clergymen in consequence of their superior education, by German merchants and artisans in consequence of their superior technical and commercial skill, by German knights in consequence of their superior military technique, and by German peasants in consequence of their superior knowledge of agriculture. Moreover, at the time of the conquest of the east, the social structure of Germany, with its political forces, had been completely feudalized. The social structure of the east was, from the very beginning, adapted to the social pre-eminence of the knight, and the German invasion only altered this slightly. The German peasant, even under the most favorable conditions of settling, had lost the support given to him in the feudal period by firm traditions, the old mutual protection, the jurisdiction of the community in the *Weistümer* [1] in the west. The Slavonian peasantry, usually more numerous, did not know anything of such traditions. Besides, in the west, the fields making up the estates of the lords were usually intermingled, even in single villages, for they had gradually arisen upon originally free land. These fields crossed the patrimonial rights of petty territorial lords everywhere and thus, by their variety and mutual conflicts, they secured his toilsome existence for the peasant. Very frequently the peasant was politically, personally, and economically subjected to quite different lords. In the east the combination of landlordship and patrimonial rights over a whole village was in the hands of one lord; the formation of a 'manor,' in the English sense, was regularly facilitated because, much more frequently than in the west, and from the very beginning, only one knight's court had been founded in a village, or had already originated from the Slavonic social structure. And finally there is an important factor, upon which Professor von Below correctly lays special stress: the estates of the knights in the east, though at first small in proportion to the entire territory of a village, were nevertheless usually much larger than was customary in the west. Therefore, the enlargement of the cultivated area of his estate was, for the lord, much easier than in the west, and also much less of a remote idea. Thus from the very beginning there existed, in the method of the distribution of the land, the first inducement to differentiation between east and west. But the cause of this difference in the size of the original estate of the landlord was connected with differences between the economic conditions of the east and those of the west. Even in the Middle Ages, considerably different conditions of life were created for the ruling social class.

The west was more densely populated, and, what is decisive in our opinion, local communication, the exchange of goods within and between the smallest local communities, was undoubtedly more developed than in the east. This was evidenced by the fact that the west was so much more thickly settled with towns. It is based partly upon the simple historical fact that the culture of the west was, in every respect, older, and partly upon a less evident, but important geographical difference, the far greater variety of the agricultural division of the west in comparison with the east. Considered from a purely technical view, communication on the extended plains of the German east must have met with fewer impediments than in the much intersected and differentiated territory of the west. Yet such technical possibilities of communication do not determine the amount of exchange. On the contrary, in the west and south the economic inducement to trade and to the development of a relatively intensive communication was much stronger than on the large plains of the east. This was due to the fact that in the west and south, bottoms, river valleys, and plateaus, are intermingled—climatic and other natural conditions of the production of goods are very noticeably differentiated within narrow districts. In the east, however, the neighboring towns have much more frequently nothing to exchange with each other (even today), because, having the same geographical situation, all of them produce the same goods. Historical and natural conditions of an intensive local trade were (and still are), for these reasons, more favorable in the west.

It is Professor von Below's merit to have pointed to the fact that in the Middle Ages the knighthood of the west was not exclusively or even predominantly founded upon territorial possession. Taxes, river tolls, rents, and imposts, which depend upon a certain amount of local traffic, played a role. This was undoubtedly much less possible in those days (as at present) in the east. Whoever wanted to live there as a knight had to found his existence upon income from his own agricultural operations. Large organizations for the production of goods and for foreign commerce, as those of the 'German Order,' are only a different phase of this same fact. The homogeneity of eastern production directed transportation into the more distant regions, and the local money economy remained considerably inferior to that of the west, according to all evidence. If the quite uncertain yet possible estimates are only approximately correct, the living conditions of the peasant in the east and the west must have been very different. It is scarcely probable that the lord would have taken up agricultural operations with their toil, risk, and the hardly gentlemanly contact with the mercantile world, if he could have lived as well in the east as in the west on the peasants' taxes, tolls, tithes, and rents. But we may ask why it was not equally possible in the east as in the west. To make it possible, peasants have to be economically able to pay taxes of considerable amount, sufficient for the wants of the landlord; it is by no means evident that the peasants could afford to do this. This would presuppose that the peasant's self-interest in the productivity of his land had reached a certain degree, that he himself had attained a certain amount of economic education. But nothing could and nothing can be substituted for that educating influence which is exerted upon the peasant by an intensive formation of urban communities, by well-developed local communication, by opportunity and inducement to sell rural products in the nearest possible local markets. This great difference may still be seen by comparing the peasant of the plain of Badenia with the peasant of the east.

It is not natural differences in the physical and chemical qualities of the soil, or differences in the economic talent of the races, but the historically established economic *milieu* that is the determining factor in the difference in the results of peasant agriculture.

A certain number of towns upon a given area was necessary to inspire the mass of the peasants with at least such a degree of interest in production that the lord was enabled to draw from them the means necessary for his sustenance, of using them as 'funds for interest.' Where these influences of culture, which cannot be replaced even by the best labor and best will, were lacking, the peasant frequently lacked the possibility and always the incentive to raise the yield of his land beyond the traditional measure of his own needs.

The cities in the east were much fewer in number, considering the size of the respective areas, than in the west and south. And the development of extensive agriculture in the east characteristically dates from an epoch in which not the rise but the decline of the cities, and a quite noticeable decline, can be observed. Because of its surplus of grain, the east was thus directed in its development as an agricultural export territory, with all the qualities of such territories. This direction reached its culmination in our century, after the abolition of the English corn laws. On the other hand, even at the end of the Middle Ages, several parts of the German west needed large importations of foodstuffs, especially cattle. The entire contrast between east and west is perhaps most evident in the difference of the prices of almost all their agricultural products in favor of the latter. This difference was only recently removed because of the hidden premiums of grain exportation, which have now been granted for a decade. Even the railroads had somewhat diminished this difference, but left it, in the middle of the last century, still very great. The unreliable condition of German numismatical history, besides many other technical difficulties, prevents us from obtaining a sufficient quantity of reliable data for the Middle Ages, but it seems well-nigh impossible that it has been different in general during that period, in spite of great fluctuations in particular cases.

If, therefore, the landlord wanted to make a more intensive use of his peasants in the east, much greater difficulties obstructed his plan to exploit them as funds for interest, on account of the peasants' traditional lack of development, the weakness of the local markets for rural products, and the less intense communication. I should like to ascribe to this circumstance a much greater importance—of course only in the form of a hypothesis yet to be proved by the sources—than has been done before. So far as I know the landlord of the east has chosen to operate his own agricultural estate, not because the gross operation was technically more rational—for this would have been also true for the west—but because it was, under the historically established conditions, the only possible economic means of obtaining a higher income. He became an operating landlord, and the peasant, bound more and more to the soil, became a serf with the duty of giving his children to the lord as menials, of furnishing his horses and wagons for husbandry, his own labor power for all sorts of work during the entire year, while his own land was considered more and more a mere reward for his labor. In spite of the opposition of the state, the lord constantly expanded the land which he cultivated. When, later on, the emancipation of the peasants came, it could not, as a Fourth of August in France, eliminate the landlords from the agrarian setup of the German east. An impecuniary state with still undeveloped industry could not easily renounce their gratuitous service in the administration and in the army. Above all, the decree abrogating feudal rights, where lord and peasants found themselves in a production community, did not at all decide the most important point: the fate of the land, which was considered to be the possession of the landlord, not of the peasant. Simply to declare it to be the peasants' property—as was done later in Russian Poland for political purposes, in order to ruin the Polish nobility—would have annihilated some twenty thousand large estates in Prussia, the only ones which the country then possessed. It would not have obliterated a mere class of rentiers, as it did in France. Therefore, only a part of the peasants, the larger holdings, and only a part of their lands were saved from being enclosed by the landlords; the remainder were appropriated by them.

The east continued to be, and henceforth became more and more, the seat of agrarian capitalism, whereas industrial capitalism took its seat primarily in the west. This development was stopped at the Russian frontier, which cut off the hinterland. A big industry, which might have arisen in the east, now developed closely behind the Russian-Poland frontier of Germany.

The Prussian landlord of the east, who originated under these conditions, was a very different social product than the English landlord. The English landlord is generally a lessor of land, not an agriculturist. His tributaries are not peasants, as in the Middle Ages, but capitalistic enterprises for cultivation of the land. He is a monopolist of the land. The estate in his possession is kept in the family by the artful juristic mechanics of 'entails,' which arose, like modern capitalist monopolies, in a constant struggle with legislation; it is withheld from communication, obligation, and division by bequest. The landlord stands outside the rural productive community. Occasionally he assists his lessee with loans of capital, but he enjoys an intangible existence as a lessor. As a social product, he is a genuine child of capitalism, arisen under the pressure of the contrasting effects, mentioned above, which capitalism produces in completely populated countries with an aristocratic social structure. The landed aristocrat wishes to live as a gentleman of leisure. Normally he strives for rents, not for profits. The technically sufficient size of the estate and the size of the property necessary for his maintenance are by no means in harmony with each other. In some areas of Germany more intensive operation, for instance, demands the diminution of property; whereas the rising luxury of the aristocratic class requires its enlargement, especially as the prices of products fall. Each purchase, each compensation of co-heirs, burdens the estate with heavy debts, while the operation of the estate becomes the more sensitive to price fluctuations the larger and more intensive it is. Only in an agrarian social structure, such as the English, is this development abolished. This, with the increased density of population and rising land values, is what endangers everywhere, nowadays, the existence of large rational agriculture, rather than the state's land monopoly, which many reformers demand. Indeed, the opposite extreme has been carried out—private monopoly of the land. But the private monopoly of the land produces, in certain economic respects, effects similar to those of the state's monopoly; it withdraws the land from the market and separates management from ownership, either of which may now go its own way. The interests of the capitalist farmer, striving for entrepreneurial profits, and the landowner's interests in rents and in the preservation of an inherited social position run side by side without being tied to each other, as is the case with the agricultural owner-operators. The practical significance of this is that the resilience of husbandry in the face of agricultural crises is powerfully increased. The shock falls upon two strong shoulders: the land monopolist and the capitalist landlord. The crisis results in lowering the rent, probably in a change of the lessee, in a gradual diminution of the cultivated soil, but not in a sudden destruction of many agricultural estates or in any sudden social degradation of many landowning families.

The conditions of the eastern Prussian Junker are quite different. He is a rural employer, a man of a thoroughly capitalist type, esteemed according to the size of his estate and income. He possesses scarcely more than one and a half to two United States 'sections,' but by tradition he is incumbered with a high life and aristocratic pretensions. He is usually the free owner of the soil he cultivates, which is sold and mortgaged, estimated for bequests, and acquired by compensating the co-heirs; hence it is always burdened with running interests. Therefore the owner alone is exposed to the fluctuation of the market prices. The Junker is involved in all economic and social conflicts, which directly menace his existence at all times. As long as the exportation of grain to England flourished, he was the strongest supporter of free trade, the fiercest opponent of the young German industry of the west that needed protection; but when the competition of younger and cheaper lands expelled him from the world market and finally attacked him at his own home, he became the most important ally of those manufacturers who, contrary to other important branches of German industry, demanded protection; he joined with them in common struggle against the demands of labor. For meanwhile capitalism had also gnawed at the social character of the Junker and his laborers. In the first half of the last century the Junker was a rural patriarch. His farm hands, the farmer whose land he had appropriated, were by no means proletarians. In consequence of the Junker's lack of funds, they did not receive wages, but a cottage, land, and the right of pasturage for their cows; during harvesttime and for threshing, a certain portion of the grain was paid to them in wheat, et cetera. Thus they were, on a small scale, agriculturists with a direct interest in their lord's husbandry. But they were expropriated by the rising valuation of the land; their lord withheld pasture and land, kept his grain, and paid them wages instead. Thus, the old community of interest was dissolved, and the farm hands became proletarians. The operation of agriculture became a seasonal operation, restricted to a few months. The lord hired migratory laborers, since the maintenance of idle hands throughout the year would be too heavy a burden.

The more German industry grew in the west, to its present size, the more the population underwent an enormous change; emigration reached its culmination in the German east, where only lords and serfs existed in far extended districts and from whence the farm laborers fled from their isolation and patriarchal dependency either across the ocean to the United States, or into the smoky and dusty but socially freer air of the German factories. On the other hand, the landlords import whatever laborers they can get to do their work: Slavs from beyond the frontier, who, as 'cheaper hands,' drive out the Germans. Today the landlord acts as any businessman, and he must act thus, but his aristocratic traditions contrast with such action. He would like to be a feudal lord, yet he must become a commercial entrepreneur and a capitalist. Other powers, rather than the Junker, endeavor to snatch the role of the landlord.

The industrial and commercial capitalists begin increasingly to absorb the land. Manufacturers and merchants who have become rich buy the knights' estates, tie their possession to their family by entailment, and use their estate as a means of invading the aristocratic class. The *fidei-commissum* of the parvenu is one of the characteristic products of capitalism in an old country with aristocratic traditions and a military monarchy. In the German east, the same thing takes place now which has been going on in England for centuries, until the present conditions were established there.

America will also experience this process in the future, though only after all free land has been exhausted and the economic pulsation of the country has slowed down. For while it is correct to say that the burden of historical tradition does not overwhelm the United States, and that the problems originating from the power of tradition do not exist here, yet the effects of the power of capitalism are the stronger, and will, sooner or later, further the development of land monopolies. When the land has become costly enough to secure a certain rent; when the accumulation of large fortunes has reached a still higher point than today; when, at the same time, the possibility of gaining proportionate profits by constant, new investments in trade and industry has been diminished so that the 'captains of industry,' as has occurred everywhere in the world, begin to strive for hereditary preservation of their possessions instead of new investments bringing both profit and risk—then, indeed, the desire of the capitalist families to form a 'nobility' will arise, probably not in form though in fact. The representatives of capitalism will not content themselves any longer with such harmless play as pedigree studies and the numerous pranks of social exclusiveness which are so startling to the foreigner. Only when capital has arrived at this course and begins to monopolize the land to a great extent, will a great rural social question arise in the United States, a question which cannot be cut with the sword, as was the slave question. Industrial monopolies and trusts are institutions of limited duration; the conditions of production undergo changes, and the market does not know any everlasting valuation. Their power also lacks the authoritative character and the political mark of aristocracies. But monopolies of the land always create a political aristocracy.

So far as Germany is concerned, in the east a certain approach to English conditions has begun in consequence of certain tendencies; whereas the German southwest shows similarity with France in its rural social structure. But, in general, the intensive English stock-breeding is not possible in the German east on account of the climate. Therefore capital absorbs only the land most favorable for agriculture. But while the inferior districts in England remain uncultivated, as pastures for sheep, in the German east they are settled by small farmers. This process has a peculiar feature, inasmuch as two nations, Germans and Slavs, struggle with each other economically. The Polish peasants, who have fewer wants than the Germans, seem to be gaining the upper hand.

Under the pressure of business cycles the frugal, Slavic small farmer gains land from the German. The advance of culture toward the east during the Middle Ages, based upon the superiority of the older and higher culture, has been reversed under the capitalistic principle of the 'cheaper hand.' Whether the United States will also have to wrestle with similar problems in the future, nobody can foretell. The diminution of the agricultural operations in the wheat-producing states results at present from the growing intensity of the operation and from division of labor. Also the number of Negro farms is growing, as is the migration from the country into the cities. If, thereby, the expansive power of the Anglo-Saxon-German settlement of the rural districts, as well as the number of children of the old, native-born population, are on the wane, and if, at the same time, the enormous immigration of untutored elements from eastern Europe grows, a rural population might soon arise here which could not be assimilated by the historically transmitted culture of this country. This population would decisively change the standard of the United States and would gradually form a community of a quite different type from the great creation of the Anglo-Saxon spirit.

For Germany, all fateful questions of economic and social politics and of national interests are closely connected with this contrast between the rural society of the east and that of the west and with its further development. I should not consider it correct to discuss here, in a foreign country, the practical problems arising from this. Destiny, which has incumbered us with a history of thousands of years, which has placed us in a country with a dense population and an intensive culture, which has forced us to maintain the splendor of our old culture, so to speak, in an armed camp within a world bristling with arms, has placed before us these problems. And we must meet them.

The United States does not yet know such problems. This nation will probably never encounter some of them. It has no old aristocracy; hence the tensions caused by the contrast between authoritarian tradition and the purely commercial character of modern economic conditions do not exist. Rightly it celebrates the purchase of this immense territory, in whose center we are here,[2] as the real historical seal imprinted upon its democratic institutions; without this acquisition, with powerful and warlike neighbors at its side, it would be forced to wear the coat of mail like ourselves, who constantly keep in the drawer of our desks the march order in case of war. But on the other hand, the greater part of the problems for whose solution we are now working will approach America within only a few generations. The way in which they will be solved will determine the character of the future culture of this continent. It was perhaps never before in history made so easy for any nation to become a great civilized power as for the American people. Yet, according to human calculation, it is also the last time, as long as the history of mankind shall last, that such conditions for a free and great development will be given; the areas of free soil are now vanishing everywhere in the world.

One of my colleagues has quoted the words of Carlyle: 'Thousands of years have passed before thou couldst enter into life, and thousands of years to come wait in silence that thou wilt do with this thy life.' I do not know if, as Carlyle believed, a single man can or will place himself, in his actions, upon the sounding-board of this sentiment. But a nation must do so, if its existence in history is to be of lasting value.

XV. National Character and the Junkers

As a carrier of political tradition, training, and balance in a polity, there is no doubt that a stratum of landlords cannot be replaced. We speak of such landlord strata as have existed in England and which, in a similar way, formed the kernel of ancient Rome's senatorial nobility.

How many such aristocrats are to be found in Germany, and especially in Prussia? Where is their political tradition? Politically, German aristocrats, particularly in Prussia, amount to almost nothing. And it seems obvious that today a state policy aimed at breeding such a stratum of large rentiers of genuinely aristocratic character is out of the question.

Even if it were still possible to let a number of great aristocratic estates emerge on woodland—land which alone qualifies socially and politically for the formation of entailed estates—it would still be impossible to obtain any significant results. *This* was precisely the abysmal dishonesty of the bill concerning entailed estates considered in Prussia at the beginning of 1917. The bill was intended to extend a legal institution appropriate for aristocratic holdings to the middle-class proprietors of the average East Elbian estate. It tried to make an 'aristocracy' out of a type which simply is not an aristocracy and never can be inflated into one.

The Junkers of the east are frequently (and often unjustly) vilified; they are just as frequently (and as often unjustly) idolized. Anyone who knows them personally will certainly enjoy their company at the hunt, over a good glass, or at cards; and in their hospitable homes, everything is genuine. But everything becomes spurious when one stylizes this essentially 'bourgeois' stratum of entrepreneurs into an 'aristocracy.' Economically, the Junkers are entirely dependent upon working as agricultural entrepreneurs; they are engaged in the struggle of economic

'Wahlrecht und Demokratie in Deutschland,' *Gesammelte Politische Schriften* (Munich, Dreimaskenverlag, 1921), pp. 277-322. This comprises a passage, pp. 307-18, from a pamphlet which 'Die Hilfe'—the book publishing department of the little magazine which Naumann edited—published in December 1917.

interests. Their social and economic struggle is just as ruthless as that of any manufacturer. Ten minutes in their circle shows one that they are plebeians. Their very virtues are of a thoroughly robust and plebeian nature. Minister von Miquel once stated (privately!) that 'Nowadays an East German feudal estate cannot support an aristocratic household,' and he was quite correct. If one tries to mold such a stratum into an aristocracy, replete with feudal gestures and pretensions, a stratum now dependent upon routine managerial work of a capitalistic nature, the only result which can be irrevocably attained is the *physiognomy of a parvenu*. Those traits of our political and general conduct in the world which bear this stamp are determined, though not exclusively, by the fact that we have fed aristocratic pretensions to strata which simply lack the qualifications.

The Junkers are only one instance of this point. Among us the absence of men of cosmopolitan education is, of course, not only due to the physiognomy of the Junkers; it is also a result of the pervasive 'petty bourgeois'[1] character of all those strata which have been the specific bearers of the Prussian polity during the time of its poverized but glorious ascendancy. The old officers' families, in their highly honorific way, cultivate in their often extremely modest economic conditions the tradition of the old Prussian army. The civil-servant families are of the same hue. It does not matter whether or not these families are of noble birth; economically, socially, and according to their horizon, they constitute a bourgeois middle-class group. In general, the social forms of the German officer corps are absolutely appropriate to the nature of the stratum, and in their decisive features they definitely resemble those of the officer corps of the democracies (of France and also of Italy). But these traits immediately become a caricature when non-military circles consider them as a model for their conduct. This holds, above all, when they are blended with social forms derived from the 'pennalism' of the schools for bureaucracy. Yet, such is the case with us.

It is well known that the student fraternities constitute the typical social education of aspirants for non-military offices, sinecures, and the liberal professions of high social standing. The 'academic freedom' of dueling, drinking, and class cutting stems from a time when other kinds of freedom did not exist in Germany and when only the stratum of literati and candidates for office was privileged in such liberties. The inroad, however, which these conventions have made upon the bearing of the 'academically certified man' of Germany cannot be eliminated even today. This type of man has always been important among us, and becomes increasingly so. Even if the mortgages on fraternity houses and the necessity for the alumni to bear their interest did not take care of the economic immortality of the student fraternities, this type would hardly disappear. On the contrary, the fraternity system is steadily expanding; for the social connections of the fraternities nowadays constitute a specific way of selecting officials. And the officers' commission with its prerequisite qualification for dueling, visibly guaranteed through the colored fraternity ribbon, gives access to 'society.'

To be sure, the drinking compulsions and dueling techniques of the fraternities are increasingly adjusted to the needs of the weaker constitutions of aspirants to the fraternity ribbon, who for the sake of connections become more and more numerous. Allegedly, there are even teetotalers in some of these dueling corps. The intellectual inbreeding of the fraternities, which has continuously increased during recent decades, is a decisive factor. Fraternities have reading rooms of their own and special fraternity papers, which the alumni provide exclusively with well-meant 'patriotic' politics of an unspeakably petty-bourgeois character. Social intercourse with classmates of a different social or intellectual background is shunned or at least made very difficult. With all this, fraternity connections are constantly expanding. A sales clerk who aspires to qualify for an officer's commission as a prerequisite of marriage into 'society' (particularly with the boss's daughter) will enroll in one of the business colleges which are frequented largely because of their fraternity life.

The yardstick of the moralist is not the yardstick of the politician. However one may judge all these student associations *per se,* they certainly do not provide an education for a cosmopolitan personality. On the contrary, their fagging system and pennalism are, after all, undeniably banal; and their subaltern social forms constitute the very opposite of such an education. The most stupid Anglo-Saxon club offers more of a cosmopolitan education, however empty one may find the organized sports in which the club often finds its fulfilment. The Anglo-Saxon club with its often very strict selection of members always rests upon the principle of the strict equality of gentlemen and not upon the principle of 'pennalism,' which bureaucracy cherishes so highly as a preparation for discipline in office. By cultivating such pennalism, the fraternities do not fail to recommend themselves to 'higher ups.' [2] In any case, formalistic conventions and the pennalism of this so-called 'academic freedom' are imposed upon the aspirant to office in Germany. The more the candidates turn out to be parvenus, boastful of a full pocketbook—from the parents—as is unavoidably the case wherever conditions allow for it, the less effective are these conventions in training aristocratic men of the world. Unless the young man who drifts into this conditioning is of an unusually independent character, a free spirit, the fatal traits of a varnished plebeian will be developed. We notice such plebeians quite often among dueling corps members, even among men who are otherwise quite excellent; for the interests cultivated by these fraternities are thoroughly plebeian and far from all 'aristocratic' interests, no matter in what sense one may interpret them. The salient point is simply that an essentially plebeian student life may formerly have been harmless; it was merely naive, youthful exuberance. But nowadays it pretends to be a means of aristocratic education qualifying one for leadership in the state. The simply incredible contradiction contained in this turns into a boomerang in that a parvenu physiognomy is the result.

We must beware of thinking that these parvenu features of the German countenance are politically irrelevant. Let us immediately consider a case. To go out for 'moral conquests' among enemies, that is, among opposed interest groups, is a vain enterprise, which Bismarck has rightly ridiculed. But does this hold for present or future allies? We and our Austrian allies are constantly depending upon one another politically. And this is known to them as well as to us. Unless great follies are committed, no danger of a break threatens. German achievement is acknowledged by them without reserve and without jealousy—the more so the less we brag about it. We do not always have a proper appreciation of difficulties which the Austrians have and which Germany is spared. Hence, we do not always appreciate Austrian achievement. But what everybody all over the world knows must also openly be said here. What could not be tolerated by the Austrians, or by any other nation with which we might ever wish to be friendly, are the manners of the parvenu as again displayed recently in an unbearable way. Such a bearing will meet with a silent and polite yet a determined rejection by any nation of good old social breeding, for instance, the Austrians. Nobody wants to be ruled by poorly educated parvenus. Any step beyond what is absolutely indispensable in foreign affairs, that is, anything which might be possible on the part of 'Central Europe' (in the inner meaning of the word), or which might be desirable for future solidarity of interests with other nations (no matter how one may feel about the idea of an economic rapprochement), may fail politically because of the absolute determination of the partner not to have imposed upon him what recently, with a boastful gesture, was proclaimed to be the 'Prussian spirit.' 'Democracy' allegedly endangers this Prussian spirit, according to the verbal assembly lines of the political phrasemongers. As is known, the same declamations have been heard, without exception, at every stage of internal reform for the last one hundred and ten years.

The genuine Prussian spirit belongs to the most beautiful blossoms of German culture. Every line we have of Scharnhorst, Gneisenau, Boyen, Moltke is inspired with this spirit, just as are the deeds and words of the great Prussian reform officials (a good many of whom, however, are of non-Prussian descent). We need not name them here. The same holds of Bismarck's eminent intellectuality, which is now so badly caricatured by the stupid and Philistine representatives of *Realpolitik*. But occasionally it seems as if this old Prussian spirit is now stronger among the officialdom of *other* federal states than in Berlin. Abuse of the term 'Prussian spirit' by present conservative demagogues is only an abuse of these great men.

To repeat, no aristocracy of sufficient weight and political tradition exists in Germany. Such an aristocracy may at best have had a place in the *Freikonservative* party and in the Center party—although no longer now—but it has had no place in the Conservative party.

It is equally important that there is no social form of German gentility. For despite the occasional boasting of our literati, it is completely untrue that individualism exists in Germany in the sense of freedom from conventions, in contrast to the conventions of the Anglo-Saxon gentleman or of the Latin salon type of man. Nowhere are there more rigid and compelling conventions than those of the German 'fraternity man.' These conventions directly and indirectly control just as large a part of the progeny of our leading strata as do the conventions of any other country. Wherever the forms of the officer corps do not hold, these fraternity conventions constitute 'the German form'; for the effects of the dueling corps conventions largely determine the forms and conventions of the dominant strata of Germany: of the bureaucracy and of all those who wish to be accepted in 'society,' where bureaucracy sets the tone. And these forms are certainly not genteel.

From a political point of view, it is still more important that, in contrast to the conventions of Latin and Anglo-Saxon countries, these German forms are simply not suited to serve as a model for the whole nation down to the lowest strata. They are not suited to mold and unify the nation in its gesture as a *Herrenvolk,* self-assured in its overt conduct in the way in which Latin and Anglo-Saxon conventions have succeeded.

It is a grave error to believe that 'race' is the decisive factor in the striking lack of grace and dignity in the overt bearing of the German. The German-Austrian's demeanor is formed by a genuine aristocracy. He does not lack these qualities, in spite of identical race, whatever else his weaknesses may be.

The forms that control the Latin type of personality, down to the lowest strata, are determined by imitation of the cavalier as evolved since the sixteenth century.

The Anglo-Saxon conventions also mold personalities down into the lower strata. They stem from the social habits of the gentry stratum, which has set the tone in England since the seventeenth century. The gentry emerged during the later Middle Ages from a peculiar blend of rural and urban notables, namely 'gentlemen,' who became the bearers of 'self-government.'

In all these cases it has been of consequence that the decisive features of the relevant conventions and gestures could be easily and universally imitated and hence could be democratized. But the conventions of the academically examined candidates for office in Germany, of those strata which they influence, and, above all, the habits for which the dueling corps conditions its men—these were and are obviously not suited for imitation by any circles outside of the examined and certified strata. In particular, they cannot be imitated by the broad masses of the people; they cannot be democratized, although, or rather precisely because, in essence these conventions are by no means cosmopolitan or otherwise aristocratic. They are thoroughly plebeian in nature.

The neo-Latin code of honor, as well as the quite different Anglo-Saxon code, has been suitable for far-reaching democratization. The specifically German concept of qualification for dueling, however, is not suited for being democratized, as one can easily see. This concept is of great political bearing, but the politically and socially important point is not—as is frequently held—that a so-called 'code of honor' in the narrower sense exists in the officer corps. It is absolutely in place there. The fact that a Prussian *Landrat*[3] must qualify himself for dueling, in the sense of the pennalist duel corps, in order to maintain himself in his post—that is what is politically relevant. This also holds for any other administrative official who is easily removable. It is in contrast, for instance, to the *Amtsrichter*,[4] who, by virtue of the law, is 'independent,' and who because of this independence is socially déclassé as compared to the *Landrat*. As with all other conventions and forms supported by the structure of bureaucracy and decisively fashioned by the idea of German student honor, from a formal point of view the concept of dueling qualification constitutes a caste convention because of its peculiar nature. None of these forms can be democratized. In substance, however, they are not of an aristocratic but of an absolutely plebeian character, because they lack all esthetic dignity and all genteel cultivation. It is this inner contradiction that invites ridicule and has such unfavorable political effects.

Germany is a nation of plebeians. Or, if it sounds more agreeable, it is a nation of commoners. Only on this basis could a specifically 'German form' grow.

Socially, democratization brought about or promoted by the new political order—and that is what should be discussed here—would not destroy the value of aristocratic forms, since there are no such forms. Nor could it deprive such values of their exclusiveness and then propagate them throughout the nation, as was done with the forms of the Latin and Anglo-Saxon aristocracies. The form values of the degree-hunter qualifying for duels are not sufficiently cosmopolitan to support personal poise even in their own stratum. As every test shows, these forms do not always suffice even to hide the actual insecurity before a foreigner who is educated as a man of the world. The endeavor to hide such insecurity often takes the form of 'pertness,' which, in the main, stems from awkwardness and appears as poor breeding.

We shall not discuss whether political 'democratization' would actually result in social democratization. Unlimited political 'democracy' in America, for instance, does not prevent the growth of a raw plutocracy or even an 'aristocratic' prestige group, which is slowly emerging. The growth of this 'aristocracy' is culturally and historically as important as that of plutocracy, even though it usually goes unnoticed.

The development of a truly cultured 'German form,' which is at the same time suitable for the character of the socially dominant stratum of commoners, lies in the future. The incipient development of such civil conventions in the Hanseatic cities has not been continued under the impact of political and economic changes since 1870. And the present war [World War I] has blessed us with a great many parvenus, whose sons will ardently acquire the usual duel corps conventions at the universities. These conventions do not raise any demands for a cultured tradition; they serve as a convenient way of taming men for qualifying as an applicant for officer commissions. Hence, for the time being there is no hope for a change. In any case, this much holds: if 'democratization' should result in eliminating the social prestige of the academically certified man—which is by no means certain and which cannot be discussed here—then no politically valuable social forms would be abolished in Germany. Since they do not exist, they cannot be eliminated. Democracy could perhaps then free the road for the development of valuable forms suitable to our civic, social, and economic structure, which therefore would be 'genuine' and cultured values. One cannot invent such values, just as one cannot invent a style. Only this much (in an essentially negative and formal way) can be said, and it holds for all values of this nature: such forms can never be developed on any other basis than upon an attitude of personal distance and reserve. In Germany this prerequisite of all personal dignity has frequently been lacking among both high and low. The latest literati, with their urge to brag about and to print their personal 'experiences'—erotical, religious, or what not—are the enemies of all dignity, no matter of what sort. 'Distance,' however, can by no means be gained exclusively on the 'cothurnus' of snobbishly setting one's self off from the 'far too many,' as is maintained by the various and misconceived 'prophecies' which go back to Nietzsche. On the contrary, when today it is in need of this inner support, distance is always spurious. Perhaps the necessity of maintaining one's inner dignity in the midst of a democratic world can serve as a test of the genuineness of dignity.

What we have said above shows that in this, as in so many other respects, the German fatherland is not and must not be the land of its fathers but rather the land of its children, as Alexander Herzen has so beautifully said of Russia. And this holds particularly for political problems.

The 'German spirit' for solving political problems cannot be distilled from the intellectual work of our past, however valuable it may be. Let us pay deference to the great shadows of our spiritual ancestors and let us make use of their intellectual work for all formal training of the mind. Our literati, in their conceit, claim from the past the title to govern the working out of our political future, like schoolmasters with a rod, simply because it is their profession to interpret the past to the nation. Should they try to lay down the law, then let us throw the old books into the nearest corner! Nothing can be learned about the future from them. The German classics, among other things, can teach us that we could be a leading cultured nation in a period of material poverty and political helplessness and even foreign domination. Even where they concern politics and economics their ideas stem from this unpolitical epoch. The ideas of the German classics, inspired by discussion of the French Revolution, were projections into a political and economic situation that lacked popular passion. But in so far as any political passion inspired them, besides wrathful rebellion against foreign domination, it was the ideal enthusiasm for moral imperatives. What lies beyond that remain philosophical ideas, which we may utilize as stimulating means of defining our own stand according to our political reality and according to the requirements of our own day, but not as guides. The modern problems of parliamentary government and democracy, and the essential nature of our modern state in general, are entirely beyond the horizon of the German classics.

There are those who reproach universal suffrage as the victory of dull mass instincts incapable of reason, in contradistinction to judicious political conviction; they hold it to be a victory of emotional over rational politics. With reference to the latter—and this must be said—Germany's foreign policy is proof of the fact that a monarchy ruling by a system of class suffrage holds the record for purely personal emotion and an irrational mood influencing leadership. Prussia holds the hegemony and is always the decisive factor in German politics. To prove this we need only compare the zigzag path of this noisy policy, unsuccessful for decades, with the calm purposiveness, for instance, of English foreign policy.

And as for irrational crowd instincts, they rule politics only where the masses are tightly compressed and exert pressure: in the modern metropolis, particularly under the conditions of neo-Latin urban forms of life. There the civilization of the café, as well as climatic conditions, permit the policy of the 'street'—as it has fittingly been called—to lord it over the country from the capital. On the other hand, the role of the English 'man of the street' is linked with very specific characteristics of the structure of the urban masses, which are totally lacking in Germany. The Russian metropolitan street policy is connected with the underground organizations which exist there. All these preconditions are absent in Germany, and the moderation of German life makes it quite improbable that Germany should fall into this *occasional* danger—for it is an occasional one in contrast to what in Imperial Germany has influenced foreign policy as a *chronic* danger. Not labor tied to workshops, but the loafers and the café intellectuals in Rome and Paris have fabricated the war-mongering policy of the street—by the way, exclusively in the service of the government and *only* to the extent to which the government intended or allowed it.

In France and Italy the balance of the industrial proletariat was lacking. When it acts with solidarity, the industrial proletariat is certainly an immense power in dominating the street. In comparison, however, with entirely irresponsible elements, it is a force at least capable of order and of orderly leadership through its functionaries and hence through rationally thinking politicians. From the point of view of state policy, all that matters is to increase the power of these leaders, in Germany of trade-union leaders, over the passions of the moment. Beyond this, what matters is to increase the importance of the responsible leaders, the importance of political leadership *per se*. It is one of the strongest arguments for the creation of an orderly and responsible guidance of policy by a parliamentarian leadership that thereby the efficacy of purely emotional motives from 'above' and from 'below' is weakened as far as possible. The 'rule of the street' has nothing to do with equal suffrage; Rome and Paris have been dominated by the street even when in Italy the most plutocratic sufferance in the world and in Paris Napoleon III ruled with a fake parliament. *Only* the orderly guidance of the masses by responsible politicians can break the irregular rule of the street and the leadership of demagogues of the moment.

XVI. India: The Brahman and the Castes

THE position of the Brahman, in classic Hinduism as well as today, can be understood only in connection with *caste,* without an understanding of which it is quite impossible to understand Hinduism. Perhaps the most important gap in the ancient Veda is its lack of any reference to caste. The Veda refers to the four later caste names in only one place, which is considered a very late passage; nowhere does it refer to the substantive content of the caste order in the meaning which it later assumed and which is characteristic only of Hinduism.[1]

Caste, that is, the ritual rights and duties it gives and imposes and the position of the Brahmans, is the fundamental institution of Hinduism. Before everything else, without caste there is no Hindu. But the position of the Hindu with regard to the authority of the Brahman may vary extraordinarily, from unconditional submission to the contesting of his authority. Some castes do contest the authority of the Brahman, but, practically, this means merely that the Brahman is disdainfully rejected as a priest, that his judgment in controversial questions of ritual is not recognized as authoritative, and that his advice is never sought. Upon first sight, this seems to contradict the fact that 'castes' and 'Brahmans' belong together in Hinduism. But as a matter of fact, if the caste is absolutely essential for each Hindu, the reverse, at least nowadays, does not hold, namely, that every caste be a Hindu caste. There are also castes among the Mohammedans of India, taken over from the Hindus. And castes are also found among the Buddhists. Even the Indian Christians have not quite been able to withhold themselves from practical recognition of the castes. These non-Hindu castes have lacked the tremendous emphasis that the specific Hinduist doctrine of salvation placed upon the caste, as we shall see later, and they have lacked a further characteristic,

From *Gesammelte Aufsaetze zur Religionssoziologie,* vol. II, pp. 32-48, 109-13. The study from which this selection is drawn was originally printed in the *Archiv,* April and December 1916, and May 1917.

namely, the determination of the social rank of the castes by the social distance from other Hinduist castes, and therewith, ultimately, from the Brahman. For this is decisive for the connection between Hindu castes and the Brahman; however intensely a Hindu caste may reject him as a priest, as a doctrinal and ritual authority, and in every other respect, the objective situation remains inescapable: in the last analysis, a rank position is determined by the nature of its positive or negative relation to the Brahman.

'Caste' is, and remains essentially, social rank, and the central position of the Brahmans in Hinduism rests more upon the fact that social rank is determined with reference to them than upon anything else. In order to understand this, we shall turn to the present condition of the Hindu castes, as described in the partly excellent scientific Census Reports. We shall also briefly consider the classical theories of caste contained in the ancient books of law and other sources.

Today the Hinduist caste order is profoundly shaken. Especially in the district of Calcutta, old Europe's major gateway, many norms have practically lost their force. The railroads, the taverns, the changing occupational stratification, the concentration of labor through imported industry, colleges, et cetera, have all contributed their part. The 'commuters to London,' that is, those who studied in Europe and who freely maintained social intercourse with Europeans, used to become outcasts up to the last generation; but more and more this pattern is disappearing. And it has been impossible to introduce caste coaches on the railroads in the fashion of the American railroad cars or waiting rooms which segregate 'White' from 'Black' in the Southern States. All caste relations have been shaken, and the stratum of intellectuals bred by the English are here, as elsewhere, bearers of a specific nationalism. They will greatly strengthen this slow and irresistible process. For the time being, however, the caste structure still stands quite firmly.

First we have to ask: with what concepts shall we define a 'caste'? * Let us ask it in the negative: what is not a caste? Or, what traits of other associations, really or apparently related to caste, are lacking in caste? What, for instance, is the difference between caste and a tribe?

* The term is of Portuguese derivation. The ancient Indian name is *varna*, 'color.'

I: CASTE AND TRIBE

As long as a tribe has not become wholly a guest or a pariah people, it usually has a fixed tribal territory. A genuine caste never has a fixed territory. To a very considerable extent, the caste members live in the country, segregated in villages. Usually in each village there is, or was, only one caste with full title to the soil. But dependent village artisans and laborers also live with this caste. In any case, the caste does not form a local, territorial, corporate body, for this would contradict its nature. A tribe is, or at least originally it was, linked together by obligatory blood revenge, mediated directly or indirectly through the sib. A caste never has anything to do with such blood revenge.

Originally, a tribe normally comprised many, often almost all, of the possible pursuits necessary for the gaining of subsistence. A caste may comprise people who follow very different pursuits; at least this is the case today, and for certain upper castes this has been the case since very early times. Yet so long as the caste has not lost its character, the kinds of pursuits admissible without loss of caste are always, in some way, quite strictly limited. Even today very often 'caste' and 'way of earning a living' are so firmly linked that a change of occupation is co-related with a division of caste. This is not the case for a 'tribe.'

Normally a tribe comprises people of every social rank. A caste may well be divided into sub-castes with extraordinarily different social ranks. Today this is almost unexceptionally the case; one caste frequently contains several hundred sub-castes. In such cases, these sub-castes may be related to one another exactly, or almost exactly, as are different castes. If this is the case, the sub-castes in reality are castes; the caste name common to all of them has a merely—or at least almost merely—historical significance and serves to support the social pretensions of degraded sub-castes towards third castes. Hence, by its very nature, caste is inseparably bound up with social ranks within a larger community.

It is decisive for a tribe that it is originally and normally a political association. The tribe either forms an independent association, as is originally always the case, or the association is part of a tribal league; or, it may constitute a *phyle,* that is, part of a political association commissioned with certain political tasks and having certain rights: franchise, holding quotas of the political offices, and the right of assuming its share or turn of political, fiscal, and liturgical obligations. A caste is never a political

association, even if political associations in individual cases have burdened castes with liturgies, as may have happened repeatedly during the
Indian Middle Ages (Bengal). In this case, castes are in the same position
as merchant and craft guilds, sibs, and all sorts of associations. By its
very nature the caste is always a purely social and possibly occupational
association, which forms part of and stands within a social community.
But the caste is not necessarily, and by no means regularly, an association
forming part of only one political association; rather it may reach beyond,
or it may fall short of, the boundaries of any one political association.
There are castes diffused over all of India.[2] Yet today, each of the sub-
castes and also most of the small castes exist only in their respective
small district. Political division has often strongly influenced the caste
order of individual areas, but precisely the most important castes have
remained interstate in scope.

With regard to the substance of their social norms, a tribe usually
differs from a caste in that the exogamy of the totem or of the villages
coexist with the exogamy of the sibs. Endogamy has existed only under
certain conditions, but by no means always, for the tribe as a whole.
Rules of endogamy, however, always form the essential basis of a caste.
Dietary rules and rules of commensality are always characteristic of the
caste but are by no means characteristic for the tribe.

We have already observed that when a tribe loses its foothold in its
territory it becomes a guest or a pariah people. It may then approximate
caste to the point of being actually indistinguishable from it.[3] The differences that remain will be discussed when we determine the positive characteristics of caste. But first, the following question arises: In contrast to
'tribe,' caste is usually intimately related to special ways of earning a
living, on the one hand, and, on the other, to social rank. Now, how is
caste related to the occupational associations (merchant and craft guilds)
and how is it related to 'status groups'? Let us begin with the former.

2: CASTE AND GUILD

'Guilds' of merchants, and of traders figuring as merchants by selling
their own produce, as well as 'craft-guilds,' existed in India during the
period of the development of cities and especially during the period in
which the great salvation religions originated. As we shall see, the salvation religions and the guilds were related. The guilds usually emerged
within the cities, but occasionally they emerged outside of the cities,

survivals of these being still in existence. During the period of the flowering of the cities, the position of the guilds was quite comparable to the position guilds occupied in the cities of the medieval Occident. The guild association (the *mahajan,* literally, the same as *popolo grasso*) faced on the one hand the prince, and on the other the economically dependent artisans. These relations were about the same as those faced by the great guilds of literati and of merchants with the lower craft-guilds (*popolo minuto*) of the Occident. In the same way, associations of lower craft guilds existed in India (the *panch*). Moreover, the liturgical guild of Egyptian and late Roman character was perhaps not entirely lacking in the emerging patrimonial states of India. The uniqueness of the development of India lay in the fact that these beginnings of guild organization in the cities led neither to the city autonomy of the Occidental type nor, after the development of the great patrimonial states, to a social and economic organization of the territories corresponding to the 'territorial economy'[4] of the Occident. Rather, the Hinduist caste system, whose beginnings certainly preceded these organizations, became paramount. In part, this caste system entirely displaced the other organizations; and in part, it crippled them; it prevented them from attaining any considerable importance. The 'spirit' of this caste system, however, was totally different from that of the merchant and craft guilds.

The merchant and craft guilds of the Occident cultivated religious interests as did the castes. In connection with these interests, questions of social rank also played a considerable role among guilds. Which rank order the guilds should follow, for instance, during processions, was a question occasionally fought over more stubbornly than questions of economic interest. Furthermore, in a 'closed' guild, that is, one with a numerically fixed quota of income opportunities, the position of the master was hereditary. There were also quasi-guild associations and associations derived from guilds in which the right to membership was acquired in hereditary succession. In late Antiquity, membership in the liturgical guilds was even a compulsory and hereditary obligation in the way of a *glebae adscriptio,* which bound the peasant to the soil. Finally, there were also in the medieval Occident 'opprobrious' trades, which were religiously déclassé; these correspond to the 'unclean' castes of India. The fundamental difference, however, between occupational associations and castes is not affected by all these circumstances.

First, that which is partly an exception and partly an occasional consequence for the occupational association is truly fundamental for the caste: the magical distance between castes in their mutual relationships. In 1901 in the 'United Provinces' roughly 10 million people (out of a total of about 40 million) belonged to castes with which physical contact is ritually polluting. In the 'Madras Presidency,' roughly 13 million people (out of about 52 million) could infect others even without direct contact if they approached within a certain, though varying, distance. The merchant and craft guilds of the Middle Ages acknowledged no ritual barriers whatsoever between the individual guilds and artisans, apart from the aforementioned small stratum of people engaged in opprobrious trades. Pariah peoples and pariah workers (for example, the knacker and hangman), by virtue of their special positions, come sociologically close to the unclean castes of India. And there were factual barriers restricting the connubium between differently esteemed occupations, but there were no ritual barriers, such as are absolutely essential for caste. Within the circle of the 'honorable' people, ritual barriers of commensalism were completely absent; but such barriers belong to the basis of caste differences.

Furthermore, caste is essentially hereditary. This hereditary character was not, and is not, merely the result of monopolizing and restricting the earning opportunities to a definite maximum quota, as was the case among the absolutely closed guilds of the Occident, which at no time were numerically predominant. Such quota restriction existed, and still exists in part, among the occupational castes of India; but restriction is strongest not in the cities but in the villages, where a quota restriction of opportunities, in so far as it has existed, has had no connection with a 'guild' organization and has had no need for it. As we shall see, the typical Indian village artisans have been the hereditary 'tied cottagers' of the village.

The most important castes, although not all castes, have guaranteed the individual member a certain subsistence, as was the case among our master craftsmen. But not all castes have monopolized a whole trade, as the guild at least strove to do. The guild of the Occident, at least during the Middle Ages, was regularly based upon the apprentice's free choice of a master and thus it made possible the transition of the children to occupations other than those of their parents, a circumstance which never occurs in the caste system. This difference is fundamental. Whereas the closure of the guilds toward the outside became stricter with diminishing income opportunities, among the castes the reverse was often observed, namely, they maintain their ritually required way of life, and hence their inherited trade, most easily when income opportunities are plentiful.

Another difference between guild and caste is of even greater importance. The occupational associations of the medieval Occident were often engaged in violent struggles among themselves, but at the same time they evidenced a tendency towards fraternization. The *mercanzia* and the *popolo* in Italy, and the 'citizenry' in the north, were regularly associations of occupational associations. The *capitano del popolo* in the south and frequently, though not always, the *Bürgermeister* in the north were heads of oath-bound organizations of the occupational associations, at least according to their original and specific meaning. Such organizations grabbed political power, either legally or illegally. Irrespective of their legal forms, the late medieval city *in fact* rested upon the fraternization of its productive citizenry. This was at least the case where the political form of the medieval city contained its most important sociological characteristics.

As a rule the fraternization of the citizenry was carried through by the fraternization of the guilds, just as the ancient *polis* in its innermost being rested upon the fraternization of military associations and sibs. Note that the base was 'fraternization.' It was not of secondary importance that every foundation of the Occidental city, during Antiquity and the Middle Ages, went hand in hand with the establishment of a cultic community of the citizens. Furthermore, it is of significance that the common meal of the *prytanes,* the drinking rooms of the merchant and craft guilds, and their common processions to the church played such a great role in the official documents of the Occidental cities, and that the medieval citizens had, at least in the Lord's Supper, commensalism with one another in the most festive form. Fraternization at all times presupposes commensalism; it does not have to be actually practiced in everyday life, but it must be ritually possible. The caste order precluded this.

Complete [5] 'fraternization' of castes has been and is impossible because it is one of the constitutive principles of the castes that there should be at least ritually irremediable barriers against complete commensalism among different castes.[6] If the member of a low caste merely looks at the meal of a Brahman, it ritually defiles the Brahman. When the last great famine [7] caused the British administration, to open public soup kitchens accessible to everyone, the tally of patrons showed that impoverished people of all castes had in their need visited the kitchens, although it was of course strictly and ritually taboo to eat in this manner in the sight of people not belonging to one's caste. At that time the strict castes were not satisfied with the possibility of cleansing magical defilement by ritual penance. Yet under threat of excommunicating the participants, they did succeed in seeing to it that high-caste cooks were employed; the hands of these cooks were considered ritually clean by all the castes concerned. Furthermore, they saw to it that often a sort of symbolic *chambre separée* was created for each caste by means of chalk lines drawn around the tables and similar devices. Apart from the fact that in the face of starvation even strong magical powers fail to carry weight, every strictly ritualist religion, such as the Indian, Hebrew, and Roman, is able to open ritualist back doors for extreme situations. Yet, from this situation to a possible commensalism and fraternization as they are known in the Occident is a very long way. To be sure, during the rise of the kingdoms, we find that the king invited the various castes, the Sudra included, to his table. They were seated, however, at least according to the classic conception, in separate rooms; and the fact that a caste that claimed to belong to the Vaisya was seated among the Sudra in the Vellala Charita occasioned a (semi-legendary) famous conflict, which we shall have to discuss later.

Let us now consider the Occident. In his letter to the Galatians (II:12, 13 ff.) Paul reproaches Peter for having eaten in Antioch with the Gentiles and for having withdrawn and separated himself afterwards, under the influence of the Jerusalemites. 'And the other Jews dissembled likewise with him.' That the reproach of dissimulation made to this very apostle has not been effaced shows perhaps just as clearly as does the occurrence itself the tremendous importance this event had for the early Christians. Indeed, this shattering of the ritual barriers against commensalism meant a shattering of the voluntary Ghetto, which in its effects is far more incisive than any compulsory Ghetto. It meant to shatter the situation of Jewry as a pariah people, a situation that was ritually imposed upon this people. For the Christians it meant the origin of Christian 'freedom,' which Paul again and again celebrated triumphantly; for this freedom meant the universalism of Paul's mission, which cut across nations and status groups. The elimination of all ritual barriers of birth for the community of the eucharists, as realized in Antioch, was, in connection with the religious preconditions, the hour of conception for the Occidental 'citizenry.' This is the case even though its birth occurred more than a thousand years later in the revolutionary *conjurationes* of the medieval cities. For without commensalism—in Christian terms, without the Lord's Supper in common—no oath-bound fraternity and no medieval urban citizenry would have been possible.

India's caste order formed an obstacle against this, which was unsurmountable, at least by its own forces. For the castes are not governed only by this eternal ritual division.[8] Even if there are no antagonisms of economic interests, a profound estrangement usually exists between the castes, and often deadly jealousy and hostility as well, precisely because the castes are completely oriented towards 'social rank.' This orientation stands in contrast to the occupational associations of the Occident. Whatever part questions of etiquette and rank have played among these associations, and often it has been quite considerable, such questions could never have gained the religiously anchored significance which they have had for the Hindu.

The consequences of this difference have been of considerable political importance. By its solidarity, the association of Indian guilds, the *mahajan,* was a force which the princes had to take very much into account. It was said: 'The prince must recognize what the guilds do to the people, whether it is merciful or cruel.' The guilds acquired privileges from the princes for loans of money, which are reminiscent of our medieval conditions. The *shreshti* (elders) of the guilds belonged to the mightiest notables and ranked equally with the warrior and the priest nobility of their time. In the areas and during the periods when these conditions prevailed, the power of the castes was undeveloped and partly hindered and shaken by the religions of salvation, which were hostile to the Brahmans. The later turn in favor of the monopoly rule of the caste system not only increased the power of the Brahmans but also that of the princes, and it broke the power of the guilds. For the castes excluded every solidarity and every politically powerful fraternization of the citizenry and of the trades. If the prince observed the ritual traditions and the social pretensions based upon them, which existed among those castes most important for him, he could not only play the castes off against one another—which he did—but he had nothing whatever to fear from them, especially if the Brahmans stood by his side. Accordingly, it is not difficult even at this point to guess the political interests which had a hand in the game during the transformation to monopoly rule of the caste system. This shift steered India's social structure—which for a time apparently stood close to the threshold of European urban development—into a course that led far away from any possibility of such development. In these world-historical differences the fundamentally important contrast between 'caste' and 'guild,' or any other 'occupational association,' is strikingly revealed.

If the caste differs fundamentally from the 'guild' and from any other kind of merely occupational association, and if the core of the caste system is connected with social rank, how then is the caste related to the 'status group,' which finds its genuine expression in social rank?

3: Caste and Status Group

What is a 'status group'? 'Classes' are groups of people who, from the standpoint of specific interests, have the same economic position. Ownership or non-ownership of material goods or of definite skills constitute the 'class-situation.' 'Status' is a quality of social honor or a lack of it, and is in the main conditioned as well as expressed through a specific style of life. Social honor can stick directly to a class-situation, and it is also, indeed most of the time, determined by the average class-situation of the status-group members. This, however, is not necessarily the case. Status membership, in turn, influences the class-situation in that the style of life required by status groups makes them prefer special kinds of property or gainful pursuits and reject others. A status group can be closed ('status by descent') or it can be open.*

Now, a caste is doubtlessly a closed status group. For all the obligations and barriers that membership in a status group entails also exist in a caste, in which they are intensified to the utmost degree. The Occident has known legally closed 'estates,' in the sense that intermarriage with non-members of the group was lacking. But, as a rule, this bar against connubium held only to the extent that marriages contracted in spite of the rule constituted *mésalliances,* with the consequence that children of the 'left-handed' marriage would follow the status of the lower partner.

Europe still acknowledges such status barriers for the high nobility. America acknowledges them between Whites and Blacks (including all mixed bloods) in the Southern States of the Union. But in America these barriers imply that marriage is absolutely and legally inadmissible,

---

* It is incorrect to think of the 'occupational status group' as an alternative. The 'style of life,' not the 'occupation,' is always decisive. This style may require a certain profession (for instance, military service), but the nature of the occupational service resulting from the claims of a style of life always remains decisive (for instance, military service as a knight rather than as a mercenary).

quite apart from the fact that such intermarriage would result in social boycott.

Among the Hindu castes at the present time, not only intermarriage between castes but even intermarriage between sub-castes is usually absolutely shunned. Already in the 'Books of Law' mixed bloods from different castes belong to a lower caste than either of the parents, and in no case do they belong to the three higher ('twice-born') castes. A different state of affairs, however, prevailed in earlier days and still exists today for the most important castes. Today one occasionally meets with full connubium among sub-castes of the same caste, as well as among castes of equal social standing.[9] In the earlier times this was undoubtedly more often the case. Above all, originally connubium was obviously not absolutely excluded, but rather hypergamy was the rule.[10] Intermarriage between a girl of higher caste to a lower-caste man was considered an offense against the status honor on the part of the girl's family. However, to own a wife of lower caste was not considered an offense, and her children were not considered degraded, or at least only partially so. According to the law of inheritance, which is certainly the product of a later period, the children had to take second place in inheritance (just as in Israel the sentence that the 'children of the servant'—and of the foreign woman—'should not inherit in Israel' has been the law of a later period, as is the case everywhere else).

The interest of upper-class men in the legality of polygamy, which they could economically afford, continued to exist, even after the acute shortage of women among the invading warriors was terminated. Such shortages have everywhere compelled conquerors to marry girls of subject populations. The result in India was, however, that the lower-caste girls had a large marriage market, and the lower the caste stood the larger was their marriage market; whereas the marriage market for girls of the highest castes was restricted to their own caste. Moreover, by virtue of the competition of the lower-caste girls, this restricted marriage market was by no means monopolistically guaranteed to upper-caste girls. And this caused the women in the lower castes, by virtue of the general demand for women, to bring high prices as brides. It was in consequence of this dearth of women, in part, that polyandry originated. The formation of marriage cartels among villages or among special associations, Golis, as frequently found, for instance, among the Vania (merchant) castes in Gujarat and also among peasant castes, is a counter-measure against the hypergamy of the wealthy and the city people, which raised the price of brides for the middle classes and for the rural population.[11]

Among the upper castes, however, the sale of girls to a bridegroom of rank was difficult, and the more difficult it became, the more was failure to marry considered a disgrace for both the girl and her parents. The bridegroom had to be bought by the parents with incredibly high dowries, and his enlistment (through professional matchmakers) became the parents' most important worry. Even during the infancy of the girl it was a sorrow for the parents. Finally it was considered an outright 'sin' for a girl to reach puberty without being married. This has led to grotesque results: for example, the marriage practice of the Kulin Brahmans, which enjoys a certain fame. The Kulin Brahmans are highly demanded as bridegrooms; they have made a business of contractually marrying girls *in absentia* upon request and for money, girls who thus escape the ignominy of maidenhood. The girls, however, remain with their families and happen to see the bridegroom only if business or other reasons accidentally bring him to a place where he has one (or several) such 'wives' in residence. Then he shows his marriage contract to the father-in-law and uses the father's house as a 'cheap hotel.' In addition, without any costs, he has the enjoyment of the girl, for she is considered his 'legitimate' wife.

Elsewhere infanticide is usually a result of restricted opportunities for subsistence among poor populations. But in India female infanticide was instituted precisely by the upper castes,[12] and existed alongside of child marriage. Child marriage has determined, first, the fact that in India some girls in the age groups of 5 to 10 years are already widowed and that they remain widowed for life. This is connected with widow celibacy, an institution which, in India as elsewhere, was added to widow suicide. Widow suicide was derived from the custom of chivalry: the burial of his personal belongings, especially his women, with the dead lord. Secondly, marriages of immature girls has brought about a high mortality rate in childbed.

All of this makes it clear that in the field of connubium, caste increases 'status' principles in an extreme manner. Today hypergamy exists as a general caste rule only within the same caste, and even there it is a specialty of the Rajput caste and of some others that stand close to the Rajput socially, or to their ancient tribal territory. This is the case, for instance, with such castes as the Bhat, Khatri, Karwar, Gujar, and Jat. However, the rule is strict endogamy of the caste and of the sub-caste;

408   SOCIAL STRUCTURES

in the case of the latter, this rule is, in the main, broken only by marriage cartels.

The norms of commensalism are similar to those of connubium: a status group has no social intercourse with social inferiors. In the Southern States of America, all social intercourse between a White and a Negro would result in the boycott of the former. As a 'status group,' 'caste' enhances and transposes this social closure into the sphere of religion, or rather of magic. The ancient concepts of 'taboo' and their social applications were indeed widely diffused in India's geographical environs and may well have contributed materials to this process. To these taboos were added borrowed totemist ritualisms and, finally, notions of the magical impurity of certain activities, such as have existed everywhere with widely varying content and intensity.

The Hinduist dietary rules are not exactly simple in nature and by no means do they concern merely the questions (1) what may be eaten, and (2) who may eat together at the same table. These two points are covered by strict rules, which are chiefly restricted to members of the same caste. The dietary rules concern above all the further questions: (3) Out of whose hand may one take food of a certain kind? For genteel houses this means above all: Whom may one use for a cook? And a further question is: (4) Whose mere glance upon the food is to be excluded? With (3) there is a difference to be noted between foods and drinks, according to whether water and food cooked in water (*kachcha*), is concerned, or whether food cooked is melted butter (*pakka*) is concerned. *Kachcha* is far more exclusive. The question with whom one may smoke is closely connected with norms of commensality in the narrower sense. Originally, one smoked out of the same pipe, which was passed around; therefore, smoking together was dependent upon the degree of ritual purity of the partner. All these rules, however, belong in one and the same category of a far broader set of norms, all of which are 'status' characteristics of ritual caste rank.

The social rank positions of all castes depend upon the question of from whom the highest castes accept *kachcha* and *pakka* and with whom they dine and smoke. Among the Hindu castes the Brahmans are always at the top in such connections. But the following questions are equal in importance to these, and closely connected with them: Does a Brahman undertake the religious services of the members of a caste? And possibly: to which of the very differently evaluated sub-castes does the Brahman belong? Just as the Brahman is the last though not the only authority in determining, by his behavior in questions of commensalism, the rank of a caste, so likewise does he determine questions of services. The barber of a ritually clean caste unconditionally serves only certain castes. He may shave and care for the 'manicure' of others, but not for their 'pedicure.' And he does not serve some castes at all. Other wage workers, especially laundrymen, behave in a similar manner. Usually, although with some exceptions, commensality is attached to the caste; connubium is almost always attached to the sub-caste; whereas usually, although with exceptions, the services by priests and wageworkers are attached to commensality.

The discussion above may suffice to demonstrate the extraordinary complexity of the rank relations of the caste system. It may also show the factors by which the caste differs from an ordinary status order. The caste order is oriented religiously and ritually, to a degree not even approximately attained elsewhere. If the expression 'church' was not inapplicable to Hinduism, one could perhaps speak of a rank order of church-estates.

4: The Social Rank Order of the Castes in General

When the Census of India (1901) attempted to order by rank contemporary Hindu castes in the presidencies—two to three thousand or even more, according to the method of counting used—certain groups of castes were established which are distinguishable from one another according to the following criteria:

First come the Brahmans, and following them, a series of castes which, rightly or wrongly, claim to belong to the two other 'twice-born' castes of classical theory: the Kshatriya and the Vaisya. In order to signify this, they claim the right to wear the 'holy belt.' This is a right which some of them have only recently rediscovered and which, in the view of the Brahman castes, who are seniors in rank, would certainly belong only to some members of the 'twice-born' castes. But as soon as the right of a caste to wear the holy belt is acknowledged, this caste is unconditionally recognized as being absolutely ritually 'clean.' From such a caste the high-caste Brahmans accept food of every kind. Throughout the system, a third group of castes follows. They are counted among the Satsudra, the 'clean Sudra' of classical doctrine. In Northern and Central India they are the Jalacharaniya, that is, castes who may give water to a Brahman and from whose *lota* (water kettle) the Brahman accepts water. Close to them are castes, in Northern and Central India, whose water a Brahman would either not always accept (that is, acceptance or non-acceptance would possibly depend on the Brahman's rank) or whose water he would never accept (Jalabyabaharya). The high-caste barber does not serve them unconditionally (no pedicure), and the laundryman does not wash their laundry. But they are not considered absolutely 'unclean' ritually. They are the Sudra in the usual sense in which the classical teachings refer to them. Finally, there are castes who are considered unclean. All temples are closed to them, and no Brahman and no barber will serve them. They must live outside the village district, and they infect either by touch or, in Southern India, even by their presence at a distance (up to sixty-four feet with the Paraiyans). All these restrictions are related to those castes which, according to the classical doctrine, originated from ritually forbidden sexual intercourse between members of different castes.

Even though this grouping of castes is not equally true throughout India (indeed there are striking exceptions), nevertheless on the whole it can be quite well sustained. Within these groupings one could proceed with further gradations of caste rank, but such gradations would present extremely varied characteristics: among the upper castes the criterion would be the correctness of life practices with regard to sib organization, endogamy, child marriage, widow celibacy, cremation of the dead, ancestral sacrifice, foods and drinks, and social intercourse with unclean castes. Among the lower caste one would have to differentiate according to the rank of the Brahmans who are still ready to serve them or who will no longer do so, and according to whether or not castes other than Brahmans accept water from them. In all these cases, it is by no means rare that castes of lower rank raise stricter demands than castes who otherwise are considered to have a higher standing. The extraordinary variety of such rules of rank order forbids here any closer treatment. The acceptance or avoidance of meat, at least of beef, is decisive for caste rank, and is therefore a symptom of it, but an uncertain one. The kinds of occupation and income, which entail the most far-reaching consequences for connubium, commensalism, and ritual rank, are decisive in the case of all castes. We shall speak of this later.

In addition to all these criteria, we find a mass of individual traits.[13] Yet even if we took them all into account, we could not establish a list of castes according to rank. This is the case simply because rank differs absolutely from place to place, because only some of the castes are univer-

sally diffused, and because a great many castes, being only locally represented, have no inter-local rank order which could be determined.
Furthermore, great rank differences appear between sub-castes of a
single caste, especially among the upper castes, but also among some of
the middle castes. One would often have to place individual sub-castes
far behind another caste, which otherwise would be evaluated as lower.

In general, the problem arose (for the census workers): Which unit
should really be considered a 'caste'? Within one and the same 'caste,'
that is, a group considered to be a caste in Hindu tradition, there is
neither necessarily connubium nor always full commensalism. Connubium is the case with only a few castes, and even with them there are
reservations. The 'sub-caste' is the predominantly endogamous unit, and
in some castes there are several hundred sub-castes. The sub-castes are
either purely local castes (diffused over districts of varying size), and/or
they constitute associations which are delimited and especially designated according to actual or alleged descent, former or present kind of
occupational pursuit, or other differences in style of life. They consider
themselves as parts of the caste and in addition to their own names carry
the name of the caste; they may be legitimated in this by a division of
the caste, or by reception into the caste, or simply by usurpation of rank.
Only the sub-castes actually live a life of unified regulation, and they
alone are organized—in so far as a caste organization exists. Caste itself
often designates merely a social claim raised by these closed associations.
Often, but not always, the caste is the womb of the sub-caste; and on
rare occasions the caste is characterized by certain organizations common
to all sub-castes. More frequently, the caste has certain characteristics of
life-conduct traditionally common to all sub-castes. Nevertheless, as a
rule the unity of caste exists side by side with the unity of sub-castes.
There are sanctions against marriage and commensalism outside the
caste which are stronger than those imposed upon members of different
sub-castes within the same caste. Also, just as new sub-castes form themselves easily, the barriers between them may be more unstable; whereas
the barriers between communities once recognized as castes are maintained with extraordinary perseverance. . .

5: Castes and Traditionalism

K. Marx has characterized the peculiar position of the artisan in the
Indian village—his dependence upon fixed payment in kind instead of

upon production for the market—as the reason for the specific 'stability of the Asiatic peoples.' In this, Marx was correct.

In addition to the ancient village artisan, however, there was the merchant and also the urban artisan; and the latter either worked for the market or was economically dependent upon merchant guilds, as in the Occident. India has always been predominantly a country of villages. Yet the beginnings of cities were also modest in the Occident, especially inland, and the position of the urban market in India was regulated by the princes in many ways 'mercantilistically'—in a similar sense as in the territorial states at the beginnings of modern times. In any case, in so far as social stratification is concerned, not only the position of the village artisan but also the caste order as a whole must be viewed as the bearer of stability. One must not think of this effect too directly. One might believe, for instance, that the ritual caste antagonisms had made impossible the development of 'large-scale enterprises' with a division of labor in the same workshop, and might consider this to be decisive. But such is not the case.

The law of caste has proved just as elastic in the face of the necessities of the concentration of labor in workshops as it did in the face of a need for concentration of labor and service in the noble household. All domestic servants required by the upper castes were ritually clean, as we have seen. The principle, 'the artisan's hand is always clean in his occupation,'[14] is a similar concession to the necessity of being allowed to have fixtures made or repair work done, personal services, or other work accomplished by wage workers not belonging to the household or by other itinerants. Likewise, the workshop[15] (ergasterium) was recognized as 'clean.' Hence no ritual factor would have been in the way of jointly using different castes in the same large workroom, just as little as the ban upon interest during the Middle Ages, as such, hindered the development of industrial capital, which did not even emerge in the form of investment for fixed interest. The core of the obstacle did not lie in such particular difficulties, which every one of the great religious systems in its way has placed, or has seemed to place, in the way of the modern economy. The core of the obstruction was rather imbedded in the 'spirit' of the whole system. In modern times it has not always been easy, but eventually it has been possible to employ Indian caste labor in modern factories. And even earlier it was possible to exploit the labor of Indian artisans capitalistically in the forms usual elsewhere in colonial areas, after the finished mechanism of modern capitalism once could be imported from Europe. Even if all this has come about, it must still be considered extremely unlikely that the modern organization of industrial capitalism would ever have *originated* on the basis of the caste system. A ritual law in which every change of occupation, every change in work technique, could result in ritual degradation is certainly not capable of giving birth to economic and technical revolutions from within itself, or even of facilitating the first germination of capitalism in its midst.

The artisan's traditionalism, great in itself, was necessarily heightened to the extreme by the caste order. Commercial capital, in its attempts to organize industrial labor on the basis of the putting-out system, had to face an essentially stronger resistance in India than in the Occident. The traders themselves in their ritual seclusion remained in the shackles of the typical Oriental merchant class, which by itself has never created a modern capitalist organization of labor. The situation is as if none but different guest peoples, like the Jews, ritually exclusive toward one another and toward third parties, were to follow their trades in one economic area. Some of the great Hinduist merchant castes, particularly, for instance, the Vania, have been called the 'Jews of India,' and, in this negative sense, rightly so. They were, in part, virtuosos in unscrupulous profiteering.

Nowadays a considerable tempo in the accumulation of wealth is singularly evident among castes which were formerly considered socially degraded or unclean and which therefore were especially little burdened with (in our sense) 'ethical' expectations addressed to themselves. In the accumulation of wealth, such castes compete with others which formerly monopolized the positions of scribes, officials, or collectors of farmed-out taxes, as well as similar opportunities for politically determined earnings typical of patrimonial states. Some of the capitalist entrepreneurs also derive from the merchant castes. But in capitalist enterprise they could keep up with the castes of literati only to the extent to which they acquired the 'education' nowadays necessary—as has been occasionally noticed above.[16] The training for trade is among them in part so intense —as far as the reports allow for insight—that their specific 'gift' for trading must by no means rest upon any 'natural disposition.'[17] But we have no indication that by themselves they could have created the rational enterprise of modern capitalism.

Finally, modern capitalism undoubtedly would never have originated from the circles of the completely traditionalist Indian trades. The Hinduist artisan is, nevertheless, notorious for his extreme industry; he is considered to be essentially more industrious than is the Indian artisan, who is of Islamic faith. And, on the whole, the Hinduist caste organization has often developed a very great intensity of work and of property accumulation within the ancient occupational castes. The intensity of work holds more for handicraft and for individual ancient agricultural castes. By the way, the Kunbis (for instance those in South India) achieve a considerable accumulation of wealth, and nowadays, as a matter of fact, it is in modern forms.

Modern industrial capitalism, in particular the factory, made its entry into India under the British administration and with direct and strong incentives. But comparatively speaking, how small is the scale and how great the difficulties! After several hundred years of English domination there are today only about 980,000 factory workers, that is, about one-third of one per cent of the population.[18] In addition, the recruitment of labor is difficult, even in those manufacturing industries with the highest wages. (In Calcutta, labor often has to be recruited from the outside. In one near-by village, hardly one-ninth of the people speak the native language of Bengal.) Only the most recent acts for the protection of labor have made factory work somewhat more popular. Female labor is found only here and there, and then it is recruited from among the most despised castes, although there are textile industries where women can accomplish twice as much as men.

Indian factory labor shows exactly those traditionalist traits which also characterized labor in Europe during the early period of capitalism. The workers want to earn some money quickly in order to establish themselves independently. An increase in wage rate does not mean for them an incentive for more work or for a higher standard of living, but the reverse. They then take longer holidays because they can afford to do so, or their wives decorate themselves with ornaments. To stay away from work as one pleases is recognized as a matter of course, and the worker retires with his meager savings to his home town as soon as possible.[19] He is simply a mere casual laborer. 'Discipline' in the European sense is an unknown idea to him. Hence, despite a fourfold cheaper wage, competition with Europe is maintained easily only in the textile industry, as two-and-a-half times as many workers and far more supervision are required. One advantage for the entrepreneurs is that the caste division of the workers has so far made any trade union organization and any real 'strike' impossible. As we have noticed, the work in the workshop is 'clean' and is performed jointly. (Only separate drinking cups at the well are necessary, at least one for the Hindus and one for the Islamites, and in sleeping quarters only men of the same caste sleep together.) A fraternization of labor, however has (so far) been as little possible as has been a *coniuratio* of the citizens.[20]

XVII. The Chinese Literati

FOR twelve centuries social rank in China has been determined more by qualification for office than by wealth. This qualification, in turn, has been determined by education, and especially by examinations. China has made literary education the yardstick of social prestige in the most exclusive fashion, far more exclusively than did Europe during the period of the humanists, or as Germany has done. Even during the period of the Warring States, the stratum of aspirants for office who were educated in literature—and originally this only meant that they had a scriptural knowledge—extended through all the individual states. Literati have been the bearers of progress toward a rational administration and of all 'intelligence.'

As with Brahmanism in India, in China the literati have been the decisive exponents of the unity of culture. Territories (as well as enclaves) not administered by officials educated in literature, according to the model of the orthodox state idea, were considered heterodox and barbarian, in the same way as were the tribal territories that were within the territory of Hinduism but not regulated by the Brahmans, as well as landscapes not organized as *polis* by the Greeks. The increasingly bureaucratic structure of Chinese polities and of their carriers has given to the whole literary tradition of China its characteristic stamp. For more than two thousand years the literati have definitely been the ruling stratum in China and they still are. Their dominance has been interrupted; often it has been hotly contested; but always it has been renewed and expanded. According to the *Annals,* the Emperor addressed the literati, and them alone, as 'My lords'[1] for the first time in 1496.

It has been of immeasurable importance for the way in which Chinese culture has developed that this leading stratum of intellectuals has never

From 'Konfuzianismus und Taoismus,' chap. 5, Der Literatenstand, in *Gesammelte Aufsaetze zur Religionssoziologie,* vol. i, pp. 395-430. This chapter was originally included in the *Archiv* series, 'Die Wirtschaftsethik der Weltreligionen'—see note to chap. 11.

had the character of the clerics of Christianity or of Islam, or of Jewish rabbis, or Indian Brahmans, or Ancient Egyptian priests, or Egyptian or Indian scribes. It is significant that the stratum of literati in China, although developed from ritual training, grew out of an education for genteel *laymen*. The 'literati' of the feudal period, then officially called *puo che,* that is, 'living libraries,' were first of all proficient in ritualism. They did not, however, stem from the sibs of a priestly nobility, as did the *Rishi* sibs of the *Rig-Veda,* or from a guild of sorcerers, as did in all likelihood the Brahmans of the *Atharva-Veda.*

In China, the literati go back, at least in the main, to the descendants, probably the younger sons, of feudal families who had acquired a literary education, especially the knowledge of writing, and whose social position rested upon this knowledge of writing and of literature. A plebeian could also acquire a knowledge of writing, although, considering the Chinese system of writing, it was difficult. But if the plebeian succeeded, he shared the prestige of any other scholar. Even in the feudal period, the stratum of literati was not hereditary or exclusive—another contrast with the Brahmans.

Until late historical times, Vedic education rested upon oral transmission; it abhorred the fixing of tradition in writing, an abhorrence which all guilds of organized professional magicians are apt to share. In contrast to this, in China the writing of the ritual books, of the calendar, and of the *Annals* go back to prehistoric times.[2] Even in the oldest tradition the ancient scriptures were considered magical objects,[3] and the men conversant with them were considered holders of a magical charisma. As we shall see, these have been persistent facts in China. The prestige of the literati has not consisted in a charisma of magical powers of sorcery, but rather in a knowledge of writing and of literature as such; perhaps their prestige originally rested in addition upon a knowledge of astrology. But it has not been their task to aid private persons through sorcery, to heal the sick, for instance, as the magician does. For such purposes there were special professions, which we shall discuss later. Certainly the significance of magic in China, as everywhere, was a self-understood presupposition. Yet, so far as the interests of the community were concerned, it was up to its representatives to influence the spirits.

The emperor as the supreme pontifex, as well as the princes, functioned for the political community. And for the family, the head of the sib and the housefather influenced the spirits. The fate of the community, above all of the harvest, has been influenced since olden times by rational means, that is, by water regulation; and therefore the correct 'order' of administration has always been the basic means of influencing the world of the spirits.

Apart from knowledge of scriptures as a means of discerning tradition, a knowledge of the calendar and of the stars was required for discerning the heavenly will and, above all, for knowing the *dies fasti* and *nefasti,* and it seems that the position of the literati has also evolved from the dignified role of the court astrologer.[4] The scribes, and they alone, could recognize this important order ritually (and originally probably also by means of horoscopes) and accordingly advise the appropriate political authorities. An anecdote of the *Annals*[5] shows the results in a striking manner.

In the feudal state of the Wei, a proved general—U KI, the alleged author of the textbook in ritually correct strategy which was authoritative until our time—and a literary man competed for the position of first minister. A violent dispute arose between the two after the literary man had been appointed to the post. He readily admitted that he could neither conduct wars nor master similar political tasks in the manner of the general. But when the general thereupon declared himself to be the better man, the literary man remarked that a revolution threatened the dynasty, whereupon the general admitted without any hesitation that the literary man was the better man to prevent it.

Only the adept of scriptures and of tradition has been considered competent for correctly ordering the internal administration and the charismatically correct life conduct of the prince, ritually and politically. In sharpest contrast to the Jewish prophets, who were essentially interested in foreign policy, the Chinese literati-politicians, trained in ritual, were primarily oriented toward problems of internal administration, even if these problems involved absolute power politics, and even though while in charge of the prince's correspondence and of the chancellery they might personally be deeply involved in the guidance of diplomacy.

This constant orientation toward problems of the 'correct' administration of the state determined a far-reaching, practical, and political rationalism among the intellectual stratum of the feudal period. In contrast to the strict traditionalism of the later period, the *Annals* occasionally reveal the literati to be audacious political innovators.[6] Their pride in education knew no limit,[7] and the princes—at least according to the lay-out of the *Annals*—paid them great deference.[8] Their intimate rela-

tions to the service of patrimonial princes existed from ancient times
and has been decisive for the peculiar character of the literati.

The origin of the literati is veiled from us in darkness. Apparently
they were the Chinese *augurs*. The pontifical Cesaro-papist character of
imperial power has been decisive for their position, and the character of
Chinese literature has also been determined by it. There were official
Annals, magically proved hymns of war and sacrifice, calendars, as well
as books of ritual and ceremony. With their knowledge the literati supported the character of the state, which was in the nature of an ecclesiastic and compulsory institution; they took the state for granted as an
axiomatic presupposition.

In their literature, the literati created the concept of 'office,' above all,
the ethos of 'official duty' and of the 'public weal.' [9] If one may trust the
Annals, the literati, being adherents of the bureaucratic organization of
the state as a compulsory institution, were opponents of feudalism from
the very beginning. This is quite understandable because, from the standpoint of their interests, the administrators should be only men who were
personally qualified by a literary education.[10] On the other hand, they
claimed *for themselves* to have shown the princes the way toward
autonomous administration, toward government manufacture of arms
and construction of fortifications, ways and means by which the princes
became 'masters of their lands.' [11]

This close relation of the literati to princely service came about during
the struggle of the prince with the feudal powers. It distinguishes the
Chinese literati from the educated laymen of Hellas, as well as from
those of Ancient India (*Kshatriya*). It makes them similar to the Brahmans, from whom, however, they differ greatly in their ritualist subordination under a Cesaro-papist pontifex. In addition, no caste order has
existed in China, a fact intimately connected with the literary education
and the subordination under a pontifex.

The relation of the literati to the *office* has changed its nature [in the
course of time]. During the Period of the Feudal States, the various
courts competed for the services of the literati, who were seeking opportunities for power and, we must not forget, for the best chances for
income.[12] A whole stratum of vagrant 'sophists' (*che-she*) emerged,
comparable to the wayfaring knights and scholars of the Occidental
Middle Ages. As we shall later see, there were also Chinese literati who,
in principle, remained unattached to any office. This free and mobile
stratum of literati were carriers of philosophical schools and antagonisms,

a situation comparable to those of India, of Hellenic Antiquity, and of the Middle Ages with its monks and scholars. Yet, the literati as such felt themselves to be a unitary status group. They claimed common status honors [13] and were united in the feeling of being the sole bearers of the homogeneous culture of China.

The relation of the Chinese literati to princely service as the normal source of income differentiated them as a status group from the philosophers of Antiquity and from at least the educated laymen of India, who, in the main, were socially anchored in fields remote from any office. As a rule, the Chinese literati strove for princely service both as a source of income and as a normal field of activity. Confucius, like Lao-tse, was an official before he lived as a teacher and writer without attachment to office. We shall see that this relation to state-office (or office in a 'church state') was of fundamental importance for the nature of the mentality of this stratum. For this orientation became increasingly important and exclusive. The opportunities of the princes to compete for the literati ceased to exist in the unified empire. The literati and their disciples then came to compete for the existing offices, and this development could not fail to result in a unified orthodox doctrine adjusted to the situation. This doctrine was to be *Confucianism.*

As Chinese prebendalism grew, the originally free mental mobility of the literati came to a halt. This development was fully underway even at the time when the *Annals* and most of the systematic writings of the literati originated and when the sacred books, which Shi-Hwang-Ti had destroyed, were 'rediscovered.' [14] They were 'rediscovered' in order that they might be revised, retouched, and interpreted by the literati and therewith gain canonical value.

It is evident from the *Annals* that this whole development came about with the pacification of the empire, or rather that it was pushed to its conclusions during this period. Everywhere war has been the business of youth, and the sentence *sexagenarios de ponte* has been a slogan of warriors directed against the 'senate.' The Chinese literati, however, were the 'old men,' or they represented the old men. The *Annals,* as a paradigmatic public confession of the prince Mu kong (of Tsin), transmitted the idea that the prince had sinned by having listened to 'youth' (the warriors) and not to the 'elders,' who, although having no strength, did have experience. [15] In fact, *this* was the decisive point in the turn toward pacifism and therewith toward traditionalism. Tradition displaced charisma.

1 : CONFUCIUS

Even the oldest sections of the classic writings connected with the name of Kung Tse, that is, with Confucius as editor, permit us to recognize the conditions of charismatic warrior kings. (Confucius died in the year 478 B.C.) The heroic songs of the hymnbook (*Shi-king*) tell of kings fighting from war chariots, as do the Hellenic and Indian epics. But considering their character as a whole, even these songs are no longer heralds of individual, and in general, purely human heroism, as are the Homeric and Germanic epics. Even when the *Shi-king* was edited, the king's army had nothing of the romance of the warrior followings or the Homeric adventures. The army already had the character of a disciplined bureaucracy, and above all it had 'officers.' The kings, even in the *Shi-king* no longer win simply because they are the greater heroes. And that is decisive for the spirit of the army. They win because before the Spirit of Heaven they are morally right and because their charismatic virtues are superior, whereas their enemies are godless criminals who, by oppression and trespass upon the ancient customs, have wronged their subjects' weal and thus have forgone their charisma. Victory is the occasion for moralizing reflections rather than heroic joy. In contrast to the sacred scriptures of almost all other ethics, one is struck at once by the lack of any 'shocking' expression, of any even conceivably 'indecent' image. Obviously, a very systematic expurgation has taken place here, and this may well have been the specific contribution of Confucius.

The pragmatic transformation of the ancient tradition in the *Annals,* produced by official historiography and by the literati, obviously went beyond the priestly paradigms performed in the Old Testament, for example, in the Book of Judges. The chronicle expressly ascribed to Confucius' authorship contains the driest and most sober enumeration of military campaigns and punitive expeditions against rebels; in this respect it is comparable to the hieroglyphic protocols of Assyria. If Confucius really expressed the opinion that his character could be recognized with special clarity from this work—as tradition maintains—then one would have to endorse the view of those (Chinese and European) scholars who interpret this to mean that his characteristic achievement was this systematic and pragmatic correction of facts from the point of view of 'propriety.' His work must have appeared in this light to his contemporaries, but for us its pragmatic meaning, in the main, has become opaque.[16]

The princes and ministers of the classics act and speak like paradigms of rulers whose ethical conduct is rewarded by Heaven. Officialdom and the promotion of officials according to merit are topics for glorification. The princely realms are still ruled hereditarily; some of the local offices are hereditary fiefs; but the classics view this system skeptically, at least the hereditary offices. Ultimately they consider this system to be merely provisional. In theory, this pertains even to the hereditary nature of the dignity of the emperor. The ideal and legendary emperors (Yao and Shun) designate their successors (Shun and Yü) without regard to birth, from the circle of their ministers and over the heads of their own sons, solely according to their personal charisma as certified by the highest court officials. The emperors designate their ministers in the same way, and only the third Emperor, Yü, does not name his first minister (Y) but his son (Ki) to become his successor.

In contrast with the old and genuine documents and monuments, one looks in vain for genuinely heroic minds in most of the classic writings. The traditional view held by Confucius is that caution is the better part of valor and that it ill behooves the wise man to risk his own life inappropriately. The profound pacification of the country, especially after the rule of the Mongols, greatly enhanced this mood. The empire became an empire of peace. According to Mencius, there were no 'just' wars within the frontiers of the empire, as it was considered as one unit. Compared to the size of the empire, the army had finally become very tiny. After having separated the training of the literati from that of the knights, the Emperors retained sport and literary contests and gave military certificates [17] in addition to the state examinations of the literati. Yet for a long time the attainment of such military certificates had hardly any connection with an actual career in the army.[18] And the fact remained that the military were just as despised in China as they were in England for two hundred years, and that a cultivated literary man would not engage in social intercourse on an equal footing with army officers.[19]

2: The Development of the Examination System

During the period of the central monarchy, the mandarins became a status group of certified claimants to office prebends. All categories of

Chinese civil servants were recruited from their midst, and their qualification for office and rank depended upon the number of examinations they had successfully passed.

These examinations consisted of three major degrees,[20] which were considerably augmented by intermediary, repetitive, and preliminary examinations as well as by numerous special conditions. For the first degree alone there were ten types of examinations. The question usually put to a stranger of unknown rank was how many examinations he had passed. Thus, in spite of the ancestor cult, how many ancestors one had was not decisive for social rank. The very reverse held: it depended upon one's official rank whether one was allowed to have an ancestral temple (or a mere table of ancestors, which was the case with illiterates). How many ancestors one was permitted to mention was determined by official rank.[21] Even the rank of a city god in the Pantheon depended upon the rank of the city's mandarin.

In the Confucian period (sixth to fifth century B.C.), the possibility of ascent into official positions as well as the system of examinations was still unknown. It appears that as a rule, at least in the feudal states, the 'great families' were in the possession of power. It was not until the Han dynasty—which was established by a parvenu—that the bestowal of offices according to merit was raised to the level of a principle. And not until the Tang dynasty, in A.D. 690, were regulations set up for the highest degree. As we have already mentioned, it is highly probable that literary education, perhaps with a few exceptions, was at first actually, and perhaps also legally, monopolized by the 'great families,' just as the Vedic education in India was monopolized. Vestiges of this continued to the end. Members of the imperial sib, although not freed from all examinations, were freed from the examination for the first degree. And the trustees, whom every candidate for examinations, until recently, had to name, had to testify to the candidate's 'good family background.' During modern times this testimony has only meant the exclusion of descendants of barbers, bailiffs, musicians, janitors, carriers, and others. Yet alongside this exclusion there was the institution of 'candidates for the mandarinate,' that is, the descendants of mandarins enjoyed a special and preferred position in fixing the maximum quota of examination candidates from each province. The promotion lists used the official formula 'from a mandarin family and from the people.' The sons of well-deserved officials held the lowest degree as a title of honor. All of which represent residues of ancient conditions.

The examination system has been fully carried through since the end of the seventh century. This system was one of the means the patrimonial ruler used in preventing the formation of a closed estate, which, in the manner of feudal vassals and office nobles, would have monopolized the rights to the office prebends. The first traces of the examination system *seem* to emerge about the time of Confucius (and Huang K'an) in the sub-state of Chin, a locality which later became autocratic. The selection of candidates was determined essentially by military merit. Yet, even the *Li Chi* and the *Chou Li*[22] demand, in a quite rationalist way, that the district chiefs examine their lower officials periodically with regard to their morals, and then propose to the emperor which of them should be promoted. In the unified state of the Han emperors, pacifism began to direct the selection of officials. The power of the literati was tremendously consolidated after they had succeeded in elevating the correct Kuang wu to the throne in A.D. 21 and in maintaining him against the popular 'usurper' Wang Mang. During the struggle for prebends, which raged during the following period and which we shall deal with later, the literati developed into a unified *status group*.

Even today the Tang dynasty irradiates the glory of having been the actual creator of China's greatness and culture. The Tang dynasty, for the first time, regulated the literati's position and established colleges for their education (in the seventh century). It also created the *Han lin yuan,* the so-called 'academy,' which first edited the *Annals* in order to gain precedents, and then controlled the emperor's correct deportment. Finally, after the Mongol storms, the national Ming dynasty in the fourteenth century decreed statutes which, in essence, were definitive.[23] Schools were to be set up in every village, one for every twenty-five families. As the schools were not subsidized, the decree remained a dead letter—or rather we have already seen which powers gained control over the schools. Officials selected the best pupils and enrolled a certain number in the colleges. In the main, these colleges have decayed, although in part they have been newly founded. In 1382, prebends in the form of rice rents were set aside for the 'students.' In 1393, the number of students was fixed. After 1370, only examined men had claims to offices.

At once a fight set in between the various regions, especially between the North and the South. The South even then supplied candidates for examinations who were more cultured, having experienced a more comprehensive environment. But the North was the military foundation stone of the empire. Hence, the emperor intervened and *punished* (!)

the examiners who had given the 'first place' to a Southerner. Separate lists for the North and the South were set up, and moreover, a struggle for the patronage of offices began immediately. Even in 1387 special examinations were given to officers' sons. The officers and officials, however, went further, and demanded the right to designate their successors, which meant a demand for re-feudalization. In 1393 this was conceded, but in the end only in a modified form. The candidates presented were preferentially enrolled in the colleges, and prebends were to be reserved for them: in 1465 for three sons, in 1482 for one son. In 1453 we meet with the purchase of college places, and in 1454 with the purchase of offices. During the fifteenth century, as is always the case, these developments arose from the need for military funds. In 1492 these measures were abolished, but in 1529 they were reintroduced.

The *departments* also fought against one another. The Board of Rites was in charge of the examinations after 736, but the Board of Civil Office appointed the officials. The examined candidates were not infrequently boycotted by the latter department, the former answering by going on strike during the examinations. Formally, the minister of rites, actually, the minister of offices (the major-domo) were in the end the most powerful men in China. Then merchants, who were expected to be less 'stingy,' came into office.[24] Of course, this hope was quite unjustified. The Manchus favored the old traditions and thus the literati and, as far as possible, 'purity' in the distribution of offices. But now, as before, three routes to office existed side by side: (1) imperial favors for the sons of the 'princely' families (examination privileges); (2) easy examinations (officially every three to six years) for the lower officials by the higher officials who controlled patronage; this inevitably led each time to advancement also to higher positions; (3) the only legal way: to qualify effectively and purely by examination.

In the main, the system of examinations has actually fulfilled the functions as conceived by the emperor. Occasionally (in 1372), it was suggested to the emperor—one can imagine by whom—that he draw the conclusion from the orthodox charisma of virtues by abolishing the examinations, since virtue *alone* legitimizes and qualifies. This conclusion was soon dropped, which is quite understandable. For after all, both parties, emperor and graduates, had a stake in the examination system, or at least they thought they had. From the emperor's standpoint, the examination system corresponded entirely to the role which the *mjestnit-shestvo,* a technically heterogeneous means, of Russian despotism played for the Russian nobility. The system facilitated a competitive struggle for prebends and offices among the candidates, which stopped them from joining together into a feudal office nobility. Admittance to the ranks of aspirants was open to everybody who was proved to be educationally qualified. The examination system thus fulfilled its purpose.

3: The Typological Position of Confucian Education

We shall now discuss the position of this educational system among the great types of education. To be sure, we cannot here, in passing, give a sociological typology of pedagogical ends and means, but perhaps some comments may be in place.

Historically, the two polar opposites in the field of educational ends are: to awaken charisma, that is, heroic qualities or magical gifts; and, to impart specialized expert training. The first type corresponds to the charismatic structure of domination; the latter type corresponds to the *rational* and bureaucratic (modern) structure of domination. The two types do not stand opposed, with no connections or transitions between them. The warrior hero or the magician also needs special training, and the expert official is generally not trained exclusively for knowledge. However, they are polar opposites of types of education and they form the most radical contrasts. Between them are found all those types which aim at cultivating the pupil for a *conduct of life,* whether it is of a mundane or of a religious character. In either case, the life conduct is the conduct of a status group.

The charismatic procedure of ancient magical asceticism and the hero trials, which sorcerers and warrior heroes have applied to boys, tried to aid the novice to acquire a 'new soul,' in the animist sense, and hence, to be reborn. Expressed in our language, this means that they merely wished to *awaken* and to test a capacity which was considered a purely personal gift of grace. For one can neither teach nor train for charisma. Either it exists *in nuce,* or it is infiltrated through a miracle of magical rebirth—otherwise it cannot be attained.

Specialized and expert schooling attempts to *train* the pupil for practical usefulness for administrative purposes—in the organization of public authorities, business offices, workshops, scientific or industrial laboratories, disciplined armies. In principle, this can be accomplished with anybody, though to varying extent.

The pedagogy of cultivation, finally, attempts to *educate* a cultivated type of man, whose nature depends on the decisive stratum's respective ideal of cultivation. And this means to educate a man for a certain internal and external deportment in life. In principle this can be done with everybody, only the goal differs. If a separate stratum of warriors form the decisive status group—as in Japan—education will aim at making the pupil a stylized knight and courtier, who despises the pen-pushers as the Japanese Samurai have despised them. In particular cases, the stratum may display great variations of type. If a priestly stratum is decisive, it will aim at making the disciple a scribe, or at least an intellectual, likewise of greatly varying character. In reality, none of these types ever occurs in pure form. The numerous combinations and intermediary links cannot be discussed in this context. What is important here is to define the position of Chinese education in terms of these forms.

The holdovers of the primeval charismatic training for regeneration, the milk name, the previously discussed initiation rites of youth, the bridegroom's change of name, and so on, have for a long time in China been a formula (in the manner of the Protestant confirmation) standing beside the testing of educational qualifications. Such tests have been monopolized by the political authorities. The educational qualification, however, in view of the educational means employed, has been a 'cultural' qualification, in the sense of a general education. It was of a similar, yet of a more specific nature than, for instance, the *humanist* educational qualification of the Occident.

In Germany, such an education, until recently and almost exclusively, was a prerequisite for the official career leading to positions of command in civil and military administration. At the same time this *humanist* education has stamped the pupils who were to be prepared for such careers as belonging socially to the *cultured* status group. In Germany, however—and this is a very important difference between China and the Occident—rational and specialized *expert* training has been added to, and in part has displaced, this educational status qualification.

The Chinese examinations did not test any special skills, as do our modern rational and bureaucratic examination regulations for jurists, medical doctors, or technicians. Nor did the Chinese examinations test the possession of charisma, as do the typical 'trials' of magicians and bachelor leagues. To be sure, we shall presently see the qualifications which this statement requires. Yet it holds at least for the technique of the examinations.

The examinations of China tested whether or not the candidate's mind was thoroughly steeped in literature and whether or not he possessed the *ways of thought* suitable to a cultured man and resulting from cultivation in literature. These qualifications held far more specifically with China than with the German humanist gymnasium. Today one is used to justifying the gymnasium by pointing to the practical value of formal education through the study of Antiquity. As far as one may judge from the assignments [25] given to the pupils of the lower grades in China, they were rather similar to the essay topics assigned to the top grades of a German gymnasium, or perhaps better still, to the select class of a German girls' college. All the grades were intended as tests in penmanship, style, mastery of classic writings,[26] and finally—similar to our lessons in religion, history, and German—in conformity with the prescribed mental outlook.[27] In our context it is decisive that this education was on the one hand purely secular in nature, but, on the other, was bound to the fixed norm of the orthodox interpretation of the classic authors. It was a highly exclusive and bookish literary education.

The literary character of education in India, Judaism, Christianity, and Islam resulted from the fact that it was completely in the hands of Brahmans and Rabbis trained in literature, or of clerics and monks of book religions who were professionally trained in literature. As long as education was Hellenic and not 'Hellenist,' the Hellenic man of culture was and remained primarily ephebe and hoplite. The effect of this was nowhere thrown into relief more clearly than in the conversation of the Symposium, where it is said of Plato's Socrates that he had never 'flinched' in the field, to use a student term. For Plato to state this is obviously at least of equal importance with everything else he makes Alcibiades say.

During the Middle Ages, the military education of the knight, and later the genteel education of the Renaissance salon, provided a corresponding though socially different supplement to the education transmitted by books, priests, and monks. In Judaism and in China, such a counterbalance was, in part altogether, and in part as good as altogether, absent. In India, as in China, the literary means of education consisted substantially of hymns, epic tales, and casuistry in ritual and ceremony. In India, however, this was underpinned by cosmogonic as well as religious and philosophical speculations. Such speculations were not entirely absent from the classics and from the transmitted commentaries in China, but obviously they have always played only a very minor role there. The

Chinese authors developed rational systems of social ethics. The educated stratum of China simply has never been an autonomous status group of scholars, as were the Brahmans, but rather a stratum of officials and aspirants to office.

Higher education in China has not always had the character it has today. The public educational institutions (*Pan kung*) of the feudal princes taught the arts of the dance and of arms in addition to the knowledge of rites and literature. Only the pacification of the empire into a patrimonial and unified state, and finally, the pure system of examinations for office, transformed this older education, which was far closer to early Hellenic education, into what has existed into the twentieth century. Medieval education, as represented in the authoritative and orthodox *Siao-Hio,* that is 'schoolbook,' still placed considerable weight upon dance and music. To be sure, the old war dance seems to have existed only in rudimentary form, but for the rest, the children, according to age groups, learned certain dances. The purpose of this was stated to be the taming of evil passions. If a child did not do well during his instruction, one should let him dance and sing. Music improves man, and rites and music form the basis of self-control.[28] The magical significance of music was a primary aspect of all this. 'Correct music'—that is, music used according to the old rules and strictly following the old measures—'keeps the spirits in their fetters.'[29] As late as the Middle Ages, archery and charioteering were still considered general educational subjects for genteel children.[30] But this was essentially mere theory. Going through the schoolbook one finds that from the seventh year of life, domestic education was strictly separated according to sex; it consisted essentially of instilling a ceremonial, which went far beyond all Occidental ideas, a ceremonial especially of piety and awe toward parents and all superiors and older persons in general. For the rest, the schoolbook consisted almost exclusively of rules for self-control.

This domestic education was supplemented by school instruction. There was supposed to be a grade school in every *Hsien.* Higher education presupposed the passing of the first entrance examination. Thus two things were peculiar to Chinese higher education. First, it was entirely non-military and purely literary, as all education established by priesthoods has been. Second, its literary character, that is, its *written* character, was pushed to extremes. In part, this appears to have been a result of the peculiarity of the Chinese script and of the literary art which grew out of it.[31]

As the script retained its pictorial character and was not rationalized into an alphabetical form, such as the trading peoples of the Mediterranean created, the literary product was addressed at once to both the eyes and the ears, and essentially more to the former. Any 'reading aloud' of the classic books was in itself a translation from the pictorial script into the (unwritten) word. The visual character, especially of the old script, was by its very nature remote from the spoken word. The monosyllabic language requires sound perception as well as the perception of pitched tone. With its sober brevity and its compulsion of syntactical logic, it stands in extreme contrast to the purely visual character of script. But in spite of this, or rather—as Grube has shown in an ingenious way —in part because of the very rational qualities of its structure, the Chinese tongue has been unable to offer its services to poetry or to systematic thinking. Nor could it serve the development of the oratorical arts as have the structures of the Hellenic, Latin, French, German, and Russian languages, each in its own way. The stock of written symbols remained far richer than the stock of monosyllabic words, which was inevitably quite delimited. Hence, all phantasy and ardor fled from the poor and formalistic intellectualism of the spoken word and into the quiet beauty of the written symbols. The usual poetic speech was held fundamentally subordinate to the script. Not speaking but writing and reading were valued artistically and considered as worthy of a gentleman, for they were receptive of the artful products of script. Speech remained truly an affair of the plebs. This contrasts sharply with Hellenism, to which conversation meant everything and a translation into the style of the dialogue was the adequate form of all experience and contemplation. In China the very finest blossoms of literary culture lingered, so to speak, deaf and mute in their silken splendor. They were valued far higher than was the art of drama, which, characteristically, flowered during the period of the Mongols.

Among the renowned social philosophers, Meng Tse (Mencius) made systematic use of the dialogue form. That is precisely why he readily appears to us as the one representative of Confucianism who matured to full 'lucidity.' The very strong impact upon us of the 'Confucian Analects' (as Legge called them) also rests upon the fact that in China (as occasionally elsewhere) the doctrine is clothed in the form of (in part, probably authentic) sententious responses of the master to questions from the disciples. Hence, to us, it is transposed into the form of speech. For the rest, the epic literature contains the addresses of the early warrior kings to the army; in their lapidar forcefulness, they are highly impressive. Part of the didactic *Analects* consists of speeches, the character of which rather corresponds to pontifical 'allocutions.' Otherwise speech plays no part in the official literature. Its lack of development, as we shall see presently, has been determined by both social and political reasons.

In spite of the logical qualities of the language, Chinese thought has remained rather stuck in the pictorial and the descriptive. The power of *logos,* of defining and reasoning, has not been accessible to the Chinese. Yet, on the other hand, this purely scriptural education detached thought from gesture and expressive movement still more than is usual with the literary nature of any education. For two years before he was introduced to their meaning, the pupil learned merely to paint about 2,000 characters. Furthermore, the examiners focused attention upon style, the art of versification, a firm grounding in the classics, and finally, upon the expressed mentality of the candidate.

The lack of all training in calculation, even in grade schools, is a very striking feature of Chinese education. The *idea* of positional numbers, however, was developed[32] during the sixth century before Christ, that is, during the period of warring states. A calculative attitude in commercial intercourse had permeated all strata of the population, and the final calculations of the administrative offices were as detailed as they were difficult to survey, for reasons mentioned above. The medieval schoolbook (*Siao-Hio* I, 29) enumerates calculation among the six 'arts.' And at the time of the warring states, there existed a mathematics which allegedly included trigonometrics as well as the rule of three and commercial calculation. Presumably this literature, apart from fragments, was lost during Shi-Hwang-Ti's burning of the books.[33] In any case, calculation is not even mentioned in later pedagogy. And in the course of history, calculation receded more and more into the background of the education of the genteel mandarins, finally to disappear altogether. The educated merchants learned calculation in their business offices. Since the empire had been unified and the tendency toward a rational administration of the state had weakened, the mandarin became a genteel literary man, who was not one to occupy himself with the 'σχολή' of calculation.

The mundane character of this education contrasts with other educational systems, which are nevertheless related to it by their literary stamp. The literary examinations in China were purely political affairs. Instruction was given partly by individual and private tutors and partly by the teaching staffs of college foundations. But no priest took part in them.

The Christian universities of the Middle Ages originated from the practical and ideal need for a rational, mundane, and ecclesiastic legal doctrine and a rational (dialectical) theology. The universities of Islam, following the model of the late Roman law schools and of Christian theology, practiced sacred case law and the doctrine of faith; the Rabbis practiced interpretation of the law; the philosophers' schools of the Brahmans engaged in speculative philosophy, in ritual, as well as in sacred law. Always ecclesiastic dignitaries or theologians have formed either the sole teaching staff or at least its basic corps. To this corps were attached mundane teachers, in whose hands the other branches of study rested. In Christianity, Islam, and Hinduism, prebends were the goals, and for the sake of them educational certificates were striven after. In addition, of course, the aspirant wished to qualify for ritual activity and the curing of souls. With the ancient Jewish teachers (precursors of the Rabbis), who worked 'gratis,' the goal was solely to qualify for instructing the laymen in the law, for this instruction was religiously indispensable. But in all this, education was always bound by sacred or cultic scriptures. Only the Hellenic philosophers' schools engaged in an education solely of laymen and freed from all ties to scriptures, freed from all direct interests in prebends, and solely devoted to the education of Hellenic 'gentlemen' (*Caloicagathoi*).

Chinese education served the interest in prebends and was tied to a script, but at the same time it was purely lay education, partly of a ritualist and ceremonial character and partly of a traditionalist and ethical character. The schools were concerned with neither mathematics nor natural sciences, with neither geography nor grammar. Chinese philosophy itself did not have a speculative, systematic character, as Hellenic philosophy had and as, in part and in a different sense, Indian and Occidental theological schooling had. Chinese philosophy did not have a rational-formalist character, as Occidental jurisprudence has. And it was not of an empirical casuist character, as Rabbinic, Islamite, and, partly, Indian philosophy. Chinese philosophy did not give birth to scholasticism because it was not professionally engaged in logic, as were the philosophies of the Occident and the Middle East, both of them being based on Hellenist thought. The very concept of logic remained absolutely alien to Chinese philosophy, which was bound to script, was not dialectical, and remained oriented to purely practical problems as well as to the status interests of the patrimonial bureaucracy.

This means that the problems that have been basic to all Occidental philosophy have remained unknown to Chinese philosophy, a fact which comes to the fore in the Chinese philosophers' manner of categorical thought, and above all in Confucius. With the greatest practical matter-of-factness, the intellectual tools remained in the form of parables, reminding us of the means of expression of Indian chieftains rather than of rational argumentation. This holds precisely for some of the truly ingenious statements ascribed to Confucius. The absence of speech is palpable, that is, speech as a rational means for attaining political and forensic effects, speech as it was first cultivated in the Hellenic *polis*. Such speech could not be developed in a bureaucratic patrimonial state which had no formalized justice. Chinese justice remained, in part, a summary Star Chamber procedure (of the high officials), and, in part, it relied solely on documents. No oral pleading of cases existed, only the written petitions and oral hearings of the parties concerned. The Chinese bureaucracy was interested in conventional propriety, and these bonds prevailed and worked in the same direction of obstructing forensic speech. The bureaucracy rejected the argument of 'ultimate' speculative problems as practically sterile. The bureaucracy considered such arguments improper and rejected them as too delicate for one's own position because of the danger of innovations.

If the technique and the substance of the examinations were purely mundane in nature and represented a sort of 'cultural examination for the literati,' the popular view of them was very different: it gave them a magical-charismatic meaning. In the eyes of the Chinese masses, a successfully examined candidate and official was by no means a mere applicant for office qualified by knowledge. He was a proved holder of magical qualities, which, as we shall see, were attached to the certified mandarin just as much as to an examined and ordained priest of an ecclesiastic institution of grace, or to a magician tried and proved by his guild.[34]

The position of the successfully examined candidate and official corresponded in important points, for example, to that of a Catholic chaplain. For the pupil to complete his period of instruction and his examinations did not mean the end of his immaturity. Having passed the 'baccalaureate,' the candidate came under the discipline of the school director and the examiners. In case of bad conduct his name was dropped from the lists. Under certain conditions his hands were caned. In the localities' secluded cells for examinations, candidates not infrequently fell seriously ill and suicides occurred. According to the charismatic interpretation of the examination as a magical 'trial,' such happenings were considered proof of the wicked conduct of the person in question. After the applicant for office had luckily passed the examinations for the higher degrees with their strict seclusion, and after, at long last, he had moved into an office corresponding to the number and rank of examinations passed and depending on his patronage, he still remained throughout his life under the control of the school. And in addition to being under the authority of his superiors, he was under the constant surveillance and criticism of the censors. Their criticism extended even to the ritualist correctness of the very Son of Heaven. The impeachment of the officials [35] was prescribed from olden times and was valued as meritorious in the way of the Catholic confession of sins. Periodically, as a rule every three years, his record of conduct, that is, a list of his merits and faults as determined by official investigations of the censors and his superiors, was to be published in the *Imperial Gazette*.[36] According to his published grades, he was allowed to retain his post, was promoted, or was demoted.[37] As a rule, not only objective factors determined the outcome of these records of conduct. What mattered was the 'spirit,' and this spirit was that of a life-long pennalism by office authority.

4: The Status-Honor of the Literati

As a status group, the literati were privileged, even those who had only been examined but were not employed. Soon after their position had been strengthened, the literati enjoyed *status privileges*. The most important of these were: first, freedom from the *sordida munera,* the *corvée;* second, freedom from corporal punishment; third, prebends (stipends). For a long time this third privilege has been rather severely reduced in its bearing, through the financial position of the state. The *Seng* (baccalaureate) still got stipends of $10.00 yearly, with the condition that they had to submit every three to six years to the *Chu jen* or Master's examination. But this, of course, did not mean anything decisive. The burden of the education *and* of the periods of nominal pay actually fell upon the sib, as we have seen. The sib hoped to recover their expenses by seeing their member finally enter the harbor of an office. The first two privileges were of importance to the very end; for the *corvée* still existed, although to a decreasing extent. The rod, however, remained the national means of punishment. Caning stemmed from the terrible pedagogy of corporal punishment in the elementary schools of China. Its unique character is said to have consisted in the following traits, which remind one of our Middle Ages but were obviously developed to even greater extremes.[38] The fathers of the sibs or of the villages compiled the 'red cards,' that is, the list of pupils (*Kuan-tan*). Then for a certain period they engaged a schoolmaster from among the over-supply of literati without office, which always existed. The ancestral temple (or other unused rooms) was the preferred schoolroom. From early until late the howling in unison of the written 'lines' was to be heard. All day long the pupil was in a condition of mental daze, which is denoted by a Chinese character, the component parts of which signify a pig in the weeds (*meng*). The student and graduate received slaps on the palm of his hand, no longer on what, in the terminology of German mothers of the old hue, was called 'the God-ordained spot.'

The graduates of high rank were entirely free from such punishment so long as they were not demoted. And in the Middle Ages freedom from the *corvée* was firmly established. Nevertheless, in spite and also because of these privileges, the development of feudal ideas of honor was impossible on their basis. Moreover, as has been observed, these privileges were precarious because they were immediately voided in the case of demotion, which frequently occurred. Feudal honor could not be developed on the bases of examination certificates as a qualification for status, possible degradation, corporal punishment during youth, and the not quite infrequent case of degradation even in old age. But *once,* in the past, such feudal notions of honor had dominated Chinese life with great intensity.

The old *Annals* praise 'frankness' and 'loyalty' as cardinal virtues.[39] 'To die with honor' was the old watchword. 'To be unfortunate and not to know how to die is cowardly.' This applied particularly to an officer who did not fight 'unto the death.'[40] Suicide was a death which a general, having lost a battle, valued as a *privilege*. To permit him to commit suicide meant to forego the right to punish him and therefore was considered with hesitation.[41] The meaning of feudal concepts was changed by the patriarchal idea of *hiao*. *Hiao* meant that one should suffer calumny and even meet death as its consequence if it served the honor of the master. One could, and in general should, compensate for *all* the mistakes of the lord by loyal service. The *kotow* before the father, the older brother, the creditor, the official, and the emperor was certainly not a symptom of *feudal* honor. For the correct Chinese to kneel before his love, on the other hand, would have been entirely taboo. All this was the reverse of what held for the knights and the *cortegiani* of the Occident.

To a great extent, the official's honor retained an element of student honor regulated by examination achievements and public censures by superiors. This was the case even if he had passed the highest examinations. In a certain sense, it is true of every bureaucracy (at least on its lower levels; and in Württemberg, with its famous 'Grade A, Fischer,' even in the highest positions of office); but it held to quite a different extent in China.

5: The Gentleman Ideal

The peculiar spirit of the scholars, bred by the system of examinations, was intimately connected with the basic presuppositions from which the orthodox and also, by the way, nearly all heterodox, Chinese theories proceeded. The dualism of the *shen* and *kwei,* of good and evil spirits, of heavenly *yang* substance as over against earthly *yin* substance, also within the soul of the individual, necessarily made the sole task of education, including self-education, to appear to be the unfolding of the *yang* substance in the soul of man.[42] For the man in whom the *yang* substance has completely gained the upper hand over the demonic *kwei* powers resting within him also has power over the spirits; that is, according to the ancient notion, he has magical power. The good spirits, however, are those who protect order and beauty and harmony in the world. To perfect oneself and thus to mirror this harmony is the supreme and the only means by which one may attain such power. During the time of the literati, the *Kiün-tse,* the 'princely man,' and once the 'hero,' was the man who had attained all-around self-perfection, who had become a 'work of art' in the sense of a classical, eternally valid, canon of psychical beauty, which literary tradition implemented in the souls of disciples. On the other hand, since the Han period at the latest,[43] it was a firmly established belief among the literati that the spirits reward 'beneficence,' in the sense of social and ethical excellence. Benevolence tempered by classical (canonical) beauty was therefore the goal of self-perfection.

Canonically perfect and beautiful achievements were the highest aspiration of every scholar as well as the ultimate yardstick of the highest qualification certified by examination. Li Hung Chang's youthful ambition was to become a perfect literary man,[44] that is, a 'crowned poet,' by attainment of the highest degrees. He was, and he remained, proud of being a calligrapher of great craftsmanship and of being able to recite the classics by heart, especially Confucius' 'Spring and Autumn.' This ability occasioned his uncle, after having tested it, to pardon the imperfections of his youth and to procure him an office. To Li Hung Chang all other branches of knowledge (algebra, astronomy) were only the indispensable means of 'becoming a great poet.' The classical perfection of the poem he conceived in the name of the Empress-Dowager, as a prayer in the temple of the tutelary goddess of silk-culture, brought him the Empress' favor.

Puns, euphemisms, allusions to classical quotations, and a refined and purely literary intellectuality were considered the conversational ideal of the genteel man. All politics of the day were excluded from such conversation.[45] It may appear strange to us that this sublimated 'salon' cultivation, tied to the classics, should enable man to administer large territories. And in fact, one did not manage the administration with mere poetry even in China. But the Chinese prebendary official proved his status quality, that is, his charisma, through the canonical correctness of his literary forms. Therefore, considerable weight was placed on these forms in official communications. Numerous important declarations of the Emperors, the high priests of literary art, were in the form of didactic poems. On the other hand, the official had to prove his charisma by the 'harmonious' course of his administration; that is, there must be no disturbances caused by the restless spirits of nature or of men. The actual administrative 'work' could rest on the shoulders of subordinate officials. We have noticed that above the official stood the imperial pontifex, his academy of literati, and his collegiate body of censors. They publicly rewarded, punished, scolded, exhorted, encouraged, or lauded the officials.

Because of the publication of the 'personal files' and all the reports, petitions, and memorials, the whole administration and the fateful careers of the officials, with their (alleged) causes, took place before the broadest public, far more so than is the case with any of our administrations under parliamentary control, an administration which puts the greatest weight upon the keeping of 'official secrets.' At least according to the official fiction, the official *Gazette* in China was a sort of running account of the Emperor before Heaven and before his subjects. This *Gazette* was the classic expression for the kind of responsibility which followed from the emperor's charismatic qualification. However dubious in reality the official argumentation and the completeness of publication may have been —that, after all, also holds for the communications of our bureaucracy to our parliaments—the Chinese procedure at least tended to open a rather strong and often a quite effective safety-valve for the pressure of public opinion with regard to the official's administrative activities.

6: The Prestige of Officialdom

The hatred and the distrust of the subjects, which is common to all patrimonialism, in China as everywhere turned above all against the lower levels of the hierarchy, who came into the closest practical contact with the population. The subjects' apolitical avoidance of all contact with 'the state' which was not absolutely necessary was typical for China as for all other patrimonial systems. But this apolitical attitude did not detract from the significance of the official education for the character formation of the Chinese people.

The strong demands of the training period were due partly to the peculiarity of Chinese script and partly to the peculiarity of the subject matter. These demands, as well as the waiting periods which were often quite long, forced those who were unable to live on a fortune of their own, on loans, or on family savings of the sort discussed above, to take up practical occupations of all sorts, from merchant to miracle doctor, before completing their educational careers. Then they did not reach the classics themselves, but only the study of the last (the sixth) textbook, the 'schoolbook' (*Siao Hioh*),[46] which was hallowed by age and contained mainly excerpts from the classic authors. Only this difference in the *level* of education and not differences in the *kind* of education set these circles off from the bureaucracy. For only classic education existed.

The percentage of candidates who failed the examinations was extraordinarily high. In consequence of the fixed quotas,[47] the fraction of graduates of the higher examinations was proportionately small, yet they always outnumbered many times the available office prebends. They competed for the prebends by personal patronage,[48] by purchase money of their own, or by loans. The sale of prebends functioned here as in Europe; it was a means of raising capital for the purposes of state, and very frequently it replaced merit ratings.[49] The protests of the reformers against the sale of offices persisted until the last days of the old system, as is shown by the numerous petitions of this sort in the *Peking Gazette*.

The officials' short terms of office (three years), corresponding to similar Islamic institutions, allowed for intensive and rational influencing of the economy through the administration as such only in an intermittent and jerky way. This was the case in spite of the administration's theoretical omnipotence. It is astonishing how few permanent officials the administration believed to be sufficient. The figures alone make it perfectly obvious that as a rule things must have been permitted to take their own course, as long as the interests of the state power and of the treasury remained untouched and as long as the forces of tradition, the sibs, villages, guilds, and other occupational associations remained the normal carriers of order.

Yet in spite of the apolitical attitude of the masses, which we have just mentioned, the views of the stratum of applicants for office exerted a very considerable influence upon the way of life of the middle classes. This resulted, first and above all, from the popular magical-charismatic conception of the qualification for office as tested by examination. By passing the examination, the graduate proved that he was to an eminent degree a holder of *shen*. High mandarins were considered magically qualified. They could always become objects of a cult, after their death as well as during their lifetime, provided that their charisma was 'proved.' The primeval magical significance of written work and of documents lent apotropaic and therapeutic significance to their seals and to their handwriting, and this could extend to the examination paraphernalia of the candidate. A province considered it an honor and an advantage to have one of its own sons selected by the emperor as the best graduate of the highest degree,[50] and all whose names were publicly posted after having passed their examinations had 'a name in the village.' All guilds and other clubs of any significance had to have a literary man as a secretary, and these and similar positions were open to those graduates for whom office prebends were not available. The officeholders and the examined candidates for office, by virtue of their magical charisma and of their patronage relations—especially when they stemmed from petty bourgeois circles—were the natural 'father confessors' and advisers in all important affairs of their sibs. In this they corresponded to the Brahmans (*Gurus*) who performed the same function in India.

Alongside the purveyor to the state and the great trader, the officeholder, as we have seen, was the personage with the most opportunities for accumulating possessions. Economically and personally, therefore, the influence on the population of this stratum, outside as well as inside their own sibs, was approximately as great as was the combined influence of the scribes and priests in Egypt. Within the sib, however, the authority of old age was a strong counterweight, as we have already emphasized. Quite independent of the 'worthiness' of the individual officials, who were often ridiculed in popular dramas, the prestige of this literary education as such was firmly grounded in the population until it came to be undermined by modern Western-trained members of the mandarin strata.

7: VIEWS ON ECONOMIC POLICY

The social character of the educated stratum determined its stand toward economic policy. According to its own legend, for millennia, the polity had the character of a religious and utilitarian welfare-state, a character which is in line with so many other typical traits of patrimonial bureaucratic structures bearing theocratic stamps.

Since olden times, to be sure, actual state policy, for reasons discussed above, had again and again let economic life alone, at least so far as production and the profit economy were concerned. This happened in China just as in the ancient Orient—unless new settlements, melioration through irrigation, and fiscal or military interests entered the picture. But military interests and interests in military finance had always called forth liturgical interventions in economic life. These interventions were monopolistically or financially determined, and often they were quite incisive. They were partly mercantilist regulations and partly in the nature of regulations of status stratification. Toward the end of national militarism, such planned 'economic policy' eventually fell into abeyance. The government, conscious of the weakness of its administrative apparatus, confined itself to the care of the tide and the maintenance of the water routes, which were indispensable for provisioning the leading provinces with rice; for the rest, to the typically patrimonial policy of dearth and consumption. It had no 'commercial policy' in the modern sense.[51] The tolls the mandarins had established along the waterways were, so far as is known, merely fiscal in nature and never served any economic policy. The government on the whole pursued only fiscal and mercantilist interests, if one disregards emergency situations which, considering the charismatic nature of authority, were always politically dangerous. So far as is known, the most grandiose attempts to establish a unified economic organization were planned by Wang An Shi, who during the eleventh century tried to establish a state trading monopoly for the entire harvest. In addition to fiscal gains, the plan was intended to serve the equalization of prices and was connected with a reform in land taxes. The attempt failed.

As the economy was left to itself to a large extent, the aversion against 'state intervention' in economic matters became a lasting and basic sentiment. It was directed particularly against monopolistic privileges,[52] which, as fiscal measures, are habitual to patrimonialism everywhere. This sentiment, however, was only one among the quite different attitudes which resulted from the conviction that the welfare of the subjects was dependent upon the charisma of the ruler. These ideas often stood in unmediated fashion beside the basic aversion to state intervention, and continually, or at least occasionally, made for bureaucratic meddling in everything, which again is typical of patrimonialism. Moreover, the administration of course reserved the right to regulate consumption in times of dearth—a policy which is also part of the theory of Confucianism [as reflected] in numerous special norms concerning all sorts of expenditures. Above all, there was the typical aversion against too sharp a social differentiation as determined in a purely economic manner by free exchange in markets. This aversion, of course, goes without saying in every bureaucracy. The increasing stability of the economic situation under conditions of the economically self-sufficient and the socially homogeneously composed world-empire did not allow for the emergence of such economic problems as were discussed in the English literature of the seventeenth century. There was no self-conscious bourgeois stratum which could not be politically ignored by the government and to whose interests the 'pamphleteers' of the time in England primarily addressed themselves. As always under patrimonial bureaucratic conditions, the administration had to take serious notice of the attitude of the merchants' guilds only in a 'static' way and when the maintenance of tradition and of the guilds' special privileges were at stake. Dynamically, however, the merchant guilds did not enter into the balance, because there were no expansive capitalist interests (*no longer!*) of sufficient strength, as in England, to be capable of forcing the state administration into their service.

8: Sultanism and the Eunuchs as Political Opponents of the Literati

The total *political* situation of the literati can be understood only when one realizes the forces against which they had to fight. We may disregard the heterodoxies here, for they will be dealt with below.

In early times the main adversaries of the literati were the 'great families' of the feudal period who did not want to be pushed out of their office monopolies. Having to accommodate themselves to the needs of patrimonialism and to the superiority of the knowledge of script, they found ways and means of paving the way for their sons by imperial favor.

Then there were the capitalist purchasers of office: a natural result of the leveling of status groups and of the fiscal money economy. Here the struggle could not lead to constant and absolute success, but only to relative success, because every demand of war pushed the impecunious central administration towards the jobbery of *office-prebends* as the *sole* means of war finance. This held until recent times.

The literati also had to fight the administration's rationalist interests in an expert officialdom. Specialist, expert officials came to the fore as early as 601 under Wen ti. During the distress of the defensive wars in 1068 under Wang An Shi, they enjoyed a short-lived and full triumph. But again tradition won out and this time for good.

There remained only one major and permanent enemy of the literati: sultanism and the eunuch-system which supported it.[53] The influence of the harem was therefore viewed with profound suspicion by the Confucians. Without insight into this struggle, Chinese history is most difficult to understand.

The constant struggle of the literati and sultanism, which lasted for two millennia, began under Shi-Hwang-Ti. It continued under all the dynasties, for of course energetic rulers continually sought to shake off their bonds to the cultured status group of the literati with the aid of eunuchs and plebeian parvenus. Numerous literati who took a stand against this form of absolutism had to give their lives in order to maintain their status group in power. But in the long run and again and again the literati won out.[54] Every drought, inundation, eclipse of the sun, defeat in arms, and every generally threatening event at once placed power in the hands of the literati. For such events were considered the result of a breach of tradition and a desertion of the classic way of life, which the literati guarded and which was represented by the censors and the 'Hanlin Academy.' In all such cases 'free discussion' was granted, the advice of the throne was asked, and the result was always the cessation of the unclassical form of government, execution or banishment of the eunuchs, a retraction of conduct to the classical schemata, in short, adjustments to the demands of the literati.

The harem system was of considerable danger because of the way in which successorship to the throne was ordered. The emperors who were not of age were under the tutelage of women; at times, this petticoat-government had come to be the very rule. The last Empress-Dowager, Tsu hsi, tried to rule with the aid of eunuchs.[55] We will not discuss at this point the roles which Taoists and Buddhists have played in these struggles, which run through all of Chinese history—why and how far they have been natural coalitionists, specifically of the eunuchs, and how far they have been coalitionists by constellation.

Let us mention in passing that, at least by modern Confucianism, astrology has been considered an unclassical superstition.[56] It has been thought to compete with the exclusive significance of the Emperor's *Tao* charisma for the course of government. Originally this had not been the case. The departmental competition of the Hanlin Academy against the collegiate body of astrologers may have played a decisive part; [57] perhaps also the Jesuit origin of the astronomic measures had a hand in it.

In the conviction of the Confucians, the trust in magic which the eunuchs cultivated brought about all misfortune. Tao Mo in his Memorial of the year 1901 reproached the Empress that in the year 1875 the true heir to the throne had been eliminated through her fault and in spite of the censors' protest, for the censor Wu Ko Tu had acknowledged this by his suicide. Tao Mo's posthumous memorial to the Empress and his letter to his son were distinguished by their manly beauty.[58] There cannot be the slightest doubt of his sincere and profound conviction. Also the belief of the Empress and of numerous princes in the magical charisma of the Boxers, a belief which alone explains her whole policy, was certainly to be ascribed to the influence of eunuchs.[59] On her death bed this impressive woman left as her counsel: (1) never again to let a woman rule in China, and (2) to abolish the eunuch system forever.[60] This counsel was fulfilled in a different way than she had undoubtedly intended—if the report is accurate. But one may not doubt that for the genuine Confucian everything that has happened since, above all the

'revolution' and the downfall of the dynasty, only confirms the correctness of the belief in the significance of the charisma of the dynasty's
classic virtue. In the improbable but possible event of a Confucian restoration, the belief would be exploited in this sense. The Confucianists, who
are ultimately pacifist literati oriented to inner political welfare, naturally
faced military powers with aversion or with lack of understanding. We
have already spoken of their relationship to the officers, and we have
seen that the whole *Annals* are paradigmatically filled with it. There
are protests to be found in the *Annals* against making 'praetorians' into
censors (and officials).[61] As the eunuchs were especially popular as
favorites and generals in the way of Narses, the enmity against the
purely sultanist patrimonial army suggested itself. The literati took pride
in having overthrown the popular military usurper Wang Mang. The
danger of ruling with plebeians has simply always been great with dictators, yet only this one attempt is known in China. The literati, however,
have submitted to *de facto* established power even when it was created
purely by usurpation, as was the power of the Han, or by conquest, as
was the power of the Mongol Manchus. They submitted even though
they had to make sacrifices—the Manchus took over 50 per cent of the
offices without having the educational qualifications. The literati have
submitted to the ruler *if* the ruler in turn submitted to their ritualist
and ceremonial demands; only *then*, in modern language, have they
accommodated themselves and taken a 'realistic' stand.

'Constitutionally'—and this was the theory of the Confucians—the
emperor could rule *only* by using certified literati as officials; 'classically'
he could rule only by using orthodox Confucian officials. Every deviation
from this rule was thought capable of bringing disaster and, in case of
obstinacy, the downfall of the emperor and the ruin of the dynasty.

Notes

I. A BIOGRAPHICAL VIEW

1. Marianne Weber, *Max Weber: ein Lebensbild* (Tübingen, 1926), pp. 57-8. This beautiful and thorough biography by Max Weber's widow is our major source for the facts as well as for several of the interpretations in this sketch of Weber's life. A second primary source of great value is Weber's *Jugendbriefe* (Tübingen, n.d.).

2. Ibid. p. 61.

3. Ibid. p. 72.

4. Ibid. p. 75.

5. Ibid. pp. 75 f.

6. Ibid. p. 77.

7. Max Weber, *Jugendbriefe*, pp. 191-2.

8. See this volume, pp. 117-28 and pp. 333-7.

9. *Jugendbriefe*, p. 221.

10. Marianne Weber, op.cit. p. 102.

11. Ibid. p. 393.

12. Ibid. p. 249.

13. Ibid. p. 254.

14. Ibid. p. 255.

15. Ibid. p. 261.

16. See this volume, 'Religious Rejections of the World,' p. 356.

17. See chap. XIV, 'Capitalism in Rural Society in Germany,' this volume.

18. *The Autobiographies of Edward Gibbon,* edited by John Murray (London, 1896), p. 270.

19. Marianne Weber, op.cit. p. 296.

20. Ibid. p. 300.

21. Ibid. p. 315.

22. The observations on American sects, pp. 303-5 of this volume, incorporate, almost literally, passages originally contained in letters Weber wrote to his mother during his travels in America.

23. Charles Sealsfield, *Lebensbilder aus beiden Hemisphaeren* (Zürich, 1835), Zweiter Teil, pp. 54, 236.

24. *Gesammelte Politische Schriften* (München, 1921), p. 483.

25. Marianne Weber, op.cit. p. 359.

26. Ibid. pp. 361-2.

27. Ibid. p. 379.

28. Ibid. p. 610.

29. Ibid. p. 527.

30. *Gesammelte Aufsaetze zur Religionssoziologie* (Tübingen, 1922-3), vol. II, p. 174.

31. Marianne Weber, op.cit. p. 360 (28 February 1906).

32. See, for example, *Gesammelte Aufsaetze zur Religionssoziologie,* vol. III, pp. 295, 319-20.

33. Marianne Weber, op.cit. p. 403 (1907).

34. 'La famille est donc, si l'on veut, le premier modèle des sociétés politiques: le chef est l'image du père, le peuple est l'image des enfants; et tous, étant nés égaux et libres, n'aliènent leur liberté que pour leur utilité. Toute la différence est que, dans la famille, l'amour du père pour ses enfants le paye des soins qu'il leur rend; et que, dans l'Etat, le plaisir de commander supplée à cet amour que le chef n'a pas pour ses peuples.' *Contrat Social,* chap. 2, par. 3.

II. POLITICAL CONCERNS

1. Marianne Weber, *Max Weber: ein Lebensbild,* pp. 124-5.

2. Ibid. p. 126. Written in the late 'eighties.

3. Ibid. pp. 129, 130.

4. Ibid. pp. 137-8.

5. *Gesammelte Politische Schriften* (München, 1921), chap. 1.

6. Ibid. pp. 24-5.

7. On these points cf. Eckart Kehr, 'Englandhass und Weltpolitik,' in *Zeitschrift für Politik,* edited by Richard Schmidt and Adolf Grabowsky (1928), vol. VII, pp. 500-26, and his more comprehensive analysis of the period in 'Schlachtflottenbau und Parteipolitik, 1894-1901' (1930). From a different point of view, Johannes Haller reaches identical conclusions. Cf. his *Die Aera Bülow* (Stuttgart und Berlin, 1922).

8. Weber's essay, 'The Protestant Sects and the Spirit of Capitalism' (chap. XII), began as a newspaper article in the *Frankfurter Zeitung;* later it was enlarged and reprinted in *Christliche Welt.* Cf. chap. XII, note 1.

9. 'We wish Social Democracy to become national. If they do not fulfil this wish it is their business. It is our business to uphold National Socialism.' Pastor Naumann, cited in Eugen Richter, *Politisches A B C Buch* (Berlin, 1903), p. 145. It is not without interest that this little party received just over 27,000 votes in 1898. More than one fourth of the total was cast in the province of Schleswig-Holstein, the one province where Hitler's National Socialists succeeded in winning the absolute majority in the last 'free' elections in 1932.

10. Marianne Weber, op.cit. p. 238.

11. Ibid. p. 413.

12. Ibid. p. 416.

13. Ibid. pp. 544, 562, 563.

14. Ibid. p. 567.

15. Ibid. p. 571. Cf. *Politische Schriften,* pp. 64-72.

16. Marianne Weber, op.cit. p. 591.

17. Ibid. pp. 664-5.

18. Carl Jentsch, ''Parlamente und Parteien in Deutschen Reiche,' *Die Neue Rundschau* (April 1906), pp. 385-412.

19. *Politische Schriften,* pp. 469 f.

20. Ernst Troeltsch, 'Das logische Problem der Geschichtsphilosophie,' *Der Historismus und seine Probleme* (Tübingen, 1922), Erstes Buch, p. 754.

21. John Stuart Mill, *Principles of Political Economy* (Boston, 1848), vol. 1, p. 379.

III. INTELLECTUAL ORIENTATIONS

1. August Bebel, *Aus meinem Leben* (Stuttgart, 1911), Zweiter Teil, p. 419.

2. Ludwig Bamberger, *Erinnerungen* (Berlin, 1899), p. 46.

3. Max Weber, 'Der Sozialismus,' in *Gesammelte Aufsaetze zur Soziologie und Sozialpolitik* (Tübingen, 1924), p. 508.

4. 'Agrargeschichte des Altertums,' *Handwörterbuch des Staatswissenschaften* (Jena, 1895-7), vol. 1, p. 182.

5. Cf. *Wirtschaft und Gesellschaft*, p. 768.

6. Cf. *Wirtschaft und Gesellschaft*, pp. 758 f.

7. W. E. H. Lecky, *History of Rationalism* (New York, 1867), vol. 1, p. 310.

8. *Wirtschaft und Gesellschaft*, vol. 1, p. 148.

9. Cf. *Gesammelte Aufsaetze zur Wissenschaftslehre* (Tübingen, 1922), pp. 132, 142.

10. *Gesammelte Aufsaetze zur Wissenschaftslehre*, p. 415; cf. also *Wirtschaft und Gesellschaft*, part 1, p. 1.

11. A. Comte, *Philosophie Positive*, vol. IV, p. 132.

12. Cf. Aroon, R., *La Sociologie Allemande* (Paris, 1935), p. 146.

13. *Wirtschaft und Gesellschaft*, vol. 1, p. 800.

14. *Religionssoziologie*, vol. 1, p. 265.

15. Ibid. vol. 1, p. 128, footnote 3.

16. *Beyond Good and Evil* (New York, 1937), chap. 4, aphorism 69.

17. *Religionssoziologie*, vol. III, pp. 321-2.

18. *Religionssoziologie*, vol. 1, p. 252. Cf. chap. XI, p. 280 of this volume.

19. Leon Trotsky, *Germany, What Next?* (New York, 1932), p. 183.

20. For a fully documented history of this controversy, see Ephraim Fischoff, 'The Protestant Ethic and the Spirit of Capitalism,' *Social Research* (vol. XI, no. 1, February 1944, pp. 53-77). The attempt of this author to dispute Weber's interest in the Protestant Ethic as an indispensable causal factor seems to point in the wrong direction. Weber indeed 'recognized that capitalism would have arisen without Protestantism, in fact, that it had done so in many culture complexes' (p. 67). But this refers only to *political* capitalism: To assert that Weber did not intend to make 'an effort to trace the causal influence of the Protestant ethic upon the emergence of capitalism' (p. 76) is to underrate Weber's interest in causal explanation in favor of a mere 'exposition of the rich congruency of such diverse aspects of a culture as religion and economics.' On the contrary, Weber held that purely economic factors were indispensable, but by themselves insufficient. He was convinced that a 'subjective factor' was also necessary for a causally sufficient explanation. That is the reason for his ceaseless inquiry into the role of ideas in the historical process. Ideas place premiums upon special psychic traits; through these premiums, and through habitual (and hence socially controlled) conduct, a special personality type is produced. Once fixed, sustained, and selected by organizations (sects), this personality type acts out conduct patterns. These patterns are religiously oriented but they lead to unforeseen economic results, namely, methodical workaday capitalism with its constant reinvestment of profits in productive enterprises. Cf. chap. XII of this book.

21. Moeller van den Bruck, *Das Dritte Reich* (Hamburg, 1931; 3rd edition), p. 189.
22. *Archiv für Socialwissenschaft und Sozialpolitik*, vol. XII, no. 1, pp. 347 ff.
23. *Wirtschaft und Gesellschaft*, p. 817.

IV. POLITICS AS A VOCATION

1. *Trachtet nach seinem Werk.*
2. A high ministerial official in charge of a special division concerning which he had to give regular reports.
3. Head of an administrative division in a ministry.
4. *Geist.*
5. The 'local agents' of the party.
6. Weber alludes to the evasion of rationing and priority rules and the developments of 'black markets' during the wartime administration of Germany, 1914 to 1918.
7. Federal Council.
8. *Landwirtschaftskammer.*
9. *Handwerkskammer.*

VI. STRUCTURES OF POWER

1. Written before 1914. (German editor's note.)
2. The custom union of the central German states since the 1830's.
3. Written before 1914. (German editor's note.)
4. Around 590 B.C.
5. Organ of Prussian Junkers.
6. The text breaks off here. Notes on the manuscript indicate that Weber intended to deal with the idea and development of the national state throughout history. The following sentence is to be found on the margin: 'There is a close connection between the prestige of culture and the prestige of power.' Every victorious war enhances the prestige of culture (Germany [1871], Japan [1905], etc.). The question of whether war contributes to the 'development of culture' cannot be answered in a 'value neutral' way. Certainly there is no unambiguous answer (Germany after 1870!), not even when we consider empirical evidence, for characteristically German art and literature did not originate in the political center of Germany. (Note of German editors.)
The supplementary passage that follows is from Max Weber's comment on a paper by Karl Barth; *Gesammelte Aufsaetze zur Soziologie und Sozialpolitik* (Tübingen, 1924), pp. 484-6. [G. & M.]
7. A war scare during the early nineteen hundreds.

VII. CLASS, STATUS, PARTY

One cross-reference footnote to a passage in *Wirtschaft und Gesellschaft*, p. 277, has been omitted, and one footnote has been placed in the text. A brief unfinished draft of a classification of status groups is appended to the German text; it has been omitted here.

VIII. BUREAUCRACY

1. Frederick II of Prussia.
2. Cf. *Wirtschaft und Gesellschaft,* pp. 73 ff. and part II. (German Editor.)
3. 'Ministerialen.'
4. Written before 1914. (German editor's note.)
5. We read 'Technische Leistung' for 'Technische Leitung.' Cf. below no. 6, pp. 214 ff.
6. *Erwerbende Schichten.*
7. We read 'Verbreitung der Einflusssphäre' instead of 'Vertreibung der Einflusssphäre.'
8. When in 1899 the German Reichstag discussed a bill for the construction of the Mittelland Kanal the conservative Junker party fought the project. Among the conservative members of the parliamentary party were a number of administrative Junker officials who stood up to the Kaiser who had ordered them to vote for the bill. The disobedient officials were dubbed *Kanalrebellen* and they were temporarily suspended from office. Cf. Bernard Fürst von Bülow, *Denkwürdigkeiten* (Berlin, 1930), vol. I, pp. 293 ff.
9. German territorial princes, since the thirteenth and fourteenth centuries, occasionally called on feudal and ecclesiastic notables for their advice. As these counselors were only visiting at court, they were called *Räte von Haus aus,* or *familiares domestici, consiliarii,* et cetera; cf. Georg Ludwig von Maurer, *Geschichte der Fronhöfe, der Bauernhöfe, und der Hofverfassung in Deutschland* (Erlangen, 1862), vol. II, pp. 237, 240 ff., 312 f.

IX. THE SOCIOLOGY OF CHARISMATIC AUTHORITY

1. Cf. *Wirtschaft und Gesellschaft,* sections 2 and 5 of part II.
2. The manuscript breaks off here. (German Editor.)

X. THE MEANING OF DISCIPLINE

1. Heavily armed footsoldier.
2. A military unit, a company.
3. The *sarissa* is the Macedonian pike, some 14 feet long, of further reach than the ordinary Greek spear.
4. A subdivision of a Roman legion, numbering either 120 or 60 men.
5. Men equipped with the halberd, a long-handled weapon.
6. Five Spartan magistrates.
7. Military colonies of the city states.

XI. THE SOCIAL PSYCHOLOGY OF THE WORLD RELIGIONS

1. At this point Weber refers the reader to *The Protestant Ethic and the Spirit of Capitalism.* Cf. also the essay, 'The Protestant Sects and the Spirit of Capitalism,' chap. 12 of the present book.
2. *Inbrünstige.*
3. A Mohammedan mysticism originating in Persia during the eighth century. It developed an elaborate symbolism, much used by poets.

4. *Wundbruehe.*

5. In these contexts every evaluative aspect must be removed from the concept of 'virtuosity,' which adheres to it nowadays. I prefer the term 'heroic' religiosity because of the loaded character of 'virtuoso,' but 'heroic' is entirely too inadequate for some of the phenomena belonging here. [M. W.]

6. The Ulema represent a body of scholars trained in Moslem religion and law. They are the guardians of sacred tradition. Opposed to them are religious leaders who claim visionary knowledge of a mystic rather than intellectual interpretation of tradition.

7. A mendicant friar.

8. In part this has been presented in the essays on Protestantism; it will be more closely discussed at a later time. [M. W.]

9. *Planmässigkeit.*

10. The *sequence* of the reflections—to mention this also—is geographical. Merely by accident it proceeds from East to West. In truth, not the external spatial distribution but internal reasons of the presentation have been decisive, as will perhaps become evident on closer attention. [M. W.]

11. For a closer discussion Weber refers to the pertinent sections in *Wirtschaft und Gesellschaft.*

12. *Anstalt.*

XII. PROTESTANT SECTS AND THE SPIRIT OF CAPITALISM

NOTE: Certain footnotes in this chapter have been placed in the text.

1. This is a new and greatly enlarged draft of an article published in the *Frankfurter Zeitung,* Eastern 1906, then somewhat enlarged in the *Christliche Welt,* 1906, pp. 558 ff., 577 ff., under the title, 'Churches and Sects.' I have repeatedly referred to this article as supplementing *The Protestant Ethic and the Spirit of Capitalism.* The present rewriting is motivated by the fact that the concept of sect as worked out by myself (as a contrasting conception to 'church') has, in the meanwhile and to my joy, been taken over and treated thoroughly by Troeltsch in his *Soziallehren der christlichen Kirchen* [*The Social Teachings of the Christian Churches,* trans. by O. Wyon, 2 vols., London, 1931]. Hence, conceptual discussions can the more easily be omitted as what is necessary has been said already in *The Protestant Ethic and the Spirit of Capitalism,* pp. 254 f., note 173. This essay contains only the barest data supplementing that essay.

2. Details are of no interest here. Reference should be made to the respective volumes of the 'American Church History Series,' which is, to be sure, of very uneven value.

3. The organization of the religious congregation during the immigration to New England often preceded the political societalization (in the fashion of the well-known pact of the Pilgrim Fathers). Thus, the Dorchester Immigrants of 1619 first bound themselves together by organizing a church congregation *before* emigrating, and they elected a parson and a teacher. In the colony of Massachusetts the church was formally a completely autonomous corporation, which admitted, however, only citizens for membership, and affiliation with which, on the other hand, was a prerequisite of citizenship. Likewise, at first, church membership and good conduct (meaning admission to the Lord's Supper) were prerequisites of citizenship in New Haven (before it was incorporated in Connecticut despite resistance against incorporation). In Connecticut, however (in 1650), the

township was obliged to maintain the church (a defection from the strict principles of Independentism to Presbyterianism).

This at once meant a somewhat laxer practice, for after the incorporation of New Haven the church there was restricted to giving out certificates stating that the respective person was religiously inoffensive and of sufficient means. Even during the seventeenth century, on the occasion of the incorporation of Maine and New Hampshire, Massachusetts had to depart from the full strictness of the religious qualification of political rights. On the question of church membership compromises had also to be made, the most famous of which is the Half-way Covenant of 1657. In addition, those who could not prove themselves to be regenerate were nevertheless admitted to membership. But, until the beginning of the eighteenth century, they were not admitted to communion.

4. Some references from the older literature which is not very well known in Germany may be listed. A sketch of Baptist history is present in: Vedder, *A Short History of the Baptists* (Second ed. London, 1897). Concerning Hanserd Knollys: Culross, *Hanserd Knollys*, vol. II of the Baptist Manuals edited by P. Gould (London, 1891).

For the history of Anabaptism: E. B. Bax, *Rise and Fall of the Anabaptists* (New York, 1902). Concerning Smyth: Henry M. Dexter, *The True Story of John Smyth, the Se-Baptist,* as told by himself and his contemporaries (Boston, 1881). The important publications of the Hanserd Knollys Society (printed for the Society by J. Hadden, Castle Street, Finsbury, 1846-54) have been cited already. Further official documents in *The Baptist Church Manual* by J. Newton Brown, D.D. (Philadelphia, American Baptist Publishing Society, 30 S. Arch Street). Concerning the Quakers, besides the cited work of Sharpless: A. C. Applegarth, *The Quakers in Pennsylvania,* ser. x, vol. VIII, IX of the Johns Hopkins University Studies in History and Political Science. G. Lorimer, *Baptists in History* (New York, 1902), J. A. Seiss, *Baptist System Examined* (Lutheran Publication Society, 1902).

Concerning New England (besides Doyle): The Massachusetts Historical Collections; furthermore, Weeden, *Economic and Social History of New England,* 1620-1789, 2 vols. Daniel W. Howe, *The Puritan Republic* (Indianapolis, Bobbs-Merrill Co.).

Concerning the development of the 'Covenant' idea in older Presbyterianism, its church discipline, and its relation to the official church, on the one hand, and to Congregationalists and sectarians on the other hand, see: Burrage, *The Church Covenant Idea* (1904), and *The Early English Dissenters* (1912). Furthermore, W. M. Macphail, *The Presbyterian Church* (1918). J. Brown, *The English Puritans* (1910). Important documents in Usher, *The Presbyterian Movement,* 1584-89 (Com. Soc., 1905). We give here only an extremely provisional list of what is relevant for us.

5. During the seventeenth century this was so much taken for granted that Bunyan, as mentioned previously, makes 'Mr. Money-Love' argue that one may even become pious *in order* to get rich, especially in order to add to one's patronage; for it should be irrelevant for what reason one had become pious. (*Pilgrims' Progress,* Tauchnitz ed., p. 114.)

6. Thomas Clarkson, *Portraiture of the Christian Profession and Practice of the Society of Friends.* Third edition (London, 1867), p. 276. (The first edition appeared around 1830.)

7. Sources are Zwingli's statements, Füssli I, p. 228, cf. also pp. 243, 253, 263, and

his *'Elenchus contra catabaptistas,' Werke* III, pp. 357, 362. In his own congregation, Zwingli characteristically had much trouble with Antipedobaptists [opposed to infant baptism]. The Antipedobaptists, in turn, viewed the Baptist 'separation,' hence voluntarism, as objectionable according to the Scriptures. A Brownist petition of 1603 to King James I demanded the exclusion of all 'wicked liars' from the church and only the admission of the 'faithful' and their children. But the (Presbyterian) Directory of Church Government of (probably) 1584 (published from the original for the first time in the Heidelberg Ph.D. thesis of A. F. Scott Pearson, 1912) demanded in article 37 that only people who had submitted to the disciplinary code, or *literas testimoniales idoneas aliunde attulcriut* [had furnished testimonial letters from elsewhere] be admitted to communion.

8. The problematic nature of the sectarian voluntarist principle follows logically from the demand for the *ecclesia pura* by the reformed (Calvinist) church. This dogmatic principle, as opposed to the sect principle, is strikingly evident in modern times in A. Kuyper (the well-known later Premier ministei). The dogmatic position in his final programmatic essay is especially obvious: *Separatie en doleantie* (Amsterdam, 1890). He sees the problem as due to the absence of the infallible doctrinal office among non-Catholic Christianity. This doctrine asserts that the *Corpus* of the visible church cannot be the *Corpus Christi* of the old Reformed Church, but that it must rather remain divided in time and space, and the shortcomings of human nature must remain peculiar to it. A visible church originates solely through an *act of will* on the part of the believers and by virtue of the authority given them by Christ. Hence the *potestas ecclesiastica* may be vested neither in Christ himself, nor in the *ministri,* but only in the believing congregation. (In this Kuyper follows Voët.) The greater community originates through the legal and voluntary association of the congregations. This association, however, must be a *religious obligation.* The Roman principle, according to which a church member is *eo ipso* a member of the parish of his local community, is to be rejected. Baptism makes him a mere passive *membrum incompletum* and grants no rights. Not baptism, but only *belijdenis en stipulatie* (confession of faith and profession of good will) gives membership in the congregation, in the legal sense. Membership alone is identical with subordination to the *disciplina ecclesiae* (again following Voët). Church law is believed to deal with the *man-made* rules of the *visible* church, which, though bound to God's order, do not represent God's order itself. (Cf. Voët *Pol. Eccles.* vol. I, pp. I and II.) All these ideas are Independentist variants of the genuine constitutional law of the reformed churches and imply an active participation of the *congregation,* hence of the laity, in the admission of new members. (Von Rieker has described this law especially well.) The co-operative participation of the whole congregation also constituted the program of the Brownist Independents in New England. They adhered to it in constant struggle against the successfully advancing 'Johnsonist' faction which advocated church government by the 'ruling elders.' It goes without saying that only 'Regenerates' were to be admitted (according to Baillie 'only one out of forty'). During the nineteenth century, the church theory of the Scotch Independents similarly demanded that admission be granted only by special resolution (Sack, loc. cit.). However, Kuyper's church theory *per se* is, of course, *not* 'congregationalist' in character.

According to Kuyper, individual congregations are religiously obliged to affiliate with and to belong to the church as a whole. There can be only one legitimate church in one place. This obligation to affiliate is only dropped, and the obligation of *separatie* emerges only when *doleantie* has failed; that is, an attempt must have been made to improve the wicked church as a whole through active protest and passive obstruction (*doleeren*, meaning to protest, occurs as a technical term in the seventeenth century). And finally, if all means have been exhausted and if the attempt has proved to be in vain, and force has prevailed, then separation is obligatory. In that case, of course, an independent constitution is obligatory, since there are no 'subjects' in the church and since the believers *per se* hold a God-given office. Revolution can be a duty to God. (Kuyper, *De conflict gekomen*, pp. 30-31). Kuyper (like Voët) takes the old independent view that only those who participate in the *communion of the Lord's Supper* by admission are full members of the church. And only the latter are able to assume the trusteeship of their children during baptism. A believer, in the *theological* sense, is one who is inwardly converted; in the legal sense a believer is only one who is *admitted* to the Lord's Supper.

9. The fundamental prerequisite for Kuyper is that it is a sin not to purge the sacramental communion of non-believers. (*Dreigend Conflict*, 1886, p. 41; reference is made to Cor. 1, 11, 26, 27, 29; Tim. 1, 5, 22; Apoc. 18, 4.) Yet according to him the church never has judged the state of grace 'before God'—in contrast to the 'Labadists' (radical Pietists). But for admission to the Lord's Supper *only belief* and *conduct* are decisive. The transactions of the Netherland Synods of the six-teenth and seventeenth centuries are filled with discussions of the prerequisites of admission to the Lord's Supper. For example, the Southern Dutch Synod of 1574 agreed that the Lord's Supper should not be given if no organized *congre-gation* existed. The elders and deacons were to be careful that no unworthy person be admitted. The Synod of Rotterdam of 1575 resolved that all those who led an obviously offensive life should not be admitted. (The elders of the congregation, not the preachers alone, decided admissions, and it is almost always the congre-gation which raises such objections—often against the more lax policy of the preachers. Cf. for instance, the case cited by Reitsma [vol. 11, p. 231].) The ques-tion of admission to the Lord's Supper included the following cases: whether the husband of an Anabaptist wife could be admitted to the Lord's Supper was decided at the Synod at Leyden in 1619, article 114; whether a Lombard's servant should be admitted, Provincial Synod at Deventer, 1595, article 24; whether men who declared their bankruptcy, Synod of Alkmaar, 1599, article 11, similarly of 1605, article 28, and men who had settled an accord, Northern Holland Synod of Enkhuizen of 1618, Grav. Class. Amstel. No. 16, should be admitted. The latter question is answered in the affirmative in case the *consistorium* finds the list of properties sufficient and judges the reservations for food and clothing made therein adequate for the debtor and his family. But the decision is especially affirmative when the creditors state themselves to be satisfied by the accord and when the failing debtor makes a confession of guilt. Concerning non-admission of Lom-bards, see above. Exclusion of spouses in case of quarrelsomeness, Reitsma 111, p. 91. The reconciliation of parties to a legal dispute is a prerequisite for admission. For the duration of the dispute they must stay away from communion. There is con-ditional admission of a person who has lost a libel suit and has appealed the case. Ibid. 111, p. 176.

Calvin may well have been the first to have forced through in the Strassborg congregation of French emigrants the exclusion of the person from the Lord's Supper whose outcome in the examination of worthiness was unsatisfactory. (But then the minister, not the congregation, made the decision.) According to Calvin's genuine doctrine (Inst. Chr. Rel. iv, chap. 12, p. 4) excommunications should legitimately apply only to reprobates. (At the quoted place excommunication is called the promulgation of the *divine* sentence.) But in the same place (cf. p. 5) it is also treated as a means of 'improvement.'

In America, nowadays, among the Baptists formal excommunication, at least in metropolitan areas, is very rare. In practice it is replaced by 'dropping,' in which case the name of the person is simply and discreetly stricken from the record. Among the sects and Independents, laymen have always been the typical bearers of discipline; whereas the original Calvinist-Presbyterian church discipline expressly and systematically strove for domination over state and church. However, even the 'Directory' of the English Presbyterians of 1584 (p. 14, note 2) summoned an equal number of lay elders and ministers to the classes and to the higher offices of the church government.

The mutual relation of the elders and the congregation has been occasionally ordered in different ways. Just as the (Presbyterian) Long Parliament placed the decision of exclusion from the Lord's Supper into the hands of the (lay) elders, so the 'Cambridge Platform' did likewise about 1647 in New England. Up to the middle of the nineteenth century the Scotch Independents, however, used to transmit notice of misconduct to a commission. After the commission's report the whole congregation decided about the exclusion, in correspondence with the stricter view of the joint responsibility of all individuals. This absolutely corresponded with the Brownist confession quoted above, which was submitted to King James I in 1603 (Dexter, loc. cit. p. 303) whereas the 'Johnsonists' considered the sovereignty of the (elected) elders to be Biblical. The elders should be able to excommunicate even against the decision of the congregation (occasion for Ainsworth's secession). Concerning the corresponding conditions among the early English Presbyterians, see the literature quoted in note 4, above, and the Ph.D. thesis of Pearson quoted in note 7, above.

10. The Dutch Pietists, by the way, believed in the same principle. Lodensteijn, for instance, held to the point of view that one must not commune with non-regenerates; and the latter are for him expressly those who do not bear the *signs* of regeneration. He even went so far as to advise against saying the Lord's Prayer with children since they had not as yet become 'children of the Lord.' In the Netherlands, Köhler still occasionally found the view that the regenerate does not sin at all. Calvinist orthodoxy and an astonishing knowledge of the Bible was found precisely among the petty bourgeois masses. Also here it was the very orthodox who, distrusting theological education and faced with the church regulation of 1852, complained of the insufficient representation of laymen in the Synod (besides the lack of a sufficiently strict '*censura morum*'). Certainly no orthodox Lutheran church party in Germany would have thought of that at the time.

11. Quoted in Dexter, *Congregationalism of the Last Three Hundred Years as Seen in its Literature* (New York, 1880), p. 97.

12. During the seventeenth century, letters of recommendation from non-resident Baptists of the local congregations were a prerequisite for admission to the Lord's Supper. Non-Baptists could only be admitted after having been examined and approved by the congregation. (Appendix to the edition of the Hanserd Knollys Confession of 1689, West Church, Pa., 1817.) Participation in the Lord's Supper was *compulsory* for the qualified member. Failure to affiliate with the legitimately constituted congregation of one's place of residence was viewed as schism. With regard to the obligatory community with other congregations, the Baptist point of view resembled that of Kuyper (cf. above, note 8). However *all* jurisdictional authority *higher* than that of the individual church was rejected. Concerning the

litterae testimoniales [testimonial letters] among the Covenanters and early English Presbyterians, see note 7 and the literature quoted in note 4.

13. Shaw, *Church History under the Commonwealth,* vol. II, pp. 152-65; Gardiner, *Commonwealth,* vol. III, p. 231.

14. This principle was expressed, for instance, in resolutions like the one of the Synod of Edam, 1585 (in the Collection of Reitsma, p. 139).

15. Baxter, *Eccles. Dir.,* vol. II, p. 108, discusses in detail the shying away of doubtful members from the Lord's Supper of the congregation (because of article 25 of the Church of England).

16. The doctrine of Predestination also represents here the purest type. Its relevance and great practical importance is evidenced in nothing so clearly as the bitter struggle over the question whether children of reprobates should be admitted to baptism after having proved themselves to be worthy. The practical significance of the doctrine of Predestination has been, however, again and again unjustly doubted. Three of the four Amsterdam Refugee congregations were in favor of admitting the children (at the beginning of the seventeenth century); but in New England only the 'Half-way Covenant' of 1657 brought a relaxation of this point. For Holland see also note 9.

17. Loc. cit. vol. II, p. 110.

18. Already at the beginning of the seventeenth century the prohibition of the conventicles (*Slijkgeuzen*) caused a general *Kulturkampf* in Holland. Elizabeth proceeded against the conventicles with frightful harshness (in 1593 with threat of capital punishment). The reason behind this was the anti-authoritarian character of asceticist religiosity or, better in this case, the competitive relationship between the religious and the secular authority (Cartwright had expressly demanded that excommunication of princes also be permitted). As a matter of fact the example of Scotland, the classic soil of Presbyterian church discipline and clerical domination against the king, had to have a deterrent effect.

19. In order to escape the religious pressure of orthodox preachers, liberal Amsterdam citizens had sent their children to neighboring congregations for their confirmation lessons. The Kerkraad [church council] of the Amsterdam congregation refused (in 1886) to acknowledge certificates of the moral conduct of the communicants made out by such ministers. The communicants were excluded from the Lord's Supper because the communion had to remain pure and because the Lord, rather than man, must be obeyed. When the synodal commission approved of the objection against this deviation, the church council refused to obey and adopted new rules. In accordance with the latter, suspension of the church council gave the council exclusive disposition over the church. It rejected community with the synod and the now suspended (lay) elders, T. Rutgers and Kuyper, seized by ruse the Nieuwe Kerk [New Church] in spite of the watchmen who had been hired. (Cf. Hogerfeil, *De kerkelijke strijd te Amsterdam,* 1886, and Kuyper's publications mentioned above.) During the 1820's the predestinarian movement had already begun under the leadership of Bilderdijk and his disciples, Isaac da Costa and Abraham Capadose (two baptized Jews). (*Because* of the doctrine of predestination it rejected, for example, the abolition of Negro slavery as 'an interference with Providence' just as it rejected vaccination!) They zealously fought the laxity of church discipline and the imparting of sacraments to unworthy persons. The movement led to separations. The synod of the 'Afgeschiedenen gereformeerten Gemeente' [Separated reformed congregation] of Amsterdam in 1840 accepted the Dordrecht Canouns and rejected any kind of domination (*gezag*) 'within or above the church.' Groen van Prinsterer was one of Bilderdijk's disciples.

20. Classical formulations are found in the 'Amsterdam Confession' of 1611 (Publ. of the Hanserd Knollys Society, vol. x). Thus, article 16 states: 'That the members of every church and congregation *ought to know one another* . . . therefore a church ought not to consist of such a multitude as cannot have practical knowledge one of another.' Hence any synodal rule and any establishment of central church authorities were considered in the last instance as principled apostasy. This happened in Massachusetts and likewise in England under Cromwell. The rules, at that time, established by Parliament in 1641, allowed every congregation to provide itself with an orthodox minister and to organize lectures. This measure was the signal for the influx of Baptists and radical Independents. The early Presbyterian Dedham Protocols, published by Usher, also presuppose the *individual* congregation (actually, at that time, in all probability, the individual minister) to be the bearer of church discipline. Admission by ballot, as evidenced by the protocol of 22 October 1582, states: 'That none be brought in as one of this company without the general consent of the whole.' But as early as 1586 these Puritans declared their opposition to the Brownists, who went in the direction of Congregationalism.

21. The 'classes' of the Methodists, as the foundation of the co-operative cure of soul, were the very backbone of the whole organization. Every twelve persons were to be organized into a 'class.' The leader of the class was to visit each member weekly, either at home or at the class meeting, during which there was usually a general confession of sins. The leader was to keep a record of the member's conduct. Among other things, this book-keeping was the basis for the writing of certificates for members who went away from the local community. By now, and for a long time, this organization has been disintegrating everywhere, including the U.S.A. The manner in which church discipline functioned in early Puritanism may be judged from the above-quoted Dedham Protocol, according to which 'admonition' was to be given in the conventicle 'if any things have been observed *or espied* by the brethren.'

22. In the Lutheran territories, especially those of Germany, either church discipline was notoriously undeveloped or else church discipline completely decayed at an early date. Church discipline was also of little influence in the reformed churches of Germany, except in Jülich-Cleve and other Rhenish areas. This was due to the influence of the Lutheran surroundings *and* to the jealousy between the state power and the competing and autonomous hierocratic forces. This jealousy had existed everywhere, but the state had remained overpowering in Germany. (Traces of church discipline are nevertheless found up to the nineteenth century. The last excommunication in the palatinate took place in 1855. However, the church rules of 1563 were there handled in an actually Erastian way from an early date.) Only the Mennonites, and later the Pietists, created effective means of discipline and disciplinary organizations. (For Menno a 'visible church' existed *only* where church discipline existed. And excommunication because of misconduct or mixed marriage was a self-understood element of such discipline. The Rynsburg Collegiants had no dogmas whatever and recognized 'conduct' alone.) Among the Huguenots, church discipline *per se* was very strict, but again and again it was relaxed through unavoidable considerations of the nobility which were politically indispensable. The adherents of Puritan church discipline in England were found especially among the bourgeois capitalist middle class, thus, for instance, in the City of London. The city was not afraid of the domination of the clergy, but intended to use church discipline as a means of mass domestication. The strata of artisan craftsmen also adhered firmly to church discipline. The political authorities

were the opponents to church discipline. Hence, in England the opponents included Parliament. Not 'class interests' but, as every glimpse into the documents shows, *primarily* religious, and, in addition, political interests and convictions played their part in these questions. The harshness not only of New England but also of the genuinely Puritan church disipline in Europe is known. Among Cromwell's major-generals and commissioners, his agents for enforcing church discipline, the proposal to exile all 'idle, debauched, and profane persons,' emerges repeatedly.

Among the Methodists the dropping of novices during the periods of probation was permissible without further ado. Full members were to be dropped after an investigation by a commission. The church discipline of the *Huguenots* (who for a long time actually existed as a 'sect') is evidenced in synodal protocols. These indicate, among other things, censure of adulteration of commodities and of dishonesty in business. Sixth Synod (Avert. Gen. xiv). Thus sumptuary laws are frequently found, and slave ownership and slave trading are *permitted,* Twenty-Seventh Synod; a rather lax practice toward fisca' demands prevails (the fiscus is a tyrant), Sixth Synod, cas de conc. dec, xiv; usury, ibid. xv (cf. Second Synod, Gen. 17; Eleventh Synod, Gen. 42). Toward the end of the sixteenth century, the English Presbyterians were designated as 'disciplinarians' in official correspondence (Quotations to be found in Pearson, loc. cit.).

23. In the 'Apologetical Narration' of the five (Independent) 'dissenting brethren' of the Westminster Synod the separation from the 'casuall and formall Christians' is placed in the foreground. This means, at first, only voluntaristic separatism, not renunciation of commercium. But Robinson, a strict Calvinist and advocate of the Dordrecht Synod (about him cf. Dexter, *Congregationalism,* p. 402) had originally held the opinion which he later softened, that the independent separatists must not have social intercourse with the others, even should they be *electi,* which was considered conceivable. However, most sects have avoided committing themselves overtly to this principle, and some have expressly rejected it, at least as a principle. Baxter, *Christian Directory,* vol. II, p. 100 (at the bottom of column 2), opines that, should not oneself but the housefather and parson, assume the responsibility, then one might acquiesce to praying together with an ungodly person. However, this is un-Puritan. The *mijdinge* [middle things] played a very important part in the radical Baptist sects in Holland during the seventeenth century.

24. This became strikingly obvious even in the discussions and struggles within the Amsterdam Refugee congregation at the beginning of the seventeenth century. Likewise in Lancashire the rejection of a *ministerial* church discipline, the demand for a lay rule in the church and for a church discipline enforced by laymen were decisive for the attitudes in the internal church struggles of Cromwell's times.

25. The appointment of the elders was the object of prolonged controversies in the Independent and Baptist communities, which will not concern us here.

26. The ordinance of the Long Parliament of 31 December 1646 was directed against this. It was intended as a stroke against the Independents. On the other hand, the principle of the liberty of prophesying had also been vindicated in literary form by Robinson. From the Episcopalian standpoint Jeremy Taylor, *The Liberty of Prophesying* (1647), made concessions to it. Cromwell's 'tryers' requested that permission to prophesy depend on the certificate of six admitted members of the congregation, among whom were four laymen. During the early period of the English Reformation the 'exercises' and 'prophesyings' had not only been frequently tolerated by ardent Anglican bishops, but had been encouraged by them.

In Scotland these were (in 1560) constituent elements of church activities; in 1571 they were introduced in Northampton. Other places were soon to follow. But Elizabeth persisted in suppressing them as a result of her proclamation of 1573 against Cartwright.

27. The charismatic revolutions of the sectarians (of the type of Fox and similar leaders) in the congregations always began with the fight against the office-holding prebendaries as 'hirelings' and with the fight for the apostolic principle of free preaching without remuneration for the speaker who is moved by the spirit. Heated disputes in Parliament took place between Goodwin, the congregationalist, and Prynne, who reproached him that, against his alleged principle, he had accepted a 'living,' whereas Goodwin declared acceptance only of what was given voluntarily. The principle that only *voluntary* contributions for the maintenance of ministers should be permissible is expressed in the petition of the Brownists to James I, in 1603 (point 71: hence the protest against 'Popish livings' and 'Jewish tithes').

28. In 1793 Methodism abolished differences between ordained and non-ordained preachers. Therewith, the non-ordained traveling preachers, and hence, the missionaries, who were the characteristic bearers of Methodism, were placed on an equal footing with the preachers still ordained by the Anglican church. But at the same time the monopoly of preaching in the whole circuit and of administering sacraments was reserved to the traveling preachers alone. (The autonomous administration of sacraments was then principally carried through, but still at hours different from those of the official church to which membership was still pretended now as before.) As, ever since 1768, preachers were forbidden to engage in ordinary civic occupations, a new 'clergy' emerged. Since 1836 formal ordination has taken place. Opposite the circuit preachers were the lay-recruited local preachers who took up preaching as a minor vocation. They had no right to administer sacraments and they had only local jurisdiction. None among these two categories of preachers donned an official garb.

29. Actually, in England at least, most of the 'circuits' have become little parishes and the travel of the preacher has become a fiction. Nevertheless, up to the very present, it has been upheld that the same minister must not serve the same circuit for more than three years. They were *professional* preachers. The 'local preachers,' from among whom the traveling preachers were recruited, were, however, people with a civic occupation and with a license to preach, which (originally) was given for one year at a time. Their existence was necessary because of the abundance of services and of chapels. But above all, they were the backbone of the 'class'-organization and its curing of souls. Hence, they were actually the central organ of church discipline.

30. Among other things Cromwell's opposition to the 'Parliament of the Saints' became acute on the question of the universities (which with the radical elimination of all tithes and prebends would have collapsed). Cromwell could not decide to destroy these cultural institutions, which, however, then were meant especially to be institutions for the education of theologians.

31. An example is given by Gardiner, *Fall of the Monarchy,* vol. I, p. 380.

32. The Westminster Confession also (xxvi, 1) establishes the principle of *inner and external* obligation to help one another. The respective rules are numerous among all sects.

33. Every case of failure to pay in early Methodism was investigated by a commission of brethren. To incur debts without the certain prospect of being able to pay them back was cause for exclusion—hence, the credit rating. Cf. the resolution

of the Dutch synods quoted in note 9. The obligation to help one's brother in emergencies is determined, for example, in the Baptist Hanserd Knollys confession (c. 28) with the characteristic reservation that this should not prejudice the sanctity of property. Occasionally, and with great harshness (as in the Cambridge platform of 1647, edition of 1653, 7, no. vi) the elders are reminded of their duty to proceed against members who live *'without a calling'* or conduct themselves *'idly in their calling.'*

34. Among the Methodists these certificates of conduct originally had to be renewed every three months. The old Independents, as noted above, gave the Lord's Supper only to holders of tickets. Among the Baptists a newcomer to the community could be admitted to the congregation only upon a letter of recommendation from his former congregation: cf. the appendix to the edition of the Hanserd Knollys Confession of 1689 (West Chester, Pa., 1827). Even the three Amsterdam Baptist Communities at the beginning of the sixteenth century had the same system, which since then recurs everywhere. In Massachusetts since 1669, a certificate from the preacher and the select men concerning orthodoxy and *conduct* has been the attestation that the holder is qualified for acquiring political citizenship. This certificate replaced the admission to the Lord's Supper, which had originally been required.

35. Again we should like to stress emphatically this absolutely decisive point of the first of these two essays. (*The Protestant Ethics and the Spirit of Capitalism.*) It has been the fundamental mistake of my critics not to have taken notice of this very fact. In the discussion of the Ancient Hebrew Ethics in relation to the *doctrines* of Egyptian, Phoenician, Babylonian ethical systems we shall hit upon a very similar state of affairs.

36. Cf. among others the statement p. 166 in the *Protestant Ethic and the Spirit of Capitalism*. The formation of congregations among ancient Jewry, just as among early Christians, worked, each in its own way, in the same direction (among Jewry the decline of the social significance of the sib, as we shall see, is conditioned thereby, and Christianity during the early Middle Ages has had similar effects).

37. Cf. The *Livre des Métiers* of the Prévôt Étienne de Boileau of 1268 (éd. Lespinasse & Bonnardot in the *Histoire générale de Paris*) pp. 211, section 8; 215, section 4. These examples may stand for many others.

38. Here, in passing, we cannot analyze this rather involved causal relationship.

XIII. RELIGOUS REJECTIONS OF THE WORLD AND THEIR DIRECTIONS

1. *'A priori* ethical rigorism' as used here refers to a belief in moral principles based on 'natural law,' or categorical imperatives deduced from reason. The ethic of the Stoics, or the cult of reason during the French Revolution, or Kantianism are examples.

2. *The Protestant Ethic and the Spirit of Capitalism* (New York, 1930).

XIV. CAPITALISM AND RURAL SOCIETY IN GERMANY

1. Judicial sentences serving as precedents in the old Germanic law.
2. St. Louis.

XV. NATIONAL CHARACTER AND THE JUNKERS

1. *Bürgerlichen.*

2. In the German *Korpszeitung*, No. 428, quoted here from Professor A. Messer's article in the *Weserzeitung* of 2 June 1917, we find the following remarks criticizing 'modern' proposals of reform: 'The proposals do not at all take into account the changing material of freshmen and active members of fraternities. To select only one item: The compulsion to drink should be abolished! There should be no compulsion to empty the glass! There should be no pumping full! Often enough I have experienced among various fraternities that kind of *Kneipen* [ceremonious drinking parties of student fraternities] without such reforms, sometimes for semesters. And later on I have spent evenings with the same fraternities when everybody was reeling drunk. Then they were simply different men who believed in drinking plenty. Quite often they even held it to be necessary. And it is necessary to provide an opportunity for drinking plenty and for making them drink a great deal. If we cancel the command for drinking "rests," any freshman who is a good drinker can at any time drink his fraternity seniors under the table, and authority is gone. Or if we abolish the obligation to honor each toast we thereby abolish the basis of *Kneipgemuetlichkeit* [tavern jollification]. If we forbid the pumping full of a member, we do away with a means of education! I beg that these words not be quoted out of their context. After all, our fraternity life shall constitute a chain of educational measures; and every member of a dueling corps will confirm that later in life he never again was told the truth so unvarnished, so incredibly bluntly as sometimes in the dueling corps. How did it happen that he took it? However ridiculous it may sound, it was due to the *Kneipe*. To us the *Kneipe* is what the often abused barrack drill and the goose step are to the soldier. Just as the command "knees bent!" repeated hundreds of times on the drill ground makes the man overcome laziness, callousness, stubbornness, rage, sluggishness, and weariness, and just as this command makes discipline emerge from the sentiment of being utterly helpless and completely devoid of initiative in the face of a superior —in the same way with us the command "drink the rest!" always gives the senior the opportunity to show the junior his absolute superiority. He may punish, he may keep a distance, and maintain the atmosphere which is absolutely required for the educational endeavor of the dueling corps—lest they become clubs! Naturally the command "drink the rest!" is not always and not with everybody advisable, but it must be an imminent·threat to the *Kneipe* as the "knees bent!" is on the drill ground. Nevertheless, in both situations men may have a jolly good time.' [M. W.]

3. County executive.

4. Judge of a lower court.

XVI. INDIA: THE BRAHMAN AND THE CASTES

1. The specialists see in the *Purusha Sukta* of the *Rig-Veda* the '*Magna Charta* of the caste system.' It is the latest product of the Vedic period. We shall discuss the *Atharva-Veda* later.

2. Of the present Hindu castes (the chief ones), one may say that 25 are diffused throughout most of the regions of India. These castes comprise about 88 million Hindus out of the total of 217 million. Among them we find the ancient priest, warrior, and merchant castes: the Brahmans (14.60 million); Rajputs (9.43 mil-

lion); Baniya (3.00 or only 1.12 million—according to whether or not one includes the split sub-castes); Cayasts (ancient caste of official scribes) (2.17 million); as well as ancient tribal castes like the Ahirs (9.50 million); Jats (6.98 million); or the great unclean occupational castes like the Chamar (leather workers) (11.50 million); the Sudra caste of the Teli (oil pressers) (4.27 million); the genteel trade caste of the goldsmiths, the Sonar (1.26 million); the ancient castes of village artisans, the Kumhar (potters) (3.42 million) and Lohar (Blacksmiths) (2.07 million); the lower peasant caste of the Koli (cooli, derived from Kul, clan, meaning something like 'kin'—*Gevatter*) (3.17 million); and other individual castes of varying origin. The great differences in caste names as well as several distinctions of social rank which, in the individual provinces, derive from castes obviously equal in descent, make direct comparisons extremely difficult.

3. The Banjaras, for instance, are partly organized as 'castes' in the Central Provinces. In Mysore, however, they are organized as an ('animist') 'tribe.' In both cases they make their living in the same way. Similar cases frequently occur.

4. 'Territorial economy' designates a stage in economic development. The term was coined by Gustav Schmoller, who distinguished between 'village economy'—'city economy'—'territorial economy'—'national economy.' [Editors.]

5. As with all sociological phenomena, the contrast here is not an absolute one, nor are transitions lacking, yet it is a contrast in 'essential' features which has been historically decisive.

6. Commensalisms existing between castes really only confirm the rule. They concern, for instance, commensalism between certain Rajput and Brahman subcastes, which rests upon the fact that the latter have of yore been the family priests of the former.

7. A separate lower caste (the Kallars) has arisen in Bengal from among people who during the famine of 1866 had infracted the ritual and dietary laws and in consequence had been excommunicated. Within this caste, in turn, the minority separate themselves as a sub-caste from the majority. The former had become guilty of the outrage only at a price of six seers for the Rupee, whereas the latter had trespassed even at a price of ten seers for the Rupee. [M. W.]

8. A nabob of Bankura, upon the request of a Chandala, wished to compel the Karnakar (metal workers) caste to eat with the Chandala. According to the legend of the origin of the Mahmudpurias, this request occasioned part of this caste to escape to Mahmudpura and to constitute itself as a separate sub-caste with higher social claims.

9. According to Gait's general report for 1911 (*Census of India,* Report, vol. 1, p. 378), this was the case for the equally genteel castes of the Baidya and Kayastha in Bengal, the Kanet and the Khas in the Punjab, and, sporadically, among the Brahmans and Rajputs, and the Sonars, Nais, and the Kanets [women]. Enriched Maratha peasants may avail themselves of Moratha women for a sufficient dowry.

10. Among the Rajputs in Punjab, hypergamy often still exists to such an extent that even Chamar girls are purchased.

11. If in India (*Census Report,* 1901, XIII, 1, p. 193) the whole village—the unclean castes included—consider themselves to be 'interrelated,' that is, if the new marriage partner is addressed by all as 'son-in-law' and the older generation is addressed by all as 'uncle,' it is evident that this has nothing whatsoever to do with derivation from a 'primitive group marriage'; this is indeed as little true in India as elsewhere.

12. Especially by the Rajputs. Despite the severe English laws of 1829, as late as 1869, in 22 villages of Rajputana there were 23 girls and 284 boys. In an 1836 count, in some Rajput areas, not one single live girl of over one year of age was found in a population of 10,000 souls!

13. Thus, for instance, the Makishya Kaibarthas (in Bengal) increasingly reject community with the Chasi Kaibarthas because the latter personally sell their (agricultural) products in the market, which the Makishya do not do. Other castes are considered *déclassé* because their women participate in selling in the stores; generally, the co-operation of women in economic pursuits is considered specifically plebeian. The social and work set-up of agriculture is very strongly determined by the fact that several performances are considered as absolutely degrading. Often caste rank determines whether or not someone uses oxen and horses or other draft and pack animals in gainful work; it determines which animals and how many of them he uses (for example, the number of oxen employed by the oil pressers is thus determined).

14. Baudhâyana's *Sacred Books of the East*, 1, 5, 9, 1. Also all commodities publicly offered for sale.

15. Baudhâyana 1, 5, 9, 3. Mines and all workshops except distilleries of alcohol are ritually clean.

16. The relations of the Indian sects and salvation religions to the banking and commercial circles of India will be discussed later.

17. Cf. *Census Report* for Bengal (1911) concerning the training for commerce among the Baniyas. That ancient castes with strong occupational mobility often drift into occupations whose demands of 'natural disposition' form the greatest psychological contrast imaginable to the previous mode of activity, but which stand close to one another through the common usefulness of certain forms of knowledge and aptitudes, acquired through training, speaks against imputations to 'natural disposition.' Thus, the frequent shift, mentioned above, from the ancient caste of surveyors—whose members naturally knew the roads particularly well—to the occupation of chauffeur may be referred to among many similar examples.

18. These figures are from the 1911 *census*.

19. v. Delden, *Die Indische Jute-Industrie*, 1915, p. 96.

20. v. Delden, ibid. pp. 114-25.

XVII. THE CHINESE LITERATI

1. Yu tsiuan tung kian kang mu, *Geschichte der Ming-Dynastie des Kaisers Kian Lung,* trans. by Delamarre (Paris, 1865), p. 417.

2. As eminent an authority as von Rosthorn disputes this point in his 'The Burning of the Books,' *Journal of the Peking Oriental Society,* vol. IV, Peking, 1898, pp. 1 ff. He believes that the sacred texts were orally transmitted until the Han period, and hence that they are in the same tradition that prevailed exclusively in early India. The outsider is not entitled to pass judgment, but perhaps the following may be said. The annalistic scriptures at least cannot rest on oral tradition and, as the calculation of the eclipses of the sun shows, they go back into the second millennium. Very much of what elsewhere is (according to the usual assumption, reliably) reported of the archives of the princes and the importance of script and the written communication of the literati could just as little be reconciled with the above, *if* one were to extend the view of the eminent expert *beyond* the ritual literature (that is, literature which has been brought into poetic form). Here, of

course, only expert sinologists have the last word, and a 'criticism' on the part of a non-expert would be presumptuous. The principle of strictly *oral* tradition has almost everywhere applied only to charismatic revelations and to charismatic commentaries of these, and not to poetry and didactics. The great age of script as such comes out in its pictorial form and also in its arrangement of the pictorial characters: at a late period the vertical columns divided by lines still referred back to the origin from scored disks of bamboo sticks which were placed side by side. The oldest 'contracts' were bamboo scores or knotted cords. The fact that *all* contracts and documents are made out in duplicate form is probably rightly considered a survival of this technique (Conrady).

3. This explains also the stereotyping of script in such an extraordinarily early stage of development, and hence it produces an after-effect even today.

4. E. de Chavannes, *Journal of the Peking Oriental Society,* vol. III, 1, 1890, p. iv, translates *Tai che ling* by 'grand astrologer,' instead of 'court annalist,' as it is usually rendered. Yet, the later, and especially the modern period knows the representatives of literary education to be sharp opponents of the astrologers. Cf. below.

5. P. A. Tschepe (S.J.), 'Histoire du Royaume de Han,' *Variétés Sinologiques,* 31 (Shanghai, 1910), p. 48.

6. During the fourth century the representatives of the feudal order, foremost among them the interested princely sibs, argued against the intended bureaucratization of the state of *Tsin* by pointing out 'that the forbears had improved the people by education, not by administrative changes' (this harmonizes fully with the later theories of Confucian orthodoxy). Thereupon the new minister Yang, belonging to the literati, comments in highly un-Confucian manner: 'the ordinary person *lives* according to tradition; the higher minds, however, *create* tradition, and for extraordinary things the rites give no precepts. The weal of the people is the highest law,' and the prince accedes to his opinion. (Cf. the passages in Tschepe's 'Histoire du Royaume de Tsin,' *Variétés Sinologiques,* 27, p. 118.) It is quite probable that when Confucian orthodoxy articulated and purified the *Annals* it very strongly erased and retouched these features in favor of the traditionalism which was later considered correct. On the other hand, one must beware of simply taking at face value all the reports referred to below which testify to the astonishing deference paid to the early literati!

7. Although the princely heir of Wei alights from the chariot he receives no response to his repeated salutations from the king's courtier and literary man, who is a parvenu. To the question 'whether the rich or the poor may be proud' the *literatus* replies 'the poor,' and he motivates this by saying that he might find employment any day at another court. (Tschepe, 'Histoire du Royaume de Han,' op. cit. p. 43.) One of the literati is seized by a great rage about a brother of the prince being preferred over him for the post of a minister. (Cf. ibid.)

8. The prince of Wei listens only in standing to the report of the court *literatus,* a disciple of Confucius (loc. cit.; cf. preceding note).

9. Cf. the statements of Tschepe, 'Histoire du Royaume de Tsin,' p. 77.

10. The hereditary transmission of the ministerial position is considered ritually objectionable by the literati (Tschepe, loc. cit.). When the prince of Chao orders his minister to scrutinize and find some land suitable as fiefs for several worthy literati the minister thrice declares after having thrice been warned, that he has as yet not found any land worthy of them. Thereupon the prince finally understands and makes them officials. (Tschepe, 'Histoire du Royaume de Han,' pp. 54-5.)

11. Cf. the passage concerning the respective question by the King of U in Tschepe, 'Histoire du Royaume de U,' *Variétés Sinologiques* 10, Shanghai, 1891.

12. That also income was an end sought goes without saying, as the *Annals* show.

13. Once when a prince's concubine laughed at one of the literati, all the prince's literati went on strike until she was executed (Tschepe, *Histoire du Royaume de Han*, loc. cit. p. 128).

14. The event reminds one of the 'finding' of the sacred law under Josiah with the Jews. The contemporary great annalist, Se ma tsien, does not mention the find.

15. Tschepe, 'Histoire du Royaume de Tsin,' loc. cit. p. 53.

16. Individual concealments are confirmed (for instance, the attack of the state U upon its own state Lu). For the rest, in view of the scantiness of the material, one may seriously raise the question as to whether one should not rather consider the great, strongly moralizing *commentary* to the *Annals* as his work.

17. In 1900 the Empress-Dowager still took very unfavorable notice of a censor's request to abolish them. Cf. the rescripts in the *Peking Gazette* concerning the 'orthodox army' (10 January 1899), concerning the 'review' during the Japanese war (21 December 1894), concerning the importance of military ranks (1 and 10 November 1898), and from an earlier period, e.g. (23 May 1878).

18. Concerning this practice cf. Etienne Zi (S.J.), 'Pratique des Examens Militaires en Chine,' *Variétés Sinologiques*, no. 9. Subjects for examination were archery and certain gymnastic feats of strength; and, formerly, the writing of a dissertation; since 1807, however, the writing of a section of one hundred characters from the U-King (theory of war), allegedly dating from the time of the Chou dynasty, was required. A great many officers did not acquire degrees and the Manchus were freed from taking them altogether.

19. A *Taotai* (prefect) for his military merits had been taken over from the officers' ranks into the civil administration. In response to a complaint an Imperial rescript (*Peking Gazette*, 17 September 1894) comments as follows: although the officer's conduct in the matter in question has substantively been found free from fault, he nevertheless has shown his 'rough soldierly manners' by his conduct, 'and we have to ask ourselves whether he possesses the *cultivated manners* which for a person of his rank and position must appear indispensable.' Therefore it is recommended that he resume a military position.

The abolition of age-old archery and of other very old sports as elements of 'military' training was made almost impossible by the rites, which in their beginnings probably were still connected with the 'bachelor house.' Thus the Empress, when rejecting the reform proposals, makes reference to these rites.

20. The French authors for the most part designate *seng yuen, siu tsai* by 'baccalaureate' [bachelor's degree], *kiu jin* by 'licentiate' [master's degree], *tien se* by 'doctorate.' The lowest degree gave a claim to a stipend only to the top graduates. The bachelors who had received a stipend were called *lin cheng* (magazine prebendaries), bachelors selected by the director and sent to Peking were called *pao kong*, those among them who were admitted to the college *yu kong,* and those who had acquired the bachelor degree by purchase were called *kien cheng.*

21. The charismatic qualities of the descendant simply were proof for those of his sib, hence of the forebears. At the time, Chi Hwang-Ti had abolished this custom, as the son was not to judge the father. But since then almost every founder of a new dynasty has bestowed ranks to his ancestors.

22. By the way, this is a rather certain symptom of its *recent origin!*

23. Cf. for this: Biot, *Essai sur l'histoire de l'instruction publique en Chine et de la corporation des Lettres* (Paris, 1847). (It is still useful.)

24. Complaints at Ma Tuan Lin, translated in Biot, p. 481.

25. Themes for them are given by Williams, cf. Zi, loc. cit.

26. This held especially for the examinations for the master's degree, where the theme of the dissertation often called for an erudite, philological, literary, and historical analysis of the respective classical text. Cf. the example given by Zi, loc. cit. p. 144.

27. This held especially for the highest degree ('doctorate') for which the emperor, often in person, gave the themes and for which he classified the graduates. Questions of administrative expediency, preferably connected with one of the 'six questions' of Emperor Tang, were customary topics. (Cf. Biot, p. 209, note 1, and Zi, loc. cit. p. 209, note 1.)

28. *Siao Hio,* ed. de Harlez, v, 11, 1, 29, 40. Cf. the quotation from Chu Tse, ibid. p. 46. Concerning the question of generations, cf. 1, 13.

29. Loc. cit. 1, 25, furthermore 2. Introduction No. 5 f.

30. There were literary prescriptions also for this.

31. It need hardly be mentioned that what is here said about language and script reproduces *exclusively* what such eminent sinologists, as especially the late W. Grube, teach the layman. It does *not* result from the author's own studies.

32. J. Edkins, 'Local Values in Chinese Arithmetical Notation,' *Journal of the Peking Oriental Society,* I, no. 4, pp. 161 f. The Chinese abacus used the (decimal) positional value. The older positional system which has fallen into oblivion seems to be of Babylonian origin.

33. de Harlez, *Siao Hio,* p. 42, note 3.

34. Also, Timkovski, *Reise durch China* (1820-21), *German by Schmid* (Leipzig, 1825), emphasizes this.

35. For such a self-impeachment of a frontier officer who had been inattentive, see No. 567 of Aurel Stein's documents, edited by E. de Chavannes. It dates from the Han period, hence long before the introduction of examinations.

36. The beginnings of the present *Peking Gazette* go back to the time of the second ruler of the Tang dynasty (618-907).

37. Actually one finds in the *Peking Gazette,* with reference to the reports partly of censors, partly of superiors, laudations and promotions (or the promise of such) for deserving officials, demotions of insufficiently qualified officials for other offices ('that he may gather experiences,' loc. cit. 31 December, 1897 and many other issues), suspension from office with half pay, expulsion of totally unqualified officials, or the statement that the good services of an official are balanced by faults which he would have to remedy before further promotion. Almost always detailed reasons are given. Such announcements were especially frequent at the end of the year but there was also a great volume at other times. There are also to be found posthumous sentences to be whipped for (obviously) posthumously demoted officials. (*Peking Gazette,* 26 May 1895.)

38. Cf. A. H. Smith, *Village Life in China* (Edinburgh, 1899), p. 78.

39. For the following see Kun Yu, *Discours des Royaumes, Annales Nationales des Etats Chinoises de X au V siècles,* ed. de Harlez [London, 1895], pp. 54, 75, 89, 159, 189, and elsewhere.

40. Tschepe, *Variétés Sinologiques,* 27, p. 38. He *begs* to be punished. Similarly in A. Stein's documents, loc. cit. no. 567.

41. See, however, the rescript in the *Peking Gazette* of 10 April 1895, by which promotions were posthumously given to officers who chose death after the surrender of Wei-hai-wei (obviously because they took the guilt *upon themselves* and thus prevented the compromise of the Emperor's charisma by the disgrace).

42. There was, however, at least in one district, also a temple of *Tai Ki*, the primary matter (chaos), from which the two substances are said to have developed by division ('Schih Luh Kuoh Kiang Yuh Tschi,' translated by Michels, p. 39).

43. According to de Groot.

44. Cf. the excerpts translated from his memoirs by Gräfin Hagen (Berlin, 1915), pp. 27, 29, 33.

45. Cf. the elegant and ingenious, though quite shallow, notes of Cheng Ki Tong, which were intended for Europeans. (*China und die Chinesen*, German by A. Schultze [Dresden und Leipzig, 1896], p. 158.) Concerning Chinese conversation, there are some observations which well agree with what has been said above in Hermann A. Keyserling, *The Travel Diary of a Philosopher*, trans. by J. Holroyd Reece (New York, 1925).

46. 'Siao Hioh' (trans. by de Harlez, *Annales du Musée, Guimet* xv, 1889) is the work of Chou Hi (twelfth century A.D.). His most essential achievement was the definitive canonization of Confucianism in the systematic form he gave to it. For Chou Hi cf. Gall, 'Le Philosophe Tchou Hi, sa doctrine etc.,' *Variétés Sinologiques*, 6 (Shanghai, 1894). It is essentially a popular commentary to the *Li Ki*, making use of historical examples. In China every grade school pupil was familiar with it.

47. The number of 'masters' was allocated to the provinces. If an emergency loan was issued—even after the Taiping rebellion—higher quotas were promised occasionally to the provinces for the raising of certain minimum sums. At every examination only ten 'doctors' were allowed to graduate, the first three of whom enjoyed an especially high prestige.

48. The paramount position of personal patronage is illustrated by the comparison between the extraction of the three highest graduates and that of the highest mandarins as given by Zi, loc. cit. Appendix ii, p. 221, note 1. Disregarding the fact that of the 748 high official positions, occupied from 1646 to 1914, 398 were occupied by Manchus although but three of them were among the highest graduates (the three *tien she* put in the first place by the Emperor), the province of Honan procured 58, that is, one sixth of all high *officials,* solely by virtue of the powerful position of the Tseng family, whereas almost two thirds of the highest *graduates* stemmed from other provinces which altogether had a share of only 30 per cent in these offices.

49. This means was first systematically used by the Ming Emperors in 1453. (But, as a financial measure, it is to be found even under Chi Hwang-Ti.) The lowest decree originally cost 108 piasters, equal to the capitalized value of the study prebends, then it cost 60 taëls. After an inundation of the Hoang-ho, the price had been reduced to about 20 to 30 taëls in order to expand the market and thereby procure ample funds. Since 1693 the purchasers of the bachelor's degree were also admitted to the higher examinations. A *Taotai* position with all secondary expenses cost about 40,000 taëls.

50. That is why the emperors under certain conditions when placing the candidates took into consideration whether or not the candidate belonged to a province which as yet had no graduate who had been put in first place.

51. Se Ma Tsien's treatise on the balance of trade (*ping shoan*) (no. 8, chap. 30, in vol. iii of Chavannes' edition) represents a rather good example of Chinese cameralism. It is also the oldest document of Chinese economics that has been preserved. Topics which in our view do not belong to the 'balance of trade' are: big trading profits during the period of the Warring States, degradation of the merchants in the unified empire, exclusion from office, fixation of salaries and, *in accordance with them,* fixation of land taxes, taxes of commerce, forest, water

(appropriated by the 'great families'), the question of private monetization, the danger of too large an enrichment of private persons (but: where there is wealth there is *virtue,* which is quite Confucian in thought), costs of transport, purchases of titles, monopolies of salt and iron, *registering* of merchants, internal tariffs, policies of price stabilization, struggles against commissions being given to wholesale purveyors to the state instead of direct commissions being given the artisans. The objective of this cameralist financial policy was *internal* order through stability, and not a favorable balance of foreign trade.

52. The Ko Hong merchants' monopoly of the trade of Canton harbor, the only one opened to foreigners, existed until 1892 and had been set up in order to choke any intercourse of the Barbarians with the Chinese. The enormous profits which this monopoly yielded caused the concerned office prebendaries to be disinclined to any voluntary change in this condition.

53. Not only the official Ming history (cf. the following note) is full of this but so is the 'Chi li kuo kiang yu chi' (*Histoire géographique des XVI Royaumes,* ed. Michels, [Paris, 1891]). Thus, in 1368 the harem is excluded from affairs of state at the request of the Hanlin Academy (p. 7); in 1498 representation of the Hanlin Academy at the occasion of the palace fire and the demand (typical for accidents) to 'speak freely' against the favorite eunuch (cf. following note).

54. Numerous cases illustrating this struggle are to be found, for instance in the 'Yu tsiuan tung kien kang mu' [*Ming History of Emperor Kien Lung*], trans. by Delamarre (Paris, 1865). Consider the fifteenth century: in 1404 a eunuch is at the head of the army (p. 155). Since then this occurs repeatedly; thus, in 1428 (p. 223). Hence, the intrusion of palace officials into the administration in 1409 (p. 168). In 1443 a Hanlin doctor demands the abolition of cabinet rule, a reduction of the *corvée,* and above all, council meetings of the Emperor, with the literati. A eunuch kills him (p. 254). In 1449 the favorite eunuch is killed at the request of the literati (p. 273), in 1457, however, *temples* are established in his honor.

In 1471 the counselors have to communicate with the Emperor through the eunuch (p. 374). The very same is reported by Hiao Kong (361-28 B.C.). In 1472 we meet eunuchs as secret policemen (p. 273), which in 1481 is abolished at the request of the censors (p. 289). In 1488 the old ritual is restored (the same occurs in numerous instances).

The removal of a eunuch in 1418 took an awkward course for the literati when the list was found on the eunuch of the literati who had bribed him. The literati were successful in having the list secreted and in seeing to it that a different pretext was found for the removal of the literati who had done the bribing (ibid. p. 422).

55. Cf. E. Backhouse and J. O. P. Bland, *China under the Empress Dowager* (Heinemann, 1910) and, against this, the famous memorial of Tao Mo from the year 1901.

56. When in 1441 a sun eclipse predicted by the astrologers failed to occur, the Board of Rites congratulated him—but the Emperor rejected this.

57. See the (previously cited) memorial, 1878, of the Hanlin Academy to the Empress.

58. Loc. cit. chap. 9, pp. 130 f.

59. See the decree of the Empress of February 1901.

60. Loc. cit. p. 457.

61. For instance, 'Yu tsiuan kien kang mu' of Emperor Kien Lung (loc. cit. pp. 167, 223), 1409 and 1428. An edict forbidding in a similar manner interference in the administration was given the military even in 1388 (ibid.).

Index

Abnegation of the world, 327-31
Absentee ownership, 366
Absolutism, princely, 230, 365; and capitalism, 230
Abstinences, 271-2
Academic career, in Germany and U.S., 129 ff.
  freedom of, 19, 387 f.
  lectures and political values, 145, 150
  role of chance in, 132-3
Academies, 134
Action, communal, and class interest, 183-4
  irrational, 254
  political, economic conditions of, 85 f.; tragedy of, 117
  societal, 228
  types of, 56
Administration, amateur, in U.S., 88
  city, 238
  concentration of means of, 221-4
  costs of, 81, 214, 224
  and economic organization, 81
  ownership of means of, 298
Administrative agencies, collegial, 89
  means, concentration of, 298
  officials, 88 f., 90-91; see also Bureaucracy
  staff, types of, 80 f.
  tasks of bureaucracy, 209-14
Adolf, Gustav, 260
Aesthetics, 144, 154
Affinity, elective, 62-3, 284-5
Agrarian institutions, history of, 10; problems, 34, 372
Agricultural proletariat, 363
Agriculture, and capitalism, 366 ff.
  medieval, 374
  separation of ownership and management in, 381
Alienation, 50; from nature, 344
America, see United States
Anabaptism, 340, 451
Anarchism, 120, 229, 334
Ancestor cult, 423

Ancient society, 19; see also Greece, Rome
Anglo-Saxon clubs, 388
  gentlemen, contrasted, 390 ff.
  society, 40
Annals, Chinese, 444; virtues praised in, 435
Anthropological types, selection of, 190; relevances of, 173, 177
Anti-intellectualism, 142 f., 152
Anti-Semitism, 19
Antiquity, Great Powers in, 161
Archilochus, 345
Archiv für Sozialwissenschaft und Sozialpolitik, 14, 46, 66
Aristocracy, 81, 386 ff.
  of education, 371 ff.
  in Germany, 390
  intellectual, 49
  landed, 373 ff.
  and rents, 369
Aristocratic forms and democratization, 392
Aristophanes, 167
Aristotle, 141
Armies, American, 9
  bureaucratization of, 222-3; in China, 421
  disintegration of, 229
  and household, separation of, 258
  organizations, their economic bases, 257, 259-60
  in politics, 227
  Roman, 222
  types of, 221 f.
Aroon, R., 447
Art, 3, 191
  of brotherliness, religious ethic, 341
  competes with salvation religion, 342
  and eroticism, 350
  of imperial Germany, 155
  and morals, 342
  and rationalization, 342
  and religion, competition between, 341 f.
  and science, 141; psychology of, 136-8